Rick Steves®

PARIS

Rick Steves, Steve Smith & Gene Openshaw

CONTENTS

Welcome to Rick Steves' Europe

Travel is intensified living—maximum thrills per minute and one of the last great sources of legal adventure. Travel is freedom. It's recess, and we need it.

I discovered a passion for European travel as a teen and have been sharing it ever since—through my bus tours, public television and radio shows, and travel guidebooks. Over the years, I've taught millions of travelers how to best enjoy Europe's blockbuster sights—and experience "Back Door" discoveries that most tourists miss.

Written with my talented co-authors, Steve Smith and Gene Openshaw, this book offers a balanced mix of Paris' blockbuster sights and lesser-known gems. It's selective: Rather than listing every sight and neighborhood in Paris, we recommend only the best ones. And it's in-depth: Our self-guided museum tours  and city walks provide insight into Paris' vibrant history and today's living, breathing culture.

We advocate traveling simply and smartly. Take advantage of our money- and time-saving tips on sightseeing, transportation, and more. Try local, characteristic alternatives to expensive hotels and restaurants. In many ways, spending more money only builds a thicker wall between you and what you traveled so far to see.

We visit Paris to experience it—to become temporary locals. Thoughtful travel engages us with the world, as we learn to appreciate other cultures and new ways to measure quality of life.

Judging by the positive feedback we receive from readers, this book will help you enjoy a fun, affordable, and rewarding vacation—whether it's your first trip or your tenth.

Bon voyage! Happy travels!

Rick Steves

PARIS

Paris—the City of Light—has been a beacon of culture for centuries. As a world capital of art, fashion, food, literature, and ideas, it stands as a symbol of all the fine things human civilization can offer—and adds a dash of romance and joie de vivre.

Two thousand years ago, Paris was a humble Celtic fishing village by the river; today it's a sprawling city, with a core population of 2.3 million. It offers sweeping boulevards, riverside book stalls, world-class art galleries, and farmers markets. Enjoy cutting-edge architecture, medieval tapestries, Gothic cathedrals, and an excellent Métro system that whisks you wherever you want to go. Sip *un café crème* with intellectuals at a sidewalk café, then step into an Impressionist painting in a tree-lined park.

Paris' sights are incomparable. Armed with a Paris Museum Pass, visit *Mona Lisa* and *Venus de Milo* at the Louvre, and marvel at the buoyant art of Monet and Renoir at the Orsay. Pay homage to beloved Notre-Dame Cathedral, still recovering from a devastating fire. Zip to the top of the Eiffel Tower, and saunter down Avenue des Champs-Elysées. Take a day trip to visit the lavish palace of Versailles to understand the inevitability of the French Rev-

People-friendly Paris: Relaxing at Luxembourg Garden; picnicking on the Seine

olution...and the rise of democracy. Few countries can equal France's impact on the global stage.

Yet Paris is also intimate and people-friendly. Prioritizing people over cars, the city turned a riverside arterial into a beach-like park, known as Paris Plages, perfect for strolling along the Seine. Waterfront pedestrian promenades run between Pont de l'Alma (near the Eiffel Tower) and the Orsay Museum on the Left Bank, and between the Louvre and Place de la Bastille on the Right Bank. The city's many lovely parks are playgrounds for all ages. Luxembourg Garden offers puppet shows, pony rides, rental toy sailboats, and a wading pool. The Esplanade des Invalides, near Napoleon's Tomb, is just right for afternoon lawn bowling *(boules)*.

As you dodge Parisians walking their poodles and pushing baby strollers on a residential market street such as Rue Cler, you'll experience real people making cozy communities in the midst of this vast, high-powered city. If you'd like to learn the fine art of living like a Parisian, a walk down a neighborhood market street provides an excellent classroom. And if you want to assemble the ultimate French picnic, there's no better place. You'll find a warm and human vibrancy you miss when just hopping from big museum to museum. Chat with the woman who makes your crêpe, pop into chic boutiques, and stop by a

The Language Barrier and That French Attitude

You may have heard that French people are cold and refuse to speak English. In my experience, the French are as friendly as other people (though a bit more formal) and many Parisians speak English well. But be reasonable in your expectations: French waiters are paid to be efficient, not chatty.

The best advice? Slow down. Impatient travelers unaware of the joys of people-watching from a café often misinterpret French attitudes. With five weeks of paid vacation and a shorter work week than ours, the French don't understand why anyone would rush through their time off.

The French view formality as being polite and prefer to avoid eye contact with strangers. When tourists stroll down the street grinning and blurting "Bonjour!" to everyone, the French find it odd rather than friendly.

Language is taken seriously, and locals place a high value on the use of pleasantries. Learn these five phrases: *bonjour* (good day), *pardon* (pardon me), *s'il vous plaît* (please), *merci* (thank you), and *au revoir* (goodbye). Begin every encounter (for instance, when entering a shop) with *"Bonjour, madame (or monsieur),"* and end every encounter with *"Au revoir, madame (or monsieur)."*

To ask a French person to speak English, say, *"Bonjour, madame (or monsieur). Parlez-vous anglais?"* They may say *"non"* (because they don't speak English fluently), but you may soon find out they speak more English than you speak French.

Practice French survival phrases (see the appendix), and have a phrase book or translator app handy. In transactions, a notepad and pen can help; have vendors write down the price. ▪

It's très *French: At sidewalk cafés, people take their time. At small shops (like this bakery), say,* "Bonjour, madame *(or* monsieur)" *when you enter.*

Provençal ratatouille with Parisian flair; street performers at Sacré-Cœur

neighborhood *fromagerie* to sniff fragrant cheese that smells like "zee feet of angels."

You'll eat very well. After all, Paris is the French capital of cuisine, offering signature dishes from all of the country's regions: ratatouille (Provence), foie gras (Dordogne), *bœuf bourguignon* (Burgundy), bouillabaisse (Riviera), and much more. Dine at a cozy bistro—the table is yours for the evening. Savor a special wine with your meal, though in France, even the table wine is fine. For dessert, crack open the caramelized crust of a crème brûlée.

Save some after-dark energy for one of the world's most romantic cities. Enjoy views over the glittering City of Light— from the Arc de Triomphe, the rooftops of stylish department stores, and the steps of Sacré-Cœur on Montmartre.

Parisians have the habit of spilling onto the river's bridges and embankments just at that magic hour when the setting sun begins to color the evening sky. Make this your habit too. It's the perfect time to share a picnic with friends, with an ambience that no restaurant can touch. Stately monuments and bridges, floodlit as darkness falls, are reflected in the waters of the Seine. Cruise the river and marvel at the nighttime light show at the sparkling Eiffel Tower. Once you've been to Paris...you'll always have Paris.

Paris by Neighborhood

Paris is a big city, but its major sights cluster in convenient zones. Thoughtfully grouping your sightseeing, walks, dining, and shopping can save you lots of time and money.

Paris is circled by a ring road and split in half by the Seine River, which runs east-west. North of the Seine is the Right Bank (Rive Droite), and to the south is the Left Bank (Rive Gauche). The bull's-eye is Notre-Dame, the heart of Paris, on an island in the middle of the Seine.

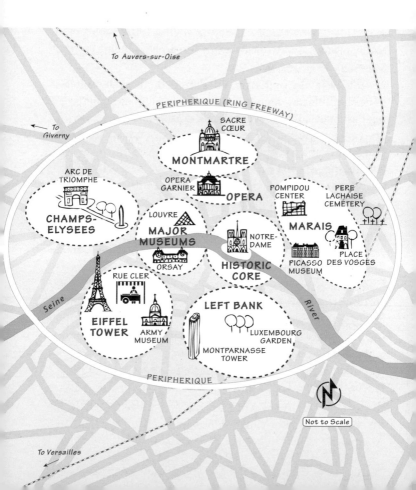

TOP NEIGHBORHOODS

Historic Core

This area centers on the Ile de la Cité ("Island of the City"), located in the middle of the Seine. On this small island, you'll find Paris' oldest sights, from Roman ruins to the medieval Notre-Dame and Sainte-Chapelle churches. Other sights in this area: Conciergerie, Archaeological Crypt, Deportation Memorial, flower market, riverside promenade and Paris Plages, and the lovely island of Ile St. Louis, with appealing shops and eateries. Paris' most historic riverside vendors, *les bouquinistes,* line both sides of the Seine as it passes Ile de la Cité.

Major Museums Neighborhood

Located just west of the historic core, this is where you'll find the art-filled Louvre, Orsay, and Orangerie museums. Other sights are the Tuileries Garden, Palais Royal courtyards, and the elegant arcades of the Galerie Vivienne.

Champs-Elysées

The greatest of the many grand 19th-century boulevards on the Right Bank, the Champs-Elysées runs northwest from Place de la Concorde to the Arc de Triomphe. Sights in this area include the Petit and Grand Palais, Hôtel Hyatt Regency Paris Etoile (for its great city view), and on the outskirts, the modern neighborhood of La Défense with La Grande Arche.

Eiffel Tower Neighborhood

Dominated by the Eiffel Tower, this area also boasts the colorful Rue Cler market street (with many recommended hotels and restaurants), Army Museum and Napoleon's Tomb, Rodin Museum, and the thriving outdoor market Marché Boulevard de Grenelle. Other sights: the pedestrian-friendly riverside

Vendor stalls (les bouquinistes) *along the Seine; Monet's* Water Lilies *at the Orangerie; Champs-Elysées with the Arc de Triomphe; Napoleon's Tomb*

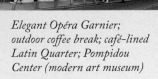

Elegant Opéra Garnier; outdoor coffee break; café-lined Latin Quarter; Pompidou Center (modern art museum)

promenade, Quai Branly Museum, National Maritime Museum, Architecture and Monuments Museum, and Sewer Museum. The Marmottan Museum is west of the Eiffel Tower on the Right Bank.

Opéra Neighborhood

Surrounding the Opéra Garnier, this classy area on the Right Bank is home to a series of impressive boulevards and sights. Though today it's busy with traffic, there are still hints of Paris circa 1870, when the city was the capital of the world. Along with elegant sights such as the Opéra Garnier, Jacquemart-André Museum, and Fragonard Perfume Museum, the neighborhood also offers high-end shopping: at Galeries Lafayette department store, around Place de la Madeleine and Place Vendôme, and at the covered passages of Choiseul and Ste. Anne.

Left Bank

The Left Bank is home to...the Left Bank. Anchored by the large Luxembourg Garden (near numerous recommended hotels and eateries), the Left Bank is the traditional neighborhood of Paris' intellectual, artistic, and café life. Other sights: the Latin Quarter, Cluny Museum, St. Germain-des-Prés and St. Sulpice churches, Panthéon, Montparnasse Tower, Catacombs, Delacroix Museum, and the Jardin des Plantes park. This is also one of Paris' best shopping areas (near Place St. Suplice). The Grande Mosquée de Paris and Muslim cultural center (Arab World Institute, with views) are just east of the Latin Quarter.

Marais

Stretching eastward from the Pompidou Center to the Bastille along Rue de Rivoli/Rue St. Antoine, this neighborhood is packed with recommended restaurants and hotels, shops, the delightful Place des Vosges, and artistic sights (Pompidou Center, Picasso Museum). The area is known for its avant-garde boutiques and residents. Other Marais sights: Jewish Art and History Museum, Holocaust Memorial, La Coulée Verte Promenade-Park, Père Lachaise Cemetery, Carnavalet Museum, Victor Hugo's House, Marché des Enfants Rouges covered market, and the outdoor markets at Bastille and Place d'Aligre.

Montmartre

This hill, topped by the bulbous white domes of Sacré-Cœur
Basilica, hovers on the northern fringes of your Paris map.
Home to recommended hotels and restaurants, Montmartre retains some of the charm that once drew Impressionist
painters and turn-of-the-century bohemians. Other sights are
the Dalí and Montmartre museums, Moulin Rouge, Pigalle
district, and nearby Puces St. Ouen flea market.

Day Trips

When you're ready to explore beyond Paris, you have good
options, all easily reached by train:

Versailles is Europe's ultimate royal palace—all others are
wannabes. It's huge, comprising the Château, Gardens, and the
Trianon Palaces and Domaine de Marie-Antoinette.

Other grand châteaux within day-tripping distance of Paris
are the exquisite **Vaux-le-Vicomte,** lavish **Fontainebleau,** and
scenically set **Chantilly.**

Chartres' historic cathedral has famous stained-glass
windows and statues that gloriously tell the entire story of the
Bible. The pedestrian-friendly town itself is worth strolling.

Giverny and **Auvers-sur-Oise** are for lovers of art and
small towns. The charming village of Giverny was the home
of Monet and his photogenic water lilies. Van Gogh spent the
end of his short life painting furiously in the rural village of
Auvers-sur-Oise.

*Sound-and-light show at Chartres
Cathedral; Versailles' Grand Trianon—
fit for a king*

Planning and Budgeting

The best trips start with good planning. Here are ideas to help you decide when to go, design a smart itinerary, set a travel budget, and prepare for your trip. For my best general advice on sightseeing, accommodations, restaurants, and more, see the Practicalities chapter.

PLANNING YOUR TIME

As you read this book and learn your options...

Decide when to go.

Late spring and fall bring the best weather and the biggest crowds. May, June, September, and October are the toughest months for hotel-hunting—don't expect many deals. Summers are generally hot and dry; if you wilt in the heat, look for a room with air-conditioning. Rooms are easy to land in August (some hotels offer deals), and though many French businesses close in August, you'll hardly notice.

Paris makes a great winter getaway (see the Paris in Winter chapter). Airfare costs less, cafés are cozy, and the city feels lively but not touristy. The only problem—weather—is solved by dressing warmly, with layers. Expect cold (even freezing lows) and rain (hats, gloves, scarves, umbrellas, and thick-soled shoes are essential). For specific temperatures, see the climate chart in the appendix.

Work out a day-by-day itinerary.

The following day plans offer suggestions for how to maximize your sightseeing, depending on how many days you have. You can adapt these itineraries to fit your own interests. To find out what days sights are open, check the "Daily Reminder" in the Orientation chapter. Note major sights where advance reservations are required (or smart) or a free Rick Steves audio tour is available.

Paris in One, Two, or Three Busy Days

Day 1

Morning   Follow my Historic Paris Walk, featuring Ile de la Cité, Notre-Dame, the Latin Quarter, and Sainte-Chapelle. If you enjoy medieval art, visit the Cluny Museum.

Afternoon   Tour the Louvre.

Evening   Enjoy a twilight ride up the Eiffel Tower and the Place du Trocadéro scene at its feet.

Day 2

Morning   Follow my Champs-Elysées Walk from the Arc de Triomphe down the grand Avenue des Champs-Elysées and into the Tuileries Garden (or take the Métro).

Midday   Cross the pedestrian bridge from the Tuileries Garden, then tour the Orsay Museum.

Afternoon   Tour the Rodin Museum or the Army Museum and Napoleon's Tomb.

Evening   Take a tour by bus, taxi/Uber, or retro-chic Deux Chevaux car. (If staying more than two days, you could save this for your last-night finale.)

Day 3

Morning   Catch RER/Train-C to Versailles, then tour the Château and sample the Gardens.

Afternoon   Versailles can take up a full sightseeing day, but if you're back in Paris, consider a sight near one of the RER/Train-C stations: the Army Museum and Napoleon's Tomb, Rodin Museum, or Orsay Museum—or enjoy my Left Bank Walk.

Evening   Cruise the Seine River or have dinner on Ile St. Louis, then take a floodlit walk by Notre-Dame.

Pyramids at the Louvre; Deux Chevaux driving tour; portico at Versailles; wintertime fun at the Eiffel Tower

Paris in Five to Seven Days Without Going In-Seine

Day 1

Morning   Follow my Historic Paris Walk, featuring Ile de la Cité, Notre-Dame, the Latin Quarter, and Sainte-Chapelle. Savor a break in Luxembourg Garden and consider a visit to the nearby Panthéon or Cluny Museum.

Afternoon   Tour the Opéra Garnier, then enjoy rooftop views at the Galeries Lafayette or Printemps department stores—or both.

Evening   Take a boat cruise on the Seine.

Day 2

Morning   Tour the Louvre.

Afternoon   Follow my Champs-Elysées Walk from the Arc de Triomphe to the Tuileries Garden, and possibly take in the Orangerie Museum. Reversing the morning and afternoon activities also works well.

Evening   Enjoy dinner on Ile St. Louis, then a floodlit walk by Notre-Dame.

Glitzy Galeries Lafayette; ready for a Seine cruise; Versailles' pastoral Domaine de Marie-Antoinette

Day 3

Morning	Tour the Orsay Museum.
Midday	Tour the Rodin Museum (café lunch in gardens).
Afternoon	Visit the Army Museum and Napoleon's Tomb, then take my Rue Cler Walk and relax at a café. Take a slow stroll along the Left Bank riverside promenade between the Orsay and Pont de l'Alma (near the Eiffel Tower), or bike along either bank.
Evening	Take one of the recommended nighttime bus/taxi/retro car tours.

Day 4

Morning	Take RER/Train-C to Versailles and tour the palace's interior.
Midday	Have lunch in the Gardens at Versailles.
Afternoon	Tour the Gardens, Trianon Palaces, and Domaine de Marie-Antoinette. (Late risers should reverse this plan and tour the palace's interior in the afternoon to minimize crowd frustrations.) Or return to Paris and do this book's Montmartre Walk.
Evening	Dine in Versailles town or back in Paris.

Day 5

Morning	Follow this book's Marais Walk and tour the Carnavalet. Have lunch on Place des Vosges or Rue des Rosiers.
Afternoon	Choose from these Marais sights: Pompidou Center, Jewish Art and History Museum, Picasso Museum, or Père Lachaise Cemetery.
Evening	Enjoy a twilight ride up the Eiffel Tower and the Place du Trocadéro scene nearby.

Day 6

Morning	Spend most of your day at Chartres or a half-day touring the château of Vaux-le-Vicomte.
Afternoon	Explore the shopping districts of Paris (follow the Left Bank Walk or see the Shopping in Paris chapter for options).
Evening	Walk the Champs-Elysées to take in the nighttime scene. Hike to the top of the Arc de Triomphe.

Day 7

There's still plenty to do: more shopping and cafés, Luxembourg Garden, Bus #69 tour followed by Père Lachaise Cemetery, Montmartre, Sacré-Cœur, Jacquemart-André and Marmottan museums, day trips to Vaux-le-Vicomte and/or Fontainebleau, and Disneyland Paris.

Spiraling up the Arc de Triomphe; winding down at peaceful Place des Vosges

PLANNING YOUR BUDGET

Run a reality check on your dream trip. You'll have major transportation costs in addition to daily expenses.

Flight: A round-trip flight from the US to Paris costs about $900-1,500, depending on where you fly from and when.

Public Transportation: For a one-week visit, allow about $50 for a Métro/bus/RER pass and a couple of day trips by

train. To get between Paris and either major airport, figure $30-130 round-trip, depending on which option you choose.

Budget Tips: To cut your daily expenses, take advantage of the deals you'll find throughout Paris and mentioned in this book.

Use public transportation, and visit sights by neighborhood for efficiency.

Buy a Paris Museum Pass and use it wisely. On days that you don't have pass coverage, visit free sights and those not covered by the pass (see the "Affording Paris' Sights" sidebar in the Sights in Paris chapter). Take advantage of free experiences (people-watching counts).

Some businesses—especially hotels and walking-tour companies—offer discounts to my readers (look for the RS% symbol in the listings in this book).

Reserve your rooms directly with the hotel and book good-value rooms early. Some hotels may offer a discount if you pay in cash and/or stay three or more nights (check online

AVERAGE DAILY EXPENSES PER PERSON

$255
Applies to Paris,
figure 20% less elsewhere.

Lodging
Based on two people
splitting the cost of
a $250 double room
$125

Meals
$20 for breakfast,
$25 for lunch, and
$45 for dinner
$90

City Transit
Buses and Métro
$10

**Sights and
Entertainment**
This daily average
works for most
people.
$30

or ask). Rooms can cost less outside of the peak season months of May, June, September, and October. And even seniors can sleep cheaply in hostels (most have private rooms) for about $30 per person ($60 for a private room). Or check Airbnb-type sites for deals.

It's no hardship to eat well on a budget in Paris. For dinner at restaurants, you can order just a *plat* (main course), and at cafés, it's fine to order only soup or a salad. You can get tasty takeout food at bakeries, street stands, delis, and grocery stores. Cultivate the art of picnicking in atmospheric settings.

When you splurge, choose an experience you'll always remember, such as a concert in Sainte-Chapelle or a cooking class. Minimize souvenir shopping; focus instead on collecting wonderful memories.

BEFORE YOU GO

You'll have a smoother trip if you tackle a few things ahead of time. For more details on these topics, see the Practicalities chapter and RickSteves.com, which has helpful travel-tip articles and videos.

Make sure your travel documents are valid. If your passport is due to expire within six months of your ticketed date of return, you need to renew it. Allow six weeks or more to renew or get a passport (www.travel.state.gov). Check for current Covid entry requirements, such as proof of vaccination or a negative Covid-19 test result.

Arrange your transportation. Book your international flights. Overall, Kayak.com is the best place to start searching for flights. If you'll be traveling beyond Paris, figure out your transportation options: bus or train (and either a rail pass or individual train tickets), rental car, or a cheap flight. (You can wing it in Europe, but it may cost more.) High-speed trains (TGVs—also called "InOui") in France require a seat reservation; book as early as possible, as seats fill fast. This is especially true if you're traveling with a rail pass.

Book rooms well in advance, especially if your trip falls during peak season or any major holidays or festivals.

Reserve ahead for key sights. At some sights (the Louvre, Sainte-Chapelle, Orangerie, and Versailles), advance reservations are required. While not technically required, advance reservations are also smart for the Eiffel Tower, Catacombs, and Conciergerie. Many of Paris' other top sights also sell tickets online. This is your best bet for avoiding long ticket-buying lines at the door.

Buy a Paris Museum Pass. If the pass makes sense for your trip (do the math), buy it online in advance, then use it to reserve timed-entry slots for covered sights.

Hire local guides in advance. Reserve ahead by email; popular guides can get booked up.

Consider travel insurance. Compare the cost of insurance to the cost of your potential loss. Check whether your existing insurance (health, homeowners, or renters) covers you and your possessions overseas.

Call your bank. Alert your bank that you'll be using your debit and credit cards in Europe. Ask about transaction fees, and, if you don't already have one, get a "contactless" credit card (request your card PIN too). You don't need to bring euros along; you can withdraw euros from cash machines in Europe.

Use your smartphone smartly. Sign up for an international service plan to reduce your costs, or rely on Wi-Fi in Europe instead. Download any apps you'll want on the road, such as maps, translators, and Rick Steves Audio Europe (see sidebar).

Pack light. You'll walk with your luggage more than you think. I travel for weeks with a single carry-on bag and a day pack. Use the packing checklist in the appendix as a guide.

Rick's Free Video Clips and Audio Tours

Travel smarter with these free, fun resources:

Rick Steves Classroom Europe, a powerful tool for teachers, is also useful for travelers. This video library contains about 500 short clips excerpted from my public television series. Enjoy these videos as you sort through options for your trip and to better understand what you'll see in Europe. Check it out at Classroom.RickSteves.com (just enter a topic to find everything I've filmed on a subject).

Rick Steves Audio Europe, a free app, makes it easy to download my audio tours and listen to them offline as you travel. For this book (look for the ∩), these audio tours include my Historic Paris Walk and Rue Cler Walk, and tours of the Louvre Museum, Orsay Museum, Père Lachaise Cemetery, and Versailles Palace. The app also offers interviews from my public radio show with experts from Europe and around the globe. Find it in your app store or at RickSteves.com/AudioEurope.

Navigating at the airport; sightseeing with a Paris Museum Pass; taking advantage of public transportation; enjoying a petite yet posh hotel room

Travel Smart

If you have a positive attitude, equip yourself with good information (this book), and expect to travel smart, you will.

Read—and reread—this book. To have an "A" trip, be an "A" student. Note opening hours of sights, closed days, crowd-beating tips, and whether reservations are required or advisable. Check the latest at RickSteves.com/update.

Be your own tour guide. As you travel in Paris and beyond, get up-to-date info on sights, reserve tickets and tours, recon-

firm hotels, and check transit connections. Visit local tourist information offices (TI).

Outsmart thieves. Pickpockets abound in crowded places where tourists congregate. Treat commotions as smoke-screens for theft. Keep your cash, credit cards, and passport secure in a money belt tucked under your clothes; carry only a day's spending money in your front pocket or wallet. Don't set valuable items down on counters or café tabletops, where they can be quickly stolen or easily forgotten.

Minimize potential loss. Keep expensive gear to a minimum. Bring copies or take photos of important documents (passport and cards) to aid in replacement if they're lost or stolen. Back up photos and files frequently.

Guard your time and energy. Taking a taxi or Uber can

be a good value if it saves you a long wait for a cheap bus or an exhausting walk across town. To avoid long lines, follow my crowd-beating tips, such as getting a Paris Museum Pass, making reservations or buying tickets in advance, or sightseeing early or late.

Be flexible. Even if you have a well-planned itinerary, expect changes, strikes, closures, sore feet, bad weather, and so on. Your Plan B could turn out to be even better.

Attempt the language. Many French people—especially in the tourist trade and in big cities like Paris—speak English, but if you learn some French, even just a few pleasantries, you'll get more smiles and make more friends. Apps such as Google Translate work for on-the-go translation help, but you

Follow the advice in this book to avoid waiting hours to get into Versailles. A small handwritten menu in French is often the sign of a good restaurant.

can get a head start by practicing the survival phrases near the end of this book.

Connect with the culture. Interacting with locals carbonates your experience. Enjoy the friendliness of the French people. The French adore enthusiastic reactions to their landscapes, sights, food, and wine. Ask questions; most locals are happy to point you in their idea of the right direction. Cheer for your favorite bowler at a *boules* match, leave no chair unturned in your quest for the best café, and find that perfect Eiffel Tower view. When an opportunity pops up, make it a habit to say "yes." Have a trip that's truly *magnifique*.

Paris...here you come!

ORIENTATION TO PARIS

Paris is magnificent, but it's also super-sized, crowded, and fast-paced. Take a deep breath, then use this orientation to the City of Light to help illuminate your trip. You'll tap into Paris' information sources for current events. Most importantly, you'll learn to navigate Paris by Métro, bus, taxi, bicycle, or on foot. With the proper approach and a measure of patience, you'll fall head over heels for Europe's cultural capital.

Paris is made up of 20 arrondissements (administrative districts) that spiral out from the center like an escargot shell. If your hotel's zip code is 75007, you know (from the last two digits) that it's in the 7th arrondissement. The city is peppered with Métro stops, and most Parisians locate addresses by the closest stop. So in Parisian jargon, the Eiffel Tower is on *la Rive Gauche* (the Left Bank) in the *7ème* (7th arrondissement),

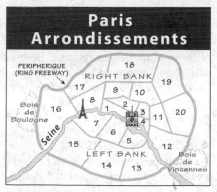

zip code 75007, Mo: Trocadéro (the nearest Métro stop).

As you're tracking down addresses, these words and pronunciations will help: arrondissement (ah-ro<u>h</u>n-dees-mah<u>n</u>), Métro (may-troh), *place* (plahs; square), *rue* (rew; road), *avenue* (ah-vuh-new), *boulevard* (bool-var), *pont* (pohn; bridge), and *carrefour* (kah-ruh-foor; intersection).

ORIENTATION

Overview

TOURIST INFORMATION

Paris' tourist offices (abbreviated as "TI" in this book, www.parisinfo.com) can provide useful information. They sell Museum Passes and individual tickets to sights but charge a small fee—but may have longer lines than the museums. TIs also sell tickets to local concerts and events.

The main TI is located at the **Hôtel de Ville** (daily 10:00-18:00, 29 Rue de Rivoli, on the north side of the building). You'll find smaller TIs at **Gare du Nord** (daily 8:00-18:00) and at the **Puces St. Ouen** flea market (Fri-Mon 9:45-13:00 & 14:00-18:00, closed Tue-Thu, 124 Rue des Rosiers). Both **airports** have handy TIs with long hours.

Event Listings: The weekly *L'Officiel des Spectacles* (available at any newsstand) is in French only but has easy-to-decipher listings of the most up-to-date museum hours, art exhibits, concerts, festivals, plays, movies, and nightclubs (for tips on deciphering the listings, see page 510). The *Paris Voice*, with snappy English-language reviews of concerts, plays, and current events, is available online-only at www.parisvoice.com.

ARRIVAL IN PARIS

For a comprehensive rundown of the city's train stations, airports, and options for parking, see the Paris Connections chapter.

HELPFUL HINTS

Theft Alert: Paris is safe in terms of violent crime but is filled with thieves and scammers who target tourists. Some are aggressive—particularly with smartphone theft. Don't be paranoid; just be smart. Keep your phone out of sight on Métro rides and in crowded places. Wherever there are crowds (especially of tourists) there are thieves at work. They thrive near famous

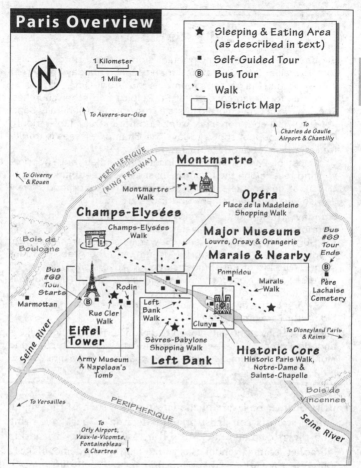

Paris Overview

Legend:
- ★ Sleeping & Eating Area (as described in text)
- ■ Self-Guided Tour
- Ⓑ Bus Tour
- Walk
- ☐ District Map

N

1 Kilometer
1 Mile

To Auvers-sur-Oise

To Giverny & Rouen

To Charles de Gaulle Airport & Chantilly

PERIPHERIQUE (RING FREEWAY)

Montmartre
Montmartre Walk

Opéra
Place de la Madeleine Shopping Walk

Champs-Elysées
Champs-Elysées Walk

Major Museums
Louvre, Orsay & Orangerie

Marais & Nearby
Pompidou
Marais Walk

Bus #69 Tour Ends

Bois de Boulogne

Bus #69 Tour Starts

Rodin

Marmottan

Rue Cler Walk

Eiffel Tower

Left Bank Walk

Cluny

Père Lachaise Cemetery

To Disneyland Paris & Reims

Army Museum & Napoleon's Tomb

Sèvres-Babylone Shopping Walk

Left Bank

Historic Core
Historic Paris Walk, Notre-Dame & Sainte-Chapelle

Bois de Vincennes

Seine River

PERIPHERIQUE

To Versailles

To Orly Airport, Vaux-le-Vicomte, Fontainebleau & Chartres

Seine River

monuments and on Métro and train lines that serve airports and high-profile tourist sights. Pickpockets work busy lines (e.g., at ticket windows at train stations). Look out for groups of young people who swarm around you (be very firm—even forceful—and walk away).

It's also smart to wear a money belt. Put your wallet in your front pocket, loop your day bag over your shoulders, and keep a tight hold on your purse or shopping bag.

Muggings are rare, but they do occur. If you're out late, avoid dark riverfront embankments and any place with dim lighting and few pedestrians.

Paris has taken action to combat crime by stationing police at monuments, on streets, and on the Métro, and installing security cameras at key sights.

Daily Reminder

Sunday: Free days at many popular sights attract hordes of visitors. Versailles is more crowded than usual on Sunday in any season, and when the garden's fountains run (April-Oct).

Look for organ concerts at St. Sulpice and other churches. The American Church often hosts a free concert (generally Sept-June at 17:30—but not every week and not in Dec). Luxembourg Garden has puppet shows today. The Champs-Elysées is traffic-free on the first Sunday of the month.

Most of Paris' stores are closed on Sunday, but shoppers will find relief along the Champs-Elysées, at street markets (until 13:00), at flea markets, and in the Marais neighborhood's lively Jewish Quarter, where many boutiques are open.

Monday: These sights are closed today: Orsay, Rodin, Cluny, Marmottan, Picasso, Carnavalet, Catacombs, Petit Palais, Victor Hugo's House, Quai Branly, Sewer Museum, Archaeological Crypt, Jewish Art and History Museum, and the Arab World Institute. Outside of Paris, most sights in Auvers-sur-Oise and all at Versailles are closed (but the gardens are open). The Louvre is jammed because of these closings.

Market streets such as Rue Cler, Rue des Martyrs, and Rue Mouffetard are dead today.

Tuesday: Many sights are closed today, including the Louvre, Orangerie, Pompidou, Delacroix, Montmartre, and Architecture and Monuments museums, as well as the châteaux of Chantilly (Nov-

Tourist Scams: Be aware of the latest tricks, such as the "found ring" scam (a con artist pretends to find a "pure gold" ring on the ground and offers to sell it to you) or the "friendship bracelet" scam (a vendor asks you to help with a demo, makes a bracelet on your arm that seems like it can't easily be removed, and then asks you to pay for it). Don't be intimidated. They are removed with the pull of a string.

Distractions by a stranger can be a smokescreen for theft. As you try to wriggle away from the pushy stranger, an accomplice picks your pocket. Be wary of a "salesman" monopolizing your attention, an "activist" asking you to sign a petition (and then bullying you into a contribution), someone posing as a deaf person to show you a small note to read, or a sidewalk hawker inviting you to play shell games (his accomplices are likely lurking nearby). Be skeptical of anything too good to be true, such as overly friendly people inviting you into impossibly friendly (or sexy) bars late at night.

Never agree to take a ride from strangers at train stations or airports. They may tell stories of problems with public transit—don't fall for it.

March) and Fontainebleau, and many sights in Auvers-sur-Oise. The Orsay and Versailles are crazy busy today. On Tuesdays in May-June, the fountains at Versailles come alive to music.

Wednesday: All sights are open. The weekly *L'Officiel des Spectacles* magazine comes out today. Most schools are closed, so kids' sights are busy, and puppet shows play in Luxembourg Garden. Some cinemas offer discounts.

Thursday: All sights are open. The Delacroix Museum is open until 21:00 on the first Thu of the month. Some department stores are open late.

Friday: All sights are open except the Grande Mosquée de Paris. Afternoon trains and roads leaving Paris are crowded. Restaurants are busy—it's smart to book ahead at popular places. Vaux-le-Vicomte hosts candlelit visits tonight (July-Aug).

Saturday: All sights are open except the Holocaust Memorial. The fountains run at Versailles (April-Oct), and Vaux-le-Vicomte hosts candlelit visits tonight (mid-May-Sept); otherwise, avoid weekend crowds at area châteaux and Impressionist sights. Department stores and popular shopping areas are jammed today. Paris' restaurants are packed; reserve in advance if you have a place in mind. Luxembourg Garden hosts puppet shows today.

Late-Night and Free Sights: For sights open late, see page 82. For free sights, see page 78.

To all these scammers, simply say "no" firmly and step away purposefully. For reports from my readers on the latest scams, go to https://community.ricksteves.com/travel-forum/tourist-scams.

Pedestrian Safety: Busy Parisian sidewalks are like freeways, so conduct yourself as if you were a foot-fueled car: Stick to your lane, look to the left before passing a slow-moving pedestrian, and if you need to stop, look for a safe place to pull over.

When crossing the street, look both ways and be careful of seemingly quiet bus/taxi/bike lanes. Parisian drivers are notorious for ignoring pedestrians. Don't assume you have the right of way, even in a crosswalk. Keep your pace constant and don't stop suddenly. By law, drivers are allowed to miss pedestrians by up to just one meter—a little more than three feet (1.5 meters in the countryside). Drivers calculate your speed so they won't hit you, provided you don't alter your route or pace. Speed limits are around 30 kilometers per hour (about 19 miles per hour) on all city streets.

Be mindful of cyclists as you cross, too. Cyclists ride in specially marked bike lanes on wide sidewalks and can also use lanes reserved for buses and taxis. Bikes commonly go against traffic, so always look both ways, even on one-way streets.

Medical Help: There are many English-speaking resources for medical help in Paris, including doctors who will visit your hotel. For a list, see the Practicalities chapter.

Smart Sightseeing: Most big Paris sights sell tickets in advance online, saving you time by not having to wait in ticket-buying lines (though you may still have to wait in a security line). At some sights, you are required to buy ahead, including the Louvre, Orangerie, Sainte-Chapelle, and Versailles. A Paris Museum Pass can also help you skip the line at some sights (and can also be purchased in advance). For more on these options, see "Sightseeing Strategies" in the Sights in Paris chapter.

Useful Apps: Gogo Paris reviews trendy places to eat, drink, relax, and sleep in Paris (www.gogocityguides.com/paris).

🎧 For free audio versions of some of the self-guided tours in this book (the Historic Paris Walk and Rue Cler Walk, and tours of the Louvre Museum, Orsay Museum, Père Lachaise Cemetery, and Versailles Palace), get the **Rick Steves Audio Europe** app (see the sidebar on page 24).

Bookstores: Paris has several English-language bookstores. My favorites include **Shakespeare and Company** (some used travel books, daily 10:00-22:00, 37 Rue de la Bûcherie, across the river from Notre-Dame, Mo: St-Michel, +33 1 43 25 40 93); **Smith&Son** (Mon-Sat 9:00-19:00, Sun 12:30-19:00, near the Tuileries at 248 Rue de Rivoli, Mo: Concorde, +33 1 44 77 88 99); **Abbey Bookshop** (Mon-Sat 10:00-19:00, closed Sun, near the Cluny at 29 Rue de la Parcheminerie, Mo: Cluny La Sorbonne, +33 1 46 33 16 24); and **San Francisco Book Company** (used books only, Thu-Tue 10:00-20:00, closed Wed), north of Luxembourg Garden at 17 Rue Monsieur le Prince, Mo: Odéon, +33 1 43 29 15 70).

Baggage Storage: Lockers are available at some train stations (see the Paris Connections chapter) and several **City Locker** locations in central Paris (daily 8:00-22:00, book ahead, details at www.citylocker.paris).

Public WCs: Some public toilets are free but you get what you pay for. If it's a pay toilet, the price will be clearly indicated, and the facility should be clean (thank the person who cleans). If there's an attendant, it's polite and sometimes required to leave a tip of €0.20-0.50. Booth-like toilets along the sidewalks provide both relief and a memory (don't leave small children inside unattended). Restrooms in museums are free and the best you'll find. Bold travelers can walk into any sidewalk café like they own the place and find the WC. Or do as the locals do—order a shot of espresso *(un café)* while standing at the café bar (then use the WC with a clear conscience). Keep toilet paper or tissues with you, as some WCs are poorly stocked.

Tobacco Stands *(Tabacs):* These little kiosks—usually just a counter inside a café—are handy and very local. Many sell public-transit passes, postage stamps (though not all sell international postage), and...oh yeah, cigarettes. (For more on this slice of Parisian life, see page 232.) To find a kiosk, just look for a *Tabac* sign and the red cylinder-shaped symbol above certain cafés.

GETTING AROUND PARIS

Paris is easy to navigate. Your basic choices are Métro (in-city subway), suburban train (commonly called RER—rapid transit tied into the Métro system), public bus, and taxi or Uber. Several tram (light rail) lines run at street level, using the same passes as the bus and Métro, but most travelers will find little use for them. Also consider the hop-on, hop-off bus and boat tours (described under "Tours in Paris," later).

Public Transit Information: The Métro, RER/suburban train, and public bus systems, all administered by RATP, share one helpful website: www.ratp.fr. The free RATP mobile app **(Bonjour RATP)** has a real-time journey planner, lets you buy and top up tickets and passes, can help you locate the best Métro station exit, and can tell you when the next bus will arrive (in English).

Public-Transit Cards and Passes

The following ticket options cover transit on the Métro, public buses, and the RER/suburban train. Paper tickets are being phased out and replaced with plastic Navigo travel cards. Transit users will need to choose one of these two good options (the Navigo Découverte weekly pass is a particularly good value):

Navigo Easy Card: This reloadable €2 card, available at any Métro station, is the easiest option for most tourists. You can add funds to your Navigo Easy card and pay as you ride (€1.90/ride, less for children under 10), or load the card with a 10-ride pass or day pass.

If your rides will be limited to central Paris (Zones 1-2), the 10-ride pass *("Navigo avec un carnet")* is a good deal at €14.90. Frequent riders may want to consider a day pass **(Navigo Jour),** which expires at midnight and costs €7.50 for Zones 1-2. To reach destinations outside Zones 1-2, you can add zones to your day pass

(€12.40 for Zones 1-4, covers regional destinations like Versailles; €17.80 for Zones 1-5, covers airports and farther-flung destinations like Fontainebleau and Vaux-le-Vicomte).

A Navigo Easy card can be shared between travelers, but not for the same journey (in other words, you can't hand the card to your travel partner across the turnstile). No photo is required, but make sure your card is loaded with enough euros to cover multiple fares.

To use your Navigo card at the Métro turnstile, touch the card to the purple pad, wait for the green validation light and the "ding," and you're on your way.

Navigo Découverte Pass: This chip-embedded card comes in weekly or monthly versions. The weekly version is an amazing value and generally pays for itself after three days of typical sightseeing. The card itself requires a one-time €5 fee and a photo (can be taken for €5 at photo booths in major Métro stations; otherwise bring a postage-stamp sized photo of yourself, such as a passport photo). The weekly unlimited pass costs about €23 and covers all forms of transit from Monday to Sunday (expires on Sunday at midnight, even if you buy it on, say, a Thursday). It's good for all zones in the Paris region, which means that you can travel anywhere within the city center, out to the châteaux of Versailles, Vaux-le-Vicomte, and Fontainebleau, to Disneyland Paris, and to Charles de Gaulle and Orly airports (except on Orlyval trains).

Buying and Loading a Navigo Card: You can buy your Navigo Easy or Découverte card at any staffed Métro station and at many *tabacs* (for locations, see the RATP website). The Vianavigo smartphone app lets you top up your Navigo Easy card, but it's just as easy to use the machines inside Métro stations. Smaller Métro stations may not have staff on hand to sell new cards, but all stations have machines to reload a Navigo Easy card. Some machines accept only credit cards and coins, though key stations have machines that take small bills of €20 or less (some American cards are accepted—try). These machines work logically, with easy-to-follow instructions in English.

RER stations sell the Découverte pass, which covers transport between Paris and many regional destinations (including airports).

Contactless Tickets and Passes: As an alternative to a physical ticket or Navigo card, you can buy a digital version on the RATP app and store it on your smartphone. You'll then hold your smartphone over the card reader to enter the Métro or board a bus. For details see www.ratp.fr.

Other Transit Passes: You'll see **Paris Visite** passes, but Navigo passes are a far better value. If you are under 26 and in Paris on a Saturday or Sunday, you can buy an unlimited daily transit pass called **Ticket Jeunes Week-end** for the unbeatable price of €4.10.

By Métro

In Paris, you're never more than a 10-minute walk from a Métro station. Europe's best subway system allows you to hop from sight to sight quickly and cheaply (runs 5:30-1:00 in the morning, Fri-Sat until 2:00 in the morning). Learn to use it. Begin by studying the color Métro map at the back of this book.

Using the Métro System: To get to your destination, determine the closest "Mo" stop and which line or lines will get you there. Lines are color-coded and numbered. You can tell their direction by the end-of-the-line stops. For example, the La Défense/Château de Vincennes line, also known as line 1 (yellow), runs between La Défense on its west end and Vincennes on its east end. Once in the Métro station, you'll see the color-coded line numbers and/or blue-and-white signs directing you to the train going in your direction (e.g., *direction: La Défense*). Scan your Navi-go card at the turnstile (watch others and imitate). Fare inspectors regularly  check for cheaters, accept absolutely no excuses, and have portable credit card machines to fine you €60 on the spot.

Be prepared to walk significant distances within Métro stations (especially when you transfer). Transfers are free and can be made wherever lines cross, provided you do so within 1.5 hours and don't exit the station. When you transfer, follow the appropriately colored line number and end-of-the-line stop to find your next train, or look for *Correspondance* (Connection) signs that lead to your next line.

When you reach your destination, blue-and-white *Sortie* signs point you to the exit. Before leaving the station, check the helpful *Plan du quartier* (map of the neighborhood) to get your bearings. At stops with several *sorties*, save time by choosing the best exit.

Métro Resources: Métro maps are in this book, free at Métro stations, online at www.ratp.fr, and included on freebie Paris maps at your hotel.

Beware of Pickpockets: Thieves dig public transit. You'll hear regular announcements in the Métro to beware of *les pickpockets* (smartphones are the most popular target). Keep nothing of value in your pockets, tuck your smartphone out of sight, and take care when buying tickets (watch your back). Be especially aware as you pass through the turnstile—if your pocket is picked, you end up stuck on the wrong side while the thief gets away. Stand away from Métro doors to avoid being a target for a theft-and-run just be-

Transit Basics

- Download the RATP app for real-time transit info.
- Buy a Navigo Easy card or Navigo Découverte pass. These are good on the Métro, RER trains (within the city), and city buses.
- Scan your card at the turnstile or on the bus: Touch it to the purple pad and wait for the green validation light.
- Beware of pickpockets, and don't buy tickets (often fake) from people roaming the stations.
- Find your train by its end-of-the-line stop.
- Safeguard your belongings; avoid standing near the train doors with luggage.
- At a stop, the door may open automatically. If it doesn't, open the door by either pushing a square button (green or black) or lifting a metal latch.
- Transfers (*correspondances*) between the Métro and RER trains are free (but not between Métro/suburban trains and buses).

Etiquette

- When your train arrives, board only after everyone leaving the car has made it out the door.
- Avoid using the hinged seats near the doors when the car is crowded; they take up valuable standing space.
- Always offer your seat to the elderly, those with disabilities, and pregnant women.
- Talk softly in cars. Notice how quietly Parisians communicate (if at all) and follow their lead.

fore the doors close. Any jostling or commotion—especially when boarding or leaving trains—is likely the sign of a thief or a team of thieves in action. Make any fare inspector show proof of identity (ask locals for help if you're not certain). Keep your bag close and never show anyone your wallet.

By Suburban Train (RER)

The RER/suburban train is an arm of the Métro, serving outlying destinations such as Versailles, Disneyland Paris, and Paris airports. Traditionally called RER (which you'll see on signage), it's also referred to as simply "Train." These routes are indicated by thick lines on your subway map and identified by the letters A-K

ORIENTATION

- When standing, hold on to the bar with one hand, leaving room for others while stabilizing yourself so you don't tumble or step on anyone.
- If you find yourself blocking the door at a stop, step out of the car to let others off, then get back on.
- Métro doors close automatically. Don't try to hold open the door for late-boarding passengers.
- On escalators and stairs, keep to the right and pass on the left.

Key Words

French	English
station de Métro (stah-see-ohn duh may-troh)	Métro stop/station
direction (dee-rehk-see-ohn)	direction
ligne (leen-yuh)	line
A, B, C, D, E, F, G, H, I, J, K (ah, bay, say, day, euh, eff, zhay, ahsh, ee, zhee, kah)	A, B, C, D, E, F, G, H, I, J, K
correspondance (koh-rehs-pohn-dahns)	connection/transfer
sortie (sor-tee)	exit
Navigo Découverte (nah-vee-goh day-coo-vehrt)	transit pass valid one week or one month
Pardon, madame/monsieur. (par-dohn, mah-dahm/muhs-yuh)	Excuse me, ma'am/sir.
Je descends. (zhuh day-sahn)	I'm getting off.
Rendez-moi mon porte-monnaie! (rahn-day-mwah mohn port-moh-nay)	Give me back my wallet!

(see pronunciations in the "Transit Basics" sidebar). Throughout this book, I refer to this train system as "RER."

Within the city center, the RER works like the Métro; it can even be speedier if it serves your destination directly, because it makes fewer stops. Unlike the Métro, not every RER train stops at every station along the way; check the sign or screen over the platform to see if your destination is listed as a stop (*"toutes les gares"* means it makes all stops along the way) or confirm with a fellow passenger before you board.

Métro passes are good on the RER; you can transfer between the Métro and RER systems with the same Navigo pass. But to travel outside the city (to Versailles or the airport, for example), you'll need to have a Navigo Découverte or Navigo Jour pass, or buy a separate ticket. The Navigo Découverte covers all area train trips, including to the airport and Versailles.

By City Bus

Paris' excellent bus system is worth figuring out. Buses require less walking and fewer stairways than the Métro, and you can see Paris unfold as you travel. Sure, they don't seem as romantic as the famous Métro and are subject to traffic jams—but savvy travelers know that buses can have you swinging through the city like Tarzan in an urban jungle.

Bus Stops: Stops are everywhere, and most come with a good city bus map, route maps for each bus that stops there, a frequency chart and schedule, live displays showing the time the next bus will arrive, a *plan du quartier* map of the immediate neighborhood, and a *soirées* map explaining night service, if available (there are even phone chargers at some locations). Bus-system maps are also available in any Métro station (and in the *Paris*  *Pratique par Arrondissement* booklet sold at newsstands). For longer stays, consider buying the *Paris Urbain* book of transit info, including bus routes.

Using the Bus System: Buses use the same Navigo cards as the Métro and RER. Be sure to buy your card before boarding the bus (available at Métro stations and *tabacs*).

When a bus approaches, wave to the driver to indicate that you want to be picked up. Board through the front door. (Families with strollers can use any doors—the ones in the center of the bus are wider. To open the middle or back doors on long buses, push the green button located by those doors.) Scan your Navigo card on the purple touchpad, then keep track of which stop is coming up next by following the onboard stop display and route diagrams or listening to recorded announcements. When you're ready to get off, push the red button to signal you want a stop, then exit through the central or rear door. Even if you're not certain you've figured out the system, do some joyriding. I always check the bus stop near my hotel to see if it's convenient to my sightseeing plans.

More Bus Tips: Avoid rush hour (Mon-Fri 8:00-9:30 & 17:30-19:30), when buses are jammed and traffic doesn't move. While the Métro shuts down at about 1:00 in the morning (even later Fri-Sat), some buses continue much later (called *Noctilien* lines, www.ratp.fr/en—select "Getting Around" from the drop-

Hop on the Bus, Gus

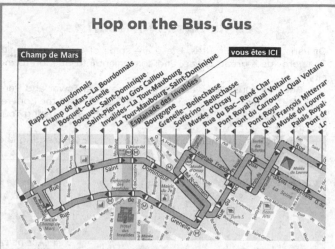

Just like the Métro, every bus stop has a name, and every bus is headed to one end-of-the-line stop or the other. This graphic shows the route map posted at the Invalides stop for bus #69.

First, find the stop on the chart—it says *"vous êtes ICI"* ("you are HERE") at Esplanade des Invalides. Next, find your destination stop—let's say Bosquet-Grenelle, located a few stops to the west. Now, find out exactly where to catch the bus going in that direction. On the route map, notice the triangle-shaped arrows pointing in the direction the bus is headed. You'll see that Esplanade des Invalides has two different bus stops—one for buses headed east, one for those going west. If you want to go west to Bosquet-Grenelle, head for that street corner to catch the bus. (One-way streets in Paris make it easy to get on the bus in the wrong direction.)

When the bus pulls up, double-check that the sign on the front of the bus has the end-of-the-line stop going in your direction—to "Champ de Mars," in this case.

down menu, then "Getting Around at Night"). Not all city buses are air-conditioned, so they can become rolling greenhouses on summer days. Navigo Easy card holders can transfer from one bus to another on the same fare (within 1.5 hours). However, you can't do a round-trip or hop on and off on the same line using the same fare. You can use the same fare to transfer between buses and trams, but you can't transfer between the bus and Métro/RER suburban train systems (it'll take two fares). Before you board the bus, check the screen on the front: If the line number appears with a slash, it means the bus does not go to the end of line (called *service partiel*).

Scenic Buses for Tourists

Of Paris' many bus routes, these are some of the most scenic. They provide a great, cheap, and convenient introduction to the city.

Bus #69 runs east-west between the Eiffel Tower and Père Lachaise Cemetery by way of Rue Cler, Quai d'Orsay, the Louvre, Ile St. Louis, and the Marais. 📖 See the Bus #69 Sightseeing Tour chapter.

Bus #63 is another good east-west route, connecting the

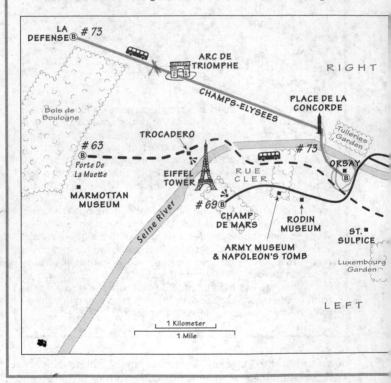

By Uber

Uber works in Paris like it does at home, and in general works better than taxis. Drivers are nicer and more flexible than taxi drivers, although prices are roughly the same as taxis. You can generally get a car wherever you are within five minutes, and you don't have to track down a taxi stand; you can also text the driver if you don't see the car. Uber is less appealing in two instances: During rush hour, when taxis can use taxi/bus lanes while Uber drivers sit in traffic, and to get from Paris' airports to the city center (taxis have flat rates

Marmottan Museum, Trocadéro (Eiffel Tower), Pont de l'Alma, Orsay Museum, St. Sulpice Church, Luxembourg Garden, Latin Quarter/Panthéon, and Gare de Lyon.

Bus #73 is one of Paris' most scenic lines, starting at the Orsay Museum and running westbound around Place de la Concorde, then up the Champs-Elysées, around the Arc de Triomphe, and down Avenue Charles de Gaulle to La Défense and beyond.

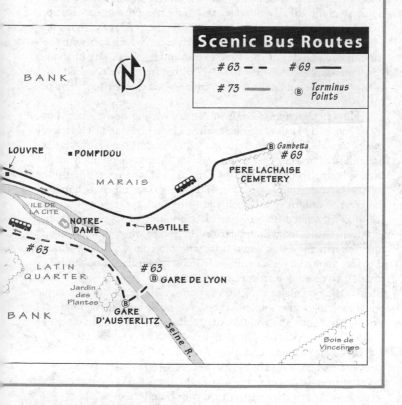

and designated pick-up areas; Uber uses dynamic pricing and you'll need to arrange a pick-up point).

By Taxi

Parisian taxis are reasonable, especially for couples and families. The meters are tamper-proof. Fares and supplements (described in English on the rear windows) are straightforward and tightly regulated. Cabbies are legally required to accept four passengers, though they don't always like it. If you have five in your group, you can book a larger taxi in advance (your hotelier can call), or try your luck at a taxi stand. A surcharge may be applied for a fifth rider. For tips on getting to and from Paris' airports by taxi, see the Paris Connections chapter.

Rates: The meter starts at €2.60 with a minimum charge of €7.30. A typical 20-minute ride (such as Bastille to the Eiffel Tower) costs about €25 (versus about €2/person on the Métro or bus). While drivers should accept credit cards, they prefer cash, and some will claim that their credit card machine isn't working in order to be paid in cash. Taxis drivers charge higher rates at rush hour, at night, all day Sunday, and for extra passengers. To tip, round up to the next euro (at least €0.50). The A, B, or C lights on a taxi's rooftop sign correspond to hourly rates, which vary with the time of day and day of the week (for example, the A rate of about €36/hour applies Mon-Sat 10:00-17:00). Tired travelers need not bother with the subtle differences in fares—if you need a cab, take it.

How to Catch *un Taxi*: You can try waving down a taxi, but it's often easier to ask someone for the nearest taxi stand (*"Où est une station de taxi?"*; oo ay ewn stah-see-ohn duh tahk-see). Taxi stands are indicated by a circled "T" on good city maps and on many maps in this book. To order a taxi in English, call the reservation line for the G7 cab company (+33 1 41 27 66 99), or ask your hotelier or server to call for you. When you summon a taxi by phone, a set fee of €4 is applied for an immediate booking or €7 for reserving in advance (this fee will appear on the meter when they pick you up). You can also book a taxi using the cab company's app, which provides approximate wait times (surcharge similar to booking by phone). To download an app, search for either "Taxi G7" or "Taxis Bleus" (the two major companies, both available in English; note when entering your mobile number, you must include the international access code and your country code—use "+1" before the area code for a US/Canadian phone number).

Taxis are tough to find during rush hour, when it's raining, on weekend nights, or on any night after the Métro closes. If you need to catch an early morning train or flight, book a taxi the day before (especially for weekday departures; your hotelier can help).

By Bike

Paris is surprisingly easy by bicycle. The city is flat, and riders have access to more than 370 miles of bike lanes and many of the priority lanes for buses and taxis (be careful on these). You can rent from a bike-rental shop or use the city-operated Vélib' bikes (best for short rides—explained later).

Though I wouldn't use bikes to get around routinely (traffic is a bit too intense), they're perfect for a joyride away from busy streets, especially on the riverside promenades. Bike-rental shops

also have good route sug-
gestions. For information
on bike tours—a safe way
to sightsee with a group—
see "Tours in Paris," later.

Urban bikers will
find Paris a breeze. First-
timers will get the hang of
it quickly enough by fol-
lowing some simple rules.
Always stay to the right in your lane, bike single-file, stay off sidewalks, watch out for opening doors on parked cars, signal with your
arm before making turns, and use bike paths when available. Obey
the traffic laws as if you were driving a car, with two exceptions:
When passing vehicles or other bikes, always pass on the left (it's
illegal to pass on the right); and where there is no stoplight, always
yield to traffic merging from the right, even if you're on a major
road and the merging driver is on a side street. Use the bell on your
bike to warn pedestrians who don't see you.

Sundays are peaceful for pedaling, when the city's "Paris Re-
spire" program opens up some streets to cyclists and rollerblad-
ers (cars are banned) from 9:00 to 18:00. Participating neighborhoods include the Marais, Montmartre, the Champs-Elysées, the
Rue Mouffetard area east of Luxembourg Garden, and the Rue
Daguerre area (near the Denfert Rochereau Métro station). Also
open exclusively to nonmotorized traffic (and described on page
67) are roads along the Seine's left and right banks. Neighborhood
bike-path maps are available at www.paris.fr/parisrespire. The TIs
have a helpful "Paris à Vélo" map, which shows all dedicated bike
paths. Many other versions are available for sale at newsstand kiosks, some bookstores, and department stores.

Rental Bikes: The following companies rent bikes to individuals and offer general tips about cycling in Paris.

Bike About Tours is your best bet for bike rental, with good
information and kid-friendly solutions such as baby seats, tandem attachments, and kid-sized bikes. Their office/café, Le Peloton, offers bikes, tours, and artisan coffee (bike rental-€20/day
if used during office hours, €25/24 hours, includes lock and helmet, daily 9:30-17:30, shop/café near Hôtel de Ville at 17 Rue du
Pont Louis Philippe—see map on page 112, Mo: St-Paul, mobile
+33 6 18 80 84 92,

Fat Tire Tours has a limited supply of bikes for rent, so call
ahead to check availability (€4/hour, €25/24 hours, includes lock
and helmet, photo ID and credit-card required for deposit; RS%—
€2/day rental discount with this book, 2-discount maximum; office
open daily 9:00-18:30, bike rental only after 11:00 as priority is

Guide to Vélib' City Bike Rental Program

Paris scatters bikes at racks across town so locals and tourists can borrow bikes and drop them off at other racks across town. Vélib' bikes are accessible 24/7 and are free for the first half-hour (designed to discourage car use for short trips); you pay a small fee for longer rentals. Most stations accept credit cards (look for a € sign), or you can reserve online.

Renting a Vélib' Bike: Though you can head straight to a ticket machine at the bike racks, it's easy to reserve bikes online on the free and easy-to-use Vélib' app or at www.velib-metropole.fr. Create an account and input your credit card information. You'll pay €3 for 45 minutes (regular or electric bike), then €0.50 per 30 minutes after that. A 24-hour rental is €5 for a regular bike and €10 for an electric bike (longer rentals possible).

When you're ready to choose a bike, check its condition (make sure it has handgrips, etc.). A seat turned backward indicates a broken bike. If you get a bad bike, return it and take another. Adjust your seat for comfort. Take advantage of the three speeds and lock (just stick it in and remove the key). Be careful riding in Paris traffic. Vélib' provides no bike helmets (and I've never seen anyone wearing one in Paris).

Returning Your Bike: Find the handiest rack with empty stalls. Simply plug your bike into an empty stall and be sure it engages. Wait 10 seconds. The station's red light will turn green and emit two beeps to indicate you've returned the bike successfully. If the machine makes rude noises, pull out the bike and stick it in again. (If the machine fails to register the bike's return, you'll be charged €150 for stealing it.)

Vélib' Biking Tips: The Vélib' app uses GPS to track nearby rack locations and shows which have available bikes and spaces (important information, since racks are often full or empty).

Bon voyage!

given to those taking a tour, near the Eiffel Tower at 24 Rue Edgar Faure—see map on page 76, Mo: Dupleix or La Motte-Picquet-Grenelle, +33 1 82 88 80 96, www.fattiretours.com/paris).

Vélib' Bikes: The city's Vélib' program (from *vélo* + *libre* = "bike freedom") scatters thousands of bikes at racks across town for use by locals and tourists alike (see sidebar). This is a great option for one-way trips or rentals of a few hours or less; pricing is structured to discourage longer use. For longer rentals, try one of the companies I list earlier.

Lime Bikes (and Scooters): You can rent bikes—and even electric scooters—with the easy-to-use Lime Bike app. Scooters also have the right to use bike and bus lanes, but be careful—the

ORIENTATION

scooters are quick to accelerate and easy to fall from. Sidewalks are off limits (€135 fine) and pickup and drop-off locations are limited.

Tours in Paris

∩ To sightsee on your own, download my **free audio tours** that illuminate some of Paris' top sights and neighborhoods, including the Historic Paris and Rue Cler walks, and tours of the Louvre Museum, Orsay Museum, Père Lachaise Cemetery, and Versailles Palace (for details, see the sidebar on page 24). Some tour companies offer a discount when you show this book (indicated in these listings with the abbreviation "RS%").

BY BUS

Paris has a variety of bus tours, but the cheapest way to see the city by bus is simply to hop on **city bus #69** and follow my Bus #69 Sightseeing Tour (see that chapter).

Hop-On, Hop-Off Bus Tours

Several companies offer double-decker bus services connecting Paris' main sights, giving you an easy once-over of the city with a basic recorded commentary. Buses normally run from about 9:30-19:00 in high season. You can hop off at any stop, tour a sight, then hop on a later bus. It's dang scenic—if you get a top-deck seat and the weather's decent. But because of traffic and stops, these buses are sloooow. (Busy sightseers will do better using the Métro.) On the plus side, because the buses move so slowly, you have time to read my sight descriptions, making this a decent orientation tour—and there's free Wi-Fi on board. Buy tickets from the driver or online.

TootBus has several ticket options with reasonably frequent service on a well-designed, 10-stop route covering central Paris. You can catch the bus at just about any major sight (look for the TootBus icon on public transit bus shelters and signs). Tickets are valid only for the days you purchase them, so get started early (1 day-€39, 2-hour "express tour"-€25, +33 1 42 66 56 56, www.tootbus.com).

Big Bus Paris runs a fleet of buses around Paris with recorded narration—or use their better free app for sight descriptions (1 day-€36, 2 days-€41 (€50 with Seine river

ORIENTATION

cruise), kids 4-12-€19, cheaper online, +33 1 53 95 39 53, www.
bigbustours.com).

Paris City Vision, TootBus, and **Big Bus Paris** all offer
nighttime bus tours. For details, see page 518 in the Entertainment
chapter.

BY BOAT
Seine Cruises

Several companies run one-hour boat cruises on the Seine. A typical cruise loops back and forth between the Eiffel Tower and Pont

d'Austerlitz, and drops you off
where you started. For a fun
experience, cruise at twilight or
after dark. (To dine while you
cruise, see page 464.) The first
three companies are convenient
to Rue Cler hotels and run daily
year-round (April-Oct 10:00-
22:30, 2-3/hour; Nov-March
shorter hours, runs hourly).
Check their websites for discounts.

Bateaux-Mouches cruises depart from Pont de l'Alma's right
bank and have the biggest open-top, double-decker boats (higher
up means better views). But this company caters to tour groups,
making their boats jammed and noisy (€14, kids 4-12-€6, +33 1 42
25 96 10, www.bateaux-mouches.fr).

Bateaux Parisiens has smaller boats with audioguides, fewer
crowds, and only one deck. Skip this cruise if the boat lacks an
outdoor deck. It leaves from right in front of the Eiffel Tower (€17,
kids 3-12-€7, +33 1 76 64 14 45, www.bateauxparisiens.com).

Vedettes de Paris boats also anchor below the Eiffel Tower
and offer good outdoor seating on most of their boats plus a small
bar onboard. Their options include a one-way trip that drops off
near Notre-Dame, or a round-trip with time to get out and explore the Notre-Dame area for a half-hour (€15 standard one-hour
cruise, €15 one-way, €18 round-trip with stop at Notre-Dame, +33
1 44 18 19 50, www.vedettesdeparis.fr).

Vedettes du Pont Neuf offers essentially the same one-hour
tour as the other companies with smaller boats; it starts and ends at
Pont Neuf, closer to recommended hotels in the Marais and Luxembourg Garden neighborhoods. The boats feature a live guide
whose delivery (in English and French) may be as stiff as a recorded
narration (€13, kids 4-12-€6, tip requested, nearly 2/hour, daily
10:30-22:30, +33 1 46 33 98 38, www.vedettesdupontneuf.com).

Canauxrama runs a variety of relaxing cruises (with live commentary) on the Seine or along the tranquil Canal St. Martin (€20, check online for routes, +33 1 42 39 15 00, www.canauxrama.com).

Hop-On, Hop-Off Boat Tour

Batobus allows you to get on and off as often as you like at any of eight popular stops along the Seine. Boats make a continuous circuit and stop in this order: Eiffel Tower, Invalides, Orsay Museum, St. Germain-des-Prés, Notre-Dame, Jardin des Plantes, Hôtel de Ville, the Louvre, and Pont Alexandre III, near the Champs-Elysées (1 day-€17, 2 days-€19, April-Aug boats run every 20 minutes 10:00-21:30, Sept-March every 25 minutes 10:00-19:00, 45 minutes one-way, 1.5-hour round-trip, www.batobus.com). This is fun as a scenic, floating alternative to the Métro, but if you just want a guided boat tour, the Seine cruises described earlier are a better choice.

ON FOOT

Walking Tours

For food-oriented walking tours, see page 450.

Paris Walks offers a variety of thoughtful and entertaining two-hour walks, led by British and American guides (€15-25, generally 2/day—morning and afternoon, private tours available, family-friendly and Louvre tours are a specialty, check current offerings online, +33 1 48 09 21 40, www.paris-walks.com, paris@paris-walks.com). Tours focus on the Marais, Montmartre, St. Germain-des-Prés, and the medieval Latin Quarter, with themes spanning the Occupation and Resistance, the Revolution, and Hemmingway's Paris (all tours must be reserved in advance, best by email). No advance payment is required for general tours, but for specialty tours—such as the Louvre, the Orsay, fashion, or chocolate—you'll prepay with a credit card when you reserve (deposits are nonrefundable).

Context Travel offers private and small group walking tours for travelers serious about learning. Led by historians, architects, and academics, tours range from traditional topics (French art history in the Louvre, Gothic architecture of Notre-Dame, etc.) to thematic explorations (immigration and the changing face of Paris, jazz in the Latin Quarter, history of the baguette, and more). Book in advance—groups are limited to six (from €120/person, does not include sight admissions, generally 3 hours but can last multiple days, US +1 800 691 6036, www.contexttravel.com). They also offer excursions to Versailles, Giverny, and the Loire Valley.

Fat Tire Tours offers high-on-fun and casual walking tours. Their two-hour Classic Paris Walking Tour covers most major sights (usually Mon, Wed, and Fri at 10:00 or 15:00). They also offer neighborhood walks of Ile de la Cité, Montmartre, Père

ORIENTATION

Connecting with the Culture

Paris hosts more visitors than any other city in the world, and with such a robust tourism industry, many travelers feel cut off from "real life" in the City of Light. Fortunately, Paris offers *beaucoup* ways for you to connect with locals—and thereby make your trip more personal...and more memorable.

Staying with a family is a simple way to experience everyday Parisian life firsthand. Several agencies set up **bed-and-breakfast** stays in private homes (listed in the Sleeping in Paris chapter). Or use a service like Airbnb to stay in a private room. Other opportunities abound:

Meeting the Locals

I'm amazed at the number of groups that help travelers meet locals. These get good reviews:

Meeting the French puts travelers in touch with Parisians who offer specialty tours, help organizing your trip—from soup to nuts— and more (fees vary by activity, +33 1 42 51 19 80, www.meetingthefrench. com).

Paris Greeter is an all-volunteer organization that connects travelers with English-speaking Parisians who want to share their knowledge of the city. These volunteer "guides" act as informal companions who can show you "their Paris"—it's like seeing Paris through the eyes of a friend. The tours are free (though donations are welcome); sign up five weeks before your visit (shorter lead times may be possible, www.greeters.paris).

The American Church and Franco-American Center, an interdenominational church in the Rue Cler neighborhood, offers many services for travelers wanting to connect with Parisian culture. The Thursday-evening English/French language exchange (18:00-19:30) is a handy way to meet locals who want to improve their English. It's free and relaxed—just show up. You'll chat with Parisians, who will respond in their best English. English-language worship services are held every Sunday (at 11:00, contemporary service at 14:00). The coffee hour after each service and the free Sunday concerts (generally Sept-June at 17:30, but not every week and not in Dec) are a good way to meet the very international congregation (church reception open Mon-Sat 9:00-12:30 & 13:30-22:00, Sun 8:30-19:00, 65 Quai d'Orsay, Mo: Invalides, +33 1 40 62 05 00, www.acparis.org).

Lost in Frenchlation offers weekly screenings of French films with English subtitles for Paris veterans looking to immerse themselves in the city's cultural scene. Venues vary from the elegant Champs-Elysées theater, Club de l'Étoile, to L'Entrepôt—a small, independent cultural space of three art-house screening rooms, a restaurant, a garden, a cocktail bar, and an art gallery. Screenings are preceded by a happy hour, during which you can connect with locals and travelers alike. After the screenings, the venue hosts Q&As with the film crews (€7-10, discounts for students and seniors, buy tickets online in advance or at the door, +33 6 67 33 39 75, www.lostinfrenchlation.com).

Cooking Schools and Wine Tastings: It's easy to hook up with small cooking schools and wine-tasting classes that provide an unthreatening and personal experience (see page 450).

Language Classes: You're at *Kilomètre Zéro* of the French language—where better to take a class? French-language classes are offered for all levels, and class size is usually small. **Alliance Française** has the best reputation and good variety of courses (101 Boulevard Raspail, +33 1 42 84 90 00, www.alliancefr.org). **France Langue** provides intensive classes on a weekly basis, some focusing on topics like wine, sports, business, or culture (+33 1 80 05 21 32 or +33 1 80 05 20 92, www.france-langue.fr). **Le Français Face à Face** runs one-on-one intensive French courses with total immersion (based in Angers, mobile +33 6 66 60 00 63, www.lefrancaisfaceaface.com).

Meeting the Americans

Long-term American residents can give you surprisingly keen insight into life in Paris.

The American Church and Franco-American Center is the community center for Americans living in Paris (see previous page).

The American Library, in the Rue Cler neighborhood, offers free programs and events for adults and children (10 Rue du Général Camou, Mo: Ecole Militaire, +33 1 53 59 12 60, www.americanlibraryinparis.org).

WICE (Women in Continuing Education) is a nonprofit association that provides an impressive array of cultural and educational programs in English for those eager to master the art of living in France. Check their schedule at www.wice-paris.org, or call +33 1 45 66 75 50.

Meetup connects people in cities around the world, whether they are in town for a day or longer. Sponsored events include picnics, group sports, museum tours, cocktail evenings, and more. This is a particularly good tool for the twentysomething traveler (www.meetup.com, search "Paris" to find groups according to your interests).

ORIENTATION

Lachaise Cemetery, as well as a themed walk on the French Revolution. Their "Skip the Line" tours get you into major sights (such as Versailles) but are most worthwhile for the Eiffel Tower and Catacombs. Reservations are required and can be made online, by phone, or in person at their office near the Eiffel Tower (€25/person for walking tours, €54-99/person for "Skip the Line" tours; RS%—€2 discount per person, 2-discount maximum; office generally open daily 9:00-18:00 or 19:00, shorter hours in winter, 24 Rue Edgar Faure, Mo: Dupleix, +33 1 82 88 80 96, www.fattiretours. com/paris).

Paris Muse Tours offers guided scavenger-hunt-like tours to explore historic areas and sights. Clever storytelling incorporates interactivity that's fun for all ages. Imagine yourself as a detective at the Louvre or a 19th-century art writer at the Orsay, or solve a real-life French Revolution murder mystery on the streets of Paris (€180-425 depending on group size, up to 8 people, 2.5 hours, mobile +33 6 73 77 33 52, www.parismuse.com, info@parismuse. com).

Local Guides

For many, Paris merits hiring a Parisian as a personal guide (€240-300 half-day, €400-500 full day). **Thierry Gauduchon** is a terrific guide and a gifted teacher (mobile +33 6 19 07 30 77, tgauduchon@ gmail.com). **Elisabeth Van Hest** is another likable and very capable guide (+33 1 43 41 47 31, mobile +33 6 77 80 19 89, elisa.guide@ gmail.com). **Vincent Cabaret** is a fun guide for Paris' city center, day trips (he's particularly terrific for Versailles), and beyond (mobile +33 6 82 19 67 23, vincentcabaret@ymail.com). **Sylvie Moreau** also leads good tours (+33 1 74 30 27 46, mobile +33 6 87 02 80 67, sylvie.ja.moreau@gmail.com). **Arnaud Servignat** is a top guide who has taught me much about Paris (also does minivan tours of the countryside around Paris, mobile +33 6 68 80 29 05, www. french-guide.com, arnotour@icloud.com). **Joelle Valette-Coat** is an effective teacher who takes her art seriously (+33 1 46 06 74 95 or +33 6 86 28 32 20, jvalettecoat@hotmail.com).

ON WHEELS
Bike Tours

A bike tour is a fun way to see Paris. Two companies—Bike About Tours and Fat Tire Tours—offer tours and bike maps of Paris and give good advice on cycling routes in the city. Their tour routes cover different areas of the city, so avid cyclists could do both without much repetition.

Bike About Tours offers easygoing 3.5-hour bike tours. The Hidden Paris tour includes a backstreet spin through the Marais, Latin Quarter, and Ile St. Louis. Their Monuments tour takes you

Rollerblading with Parisians

Inline skaters take to the streets most Sunday afternoons and Friday evenings. It's serious skaters only on Fridays (they meet at 21:30 and are ready to roll at 22:00), but anyone can join in on Sundays (at 14:30). Police close off different routes each week to keep locals engaged.

On Sunday, skaters leave from the south side of Place de la Bastille (for the route, see www.rollers-coquillages.org); the Friday start point varies by week (see www.pari-roller.com). You can rent skates near the Sunday starting point at Nomades (about €10/day, closed Mon, 37 Boulevard Bourdon, near Place de la Bastille, Mo: Bastille, +33 1 44 54 07 44).

past the Louvre, Eiffel Tower, and other classics (€45, RS%—10 percent discount, helmets on request, 12-person maximum group size—reserve online to guarantee a spot or show up and take your chances, meet at their Le Peloton office/café in the Marais; for address and contact info see listing earlier, under "Getting Around Paris—By Bike").

Over at **Fat Tire Tours,** a gang of Anglophone expats offers an extensive program of bike, Segway (see next), and walking tours (see earlier). Their young guides run three-hour bike tours of Paris day and night (adults-€39, students-€32, infants-€5; RS%—€4 discount per person, 2-discount maximum; reservations recommended but not required, especially in off-season). Kid-size bikes are available, as are tandem attachments and baby seats. On the day tour, you'll pedal with a pack of up to 20 riders, mostly in parks and along bike lanes, with a lunch stop in the Tuileries Garden (tours leave daily rain or shine at 10:30, April-Oct also at 15:00). Livelier night tours follow a route past floodlit monuments and include a boat cruise on the Seine (€44, May-Aug daily at 18:30, less frequent off-season). Both tours meet at Fat Tire's office at 24 Rue Edgar Faure, near the Eiffel Tower (helmets available on request; for contact info, see listing earlier, under "Getting Around Paris—By Bike"). They also run bike tours to Versailles and Giverny (reservations required, see website for details).

Segway Tour

Fat Tire offers pricey two-hour **City Segway Tours.** Learn to ride these stand-up motorized scooters while exploring Paris (you'll get the hang of it after about a half-hour). These tours take no more than eight people at a time, so reservations are required. Kids must be at least 12 years old and 100 pounds (€59, April-Oct daily at 14:30; see Fat Tire Tours listing under "Getting Around Paris—By Bike," earlier).

Pedal Cab Tour

You'll find these three-wheeled, pedal-powered vehicles at key sights in Paris. **Cyclopolitain Paris** can usually be found outside the Shakespeare and Company bookstore, on Place du Parvis de Notre-Dame. Grab one for anything from a short taxi trip to a night tour (allow €60/hour, 3-person maximum).

EXCURSIONS FROM PARIS

You'll never run out of things to do in Paris, but the outlying areas may lure you out of the city. The grand châteaux at **Versailles, Vaux-le-Vicomte,** and **Fontainebleau,** the cathedral at **Chartres,** Monet's garden at **Giverny,** and the artist town of **Auvers-sur-Oise** are all within reach as day trips. Go on your own, with a bus or minivan tour, or with a local guide: Most of the guides listed earlier will do excursion tours from Paris using your rental car. For details on doing these trips on your own or by bus or minivan tour, see the individual destination chapters.

Farther from Paris

It's easy to arrange day trips from Paris to places around northern France, such as Reims, the Loire Valley, and the D-Day beaches of Normandy (all beyond the scope of this book, but well covered in *Rick Steves France*). Thanks to bullet trains and good local guides who can help you maximize your time, well-coordinated blitz-tour trips to these places are doable (though hardly relaxing). To see these places in a day, I recommend using a guide from the region who will meet you at the train station (most have cars) and show you the highlights before getting you back on your return train to Paris. Book well in advance, especially for the D-Day beaches.

Reims: For a day trip to Reims, check out **France Bubbles Tours** (www.france-bubbles-tours.com). The wine gurus at **Ô Château** in Paris offer day trips and tastings to Reims and Champagne (see page 451 for contact info).

Loire Valley: Pascal Accolay runs **Acco-Dispo,** which offers good all-day château tours from the city of Tours—an hour from Paris by train (mobile +33 6 82 00 64 51, www.accodispo-tours.com).

D-Day Beaches: An army of small companies offers all-day excursions to the D-Day beaches from Bayeux or Caen, both reachable by train from Paris in 2.5 hours or less. These guides are top notch: **Dale Booth Normandy Tours** (Dale Booth, +33 2 14 16 66 14, www.dboothnormandytours.com, dboothholidays@aol.com), **D-Day Experience Tours** (Sylvain Kast, +33 6 17 44 04 46, www.d-day-experience-tours.com), **Normandy American Heroes Tours** (Rodolphe Passera, mobile +33 6 30 55 63 39, www.normandyamericanheroes.com, rudy@normandyamericanheroes.com), and **D-Day Guided Tours** (Mathias Leclere, www.ddayguidedtours.com).

Bayeux Shuttle takes individual signups for their minivan tours and has an easy booking calendar online (mobile +33 2 31 78 88 88, www.bayeuxshuttle.com).

Other Day-Trip Options

If you'd be happier letting someone else arrange the logistics, the following companies offer convenient transportation and a smidgen of guiding to destinations outside Paris.

Paris Webservices, a reliable outfit, offers private group day trips to Giverny and Versailles with well-trained, English-speaking chauffeur-guides in cushy minivans (figure €95-140/person for groups of 4 or more, RS%—use code RICK-23-STEVES, +33 1 45 56 91 67 or +33 9 52 06 02 59, www.pariswebservices.com, reservation@pariswebservices.fr).

Paris City Vision runs bus tours to several popular regional destinations, including the Loire Valley, Champagne region, D-Day beaches, and Mont St-Michel (3 Place des Pyramides, Mo: Pyramides, www.pariscityvision.com). Their full-size bus tours are multilingual, mass-marketed, and mediocre at best, but can be worthwhile simply for the ease of transportation to the sights (about €50-170, destinations include Versailles, Giverny, Mont St-Michel, and more).

SIGHTS IN PARIS

Paris is blessed with world-class museums and monuments—more than anyone could see in a single visit. To help you prioritize your limited time and money, I've chosen what I think are the best of Paris' many sights. I've clustered them into walkable neighborhoods for more efficient sightseeing.

In this chapter, some of Paris' most important sights have the shortest listings and are marked with a 📖. That's because they are described in much more detail in one of my self-guided walks or tours. A 🎧 means the walk or tour is available as a free audio tour (via my Rick Steves Audio Europe app—see page 24). Some walks and tours are available in both formats—take your pick.

To connect some of the most central sights, follow my Historic Paris Walk (see the next chapter), which takes you from Notre-Dame to Saint-Chapelle, and ends on Pont Neuf, very near the Louvre and Orsay.

For general tips on sightseeing, see page 656 in the Practicalities chapter. For advice on saving money, see "Affording Paris' Sights" on page 78.

Sightseeing Strategies

ADVANCE TICKETS

Virtually all sights of any importance in Paris sell tickets online for no additional fee. At a few key sights, you can't get in without a timed-entry ticket bought in advance: the **Louvre, Orangerie, Sainte-Chapelle,** and **Versailles.** Although advance tickets are not technically required for the **Eiffel Tower, Catacombs,** and **Conciergerie,** I recommend booking ahead to assure you get your preferred date and time. At some sights, you can drop in and take your chances (but I wouldn't—unless it's the off-season).

Even where advance tickets are not required, buying ahead lets you avoid the long ticket-buying lines that many tourists suffer through in Paris (though you'll still likely have to wait in a security line). Better yet, combine this strategy with a **Paris Museum Pass** (described below), and you'll save both time and money.

You can also buy advance tickets for activities and cultural events such as the Bateaux-Mouches river cruises, Sainte-Chapelle concerts, and performances at the Opéra Garnier.

Booking Tickets in Advance

Buy your ticket online, save the digital ticket to your phone (or keep it in your email), and bypass any ticket-buying lines when you get to the sight.

Always book directly on the sight's official website. The process can be cumbersome, as you may need to create an account and go through several tedious steps. If you're already in Paris, ask your hotelier for help.

You'll select your preferred date and entry time (usually with a 30-minute window to enter), then make the purchase with your credit card. If you have a Paris Museum Pass and are reserving a sight covered by the pass, look for the pass holder option (sometimes called *free ticket option*), which lets you book an entry time for free. You'll need to input your Museum Pass number.

Once you've booked, you'll receive an email—usually with a QR code—that acts as your digital ticket. (If you don't get the email, check your junk folder.) When you arrive at the sight, look for a line marked "ticket holders" *(avec billet)*. There may still be a wait to enter, but when you get to the front, pull up the digital ticket on your phone, let the attendant scan it, and walk right in.

PARIS MUSEUM PASS

The Paris Museum Pass admits you to many of Paris' most important sights on two, four, or six consecutive days—saving you money if you visit several included sights (2 days-€52, 4 days-€66, 6 days-€78; no youth or senior discounts, but many museums offer free admission to those under age 18—see below). The pass pays for itself with four key admissions in two days (for example, the  Louvre, Orsay, Sainte-Chapelle, and Rodin Museum).

Pertinent details about the pass are outlined here. For more info, and to purchase the pass, visit www.parismuseumpass.com.

SIGHTS

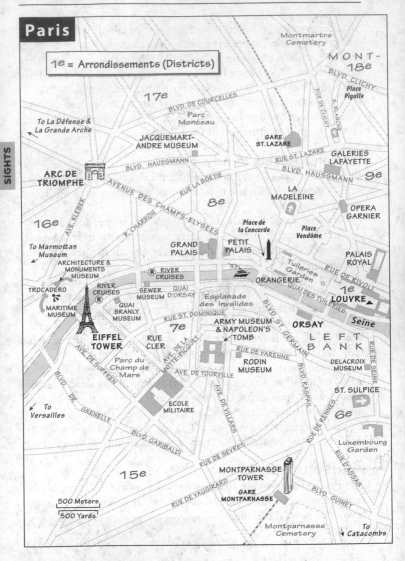

Paris

1e = Arrondissements (Districts)

Montmartre Cemetery

MONT- 18e

BLVD. CLICHY

Place Pigalle

R. BLANCHE

RUE DE CLICHY

17e

BLVD. DE COURCELLES

Parc Monceau

To La Défense & La Grande Arche

JACQUEMART-ANDRE MUSEUM

GARE ST. LAZARE

RUE ST. LAZARE

GALERIES LAFAYETTE

BLVD. HAUSSMANN

9e

BLVD. HAUSSMANN

ARC DE TRIOMPHE

AVENUE DES CHAMPS-ELYSEES

RUE LA BOETIE

LA MADELEINE

OPERA GARNIER

AVE. KLEBER

16e

8e

Place de la Concorde

Place Vendôme

PALAIS ROYAL

To Marmottan Museum

R. CHARRON

GRAND PALAIS

PETIT PALAIS

RUE DE RIVOLI

ARCHITECTURE & MONUMENTS MUSEUM

RIVER CRUISES

Tuileries Garden

ORANGERIE

1e LOUVRE

TROCADERO

RIVER CRUISES R

SEWER MUSEUM

QUAI D'ORSAY

QUAIS TUILERIES

MARITIME MUSEUM

QUAI BRANLY MUSEUM

Esplanade des Invalides

ORSAY

Seine

EIFFEL TOWER

RUE CLER

RUE ST. DOMINIQUE

7e

RUE DE LA MOTTE-PICQUET

ARMY MUSEUM & NAPOLEON'S TOMB

BLVD. ST. GERMAIN

LEFT BANK

RUE DE SEINE

Parc du Champ de Mars

RUE DE VARENNE

RODIN MUSEUM

DELACROIX MUSEUM

AVE. DE SUFFREN

AVE. DE TOURVILLE

BLVD. RASPAIL

ST. SULPICE

BLVD. DE GRENELLE

ECOLE MILITAIRE

AVE. DE VILLARS

6e

To Versailles

BLVD. GARIBALDI

RUE DE RENNES

Luxembourg Garden

RUE DE SEVRES

RUE D'ASSAS

15e

RUE DE VAUGIRARD

MONTPARNASSE TOWER

GARE MONTPARNASSE

BLVD. GUINET

500 Meters
500 Yards

Montparnasse Cemetery

To Catacombs

Buying the Pass

If you buy the pass online in advance, you can either download and print a hard copy to show as you enter museums, or keep it on your smartphone (take a screenshot and save it in your Favorites photo album for quick access).

If you wait to buy a pass until you arrive in Paris, it is sold at participating museums, monuments, TIs (small fee added)—including TIs at Paris airports and some souvenir stores near major

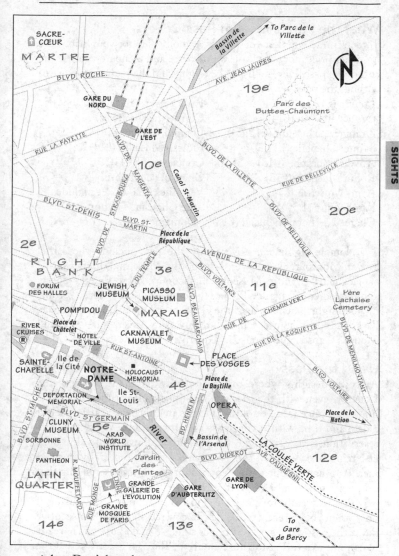

sights. Don't buy the pass at a major museum (such as the Louvre), where the supply can be spotty and lines long.

Families: The pass isn't worth buying for children and teens, as most museums are free or discounted for those under age 18 (teenagers may need to show ID as proof of age). If parents have a Museum Pass, kids can usually skip the ticket lines as well. A few places may require everyone—even pass holders—to stand in line to collect your child's free ticket.

What the Paris Museum Pass Covers

To determine whether the pass is a good value for your trip, tally up ticket prices for what you want to see and compare against the cost of the pass. Here's a list of key sights and their admission prices without the pass:

Louvre (€17)	Paris Sewer Museum (€9)
Orsay Museum (€14)	Cluny Museum (€12)
Orangerie Museum (€12.50)	Pompidou Center (€14)
Sainte-Chapelle (€11.50)	Picasso Museum (€14)
Arc de Triomphe (€13)	Conciergerie (€11.50)
Rodin Museum (€13)	Château de Chantilly (€17)
Army Museum (€14)	Versailles (€20 ticket includes
Panthéon (€11.50)	the Château, Trianon, and
Château de Fontainebleau (€13)	Domaine)

Notable sights *not* covered by the pass include the Eiffel Tower, Montparnasse Tower, Marmottan Museum, Opéra Garnier, Jacquemart-André Museum, Catacombs, Sacré-Cœur's dome, and the ladies of Pigalle. The pass also does not cover these recommended sights outside Paris: the Gardens at Versailles on Spectacle days, Vaux-le-Vicomte, Château d'Auvers in Auvers-sur-Oise, and Monet's Garden and House in Giverny.

Using the Pass

At covered sights where reservations are required—such as the Louvre—even with the pass you must book a free timed entry online in advance (see "Booking Tickets in Advance," earlier; select a date and time within your pass validity period). At sights where reservations aren't required, the pass often allows you to skip ticket-buying lines—which can save some waiting, especially in summer. Another benefit is that you might pop into lesser sights that otherwise may not be worth the expense.

Plan carefully to make the most of your pass. Start using it only when you're ready to tackle the covered sights on consecutive days. The pass allows one entry per sight, so make sure you're ready to commit to a full visit before entering. The pass is activated at the time of first use and is time-based (not days-based). For example, a two-day pass gives you 48 hours of use from the time you activate it (so if your first entry is at 13:00, you get 48 hours from 13:00). Make sure the sights you want to visit will be open when you want to go (many museums are closed Mon or Tue).

The pass provides the best value on days when sights close later, letting you extend your sightseeing day. Take advantage of late hours on selected evenings or times of year at the Arc de Triomphe, Pompidou, Sainte-Chapelle, Orsay, and Napoleon's Tomb (see the "Paris for Early Birds and Night Owls" sidebar on page

82). After your pass expires, visit free sights (many are free every day; see the "Affording Paris' Sights" sidebar, later) and those not covered by the pass.

You can't skip security lines, though at a few sights (such as the Orsay Museum) pass holders may enjoy "priority lines." Once you pass security, look for signs designating the entrance for reserved ticket holders. If it's not obvious, don't be shy—boldly walk to the front of the ticket line, hold up your pass, and ask the ticket taker: *"Entrez, pass?"* (ahn-tray pahs). For some sights, such as the Orsay Museum, I've identified pass-holder entrances on the maps in this book.

LAST-DITCH TICKET TIPS

If you can't get an online reservation for the date you want, you can buy skip-the-line *"coupe-file"* tickets (pronounced "koop feel") through third party vendors—usually for a high fee. You'll find *coupe-file* tickets at TIs, FNAC department stores, and travel-service companies such as Paris Webservices and Fat Tire Tours. Compare your options: Some allow you to skip the ticket-buying line, while others provide a "host" to escort you into the sight (small fee at TIs, 10-20 percent surcharge elsewhere). FNAC stores are common, even on the Champs-Elysées (www.fnactickets.com, ask your hotelier for the nearest one); for Paris Webservices, see page 55; for Fat Tire Tours, see page 49.

Sights

HISTORIC CORE OF PARIS

📖 Connect the following sights with my Historic Paris Walk chapter and 🎧 free audio tour, which also provide more detailed visiting information and descriptions for Notre-Dame, the Deportation Memorial, Ile St. Louis, Sainte-Chapelle, and the Conciergerie.

▲▲▲Notre-Dame Cathedral
(Cathédrale Notre-Dame de Paris)

This 850-year-old cathedral, packed with history, is recovering from a devastating fire in 2019 (though thankfully, much of what made the church's interior famous was salvaged). While the interior and some of the surrounding areas will be closed for several years, you can still appreciate its monumental exterior. With a pair of 200-foot-tall bell towers, a facade studded with ornate statuary, beautiful stained-glass rose windows, famous gargoyles, a picture-perfect Seine-side location, and textbook flying buttresses, there's a good reason that this cathedral of "Our Lady" *(Notre-Dame)* is France's most famous church.

Check out the facade: Mary with the Baby Jesus (in rose

Paris at a Glance

▲▲▲**Notre-Dame Cathedral** Paris' most beloved church is closed indefinitely. See page 61.

▲▲▲**Sainte-Chapelle** Gothic cathedral with peerless stained glass. **Hours:** Daily 9:00-19:00, Oct-March until 17:00. See page 65.

▲▲▲**Louvre** Europe's oldest and greatest museum, starring *Mona Lisa* and *Venus de Milo*. **Hours:** Wed-Mon 9:00-18:00, closed Tue. See page 68.

▲▲▲**Orsay Museum** Nineteenth-century art, including Europe's greatest Impressionist collection. **Hours:** Tue-Sun 9:30-18:00, Thu until 21:45, closed Mon. See page 71.

▲▲▲**Eiffel Tower** Paris' soaring exclamation point. **Hours:** Daily mid-June-Aug 9:00-24:45, Sept-mid-June 9:30-23:45. See page 74.

▲▲▲**Champs-Elysées** Paris' grand boulevard. See page 95.

▲▲▲**Versailles** The ultimate royal palace (Château), with a Hall of Mirrors, vast gardens, a grand canal, plus a queen's playground (Trianon Palaces and Domaine de Marie-Antoinette). **Hours:** Château Tue-Sun 9:00-18:30, Nov-March until 17:30; Trianon/Domaine Tue-Sun 12:00-18:30, Nov-March until 17:30; gardens generally daily 8:00-20:30, Nov-March until 18:00; entire complex closed Mon year-round except the Gardens. See the Versailles chapter.

▲▲**Riverside Promenades and Paris Plages** Traffic-free riverside areas for recreation and strolling; in summer, "beaches" add more fun. **Hours:** Promenades—always strollable; Plages—mid-July-mid-Aug 8:00-24:00. See page 66.

▲▲**Orangerie Museum** Monet's water lilies and modernist classics in a lovely setting. **Hours:** Wed-Mon 9:00-18:00, closed Tue. See page 72.

▲▲**Rue Cler** Ultimate Parisian market street. **Hours:** Stores open Tue-Sat 8:30-13:00 & 15:00-19:30, Sun 8:30-12:00, dead on Mon. See page 80.

▲▲**Army Museum and Napoleon's Tomb** The emperor's imposing tomb, flanked by museums of France's wars. **Hours:** Daily 10:00-18:00; Napoleon's Tomb open until 21:00 on Tue. See page 81.

▲▲**Rodin Museum** Works by the greatest sculptor since Michelangelo, with many statues in a peaceful garden. **Hours:** Tue-Sun 10:00-18:30, closed Mon. See page 81.

▲▲**Marmottan Museum** Art museum focusing on Monet. **Hours:** Tue-Sun 10:00-18:00, Thu until 21:00, closed Mon. See page 83.

▲▲**Cluny Museum** Medieval art with unicorn tapestries. **Hours:** Tue-Sun 9:30-18:15, first and third Thu of the month until 21:00, closed Mon. See page 86.

▲▲**Arc de Triomphe** Triumphal arch marking start of Champs-Elysées. **Hours:** Interior daily 10:00-23:00, Oct-March until 22:30. See page 96.

▲▲**Opéra Garnier** Grand belle époque theater with a modern ceiling by Chagall. **Hours:** Generally daily 10:00-16:15, mid-July-Aug until 17:15. See page 104.

▲▲**Jacquemart-André Museum** Art-strewn 19th-century mansion. **Hours:** Daily 10:00-18:00, Mon until 20:30 during special exhibits. See page 110.

▲▲**Pompidou Center** Modern art in colorful building with city views. **Hours:** Permanent collection open Wed-Mon 11:00-21:00, closed Tue. See page 117.

▲▲**Père Lachaise Cemetery** Final home of Paris' illustrious dead. **Hours:** Mon-Fri 8:00-18:00, Sat from 8:30, Sun from 9:00, closes at 17:30 in winter. See page 118.

▲▲**Montmartre and Sacré-Cœur** Bohemian, hill-top neighborhood capped with a stunning white basilica and spectacular views. **Hours:** Daily 6:30-22:30; dome climb daily 10:00-20:00, Oct-May 10:00-18:00, Jan-Feb until 17:00. See page 119.

▲▲**Carnavalet Museum** Paris' history wrapped up in a 16th-century mansion. **Hours:** Tue-Sun 10:00-18:00, closed Mon. See page 112.

▲**Picasso Museum** Rotating Picasso exhibits filling a three-floor mansion. **Hours:** Tue-Fri 10:30-18:00, Sat-Sun from 9:30, closed Mon. See page 114.

▲**Panthéon** Neoclassical monument/burial place of the famous. **Hours:** Daily 10:00-18:30, Oct-March until 18:00. See page 88.

▲**Ile St. Louis** Residential island behind Notre-Dame known for its restaurants. See page 65.

window) above the 28 Kings of Judah (statues that were beheaded during the Revolution). Then wander around the exterior with
its forest of frilly buttresses, watched over by
a fleet of whimsical gargoyles.

During the closure, you can view the
church from three spots: across the river
(where you'll find what seems like a pur-
pose-built viewpoint between the green
bookstalls); from the plaza facing the facade (worthwhile even if looking over the
construction fence); and walking along the
left side (where you won't see much of the
architecture, but you can follow a fascinat-
ing outdoor photo exhibit that describes the demanding restoration
process in English).

For up-to-date information, see www.notredamedeparis.fr
(select "Visiter"—website is in French only) or https://en.parisinfo.
com/practical-paris/info/guides. To experience the interior of another Gothic church that's roughly the size of Notre-Dame, visit
St. Eustache Church (listed on page 73).

▲Paris Archaeological Crypt

This intriguing 20-minute stop lets you view Roman ruins from
Emperor Augustus' reign (when this island became the birthplace
of Paris), trace the street plan of the medieval village, and see diagrams of how early Paris grew. It's all thoughtfully explained in
English (pick up the floor plan with some background info) and
well presented with videos and touchscreens. This (along with the
Cluny Museum) gives the best view of ancient Roman Paris.

Cost and Hours: €8, covered by Museum Pass, Tue-Sun
10:00-18:00, closed Mon, good audioguide-€5, enter 100 yards in
front of cathedral, +33 1 55 42 50 10, www.crypte.paris.fr.

Visiting the Crypt: The first few displays put the ruins in historical context. Three models show the growth of Paris—from an
uninhabited riverside plot to the grid-planned Roman town of Lutèce, then to an early medieval city with an enclosing wall and the
church that preceded Notre-Dame. A fourth model (off to the left)
shows the current Notre-Dame surrounded by buildings, along
with the old, straight road—Rue Neuve de Notre-Dame—that led
up to the church and now runs right down the center of the museum. The ruins in the middle of the museum are a confusing mix
of foundations from all these time periods, including parts of the
old Rue Neuve.

As you circle the ruins counterclockwise, note some highlights: Along the right side of the museum, you can see big stone

blocks from the old Roman wall. At the back, you can step onto the remains of a Roman dock, made lively with audio and video. Farther along, play with the touchscreen for a chance to appreciate the 200-year-long construction process of Notre-Dame Cathedral, and a view of the Rue Neuve ruins. On the museum's far side, find the thermal baths, where you can see a Roman building with "hypocaustal" heating—narrow passages pumped full of hot air to heat the room.

▲Deportation Memorial (Mémorial de la Déportation)

Climb down the steps into this memorial dedicated to the 200,000 French victims of the Nazi concentration camps. As Paris disappears above you, this monument draws you into the victims' experience. Once underground you enter a one-way hallway studded with tiny lights commemorating the dead, leading you to an eternal flame. For a small and moving exhibit about the Holocaust, don't miss the rooms upstairs.

Cost and Hours: Free, daily 10:00-19:00, Oct-March until 17:00, may close at random times, free 45-minute audioguide and guided tours may be available; at the east tip of Ile de la Cité, behind Notre-Dame and near Ile St. Louis (Mo: Cité); +33 6 14 67 54 98.

▲Ile St. Louis

The residential island behind Notre-Dame is known for its restaurants (see the Eating in Paris chapter), great ice cream, and shops (along Rue St. Louis-en-l'Ile).

▲▲▲Sainte-Chapelle

The interior of this 13th-century chapel is a triumph of Gothic church architecture. Built to house Jesus' Crown of Thorns, Sainte-Chapelle is jam-packed with stained-glass windows, bathed in colorful light, and slippery with the drool of awestruck tourists. Ignore the humdrum exterior and climb the stairs into the sanctuary, where more than 1,100 Bible scenes—from  the Creation to the Passion to Judgment Day—are illustrated by light and glass.

Cost and Hours: €11.50 for timed-entry ticket, €18.50 combo-ticket with Conciergerie, free for kids under age 18, covered by Museum Pass, reserve online in advance to ensure entry (limited tickets available in person); open daily 9:00-19:00, Oct-March until 17:00; audioguide-€3, evening concerts—see page 512, 4 Boulevard du Palais, Mo: Cité, +33 1 53 40 60 80, www.sainte-chapelle.fr. For tips on avoiding long lines here, see page 122.

▲Conciergerie

Marie-Antoinette was imprisoned here, as were Louis XVI, Robespierre, Danton, and many others on their way to the guillotine. Exhibits with good English descriptions trace the history of the building and give some insight into prison life.

Cost and Hours: €11.50 for timed-entry ticket, €18.50 combo-ticket with Sainte-Chapelle, covered by Museum Pass, daily 9:30-18:00, multimedia guide-€5, 2 Boulevard du Palais, Mo: Cité, +33 1 53 40 60 80, www.paris-conciergerie.fr.

▲▲Riverside Promenades and Paris Plages

At the cost of closing down two busy expressways along the Seine, Paris has reclaimed sections of the embankment in a fun-loving project stretching several miles.  These traffic-free areas are a new world for strolling, biking, having fun with the kids, dining (in pop-up drinking and eating establishments or at extravagant picnics complete with tablecloths and Champagne)—or, simply dangling one's feet over the water and being in the moment. One section runs along the Left Bank between Pont de l'Alma (near the Eiffel Tower) and the Orsay, and another runs along the Right Bank between the Louvre and Place de la Bastille. In balmy weather, the embankment takes on a special energy. The gaggle of bars and fun eating spots at Pont Alexandre III (Left Bank) and across from Ile St. Louis (Right Bank) are particularly lively. The riverside promenade is fine for strolling or biking.

The **Paris Plages** (beaches) add lots of beach activities each summer. The Riviera it's not, but this string of fanciful faux beaches—assembled along a one-mile stretch of the Right Bank of the Seine—is a fun place to stroll, play, and people-watch. Each summer, the Paris city government trucks in potted palm trees, hammocks, and lounge chairs to create colorful urban beaches. You'll also find "beach cafés," climbing walls, prefab pools, trampolines, a library, beach volleyball, badminton, and Frisbee areas. (Other less-central areas of town, such as Bassin de la Vilette, have their own *plages*.)

Cost and Hours: Free, promenades always open, Plages run mid-July-mid-Aug daily 8:00-24:00, on Right Bank of Seine, just north of Ile de la Cité, between Pont des Arts and Pont de Sully.

▲▲Bike Ride on Riverside Promenade

While Paris is crisscrossed with bike lanes, most are adjacent to regular traffic or mixed with bus-only lanes (ouch). The most relaxing and scenic Parisian joyride on two wheels is along its riverside promenades (described above), with nary a car in sight. A four-mile stretch runs through the heart of the city, from near the Eiffel Tower to below the Bastille; the round-trip ride makes a wonderful experience of about an hour or so. (It could be much longer if you succumb to the temptations of the lounge chairs, hammocks, outdoor cafés, and simple delights of riverside Parisian life.)

I like starting at Pont de l'Alma, near the Eiffel Tower on the Left Bank. Head east, passing under four bridges (about 1.5 miles) to the Orsay Museum. Just past the Orsay, turn left, crossing to the Right Bank on Pont Royal. Now on the Right Bank, continue east on Quai Mitterand (with a broad sidewalk), passing the Louvre Museum. Find the cobbled ramp down to the river near the Pont des Arts. You'll bump along cobbles for a few blocks before merging with the smooth-as-silk road. You'll pass the two islands and finally reach the end of our ride (and turn around) at the tunnel entrance. (To trace this bike route, set out with the "Eiffel Tower & Nearby" map on page 76, pedal across the "Major Museums Neighborhood" map on page 68, and gear down on the "Marais Neighborhood & Nearby" map on page 112).

Avoid pedestrians or pedaling into the river—you'll be distracted by many iconic buildings and sights. You can extend your ride by side-tripping through grand Parisian parks like the Champs de Mars (under the Eiffel Tower) and Tuileries Garden (the Louvre's front yard—bikes allowed only in section closest to river).

Renting Your Bike: To do this as a one-way trip, use a Vélib' or other city bike-share option (see details on page 46 and check the Vélib' app or website for locations, www.velib-metropole.fr). You can also pop into a bike rental shop (Fat Tire Bike Tours near the west end, Bike About Tours at the east end—see page 45).

MAJOR MUSEUMS NEIGHBORHOOD

Paris' grandest park, the Tuileries Garden, was once the private property of kings and queens. Today it links the Louvre, Orangerie, and Orsay museums. And across from the Louvre are the tranquil, historic courtyards of the Palais Royal.

SIGHTS

Major Museums Neighborhood

▲▲▲Louvre (Musée du Louvre)

This is Europe's oldest, biggest, greatest, and second-most-crowded museum (after the Vatican). Housed in a U-shaped, 16th-century palace (accentuated by a 20th-century glass pyramid), the Louvre is Paris' top museum and one of its key landmarks. It's home to *Mona Lisa*, *Venus de Milo*, and hall after hall of Greek and Roman masterpieces, medieval jewels, Michelangelo statues, and paintings by the greatest artists from the Renaissance to the Romantics. When

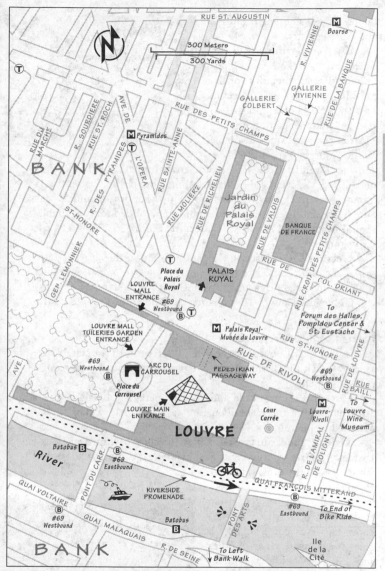

it's crowded—and that's most of the year—woe to those who show up without a timed-entry ticket (buy online in advance).

Touring the Louvre can be overwhelming, so be selective. Focus on the Denon wing, with Greek sculptures, Italian paintings (by Raphael and Leonardo), and—of course—French paintings (Neoclassical and Romantic), and the adjoining Sully wing, with Egyptian artifacts and more French paintings. For extra credit, tackle the Richelieu wing, displaying works from ancient Mesopotamia, as well as French, Dutch, and Northern art.

Cost and Hours: €17 for timed-entry ticket—book online in advance, includes special exhibits, covered by Museum Pass (but pass holders must still reserve time slot in advance); €15 tickets sometimes available at the door but it's unlikely—

and you'll wait in a long line; open Wed-Mon 9:00-18:00, possibly until 21:45 Wed and Fri—check online, closed Tue, last entry 45 minutes before closing; crowds worst in the morning and all day Sun, Mon, and Wed; multimedia guide-€5, guided tours available, several cafés, +33 1 40 20 53 17, recorded info +33 1 40 20 51 51, www.louvre.fr.

Getting There: Use the Palais Royal-Musée du Louvre Métro stop. (The old Louvre Métro stop, called Louvre-Rivoli, is farther from the entrance.) Bus #69 also runs past the Louvre.

📖 See the Louvre Tour chapter or 🎧 download my free audio tour.

Palais Royal Courtyards

Across from the Louvre are the lovely courtyards of the stately Palais Royal. Although the palace is closed to the public, the courtyards are open.

Cost and Hours: Free and always open. The Palais Royal is directly north of the Louvre on Rue de Rivoli (Mo: Palais Royal-Musée du Louvre).

Visiting the Courtyards: Enter through a whimsical (locals say tacky) courtyard filled with stubby, striped columns and playful fountains (with fun, reflective metal balls). Next, you'll pass into another, perfectly Parisian garden. This is where in-the-know Parisians come to take a quiet break, walk their poodles and kids, or enjoy a rendezvous—amid flowers and surrounded by a serene arcade and a handful of historic restaurants.

Bring a picnic and create your own quiet break, or have a drink at one of the outdoor cafés at the courtyard's northern end. This is Paris.

Though tranquil today, this was once a hotbed of political activism. The palace was built in the 17th century by Louis XIII and

eventually became the headquarters of the powerful Dukes of Orléans. Because the Dukes' digs were off-limits to the police, some
shocking free-thinking took root here. This was the meeting place
for the debating clubs—the precursors to modern political parties.
During the Revolution, palace resident Philippe, duc d'Orléans,
(nicknamed Philippe Egalité for his progressive ideas) advocated
a constitutional monarchy, and voted in favor of beheading Louis
XVI—his own cousin. Philippe hoped his liberal attitudes would
spare him from the Revolutionaries, but he, too, was guillotined.
His son, Louis-Philippe, became France's first constitutional monarch (r. 1830-1848). The palace's courtyards were backdrops for a
riotous social and political scene, filled with lively café culture, revolutionaries, rabble-rousers, scoundrels, and...Madame Tussaud's
first wax shop (she used the severed heads of guillotine victims to
model her sculptures).

Nearby: Exiting the courtyard at the side facing away from
the Seine brings you to the Galeries Colbert and Vivienne, attractive examples of shopping arcades from the early 1800s (see page
70).

▲▲▲Orsay Museum (Musée d'Orsay)

The Orsay boasts Europe's greatest collection of Impressionist
works. It might be less important than the Louvre—but it's more
purely enjoyable.

The Orsay, housed in
an atmospheric old train
station, picks up where
the Louvre leaves off: the
second half of the 19th
century. This is art from
the tumultuous time that
began when revolutions
swept across Europe in
1848 and ended when World War I broke out in 1914. Begin with
the conservative art of the mid-1800s—careful, idealized Neoclassicism (with a few rebels mixed in). Then tour the late 1800s, when
the likes of Manet, Monet, Degas, and Renoir jolted the art world
with their colorful, lively invention, Impressionism. (Somewhere
in there, *Whistler's Mother* sits quietly.) The Orsay also displays the
works of their artistic descendants, the Post-Impressionists: Cézanne, Van Gogh, Gauguin, Seurat, and Toulouse-Lautrec. On the
mezzanine level, waltz through Rodin sculptures and Art Nouveau
exhibits, and finish in the Grand Ballroom, which shows the chandeliered elegance of this former train station.

Cost and Hours: €14, free on first Sun of month, covered by
Museum Pass, combo-tickets with Orangerie Museum (€18) or

Rodin Museum (€24) are sold only at those museums—not the Orsay, keep Orsay ticket for discount at Opéra Garnier. Museum open Tue-Sun 9:30-18:00, Thu until 21:45, closed Mon, last entry one hour before closing (45 minutes before on Thu), Impressionist galleries start shutting 45 minutes before closing; museum especially crowded on Sun and Tue; audioguide-€6, guided tours-€6; cafés and restaurant, +33 1 40 49 48 14, www.musee-orsay.fr.

Getting There: The museum, at 1 Rue de la Légion d'Honneur, sits above the RER/Train-C Musée d'Orsay stop; the nearest Métro stop is Solférino, three blocks southeast of the Orsay. Buses #69 and #87 stop near the Orsay. From the Louvre, it's a lovely 15-minute walk through the Tuileries Garden and across the pedestrian bridge.

☐ See the Orsay Museum Tour chapter (which includes more tips on avoiding lines) or ∩ download my free audio tour.

▲▲Orangerie Museum (Musée de l'Orangerie)

Located in the Tuileries Garden and drenched by natural light from skylights, the Orangerie (oh-rahn-zhuh-ree) is the closest you'll come to stepping into an Impressionist painting. Start with the museum's claim to fame: Monet's *Water Lilies*. Then head downstairs to enjoy the manageable collection of select works by Utrillo, Cézanne, Renoir, Matisse, and Picasso.

Cost and Hours: €12.50 for timed-entry ticket—reserve online in advance, free for those under age 18, free on first Sun of the month, €18 combo-ticket with Orsay Museum, ask about combo-ticket with Monet's garden and house at Giverny, covered by Museum Pass; Wed-Mon 9:00-18:00, closed Tue; audioguide-€5, English guided tours available-€6, located in Tuileries Garden near Place de la Concorde (Mo: Concorde), 15-minute stroll from the Orsay, +33 1 44 77 80 07, www.musee-orangerie.fr.

☐ See the Orangerie Museum Tour chapter.

Forum des Halles

Today's modern shopping mall and esplanade covers what was, since the Middle Ages, the center of all food distribution in Paris. For eight centuries, Les Halles (*lay all*, the halls) functioned as a gargantuan open market where fish, meats, and vegetables were sold and distributed. By the late 1800s the market was covered with muscular steel arches and looked something like Paris' older train stations. The area buzzed 24/7—meats were butchered and fish were cleaned until late at night, farmers and fishermen arrived with their goods early in the mornings, and deals were made throughout the day. In 1971 the market was torn down: Increased traffic, smells, and higher land values had forced its relocation to near Orly airport (in the town of Rungis).

Today's incarnation of the huge market—Forum des Halles—is a multilevel shopping center. It's famous for its canopy with louvers to maximize the shade and is designed to collect rainwater, which powers a fountain that cascades from its peak down to a babbling man-made brook. The mall is the embodiment of 21st-century urban design: It quietly rests over a massive underground transportation hub and faces a pleasant city park (with a fun kids' zone) and esplanade. The park is overlooked by the spindly Gothic St. Eustache Church (described next) and the stately old Bourse de Commerce building, which now houses a contemporary art collection (www.pinaultcollection.com).

Nearby: Rue Montorgueil and Rue Montmartre are delightful café-lined streets a *macaron* toss from the shopping mall (described in the Shopping in Paris chapter).

St. Eustache Church

This impressive Gothic church is a worthy alternative to Notre-Dame during the famous cathedral's closure. Built 300 years after Notre-Dame (and similar in size), St. Eustache is a testament to the enduring appeal of the Gothic style. From the exterior, St. Eustache's forest of flying buttresses makes Notre-Dame's seem tame by comparison. Inside you'll notice Renaissance details, but its Gothic style resonates. St. Eustache served the community of vendors of the once-magnificent outdoor market of Les Halles. After the market relocated in 1971, this "church of the market people" fell silent. Today, in the rear of the church, you'll find a delightful sculpture honoring the market tradition of this neighborhood: *The Departure of Fruit and Vegetables from the Heart of Paris*, by Raymond Mason.

Cost and Hours: Free, Sun-Fri 9:30-19:00, Sat from 10:00, 146 Rue Rambuteau, Mo: Les Halles, +33 1 42 36 31 05, www.saint-eustache.org.

Louvre Wine Museum (Les Caves du Louvre)

This free, scratch-and-sniff wine museum has engaging exhibits describing everything from *terroir* (the qualities that come from soil, climate, etc.) to grape varieties to corks to bottle labels (using a free "Wines in Paris" app that can serve you well long after your visit). Your self-guided tour ends with an optional wine tasting (€19/3 wines). They also offer €32 guided tours in English with wine tasting and a €75 hands-on workshop in wine blending that includes a bottle of your very own blend.

Cost and Hours: Museum-free, tastings-€19-34; daily 14:00-18:00, last entry one hour before closing; between Forum des Halles and the Louvre at 52 Rue de l'Arbre Sec, Mo: Louvre-Rivoli, +33 1 40 28 13 11, www.cavesdulouvre.com.

EIFFEL TOWER AND NEARBY
▲▲▲Eiffel Tower (La Tour Eiffel)

Built on the 100th anniversary of the French Revolution (and in the spirit of the Industrial Revolution), the tower was the center-

piece of a World Expo designed simply to show off what people could build in 1889. For decades it was the tallest structure the world had ever known, and though it's since been eclipsed, it's still the most visited monument. Ride the elevators to the top of its 1,063 feet for expansive views that stretch 40 miles. Then descend to the two lower levels, where the views are arguably even better, since the monuments are more recognizable.

Cost and Hours: €27 to ride all the way to the top, €17.50 for just the two lower levels, €11 to climb the stairs to the first or second level, €21 to climb the stairs to the second level and take the elevator to the summit, 50 percent cheaper for those under 25, 75 percent cheaper for those under 12, book online in advance (see below), not covered by Museum Pass; open daily mid-June-Aug 9:00-24:45, Sept-mid-June 9:30-23:45, last ascent to top by elevator at 22:30 and to lower levels at 23:00 all year (stairs same except Sept-mid-June last ascent 18:30); cafés and great view restaurants, Mo: Bir-Hakeim or Trocadéro, RER/Train-C: Champ de Mars-Tour Eiffel (all a 10-minute walk away). Recorded information +33 8 92 70 12 39, www.toureiffel.paris.

Reservations Smart: Make a reservation well in advance of your visit—or be ready to wait in long lines. At www.toureiffel.paris, you can book a time slot for your ascent; this allows you to skip the long initial entry line. Tickets go on sale about 60 days in advance and sell out quickly for visits from April through September, so don't dally.

📖 See the Eiffel Tower Tour chapter (which includes more tips on getting in).

▲Place du Trocadéro

This fountain-fronted square just across the river and uphill from the Eiffel Tower delivers the greatest views of that landmark. Trocadéro's view plaza is a circus of tourists from early to late (watch for pickpockets). The construction you see is the beginnings of a new pedestrian-friendly garden connecting the Place du Trocadéro with the Ecole Militaire across the Seine. The busy Pont d'Iéna bridge will be made traffic-free, and a series of mini-parks will delight walkers as they explore this area.

Place du Trocadéro is named for a 19th-century battle victory by *Les* French over Spain and is overseen by a statue of WWI Supreme Allied Commander Ferdinand Foch on his horse. Two interesting museums, described next, flank the plaza as wings of the curved Palais de Chaillot, built for the 1937 World's Fair.

National Maritime Museum (Musée National de la Marine)

This kid-friendly museum, closed until at least 2023, anchors a dazzling collection of ship and submarine models, torpedoes, cannonballs, *beaucoup* bowsprits, and naval you-name-it. Enjoy the full-sized party barge made for Napoleon in 1810 and look up at the elaborate stern of the 1694 *Réale de France* royal galley (don't miss the scale model). Exhibits describe ship construction, from Roman vessels to modern cruise ships to aircraft carriers. Few English explanations make the free audioguide essential.

Cost and Hours: Likely €8.50, includes audioguide, free for those age 26 and under, covered by Museum Pass; Mon and Wed-Fri 11:00-18:00, Sat-Sun until 19:00, closed Tue; on left side of Place du Trocadéro with your back to Eiffel Tower, tel. +33 1 53 65 69 69, www.musee-marine.fr.

Architecture and Monuments Museum (Cité de l'Architecture et du Patrimoine)

This museum, on the east side of Place du Trocadéro, takes you through 1,000 years of French architecture, starring some of France's greatest Gothic churches—all brought to life through full-sized casts and scale models.

Cost and Hours: €9, covered by Museum Pass, free on first Sun of the month; open Wed-Mon 11:00-19:00, Thu until 21:00, closed Tue; helpful audioguide-€5, 1 Place du Trocadéro, Mo: Trocadéro, RER/Train-C: Champ de Mars-Tour Eiffel, +33 1 58 51 52 00, www.citechaillot.fr.

Visiting the Museum: Pick up the museum plan, augment it with the English info posted in many rooms, and focus most of your time on the ground floor. Walk the length of the floor, passing under tympanum arches and pondering how many ways you can envision the Last Judgment. Gaze into the eyes of medieval statues from Cluny Abbey, Chartres Cathedral, Château de Chambord,

SIGHTS

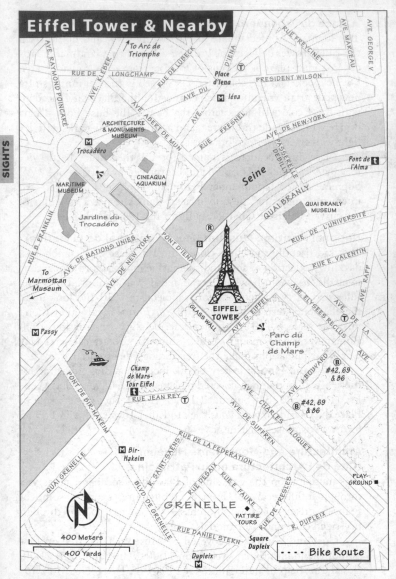

Eiffel Tower & Nearby

and much more. You'll find an exhibit on Notre-Dame and its fire, along with some original statues (removed from the cathedral for cleaning just before the fire), a worthwhile exhibit on the destroyed spire, and models of the timber-frame roof support that burned. A U-turn at the end of the hall leads to the Renaissance and the screaming passion of the Revolution.

Take the elevator up a floor (level N-2) to see thought-provoking designs for modern projects, including sports arenas, suspen-

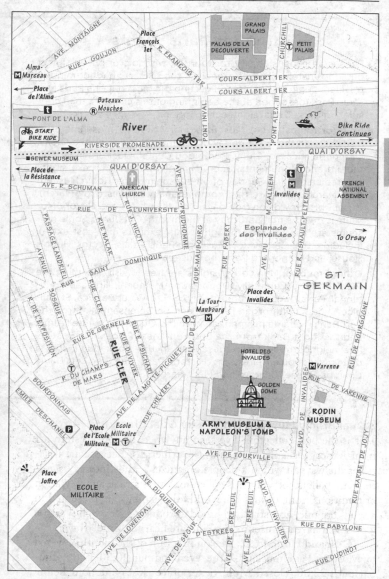

sion bridges, and low-income housing. You can walk into a room from Le Corbusier's 1952 Habitation Unit from Marseille and appreciate what a forward thinker he was. Farther along, you'll see how colorfully painted the chapels were in medieval churches. The views to the Eiffel Tower are sensational. The attached café makes for a classy break in your sightseeing, with more views of the Eiffel Tower.

Affording Paris' Sights

Paris is an expensive city for tourists, with lots of pricey sights, but—fortunately—lots of freebies, too. Smart, budget-minded travelers begin by buying and getting the most out of a Paris Museum Pass (described at the beginning of this chapter), then considering these frugal sightseeing options.

Free (or Almost Free) Museums: Many of Paris' museums offer free entry on the first Sunday of the month, including the Orsay, Orangerie, Picasso, Cluny, Pompidou Center, Quai Branly, Architecture and Monuments, and Delacroix museums. These sights are free on the first Sunday of off-season months: Rodin Museum (Oct-March), plus Arc de Triomphe and Versailles (Nov-March). Expect big crowds on free days. The Jewish Art and History Museum is free the first Saturday of the month (Oct-June). Some museums are always free (though special exhibits may cost extra), including the Carnavalet Museum, Petit Palais, Victor Hugo's House, and Fragonard Perfume Museum.

Other Freebies: Many other sights are free to visit, including the Père Lachaise Cemetery, Deportation Memorial, Holocaust Memorial, Paris Plages (summers only), Sacré-Cœur Basilica, St. Sulpice Church (with organ recital), and La Défense mall. Stroll the Left Bank riverside promenade from the Orsay to Pont de l'Alma, and the Right Bank from the Louvre to near Place de la Bastille. The neighborhood walks described in this book don't cost a dime unless you enter a sight (Historic Paris, Rue Cler, Left Bank, Champs-Elysées, Marais, and Montmartre).

▲Quai Branly Museum (Musée du Quai Branly)

This is the best collection I've seen anywhere of non-Western art from Africa, Oceania, Asia, and the Americas. Because art illustrates the ways in which a people organizes and delineates its culture and beliefs, viewing this collection offers a richer appreciation of traditions from around the world. The exhibits are presented in a wild, organic, and strikingly modern building. It's well worth a look if you have a Museum Pass and are near the Eiffel Tower.

Cost and Hours: €12, free on first Sun of the month, covered by Museum Pass; museum—Tue-Wed and Sun 10:30-19:00, Thu-Sat until 22:00, closed Mon, ticket office closes one hour before closing; gardens—Tue-Wed and Sun 9:15-19:30, Thu-Sat until 21:15, closed Mon; audioguide-€5, 37 Quai Branly, 10-minute walk east (upriver) of Eiffel Tower, along the river, RER/Train-C: Champ de Mars-Tour Eiffel or Pont de l'Alma, +33 1 56 61 70 00, www.quaibranly.fr.

Visiting the Museum: After passing the security check and the ticket taker, pick up the museum map, then follow a ramp upstream along a projected river of the 1,657 names of the peoples

Paris' glorious, entertaining parks are free, *bien sûr.* These include Luxembourg Garden, Champ de Mars (under the Eiffel Tower), Tuileries Garden (between the Louvre and Place de la Concorde), Palais Royal Courtyards, Jardin des Plantes, Parc Monceau, and La Coulée Verte. Versailles' gardens are free most weekdays in peak season and daily in winter (Nov-March).

Reduced Prices: The Eiffel Tower costs less if you restrict your visit to the two lower levels—and even less if you use the stairs.

Free Concerts: Venues offering free or cheap (€10-20) concerts include the American Church, Army Museum, St. Sulpice Church, Quai Branly Museum, and La Madeleine Church. For a listing of free concerts, check *L'Officiel des Spectacles* magazine (under the Concerts section) and look for events marked *entrée libre.*

Good-Value Tours: At €15-25, Paris Walks' tours are a good value. The Seine River cruises (allow €15), best after dark, are also worthwhile. My Bus #69 Sightseeing Tour, which costs only the price of a transit fare (€2), could be the best deal of all. The Paris audio tours covered on the Rick Steves Audio Europe app are all free (see page 24).

Pricey...But Worth It? Certain big-ticket items—primarily the top of the Eiffel Tower, the Louvre, and Versailles—are expensive and crowded, but offer once-in-a-lifetime experiences. All together they amount to less than the cost of a ticket to Disneyland—only these are real.

covered in the museum. The permanent collection occupies the first floor up. Masks, statuettes, musical instruments, textiles, clothes, voodoo dolls, and a variety of temporary exhibitions and activities are artfully presented and exquisitely lit (the dim lighting also helps to preserve the fragile works). There's no need to follow a route: Wander at whim. Helpful English explanations are posted in most rooms and provide sufficient description for most visitors, though serious students will want to rent the audioguide.

Eiffel Tower Views: Even if you skip the museum, drop by its peaceful garden Café Jacques for fine Eiffel Tower views and enjoy the intriguing gardens. The pedestrian bridge that crosses the river and runs up to the museum also has sensational tower views.

▲Paris Sewer Museum (Les Egouts de Paris)

Discover what happens after you flush. This quick, interesting, and slightly stinky visit (a perfumed hanky helps) takes you along a few hundred yards of water tunnels in the world's first underground sewer system.

Cost and Hours: €9, covered by Museum Pass, ask about free entry for those under 26; Tue-Sun 10:00-17:00, closed Mon, last entry one hour before closing; audioguide may be available-€3, located where Pont de l'Alma greets the Left Bank—on the right side of the bridge as you face the river, Mo: Alma-Marceau, RER/Train-C: Pont de l'Alma, +33 1 53 68 27 81.

Visiting the Sewer: With nary a word in English throughout the museum, the loaner booklet, map, and audioguide (if available) are essential. Grab these as you enter, then drop down into Jean Valjean's world of tunnels, rats, and manhole covers. (Victor Hugo was friends with the sewer inspector when he wrote *Les Misérables*.) Well-organized displays explain the history of water distribution and collection in Paris, from Roman times to the present.

Sens de la Visite ("direction of visit") signs and numbered stops guide you along open sewers and through exhibits that explain the evolution of this amazing network of sewers. More than 1,500 miles of tunnels carry 317 million gallons of water daily through this underworld. It's the world's longest sewer system—so long, they say, that if it were laid out straight, it would stretch from Paris all the way to Istanbul.

It's enlightening to see how much work goes into something we take for granted. Sewage didn't always disappear so readily. In the Middle Ages, wastewater was tossed from windows to a center street gutter, then washed into the river (which also supplied locals' drinking water). In castles, sewage ended up in the moat (enhancing the moat's defensive role). In the 1500s, French Renaissance King François I moved from château to château (he had several) when the moat-muck became too much. The museum illustrates how, over time, sewage became separated from drinking water and explains the intricate systems in place today that sustain that separation.

▲▲Rue Cler

Paris is always changing, but a stroll down this market street introduces you to a thriving, traditional Parisian neighborhood and offers insights into the local culture. Although this is a wealthy district, Rue Cler retains the workaday charm still found in most neighborhoods throughout Paris. The shops lining the street are filled with the freshest produce, the stinkiest cheese, the tastiest chocolate, and the finest wines (markets generally open  Tue-Sat 8:30-13:00 & 15:00-19:30, Sun 8:30-12:00, dead Sun afternoon and Mon). I'm still far from a gourmet eater, but my time spent tasting my way along Rue Cler has heightened my appreciation of good cuisine (as well as the French knack for good living).

☐ See the Rue Cler Walk chapter or ∩ download my free audio tour.

▲▲Army Museum and Napoleon's Tomb (Musée de l'Armée)

Europe's greatest military museum, in the Hôtel des Invalides, provides interesting coverage of several wars, particularly World Wars

I and II. At the center of the complex, Napoleon lies majestically dead inside several coffins under a grand dome—a goosebump inducing pilgrimage for historians. The dome overhead glitters with 26 pounds of thinly pounded gold leaf.

Cost and Hours: €14, free for military personnel in uniform, free for kids but they must wait in line for ticket, covered by Museum Pass; daily 10:00-18:00, Napoleon's Tomb until 21:00 on Tue; multimedia guide-€5, cafeteria, +33 1 44 42 38 77, www.musee-armee.fr.

Getting There: The Hôtel des Invalides is at 129 Rue de Grenelle, a 10-minute walk from Rue Cler (Mo: La Tour Maubourg, Varenne, or Invalides). You can take bus #69 (from the Marais and Rue Cler) or bus #6 from the St. Germain-des-Prés area. Buses #82 or #92 also take you there.

☐ See the Army Museum & Napoleon's Tomb Tour chapter.

▲▲Rodin Museum (Musée Rodin)

This user-friendly museum with gardens is filled with passionate works by Auguste Rodin (1840-1917), the greatest sculptor since

Michelangelo. You'll see *The Kiss, The Thinker, The Gates of Hell,* and many more, well displayed in the mansion where the sculptor lived and worked. Exhibits trace Rodin's artistic development, explain how his bronze statues were cast, and show some of the studies he created to work up to his masterpiece, the unfinished *Gates of Hell.* Learn about Rodin's tumultuous relationship with his apprentice and lover, Camille Claudel. Mull over what makes his

SIGHTS

Paris for Early Birds and Night Owls

Most major sights in Paris are open between 9:00 and 18:00, but some open even earlier and/or stay open late. Parks such as Luxembourg Garden are a good option for early or late sightseeing (open from dawn to dusk). The Champs-Elysées is best at night.

Sights Open Early

Sacré-Cœur: Basilica daily at 6:30 (dome sleeps in until 10:00)

St. Sulpice Church: Daily at 7:30

Paris Plages (Paris Beaches): Mid-July–mid-Aug daily (24/7)

Père Lachaise Cemetery: Mon-Fri at 8:00, Sat at 8:30, Sun at 9:00

Gardens at Versailles: Daily at 8:00

Sights Open Late

Every night in Paris, at least one sight is open late. Keep in mind that sights may stop admitting visitors well before posted closing times.

Jacquemart-André Museum: Mon until 20:30 during special exhibits

Gardens at Versailles: April-Oct daily until 20:30 (may close earlier for special events)

Marmottan Museum: Thu until 21:00

Napoleon's Tomb: Tue until 21:00

Pompidou Center: Wed-Mon until 21:00, special exhibits until 22:00 and Thu until 23:00

Architecture and Monuments Museum: Thu until 21:00

Jewish Art and History Museum: Wed until 21:00 during special exhibits

Delacroix Museum: First Thu of the month until 21:00

Holocaust Memorial: Thu until 22:00

Cluny Museum: First and third Thu of the month until 21:00

Quai Branly: Thu-Sat until 22:00 (gardens until 21:15)

Louvre: Possibly Wed and Fri until 21:45; check online

Orsay Museum: Thu until 21:45

Sacré-Cœur: Basilica daily until 22:30

Arc de Triomphe: Daily until 23:00, Oct-March until 22:30

Paris Plages (Paris Beaches): Mid-July–mid-Aug daily (24/7)

Eiffel Tower: Daily mid-June-Aug until 24:45, Sept-mid-June until 23:45

sculptures some of the most evocative since the Renaissance. And stroll the beautiful gardens, packed with many of his greatest works (including *The Thinker*) and ideal for artistic reflection.

Cost and Hours: €13, free for those under age 18, free on first Sun of the month Oct-March, €24 combo-ticket with Orsay Museum, both museum and garden covered by Museum Pass; Tue-Sun 10:00-18:30, closed Mon, Oct-March garden closes at dusk; audioguide-€6, mandatory baggage check, self-service café in garden, 77 Rue de Varenne, Mo: Varenne, +33 1 44 18 61 10, www.musee-rodin.fr.

☐ See the Rodin Museum Tour chapter.

▲▲Marmottan Museum (Musée Marmottan Monet)

In this private, intimate, and untouristy museum, you'll find the best collection anywhere of works by Impressionist headliner Claude Monet. Follow Monet's life through more than a hundred works, from simple sketches to the *Impression: Sunrise* painting that gave his artistic movement its start—and a name. The museum also displays some of the enjoyable large-scale canvases featuring the water lilies from his garden at Giverny.

Cost and Hours: €12, not covered by Museum Pass, ask about combo-ticket with Monet's garden and house at Giverny (see page 627; lets you skip the line at Giverny); Tue-Sun 10:00-18:00, Thu until 21:00, closed Mon; audioguide-€4 (includes temporary exhibits), 2 Rue Louis-Boilly, Mo: La Muette, +33 1 44 96 50 33, www.marmottan.fr.

☐ See the Marmottan Museum Tour chapter.

LEFT BANK

▲Latin Quarter (Quartier Latin)

This Left Bank neighborhood, immediately across the river from Notre-Dame, was the center of Roman Paris. But the Latin Quarter's touristy fame relates to its intriguing, artsy, bohemian character. This was perhaps Europe's leading university district in the Middle Ages, when Latin was the language of higher education. The neighborhood's main boulevards (St. Michel and  St. Germain) are lined with cafés—once the haunts of great poets and philosophers, now the hangouts of tired tourists. Though still youthful and artsy, much of this area is touristy and filled with

SIGHTS

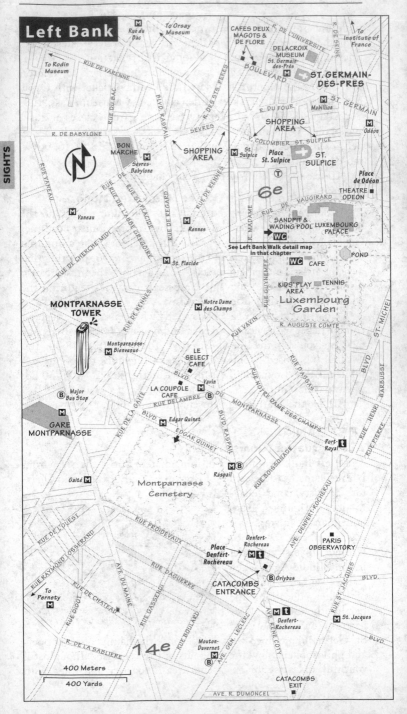

Left Bank

To Orsay Museum
Rue du Bac

To Rodin Museum

RUE DE VARENNE

R. DE BABYLONE

RUE DU BAC

BLVD. RASPAIL

SÈVRES

SHOPPING AREA

BON MARCHE

Sèvres-Babylone

RUE YANEAU

RUE DE SÈVRES

RUE DE ST-PLACIDE

RUE DE L'ABBÉ GREGOIRE

RUE DE CHERCHE-MIDI

RUE DE REGARD

RUE DE RENNES

Vaneau

Rennes

St. Placide

CAFES DEUX MAGOTS & DE FLORE

DELACROIX MUSEUM

St. Germain-des-Prés

BOULEVARD

R. DES STS-PÈRES

R. DE L'UNIVERSITÉ

R. DE SEINE

To Institute of France

ST. GERMAIN-DES-PRES

R. DU FOUR

ST. GERMAIN

Mabillon

SHOPPING AREA

V. COLOMBIER   ST. SULPICE

St. Sulpice

Place St. Sulpice

ST. SULPICE

Odeon

Place de Odéon

THEATRE ODEON

6e

RUE   DE   VAUGIRARD

R. MADAME

SANDPIT & WADING POOL

WC

LUXEMBOURG PALACE

See Left Bank Walk detail map in that chapter

WC   CAFE

POND

KIDS' PLAY AREA

TENNIS

Luxembourg Garden

R. AUGUSTE COMTE

RUE GUYNEMER

BLVD.   ST-MICHEL

MONTPARNASSE TOWER

RUE DE RENNES

Notre Dame des Champs

RUE VAVIN

RUE D'ASSAS

RUE NOTRE-DAME-DES-CHAMPS

BLVD. RASPAIL

Montparnasse-Bienvenue

LE SELECT CAFE

BLVD.   Vavin

LA COUPOLE CAFE

RUE DELAMBRE

RUE DE LA GAITE

BLVD.   Edgar Quinet

EDGAR QUINET

BLVD.   DU   MONTPARNASSE

Raspail

RUE   BOISSONADE

RUE HENRI BARBUSSE

RUE PIERRE

Port-Royal

Major Bus Stop

GARE MONTPARNASSE

Gaité

Montparnasse Cemetery

RUE DE L'OUEST

RUE FROIDEVAUX

RUE DAGUERRE

Denfert-Rochereau

Place Denfert-Rochereau

CATACOMBS ENTRANCE

Orlybus

PARIS OBSERVATORY

AVE. DENFERT-ROCHEREAU

RUE ST-JACQUES

BLVD.

To Pernety

RUE RAYMOND LOSSERAND

AVE. DU MAINE

RUE DE CHATEAU

RUE DIDOT

RUE GASSENDI

RUE BOULARD

AVE. DU MAINE

Denfert-Rochereau

St. Jacques

AVE. RENÉ COTY

BLVD.

14e

R. DE LA SABLIERE

Mouton-Duvernet

AVE. GEN. LECLERC

400 Meters

400 Yards

CATACOMBS EXIT

AVE. R. DUMONCEL

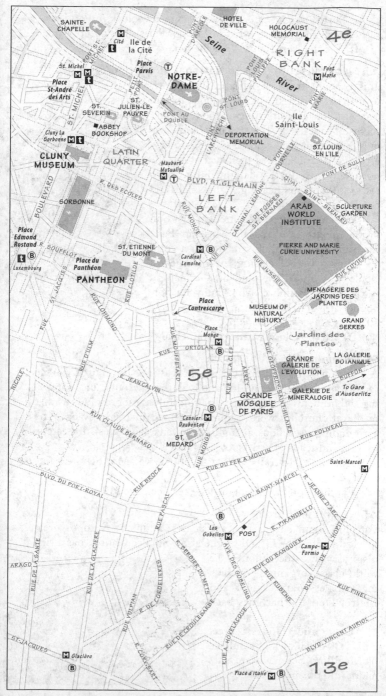

SIGHTS

cheap North African eateries. Exploring a few blocks up or down-river reveals the pulse of what survives of Paris' classic Left Bank.

ロ See the Left Bank Walk chapter.

▲▲Cluny Museum (Musée National du Moyen Age)

This treasure trove of Middle Ages (Moyen Age) art fills old Roman baths, offering close-up looks at stained glass, Notre-Dame carvings, fine goldsmithing and jewelry, and rooms of tapestries. The star here is the ex-quisite series of six *Lady and the Unicorn* tap-estries: A delicate, as-medieval-as-can-be noble lady introduces a delighted unicorn to the senses of taste, hearing, sight, smell, and touch.

Cost and Hours: €12, free on first Sun of the month, covered by Museum Pass; Tue-Sun 9:30-18:15, closed Mon, last entry 45 minutes before closing; near corner of Boulevards St. Michel and St. Germain at 6 Place Paul Painlevé; Mo: Cluny La Sor-bonne, St-Michel, or Odéon; +33 1 53 73 78 10, www.musee-moyenage.fr.

ロ See the Cluny Museum Tour chapter.

St. Germain-des-Prés Church

A church was first built on this site in AD 558. The church you see today was constructed in 1163 and is all that's left of a once sprawl-ing and influential monastery. The colorful interior reminds us that medieval churches were originally painted in bright colors. The surrounding area hops at night with venerable cafés, fire-eaters, mimes, and scads of artists.

Cost and Hours: Free, daily 8:00-19:45, Mo: St-Germain-des-Prés.

For more on St. Germain-des-Prés, see page 313.

▲St. Sulpice Church

For pipe-organ enthusiasts, a visit here is one of Europe's great musical treats. The Grand Orgue at St. Sulpice Church has a rich history, with a succession of 12 world-class organists—includ-ing Charles-Marie Widor and Marcel Dupré—that goes back 300 years.

Cost and Hours: Free, daily 7:30-19:30, Mo: St-Sulpice or Mabillon. See www.aross.fr/en for info on special concerts.

Sunday Organ Recitals: You can hear the organ played before and after Sunday Mass (10:45-11:00, 12:00-12:30, and 18:35; come appropriately dressed). The post-Mass offering is a high-powered 25-minute recital, usually performed by talented organist Daniel Roth.

Visiting the Church: Patterned after St. Paul's Cathedral in London, the church has a Neoclassical arcaded facade and two round towers. Inside, in the first chapel on the right, are three murals of fighting angels by Delacroix: *Jacob Wrestling the Angel, Heliodorus Chased from the Temple,* and *The Archangel Michael* (on the ceiling). The fourth chapel on the right has a statue of Joan of Arc and wall plaques listing hundreds from St. Sulpice's congregation who died during World War I. The north transept wall features an Egyptian-style obelisk used as a gnomon on a sundial. The last chapel before the exit has a display on the Shroud of Turin.

For more on St. Sulpice, see page 314.

Nearby: Tempting boutiques surround the church (see the Shopping in Paris chapter), and Luxembourg Garden is nearby.

Delacroix Museum (Musée National Eugène Delacroix)

This quaint and quiet museum celebrating the Romantic artist Eugène Delacroix (1798-1863) was once his home and studio. A friend of bohemian artistic greats—including George Sand and Frédéric Chopin—Delacroix is most famous for his monumental painting of flag-waving *Liberty Leading the People* (displayed at the Louvre). He moved to this studio in 1857 to be within walking distance of St. Sulpice Church (described earlier), where he was furiously working on its chapel of St. Agnes.

Cost and Hours: €7, free on first Sun of the month, covered by Museum Pass; Wed-Mon 9:30-17:30, first Thu of the month until 21:00, closed Tue; 6 Rue de Furstenberg, Mo: St-Germain-des-Prés, +33 1 44 41 86 50, www.musee-delacroix.fr.

Visiting the Museum: The tiny museum—with a few of Delacroix's paintings and a smattering of memorabilia—is three rooms on one floor in the main building, the artist's studio in back, and his oasis-like garden. Most rooms have good posted explanations in English.

Delacroix's living room is decorated with original furniture and paintings. The bedroom (with fireplace) is where Delacroix died in 1863, nursed by his longtime servant, Lucile Virginie "Jenny" Le Guillou (her portrait may be on display). Look for Delacroix's small worktable (where he kept his paints). Outside is his small-but-peaceful walled garden where you can visit his studio *(atelier)*.

Delacroix built the studio to his own specifications, with high ceilings, big windows, and a skylight, ideal for an artist working prior to electric lights. It's easy to imagine him working at his easel.

While there are a few "permanent" paintings here, the collection is shuffled annually. Still, you'll always find good examples of his dramatic style in paintings and sketches. Some of Delacroix's most popular works were book illustrations (lithographs for Goethe's *Faust*, Revolutionary history, and Shakespeare). Admire Delacroix's artistic range—from messy, colorful oils to meticulously detailed lithographs.

For more on Delacroix's life, see page 310.

SIGHTS

▲Luxembourg Garden (Jardin du Luxembourg)

This lovely 60-acre garden is an Impressionist painting brought to life. Slip into a green chair pondside, enjoy the radiant flower beds, go jogging, play tennis or basketball, sail a toy sailboat, or take in a chess game or puppet show. Some of the park's prettiest (and quietest) sections lie around its perimeter. Notice any pigeons? The story goes that a very poor Ernest Hemingway used to hand-hunt (read: strangle) them here.

Cost and Hours: Free, daily dawn until dusk, Mo: Odéon, RER/Train-B: Luxembourg.

For more on the garden and nearby sights, see page 316. Also see the Paris with Children chapter for kid-friendly activities in the garden and the Left Bank Walk chapter for café recommendations.

Other Parks: If you enjoy Luxembourg Garden and want to see more green spaces, you could visit the more elegant **Parc Monceau** (Mo: Monceau), the colorful **Jardin des Plantes** (Mo: Jussieu or Gare d'Austerlitz, RER/Train-C: Gare d'Austerlitz), the **Tuileries Garden** (between the Louvre and Place de la Concorde, Mo: Concorde or Tuileries), or the hilly and bigger **Parc des Buttes-Chaumont** (Mo: Buttes-Chaumont).

▲Panthéon

This state-capitol-style Neoclassical monument celebrates France's illustrious history and people, balances a Foucault pendulum, and is the final resting place of many French VIPs.

In 1744, an ailing King Louis XV was miraculously healed by St. Geneviève, the city's patron saint, and he thanked her by replacing her ruined church with a more fitting tribute. By the time the church

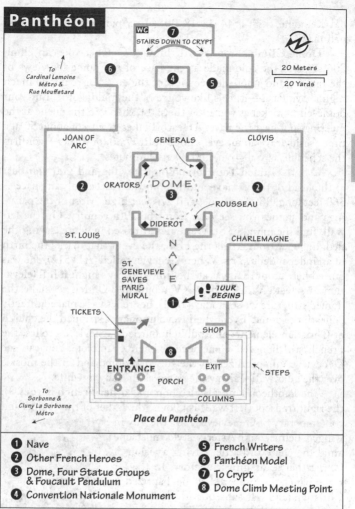

Panthéon

WC

7

STAIRS DOWN TO CRYPT

To Cardinal Lemoine Métro & Rue Mouffetard

6

4

5

20 Meters
20 Yards

JOAN OF ARC

GENERALS

CLOVIS

2

ORATORS

D O M E

3

ROUSSEAU

DIDEROT

ST. LOUIS

N A V E

CHARLEMAGNE

ST. GENEVIEVE SAVES PARIS MURAL

1

TOUR BEGINS

TICKETS

SHOP

8

ENTRANCE

EXIT

STEPS

PORCH

To Sorbonne & Cluny La Sorbonne Métro

COLUMNS

Place du Panthéon

- **1** Nave
- **2** Other French Heroes
- **3** Dome, Four Statue Groups & Foucault Pendulum
- **4** Convention Nationale Monument
- **5** French Writers
- **6** Panthéon Model
- **7** To Crypt
- **8** Dome Climb Meeting Point

SIGHTS

was completed (1791), however, the secular-minded Revolution was in full swing, and the church was converted into a nonreligious mausoleum honoring the "Champions of French liberty": Voltaire, Rousseau, and others. On the entrance pediment (inspired by the ancient Panthéon in Rome), the Revolutionaries carved the inscription, "To the great men of the Fatherland." The audioguide is worthwhile for a longer description of the many painted scenes.

Cost and Hours: €11.50, free for those under age 18, covered by Museum Pass, €3.50 for "panorama" dome climb (not covered by Museum Pass); daily 10:00-18:30, Oct-March until 18:00, last entry 45 minutes before closing; audioguide €3, Mo: Cardinal Lemoine, +33 1 44 32 18 00, http://pantheon.monuments-nationaux.fr.

Dome Climb: From April through October you can climb 206 steps to the colonnade at the base of the dome for views of the interior and a 360-degree view of the city. You're not so much high above Paris—it feels like you're in the middle of it. Buy your dome-climb ticket as you enter the sight, then join the queue at the meeting spot near the nave. An escort takes groups of about 50 at a time. Visits leave about every hour until 17:30 (or earlier—confirm the schedule as you go in) and take 40 minutes.

◐ Self-Guided Tour: Stand on the white-and-gray star bust at the head of the **❶ nave** and take in the vast, evenly lit space—360 feet long, 280 feet wide, and 270 feet high. Most of the paintings and statues you see date from the 19th century. On the left wall, find the mural of **St. Geneviève** dressed in white, saving the fledgling city from Attila the Hun, the event that marks the birth of an independent Paris. When Geneviève died (AD 512), she was buried here atop what was at the time the city's highest hill (elevation 200 feet). When Louis XV rebuilt her church to make the domed structure we see today (1791), her relics were placed directly beneath the dome. Even when Revolutionaries stripped the church of Christian elements and publicly burned Geneviève's relics, the French still honored Geneviève as their champion. You can see Geneviève immortalized in the frescoed dome and in the mosaic over the altar wall—always depicted as the lady in white.

The Panthéon's murals also honor **❷ other French heroes.** In the right transept (left wall) is Clovis, the father of the Franks and contemporary of Geneviève. He's the guy in winged helmet and Asterix-style mustache amid the chaos of battle, having a vision of Christ that leads him to victory. In the far right panel, he prepares to be baptized a Christian (and was subsequently buried here on Geneviève's hill).

On the opposite wall is **Charlemagne** being crowned Emperor of the Franks (c. 800), marking the symbolic birth of France.

In the left transept (right wall) are scenes of Joan of Arc, who rallied the French in the 1420s to rid the country of the English, and was then burnt at the stake (far left).

Return to the nave. The 15,000-ton **❸ dome** is made of a core of iron ribs covered with stone. Under the dome stand **four statue groups** that mark the next phase of French history, the Revolution. Check them out counterclockwise: **Denis Diderot** created the *Encyclopédie* that championed secular knowledge. **Jean-Jacques**

Rousseau promoted the idea of a social contract between government and the people. **Napoleon** (on horseback) is surrounded by his generals. The **Restoration** is a statue of orators and bureaucrats who served the state as it sorted through the tumult of the Revolution and Napoleonic era and finally restored the monarchy—but this time kings were somewhat limited by a constitution.

A **Foucault pendulum** swings gracefully at the end of a cable suspended from the towering dome. It was here in 1851 that the scientist Léon Foucault first demonstrated the rotation of the earth. The great length of the cable (220 feet) produces a slow enough oscillation to make the rotation more obvious. Stand a few minutes and watch the pendulum's arc appear to shift as you and the earth rotate beneath it. It's easier to visualize if you picture the pendulum suspended directly above the North Pole, with the earth spinning beneath it. Every time the pendulum swings back to the same spot, the earth will have shifted. The pendulum can also be used to tell time: Check your watch against the 24-hour dial that surrounds the pendulum.

At the altar end of the church stands the massive ❹ **Convention Nationale Monument.** "Marianne," the fictional woman who

symbolized the Revolution, stands in the center, flanked by soldiers who fight for her and citizens who pledge allegiance to her. The inscription below reads "Live free or die." Marianne embodies liberty, reason, and the nation of France. Above her is a mosaic in which Christ (accompanied by Geneviève and Joan of Arc) seems to give his blessing. From Geneviève to Joan of Arc to Marianne, France has always incarnated its national spirit in the female form.

To the right of the monument, ❺ **French writers** have their names inscribed onto the walls.

To the far left of the monument is a room displaying a ❻ **model of the Panthéon.** This cross-section model allows you to look inside and see the structural elements. The dome is actually made of three domes-within-a-dome, and it's supported by flying buttresses. Also, notice that there's no patriotic inscription over the entrance, as the model was built before the Revolution.

A staircase behind the monument leads down to the ❼ **crypt,** where a panoply of greats is buried. Rousseau is along the right wall as you enter, while Voltaire faces him impishly from across the hall. Behind Voltaire is Soufflot (the architect who built the Panthéon). Straight ahead up a few steps and through the small central rotunda are more greats (all to the left): Victor Hugo *(Les Misérables, The Hunchback of Notre-Dame),* Alexandre Dumas *(The Three Musketeers, The Count of Monte Cristo),* and Louis Braille (who invented the script for the blind). Double back to the central rotunda and turn left to find scientist Marie Curie (follow the glow), and various WWII dead (from Holocaust victims to the hero of the Resistance, Jean Moulin). This building is a fitting monument to those who've forged France's freedom and defended freedom of thought.

Montparnasse Tower

This sadly out-of-place 59-story superscraper has one virtue: If you can't make it up the Eiffel Tower, the sensational views from this tower are cheaper, far easier to access (a 40-second elevator ride), and make for a fair consolation prize. Come early in the day for clearest skies and shortest lines and be treated to views from a comfortable interior and from up on the rooftop (consider their breakfast with a view). Sunset is great but views are disappointing after dark. Some say it's the very best view in Paris, as you can see the Eiffel Tower clearly...and you can't see the Montparnasse Tower at all.

Cost and Hours: €20, RS%—30 percent discount (2 people per book), not covered by Museum Pass; daily 10:00-23:30, Oct-March 11:00-22:30; entrance on Rue de l'Arrivée, Mo: Montparnasse-Bienvenüe—from the Métro, stay inside the station and follow signs to exit #1, +33 1 45 38 52 56, www.tourmontparnasse56.com.

Visiting the Tower: Find the elevator entrance near the skyscraper's main entry on the northwest side of the tower (with the train station to your back, it's around to the left side of the building; look for orange signs). Exit the elevator at the 56th floor to buy your ticket. Here you can marvel at the views of *tout Paris* (good even if cloudy), have a drink or a light lunch (reasonable prices), and peruse the gift shop. Exhibits identify highlights of the star-studded vista.

Next, climb three flights of steps to the open terrace on the 59th floor to enjoy magnificent views in all directions (good

English information posted and a surprise bar in summer). Here, 690 feet above Paris, you can scan the city through glass panels that limit wind. The view over Luxembourg Garden is terrific, as is the view up the Champ de Mars to the Eiffel Tower. Montparnasse Cemetery is right below, and the high-rise suburbs lie immediately to the west. From this vantage, it's easy to admire Baron Georges-Eugène Haussmann's grand-boulevard scheme (see sidebar later in this chapter). Notice the lush courtyards hiding behind grand street fronts.

Sightseeing Tip: The tower is an efficient stop when combined with a day trip to Chartres, which begins at the Montparnasse train station (see the Chartres chapter).

▲Catacombs

Spiral down 60 feet below the street and walk a one-mile route through tunnels containing the anonymous bones of six million permanent Parisians. Once inside, allow an hour if you dawdle.

Cost and Hours: €29 for timed-entry ticket, book online in advance, includes audioguide, not covered by Museum Pass; open Tue-Sun 10:00-20:30, closed Mon; €15 same-day tickets sometimes available online and at the door (limited availability; ticket booth closes at 19:30), otherwise consider Fat Tire Tours' "Skip the Line" tour (see page 49); +33 1 43 22 47 63, www.catacombes. paris.fr.

Getting There: It's at 1 Place Denfert-Rochereau. Take the Métro to Denfert-Rochereau and follow *Sortie 1*, then find the lion in the big traffic circle; if he looked left rather than right, he'd stare right at the green entrance to the Catacombs.

Background: In 1785, health-conscious Parisians looking to relieve congestion and improve the city's sanitary conditions emptied the church cemeteries and moved the bones here, to former limestone quarries, where incidentally, plaster of Paris was made. Then, in the mid-19th century, Baron Haussmann's many urban projects required the relocation of cemeteries, and these ancient, hand-dug quarries fit the bill. For decades, priests led ceremonial processions of black-veiled, bone-laden carts into the quarries, where the bones were stacked in piles five feet high and as much as 80 feet deep.

Visiting the Catacombs: You'll descend 130 steps and land in a room with English posters describing 45 million years of ancient geology, then walk for 10 minutes through tunnels to reach the bones. Appreciate that some of these tunnels were originally built sans mortar. The sign, "Halt, this is the empire of the dead," announces your arrival at the bones. From here, shuffle along passageways of artfully arranged, skull-studded tibiae; admire 300-year-old sculptures cut into the walls of the catacombs; and see more cheery signs: "Happy is he who is forever faced with the hour of his death and prepares himself for the end every day." The highlight for me is the Crypt of the Passion (a.k.a. "the Barrel"), where bones are meticulously packed in a barrel shape hiding a support pillar.

Climb many steps to emerge far from where you entered and find a good WC and a ghoulish gift shop selling skulls and more. Note to wannabe Hamlets: An attendant checks your bag at the exit for stolen souvenirs.

After Your Visit: You'll exit 10 minutes from where you started on Avenue René Coty (see the "Left Bank" map, earlier). From the exit, turn right and walk to the Denfert-Rochereau Métro station. Traffic-free Rue Daguerre, a pleasing pedestrian street (see the Shopping in Paris chapter), is a block from the Denfert-Rochereau Métro off Avenue du Général Leclerc (a block from where you entered the Catacombs).

Jardins des Plantes

For a review of sights within this kid-friendly gardener's mecca, see the Paris with Children chapter.

Muslim Paris

The Paris region is home to 1.7 million Muslims, many from France's former North African colonies (Algeria, Morocco, and Tunisia)—though most live in vast suburbs where tourists rarely venture. But just next to the Latin Quarter, a handy and inviting bit of Muslim Paris offers an intriguing glimpse at that world, with a mosque, a cultural center, and a popular teahouse.

Grande Mosquée de Paris

This mosque was founded in 1926 in gratitude for the sacrifices made by Muslims from France's colonial empire, who fought the Germans alongside the French in World War I (100,000 Muslims died in this effort). During World War II, the mosque provided refuge for Algerian and European Jews. Today's mosque is busy with worshippers, yet still welcomes non-Muslim visitors (be considerate and dress modestly; women don't need head scarves).

Cost and Hours: €3, Sat-Thu 9:00-12:00 & 14:00-18:00, closed to visitors Fri and on Muslim holidays, 2 bis Place du Puits de l'Ermite, Mo: Censier-Daubenton, Jussieu, or Place Monge, www.mosqueedeparis.net.

Eating at the Mosque: The Restaurant La Mosquée hides at the back of the mosque with wonderful Arabic ambience, a tea room with tasty baked goods and teas, and delicious meals (see listing on page 462).

Visiting the Mosque: The entrance is next to the tall minaret. Loop through its rooms and appreciate intricate wood-carved arches over whitewashed walls and elaborate tile work, with no images of humans anywhere. You'll start in the main courtyard (called a *sahn*) with a central fountain (for ablutions before prayer, which now take place below), and tour the mosque counterclockwise. Admire the exquisite detail in the capitals and wall sculptures. Peer into the large prayer hall (which non-Muslims and all women are prohibited from entering—Muslim women worship in a basement room). Exit the courtyard through the doorway at the far right corner and find a sumptuous library and meeting rooms, all surrounding a peaceful garden patio.

Arab World Institute (Institut du Monde Arabe)

Founded in 1980 to improve understanding of the Arab world in France with a museum and special exhibits, the Arab World Institute's striking, modern building also has free, 180-degree views over the river from its roof terrace.

Cost and Hours: Terrace—free, Sat-Sun until 19:00; museum—€8, not covered by Museum Pass; Tue-Fri 10:00-18:00, closed Mon; for terrace view don't wait in special exhibit line—ask for entrance for "*la terrasse*," 1 Rue des Fossés Saint-Bernard, Place Mohammed V, Mo: Jussieu, +33 1 40 51 38 38, www.imarabe.org.

CHAMPS-ELYSEES AND NEARBY
▲▲▲Champs-Elysées

This famous boulevard is Paris' backbone, with its greatest concentration of traffic (although it's delightfully traffic-free on the first Sun of the month).

From the Arc de Triomphe down Avenue des Champs-Elysées, all of France seems to converge on Place de la Concorde, the city's largest square. And though the Champs-Elysées has become as international as it is Parisian, a walk down the two-mile boulevard is still a must.

To reach the top of the Champs-Elysées, take the Métro to the Arc de Triomphe (Mo: Charles de Gaulle-Etoile), then saunter down the grand boulevard (Métro stops every few blocks, including George V and Franklin D. Roosevelt).

📖 See the Champs-Elysées Walk chapter.

SIGHTS

▲▲Arc de Triomphe

Napoleon had the magnificent Arc de Triomphe commissioned to commemorate his victory at the 1805 battle of Austerlitz. The foot

of the arch is a stage on which the last two centuries of Parisian history have played out—from the funeral of Napoleon to the goose-stepping arrival of the Nazis to the triumphant return of Charles de Gaulle after the Allied liberation. Examine the carvings on the pillars, featuring a mighty Napoleon and excitable Lady Liberty. Pay your respects at the Tomb of the Unknown Soldier. Then climb the 284 steps to the observation deck up top, with sweeping skyline panoramas and a mesmerizing view down onto the traffic that swirls around the arch.

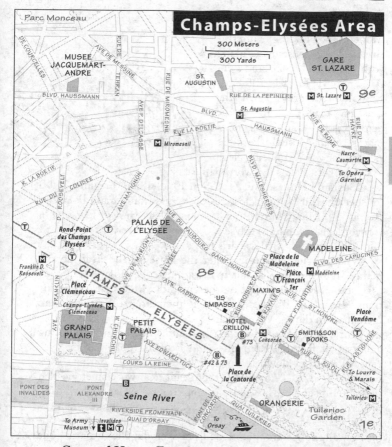

Cost and Hours: Free to view exterior; steps to rooftop-€13, timed-entry tickets available online, free for those under age 18, free on first Sun of the month Nov-March, covered by Museum Pass—pass holders do not need to reserve a time slot; daily 10:00-23:00, Oct-March until 22:30, last entry 45 minutes before closing; Place Charles de Gaulle, use underpass to reach arch, Mo: Charles de Gaulle-Etoile, +33 1 55 37 73 77, www.paris-arc-de-triomphe.fr.

📖 See the Champs-Elysées Walk chapter.

▲Petit Palais (and Musée des Beaux-Arts)

This free museum displays a broad collection of paintings and sculpture from the 1600s to the 1900s on its ground floor, and an easy-to-appreciate collection of art from Greek antiquities to Art Nouveau in its basement. While the collection can be shuffled about for special exhibits, the part I describe is usually unaffected. Though it houses mostly second-tier art, there are a few diamonds in the rough (including works by Rembrandt, Courbet, Cézanne,

Sisley, Pissarro, Degas, and Monet). The building is impressive, and was constructed along with the Grand Palais and Pont Alexandre III for the 1900 Paris Exhibition (World's Fair). The museum's classy café merits the detour alone—and if it's raining and your Museum Pass has expired, or you just need a clean WC, the Petit Palais is a worthwhile stop.

Cost and Hours: Free, Tue-Sun 10:00-18:00, Fri until 21:00 for special exhibits (fee), closed Mon; across from Grand Palais on Avenue Winston Churchill, a looooong block west of Place de la Concorde, Mo: Champs-Elysées Clemenceau; lovely café, +33 1 53 43 40 00, www.petitpalais.paris.fr.

Visiting the Museum: Enter the museum and head up the main hall to the left, passing an intriguing collection of 19th-century statues commissioned by the city, all with English descriptions. These are all plaster casts, as their bronze brothers were melted down during World War II.

Turn right into the second hall and find the large painting gallery that features Romantics and Realists from the late 19th century. Midway down the main hall on the left, Courbet's soft-porn *The Sleepers* (*Le Sommeil*, 1866) captures two women nestled in post-climactic bliss. A few paintings down, his large, dark *Firefighters (Pompiers courant à un incendie)* is a Realist's take on an everyday scene—firefighters rushing to put out a blaze. On the opposite wall, notice another scene from everyday life in Paris—the massive produce market that once thrived at Les Halles (now a modern mall).

Turning the corner, you'll see artwork by Gustave Doré (1832-1883), best known as the 19th century's greatest book illustrator. In his enormous *La Vallée de Larmes* (1883), Christ and the cross are the only salvation from this "valley of tears." (The doorway behind the painting leads directly to the museum café.)

Walk left into the bright room, then make a right to find Claude Monet's *Sunset on the Seine at Lavacourt* (*Soleil couchant sur la Seine a Lavacourt*, 1880). Painted the winter after his wife died, it looks across the river from Monet's home to two lonely boats in the distance, with the hazy town on the far bank. The sun's reflection is a vertical smudge down the water. Nearby you should find works by Alfred Sisley, Edgar Dégas, Camille Pissarro, Eugène Boudin, and the American painter Mary Cassatt. Boudin's gray, luminous seascape recalls his Normandy upbringing (Honfleur), and reminds us that he was an early mentor of Claude Monet. He urged Monet to accompany him in Normandy, telling him, "I want you to see the light." Claude listened.

On the back side of Monet's *Sunset*, Paul Cézanne's *Portrait d'Ambroise Vollard* depicts his agent (art dealer), whose job it was to make his paintings go viral—though Cézanne was unknown for most of his life. While Vollard looks somewhat dejected (this painting took 115 sessions to complete), he provided exposure for Cézanne's work and gave him essential moral support. Notice how Cézanne used blocks of paint rather than brush strokes to create chunkier, geometrical shapes in his works. Continuing into the yellow room, you're greeted by a few smaller paintings by Paul Cézanne and a Cézanne-looking early work by Paul Gauguin *(Vieil Homme au Bâton)*, painted during his time with Vincent van Gogh in Arles.

Before heading downstairs, double back to the side rooms adjoining the large painting gallery you just visited to find exquisite furniture in the Louis XIV, XV, and XVI styles.

The museum's overlooked basement features a surprising collection of art, with Greek antiquities, a gorgeous room of medieval iconography, rooms filled with art by Dutch masters, and beautiful displays of Art Nouveau furniture. English explanations in every room help bring these works to life.

Grand Palais

This grand exhibition hall, built for the 1900 World's Fair, is used for temporary exhibits (closed for renovation until 2024; temporary exhibits are set up at the south end of the Champ de Mars park). The building's Industrial Age, erector-set, iron-and-glass exterior is striking (Avenue Winston Churchill, Mo: Champs-Elysées Clemenceau or Franklin D. Roosevelt, tel. +33 01 44 13 17 17, www.grandpalais.fr).

▲Paris Ferris Wheel (Roue de Paris)

In summer, the Paris Ferris Wheel offers a sensational 200-foot-high view of the city from the northern side of the Tuileries Garden. The towering wheel is the centerpiece of a funfair complete with kid-pleasing rides and games.

Cost and Hours: €12 ticket covers two slow revolutions, two passengers per gondola, open long hours daily late June-late Aug.

View from Hôtel Hyatt Regency

For a remarkable Parisian panorama, head to Hôtel Hyatt Regency Paris Etoile and its Windo Skybar on the 34th floor. Ride the free elevators to floor 33 and walk up one flight to the bar. You'll enter a sky-high world of comfy chairs, glass walls, expensive drinks, and jaw-dropping views that are best before dark and not worthwhile in poor weather (bar open daily 17:00-late, +33 1 40 68 51 31, www.windoparis.com).

Getting There: It's at Porte Maillot (3 Place du Général Koenig). Take the Métro to the pedestrian-unfriendly Porte Maillot stop. Follow signs to *Palais des Congrès* and enter the underground mall, turn right at the small sign for *Hôtel Hyatt Regency,* and walk straight until you arrive at the hotel (don't take escalator up from mall—if you get lost there are maps everywhere in the mall). If you're coming from the Rue Cler area, take RER/Train-C from Invalides or Pont de l'Alma to Porte Maillot (direction: Pontoise). If you're pooped or strapped for time, the skies are clear, and the sun's about to set, spring for a taxi or Uber.

La Défense and La Grande Arche

Though Paris keeps its historic center classic and skyscraper-free, this district, nicknamed *"le petit Manhattan,"* offers an impressive excursion into a side of Paris few tourists see: that of a modern-day economic superpower. La Défense was first conceived more than 60 years ago as a US-style forest of skyscrapers that would accommodate the business needs of the modern world. Today La Défense is a thriving commercial and shopping center, home to 150,000 employees and 55,000 residents. It's also the single largest concentration of skyscrapers in all of Europe.

For a worthwhile visit, take the Métro to the La Défense Grande Arche stop, carefully follow *Sortie Grande Arche* signs (there are many), and climb to the base of La Grande Arche for distant city views. Then stroll about three-quarters of a mile gradually downhill among the glass buildings to the Esplanade de la Défense Métro station, and return home from there. Mall stores are open every day.

Visiting La Défense: The centerpiece of this ambitious complex is the mammoth **La Grande Arche de la Fraternité.** Inaugurated in 1989 on the 200th anniversary of the French Revolution, it was, like the Revolution, dedicated to human rights and brotherhood. The place is big—Notre-Dame Cathedral could fit under its arch. The four-sided structure sits on enormous underground pillars and is covered with a veneer of beautiful white Carrara marble. The arch is a 38-story office building for 30,000 people on more than 200 acres. The left side houses gov-

ernment ministries, the right side corporate offices, and the top is dedicated to human rights. The "cloud"—a huge canvas canopy under the arch—is an attempt to cut down on the wind-tunnel effect this gigantic building creates. You can take a pricey elevator to the **panoramic rooftop** for a view over the skyscrapers and Parisian suburbs, but I wouldn't as you're too far from the city center for worthwhile views (€15, daily 10:00-18:30).

Wander behind the arch, past freestanding glass sheets that help to deflect wind, to see an unusual mix of glassy skyscrapers and a cemetery (in the orchard). Study the Le Corbusier-style planning, where motor traffic (the freeway and trains that tunnel underneath) is separated from pedestrian traffic (the skybridges).

Back on the mall side, notice the Arc de Triomphe in the distance, bull's-eye down the Esplanade. La Grande Arche aligns perfectly with the Arc de Triomphe, the Obelisk on Place de la Concorde, and the Arc de Triomphe du Carrousel in front of the Louvre.

Drop down the arch's steps and glide onto the vast **Esplanade** (a.k.a. "le Parvis"). Survey the skyscraping scene. La Défense is much more than its eye-catching arch—it's an international power broker. Check out the skyscrapers clockwise: Engie (almost behind you to the left) deals in electricity, Areva is a global energy company that is big into nuclear power, and EDF is France's national electric company. Back to the left, that tall brass thing in front of the small trees is one of French artist César Baldaccini's famous thumb statues (40 feet high).

Continue down the Esplanade back toward the city center to about where the skyscrapers end (and to the next Métro stop). Take in the monumental structures around you: Les 4 Temps is a giant shopping mall of 250 stores, and like malls at home, it's a teenage wasteland when school is out and eerily quiet at night. Go ahead, have a peek and compare with your shopping mall.

Opposite Les 4 Temps, the half-dome Center of New Industries and Technologies (better known as CNIT) was built in 1958 and looks like it. It's now a congress center and remains a feat of architecture: It's the largest concrete vault anywhere that rests on

Best Views over the City of Light

Your trip to Paris is played out in the streets, but the brilliance of the City of Light is best appreciated by rising above it all. Invest time to marvel at all the man-made beauty, seen best in the early morning or around sunset. Many of the viewpoints listed here are free or covered by the Museum Pass; otherwise, expect to pay €8-20.

Eiffel Tower: It's hard to find a grander view of Paris than from the tower's second level (for most, it's better than from the top level).

Go around sunset and stay after dark to see the tower illuminated; or go in the early morning to avoid the midday haze and crowds (not covered by Museum Pass, see the Eiffel Tower Tour chapter).

Paris Ferris Wheel: The Roue de Paris offers a 200-foot-high view of Paris (not covered by Museum Pass, summer only, two slow and scenic loops, see page 99).

Arc de Triomphe: This is the perfect place to see the glamorous Champs-Elysées (if you can manage the 284 steps). It's great during the day, but even greater at night, when the boulevard positively glitters (covered by Museum Pass, see page 96).

Steps of Sacré-Cœur: Join the party on Paris' only hilltop. Walk uphill, or take the funicular or bus, then hunker down on Sacré-Cœur's steps to enjoy the sunset and territorial views over Paris. Stay in Montmartre for dinner, then see the view again after dark (free, see page 119).

Galeries Lafayette or **Printemps:** Take the escalator to the top

only three points. Enter the vault to see a semicircle of dazzling offices and shops that recede as they rise, like the seating in an opera house.

In France, getting a building permit often comes with a requirement to dedicate two percent of the construction cost to art. Hence, the Esplanade is a virtual open-air modern art gallery, sporting pieces by Joan Miró (blue, red, and yellow), Alexander Calder (red), Anthony Caro (long, brown, folded-steel sculpture that resembles the meltdown of a bridge support), and Yaacov Agam (the fountain with colorful stripes and rhythmically dancing spouts), among others. Just behind Yaacov's fountain, find *La Défense de Paris*, the statue that gave the area its name; it recalls the

floor of either department store (they sit side by side) for a stunning overlook of the old Opéra district (free, see page 488).

Montparnasse Tower: The top of this solitary skyscraper has some of the best views in Paris, though they're too high to be worthwhile after dark. Zip up 56 floors on the elevator, then walk to the rooftop (not covered by Museum Pass, see page 92).

Pompidou Center: Take the escalator up and admire the beautiful cityscape along with the exciting modern art (the sixth floor is the top, but the fifth-floor outdoor terrace is more enjoyable). There may be better views over Paris, but this is the best one from a museum (covered by Museum Pass, see the Pompidou Center Tour chapter).

Place du Trocadéro: This square, a 20-minute walk from the Eiffel Tower, is *the* place to see the tower. Come for a look at Monsieur Eiffel's festive creation day or night (when the tower is lit up), before or after your tower visit.

Arab World Institute: This building near Ile St. Louis has 180-degree views over the river from its roof terrace (free for views, see page 95).

Windo Skybar at Hôtel Hyatt Regency Paris Etoile: This otherwise unappealing hotel is noteworthy for its razzle-dazzle 34th-floor bar, where you can sip wine and enjoy a stunning Parisian panorama (free elevator but pricey drinks, see page 100).

1870 Franco-Prussian war—a rare bit of old Paris out here in the 'burbs.

As you descend the Esplanade, notice how the small gardens with benches and areas for *boules* are designed to integrate tradition into this celebration of modern commerce. Note also how the buildings tend to decrease in height and increase in age as you approach Paris' center. Your walk ends at the amusing fountain of Bassin Takis, where you'll find the Esplanade de la Défense Métro station that zips you out of all this modernity and directly back into town. Near this station, look in the middle of the esplanade for the giant green bench—a fun photo op. Before descending into the Métro, take one last look (perhaps from a perch on that big green bench) back to La Grande Arche to appreciate how far you've come.

OPERA NEIGHBORHOOD

The glittering Garnier opera house anchors this neighborhood of broad boulevards and grand architecture. This area is also nirvana for high-end shoppers, with the opulent Galeries Lafayette and Printemps stores, the delicate Fragonard Perfume Museum, and the sumptuous shops that line Place Vendôme and Place de la Madeleine (see the Shopping in Paris chapter for a shopping walk of this area). Key Métro stops include Opéra, Madeleine, and Havre-Caumartin (RER/Train-A: Auber).

▲▲Opéra Garnier
(Opéra National de Paris—Palais Garnier)

A gleaming grand theater of the belle époque, the Palais Garnier was built for Napoleon III and finished in 1875. From Avenue de l'Opéra, once lined with Paris' most fashionable haunts, the facade suggests "all power to the wealthy." In the 1980s, that elitism prompted the call for a new opera house built for the people, and the larger Opéra Bastille was situated symbolically on Place de la Bastille, where the French Revolution started in

1789. The smaller Opéra Garnier is now home to ballet, some opera, and other performances.

To see the interior, you have several choices: Take a guided tour (your best look), tour the public areas on your own (using the audioguide and/or my self-guided tour, later), or attend a performance. Note that the auditorium is sometimes off-limits due to performances and rehearsals. Highlights of the interior include the Grand Staircase, the various chandeliered reception halls, the 2,000-seat auditorium, and a few exhibits on the building and opera.

Cost and Hours: €14, €4 off if you show your Orsay Museum ticket (within 8 days of Orsay visit), not covered by Museum Pass; generally daily 10:00-16:15, mid-July-Aug until 17:15, closes for rehearsals and performances—most reliably open 10:00-13:00; 8 Rue Scribe, Mo: Opéra, RER/Train-A: Auber, www.operadeparis.fr/en/visits/palais-garnier.

Tours: The €6.50 multimedia guide gives a good self-guided tour. Guided tour in English usually runs daily at 14:00, check website to reserve a spot, arrive 30 minutes early for security screening (€18.50, after-hours tours-€22, tours include entry, +33 1 42 46 72 40 or +33 1 42 46 92 10).

Ballet and Concert Tickets: To find out about upcoming

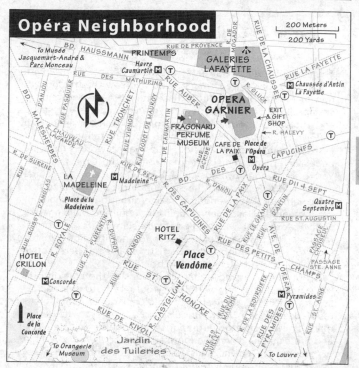

Opéra Neighborhood

performances, ask for a schedule at the information booth, consult *L'Officiel des Spectacles* magazine (see page 510), or see the Paris Opera website (www.operadeparis.fr). There are usually no performances mid-July-Sept. It's easiest to reserve online but cheaper to buy on performance day. To buy tickets by phone, call +33 1 71 25 24 23 (office closed Sun). You can also go directly to the ticket office (open Mon-Sat 11:30–18:30 and an hour before the show, closed Sun).

➋ **Self-Guided Tour:** First, take in the best ➊ **view of the facade** from the traffic island of the Opéra Métro. The building is huge. Its massive foundations straddle an underground lake (inspiring the mysterious world of *The Phantom of the Opera*). It's the masterpiece of architect Charles Garnier, who oversaw every element, from laying the foundations to what color the wallpaper should be. His cohesive design was so admired that the building came to be known as the Palais Garnier. (To better understand what you're seeing, read the "Baron Georges-Eugène Haussmann" sidebar.)

Garnier's classically inspired facade is a celebration of opera—the art form that combines all the arts. Atop the green dome, a shimmering Apollo, the god of music, holds aloft his shining

SIGHTS

Baron Georges-Eugène Haussmann
(1809-1891)

The elegantly uniform streets that make Paris so Parisian are the work of Baron Haussmann, who oversaw the modernization of the city in the mid-19th century. He cleared out the cramped, higgledy-piggledy, unhygienic medieval cityscape and replaced it with broad, straight boulevards lined with stately buildings and linked by modern train stations.

The quintessential view of Haussmann's work is from the pedestrian island immediately in front of the Opéra Garnier. You're surrounded by Paris circa 1870, when it was the capital of the world. Gaze down the surrounding boulevards to find the column of Place Vendôme in one direction, and the Louvre in another. Haussmann's uniform, cohesive buildings are all five stories tall, with angled, black slate roofs and formal facades. The balconies on the second and fifth floors match those of their neighbors, creating strong lines of perspective as the buildings stretch down the boulevard.

But there was more than aesthetics to the plan. In pre-Haussmann Paris, angry rioters would take to the narrow streets, setting up barricades to hold back government forces (as made famous in Victor Hugo's *Les Misérables*). With Haussmann's new design, government troops could circulate easily and fire cannons down the long, straight boulevards. A whiff of "grapeshot"—chains, nails, and other buckshot-type shrapnel—could clear out any revolutionaries in a hurry.

The 19th century was a great time to be wealthy, thanks to the city's fancy covered market halls, civilized sidewalks, and even elevators. With the coming of elevators, the wealthy took the higher floors and enjoyed the view.

bronze lyre, as if to declare, "This is a temple of the highest arts." (You'll see lyres and Apollos all over the building, outside and in.) Running across the middle of the facade are (smallish) bronze busts of famous composers. The medallions with "E" and "N" honor the Emperor Napoleon III. On the lower right (second statue from the right) is a copy of the well-known *Dance* by Carpeaux (whose original is in the Orsay).

The ❷ **tourist entrance** is around the left side of the building, between the two curved ramps. In fact, this was once the rich patrons' entrance, as they could drive their carriages right up the ramps and slip in, away from the riff-raff. Before the entrance stands a bust of Garnier and a bronze plaque showing the building's footprint. Find the horseshoe-shaped seating area (in the center), the rectangular stage (to the left), and the rectangular Grand Staircase (to the right). Notice how little space was given to the seating area itself—the public spaces were paramount.

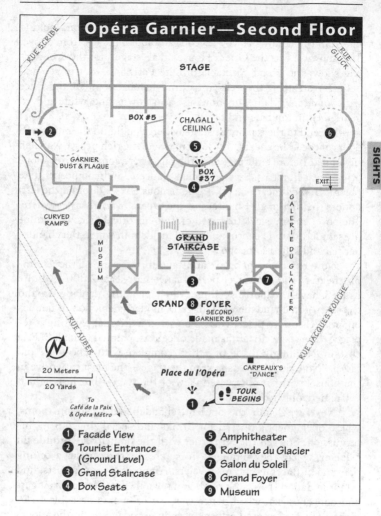

Opéra Garnier—Second Floor

RUE SCRIBE

RUE GLÜCK

STAGE

BOX #5

CHAGALL CEILING

GARNIER BUST & PLAQUE

BOX #37

CURVED RAMPS

MUSEUM

GRAND STAIRCASE

GALERIE DU GLACIER

EXIT

GRAND FOYER

SECOND GARNIER BUST

RUE JACQUES ROUCHE

RUE AUBER

20 Meters

20 Yards

CARPEAUX'S "DANCE"

Place du l'Opéra

TOUR BEGINS

To Café de la Paix & Opéra Métro

SIGHTS

- ① Facade View
- ② Tourist Entrance (Ground Level)
- ③ Grand Staircase
- ④ Box Seats
- ⑤ Amphitheater
- ⑥ Rotonde du Glacier
- ⑦ Salon du Soleil
- ⑧ Grand Foyer
- ⑨ Museum

Enter, buy your ticket, and make your way (up a small curving staircase) to the foot of the ❸ **Grand Staircase.** Gaze up into this vast hall, where the whole building is united by the set of stairs that branches into a Y midway up. Take in the columns, statues, railings, lanterns, chandeliers, and the different colors of marble, as your eye goes up to a ceiling fresco featuring Apollo. Check

out the Grand Staircase from all angles: from the bottom looking up, from the landing as you ascend, and looking back from above. This staircase was the Opera House's real "stage," for the evening's real show: the grand spectacle of elite Parisians—out to see and be seen—strutting their elegant stuff. Mentally populate the space with *fin de siècle* ladies in flowing satin gowns and white-gloved gentlemen in top hats and tuxes.

Ascend to the top of the stairs, where you'll find the numbered doors of the ❹ box seats. These were where the rich people watched the opera. Before entering, note the busts between the boxes, honoring great librettists, set designers, dancers, and composers, like Hector Berlioz (near box #37). The famous box #5 (around the left) honors the (fictional) Phantom of the Opera, who always sat here. The novel and musical are based on two historical facts: the building's underground cistern, and a real incident in which the chandelier fell and killed someone.

Now enter an open box and take in the view of the ❺ amphitheater. The red-velvet performance hall seats 2,000. Admire Marc Chagall's colorful ceiling (1964) playfully dancing around the seven-ton chandelier. If Chagall's modern depiction of famous operas feels out of place, we'll soon see the original painting it replaced. The stage curtain is made of canvas, painted to look like...a curtain, seemingly made of velvet, complete with fake folds and tassels. Note the box seats next to the stage—the most expensive in the house, with an obstructed view of the stage—but just right if you're here only to be seen.

Next, we'll tour the opulent, chandeliered reception rooms, where operagoers gathered for drinks and socializing during intermission. Start in the far corner with the domed ❻ **Rotonde du Glacier,** where they indulged in ice cream treats under a ceiling painting of Bacchus and his revelers. Among the room's busts, find Antonio Salieri (Mozart's rival) and several "divas"—noted singers and dancers, back when dance was one of opera's best-loved elements. (In fact, most performances here today are by the Opéra Garnier's dance company.)

Head down the long, chandelier-strewn Galerie du Glacier, and turn right (just before the end) into the tiny ❼ **Salon du Soleil.** This Room of the Sun dazzles the eye with a black-and-gold sunray ceiling and walls fitted with infinity mirrors.

Continue straight to the Grand Staircase and turn left, entering the large and over-the-top opulent ❽ **Grand Foyer.** This long, high-ceilinged Hall-of-Mirrors-esque space was the main gathering place at intermission. Its golden decor (mostly gold paint, not gilding) features statues, columns, and chandeliers, all set off by colorful ceiling paintings. Find 20 lyres in a minute. The statues at either end, by the fireplaces, are 24-carat gold, and visibly shinier than the gold-painted statues. Garnier proudly put his own bust here (halfway down the foyer on the left), eternally admiring his fine work. (Garnier's next major project was the famous Monte Carlo casino and opera house.) Step outside onto the balcony (or look out the windows), and you realize this room sits in the middle story of the facade, overlooking Place de l'Opéra.

Exit the Grand Foyer at the far end, pass through the tiny Salon de la Lune (Soleil's nocturnal counterpart), and turn left into the ❾ **museum.** Browse the long hallway of exhibits, starting with a cutaway model of the stage (with two subterranean levels below and elaborate pulleys above), followed by paintings of famous singers, dancers, composers, and set designers. Farther down on the right is a round gold-framed work depicting the original ceiling painting that graced the auditorium before Chagall came along. Muses spin and cavort among the fluffy clouds of heaven. The museum leads into the library, with dioramas of set designs for famous operas, including *Faust*, by Paris' hometown boy Charles Gounod.

Head downstairs (where there are often other exhibits) and enjoy one more view from the foot of the Grand Staircase. Exit through the appropriately elegant gift shop on the opposite side from where you entered.

Nearby: The illustrious **Café de la Paix** faces the Opera's front and has been a meeting spot for the local glitterati for generations. If you can afford the coffee, this spot offers a delightful break.

Fragonard Perfume Museum

Near Opéra Garnier, this perfume shop (often congested with tour groups) masquerades as a museum. Housed in a beautiful 19th-century mansion, it's the best-smelling museum in Paris—and you'll learn a little about how perfume is made, too (well-described in English).

Cost and Hours: Free, daily 9:00-17:00, 3 Square Louis Jouvet, Mo: Opéra, RER/Train-A: Auber, +33 1 47 42 04 56, http://musee-parfum-paris.fragonard.com/en/.

High-End Shopping

The upscale Opéra neighborhood hosts some of Paris' best shopping. Even window shoppers can appreciate this as a ▲ "sight." Just behind the Opéra, the **Galeries Lafayette** department store is a magnificent cathedral to consumerism, under a stunning stained-glass dome. The area between **Place de la Madeleine,** dominated by the Madeleine Church (looking like a Roman temple), and the octagonal **Place Vendôme,** is filled with pricey shops and boutiques, giving travelers a whiff of the exclusive side of Paris (for more on Galeries Lafayette or for a boutique-to-boutique stroll through this area, see the Shopping in Paris chapter).

▲▲Jacquemart-André Museum (Musée Jacquemart-André)

This enjoyable (if somewhat faded) museum-mansion, with an elegant café, showcases the lavish home of a wealthy, art-loving, 19th-century Parisian couple. After visiting the Opéra Garnier and wandering Paris' grand boulevards, get inside for an intimate look at the lifestyles of the Parisian rich and fabulous. Edouard André and his wife Nélie Jacquemart spent their lives and fortunes designing, building, and then decorating this sumptuous mansion. What makes the visit worthwhile is the helpful audioguide tour (included with admission, plan on spending an hour with the audioguide). The place is strewn with paintings by Rembrandt, Botticelli, Uccello, Mantegna, Bellini, Boucher, and Fragonard. Though there are no must-see masterpieces, the art gathered here would still be enough to make any gallery famous.

Cost and Hours: €12, €3-5 more for special exhibits (which are common), includes audioguide, not covered by Museum Pass; daily 10:00-18:00, Mon until 20:30 during special exhibits; avoid lines on weekends and during the first week of special exhibits by purchasing skip-the-line tickets online in advance (€2 fee), 158 Boulevard Haussmann, Mo: St-Philippe-du-Roule, bus #80 connects conveniently with Ecole Militaire; +33 1 45 62 11 59, www.musee-jacquemart-andre.com.

Visiting the Museum: While you follow the audioguide, keep an eye out for these highlights.

The **Antechamber** introduces you to the museum's winning formula: opulent decor (chandeliers, red velvet walls, gilded trim) + semi-famous paintings (two Boucher nudes and two Canaletto scenes of Venice) + the lifestyle of Edouard and Nélie (who received visitors here) = an immersive aesthetic experience. Next, you enter the Versailles-like **Grand Salon,** the central focus for their parties, with a guest list of up to 1,000.

After passing through several rooms of Edouard's collection of beautiful things—furniture, tapestries, exotic curios, and Tiepolo paintings on the ceiling—you'll reach the **Library,** displaying portraits by Rembrandt, Hals, and Van Dyck, and Rembrandt's *Supper at Emmaus.*

Backtracking, you reach the spacious **Music Room,** used for candlelit parties and concerts. (The band was perched on the balconies above, so the music seemed to waft down from heaven.) Find the bronze bust of Edouard, age 57, done by his wife, Nélie. They'd met when he hired her to do his portrait. The **Winter Room** is fitted with skylights and exotic plants, to brighten a sunny day. It leads into the **Smoking Room**—the belle époque man cave.

Upstairs, you enter the world of Italian art. You pass a mural by Tiepolo and enter the **Studio,** which Edouard made for his artist wife to work in. Among the many (minor) sculptures displayed now, locate Luca della Robbia's ceramic Madonna and Donatello's small bronze torchbearer. The **Florentine and Venetian Painting Rooms** have Botticelli's *Virgin and Child,* a Giovanni Bellini *Madonna,* Mantegna's *Ecce Homo,* and works by Uccello, Guardi, and Carpaccio.

Downstairs are the couple's **Private Apartments.** They kept separate bedrooms (one for "Madame," one for "Monsieur") but met in the room in between for breakfast. There you'll see the portrait that Nélie painted of Edouard when they first met—the spark that brought about their marriage, their mutual passion for art, and eventually the Jacquemart-André Museum.

After Your Visit: Consider a break in the sumptuous museum tearoom, with delicious cakes and tea (daily 11:45-17:30). From here walk north on Rue de Courcelles to see Paris' most beautiful park, Parc Monceau.

MARAIS NEIGHBORHOOD AND NEARBY

The Marais neighborhood extends along the Right Bank of the Seine, from the Bastille to the Pompidou Center. The main east-west axis is formed by Rue St. Antoine, Rue des Rosiers (the heart of Paris' Jewish community), and Rue Ste. Croix de la Bretonnerie. The centerpiece of the neighborhood is the stately Place des Vosges. Helpful Métro stops are Bastille, St-Paul, and Hôtel de Ville.

Don't waste time looking for the Bastille, the prison of Revolution fame. It's Paris' most famous nonsight. The building is long gone, and just the square remains, good only for its nightlife and as a jumping-off point for the Marais Walk or a stroll through La Coulée Verte.

Ⓜ The Marais Walk chapter connects the following sights with a fun, fact-filled stroll.

SIGHTS

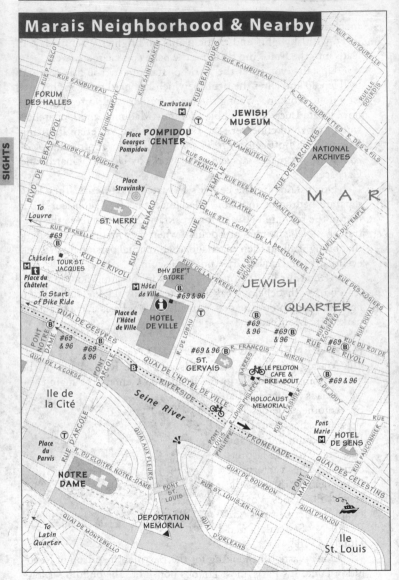

Marais Neighborhood & Nearby

▲▲Carnavalet Museum (Musée Carnavalet)

Housed in three floors of an elegant mansion, this museum delves into the history of Paris—all wonderfully explained with English descriptions, making it quite user-friendly (once you figure out the confusing floorplan). A fine statue of Louis XIV greets you in the elegant courtyard, as if saying, "Hey, this place is underrated, free, and gives the best history lesson anywhere for those wanting to better understand Paris."

SIGHTS

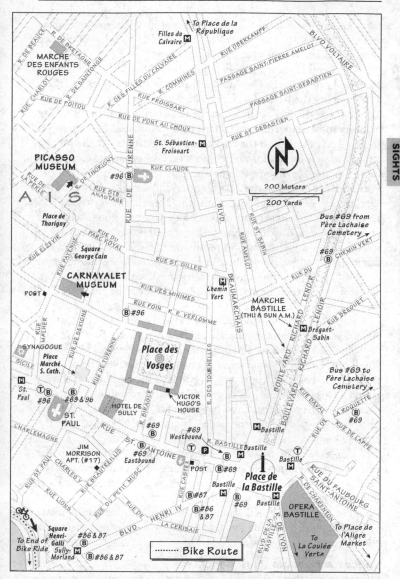

Inside, French history unfolds in a series of stills—like a Ken Burns documentary, except you have to walk. You get a good overview of everything—from Louis XIV-period rooms, to Napoleon, to the belle époque. There's even a delightful basement exhibit on prehistoric, ancient Roman, and medieval Paris. But I'd focus on the museum's highlight: the French Revolution and the 19th century. In fact, the museum was established on the 100th anniversary of the French Revolution, and it features surviving treasures and artifacts from that turning point in Western democracy. A thoughtful visit here gives valuable context to what you'll see throughout the rest of your Paris sightseeing.

Cost and Hours: Free, Tue-Sun 10:00-18:00, closed Mon, 16 Rue des Francs Bourgeois, Mo: St-Paul, www.carnavalet.paris.fr.

Visiting the Museum: Upon entry, lock up your coat and bag. While there are other sections in the museum, I find the following exhibits most important and interesting. From the first room on the ground floor, climb the curvy wooden staircase. At the top, go straight down a corridor and climb a second curvy wooden staircase. On the top floor, straight ahead is the section called **"The French Revolution to the 21st Century."** A small painting of the Declaration of the Rights of Man (the French answer to the US Declaration of Independence) welcomes you to a long, winding, and chronological exhibit on the French Revolution. Each room starts with a concise historic recap, with displays that are both fascinating and well-described in English. You'll see the roots of revolution, divine monarchs and angry masses, the Bastille prison, royals who lost their heads, revolutionary heroes, the Reign of Terror, and Napoleon.

Popping out the other end, you've survived the Revolution. Another curvy wooden staircase leads down to another fascinating era: **"Paris 1852 to Today."** Following *Sens de la Visite* signs, you'll wind through a series of rooms that illustrate the foundations of the Paris we know and love today. The exhibit starts with Baron Haussmann and his late-19th-century redesign of the city, then traces the *fin de siècle* and beyond: can-can dancers, the Eiffel Tower, hot-air balloons, the belle époque, Art Nouveau, and the Impressionists.

Cap your visit with some ancient history. Signs lead to the exit *(sortie)* and a humble staircase leading into a **medieval cellar.** Here you'll find artifacts, art, and carvings from megalithic Paris (4000 BC), helping you envision the tribes that first settled on the island in the Seine. You'll also learn about the ancient Roman city of Lutetia (which became Paris) and medieval life here, illustrating the rise of this great city.

▲Picasso Museum (Musée Picasso)

Whatever you think about Picasso the man, as an artist he was unmatched in the 20th century for his daring and productivity. This museum rotates its huge collection of Picasso works to host an ever-changing calendar of Picasso-themed exhibits.

Cost and Hours: €14, covered by Museum Pass, free on first Sun of month; open Tue-Fri 10:30-18:00, Sat-Sun from 9:30, closed Mon, last entry 45 minutes before closing; 5 Rue de Thorigny, Mo: St-Sébastien-Froissart, St-Paul, or Chemin Vert, +33 1 42 71 25 21, www.museepicassoparis.fr.

▲Jewish Art and History Museum
(Musée d'Art et Histoire du Judaïsme)

This is a fine museum of historical artifacts and rare ritual objects spanning the Jewish people's long cultural heritage. It emphasizes the cultural unity maintained by this continually dispersed population. You'll learn about Jewish traditions and see exquisite costumes and objects central to daily life and religious practices. Novices may find the displays beautiful and thought-provoking but not especially meaningful. Those with a background in Judaism or who take the time with the thoughtful audioguide and posted information will be rewarded.

Cost and Hours: €10, includes audioguide, covered by Museum Pass, free on first Sat of month Oct-June; Tue-Fri 11:00-18:00, Sat-Sun from 10:00, open later during special exhibits—Wed until 21:00 and Sat-Sun until 19:00, closed Mon year-round, last entry 45 minutes before closing; 71 Rue du Temple, Mo: Rambuteau or Hôtel de Ville a few blocks farther away, RER/Train-B: Châtelet-Les Halles; +33 1 53 01 86 60, www.mahj.org.

Visiting the Museum: Before entering, visitors undergo a thorough security check. Once inside, your visit starts with a black-and-white display of Jewish life in Paris just before World War II. One floor up, you're greeted by a centuries-old Torah scroll that introduces the exhibit. The next room covers the early Middle Ages (AD 500-1000), when Judaism flourished in France. A row of excavated gravestones attests to Jews living peacefully on the Ile de la Cité. Then came the Crusade of 1096 and several centuries of persecution, pogroms, and expulsions under Christian kings like "Saint" Louis IX. Continuing on, you'll see displays on Jewish rituals—getting married under a canopy, menorahs lit during Hanukkah, and gift-giving during Purim. There's a full-size sukkah (tabernacle), a structure for celebrating the harvest festival, and models of various synagogue styles.

Upstairs, you'll find many exquisite silver-and-jeweled ritual objects: Torah scrolls and their rich cloth coverings, pointers for reading the Torah, and rams' horns blown at Rosh Hashanah and Yom Kippur. You'll see a few paintings by famous Jewish artists, including Marc Chagall, Amedeo Modigliani, and Chaïm Soutine. The museum brings the Jewish story up to modern times. French Jews were "Emancipated" during the Enlightenment of the 1700s. But anti-Semitism lingered, as illustrated by the final exhibit: the Dreyfus Affair (c. 1900). A French officer was accused of treason. Was he guilty, or merely guilty of being Jewish?

Holocaust Memorial (Mémorial de la Shoah)

This sight, commemorating the lives of the more than 76,000 Jews deported from France in World War II, has several facets: a WWII deportation memorial, a museum on the Holocaust, and a Jewish resource center. Display-ing original deportation records, the museum takes you through the history of Jews in Europe and France, from medieval po-groms to the Nazi era. But its focal point is underground, where victims' ashes are buried.

Cost and Hours: Free, Sun-Fri 10:00-18:00, Thu until 22:00, closed Sat and certain Jewish holidays, 17 Rue Geoffroy l'Asnier, +33 1 42 77 44 72, www.memorialdelashoah.org.

Visiting the Memorial: To the right of the entrance, on the Allée des Justes, notice the large bronze wall plaque honoring those who risked their lives for Jewish people. The entry courtyard (after the security check) contains a cylinder evoking concentration camp smokestacks. Down three steps, large stone walls are engraved with the names of French Jews deported during the war.

Enter the building (with an information desk, bookstore, and exhibits), and pick up the Mémorial de la Shoah brochure. Go downstairs one floor to the crypt, which has a large Star of David in black marble. Ashes from some of the six million victims of Nazi brutality are buried underneath the star, in soil brought from Is-rael. Behind you is a small corridor containing the original French police files from the arrest, internment, and deportation of Paris' Jews. (Since 1995, the French have acknowledged the Vichy gov-ernment's complicity in the Nazis' local ethnic cleansing.)

Go downstairs another floor to the permanent exhibition. Photos and videos (most with English explanations) present an in-troduction to Judaism and the history of Jews in Europe (including pogroms) and in France (including the notorious Dreyfus affair, concerning a Jewish officer unjustly imprisoned for treason). The well-devised displays start with a floor map showing the distri-bution of the Jewish population in Europe before World War II. Next, you'll trace the rise of Nazism, the deportations and France's collaboration with them (12,884 Parisians were once rounded up in a single day and 76,000 were deported from throughout France), the death camps, and the liberation at the end of the war. The mov-ing finale is a brightly lit collage of children lost to the Holocaust.

▲▲Pompidou Center (Centre Pompidou)

One of Europe's greatest collections of far-out modern art is housed in the Musée National d'Art Moderne. While this sprawl-ing arts center is huge, most visitors focus on the fourth and fifth floors of this colorful exoskeletal building. Created ahead of its time, the modern and contemporary art in this collection is still waiting for the world to catch up. After so many Madonnas-and-children, a piano smashed to bits and glued to the wall can be refreshing.

The Pompidou Center and the square that fronts it are lively, with lots of people, street theater, and activity inside and out—a perpetual street fair. Kids of any age enjoy the fun, colorful foun-tain (an homage to composer Igor Stravinsky) next to the Pompi-dou Center. The exterior escalators lead to a great city view from the top (ticket or Museum Pass required).

Cost and Hours: €14, €11 for those 18-25, free for kids 17 and under, free on first Sun of the month, €5 for escalator to sixth-floor view (but no museum entry); Museum Pass covers permanent col-lection and sixth-floor panoramic views (plus occasional special ex-hibits); permanent collection open Wed-Mon 11:00-21:00, closed Tue, ticket counters close at 20:00; rest of the building open until 22:00 (Thu until 23:00); arrive after 17:00 to avoid crowds (mainly for special exhibits); café on mezzanine, pricey view restaurant on level 6, Mo: Rambuteau or Hôtel de Ville, +33 1 44 78 12 33, www.centrepompidou.fr.

📖 See the Pompidou Center Tour chapter.

La Coulée Verte Promenade-Park

This elevated viaduct was used for train tracks from 1853 to 1969 and is now a three-mile narrow garden walk and a delightful place for a refreshing stroll or run. Botanists appreciate the well-main-tained and varying vegetation. From west (near Opéra Bastille) to east, the first half of the path is elevated until the midway point, the pleasant Jardin de Reuilly (a good stopping point for most, near Mo: Dugommier), then it continues at street level—with separate paths for pedestrians and cyclists—out to Paris' ring road, the *péri-phérique*.

Cost and Hours: Free, opens Mon-Fri at 8:00, Sat Sun at 9:00, closes at sunset (17:30 in winter, 20:30 in summer). It runs from Place de la Bastille (Mo: Bastille) along Avenue Daumesnil to the suburb of St. Mandé (Mo: Michel Bizot or Porte Dorée), passing within a block of Gare de Lyon.

Getting There: To get to the park from Place de la Bastille (exit the Métro following *Sortie Rue de Lyon* signs), walk a looooong block down Rue de Lyon, hugging the Opéra on your left. Find the low-key entry and steps up the red-brick wall a block after the Opéra.

▲▲Père Lachaise Cemetery (Cimetière du Père Lachaise)

Littered with the tombstones of many of the city's most illustrious dead, this is your best one-stop look at Paris' fascinating, romantic past residents. More like a small city, the cemetery is big and confusing, but my self-guided tour directs you to the graves of Frédéric Chopin, Molière, Edith Piaf, Oscar Wilde, Gertrude Stein, Jim Morrison, Héloïse and Abélard, and many more.

Cost and Hours: Free, Mon-Fri 8:00-18:00, Sat from 8:30, Sun from 9:00, closes at 17:30 in winter; two blocks from Mo: Gambetta (do not go to Mo: Père Lachaise) and two blocks from bus #69's last stop (see the Bus #69 Sightseeing Tour chapter); +33 1 55 25 82 10, searchable map available at unofficial website: www.pere-lachaise.com.

📖 See the Père Lachaise Cemetery Tour chapter or 🎧 download my free audio tour for a tomb-by-tomb tour of the most illustrious of these permanent Parisians.

Victor Hugo's House (Maison Victor Hugo)

France's literary giant lived in this house on Place des Vosges from 1832 to 1848. Hugo stayed in many places during his life, but he was here the longest. He moved to this apartment after the phenomenal success of *The Hunchback of Notre-Dame*, and it was while living here that he wrote much of *Les Misérables* (when he wasn't entertaining Paris' elite). After climbing up two floors, you'll visit well-decorated rooms re-creating different phases of Hugo's life and passions, from his celebrity years, to his 19-year exile during the repressive reign of Napoleon III (Hugo said "When freedom returns, I will return"), to his final years as a national treasure. Rooms are littered with personal possessions and paintings of Hugo and his

family and of some of his most famous character creations. Posted explanations in English provide sufficient context to grasp the importance of Hugo to France.

Cost and Hours: Free, fee for optional special exhibits, Tue-Sun 10:00-18:00, closed Mon, peaceful courtyard café, good WCs, 6 Place des Vosges; Mo: Bastille, St-Paul, or Chemin Vert; +33 1 42 72 10 16, http://maisonsvictorhugo.paris.fr.

MONTMARTRE

Paris' highest hill, rated ▲▲ and topped by Sacré-Cœur Basilica, is best known as the home of cabaret nightlife and bohemian artists. Struggling painters, poets, dreamers, and drunkards came here for cheap rent, untaxed booze, rustic landscapes, and views of the underwear of high-kicking cancan girls at the Moulin Rouge. These days, the hill is equal parts charm and kitsch—still vaguely village-like but mobbed with tourists and pickpockets—especially on sunny weekends. Come for a bit of history, a getaway from Paris' noisy boulevards, and the view.

📖 Connect the following sights with this book's Montmartre Walk (to locate the sights, see the map in that chapter).

▲Sacré-Cœur

You'll spot Sacré-Cœur (Sacred Heart), the onion-domed white basilica atop Montmartre, from most viewpoints in Paris. Though

it looks ancient, the impressive and iconic basilica is less than 150 years old (built 1875-1919). With a climbable dome, Sacré-Cœur sits atop Paris' highest natural point (430 feet).

After the disastrous Franco-Prussian war and subsequent bloodshed between the monarchist French government and Parisian insurgents (Communards), France was humbled and devastated. This basilica was built by Roman Catholics as penance for years of rebellion violence centered in the Montmartre area. The exterior of the basilica is laced with gypsum, which gives it its bleached-bone pallor. Inside, you'll enjoy wonderful mosaics, a statue of St. Thérèse, a scale model of the church, and three stained-glass windows dedicated to Joan of Arc. Pause near the Stations of the Cross mosaic to give St. Peter's bronze foot a rub, or for a panoramic view of Paris, climb 260 feet up the tight spiral stairs to the top of the dome.

Cost and Hours: Church—free, daily 6:30-22:30; dome—€7, not covered by Museum Pass, daily 10:00-18:00, June-Sept until

20:00, Jan-Feb until 17:00; modest dress required, +33 1 53 41 89 00, www.sacre-coeur-montmartre.com.

Getting There: You can take the Métro to the Anvers stop (to avoid the stairs up to Sacré-Cœur, use your Navigo transit pass and ride up on the funicular). Or, from Place Pigalle, you can take bus #40, which drops you right by Sacré-Cœur (Funiculaire stop, costs one Métro ticket, 4/hour). A taxi from near the Seine saves time and avoids sweat (about €20, €25 at night).

Nearby: To lose the crowd and feel Montmartre's pulse, explore a few blocks behind Place du Tertre. Go down Rue du Mont Cenis and turn left on Rue Cortot (past the Montmartre Museum). At Rue des Saules take a few steps downhill to see the vineyards that still supply cheap wine, then backtrack up Rue des Saules to the hilltop.

▲Montmartre Museum (Musée de Montmartre)

This 17th-century home re-creates the traditional cancan-and-cabaret Montmartre scene, with paintings, posters, photos, music, videos, and memorabilia. It offers the best look at the history of Montmartre and the amazing period from 1870 to 1910 when so much artistic action was percolating in this neighborhood, plus a chance to see the studio of Maurice Utrillo.

Cost and Hours: €14, includes good 45-minute audioguide, not covered by Museum Pass; Wed-Mon 10:00-18:00, closed Tue, last entry 45 minutes before closing; 12 Rue Cortot, +33 1 49 25 89 39, www.museedemontmartre.fr.

Pigalle

Paris' red light district, the infamous "Pig Alley" to WWII servicemen, is at the foot of Butte Montmartre. *Oh là là.* It's more racy than dangerous. Walk from Place Pigalle to Place Blanche, teasing desperate barkers and fast-talking temptresses. In bars, a €150 bottle of (what would otherwise be) cheap Champagne comes with a friend. Stick to the bigger streets, hang on to your wallet, and exercise good judgment. Cancan can cost a fortune, as can con artists in topless bars. After dark, countless tour buses line the streets, reminding us that tour guides make big bucks by bringing their groups to touristy nightclubs like the famous Moulin Rouge (Mo: Pigalle or Abbesses).

HISTORIC PARIS WALK

Ile de la Cité and the Latin Quarter

Paris has been the cultural capital of Europe for centuries. We'll start where it did, on Ile de la Cité, with a foray onto the Left Bank, on a walk that laces together 80 generations of history—from Celtic fishing village to Roman city, bustling medieval capital, birthplace of the Revolution, bohemian haunt of the 1920s café scene, and the working world of modern Paris. Along the way, we'll marvel at two of Paris' greatest sights—Notre-Dame and Sainte-Chapelle. Expect changes in the area around Notre-Dame as the cathedral undergoes reconstruction in the wake of the 2019 fire.

Orientation

Length of This Walk: Allow 2 hours to do justice to this three-mile walk (allow 4 hours if you go into the Sainte-Chapelle and the Conciergerie). This is the most historically important walk you'll do in Paris, so don't rush it. Take breaks at any number of appealing cafés and bistros along the way.

Getting There: The closest Métro stop is Cité (actually on the island).

Paris Museum Pass: Some sights on this walk are covered by the time- and money-saving Paris Museum Pass (see page 57). On Ile de la Cité, you can buy a pass at the tourist-friendly tabac/souvenir store (5 Boulevard du Palais) across the street from the Sainte-Chapelle entrance.

Notre-Dame: Due to the 2019 fire, only the cathedral's exterior is viewable. The interior and tower climb are closed for repair, and some surrounding areas may also be blocked off. For updates, see www.notredamedeparis.fr (select "Visiter"—website is in French only). Binoculars are helpful to view the church exterior (as well as Sainte-Chapelle's stained-glass windows).

Paris Archaeological Crypt: €8, covered by Museum Pass, Tue-Sun 10:00-18:00, closed Mon, enter 100 yards in front of cathedral, http://www.crypte.paris.fr.

Deportation Memorial: Free, daily 10:00-19:00, Oct-March until 17:00, may close at random times, free 45-minute audioguide and guided tours may be available, Mo: Cité, +33 6 14 67 54 98.

Shakespeare and Company Bookstore: Daily 10:00-22:00, 37 Rue de la Bûcherie, across the river from Notre-Dame, Mo: St-Michel, +33 1 43 25 40 93.

Sainte-Chapelle: €11.50 timed-entry ticket, €18.50 combo-ticket with Conciergerie, free for kids under age 18, covered by Museum Pass, reserve online in advance to ensure entry (limited tickets may be available in person); open daily 9:00-19:00, Oct-March until 17:00; audioguide-€3, frequent evening concerts—see page 512, 4 Boulevard du Palais, Mo: Cité, +33 1 53 40 60 80, www.sainte-chapelle.fr.

Expect long lines to get in. First comes the **security line** (sharp objects and glass confiscated). Next, you'll encounter the **ticket-buying line**—Museum Pass, combo, and advance ticket holders can skip this queue.

Conciergerie: €11.50 timed-entry ticket, €18.50 combo-ticket with Sainte-Chapelle, covered by Museum Pass, book online, daily 9:30-18:00, multimedia guide-€5, 2 Boulevard du Palais, Mo: Cité, +33 1 53 40 60 80, www.paris-conciergerie.fr.

Avoiding Crowds: This area is most crowded from midmorning to midafternoon, especially on Tue (when the Louvre is closed) and on weekends. Generally, come early or as late in the day as possible (while still leaving enough time to visit all the sights).

Sainte-Chapelle has limited space, and bottlenecks to get in are the norm. Its security lines are shortest first thing in the morning, so try for an early reservation. Lacking a reservation, arrive by 9:00 to inquire about available entry times, or arrive late and cross your fingers.

Tours: ∩ Download my free Paris Historic Walk audio tour.

Services: Find WCs at Sainte-Chapelle, the Conciergerie, and at cafés.

The Walk Begins

NOTRE-DAME AND NEARBY

• *Start in front of Notre-Dame Cathedral, the physical and historic bull's-eye of your Paris map. Some areas around the cathedral are blocked off as reconstruction continues. Find a place where you can take in the whole scene: the church, the square (Place du Parvis), the cityscape, and visitors from around the globe. You're standing near the center of France: The small bronze plaque called "Point Zero" (embedded in the ground,*

30 yards in front of the church) is the point from which all distances are measured. And you're looking at the symbolic heart of France. As you take it all in, ponder this spot's long and venerable history.

Notre-Dame through the Ages

Centuries from now, people standing here will still talk about the night of April 15, 2019, when Notre-Dame Cathedral went up in flames. That disastrous event is just one more episode in the long and fascinating story of Paris.

Think of the changes this site has seen over the years. About 2,300 years ago, there was virtually nothing here at all. This was the humble island where the Parisii tribe lived, caught fish, and sold their catch at the place where the east-west river crossed a north-south road. When the Romans conquered the Parisii, they built their Temple of Jupiter where Notre-Dame stands today (52 BC). When Rome fell, the Germanic Franks sealed their victory by replacing the temple with the Christian church of St. Etienne. Around the year 800, the Frankish King Charlemagne (see his big equestrian statue to the right of the church) established the first glimmers of modern "France."

By the year 1200, visitors standing here would have seen (as we do today) a construction zone. The old Frankish church was being torn down and replaced with a more glorious structure renamed "Notre-Dame." Soon it was topped with a pointy spire atop the roof and two never-completed steeples in front (the two stubby bell towers we see today).

By 1800, if you were still standing here, you'd be exhausted, but you'd also see a crumbling church weathered by the ages and neglect. The central spire had been removed (for fear it would fall over), and there were virtually no statues on the facade (having been damaged during the Revolution). The square in front was a tangle of ramshackle medieval buildings, with Notre-Dame's bell towers rising above, inspiring Victor Hugo's story of a deformed bell-ringer who could look down on all of Paris. (The instant success of that book helped rally public interest in saving the building.)

In 1844, a 30-year-old architect named Eugène-Emmanuel Viollet-le-Duc began a massive renovation in the Neo-Gothic

HISTORIC PARIS

HISTORIC PARIS

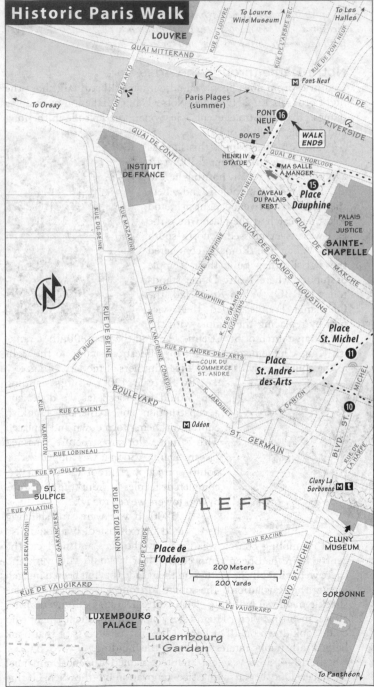

Historic Paris Walk

To Louvre
Wine Museum

To Les
Halles

LOUVRE

RUE DU LOUVRE

RUE DE L'ARBRE SEC

RUE DE PONT NEUF

QUAI MITTERAND

M Pont Neuf

QUAI DE

PONT DES ARTS

Paris Plages
(summer)

PONT
NEUF **16**

RIVERSIDE

To Orsay

WALK
ENDS

QUAI DE CONTI

BOATS

QUAI DE L'HORLOGE

HENRI IV
STATUE

MA SALLE
À MANGER

INSTITUT
DE FRANCE

CAVEAU
DU PALAIS
REST.

15
*Place
Dauphine*

PALAIS
DE
JUSTICE

RUE DU SEINE

RUE MAZARINE

RUE DAUPHINE

PONT NEUF

QUAI DES GRANDS AUGUSTINS

QUAI DE
MARCHÉ

SAINTE-
CHAPELLE

PSG.

DAUPHINE

RUE DE SEINE

RUE BUCI

RUE L'ANCIENNE COMÉDIE

R. DES GRANDS AUGUSTINS

RUE ST. ANDRÉ-DES-ARTS

*Place
St. André-
des-Arts*

**Place
St. Michel**

11

COUR DU
COMMERCE
ST. ANDRÉ

R. JARDINET

R. DANTON

10

BLVD. ST. MICHEL

RUE DE LA HARPE

BOULEVARD

RUE CLÉMENT

M Odéon

ST. GERMAIN

RUE MABILLON

RUE LOBINEAU

RUE ST. SULPICE

ST.
SULPICE

Cluny La
Sorbonne M t

RUE PALATINE

L E F T

CLUNY
MUSEUM

RUE SERVANDONI

RUE GARANCIÈRE

RUE DE TOURNON

RUE DE CONDÉ

*Place de
l'Odéon*

RUE RACINE

SORBONNE

200 Meters

200 Yards

RUE DE VAUGIRARD

R. DE VAUGIRARD

BLVD. ST.-MICHEL

LUXEMBOURG
PALACE

*Luxembourg
Garden*

To Panthéon

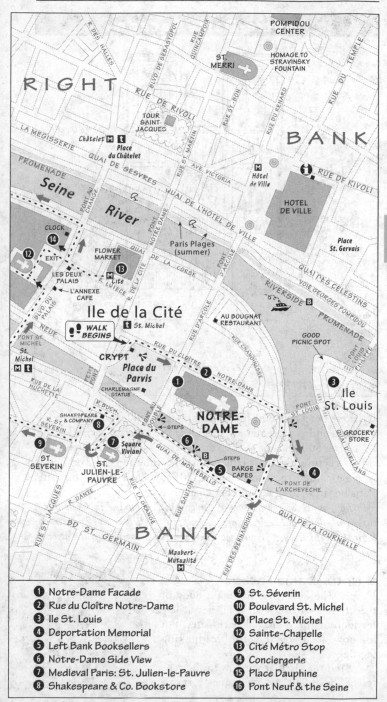

1 Notre-Dame Facade
2 Rue du Cloître Notre-Dame
3 Ile St. Louis
4 Deportation Memorial
5 Left Bank Booksellers
6 Notre-Dame Side View
7 Medieval Paris: St. Julien-le-Pauvre
8 Shakespeare & Co. Bookstore

9 St. Séverin
10 Boulevard St. Michel
11 Place St. Michel
12 Sainte-Chapelle
13 Cité Métro Stop
14 Conciergerie
15 Place Dauphine
16 Pont Neuf & the Seine

HISTORIC PARIS

Notre-Dame Facade

BORED GARGOYLE

GARGOYLES

MARY IN ROSE WINDOW

Seine

28 KINGS OF JUDAH

ST. DENIS (HOLDING HIS HEAD)

NOTRE-DAME

PORTAL OF MARY

LAST JUDGMENT

PORTAL OF ST. ANNE

To Left Bank & Latin Quarter

To Right Bank

RUE D'ARCOLE

EXIT

ENTER

STAIRS DOWN TO RIVERSIDE PROMENADE

PONT AU DOUBLE

DRINKING FOUNTAIN

HOTEL DIEU

RUE DU CLOÎTRE NOTRE-DAME

POINT ZERO

WC

CHARLEMAGNE STATUE

River

Place du Parvis

To Sainte-Chapelle & 🇹

To Crypt & Place St. Michel

style. He put a new 300-foot spire atop the roof (echoing the original), and added more statues, including the fanciful gargoyles.

After 800 years of work, Notre-Dame had become a truly glorious structure, the most famous Gothic church in the world. That was the church that stood here in 2019 when it caught fire...and Paris began writing yet another chapter in its story.

• *In fact, much of the history of Paris still lies buried in front of the cathedral. Some has been unearthed and put on display in the **Archaeological Crypt** (to your right; see page 64). Now turn your attention to the church.*

❶ Notre-Dame Facade

Despite the 2019 fire, the main body of the church still stands. We'll get a better look at the damaged parts later, but for now, focus on the still-breathtaking facade.

Find the circular window in the center of the facade, which frames a statue

of a woman holding a baby. For centuries, the main figure in the Christian pantheon has been Mary, the mother of Jesus. Catholics petition her in times of trouble to gain comfort, and to ask her to convince God to be compassionate with them. This church is dedicated to "Our Lady" (Notre Dame), and there she is, cradling God, right in the heart of the facade, surrounded by the halo of the rose window. Though the church is massive and imposing, it has always stood for the grace and compassion of Mary, the "mother of God."

Imagine the faith of the people who built this cathedral. They broke ground in 1163 with the hope that someday their great-great-great-great-great-great grandchildren might attend the dedication Mass, which finally took place two centuries later, in 1345. Look up the 200-foot-tall bell towers and imagine a tiny medieval community mustering the money and energy for construction. Master masons supervised, but the people did much of the grunt work themselves for free—hauling the huge stones from distant quarries, digging a 30-foot-deep trench to lay the foundation, and treading like rats on a wheel designed to lift the stones up, one by one. This kind of backbreaking, arduous manual labor created the real hunchbacks of Notre-Dame.

• *Looking two-thirds of the way up Notre-Dame's left tower, you might spot Paris' most photographed gargoyle (see drawing on page 126). Propped on his elbows on the balcony rail, he watches all the tourists below.*

Now, approach closer to the cathedral (as best you can with the construction barriers) to view the statues adorning the church's left portal.

St. Denis

Flanking the left doorway is a man with a misplaced head—that's St. Denis, the city's first bishop and patron saint. He stands among statues of other early Christians who helped turn pagan Paris into Christian Paris.

Sometime in the third century, Denis came here from Italy to convert the Parisii. He settled here on the Ile de la Cité, back when there was a Roman temple on this spot and Christianity was suspect. Denis proved so successful at winning converts that the Romans' pagan priests beheaded him as a warning to those forsaking the Roman gods. But those early Christians were hard to keep down. The man who would become St. Denis got up, tucked his head under his arm, headed north, paused at a fountain to wash it off, and continued

The Fire, the Damage, and the Rebuild

At 18:50 on April 15, 2019, a fire ignited in the attic of Notre-Dame and quickly grew to an inferno.

Paris came to a standstill, transfixed with horror at the sight of its beloved church in flames. Crowds flooded the streets while fire crews waged a desperate battle to save the landmark and its precious relics. Within an hour, the 300-foot-long roof was reduced to cinders.

Inside the church, parts of the stone ceiling broke apart and dropped to the floor far below, followed by massive, fiery, wooden roof beams. Soon after, the cathedral's soaring spire teetered, broke in two, and collapsed. That steeple—known as *la flèche* to Parisians ("the arrow")—was the needle around which this city spins. Remarkably, the Gallic rooster (France's unofficial symbol) crowning the top of the steeple was found undamaged with three relics tucked safely inside—including a piece from the Crown of Thorns. It seemed like a miracle...though the real miracle may be that the fire was extinguished within nine hours, thanks to the heroic work of more than 400 firefighters, mounting cranes while pumping water from the Seine.

How could a stone building like Notre-Dame catch fire? Although the cathedral's main body is stone, its roof and spire were made of wood coated with sheets of lead. The fire (likely started by an electrical short circuit) ignited some 1,300 huge 13th-century oak beams that supported the triangular roof. Once alight, such intense heat can cause stone to expand and crack, weaken the mortar that holds the stones together—and cause ceilings, arches, and entire walls to fail. Fortunately, at Notre-Dame, the fire was contained quickly enough that damage was limited. Many other cathedrals have fared far worse from fires—like Chartres (1194), London (1666), Reims (1917), Barcelona (1936), and Cologne (1945). Yet Notre-Dame, even with no firewalls or sprinkler

until he found just the right place to meet his maker: Montmartre. The Parisians were convinced by this miracle, Christianity gained ground, and a church soon replaced the pagan temple.

Medieval art was OK if it embellished the house of God and told biblical stories. Find the base of the central column (at the foot of Mary, about where the head of St. Denis could spit if he were really good). Working around from the left, find God telling a barely created Eve, "Have fun, but no apples." Next, the sexiest serpent I've ever seen makes apples à la mode. Finally, Adam and Eve, now

systems (an intentional choice to maintain its original look), survived.

Once the fire was out, city and church leaders assessed the damage. The 13th-century lead roof and 19th-century spire were gone (400 tons of lead were lost in the fire). The roof's copper statues (by Viollet-le-Duc in the 19th century) survived, ironically, because they had been previously removed for restoration. Inside the church, the

nave was littered with fallen stones, the remains of the steeple, and charred beams. Although most of the rib-arched stone ceiling support was intact, gaping holes opened to the sky. The falling debris caused some damage to the church's furnishings, but rescuers had managed to retrieve scores of priceless artifacts, including the Crown of Thorns, before the fire could reach them. The Grand Organ, one of Notre-Dame's most revered objects, with multiple keyboards and almost 8,000 pipes, was spared major damage (albeit covered in ash). And finally, three big beehives located just below the south transept's rose window, and home to over 180,000 bees, managed to survive the fire. *C'est incroyable.*

No sooner had the smoke cleared than the French vowed to rebuild. Still undecided is exactly what form the rebuilt Notre-Dame roof will take. Will builders replicate Viollet-le-Duc's 19th-century spire...or return to its 14th-century look? (President Macron dropped the idea of using a modern spire after it proved extremely unpopular.) Whatever this great cathedral becomes, it's clear that Notre-Dame—like its bees and the people of Paris—is a survivor. The latest goal? To have the church open in time for the 2024 Olympic Games in Paris.

ashamed of their nakedness, are expelled by an angel. This is a tiny example in a church covered with meaning.

• *Now, get as close as you can to the central doorway. Over the door are scenes from the Last Judgment.*

Central Portal

It's the end of the world, and Christ sits on the throne of judgment (just under the arches, holding both hands up). Beneath him an angel and a demon weigh souls in the balance; the demon cheats

Paris Through History

250 BC: Small fishing village of the Parisii, a Celtic tribe.

52 BC: Julius Caesar conquers the Parisii capital of Lutetia (near Paris); Romans replace it with a new capital on the Left Bank.

AD 497: Roman Paris falls to the Germanic Franks. King Clovis (482-511) converts to Christianity and makes Paris his capital.

885-886: Paris under siege by Viking Norsemen = Normans.

1163: Notre-Dame cornerstone laid.

c. 1250: Paris is a bustling commercial city with a university and new construction, such as Sainte-Chapelle and Notre-Dame.

c. 1600: King Henry IV beautifies Paris with buildings, roads, bridges, and squares.

c. 1700: Louis XIV makes Versailles his capital. Parisians grumble.

1789: Paris is the heart of France's Revolution, which condemns thousands to the guillotine.

1804: Napoleon Bonaparte crowns himself emperor in a ceremony at Notre-Dame.

1830 & 1848: Parisians take to the streets again in revolutions, fighting the return of royalty.

c. 1860: Napoleon's nephew, Napoleon III, commissions Baron Haussmann to build Paris' wide boulevards.

1889: The centennial of the Revolution is celebrated with the Eiffel Tower. Paris enjoys wealth and middle-class prosperity in the belle époque (beautiful age).

1920s: After the draining Great War, Paris is a cheap place to live, attracting expatriates such as Ernest Hemingway.

1940-1944: Occupied Paris spends the war years under gray skies and gray Nazi uniforms.

by pressing down. It's a sculptural depiction of the good, the bad, and the ugly. The good souls stand to the left, gazing up to heaven. The bad souls to the right are chained up and led off to a six-hour tour of the Louvre with a lousy guide on a hot summer day. The ugly souls must be the crazy, sculpted demons just below.

On the arch to the right there's a flaming cauldron with the sinner diving into it headfirst. The lower panel (beneath the chain of souls) shows angels with trumpets waking the dead from their

1968: Student protests and civil unrest pervade Paris.

1981: High-speed rail service (TGV) links Paris to Lyon, changing travel patterns in France (and making it easier for tourists to see more of the country).

1981-1995: Under President François Mitterrand, Paris' cityscape is enriched by the Louvre Pyramid, Musée d'Orsay, La Grande Arche de la Défense, and Opéra Bastille.

2000: Sparkly new lights brighten the Eiffel Tower.

2007: The Vélib' bike-rental system is the first step in an initiative to reduce Paris' car traffic, open riverside *quais* to pedestrians, and make the city more "green."

2008: All bars, cafés, and restaurants in France become smoke-free, ending the era of the smoky Parisian café.

2014: Socialist Anne Hidalgo becomes Paris' first female mayor.

2015: Separate terrorist attacks target the Paris offices of satirical magazine *Charlie Hebdo* and concertgoers at the Bataclan Theater. Free-speech supporters worldwide respond to the magazine attack with a slogan of solidarity: *Je suis Charlie* ("I am Charlie").

2017: President Emmanuel Macron and his wife, Brigitte, settle into Paris' Elysée Palace—the "French White House."

2018: Hundreds of thousands of Parisians swarm the Champs-Elysées to celebrate France's victory in the World Cup.

2019: Parisians are shocked to see their beloved Notre-Dame catch fire. Undaunted, they vow to rebuild.

2020: Work on the cathedral stalls as the coronavirus pandemic brings construction—and life as Parisians knew it—to a halt.

2022: Cathedral reconstruction continues with the goal of re-opening to the public in time for the 2024 Paris Olympic Games.

graves. The souls are from every class of French society—knights, ladies, peasants, clergy, even royalty—reminding all who entered these doors that everyone will be judged. Fortunately, Jesus (who stands below, between the double doors) can lead the way to salvation, along with his 12 apostles—each barefoot and with his ID symbol (such as Peter with his keys).

• *Now look higher. Above the doorway arches is a row of 28 statues, known as...*

The Kings of Judah

In the days of the French Revolution (1789-1799), these biblical kings were mistaken for the hated French kings, and Notre-Dame represented the oppressive Catholic hierarchy. The citizens stormed the church, crying, "Off with their heads!" Plop—they lopped off the crowned heads of these kings with glee, creating a row of St. Denises that weren't repaired for decades.

But the story doesn't end there. A schoolteacher who lived nearby collected the heads and buried them in his backyard for safekeeping. There they slept until 1977, when they were accidentally unearthed. Today, you can stare into the eyes of the original kings in the Cluny Museum, a few blocks away.

• *Remember that Notre-Dame is more than a tourist sight—it's been a place of worship for nearly a thousand years. Close your eyes and imagine the church in all its glory. Since the interior is currently closed to visitors, let's remove our metaphorical hats and mentally "step inside" the church, to take a...*

Virtual Tour of Notre-Dame's Interior

"Enter" the church like a simple bareheaded peasant of old (referring to the modern "Notre-Dame Interior" map). Imagine stepping

into a dark, earthly cavern lit with an unearthly light from the stained-glass windows. The priest intones the words of the Mass that echo through the hall. Your eyes follow the slender columns up 10 stories to the praying-hands arches of the ceiling. Walk up the long central **nave** lined with columns and flanked by side aisles. The place is huge—it can hold up to 10,000 faithful for a service.

When you reach the altar, you're at the center of this cross-shaped church, where the faithful receive the bread and wine of Communion. This was the holy spot for Romans, Christians...and even atheists. When the Revolutionaries stormed the church, they gutted it and turned it into a "Temple of Reason," complete with a woman dressed like Lady Liberty holding court at the altar.

If you were able to browse around the church, you'd see it's become a kind of Smithsonian for **artifacts** near and dear to the heart of the Parisian people. There's the venerated Crown of Thorns that supposedly Jesus wore (kept safely in the Treasury). There's the gilded-and-enameled reliquary dedicated to St. Geneviève (fifth century), whose prayers saved Paris from Attila the Hun. A painting honors the scholar Thomas

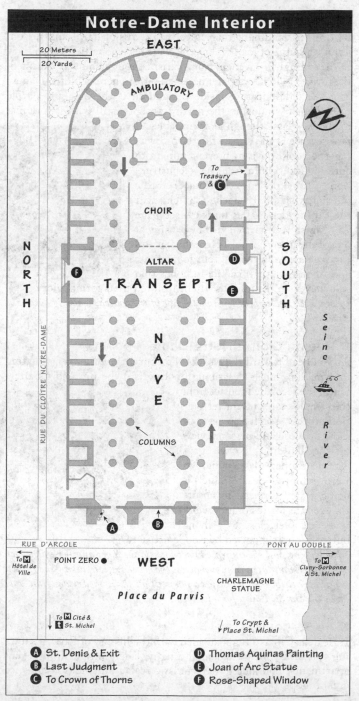

Notre-Dame Interior

EAST

20 Meters
20 Yards

AMBULATORY

CHOIR

To Treasury & C

ALTAR

T R A N S E P T

F

D

E

**N
A
V
E**

COLUMNS

**N
O
R
T
H**

RUE DU CLOÎTRE NOTRE-DAME

**S
O
U
T
H**

Seine River

A

B

HISTORIC PARIS

RUE D'ARCOLE

PONT AU DOUBLE

To M Hôtel de Ville

POINT ZERO ●

WEST

To M Cluny-Sorbonne & St. Michel

CHARLEMAGNE STATUE

Place du Parvis

To M Cité & t St. Michel

To Crypt & Place St. Michel

A St. Denis & Exit	**D** Thomas Aquinas Painting
B Last Judgment	**E** Joan of Arc Statue
C To Crown of Thorns	**F** Rose-Shaped Window

Aquinas (1225-1274), who studied at the University of Paris while writing his landmark theological works fusing faith and reason. There's a statue of Joan of Arc, the teenager who rallied her country to drive English invaders from Paris. (Though she was executed, the former "witch" was later beatified—right here in Notre-Dame.)

The oldest feature inside the church is the blue-and-purple rose-shaped window in the north transept—still with its original medieval glass, though not viewable. A new feature is the huge white tarp covering the roof above to prevent rain from entering the church during reconstruction. (To experience an intact Gothic interior, visit St. Eustache Church, near the Forum des Halles market—see page 73.) Finish your virtual visit by pausing at one of the many chapels. Here the faithful can pause in your mental tour to meditate and light a (virtual) candle in hopes that someday soon the interior will be restored to its former glory.

• *Let's circle around the left (north) side of the church, walking down the street called...*

❷ Rue du Cloître Notre-Dame

As you head toward the back of the church, you'll pass fascinating information panels describing (in English) the fire and its after-math, the recovered rooster from the steeple's top, and the restoration process. You'll also get your most up close and personal view of the building. Notice gaps where stained-glass windows were removed—each panel is being tested for lead to ensure they're safe for restoration work to begin. Get close to a flying

buttress, now supported by wooden structures.

• *Keep going past the church. (Don't worry, we'll get another classic look at Notre-Dame later, from just across the river.) After passing the garden behind the cathedral, pause for a moment on the arched pedestrian-only bridge, Pont St. Louis, for a look at...*

❸ Ile St. Louis

If Ile de la Cité is a tugboat laden with the history of Paris, it's towing this classy little residential dinghy, laden only with high-rent apartments, boutiques, characteristic restaurants, and famous ice cream shops.

Ile St. Louis wasn't developed until much later than Ile de la Cité (17th century). What was a swampy mess is now harmonious Parisian architecture and one of Paris' most exclusive neighborhoods.

Now look upstream (east) to the bridge (Pont Tournelle) that links Ile St. Louis with the Left Bank (which is now on your right). Where the bridge meets the Left Bank, you'll find one of Paris' most exclusive restaurants, La Tour d'Argent (with a flag flying from the rooftop). This restaurant was the inspiration for the movie *Ratatouille*. Because the top floor has floor-to-ceiling windows, your evening meal comes with glittering views—and a golden price (allow €200 minimum, though you get a photo of yourself dining elegantly with Notre-Dame floodlit in the background).

Ile St. Louis is a lovely place for an evening stroll (for details, see the Entertainment in Paris chapter). If you won't have time to come back later, consider taking a brief detour across the pedestrian bridge, Pont St. Louis, to explore this little island.

• *Let's head toward the Left Bank. Do an about face and start walking south (with the backside of Notre-Dame on your right). Enter the little grassy park to your left, where (behind a tall green hedge) you'll find the...*

❹ Deportation Memorial (Mémorial de la Déportation)

This memorial to the 200,000 French victims of the Nazi concentration camps (1940-1945) draws you into their experience. France was quickly overrun by Nazi Germany, and Paris spent the war years under Nazi occupation. Jews and dissidents were rounded up and deported—many never returned.

As you descend the steps, the city around you disappears. Surrounded by walls, you have become a prisoner. Your only freedom is your view of the sky and the tiny glimpse of the river below. Enter the dark, single-file chamber up ahead. Inside, the circular plaque in the floor reads, "They went to the end of the earth and did not return."

The hallway stretching in front of you is lined with 200,000 lighted crystals, one for each French citizen who died. Flickering at the far end is the eternal flame of hope. The tomb of the unknown deportee lies at your feet. Above, the inscription reads, "Dedicated to the living memory of the 200,000 French deportees shrouded by the night and the fog, exterminated in the Nazi concentration camps." The side rooms are filled with triangles—reminiscent of the identification patches inmates were forced to wear—each bearing the name of a concentration camp.

From the side room on the left, stairs lead up to Rooms 1 and 2, where you'll find a powerful exhibit on life in a concentration camp (vividly described in English). You'll circle around to where stairs lead back to the room of 200,000 crystals.

Above the exit as you leave is the message you'll find at many other Holocaust sites: "Forgive, but never forget."

• *Return to ground level. Exit the garden, turn left, and cross the bridge (Pont de l'Archevêché). When you reach the Left Bank, turn right along the river and work your way along the south side of Notre-Dame. We're now turning our attention to the neighborhood around us, the...*

LEFT BANK
❺ Left Bank Booksellers
You're now on the Left Bank.

The Rive Gauche, or the Left Bank of the Seine—"left" if you were floating downstream—is old Paris at its most atmospheric. This side of the river still has many of the twisting lanes and narrow buildings of medieval times. (The Right Bank near the Seine is more modern and business-oriented, with wide boulevards and stressed Parisians in suits.)

Here along the riverbank, the "big business" is secondhand books, displayed in the green metal stalls on the parapet. These literary entrepreneurs pride themselves on their easygoing style. With flexible hours and virtually no overhead, they run their businesses as they have since medieval times.

These booksellers (or *bouquinistes;* boo-keen-eest) have been a Parisian fixture since the mid-1500s, when such shops and stalls lined most of the bridges in Paris. In 1557, these merchants ran afoul of the authorities for selling forbidden Protestant pamphlets

Eateries Along This W

The following spots make for a nice lunch or snack break

Ile St. Louis: Stop for gelato at **Berthillon** or **Amorino Gelati,** for crêpes and a view at the recommended **Café Med,** or select another of the island's atmospheric eateries (see page 455).

Ile de la Cité: Conveniently located across from Sainte-Cha-pelle's entrance, **L'Annexe Café** offers reasonably priced café fare (and takeout coffee to sip while you wait in the church's security line). For a full meal, consider **Les Deux Palais,** across from Sainte-Chapelle's exit, or **Au Bougnat,** near Notre-Dame (for listings, see page 456).

A few peaceful food refuges on dreamy Place Dauphine, near the end of this walk, are worth the wait if you have the time: The **$$$ Caveau du Palais** restaurant is a refined spot for a drink (cool bar/café) or a fine meal, inside or out (daily, 17 Place Dauphine, +33 1 43 26 04 28). If you feel more like plotting a revolution (while saving a few euros), try the funky **$$ Ma Salle à Manger** (closed Mon, across the square at #26, +33 1 43 29 52 34).

Barges in the Seine: Docked near Notre-Dame are barges, some housing cafés with stunning views.

Picnics: The small park behind Notre-Dame, at the Deporta-tion Memorial, is good for a picnic, as is the tip of the Ile St. Louis. A short walk up the main drag on Ile St. Louis leads to a small grocery store.

Place St. André-des-Arts: Two nice outdoor restaurants sit amid the bustle on this tree-filled square near Place St. Michel.

in then-Catholic Paris. After the Revolution, business boomed when entire libraries were liberated from rich nobles.

Today, the waiting list to become one of Paris' 250 *bouquinistes* is eight years. Each *bouquiniste* is allowed four boxes, and the most-coveted spots are awarded based on seniority. Rent is around €100 per year. *Bouquinistes* are required to paint their boxes a standard green and stay open at least four days a week, or they lose their spot. Notice how they guard against the rain by wrapping everything in plastic. And yes, they do leave everything inside when they lock up at night; metal bars and padlocks keep things safe. Though their main items may be vintage books, these days tourists prefer posters and magnets.

• *At a gap in the green stalls directly across from Notre-Dame, find stairs leading down to the river—good for losing crowds and for a terrific...*

❻ Notre-Dame Side View

From this side, you can really appreciate both the church architec-ture and the devastation wrought by the 2019 fire. Before the fire,

It takes 13 tourists to build a Gothic church: one steeple, six columns, and six buttresses.

you'd have seen a green lead-covered roof topped with Viollet-le-Duc's 300-foot steeple, and several statues adorning its base.

Those are gone completely, as is the lead roof and all windows—save for the three massive rose windows (now covered for protection). But what's surprising is how much of the church survived. That's a testament to the medieval architects who designed this amazing structure. Their great technological innovation is what we've come to call the **Gothic style.**

In a glance, you can spot many of the elements of Gothic: pointed arches, the lacy stone tracery of the windows, pinnacles, statues on rooftops, and pointed steeples covered with the prickly "flames" (Flamboyant Gothic) of the Holy Spirit. Most distinctive of all are the **flying buttresses.** These 50-foot stone "beams" that stick out of the church were the key to the complex Gothic architecture. The pointed arches built inside the church cause the

weight of the roof to push outward rather than downward. The "flying" buttresses support the roof by pushing back inward. Gothic architects were masters at playing architectural forces against each other to build loftier and loftier churches, opening the walls for stained-glass windows. The Gothic style was born here in Paris. Those wooden structures you see supporting the flying buttresses show how they were originally raised.

Picture Quasimodo (the fictional hunchback) limping around along the railed balcony at the base of the roof among the "gargoyles." These grotesque beasts sticking out from pillars and buttresses represent souls caught between heaven and earth. They also function as rainspouts (from the same French root word as "gargle") when there are no evil spirits to battle.

• *Continue walking along the river. When you reach the bridge (Pont au Double) at the front of Notre-Dame, head back up the stairs, veer left across the street, and find a small park called Square Viviani (fill your water bottle from fountain on left). Angle across the square and pass by Paris' oldest inhabitant—an acacia tree nicknamed Robinier, after the guy who planted it in 1602. Imagine that this same tree might once have shaded the Sun King, Louis XIV. Just beyond the tree you'll find the small rough-stone church of St. Julien-le-Pauvre. Leave the park, walking past the church, to tiny Rue Galande.*

❼ Medieval Paris

Picture Paris in 1250, when the church of St. Julien-le-Pauvre was still new. You can pop into the church for a trip east a few hundred miles and back a few centuries. Back outside, continue around the church a few steps. Notre-Dame was nearly built, Sainte-Chapelle had just opened, the university was expanding human knowledge, and Paris was fast becoming a prosperous industrial and commercial center. The area around the church and along Rue Galande gives you some of the medieval feel of ramshackle architecture and old houses leaning every which way. In medieval days, people were piled on top of each other, building at all angles, as they scrambled for this prime real estate near the main commercial artery of the day—the Seine. The smell of fish competed with the smell of neighbors in this knot of humanity.

Narrow dirt (or mud) streets sloped from here down into the mucky Seine until the 19th century, when modern quays and embankments cleaned everything up.

• *Return toward the river, walking past the church and park on the cobbled lane. Turn left on Rue de la Bûcherie and drop into the...*

❽ Shakespeare and Company Bookstore

In addition to hosting butchers and fishmongers, the Left Bank has been home to scholars, philosophers, and poets since medieval times. This funky bookstore—a reincarnation of the original shop from the 1920s on Rue de l'Odéon—has picked up the literary torch. Sylvia Beach, an American with a passion for free thinking, opened Shakespeare and Company for the post-WWI Lost Generation, who came to Paris to find themselves. American writers flocked to the city for the cheap rent, fleeing the uptight, Prohibition-era United States. Beach's bookstore

was famous as a meeting place for Paris' expatriate literary elite. Ernest Hemingway borrowed books from it regularly. James Joyce struggled to find a publisher for his now-classic novel *Ulysses*—until Sylvia Beach published it. George Bernard Shaw, Gertrude Stein, and Ezra Pound also got their English fix at her shop.

Today, the bookstore carries on that literary tradition—the owner, Sylvia, is named after the original store's founder. Struggling writers are given free accommodations in tiny rooms with views of Notre-Dame. Explore—the upstairs has a few seats, cots, antique typewriters, and cozy nooks. Downstairs, travelers enjoy a great selection of used English books—including my Paris and France guidebooks. Their cozy coffee shop sits next door.

Notice the green water fountain (1900) in front of the bookstore, one of the many in Paris donated by the English philanthropist Sir Richard Wallace. The hooks below the caryatids once held metal mugs for drinking the water before the age of plastic (the mugs were removed in the 1950s). Wallace donated the fountains after the Franco-Prussian War to give residents free access to water as aqueducts had been destroyed. The four nymphs represent sobriety, simplicity, kindness, and charity.

• *Continue to Rue du Petit-Pont and turn left. This bustling north-south boulevard (which becomes Rue St. Jacques) was the Romans' busiest street 2,000 years ago, with chariots racing in and out of the city. (Roman-iacs can view remains from the third-century baths, and a fine medieval collection, at the nearby Cluny Museum).*

A block south of the Seine, turn right at the Gothic church of St. Séverin and walk into the Latin Quarter.

❾ St. Séverin

Don't ask me why, but building this church took a century longer than building Notre-Dame. This is Flamboyant, or "flame-like,"

Gothic, and you can see how the short, prickly spires are meant to make this building flicker in the eyes of the faithful. The church gives us a close-up look at gargoyles, the decorative drain spouts that also functioned to keep evil spirits away.

Inside you can see the final stage of Gothic, on the cusp of the Renaissance. It's also notable for carrying on the medieval tradition of stained-glass windows into more modern times, while keeping the dominant blues, greens, and reds popular in St. Séverin's heyday. Walk to the apse and admire the lone twisted Flamboyant Gothic column and the fan vaulting. The apse's windows (by Jean Bazaine, c. 1960) echo the fan-vaulting effect in a modern, abstract way. Each colorful window represents one of the seven sacraments—blue for baptism, yellow for marriage, etc. The impressive organ filling the entrance wall is a reminder that this church is still a popular venue for evening concerts (see gate for information posters, buy tickets at door).

• *At #22 Rue St. Séverin, you'll find the skinniest house in Paris, two windows wide. Rue St. Séverin leads right through the...*

Latin Quarter

Although it may look more like the Greek Quarter today (cheap gyros abound), this area is the Latin Quarter, named for the language you'd have heard on these streets if you walked them in the Middle Ages. The University of Paris (founded 1215), one of the leading educational institutions of medieval Europe, was (and still is) nearby.

A thousand years ago, the "crude" or vernacular local languages were sophisticated enough to communicate basic human needs, but if you wanted to get philosophical, the language of choice was Latin. Medieval Europe's class of educated elite transcended nations and borders. From Sicily to Sweden, they spoke and corresponded in Latin. Now the most "Latin" thing about this area is the beat you may hear coming from some of the subterranean jazz clubs.

Walking along Rue St. Séverin, you can still see the shadow of the medieval sewer system. The street slopes into a central channel of bricks. In the days before plumbing and toilets, when people still went to the river or neighborhood wells for their water, flushing meant throwing it out the window. At certain times of day, maids on the fourth floor would holler, *"Garde de l'eau!"* ("Watch out for the water!") and heave it into the streets, where it would eventually wash down into the Seine.

As you wander, remember that before Napoleon III commissioned Baron Haussmann to modernize the city with grand boulevards (19th century), Paris was just like this—a medieval tangle. The ethnic feel of this area is nothing new—it's been a melting pot and university district for almost 800 years.

• *At the fork with Rue de la Harpe, bear slightly right to continue down Rue St. Séverin another block until you come to...*

⑩ Boulevard St. Michel

Busy Boulevard St. Michel (or "boul' Miche") is famous as the main artery for Paris' café and arts scene, culminating a block away

(to the left) at the intersection with Boulevard St. Germain. Although nowadays you're more likely to find leggings at 30 percent off, there are still many cafés, boutiques, and bohemian haunts nearby.

The Sorbonne—the University of Paris' humanities department—is also nearby, if you want to make a detour, though visitors are not allowed to enter. (Turn left on Boulevard St. Michel and walk two blocks south. Gaze at the dome from the Place de la Sorbonne courtyard.) Originally founded as a theological school, the Sorbonne began attracting more students and famous professors—such as St. Thomas Aquinas and Peter Abélard—as its prestige grew. By the time the school expanded to include other subjects, it had a reputation for bold new ideas. Nonconformity is a tradition here, and Paris remains a world center for new intellectual trends.

• *Also to the left is the Cluny Museum, which brings the era of Aquinas and Abélard to life (*☐ *see the Cluny Museum Tour chapter). But to continue this walk, cross Boulevard St. Michel. Just ahead is...*

Place St. André-des-Arts

This tree-filled square is lined with cafés. In Paris, most serious thinking goes on in cafés. For centuries these have been social watering holes, where you can get a warm place to sit and stimulating conversation for the price of a cup of coffee. Every great French

writer—from Voltaire and
Jean-Jacques Rousseau
to Jean-Paul Sartre and
Jacques Derrida—had a
favorite haunt.

Paris honors its intel-
lectuals. If you visit the
Panthéon (described on
page 88)—several blocks
south on Boulevard St.
Michel and to the left—you'll find French writers (Voltaire, Victor
Hugo, Emile Zola, and Rousseau), inventors (Louis Braille), and
scientists (including Marie and Pierre Curie) buried in a setting
usually reserved for warriors and politicians.

• *Adjoining this square toward the river is the triangular Place St. Michel, with a Métro stop and a statue of St. Michael killing a devil. Note:
If you were to continue west along Rue St. André-des-Arts, you'd find
more Left Bank action (* 📖 *see the Left Bank Walk chapter).*

⓫ Place St. Michel

You're standing at the traditional core of the Left Bank's artsy, liberal, hippie, bohemian district of poets, philosophers, winos, and
*baba cool*s (neo-hippies).
Nearby, you'll find international eateries, far-out
bookshops, street singers,
pale girls in black berets,
jazz clubs, and—these
days—tourists. Small cin-
emas show avant-garde
films, almost always in the
version originale (v.o.). For
colorful wandering and café-sitting, afternoons and evenings are
best. In the morning, it feels sleepy. The Latin Quarter stays up late
and sleeps in.

In less commercial times, Place St. Michel was a gathering
point for the city's malcontents and misfits. In 1830, 1848, and
again in 1871, the citizens took the streets from the government
troops, set up barricades *Les Miz*-style, and fought against royalist
oppression. During World War II, the locals rose up against their
Nazi oppressors (read the plaques under the dragons at the foot of
the St. Michel fountain).

In the spring of 1968, a time of social upheaval all over the
world, young students battled riot batons and tear gas by digging
up the cobblestones on the street and hurling them at police. They
took over the square and declared it an independent state. Factory

workers followed their call to arms and went on strike, challenging the de Gaulle government and forcing change. Eventually, the students were pacified, the university was reformed, and the Latin Quarter's original cobblestones were replaced with pavement, so future scholars could never again use the streets as weapons. Even today, whenever there's a student demonstration, it starts here.

• *From Place St. Michel, look across the river and find the prickly steeple of the Sainte-Chapelle church. Head toward it. Cross the river on Pont St. Michel and continue north along the Boulevard du Palais. On your left, you'll see the doorway to Sainte-Chapelle.*

SAINTE-CHAPELLE AND NEARBY

Security is strict at the Sainte-Chapelle complex because this is more than a tourist attraction: France's Supreme Court meets to the right of Sainte-Chapelle in the Palais de Justice.

You'll need a timed-entry ticket to go inside (see details at the beginning of this chapter), and the church entry may be hidden behind a line of ticket buyers. Once past security, you'll enter the courtyard outside Sainte-Chapelle, where you'll find information about upcoming church concerts.

• *Enter the humble ground floor.*

⓲ Sainte-Chapelle

This triumph of Gothic church architecture is a cathedral of glass like no other. It was speedily built between 1242 and 1248 for King Louis IX—the only French king who is now a saint—to house the supposed Crown of Thorns (later moved to Notre-Dame's treasury and now in safekeeping since the fire). Its architectural harmony is due to the fact that it was completed under the direction of one architect and in only six years—unheard of in Gothic  times. Recall that Notre-Dame took more than 200 years.

Though the inside is beautiful, the exterior is basically functional. The muscular buttresses hold up the stone roof, so the walls are essentially there to display stained glass. The lacy spire is Neo-Gothic—added in the 19th century. Inside, the layout clearly shows an *ancien régime* approach to worship. The low-ceilinged basement was for staff and other common folks—worshipping under a sky filled with painted fleurs-de-lis, a symbol of the king. Royal Christians worshipped upstairs. The paint job, a 19th-century restoration, helps you imagine how grand this small, painted, jeweled

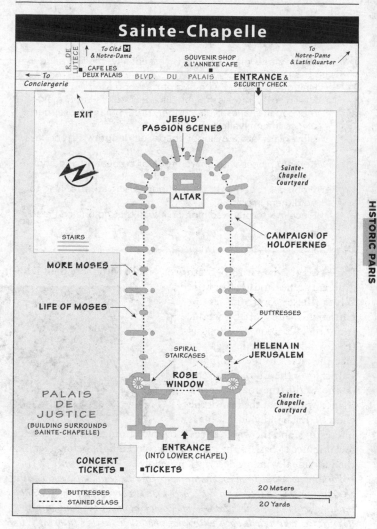

Sainte-Chapelle

(Map labels:)

To Cité Ⓜ & Notre-Dame

R. DE LUTECE

SOUVENIR SHOP & L'ANNEXE CAFE

To Notre-Dame & Latin Quarter

CAFE LES DEUX PALAIS

← To Conciergerie

BLVD. DU PALAIS

ENTRANCE & SECURITY CHECK

EXIT

JESUS' PASSION SCENES

ALTAR

Sainte-Chapelle Courtyard

STAIRS

CAMPAIGN OF HOLOFERNES

MORE MOSES

LIFE OF MOSES

BUTTRESSES

SPIRAL STAIRCASES

HELENA IN JERUSALEM

ROSE WINDOW

PALAIS DE JUSTICE (BUILDING SURROUNDS SAINTE-CHAPELLE)

Sainte-Chapelle Courtyard

ENTRANCE (INTO LOWER CHAPEL)

CONCERT TICKETS ■

■TICKETS

BUTTRESSES

STAINED GLASS

20 Meters

20 Yards

HISTORIC PARIS

chapel was. (Imagine Notre-Dame painted like this...) Each capital is playfully carved with a different plant's leaves.

• *Climb the spiral staircase to the Chapelle Haute. Leave the rough stone of the earth and step into the light.*

Stained Glass

Fiat lux. "Let there be light." From the first page of the Bible, it's clear: Light is divine. Light shines through stained glass like God's grace shining down to earth. Gothic architects used their new technology to turn dark stone buildings into lanterns of light. The glory of Gothic shines brighter here than in any other church.

There are 15 separate panels of stained glass (6,500 square

Stained Glass Supreme

Craftsmen made glass—which is, essentially, melted sand—using this recipe:

- Melt one part sand with two parts wood ash.
- Mix in rusty metals to get different colors—iron makes red; cobalt makes blue; copper, green; manganese, purple; cadmium, yellow.
- Blow glass into a cylinder shape, cut lengthwise, and lay flat to cool.
- Cut into pieces with an iron tool, or by heating and cooling a select spot to make it crack.
- Fit pieces together to form a figure, using strips of lead to hold them in place.
- Place masterpiece so high on a wall that no one can read it.

feet—two-thirds of it 13th-century original), with more than 1,100 different scenes, mostly from the Bible. These cover the entire Christian history of the world, from the Creation in Genesis (first window on the left, as you face the altar), to the coming of Christ (over the altar), to the end of the world (the round "rose"-shaped window at the rear of the church). Each individual scene is

interesting, and the whole effect is overwhelming. Allow yourself a few minutes to bask in the glow of the colored light before tackling the individual window descriptions below.

• *Working clockwise from the entrance, look for these notable scenes, using the map in this chapter as a reference. Don't worry if you have trouble making sense of the windows—you're not alone. (The souvenir shop downstairs sells a little book with color photos for further tutoring.) The sun lights up different windows at various times of day. Overcast days give the most even light. On bright, sunny days, some sections are glorious, while others look like sheets of lead.*

The first window on the left (with scenes from Genesis) is always dark because of a building butted up against it. Let's pass over that one and turn to the second window on the left.

Life of Moses (second window, dark bottom row of diamond panels): The first panel shows baby Moses in a basket, placed by his sister in the squiggly brown river. Next he's found by the pharaoh's daughter. Then he grows up. And finally, he's a man, a prince of Egypt on his royal throne.

More Moses (third window, in middle and upper sections): See how many guys with bright yellow horns you can spy. Moses is shown with horns as the result of a medieval mistranslation of the Hebrew word for "rays of light," or halo.

Jesus' Passion Scenes (directly over the altar and behind the canopy): These scenes from Jesus' arrest and Crucifixion were the backdrop for this chapel's *raison d'être*—the Crown of Thorns, which was originally displayed on this altar. Stand close to the steps of the altar—about five paces away—and gaze through the canopy where, if you look just above the altar table, you'll see Jesus, tied to a green column, being whipped. To the immediate right is the key scene in this relic chapel—Jesus (in purple robe) being fitted with the painful Crown of Thorns.

• *Continuing clockwise, find the window on the right wall that's four circular scenes wide.*

Campaign of Holofernes: On the bottom row, focus on the second circle from the left. It's a battle scene (the campaign of Holofernes) showing three soldiers with swords slaughtering three men. Examine the details. The background is blue. The men have different-colored clothes—red, blue, green, mauve, and white. You can actually see the folds in the robes, the hair, and facial features. Look at the victim in the center—his head is splotched with blood. Details like these were created either by scratch-

ing on the glass or by baking on paint. It was a painstaking process of finding just the right colors, fitting them together to make a scene...and then multiplying by 1,100.

Helena in Jerusalem (first window on the right wall, at the rear of the nave near where you'll exit): This window tells the story of how Christ's Crown of Thorns found its way from Jerusalem to Constantinople to this chapel. Start in the lower-left corner, where the Roman emperor Constantine (in blue, on his throne) waves goodbye to his Christian mom, Helena. She arrives at the gate of Jerusalem (next panel to the right). The other panels (though almost impossible for 21st-century eyes to follow) tell the rest of the story: Helena discovers the Crown of Thorns and brings it back to Constantinople. Nine hundred years later, French Crusader knights invade the Holy Land and visit Constantinople. Finally, King Louis IX returns to France with the sacred relic, and builds this church to house it.

Rose Window (above entrance): This window (added 200 years later) is the chapel's climax, showing the final scene in human history. It's Judgment Day, with a tiny Christ in the center, presiding over a glorious moment of wonders and miracles.

Altar

The altar was raised up high to better display the Crown of Thorns, the relic around which this chapel was built. Notice the staircase: Access was limited to the priest and the king, who wore the keys to the shrine around his neck. Also note that there is no high-profile image of Jesus anywhere—this chapel was all about the Crown.

King Louis IX, convinced he'd found the real McCoy, spent roughly the equivalent of €500 million for the Crown, €370 million for the gem-studded shrine to display it in (later destroyed in the French Revolution), and a mere €150 million to build Sainte-Chapelle to house it.

Lay your camera on the ground and shoot the ceiling. Those pure and simple ribs growing out of the slender columns are the essence of Gothic structure.

• *Exit Sainte-Chapelle. Back outside, as you walk around the church exterior, look down to see the foundation and take note of how much Paris has risen in the 750 years since Sainte-Chapelle was built. As you head toward the exit of the complex, you'll pass by the...*

Palais de Justice

Sainte-Chapelle sits within a huge complex of buildings that has housed the local government since ancient Roman times. It was the site of the original Gothic palace of the early kings of France. The only surviving medieval parts are Sainte-Chapelle and the Conciergerie prison.

Most of the site is now covered by the giant Palais de Justice, built in 1776, home of the French Supreme Court. The motto *Liberté, Egalité, Fraternité* over the doors is a reminder that this was also the headquarters of the Revolutionary government. Here they doled out justice, condemning many to imprisonment in the Conciergerie downstairs—or to the guillotine.

• *Now pass through the big iron gate to the noisy Boulevard du Palais. Cross the street to the wide, pedestrian-only Rue de Lutèce and walk about halfway down.*

⑬ Cité "Metropolitain" Métro Stop

Of the 141 original early-20th-century subway entrances, this is one of only a few survivors—now preserved as a national art treasure.

(New York's Museum of Modern Art even exhibits one.) It marks Paris at its peak in 1900—on the cutting edge of Modernism, but with an eye for beauty. The curvy, plantlike ironwork is a textbook example of Art Nouveau, the style that rebelled against the erector-set squareness of the Industrial Age. Other similar Métro stations in Paris are Abbesses and Porte Dauphine.

The flower and plant market on Place Louis Lépine is a pleasant detour. On Sundays this square flutters with a busy bird market. And across the way is the Préfecture de Police, where Inspector Clouseau of *Pink Panther* fame used to work, and where the local Resistance fighters took the first building from the Nazis in August 1944, leading to the Allied liberation of Paris a week later.

• *Pause here to admire the view. Sainte-Chapelle is a pearl in an ugly architectural oyster. Double back to the Palais de Justice, turn right onto Boulevard du Palais, and enter the Conciergerie (sidestep the ticket-buying bottleneck with a Museum Pass or ticket bought in advance).*

⑭ Conciergerie

Though barren inside, this former prison echoes with history. The Conciergerie was the last stop for 2,780 victims of the guillotine,

including France's last *ancien régime* queen, Marie-Antoinette. Before then, kings had used the building to torture and execute failed assassins. (One of its towers along the river was called "The Babbler," named for the pain-induced sounds that leaked from it.) When the Revolution (1789) toppled the king, the progressive Revolutionaries proudly unveiled a modern and more humane way to execute people—the guillotine. The Conciergerie was the epicenter of the Reign of Terror—the year-long period of the Revolution (1793-94) during which Revolutionary fervor spiraled out of control and thousands were killed. It was here at the Conciergerie that "enemies of the Revolution" were imprisoned, tried, sentenced, and marched off to Place de la Concorde for decapitation.

Inside the Conciergerie

Pick up a free map and breeze through the one-way, well-described circuit. You'll start in the spacious, low-ceilinged Hall of Men-at-Arms (Room 1), originally a guards' dining room warmed by four big fireplaces (look up the chimneys). During the Reign of Terror, this large hall served as a holding tank for the poorest prisoners. Then they were taken upstairs (in an area not open to visitors), where the Revolutionary tribunals grilled scared prisoners on their political correctness.

Continue to the raised area at the far end of the room (Room 4, today's bookstore). This was the walkway of the executioner, who was known affectionately as "Monsieur de Paris." Just past the bookstore, pause in rooms (to the right) with displays on Revolutionary history. Continuing on, you'll pass the cell (on the left) where shackled suspects were processed by the Office of the Keeper (or "Concierge"), who admitted prisoners, monitored torture... and recommended nearby restaurants. The next cell is where condemned prisoners combed their hair or touched up their lipstick before their final public appearance—waiting for the open-air cart (tumbrel) to pull up outside. The tumbrel would carry them to the guillotine, which was on Place de la Concorde.

Upstairs is a memorial room with the names of the 2,780 citizens condemned to death by the guillotine. While most of the famous names have been vandalized (Charlotte Corday, Robespierre, Louis XVI—who was called "Capet: last king of France"), you may see Marie-Antoinette (opposite the entry, 10 rows down, look for Capet Marie-Antoinette). Head down the hallway past more cells that give a sense of the poor and cramped conditions. Then comes a small set of displays. You'll see old paintings of the Conciergerie and some of the famous prisoners.

Next, go downstairs, where—tucked behind heavy gray cur-

Marie-Antoinette

In 1789, as the Revolution was coming to a head, it was Queen Marie-Antoinette—even more than her husband, King Louis XVI—who became the focus of the citizens' disgust.

First off, she was foreign-born, known simply as "The Austrian." Reports flew that she spent extravagantly, plunging France into debt. She was seen as a dragon lady who'd manipulated her husband against the Revolution. Worst of all, a rumor spread (probably false) that when Marie was told that the Parisians had no bread, she sneered, "Let them eat cake!" ("Cake" was the burnt crusts of the bread oven.)

Enraged and hungry, 6,000 Parisian women (backed by armed men) marched through the rain to the royal palace at Versailles. The Revolutionaries stormed the château, kidnapped the royal family, and brought them back to Paris. They were placed under house arrest in the Tuileries Palace (which once stood in the Tuileries Garden).

In 1791, Marie and Louis engineered an escape to Austria to begin a counterrevolution. They had one of their servants pretend to be a German baroness, while Louis disguised himself as her servant. (The irony must have been killing him.) But someone recognized Louis from his portrait on a franc note. The family was captured, put on trial as traitors to France, and the monarchy was abolished.

Louis, Marie-Antoinette, and their eight-year-old son were tearfully split up and sent to separate prisons. Marie-Antoinette was taken to the Conciergerie.

On January 21, 1793, King Louis XVI (excuse me, that's "Citizen Capet") was led to Place de la Concorde and laid face down on a slab. *Shoop!*—a thousand years of monarchy that dated back to before Charlemagne was decapitated. On October 16, Marie-Antoinette was also carted to Place de la Concorde. Genteel to the end, she apologized to the executioner for stepping on his foot. The blade fell, the blood gushed, and her head was shown to the crowd on a stick—an exclamation point for the new rallying cry: *Vive la nation!*

tains—is a tiny chapel built on the site where Marie-Antoinette's prison cell originally stood. The chapel's three paintings tell her sad story: First, Marie (dressed in widow's black) stoically says goodbye to her grieving family as she's led off to prison. Next, still stoic, she awaits her fate. Finally, she piously kneels in her cell to receive the Last Sacrament on the night before her beheading. The chapel's walls drip with silver-embroidered tears. It was made in

Marie's honor by Louis XVIII, the brother of beheaded Louis XVI and the first king to reclaim the throne after the Revolution.

The tour concludes outside in the "Cour de Femmes" courtyard, where female prisoners were allowed a little fresh air. Look up and notice the spikes still guarding from above...and be glad you can leave this place with your head intact. It wasn't so easy for enemies of the state. On October 16, 1793, Marie-Antoinette was awakened at 4:00 in the morning and led away. She walked the corridor, stepped onto the cart, and was slowly carried to Place de la Concorde, where she had her date with "Monsieur de Paris."

• *Back outside, turn left on Boulevard du Palais. On the corner is the city's oldest public clock. The mechanism of the present clock is from 1334, and even though the case is Baroque, it keeps on ticking.*

Turn left onto Quai de l'Horloge and walk along the river, past the "Babbler" tower. The bridge up ahead is Pont Neuf, where we'll end this walk. At the first corner, veer left into a sleepy triangular square called...

⓯ Place Dauphine

It's amazing to find such coziness in the heart of Paris. This city of more than two million is still a city of neighborhoods, a collection of villages. The French Supreme Court building looms behind like a giant marble gavel. Enjoy the village-Paris feeling in the park (young Parisians flock to the square on weekend afternoons for *pétanque* and more). For eating recommendations on this square, see the "Eateries Along this Walk" sidebar, earlier.

• *Continue through Place Dauphine. As you pop out the other end, you're face-to-face with a...*

Statue of Henry IV

Henry IV (1553-1610) is not as famous as his grandson, Louis XIV, but Henry helped make Paris what it is today—a European capital of elegant buildings and quiet squares. He built the Place Dauphine (behind you), the Pont Neuf (to the right), residences (to the left, down Rue Dauphine), the Louvre's long Grand Gallery (downriver on the right), and the tree-filled Square du Vert-Galant (directly behind the statue, on the tip of the island). The square is one of Paris' make-out spots; its name comes from Henry's nickname, the Green Knight, as Henry was a notorious ladies' man. The park is a great place to relax, dangling your legs over the concrete prow of this boat-shaped island.

• *From the statue, turn right onto the old bridge. Pause at the little nook halfway across.*

⓰ Pont Neuf and the Seine

This "new bridge" is now Paris' oldest. Built during Henry IV's reign (about 1600), its arches span the widest part of the river.

Unlike other bridges, this one never had houses or buildings growing on it. The turrets were originally for vendors and street entertainers. In the days of Henry IV, who promised his peasants "a chicken in every pot every Sunday," this would have been a lively scene. From the bridge, look downstream (west) to see the next bridge, the pedestrian-only Pont des Arts. Ahead on the Right Bank is the long Louvre museum. Beyond that, on the Left Bank, is the Orsay. And what's that tall black tower in the distance?

Our walk ends where Paris began—on the **Seine River.** From Dijon to the English Channel, the Seine meanders 500 miles, cutting through the center of Paris. The river is shallow and slow within the city, but still dangerous enough to require steep stone embankments (built 1910) to prevent occasional floods.

In summer, the riverside *quais* are turned into beach zones with beach chairs and tanned locals, creating the Paris Plages (see page 66). The success of the Paris Plages helped motivate the city to take the next step: to permanently banish cars from long stretches of the riverside (between the Orsay and Pont de l'Alma on the Left Bank and between the Louvre and Place de la Bastille on the Right Bank), turning them into parks instead.

The Seine is still the main artery of Paris. Besides tourist boats, it also carries commercial barges with 20 percent of Paris' transported goods. And on the banks, sportsmen today cast into the waters once fished by Paris' original Celtic inhabitants 2,000 years ago.

• We're done. You can take a boat tour that leaves from near the base of Pont Neuf on the island side (Vedettes du Pont Neuf; see page 48). Or you could take our Left Bank Walk, which begins one bridge downriver.

The nearest Métro stop is Pont Neuf, across the bridge on the Right Bank. Bus #69 heads east along Quai du Louvre (at the north end of the bridge) and west along Rue de Rivoli (a block farther north). Below the bridge is the riverside promenade—filled with people, for good reason, on a sunny day. In fact, from here you can go anywhere—you're standing in the heart of Paris.

LOUVRE TOUR

Musée du Louvre

Paris walks you through world history in three world-class museums—the Louvre (ancient world to 1850), the Orsay (1848-1914, including Impressionism), and the Pompidou (20th century to today). Start your "art-yssey" at the Louvre. With more than 30,000 works of art on display, the Louvre is a full inventory of Western civilization. To cover it all in one visit is impossible. Let's focus on the Louvre's specialties—Greek sculpture, Italian painting, and French painting.

We'll see "Venuses" through history, from prehistoric stick figures to the curvy *Venus de Milo* to the wind-blown *Winged Victory of Samothrace,* and from placid medieval Madonnas to the *Mona Lisa* to the symbol of modern democracy. Those with a little more time can visit some impressive chunks of stone from Mesopotamia—the "Cradle of Civilization" (modern-day Iraq). As we traverse the centuries, we'll see how each generation defined beauty differently, and gain insight into long-ago civilizations by admiring what they found beautiful.

Orientation

Cost: €17 timed-entry ticket required (purchase online in advance), covered by Museum Pass. Tickets are good all day and include special exhibits; reentry is not allowed (don't leave the security check area as you travel between the wings of the museum).

Hours: Wed-Mon 9:00-18:00, closed Tue. Galleries start shutting down 30 minutes before closing; last entry is 45 minutes before closing. The museum may stay open into the evening on Wed and Fri (until 21:45—check online for the latest).

Information: +33 1 40 20 53 17, recorded info +33 1 40 20 51 51, www.louvre.fr.

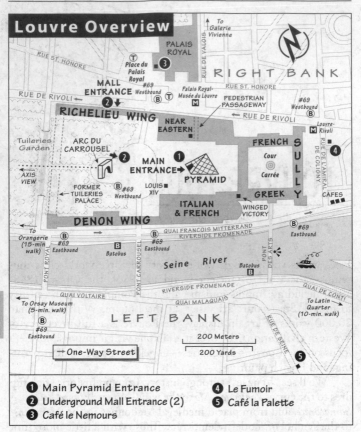

Louvre Overview

1 Main Pyramid Entrance
2 Underground Mall Entrance (2)
3 Café le Nemours
4 Le Fumoir
5 Café la Palette

Reserved Entry Time Required: The Louvre requires all visitors—including Museum Pass holders—to reserve a time slot for your visit. You can generally book a reservation time up to a few hours before your visit; a day or more before is better in peak season. You'll be able to enter at the pyramid up to 30 minutes before your assigned time.

Buying Tickets at the Louvre: If you arrive sans ticket or reservation (bad idea) and are allowed in (unlikely), in very quiet times it may be possible to buy a €15 timed-entry ticket at the door. When available, these tickets are sold in a side room under the pyramid. Line up for the next available self-service machine (machines only accept credit cards with a PIN) or ticket window. You'll generally wait in a long ticket line.

Buying Museum Passes at the Louvre: The "Museum Pass Tabac" (a.k.a. La Civette du Carrousel) sells the Museum Pass for no extra charge (cash only). It's just outside the Louvre entrance in the underground Carrousel du Louvre mall—to find it, follow *Museum Pass* signs inside the mall.

Renovations: Due to renovations, some sections are routinely closed one day a week (for example, the Near Eastern Antiquities section may be closed Wed; get the latest on the website or at the info desk). Other renovations affect room numbers—expect changes to the room numbers provided in this tour.

When to Go: Crowds can be miserable on Sun, Mon (the worst day), Wed, and in the morning (arrive 30 minutes before opening to secure a good place in line). Evening visits (when available) are quieter, and the glass pyramid glows after dark.

Getting There: Métro stop Palais Royal-Musée du Louvre is the closest. From the station, you can either exit above ground to go in the pyramid entrance or stay underground to use the Carrousel du Louvre entrance. Eastbound bus #69 stops along the Seine River; the best stop is labeled Quai François Mitterrand. Westbound #69 stops in front of the pyramid (see the "Louvre Overview" map for stop locations). You'll find a taxi stand on Rue de Rivoli, next to the Palais Royal-Musée du Louvre Métro station.

Getting In: There are two entrances. Everyone must pass through security at the entrances.

  Main Pyramid Entrance: There is no grander entry than through the main entrance at the pyramid in the central courtyard. With your timed-entry ticket, you'll scoot right in (find the line that corresponds to your ticket type). Avoid the long line for those hoping to get a same-day reservation.

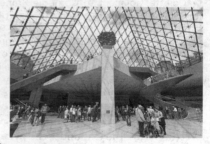

  Underground Mall Entrance: The less crowded underground entrance is accessed through the Carrousel du Louvre shopping mall. Enter the mall at 99 Rue de Rivoli (the door with the shiny metal awning), directly from the Métro stop Palais Royal-Musée du Louvre (stepping off the train, exit to *Musée du Louvre–Le Carrousel du Louvre*), or via the Tuileries Garden entrance close to the arch. Once inside the mall, continue toward the inverted pyramid next to the Louvre's security entrance. (Don't follow signs to the *Passholders* entrance, which is a long detour away.)

  After passing through security, everyone proceeds to the grand space beneath the glass pyramid with all the services.

LOUVRE

Eating at or near the Louvre

The Louvre has plenty of good eating options. The tiny **$$ Café Mollien** is located near the end of our tour (on the terrace overlooking the pyramid, closes at 16:45). The practical and economic self-service **$ Goguette cafeteria** (with a Starbucks and a couple of satellites selling sandwiches and salads on the mezzanine) is up the escalator near the pyramid on the Richelieu wing side. **$$$ Bistrot Benoit** is under the pyramid. Some visitors discreetly munch a sandwich or snack at the tiny "fast-food tables" lining the wall on the mezzanine level.

For more selection (after exiting the Louvre), walk to the underground shopping mall, the **Carrousel du Louvre** (daily 8:30-19:00), which has a food court upstairs with decent-value fast-food eateries, including—*quelle horreur*—a McDonald's. The mall also has glittering boutiques, a post office, two Starbucks (*vive* globalization), a Métro stop (Mo: Palais Royal-Musée du Louvre), and a convenient exit (*sortie*) directly into the Tuileries Garden.

Picnics are painting-perfect in the adjacent Palais Royal gardens, a block north of the museum (enter from Place du Palais Royal).

For a post-Louvre lunch/retreat, head to the venerable **$$ Café le Nemours,** with elegant brass-and-Art Deco style and outdoor tables that get good afternoon sun (daily; leaving the Louvre, cross Rue de Rivoli and veer left to 2 Place Colette, adjacent to Comédie Française; +33 1 42 61 34 14). **$$$ Le Fumoir** is another classy place, with brown leather couches perfect for kicking back with a coffee or cocktail (good-value two-course lunch *menu*, daily, 6 Rue de l'Amiral de Coligny, near Louvre-Rivoli Métro stop, +33 1 42 92 00 24). **$$ Café la Palette** is a 15-minute walk on the other side of the river, but worth it if you're doing my Left Bank Walk (daily, 43 Rue de Seine, +33 1 43 26 68 15).

Getting Out: The exit under the pyramid is usually closed. Leave via the Richelieu wing (leading to Rue de Rivoli and the Palais Royal-Musée du Louvre Métro stop) or via the Carrousel du Louvre shopping mall.

Tours: Ninety-minute English-language **guided tours** leave from inside the *Accueil des Groupes* area, under the pyramid normally at 11:00 (and possibly at 14:00 in peak season); book in advance online, €12 plus admission, tour +33 1 40 20 52 63). **Multimedia guides** (€5) provide commentary on about 700 masterpieces.

🎧 Download my free Louvre Museum **audio tour,** which complements the text in this chapter.

Length of This Tour: Allow at least two hours. With less time, string together the *Venus de Milo, Winged Victory, Mona Lisa,* and *Coronation of Emperor Napoleon*...and whatever else catches your eye along the way.

Baggage Check: It's free to store your bag in slick self-service lockers under the pyramid. No bags bigger than a small day bag are allowed in the galleries. No bags bigger than airline carry-on size are allowed anywhere in the Louvre. Consider checking whatever you don't need—even if it's just a small bag—to make your visit more pleasant.

Services: WCs are located under the pyramid. Once you're in the galleries, WCs are scarce.

Starring: *Venus de Milo, Winged Victory, Mona Lisa,* Leonardo da Vinci, Raphael, Michelangelo, the French painters, and many of the most iconic images of Western civilization.

SURVIVING THE LOUVRE

Start by picking up the free map *(Plan/Information)* at the information desk beneath the **glass pyramid** as you enter and take a moment to orient yourself.

The Louvre, the largest museum in the Western world, fills three wings of this immense, U-shaped palace. The **Richelieu wing** (north side) houses Near Eastern antiquities (covered in the last part of this tour), decorative arts, and French, German, and Northern European art. The **Sully wing** (east side) has extensive French painting and collections of ancient Egyptian and Greek art. The **Denon wing** (south side) houses Greek and Roman antiquities, as well as Italian, French, and Spanish paintings—plus an Islamic art exhibit.

We'll concentrate on the Denon and Sully wings, which hold many of the superstars, including ancient Greek sculpture, Italian Renaissance painting, and French Neoclassical and Romantic painting.

The Louvre's Map: The Louvre's free map is detailed but confusing. To get oriented, find the *Mona Lisa:* She's on level 1 (first floor), in the Denon wing's Room 711. Our tour starts on level -1, under the pyramid. Then we enter the Denon wing and turn left into the Greek antiquities in Room 170.

Expect Changes: The sprawling Louvre is constantly shuffling its deck. Rooms close, room numbers change, and pieces can be on loan or in restoration. If you can't find the artwork you're looking for, ask the nearest guard for its new location. Point to the photo in your book and ask, *"Où est, s'il vous plaît?"* (oo ay, see voo play).

The Bottom Line: You could spend a lifetime here. Zero in on the biggies, and try to finish the tour with enough energy left to browse.

The Tour Begins

• *From inside the big glass pyramid, head for the Denon wing. Ride the escalator up one floor. After showing your ticket, continue ahead 25 paces, take the first left, follow the* Antiquités Grecques *signs, and climb a set of stairs to the brick-ceilinged Salle (Room) 170: Grèce Préclassique. Enter prehistory.*

GREECE (3000 BC-AD 1)
Pre-Classical Greek Statues

These statues are noble but crude. In the first glass cases, find Greek Barbie dolls (3000 BC) that are older than the pyramids—as old as writing itself. These prerational voodoo dolls whittle women down to their life-giving traits. Halfway down the hall, a miniature woman *(Dame d'Auxerre)* pledges allegiance to stability. Nearby, another woman *(Core)* is essentially a column with breasts. These statues  stand like they have a gun to their backs—hands at sides, facing front, with sketchy muscles and mask-like faces. "Don't move."

The early Greeks, who admired statues like these, found stability more attractive than movement. Like their legendary hero Odysseus, the Greek people spent genera-tions wandering, war-weary and longing for the comforts of a secure home. The strength and sturdiness of these works looked beauti-ful.

• *Before moving on, note that the Islamic rooms are to the right. But we'll continue on with an-cient Greece.*

Exit at the far end of the pre-Classical Greece galleries, and climb the stairs one flight. At the top, veer left (toward 11 o'clock, cross-through the domed room), and continue into the Sully wing. After about 50 yards, turn right into Salle 345, where you'll find Venus de Milo  *floating above a sea of worshipping tourists. It's been said that among the warlike Greeks, this was the first statue to unilaterally disarm.*

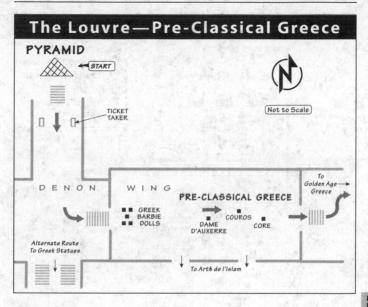

The Louvre—Pre-Classical Greece

PYRAMID

← START

TICKET TAKER

N

Not to Scale

DENON   WING

PRE-CLASSICAL GREECE

To Golden Age → Greece

GREEK BARBIE DOLLS

DAME D'AUXERRE

COUROS

CORE

Alternate Route To Greek Statues

To Arts de l'Islam

LOUVRE

Golden Age Greece

The great Greek cultural explosion that changed the course of history unfolded over 50 years (starting around 450 BC) in Athens, a town smaller than Muncie, Indiana. Having united Greece to repel a Persian invasion, Athens rebuilt, with the Parthenon as the centerpiece of the city.

The Greeks dominated the ancient world using brains, not brawn, and their art shows their love of rationality, order, and balance. The ideal Greek was well rounded—an athlete and a bookworm, a lover and a philosopher, a carpenter who played the lyre, a warrior and a poet. In art, the balance between timeless stability and fleeting movement made beauty.

In a sense, we're all Greek: Democracy, mathematics, theater, philosophy, literature, and science were practically invented in ancient Greece. Most of the art that we'll see in the Louvre either came from or was inspired by Greece.

Venus de Milo, a.k.a. *Aphrodite,* late second century BC

This goddess of love created a sensation when she was discovered in 1820 on the Greek island of Melos. Europe was already in the grip of a classical fad, and this statue seemed to sum up all that ancient Greece stood for. The

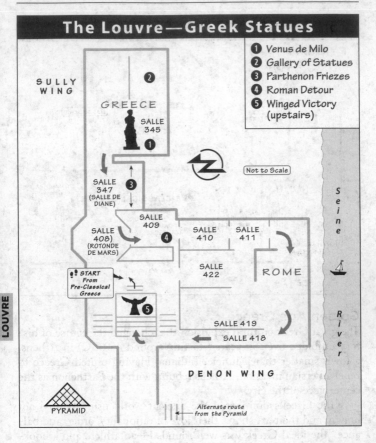

The Louvre—Greek Statues

1. Venus de Milo
2. Gallery of Statues
3. Parthenon Friezes
4. Roman Detour
5. Winged Victory (upstairs)

SULLY WING

GREECE

SALLE 345

SALLE 347 (SALLE DE DIANE)

SALLE 409

SALLE 408 (ROTONDE DE MARS)

SALLE 410

SALLE 411

SALLE 422

ROME

START From Pre-Classical Greece

SALLE 419

SALLE 418

Not to Scale

Seine River

DENON WING

PYRAMID

Alternate route from the Pyramid

LOUVRE

Greeks pictured their gods in human form (meaning humans are godlike), telling us they had an optimistic view of the human race. Venus' well-proportioned body captures the balance and orderliness of the Greek universe.

Split *Venus* down the middle from nose to toes and see how the two halves balance each other. Venus rests on her right foot (a position called *contrapposto*, or "counterpoise"), then lifts her left leg, setting her whole body in motion. As the left leg rises, her right shoulder droops down. And as her knee points one way, her head turns the other. *Venus* is a harmonious balance of opposites, orbiting slowly around a vertical axis. The twisting pose gives a balanced S-curve to her body (especially noticeable from the back view) that Golden Age Greeks and succeeding generations found beautiful.

Other opposites balance as well, like the smooth skin of her upper half that sets off the rough-cut texture of her dress (size 14). She's actually made from two different pieces of stone plugged together at the hips (the seam is visible). The face is realistic and anatomically accurate, but it's also idealized, a goddess, too generic and too perfect. This isn't any particular woman, but Everywoman—all the idealized features that appealed to the Greeks.

Most "Greek" statues are actually later Roman copies. This is a rare Greek original. This "epitome of the Golden Age" was sculpted three centuries after the Golden Age, though in a retro style.

What were her missing arms doing? Some say her right arm held her dress, while her left arm was raised. Others say she was hugging a male statue or leaning on a column. I say she was picking her navel.

• *Orbit* Venus. *This statue is interesting and different from every angle. Remember the view from the back—we'll see it again later. Now make your reentry to earth. Follow* Venus' *gaze and browse around this long hall.*

Gallery of Statues

Greek statues feature the human body in all its splendor. The anatomy is accurate, and the poses are relaxed and natural. Around the fifth century BC, Greek sculptors learned to capture people in motion and to show them from different angles, not just face-forward. The undoubted master was Praxiteles, whose lifelike statues set the tone for later sculptors. He pioneered the classic *contrapposto* pose—with the weight resting on one leg—capturing a balance between timeless stability and fleeting

motion. The stance is not only more lifelike, but also intrinsically beautiful. If the statue has clothes, the robes drape down naturally, following the body's curves. The intricate folds become part of the art.

In this gallery, you'll see statues of gods, satyrs, soldiers, athletes, and everyday people engaged in ordinary activities. For Athenians, the most popular goddess was their patron, Athena. She's usually shown as a warrior, wearing a helmet and carrying a (missing) spear, ready to fight for her city. A monumental version of Athena stands at one end of the hall—the goddess of wisdom facing the goddess of love *(Venus de Milo)*.

Whatever the statue, Golden Age artists sought the perfect balance between down-to-earth humans (with human flaws and quirks) and the idealized perfection of Greek gods.

• *Head to Salle 347 (also known as Salle de Diane), located behind the* Venus de Milo. *(Facing* Venus, *find Salle 347 to your right, back the way you came.) You'll find two carved panels on opposite walls.*

Parthenon Friezes, mid-fifth century BC

These stone fragments once decorated the exterior of the greatest Athenian temple, the Parthenon (see the scale model). Built at the peak of the Greek Golden Age, the temple glorified the city's divine protector, Athena, and the superiority of the Athenians, who were feeling especially cocky, having just crushed their archrivals, the Persians. A model of the Parthenon shows where the panels might have hung. The centaur panel would have gone above the entrance. The panel of young women was placed under the covered colonnade, but above the doorway (to see it in the model, you'll have to crouch way down and look up).

The panel on the right side of the room shows a centaur (half-human/half-horse) sexually harassing a woman, as these rude creatures crashed a party of regular people. But the humans fought back and threw out their enemy. The panel was meant to represent Athens defeating its Persian invaders.

The other relief shows the sacred procession of young women who marched up the temple hill every four years with an embroi-

dered shawl for the 40-foot-high statue of Athena, the goddess of wisdom (statue pictured at bottom of previous page). Though headless, the maidens speak volumes about Greek craftsmanship. Carved in only a couple of inches of stone, they're amazingly realistic—more so than anything seen in the pre-Classical period. They glide along horizontally (their belts and shoulders all in a line), while the folds of their dresses drape down vertically. The man in the center is relaxed, realistic, and *contrapposto*. Notice the veins in his arm. The maidens' pleated dresses make them look as stable as fluted columns, but their arms and legs step out naturally—their human forms emerging gracefully from the stone.

• *Keep backtracking another 20 paces, turning left into Salle 409, the Roman Antiquities room* (Antiquités Romaines), *for a...*

Roman Detour (Salles 409-418)

Stroll among the Caesars and try to see the person behind the public persona. Besides the many faces of the ubiquitous Emperor

Inconnu ("unknown"), you might spot Augustus (Auguste), the first emperor, and his wily wife, Livia (Livie). Her son Tiberius (Tibère) was the Caesar that Jesus Christ "rendered unto." Caligula was notoriously depraved, curly-haired Domitia murdered her husband, Hadrian popularized the beard, Trajan ruled the Empire at its peak, and Marcus Aurelius (Marc Aurèle) presided stoically over Rome's slow fall.

The pragmatic Romans (500 BC-AD 500) were great conquerors but bad artists. One area in which they excelled was realistic portrait busts, especially of their emperors, who were worshipped as gods on earth. Fortunately for us, the Romans also had a huge appetite for Greek statues and made countless copies. They took the Greek style and wrote it in capital letters, adding a veneer of sophistication to their homes, temples, baths, and government buildings.

You'll wander past several impressive sarcophagi while looping around a massive courtyard (Salle 419) with an impressive mosaic floor and beautiful wall-mounted mosaics from the ancient city of Antioch.

• *To reach the* Winged Victory *continue clockwise through the Roman collection, which eventually spills out at the base of the stairs leading up to the first floor and the dramatic...*

Winged Victory of Samothrace (Victoire de Samothrace), c. 190 BC

This woman with wings, poised on the prow of a ship, once stood on an island hilltop to commemorate a naval victory. Her clothes are windblown and seasprayed, clinging to her body. (Look at the detail in the folds of her dress around the navel, curving down to her hips.) Originally, her right arm was stretched high, celebrating the victory like a Super Bowl champion, waving a "we're number one" finger.

This is the *Venus de Milo* gone Hellenistic, from the time after the culture of Athens was spread around the Mediterranean by Alexander the Great (c. 325 BC). As *Victory* strides forward, the wind blows her and her wings back. Her feet are firmly on the ground, but her wings (and missing arms) stretch upward. She is a pillar of vertical strength, while the clothes curve and whip around her. These opposing forces create a feeling of great energy, making her the lightest two-ton piece of rock in captivity.

The earlier Golden Age Greeks might have considered this statue ugly. Her rippling excitement is a far cry from the dainty Parthenon maidens and the soft-focus beauty of *Venus*. And the statue's off-balance pose, like an unfinished melody, leaves you hanging. But Hellenistic Greeks loved these cliff-hanging scenes of real-life humans struggling to make their mark.

In the glass case nearby is *Victory*'s open right hand with an outstretched finger, found in 1950, a century after the statue itself was unearthed. When the French learned the hand was in Turkey, they negotiated with the Turkish government for the rights to it. Considering all the other ancient treasures that France had looted from Turkey in the past, the Turks thought it only appropriate to give the French the finger.

• *Enter the octagonal room to the left as you face the* Winged Victory, *with Icarus bungee-jumping from the ceiling. Find a friendly window and look out toward the pyramid.*

THE LOUVRE AS A PALACE

Formerly a royal palace, the Louvre was built in stages over eight centuries. The original medieval fortress was the part over your right shoulder (as you face the pyramid), which is today's Sully wing. Then the Tuileries Palace was built about 500 yards away, in the now-open area past the pyramid and the triumphal arch. Succeeding kings tried to connect these two palaces, each monarch adding another section onto the long, skinny north and south wings. Finally, in 1852, after three centuries of building, the two palaces were connected, creating a rectangular Louvre. Nineteen years later, the Tuileries Palace burned down during a riot, leaving the U-shaped Louvre we see today.

The glass pyramid was designed by the Chinese-born American architect I. M. Pei (1989). Many Parisians initially hated the pyramid, just as they had hated another new and controversial structure 100 years earlier—the Eiffel Tower.

In the octagonal room, find the plaque at the base of the dome. The inscription reads: *"Le Musée du Louvre, fondé le 16 Septembre, 1792."* The museum was founded by France's Revolutionary National Assembly—the same people who brought you the guillotine. What could be more logical? You behead the king, inherit his palace and art collection, open the doors to the masses, and *voilà!* You have Europe's first public museum.

• From the octagonal room, enter the Apollo Gallery (Galerie d'Apollon).

Apollo Gallery

This gallery gives us a feel for the Louvre as the glorious home of French kings (before Versailles). Imagine a candlelit party in this room, drenched in stucco and gold leaf, with tapestries of leading Frenchmen and paintings featuring mythological and symbolic themes. The crystal vases, the inlaid tables made from marble and semiprecious stones, and many other art objects show the wealth of France, Europe's number-one power for two centuries. Portraits on the walls depict great French kings: Henry IV, who built the Pont Neuf; Louis XIV, the Sun King; and François I, who brought Leonardo da Vinci (and the Italian Renaissance) to France.

Stroll past glass cases of royal dinnerware to the far end of the room. In a glass case are the crown jewels. The display varies, but you may see the jewel-studded crowns of Louis XV and the less flashy Crown of Charlemagne (the only crowns to escape destruction in the Revolution), along with the 140-carat Regent Diamond, which once graced crowns worn by Louis XV, Louis XVI, and Napoleon.

• A rare WC is a half-dozen rooms away, near Salle 650 in the Sully wing. *The Italian collection* (Peintures Italiennes) *is on the other side of* Winged Victory. *Cross back in front of* Winged Victory *and enter the Denon wing and Salle 706, where you'll find...*

Two Botticelli Frescoes

Look at the paintings on the wall to the left. These pure maidens, like colorized versions of the Parthenon frieze, give us a preview of how ancient Greece would be "reborn" in the Renaissance.

• But first, the Medieval World. Continue into the large Salle 708.

THE MEDIEVAL WORLD (1200-1500)

Cimabue, *The Madonna and Child in Majesty Surrounded by Angels (La Vierge et l'Enfant en Majesté Entourés de Six Anges)*, c. 1280

During the Age of Faith (1200s), almost every church in Europe had a painting like this one. Mary was a cult figure—even bigger than the late-20th-century Madonna—adored and prayed to by the faithful for bringing Baby Jesus into the world. After the collapse of the Roman Empire (c. AD 500), medieval Europe was a poor and violent place, with the Christian Church as the only constant in troubled times.

Altarpieces tended to follow the same formula: somber iconic faces, stiff poses, elegant folds in the robes, and generic angels. Violating the laws of perspective, the angels at the "back" of Mary's throne are the same size as those holding the front. These holy figures are laid flat on a gold background like cardboard cutouts, existing in a golden never-never land, as though the faithful couldn't imagine them as flesh-and-blood humans inhabiting our dark and sinful earth.

• *Do a 180 and find...*

Giotto, *St. Francis of Assisi Receiving the Stigmata (Saint François d'Assise Recevant les Stigmates)*, c. 1295-1300

Francis of Assisi (c. 1181-1226), a wandering Italian monk of renowned goodness, kneels on a rocky Italian hillside, pondering the pain of Christ's torture and execution.

Suddenly, he looks up, startled, to see Christ himself, with six wings, hovering above. Christ shoots lasers from his wounds to the hands, feet, and side of the empathetic monk, marking him with the stigmata. Francis went on to breathe the spirit of the Renaissance into medieval Europe. His humble love of man and nature inspired artists like Giotto to portray real human beings with real emotions, living in a physical world of beauty.

Like a good filmmaker, Giotto (c. 1266-1337) doesn't just *tell* us what happened, he *shows* us in the present tense, freezing the scene at its most dramatic moment. Though the perspective is crude—Francis' hut is smaller than he is, and Christ is somehow shooting at Francis while facing us—Giotto creates the illusion of three dimensions, with a foreground (Francis), middle ground (his hut), and background (the hillside). Painting a 3-D world on a 2-D surface is tough, and after a millennium of Dark Ages, artists were rusty.

In the predella (the panel of paintings beneath the altarpiece), birds gather at Francis' feet to hear him talk about God. Giotto catches the late arrivals in

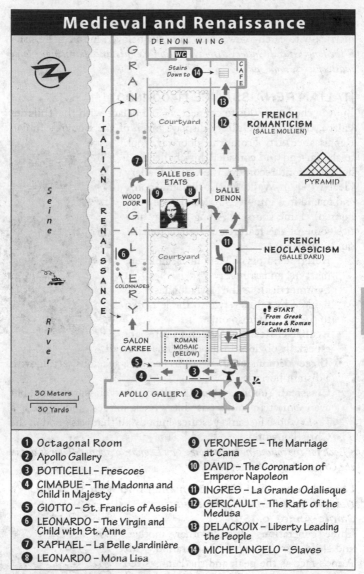

Medieval and Renaissance

DENON WING

GRAND GALLERY

ITALIAN RENAISSANCE

Seine River

WC

Stairs Down to ❶❹

CAFE

Courtyard

❼

SALLE DES ETATS

WOOD DOOR ❾ ❽

SALLE DENON

❻

Courtyard

COLONNADES

SALON CARREE

ROMAN MOSAIC (BELOW)

❺

❹ ❸

APOLLO GALLERY ❷ ❶

FRENCH ROMANTICISM (SALLE MOLLIEN)

❶❸

❶❷

PYRAMID

FRENCH NEOCLASSICISM (SALLE DARU)

❶❶

❶❶❶❶

❶❶ ❶❶

START From Greek Statues & Roman Collection

30 Meters
30 Yards

LOUVRE

❶ Octagonal Room
❷ Apollo Gallery
❸ BOTTICELLI – Frescoes
❹ CIMABUE – The Madonna and Child in Majesty
❺ GIOTTO – St. Francis of Assisi
❻ LEONARDO – The Virgin and Child with St. Anne
❼ RAPHAEL – La Belle Jardinière
❽ LEONARDO – Mona Lisa

❾ VERONESE – The Marriage at Cana
❿ DAVID – The Coronation of Emperor Napoleon
⓫ INGRES – La Grande Odalisque
⓬ GERICAULT – The Raft of the Medusa
⓭ DELACROIX – Liberty Leading the People
⓮ MICHELANGELO – Slaves

midflight, an astonishing technical feat for an artist working more than a century before the Renaissance. The simple gesture of Francis' companion speaks volumes about his amazement. Breaking the stiff, iconic mold for saints, Francis bends forward at the waist to talk to his fellow creatures. The diversity of the birds—"red and yellow, black and white"—symbolizes how all humankind is equally precious in God's sight. Meanwhile, the tree bends down symmetrically to catch a few words from the beloved hippie of Assisi.

• *The long Grand Gallery displays Italian Renaissance painting—some masterpieces, some not.*

ITALIAN RENAISSANCE (1400-1600)

Built in the late 1500s to connect the old palace with the Tuileries Palace, the **Grand Gallery** displays much of the Louvre's Italian Renaissance art. From the doorway, look to the far end and consider this challenge: I hold the world record for the Grand Gallery Heel-Toe-Fun-Walk-Tourist-Slalom, going end to end in 1 minute, 58 seconds (only two injured). Time yourself. Along the way, notice some of the features of Italian Renaissance painting:

- **Religious:** Lots of Madonnas, children, martyrs, and saints.
- **Symmetrical:** The Madonnas are flanked by saints—two to the left, two to the right, and so on.
- **Realistic:** Real-life human features are especially obvious in the occasional portrait.
- **Three-Dimensional:** Every scene gets a spacious setting with a distant horizon.
- **Classical:** You'll see some Greek gods and classical nudes, but even Christian saints pose like Greek statues, and Mary is a *Venus* whose face and gestures embody all that was good in the Christian world.

• *Look for the following masterpieces by Leonardo about 50 yards down the Grand Gallery, on the left.*

Leonardo da Vinci, *The Virgin and Child with St. Anne (La Vierge à l'Enfant Jésus avec Sainte-Anne),* c. 1510

Three generations—grandmother, mother, and child—are arranged in a pyramid, with Anne's face as the peak and the lamb as the lower right corner. Within this balanced structure, Leonardo sets the figures in motion. Anne's legs are pointed to our left. (Is Anne *Mona*? Hmm.) Her daughter Mary, sitting on her lap, reaches to the right. Jesus looks at her playfully while turning away. The lamb pulls away from him. But even with all the twisting and turning, this is still a placid scene. It's as orderly as the geometrically perfect universe created by the Renaissance god.

There's a psychological kidney punch in this happy painting. Jesus, the picture of childish joy, is innocently playing with a lamb—the symbol of his inevitable sacrificial death.

The Louvre has the greatest collection of Leonardos in the world—five of them. Look for the neighboring *Virgin of the Rocks* and *John the Baptist.* Leonardo was the consummate Renaissance Man; a musician, sculptor, engineer, scientist, and sometime painter, he combined knowledge from all these areas to create beauty. If he were alive today, he'd create a Unified Field Theory in physics—and set it to music.

• *Continue about 20 yards (past the crowded* Mona Lisa *room—where we'll head in a moment). On the right side, look for a masterpiece by Raphael.*

Raphael, *La Belle Jardinière,* c. 1507

Raphael perfected the style Leonardo pioneered. This configuration of Madonna, Child, and John the Baptist is also a balanced pyramid with hazy grace and beauty. Mary is a mountain of maternal tenderness (the title translates as "The Beautiful Gardener") as she eyes her son with a knowing look and holds his hand in a gesture of union. Jesus looks up innocently, standing *contrapposto* like a chubby Greek statue. Baby John the Baptist kneels lovingly at Jesus' feet, holding a cross that hints at his playmate's sacrificial death. The interplay of gestures and gazes gives the masterpiece both intimacy and cohesiveness, while Raphael's blended brushstrokes varnish the work with an iridescent smoothness.

With Raphael, the Greek ideal of beauty—reborn in the Renaissance—reached its peak. His work spawned so many imitators who cranked out sickly sweet, generic Madonnas that we often take him for granted. Don't. This is the real thing.

• *The* Mona Lisa (La Joconde) *is a few steps away, in the room just behind that tall wooden door—Salle 711.* Mona *is alone behind glass on her own false wall. Six million heavy-breathing people crowd in each year to glimpse the most ogled painting in the world. (You can't miss her. Just follow the signs and the people...it's the only painting you can hear. With all the crowds, you can even smell it.) Choose your strategy: You can either linger on the fringes and view* Mona *from a distance, or patiently press forward awaiting your turn up front.*

Leonardo da Vinci, *Mona Lisa,* a.k.a. *La Joconde,* 1503-1506

Leonardo was already an old man when François I invited him to France. Determined to pack light, he took only a few paintings with him. One was a portrait of Lisa del Giocondo, the wife of a wealthy Florentine merchant. When Leonardo arrived, François immediately fell in love with the painting, making it the centerpiece of the small collection of Italian masterpieces that would, in three centuries, become the Louvre museum. He called it *La Gioconda* (*La Joconde* in French)—a play on both her last name and the Italian word for "happiness." We know it as the *Mona Lisa*—a contraction of the Italian for "my lady Lisa."

Mona may disappoint you. She's smaller than you'd expect, darker, engulfed in a huge room, and hidden behind a glaring pane of glass. So, you ask, "Why all the hubbub?" Let's take a closer look. As you would with any lover, you've got to take her for who she is, not what you'd like her to be.

The famous smile attracts you first. Leonardo used a hazy technique called *sfumato,* blurring the edges of her mysterious smile. Try as you might, you can never quite see the corners of her mouth. Is she happy? Sad? Tender? Or is it a cynical supermodel's smirk? All visitors read it differently, projecting their own moods onto her enigmatic face. *Mona* is a Rorschach inkblot...so, how are you feeling?

Now look past the smile and the eyes that really do follow you (most eyes in portraits do) to some of the subtle Renaissance elements that make this painting work. The body is surprisingly massive and statue-like, a perfectly balanced pyramid turned at an angle, so we can see its mass. Her arm rests lightly on the armrest of a chair, almost on the level of the frame itself, as if she's sitting in a window looking out at us. The folds of her sleeves and her gently folded hands are remarkably realistic and relaxed. The typical Leonardo landscape shows distance by getting hazier and hazier.

Though the portrait is generally accepted as a likeness of Lisa del Giocondo, other hypotheses about the sitter's identity have been suggested, including the idea that it's Leonardo himself. Or she might be the Mama Lisa. A recent infrared scan revealed that she has a barely visible veil over her dress, which may mean (in the custom of the day) that she had just had a baby.

The overall mood is one of balance and serenity, but there's

Italian Renaissance

A thousand years after Rome fell, plunging Europe into the Dark Ages, the Greek ideal of beauty was reborn in 15th-century Italy. The Renaissance—or "rebirth" of the culture of ancient Greece and Rome—was a cultural boom that changed people's thinking about every aspect of life. In politics, it meant democracy. In religion, it meant a move away from Church dominance and toward the assertion of man (humanism) and a more personal faith. Science and secular learning were revived after centuries of superstition and ignorance. In architecture, it was a return to the balanced columns and domes of Greece and Rome.

In painting, the Renaissance meant realism, and for the Italians, realism was spelled "3-D." Artists rediscovered the beauty of nature and the human body. With pictures of beautiful people in harmonious 3-D surroundings, they expressed the optimism and confidence of this new age.

also an element of mystery. *Mona*'s smile and long-distance beauty are subtle and elusive, tempting but always just out of reach, like strands of a street singer's melody drifting through the Métro tunnel. *Mona* doesn't knock your socks off, but she winks at the patient viewer.

• *Before leaving* Mona, *step back and just observe the paparazzi scene. The huge canvas opposite* Mona *is...*

Paolo Veronese, *The Marriage at Cana* (*Les Noces de Cana*), 1562-1563

Stand 10 steps away from this enormous canvas to where it just fills your field of vision, and suddenly...you're in a party! Help yourself to a glass of wine. This is the Renaissance love of beautiful things gone hog-wild. Venetian artists like Veronese painted the good life of rich, happy-go-lucky Venetian merchants.

In a spacious setting of Renaissance architecture, colorful lords and ladies, decked out in their fanciest duds, feast on a great spread of food and drink, while the musicians fuel the fires of good fun. Servants prepare and serve the food, jesters play, and animals roam. In the upper left, a dog and his master look on. A sturdy linebacker in yellow pours wine out of a jug (right foreground). The man in white samples some and thinks, "Hmm, not bad," while nearby a ferocious cat battles a lion. The wedding couple at the far left is almost forgotten.

Believe it or not, this is a religious work showing the wedding celebration in which Jesus turned water into wine. And there's Jesus in the dead center of 130 frolicking figures, wondering if maybe a nonalcoholic beverage might have been a better choice. With true Renaissance optimism, Venetians pictured Christ as a party animal, someone who loved the created world as much as they did.

Now, let's hear it for the band! On bass—the bad cat with the funny hat—Titian the Venetian! And joining him on viola—Crazy Veronese!

• *Exit behind* Mona *into the Salle Denon (Room 701). The dramatic Romantic room is to your left, and the grand Neoclassical room is to your right. These two rooms feature the most exciting French canvases in the Louvre. Turn right into the Neoclassical room (Salle Daru, Room 702) and kneel before the largest canvas in the Louvre.*

FRENCH PAINTING (1780-1850)
Jacques-Louis David, *The Coronation of Emperor Napoleon (Sacre de l'Empereur Napoléon),* 1806-1807

Napoleon holds aloft an imperial crown. This common-born son of immigrants is about to be crowned emperor of a "New Rome." He has just made his wife, Josephine, the empress, and she kneels at his feet. Seated behind Napoleon is the pope, who journeyed from Rome to place the imperial crown on his head. But Napoleon feels that no one is worthy of the task. At the last moment, he shrugs the pope aside, grabs the crown, holds it up for all to see...and crowns himself. The pope looks p.o.'d.

After the French people decapitated their king during the Revolution (1793), their fledgling democracy floundered in chaos. France was united by a charismatic, brilliant, temperamental, upstart general who kept his feet on the ground, his eyes on the horizon, and his hand in his coat—Napoleon Bonaparte. Napoleon quickly conquered most of Europe and insisted on being made emperor (not merely king). The painter David (dah-VEED) recorded the coronation for posterity.

The radiant woman in the gallery in the background center wasn't actually there. Napoleon's mother couldn't make it to see her boy become the most powerful man in Europe, but he had David

paint her in anyway. (There's a key on the frame telling who's who in the picture.)

The setting for the coronation was the ultra-Gothic Notre-Dame Cathedral. But Napoleon wanted a location that would reflect the glories of Greece and the grandeur of Rome. So, interior decorators erected stage sets of Greek columns and Roman arches to give the cathedral the architectural political correctness you see in this painting. (The *pietà* statue on the right edge of the painting remains in Notre-Dame to this day.)

David was the new emperor's official painter and propagandist, in charge of color-coordinating the costumes and flags for public ceremonies and spectacles. (Find his self-portrait with curly gray hair in the *Coronation,* way up in the second balcony, peeking around the tassel directly above Napoleon's crown.) His "Neoclassical" style influenced French fashion. Take a look at his *Madame Juliet Récamier* portrait on the opposite wall, showing a modern Parisian woman in ancient garb and Pompeii hairstyle reclining on a Roman couch. Nearby paintings, such as *The Oath of the Horatii (Le Serment des Horaces),* are fine examples of Neoclassicism, with Greek subjects, patriotic sentiment, and a clean, simple style.

• *As you double back toward the Romantic room, stop at...*

Jean-Auguste-Dominique Ingres, *La Grande Odalisque,* 1814

Take *Venus de Milo,* turn her around, lay her down, and stick a hash

pipe next to her, and you have the *Grande Odalisque.* OK, maybe you'd have to add a vertebra or two.

Using clean, polished, sculptural lines, Ingres (ang-gruh) exaggerates the S-curve of a standing Greek nude. As in the *Venus de Milo*, rough folds of cloth set off her smooth skin. Ingres gave the face, too, a touch of *Venus'* idealized features, taking nature and improving on it. Contrast the cool colors of this statue-like nude with Titian's golden girls. Ingres preserves *Venus'* backside for posterior—I mean, posterity.

• *Cross back through the Salle Denon and into Room 700, gushing with French Romanticism.*

Théodore Géricault, *The Raft of the Medusa* (*Le Radeau de la Méduse*), 1819

In the artistic war between hearts and minds, the heart style was known as Romanticism. Stressing motion and emotion, it was the flip side of cool, balanced Neo-classicism, though they both flourished in the early 1800s.

What better setting for an emotional work than a ship-wreck? Clinging to a raft is a tangle of bodies and lunatics sprawled over each other. The scene writhes with agitated, ominous motion—the ripple of muscles, churning clouds, and choppy seas. On the right is a deathly green corpse dangling overboard. The face of the man at left, cradling a dead body, says it all—the despair of spending weeks stranded in the middle of nowhere.

This painting was based on the actual sinking of the ship *Medusa* off the coast of Africa in 1816. About 150 people packed onto the raft. After floating on the open seas for 12 days—suffering hardship and hunger, even resorting to cannibalism—only 15 survived. The story was made-to-order for a painter determined to shock the public and arouse its emotions. That painter was young Géricault (ZHAIR-ee-ko). He interviewed survivors and honed his craft, sketching dead bodies in the morgue and the twisted faces of lunatics in asylums, capturing the moment when all hope is lost.

But wait. There's a stir in the crowd. Someone has spotted something. The bodies rise up in a pyramid of hope, culminating in a flag wave. They signal frantically, trying to catch the attention of the tiny ship on the horizon, their last desperate hope...which did finally save them. Géricault uses rippling movement and powerful colors to catch us up in the excitement. If art controls your heartbeat, this is a masterpiece.

Eugène Delacroix, *Liberty Leading the People* (*La Liberté Guidant le Peuple*), 1831

The year is 1830. King Charles has just issued the 19th-century equivalent of the Patriot Act, and his subjects are angry. Parisians

take to the streets once again, *Les Miz*-style, to fight royalist oppressors. The people triumph—replacing the king with Louis-Philippe, who is happy to rule within the constraints of a modern constitution. There's a hard-bitten proletarian with a sword (far left), an intellectual with a top hat and a sawed-off shotgun, and even a little boy brandishing pistols.

Leading them on through the smoke and over the dead and dying is the figure of Liberty, a strong woman waving the French flag. Does this symbol of victory look familiar? It's the *Winged Victory*, wingless and topless.

To stir our emotions, Delacroix (del-ah-kwah) uses only three major colors—the red, white, and blue of the French flag. France is the symbol of modern democracy, and this painting has long stirred its citizens' passion for liberty. The French weren't the first to adopt democracy in its modern form (Americans were), nor are they the best working example of it, but they've had to try harder to achieve it than any other country. No sooner would they throw one king or dictator out than they'd get another. They're now working on their fifth republic.

This symbol of freedom is a fitting tribute to the Louvre, the first museum ever opened to the common rabble of humanity. The good things in life don't belong only to a small, wealthy part of society, but to everyone. The motto of France is *Liberté, Egalité, Fraternité*—liberty, equality, and brotherhood for all.

• *Exit the room at the far end (past the Café Mollien) and go downstairs, where you'll bump into the bum of a large, twisting male nude looking like he's just waking up after a thousand-year nap.*

MORE ITALIAN RENAISSANCE
Michelangelo, *Slaves (Esclaves)*, 1513-1515

These two statues by the earth's greatest sculptor are a bridge between the ancient and modern worlds. Michelangelo, like his fellow Renaissance artists, learned from the Greeks. The perfect anatomy, twisting poses, and idealized faces appear as if they could have been created 2,000 years earlier.

The so-called *Dying Slave* (also called the *Sleeping Slave*, looking like he should be stretched out on a sofa) twists listlessly against his T-shirt-like bonds, revealing his smooth skin. Compare the polished detail of the rippling, bulging left arm with the sketchy details of the face and neck. With Michelangelo, the body does the talking. This is probably the most sensual nude that Michelangelo, the master of the male body, ever created.

The *Rebellious Slave* fights against his bondage. His shoulders rotate one way, his head and leg turn the other. He looks upward, straining to get free. He even seems to be trying to release himself from the rock he's made of. Michelangelo said that his purpose was to carve away the marble to reveal the figures God put inside. This slave shows the agony of that process and the ecstasy of the result.

• *Tour over! These two may be slaves of the museum, but you are free to go. You've seen the essential Louvre. But no Louvre visit is complete without first taking a photo alongside the statue located 20 paces away, which I believe is titled "Apollo Taking Selfie." Or, for romantics, continue to the far corner of the room (on the right), and swoon at Antonio Canova's sculpture* Psyche Revived by Cupid's Kiss.

To leave the museum, continue out this hall, take four steps down, notice the iconic pyramid outside the windows on the left (where you're heading), and turn right, following signs down the stairs to the Sortie.

But, of course, there's so much more. After a break (or on a second visit—and a second entry fee, even with the Museum Pass), consider a stroll through a few rooms of the Richelieu wing, which contain some of the Louvre's most ancient pieces. Bible students, amateur archaeologists, and veterans of the Iraq conflict may find the collection especially interesting.

NEAR EASTERN ANTIQUITIES

Saddam Hussein was only the latest iron-fisted, palace-building conqueror to fall in the long history of the region that roughly corresponds with modern Iraq. Its origins stretch back to the dawn of time. Civilization began 6,000 years ago between the Tigris and Euphrates rivers, in the area called the Fertile Crescent.

In the Richelieu wing, you can quickly sweep through 2,000 years of this area's ancient history, enjoying some of the Louvre's biggest and oldest artifacts. See how each new civilization toppled the previous one—pulling down its statues, destroying its palaces, looting its cultural heritage, and replacing it with victory monuments of its own...only to be toppled again by the next wave of history.

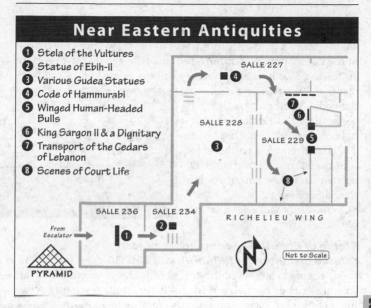

Near Eastern Antiquities

1. Stela of the Vultures
2. Statue of Ebih-Il
3. Various Gudea Statues
4. Code of Hammurabi
5. Winged Human-Headed Bulls
6. King Sargon II & a Dignitary
7. Transport of the Cedars of Lebanon
8. Scenes of Court Life

SALLE 227

SALLE 228

SALLE 229

SALLE 236 SALLE 234

From Escalator

RICHELIEU WING

PYRAMID

Not to Scale

The iconoclasm continues to this day, as Islamist militants have vandalized ancient artifacts at Nineveh and elsewhere—making the Louvre's collection all the more priceless. It's interesting to note that while Westerners make pilgrimages to the Greek and Renaissance sections of the Louvre, visitors from the Middle East are drawn to this part of the museum's collection.

• *From under the pyramid, enter the Richelieu wing. Show your ticket, then take the first right. Go up one flight of stairs and one escalator to the ground floor* (rez-de-chaussée), *where you'll find the Near Eastern antiquities. Walk straight off the escalator, enter Salle 236* (Mesopotamie Archaïque), *and come face-to-face with fragments of the broken...*

Stela of the Vultures (Stèle des Vautours), 2600-2330 BC

As old as the pyramids, this Sumerian stela (ceremonial stone pillar) is thought to be the world's oldest surviving historical document.

Its images and words record the battle between the city of Lagash (100 miles north of modern Basra) and its neighboring archrival, Umma.

Circle around the partition to the other side of the stela. "Read" the stela from top to bottom.

Top level: Behind a wall of shields, a phalanx of helmeted soldiers advances, trampling the enemy underfoot. They pile the corpses (right), and vultures swoop down from above to pluck the remains. Middle level: King Eannatum waves to the crowd from his chariot in the victory parade. Bottom level: They dig a mass grave—one of 20 for the 36,000 enemies dead—while a priest (top of the fragment, in a skirt) gives thanks to the gods. A tethered ox (see his big head tied to a stake) is about to become a burnt sacrifice.

The inscription on the stela is in cuneiform, the world's first written language, invented by the Sumerians.

• *Continue into Salle 234, with the blissful...*

Statue of Ebih-il, Superintendent of Mari (Statue de l'Intendant Ebih-il), c. 2400 BC

Bald, bearded, blue-eyed Ebih-il (his name is inscribed on his shoulder) sits in his fleece skirt, folds his hands reverently across his chest, and gazes rapturously into space, dreaming of...Ishtar. A high-ranking dignitary, Ebih-il placed this statue of himself in the goddess Ishtar's temple to declare his perpetual devotion to her.

Ishtar was the chief goddess of many Middle Eastern peoples. As goddess of both love and war, she was a favorite of horny soldiers. She was a giver of life (this statue is dedicated "to Ishtar the virile"), yet also miraculously a virgin. She was also a great hunter with bow and arrow, and a great lover ("Her lips are sweet...her figure is beautiful, her eyes are brilliant...women and men adore her," sang the *Hymn to Ishtar,* c. 1600 BC).

Ebih-il adores her eternally with his eyes made of seashells and lapis lazuli. The smile on his face reflects the pleasure the goddess has just given him, perhaps through one of the sacred prostitutes who resided in Ishtar's temple.

• *Go up the five steps behind Ebih-il, and turn left into Salle 228, containing a dozen statues of the same man.*

Statue of Gudea, Prince of Lagash (Statue de Gudea, Prince de Lagash), c. 2120 BC

Gudea (r. 2141-2122 BC), in his wool stocking cap (actually a royal turban), folds his hands and prays to the gods to save his people from invading barbarians. One of Sumeria's last great rulers, the peaceful and pious Gudea (his name means "the destined") rebuilt temples (where these statues once stood) to thank the gods for their help.

• *Exit Salle 228 at the far end and enter Salle 227, with the large black stela of Hammurabi.*

Code of Hammurabi, King of Babylon (Code de Hammurabi, Roi de Babylone), 1792-1750 BC

King Hammurabi (r. c. 1792-1750 BC) extended the reach of the great Babylonian empire, which joined Sumer and Akkad (stretching from modern-day Baghdad to the Persian Gulf). He proclaimed 282 laws, all inscribed on this eight-foot black basalt stela—one of the first formal legal documents, four centuries before the Ten Commandments. Stelas such as this likely dotted Hammurabi's empire, and this one may have stood in Babylon before being moved to Susa, Iran.

At the top of the stela, Hammurabi (standing and wearing Gudea's hat of kingship) receives the scepter of judgment from the god of justice and the sun, who radiates flames from his shoulders. The inscription begins, "When Anu the Sublime...called me, Hammurabi, by name...I did right, and brought about the well-being of the oppressed."

Next come the laws, scratched in cuneiform down the length of the stela, some 3,500 lines reading right to left. The laws cover very specific situations, everything from lying, theft, and trade to marriage and medical malpractice. The legal innovation was the immediate retribution for wrongdoing, often with poetic justice. Here's a sample:

#1: If any man ensnares another falsely, he shall be put to death.

#57: If your sheep graze another man's land, you must repay 20 *gur* of grain.

#129: If a couple is caught in adultery, they shall both be tied up and thrown in the water.

#137: If you divorce your wife, you must pay alimony and child support.

#218: A surgeon who bungles an operation shall have his hands cut off.

Just Enough Geography and History for This Tour

The ancient region of Mesopotamia generally matches the contours of present-day Iraq. Modern Baghdad sits roughly

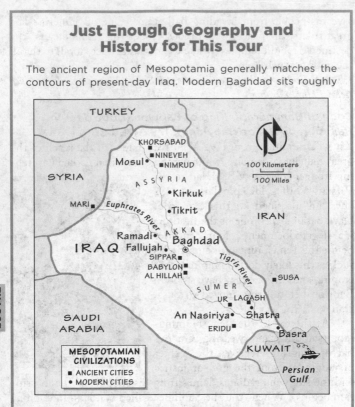

in the middle, along the Tigris. The Sumerians inhabited the south, the Assyrians the north, and the Akkadians and Babylonians the center, around Baghdad. Here's a brief timeline:

3500-2400 BC: Sumerian city-states flourish between the Tigris and Euphrates rivers. Sumerians invent cuneiform writing.

2300 BC: Akkadians invade Sumer.

1750 BC: Hammurabi establishes the first Babylonian empire.

710 BC: Sargon II rules over a vast Assyrian-controlled empire, encompassing modern Iraq, Israel, Syria, and Egypt.

612 BC: Babylonians revolt against the Assyrians and destroy their capital of Nineveh, then build their own—Babylon.

#282: If a slave shall say, "You are not my master," the master can cut off the slave's ear.

The most quoted laws—summing up the spirit of ancient Near Eastern justice—are #196 ("If a man put out the eye of another man, his eye shall be put out") and #200 ("a tooth for a tooth").

• *Facing the front of the stela, veer ahead to the left and enter the large,*

The Assyrians

This Semitic people from the agriculturally challenged hills of northern Mesopotamia became traders and conquerors, not farmers. They conquered their southern neighbors and dominated the Near East for 300 years (c. 900-600 BC).

Their strength came from a superb army (chariots, mounted cavalry, and siege engines), a policy of terrorism against enemies ("I tied their heads to tree trunks all around the city," reads a royal inscription), ethnic cleansing and mass deportations of the vanquished, and efficient administration (roads and express postal service). They have been called "The Romans of the East."

bright Salle 229, dominated by colossal winged bulls with human heads. These sculptures—including five winged bulls and many relief panels along the walls—are from the...

Palace of Sargon II

Sargon II, the Assyrian king (r. 721-705 BC), spared no expense on his palace (see various reconstructions of the palace on plaques around the room). In Assyrian society, the palace of the king—not the temple of the gods—was the focus of life, and each ruler demonstrated his authority with large residences.

Sargon II actually built a whole new city for his palace, just north of the traditional capital of Nineveh (modern-day Mosul). He called it Dur Sharrukin ("Sargonburg"), and the city's vast dimensions were 4,000 cubits by—oh, excuse me—it covered about 150 football fields pieced together. The whole city was built on a raised, artificial mound, and the 25-acre palace itself sat even higher, surrounded by walls, with courtyards, temples, the king's residence, and a wedding cake-shaped temple (called a ziggurat) dedicated to the god Sin.

• *Start with the two big bulls supporting a (reconstructed) arch.*

Winged Human-Headed Bulls (Taureau Androcéphale Ailé), c. 721-704 BC

These 30-ton, 14-foot alabaster bulls with human faces once guarded the entrance to the throne room of Sargon II. A visitor to the palace back then could have looked over the bulls' heads and seen a 15-story ziggurat (stepped-pyramid temple) towering overhead.

LOUVRE

The winged bulls were guardian spirits, warding off demons and intimidating liberals.

Between their legs are cuneiform inscriptions such as: "I, Sargon, King of the Universe, built palaces for my royal residence...I had winged bulls with human heads carved from great blocks of mountain stone, and I placed them at the doors facing the four winds as powerful divine guardians...My creation amazed all who gazed upon it."

• *We'll see a few relief panels from the palace, working counterclockwise around the room. Start with the panel just to the left of the two big bulls (as you face them). Find the bearded, earringed man in whose image the bulls were made.*

King Sargon II and a Dignitary
(Le Roi Sargon II et un Haut Dignitaire), c. 710 BC

Sargon II, wearing a fez-like crown with a cone on the top and straps down the back, cradles his scepter and raises his staff to re-

ceive a foreign ambassador who has come to pay tribute. Sargon II controlled a vast empire, consisting of modern-day Iraq and extending westward to the Mediterranean and Egypt.

Before becoming emperor, Sargon II was a conquering general who invaded Israel (2 Kings 17:1-6). After a three-year siege, he took Jerusalem and deported much of the population, inspiring the legends of the "Lost" Ten Tribes. The proph-

et Isaiah saw him as God's tool to punish the sinful Israelites, "to seize loot and snatch plunder, and to trample them down like mud in the streets" (Isaiah 10:6).

• *On the wall to the left of Sargon are four panels depicting the...*

Transport of the Cedars of Lebanon
(Transport du Bois de Cèdre du Liban), c. 713-706 BC

Boats carry the finest quality logs for Sargon II's palace, crossing

a wavy sea populated with fish, turtles, crabs, and mermen. The transport process is described in the Bible (1 Kings 5:9): "My men will haul them down from Lebanon to the sea, and I will float them in rafts to the place you specify."

• *Continue counterclockwise around the room—past more big, winged animals, past the huge hero, Gilgamesh, crushing a lion—until you reach more relief panels. These depict...*

Scenes of Court Life

The brown, eroded gypsum panels we see here were original-ly painted and varnished. Placed side by side, they would have stretched over a mile. The panels read like a comic strip, showing the king's men parading in to serve him.

First, soldiers sheathe their swords and fold their hands rever-ently. A winged spirit prepares them to enter the king's presence

by shaking a pine cone to anoint them with holy perfume. Next, servants hurry to the throne room with the king's dinner, carrying his table, chair, and bowl. Other servants ready the king's horses and chariots. They all proceed forward, ready to serve

their master—the all-powerful ruler of the civilized world.

From Sargon to Saddam

Sargon II's palace remained unfinished and was later burned and buried. Sargon's great Assyrian empire dissolved over the next few generations. When the Babylonians revolted and conquered their northern neighbors (612 BC), the whole Middle East applauded. As the Bible put it: "Nineveh is in ruins—who will mourn for her?... Everyone who hears the news claps his hands at your fall, for who has not felt your endless cruelty?" (Nahum 3:7, 19).

The new capital was Babylon (50 miles south of modern Bagh-dad), ruled by King Nebuchadnezzar, who conquered Judea (586 BC, the Bible's "Babylonian Captivity") and built a palace with the Hanging Gardens, one of the Seven Wonders of the World.

Over the succeeding centuries, Babylon/Baghdad fell to Per-sians (539 BC), Greeks (Alexander the Great, 331 BC), Persians again (second century BC), Arab Muslims (AD 634), Mongol hordes (Genghis Khan's grandson, 1258), Iranians (1502), Otto-man Turks (1535), British-controlled kings (1921), and military regimes (1958), the most recent headed by Saddam Hussein (1979).

After toppling Saddam Hussein in 2003, President George W. Bush declared, "Mission accomplished!" After five thousand years of invasions, violence, and regime change, Iraq was finally... well, maybe not.

ORSAY MUSEUM TOUR

Musée d'Orsay

The Musée d'Orsay (mew-zay dor-say) houses French art of the 1800s and early 1900s (specifically, 1848-1914), picking up where the Louvre's art collection leaves off. For us, that means Impressionism, the art of sun-dappled fields, bright colors, and crowded Parisian cafés. The Orsay houses the best general collection anywhere of Manet, Monet, Renoir, Degas, Van Gogh, Cézanne, and Gauguin. If you like Impressionism, visit this museum. If you don't like Impressionism, visit this museum. I find it a more enjoyable and rewarding place than the Louvre. Sure, ya gotta see the *Mona Lisa* and *Venus de Milo,* but after you get your gottas out of the way, enjoy the Orsay.

Keep in mind that the collection is always on the move—paintings on loan, in restoration, or displayed in different rooms. The museum updates its website daily with the latest layout, so with a little flexibility, you should be able to see most of the Orsay's masterpieces.

Orientation

Cost: €16, free on first Sun of month, covered by Museum Pass; combo-tickets with the Orangerie (€18) or Rodin Museum (€24) are sold only at those museums—not at the Orsay; keep ticket for discount at the Opéra Garnier.

Hours: Tue-Sun 9:30-18:00, Thu until 21:45, closed Mon, last entry one hour before closing (45 minutes on Thu). The top-floor Impressionist galleries begin closing 45 minutes early, frustrating unwary visitors.

Information: +33 1 40 49 48 14, www.musee-orsay.fr.

When to Go: For shorter lines and fewer crowds, visit on Wed, Fri, or Thu evening (when the museum is open late). You'll battle the biggest hordes on Sun, as well as on Tue, when the Louvre is closed.

Avoiding lines: While everyone must wait to go through security, avoid the long ticket-buying lines with a Museum Pass, a combo-ticket, or by purchasing tickets in advance on the Orsay website; any of these entitle you to use a separate entrance.

You can also buy tickets and Museum Passes (no markup; tickets valid 3 months) at the newspaper kiosk just outside the Orsay entrance (along Rue de la Légion d'Honneur).

Getting There: The museum sits at 1 Rue de la Légion d'Honneur, above the Musée d'Orsay RER/Train-C stop. The Solférino Métro stop is three blocks southeast of the Orsay. Bus #69 from the Marais neighborhood stops at the museum on the river side (Quai Anatole France); from the Rue Cler area, it stops behind the museum on Rue du Bac. From the Louvre, catch bus #69 along Rue de Rivoli. Bus #87, running west from the Marais, shares a riverside stop with bus #69; the return stop eastbound is along Rue du Bac.

From the Louvre or Orangerie museums, the Orsay is a lovely 15-minute walk through the Tuileries Garden and across the river on the pedestrian bridge. A taxi stand is in front of the entry on Quai Anatole France. The Batobus boat stops here (see page 49).

Getting In: As you face the entrance, pass and ticket holders enter on the right (Entrance C). Ticket purchasers enter on the left (Entrance A). Security checks slow down all entrances.

Tours: Audioguides cost €6. English-language **guided tours** are available; confirm times—usually Mon-Sat at 11:00 (€6/1.5 hours, none on Sun, may also run at 14:30 and Thu at 18:30 in high season).

🎧 Download my free Orsay Museum **audio tour.**

Length of This Tour: Allow two hours. With less time, focus on the Impressionists and Post-Impressionists on the top floor.

Cloakroom *(Vestiaire):* Checking bags or coats is free (look to the far right, before the ticket checkers). Day bags (but nothing bigger) are allowed in the museum. No valuables can be stored in checked bags (the clerk might ask you in French not to check cameras, passports, or anything particularly precious).

Cuisine Art: The *très* elegant **$$$ Le Restaurant** on the museum's second floor is worth a peek just to admire the grand setting and

ORSAY

The Orsay's "19th Century" (1848-1914)

Einstein and Geronimo. Abraham Lincoln and Karl Marx. The train, the bicycle, the horse and buggy, the automobile, and the balloon. Freud and Dickens. Darwin's *Origin of Species* and the Church's Immaculate Conception. Louis Pasteur and Billy the Kid. Ty Cobb and V. I. Lenin.

The 19th century was a mix of old and new, side by side. Europe was entering the modern Industrial Age, with cities, factories, rapid transit, instant communication, and global networks. At the same time, it clung to the past with traditional, rural—almost medieval—attitudes and morals.

According to the Orsay, the "19th century" began in 1848 with the socialist and democratic revolutions (Marx's *Communist Manifesto*). It ended in 1914 with the pull of an assassin's trigger, which ignited World War I and ushered in the modern world. The museum shows art that is also both old and new, conservative and revolutionary.

lovely views. In addition to lunch (served Tue-Sun 11:45-14:45), an affordable tea and coffee service is available daily (15:00-17:30) except Thursday, when dinner is served (19:00-21:00). Stylish **$$ Café Campana** serves simpler meals to crowds on the fifth floor beyond the Impressionist galleries (Tue-Sun 10:30-17:00). Outside, behind the museum, several classy eateries line Rue du Bac. If the weather is even close to good, drop down to the riverside promenade just below the museum, where you'll find food stands and more (closed in winter).

Starring: Manet, Monet, Renoir, Degas, Van Gogh, Cézanne, and Gauguin.

The Tour Begins

• *Pick up a free map at the booth inside the entrance and belly up to the stone balustrade overlooking the ground floor.*

Trains used to run right under our feet down the center of the gallery. This former train station, the Gare d'Orsay, barely escaped the wrecking ball in the 1970s, when the French realized it'd be a great place to house the enormous collections of 19th-century art scattered throughout the city.

From this perch, survey our tour route. We'll do two laps around three floors of this grand

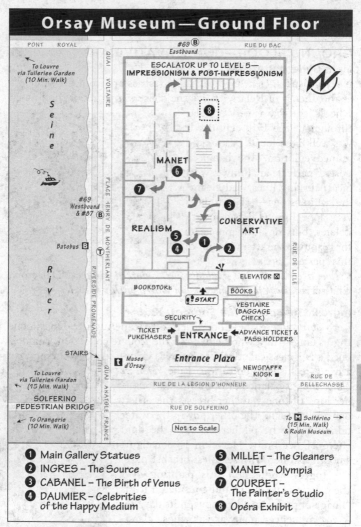

Orsay Museum—Ground Floor

PONT ROYAL • QUAI VOLTAIRE • RUE DU BAC

#69 (B) Eastbound

← To Louvre via Tuileries Garden (10 Min. Walk)

S e i n e

ESCALATOR UP TO LEVEL 5— IMPRESSIONISM & POST-IMPRESSIONISM

8

MANET 6

7

#69 Westbound & #87 (B)

Batobus (B) (T)

PLACE HENRY DE MONTHERLANT

RIVERSIDE PROMENADE

R i v e r

REALISM 5 1

3

CONSERVATIVE ART

4 2

RUE DE LILLE

BOOKSTORE

ELEVATOR ⓜ

BOOKS

START

VESTIAIRE (BAGGAGE CHECK)

SECURITY

TICKET PURCHASERS

ENTRANCE

ADVANCE TICKET & PASS HOLDERS

STAIRS →

QUAI ANATOLE FRANCE

t Musée d'Orsay

Entrance Plaza

NEWSPAPER KIOSK ■

To Louvre via Tuileries Garden (15 Min. Walk)

RUE DE LA LÉGION D'HONNEUR

RUE DE BELLECHASSE

SOLFÉRINO PEDESTRIAN BRIDGE

RUE DE SOLFÉRINO

← To Orangerie (10 Min. Walk)

To ⓜ Solférino (15 Min. Walk) & Rodin Museum →

Not to Scale

ORSAY

- ❶ Main Gallery Statues
- ❷ INGRES – The Source
- ❸ CABANEL – The Birth of Venus
- ❹ DAUMIER – Celebrities of the Happy Medium
- ❺ MILLET – The Gleaners
- ❻ MANET – Olympia
- ❼ COURBET – The Painter's Studio
- ❽ Opéra Exhibit

museum: Stretching before you on the ground floor is conservative art of the Academy and Salon, with some early rebels mixed in. At the far end, we'll ride escalators to the top floor, where we'll enjoy the Impressionists and Post-Impressionists like Van Gogh (if you're pressed for time, go directly there). Then, we'll descend to the mezzanine level for a wander through Rodin's statues and some prime examples of Art Nouveau. Ready? *Bien.*

Remember that the museum rotates its large collection often, so find the latest arrangement on your current Orsay map and be ready to go with the flow.

• *Walk down the steps to the main floor, a gallery filled with statues.*

GROUND FLOOR—CONSERVATIVE ART
Main Gallery Statues

No, this isn't ancient Greece. These statues are from the same era as the Theory of Relativity. It's the conservative art of the French

schools, and it was very popular throughout the 19th century. It was well liked for its beauty and refined emotion. The balanced poses, perfect anatomy, sweet faces, curving lines, and gleaming white stone—all of this is very appealing. (I'll bad-mouth it later, but for now appreciate the exquisite craftsmanship of this "perfect" art.)

• *Take a right into the small Room 1, marked* Ingres, Delacroix, Chassériau. *Look for a nude woman with a pitcher of water.*

Ingres, *The Source (La Source),* 1856

Let's start where the Louvre left off. Jean-Auguste-Dominique Ingres (ang-gruh), who helped cap the Louvre collection, championed a Neoclassical style. *The Source* is virtu-

ally a Greek statue on canvas. Like *Venus de Milo,* she's a balance of opposite motions—her hips tilt one way, her breasts the other; one arm goes up, the other down; the water falling from the pitcher matches the fluid curve of her body. Her skin is porcelain-smooth, painted with seamless brushstrokes.

Ingres worked on this painting over the course of 35 years and considered it his "image of perfection." Famous in its day, *The Source* influenced many artists whose classical statues and paintings are in this museum.

In the Orsay's first few rooms, you're surrounded by visions of idealized beauty—nude women in languid poses, Greek mythological figures, and anatomically perfect statues. This was the art adored by French academics and the middle-class *(bourgeois)* public. The 19th-century art world was dominated by two conservative institutions: the Academy (the state-funded art school) and the Salon, where works were exhibited to the buying public. The art they produced was technically perfect, refined, uplifting, and heroic. Some might even say...boring.

ORSAY

• *Continue to Room 3 to find a pastel blue–green painting of a swooning Venus.*

Cabanel, *The Birth of Venus*
(La Naissance de Vénus), 1863

This painting and others nearby were popular items at the art market called the Salon. The public loved Alexandre Cabanel's *Venus*. Emperor Napoleon III purchased it.

Cabanel lays Ingres' *The Source* on her back. This goddess is a perfect fantasy, an orgasm of beauty. The Love Goddess stretches

back seductively, recently birthed from the ephemeral foam of the waves. This is art of a pre-Freudian society, when sex was dirty and mysterious and had to be exalted into a more pure and divine form. The sex drive was channeled into an acute sense of beauty. French folk would literally swoon in ecstasy before these works of art. Like it? Go ahead, swoon. If it feels good, enjoy it. (If you feel guilty, get over it.) Now, take a mental cold shower, and get ready for a Realist's view.

• *Cross the main gallery of statues, backtrack toward the entrance, and enter Room 4 (directly across from Ingres), marked* Daumier.

ORSAY

GROUND FLOOR—REALISM, EARLY REBELS, AND THE BELLE EPOQUE
Daumier, *Celebrities of the Happy Medium*
(Célébrités du Juste Milieu), 1832-1835

This is a liberal's look at the stuffy bourgeois establishment that controlled the Academy and the Salon.

In these 36 bustlets, Honoré Daumier, trained as a political cartoonist, exaggerates each subject's most distinct characteristic to capture with vicious precision the pomposity and self-righteousness of these self-appointed arbiters of taste (most were members of the French parliament). Daumier gave insulting nicknames for the person being caricatured, like "gross, fat, and satisfied" or Monsieur "Platehead." Give a few nicknames yourself. Can you find Reagan, Clinton, Kerry, Sarkozy, Al

Sharpton, Gingrich, Trump, and Paul Ryan with sideburns? How about Margaret Thatcher...or is that a dude?

These people hated the art you're about to see. Their prudish faces tightened as their fantasy world was shattered by the Realists.

• *Nearby, find Millet's* Gleaners. *(Reminder: Paintings often move around, so you may need to use your Orsay map to find specific works.)*

Millet, *The Gleaners (Les Glaneuses)*, 1867

Jean-François Millet (mee-yay) shows us three gleaners, the poor women who pick up the meager leftovers after a field has already

been harvested for the wealthy. Millet grew up on a humble farm. He didn't attend the Academy and despised the uppity Paris art scene. Instead of idealized gods, goddesses, nymphs, and winged babies, he painted simple rural scenes. He was strongly affected by the socialist revolution of 1848, with its affirmation of the working class. Here he captures the innate dignity of these stocky, tanned women who bend their backs quietly in a large field for their small reward.

This is "Realism" in two senses. It's painted "realistically," not prettified. And it's the "real" world—not the fantasy world of Greek myth, but the harsh life of the working poor.

• *For a Realist's take on the traditional Venus, walk farther up the gallery and find Manet's* Olympia *in Room 14.*

Manet, *Olympia*, 1863

"This brunette is thoroughly ugly. Her face is stupid, her skin cadaverous. All this clash of colors is stupefying." So wrote a critic

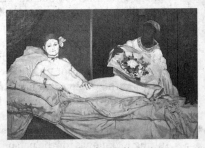

when Edouard Manet's nude hung in the Salon. The public hated it, attacking Manet (manay) in print and literally attacking the canvas.

Compare this uncompromising nude with Cabanel's idealized, pastel, Vaseline-on-the-lens beauty in *The Birth of Venus*. Cabanel's depiction was basically soft-core pornography, the kind you see today selling lingerie and perfume.

Manet's nude doesn't gloss over anything. The pose is classic, used by Titian, Goya, and countless others. But the traditional pose is challenged by the model's jarring frankness. The sharp outlines and harsh, contrasting colors are new and shocking. The woman is Manet's favorite model, a sometime painter and free spirit who also appears in his *Déjeuner* (described later). Her hand is a clamp, and her stare is shockingly defiant, with not a hint of the seductive, hey-sailor look of most nudes. This prostitute, ignoring the flowers sent by her last customer, looks out as if to say, "Next." Manet replaced soft-core porn with hard-core art.

• *Exit Room 14 up a few steps, hook left, and then right to see a huge canvas at the end of a large open space...*

Courbet, *The Painter's Studio (L'Atelier du Peintre)*, 1855

The Salon of 1855 rejected this dark-colored, sprawling, monumental painting that perplexed casual viewers. (It may be under-

going restoration in situ when you visit.) In an age when "Realist painter" was equated with "bomb-throwing Socialist," it took courage to buck the system. Dismissed by the so-called experts, Gustave Courbet (coor-bay) held his own one-man exhibit.

He built a shed in the middle of Paris, defiantly hung his art out, and basically mooned the shocked public.

Courbet's painting takes us backstage, showing us the gritty reality behind the creation of pretty pictures. We see Courbet himself in his studio, working diligently on a Realistic landscape, oblivious to the confusion around him. Milling around are ordinary citizens, not Greek heroes. The woman who looks on is not a nude Venus but a naked artist's model. And the little boy with an adoring look on his face? Perhaps it's Courbet's inner child, admiring the artist who sticks to his guns, whether it's popular or not.

• *Return to the main corridor, turn left, and head to the far end of the gallery, where you'll walk on a glass floor over a model of Paris.*

Opéra Exhibit

Expand to 100 times your size and hover over this scale-model section of the city. In the center sits the 19th-century Opéra Garnier, with its green-domed roof.

Nearby, you'll also see a cross-section model

ORSAY

of the Opéra. You'd enter from the right end, buy your ticket in the foyer, then move into the entrance hall with its grand staircase, where you could see and be seen by *tout* Paris. At curtain time, you'd find your seat in the red-and-gold auditorium, topped by a glorious painted ceiling. Notice that the stage, with elaborate riggings to raise and lower scenery, is as big as the seating area. Nearby are models of set designs from some famous productions. These days, Parisians enjoy their Verdi and Gounod at the modern opera house at Place de la Bastille.

The Opéra Garnier—opened in 1875—was the symbol of the belle époque, or "beautiful age." Paris was a global center of prosperity, new technology, opera, ballet, painting, and joie de vivre. But behind Paris' gilded and gas-lit exterior, a counterculture simmered. Revolutionaries battled to allow labor unions and give everyone the right to vote. Realist painters captured scenes of a grittier Paris, and Impressionists chafed against middle-class tastes, rejecting the careers mapped out for them to follow their artistic dreams.

Next up—the Orsay's Impressionist collection. (Consider reading ahead on Impressionism while you're still on the ground floor, as the Impressionist rooms can be very crowded.)

• *Take the escalator up to the top floor (follow signs for* 5th floor *and* Impressionisme*). Pause to take in a commanding* **view** *of the vast interior of the Orsay. The* **grand clock** *at the far end is a reminder that when this building opened in 1900, train travel was king and schedules to the minute actually mattered. Follow the crowds, pass through the bookstore, glance at the backward clock, skip the temporary exhibits, and enter the Impressionist rooms.*

LEVEL 5—IMPRESSIONISM

Light! Color! Vibrations! You don't hang an Impressionist canvas—you tether it. Impressionism features bright colors, easygoing open-air scenes, spontaneity, broad brushstrokes, and the play of light.

The Impressionist collection is scattered chronologically through Rooms 29-36. You'll see Monet hanging in many rooms, Manet sprinkled among Pissarro and Sisley, and a few Renoir here and a lot of Renoir there. Shadows dance and the displays mingle. Where they're hung is a lot like their brushwork...delightfully sloppy. If you don't see a described painting, just move on.

The Impressionists made their canvases shimmer by using a simple but revolutionary technique. Let's say you mix red, yellow, and green together—you'll get brown, right? But Impressionists didn't bother to mix them. They'd slap a thick brushstroke of yellow down, then a stroke of green next to it, then red next to that. Up close, all you see are the three messy strokes, but as you back up...*voilà!* Brown! The colors blend in the eye, at a distance. But while your eye is saying "bland old brown," your subconscious is shouting, "Red! Yellow! Green! Yes!"

There are no lines in nature, yet someone in the classical tradition (Ingres, for example) would draw an outline of his subject, then fill it in with color. Instead the Impressionists built a figure with dabs of paint...a snowman of color.

Although this top floor displays the Impressionists, you'll find a wide variety of styles. What united these artists was their commitment to everyday subjects (cafés, street scenes, landscapes, workers), their disdain for the uptight Salon, their love of color, and a

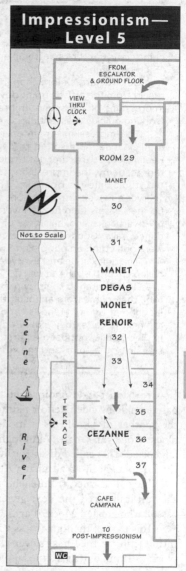

sense of artistic rebellion. These painters had a love-hate relationship with the "Impressionist" label. Later in their careers, they all went their own ways and developed their own individual styles.

The Impressionists all seemed to know each other. You may have seen a group portrait by Henri Fantin-Latour (on the main floor) depicting the circle of Parisian artists and intellectuals. Manet first met Degas while copying the same painting at the

Painting "in the Open Air"

The camera threatened to make artists obsolete. Now a machine could capture a better likeness faster than you could say "Etch-a-Sketch."

But true art is more than just painting reality. It gives us reality from the artist's point of view, with the artist's personal impressions of the scene. Impressions are often fleeting, so working quickly is essential.

The Impressionist painters rejected camera-like detail for a quick style more suited to capturing the passing moment. Feeling stifled by the rigid rules and stuffy atmosphere of the Academy, the Impressionists took as their motto, "Out of the studio, into the open air." They grabbed their berets and scarves and went on excursions to the country, where they set up their easels (and newly invented tubes of premixed paint) on riverbanks and hillsides, or they sketched in cafés and dance halls. Gods, goddesses, nymphs, and fantasy scenes were out; common people and rural landscapes were in.

The quick style and everyday subjects were ridiculed and called childish by the "experts." Rejected by the Salon, the Impressionists staged their own exhibition in 1874. They brashly took their name from an insult thrown at them by a critic who laughed at one of Monet's "impressions" of a sunrise. During the next decade, they exhibited their own work independently. The public, opposed at first, was slowly won over by the simplicity, the color, and the vibrancy of Impressionist art.

ORSAY

Louvre. Monet and Renoir set up their canvases in the country and painted side by side. Renoir painted with Cézanne and employed the mother of Utrillo as a model. Toulouse-Lautrec lived two blocks from Van Gogh. Van Gogh painted in Arles with Gauguin (an episode that ended disastrously). Van Gogh's work was some of the first bought by an admiring Rodin.

They all learned from each other and taught each other, and they all influenced the next generation's artists (Matisse and Picasso), who created Modern art.

This part of the tour is less a room-by-room itinerary than an introduction to the Orsay's ever-changing collection. Have fun exploring: Think of it as a sun-dappled treasure hunt.

• *Start with the Impressionists' mentor, Manet, whose work is usually found in Room 29. The Orsay loves to mix up the Impressionist paintings. Review the art and photos on the next five or so pages so you will know which paintings to look for as you stroll.*

Edouard Manet (1832-1883)

Manet had an upper-class upbringing and some formal art training and had been accepted by the Salon. He could have cranked out pretty nudes and been a successful painter, but instead he surrounded himself with a group of young artists experimenting with new techniques. His reputation and strong personality made him their master, but he also learned equally from them.

Manet's thumbnail bio is typical of almost all the Impressionists: They rejected a "normal" career (lawyer, banker, grocer) to become artists, got classical art training, exhibited in the Salon, became fascinated by Realist subjects, but grew tired of the Salon's dogmatism. They joined the Impressionist exhibition of 1874, experimented with bright colors and open-air scenes, and moved on to forge their unique styles in later years.

Manet's starting point was Realism. Rather than painting Madonnas, Greek gods, and academic warhorses, he hung out in cafés, sketchbook in hand, capturing the bustle of modern Paris. His painting style was a bit messy with its use of rough brushstrokes—a technique that drew the attention of budding painters like Monet and Renoir. Manet was never a full-on Impressionist. He tried but disliked open-air painting, preferring to sketch on the spot, then do his serious painting in the studio. And his colors remained dark, with plenty of brown and figures outlined in black. But when Manet's paintings were criticized by the art establishment, the Impressionists rallied to his defense, and Manet became the best-known champion of the new movement.

Manet's ***Luncheon on the Grass*** (*Le Déjeuner sur l'Herbe,* 1863) shocked Paris. The staid citizens looked at this and wondered: What are these scantily clad women doing with these men? Or rather, what will they be doing after the last baguette is eaten? It isn't the nudity, but the presence of the men in ordinary clothes

that suddenly makes the nudes look naked. The public judged the painting on moral rather than artistic terms. Here, too, the pose is classical (as seen in works by Titian), but it's presented as though it were happening in a Parisian park in 1863.

A new revolutionary movement was starting to bud—Impressionism. Notice the background: the messy brushwork of trees and leaves, the play of light on the pond, and the light that filters through the trees onto the woman who stoops in the haze. Also note the strong contrast of colors (white skin, black clothes, green grass).

Let the Impressionist revolution begin!

• *Scattered in the next galleries are works by two Impressionist masters at their peak, Monet and Renoir (with a bit of Degas in the mix too).*

You're looking at the quintessence of Impressionism. Monet and Renoir were good friends, often working side-by-side, and their canvases sometimes hang next to each other in these rooms.

Claude Monet (1840-1926)

Monet (mo-nay) is the father of Impressionism. He fully explored the possibilities of open-air painting and tried to faithfully reproduce nature's colors with bright blobs of paint. Throughout his long career, more than any of his colleagues, Monet stuck to the Impressionist credo of creating objective studies in color and light.

In the 1860s, Monet (along with Renoir) began painting landscapes in the open air. Although Monet did the occasional urban scene, he was most at home in the countryside, painting farms, rivers, trees, and passing clouds. He studied optics and pigments to know just the right colors he needed to reproduce the shimmering quality of reflected light. The key was to work quickly—at that "golden hour" (to use a modern photographer's term) when the light was just right. Then he'd create a fleeting "impression" of the scene. In fact, that was the title of one of Monet's canvases (now hanging in the Marmottan Museum); it gave the movement its name.

Monet is known for his series of paintings on the same subject. For example, you may see several canvases of the **cathedral in Rouen.** In 1893, Monet went to Rouen, rented a room across from the cathedral, set up his easel...and waited. He wanted to catch "a series of differing impressions" of the cathedral facade at various times of day and year. He often had several canvases going at once.

In all, he did 30 paintings of the cathedral, and each is unique. The time-lapse series shows the sun passing slowly across the sky, creating different-colored light and shadows. The labels next to the art describe the conditions: in gray weather, in the morning, morning sun, full sunlight, and so on.

As Monet zeroed in on the play of colors and light, the physical subject—the cathedral—dissolved. It's only a rack upon which to hang the light and color. Later artists would boldly throw away the rack, leaving purely abstract modern art in its place.

One of Monet's favorite places to paint was the garden he landscaped at his home in **Giverny,** west of Paris (and worth a visit, provided you like Monet more than you hate crowds—see the Giverny & Auvers-sur-Oise chapter). The Japanese bridge and the water lilies floating in the pond were his two favorite subjects. As Monet aged and his eyesight failed, he made bigger canvases of smaller subjects. The final water lilies are monumental smudges of thick paint surrounded by paint-splotched clouds that are reflected on the surface of the pond.

Monet's most famous water lilies are in full bloom at the Orangerie Museum, across the river in the Tuileries Garden. You can also see more Monet at the Marmottan Museum.

Pierre-Auguste Renoir (1841-1919)

Renoir (ren-wah) started out as a painter of landscapes, along with Monet, but later veered from the Impressionist's philosophy and painted images that were unabashedly "pretty." He populated his canvases with rosy-cheeked, middle-class girls performing happy domestic activities, rendered in a warm, inviting style. As Renoir himself said, "There are enough ugly things in life."

He did portraits of his friends (such as Monet) and his own kids, including his son Jean (who grew up to make the landmark film *Grand Illusion*). But his specialty was always women and girls, emphasizing their warm femininity.

Renoir's lighthearted work uses light colors—no brown or black. The paint is thin and translucent, and the outlines are soft, so the figures blend seamlessly with the background. He seems to be searching for an ideal, the sort of pure beauty we saw in paintings on the ground floor.

In his last years (when he was confined to a wheelchair with arthritis), Renoir turned to full-figured nudes—like those painted by Old Masters such as Rubens or Boucher. He introduced more and more red tones, as if trying for even greater warmth.

Renoir's best-known work is ***Dance at the Moulin de la Galette*** (*Bal du Moulin de la Galette*, 1876). On Sunday afternoons, working-class folk would dress up and head for the fields on Butte Montmartre (near Sacré-Cœur basilica) to dance, drink, and eat little crêpes (galettes) till dark. Renoir liked to go there to paint the common Parisians living and loving in the afternoon sun. The sunlight filtering through the trees creates a kaleidoscope of colors, like the 19th-century equivalent of

ORSAY

a mirror ball throwing darts of light onto the dancers. While the dance hall is long gone, you can still see the windmill and original entrance to the Moulin de la Galette (now a recommended restaurant) along our Montmartre Walk.

He captured the dappled light with quick blobs of yellow staining the ground, the men's jackets, and the sun-dappled straw hat (right of center). Smell the powder on the ladies' faces. The painting glows with bright colors. Even the shadows on the ground, which should be gray or black, are colored a warm blue. Like a photographer who uses a slow shutter speed to show motion, Renoir paints a waltzing blur.

Edgar Degas (1834-1917)

Degas (day-gah) was a rich kid from a family of bankers, and he got the best classical-style art training. Adoring Ingres' pure lines and cool colors, Degas painted in the Academic style. His work was exhibited in the Salon, he gained success and a good reputation, and then...he met the Impressionists.

Degas blends classical lines and Realist subjects with Impressionist color, spontaneity, and everyday scenes from urban Paris. He loved the unposed "snapshot" effect, catching his models off guard. Dance students, women at work, and café scenes are approached from odd angles that aren't always ideal but make the scenes seem more real. He gives us the backstage view of life.

Although Degas participated in the Impressionist exhibitions, he disdained open-air painting, preferring to perfect his meticulous paintings in the studio. He painted few landscapes, focusing instead on people. And he created his figures not as a mosaic of colorful brushstrokes, but with a classic technique—outline filled in with color. His influence on Toulouse-Lautrec is clear.

Degas loved dance and the theater. The play of stage lights off his dancers, especially the halos of ballet skirts, is made to order for an Impressionist. A dance rehearsal let Degas capture a behind-the-scenes look at bored, tired, restless dancers (*The Dance Class*, *La Classe de Danse*, c. 1873-1875). Pirouetting near his oil paintings of dancers, you'll see his small and life-size statues of them—he first modeled the figures in wax, then cast them in bronze.

Degas hung out with low-life Impressionists, discussing art, love, and life in the cheap cafés and bars in Montmartre. In the painting *In a Café* (*Dans un Café*, 1875-1876), a weary lady of the evening meets morning with a last, lonely, nail-in-the-coffin drink in the glaring light of a four-in-the-morning café. The pale green drink at the center of the composition is the toxic substance absinthe, which fueled many artists and burned out many more.

Camille Pissarro, Alfred Sisley, and Others

The Orsay features some of the "lesser" pioneers of the Impressionist style. Browse around and discover your own favorites. Pissarro is one of mine. His grainy landscapes are more subtle and subdued than those of the flashy Monet and Renoir—but, as someone said, "He did for the earth what Monet did for the water."

Paul Cézanne (1839-1906)

Paul Cézanne (say-zahn) brought Impressionism into the 20th century. After the color of Monet and the warmth of Renoir, Cézanne's rather impersonal canvases can be difficult to appreciate. Bowls of fruit, landscapes, and a few portraits were Cézanne's passion (see *The Card Players*, *Les Joueurs de Cartes*, 1890-1895). Be-

cause of his style (not the content), he is often called the first modern painter.

Cézanne was virtually unknown and unappreciated in his lifetime. He worked alone, lived alone, and died alone, ignored by all but a few revolutionary young artists who understood his genius.

Unlike the Impressionists, who painted what they saw, Cézanne reworked reality. He simplified it into basic geometric forms—circular apples, rectangular boulders, cone-shaped trees, triangular groups of people. He might depict a scene from multiple angles—showing a tabletop from above but the bowl of fruit resting on it from the side. He laid paint down with heavy brushstrokes, blending the background and foreground to obliterate traditional 3-D depth. He worked slowly, methodically, stroke by stroke—a single canvas could take months.

Where the Impressionists built a figure out of a mosaic of individual brushstrokes, Cézanne used blocks of paint to create a more solid, geometrical shape. These chunks are like little "cubes." It's no coincidence that his experiments in reducing forms to their geometric basics inspired the...Cubists.

Taking Cézanne's "slabism" a step further, the last room in this gallery is dedicated to Pointillism and the vibrant dots of Seurat and Signac.

• *Break time. Continue to the jazzy Café Campana, which serves small-plate fare with savoir faire. In good weather, venture out on the terrace for fresh air and great views. WCs are nearby (upstairs on level 6).*

LEVEL 5—POST-IMPRESSIONISM

The Impressionists were like a tribe. They spoke the same artistic language. But, after that, more than ever, artists went in different directions, creating art that was uniquely their own. Van Gogh, Gauguin, and Toulouse-Lautrec are fine examples of these Post-Impressionists, and their paintings line the walls of the next string of rooms (Rooms 43-45 especially).

• *You'll find the Post-Impressionists in a series of rooms behind the café. Just follow the signs to Van Gogh.*

Vincent van Gogh (1853-1890)

Impressionists have been accused of being "light"-weights. The colorful style lends itself to bright country scenes, gardens, sunlight on the water, and happy crowds of simple people. It took a remarkable genius to add profound emotion to the Impressionist style.

Like Michelangelo, Beethoven, and a select handful of others, Vincent van Gogh (pronounced "van-go," or van-HOCK by the Dutch and the snooty) put so much of himself into his work that art and life became one. In the Orsay's collection of paintings, you'll see both Van Gogh's painting style and his life unfold.

Vincent was the son of a Dutch minister. He too felt a reli-

ORSAY

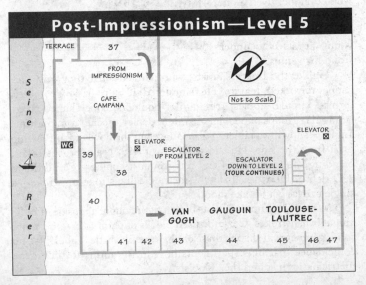

Post-Impressionism—Level 5

gious calling, and he spread the gospel among the poorest of the poor—peasants and miners in overcast Holland and Belgium. He painted these hardworking, dignified folks in a crude, dark style reflecting the oppressiveness of their lives...and his own loneliness as he roamed northern Europe in search of a calling.

Encouraged by his art-dealer brother, Van Gogh moved to Paris, and *voilà!* The color! He met Monet, drank with Gauguin and Toulouse-Lautrec, and soaked up the Impressionist style. (For example, see how he might build a bristling brown beard using thick strokes of red, yellow, and green side by side.)

At first, he painted like the others, but soon he developed his own style. By using thick, swirling brushstrokes, he infused life into even inanimate objects. Van Gogh's brushstrokes curve and thrash like a garden hose pumped with wine.

The social life of Paris became too much for the solitary Van Gogh, and he moved to the south of France. At first, in the glow of the bright spring sunshine, he had a period of incredible creativity and happiness. He was overwhelmed by the bright colors, landscape vistas, and common people. It was an Impressionist's dream (see **Midday, La Méridi-enne**, 1889-90).

But being alone in a strange country began to wear on him. An ugly man, he found it hard to get a date. A painting of his rented bedroom in Arles shows a cramped, bare-bones place (**Van Gogh's Bedroom in Arles**, *La Chambre de Van Gogh à Arles*, 1889). He invited his friend Gauguin to join him, but after two months together arguing passionately about art, nerves got raw. Van Gogh threatened Gauguin with a razor, which drove his friend back to

Paris. In crazed despair, Van Gogh cut off a piece of his own ear.

The people of Arles realized they had a mad-man on their hands and convinced Vincent to seek help at a mental hospital. The paintings he finished in the peace of the hospital are more meditative—there are fewer bright landscapes and more closed-in scenes with deeper, almost surreal colors.

Van Gogh, the preacher's son, saw painting as a calling, and he approached it with a spiritual intensity. In his last days, he wavered between happiness and madness. He despaired of ever being sane enough to continue painting.

His final self-portrait shows a man engulfed in a confused background of brushstrokes that swirl and rave (**Self-Portrait**, *Portrait de l'Artiste*, 1889). But in the midst of this rippling sea of mystery floats a still, detached island of a face. Perhaps his troubled eyes know that in only a few months, he'll take a pistol and put a bullet through his chest.

You can ponder his tragic life from outside his former Montmartre apartment (along the route of our Montmartre Walk) or on a day trip to the village where he took his life, Auvers-sur Oise (see the Giverny & Auvers-sur-Oise chapter).

• *Carry on to the next room, where you'll find works by...*

Paul Gauguin (1848-1903)

Gauguin (go-gan) got the travel bug early in childhood and grew up wanting to be a sailor. Instead, he became a stockbroker. In his spare time, he painted, and he was introduced to the Impressionist circle. He learned their bright clashing colors but diverged from their path about the time Van Gogh waved a knife in his face. At the age of 35, he got fed up with it all, quit his job, abandoned his wife and family, and took refuge in his art. (Look for his self-portrait with the travel-dreams background.)

Gauguin traveled to the South Seas in search of the exotic, finally settling on Tahiti. There he found his Garden of Eden. He simplified his life into a routine of eating, sleeping, and painting. He simplified his paintings still more, to flat images with heavy black outlines filled with bright, pure colors. The background and foreground colors are equally bright, producing a flat, stained-glass-like surface.

Gauguin also carved statuettes in the style of Polynesian pagan idols. His fascination with indigenous peoples and Primitive art had a great influence on later generations. Matisse and the Fauves (or "Wild Beasts") loved Gauguin's bright, clashing colors. Picasso used his tribal-mask faces for his groundbreaking early Cubist works.

Gauguin's best-known works capture an idyllic Tahitian landscape peopled by exotic women engaged in simple tasks and making music (*Arearea*, 1892). The local girls lounge placidly in unselfconscious innocence (so different from Cabanel's seductive,

ORSAY

melodramatic *Venus*). The style is intentionally "primitive," collapsing the three-dimensional landscape into a two-dimensional pattern of bright colors. Gauguin intended that this simple style carry a deep undercurrent of symbolic meaning. He wanted to communicate to his "civilized" colleagues back home that he'd found the paradise he'd always envisioned.

• *The next section features an artist who found his travel thrills closer to home, in the Paris underworld.*

Henri de Toulouse-Lautrec (1864-1901)

Henri de Toulouse-Lautrec was the black sheep of a noble family. At age 14 he broke both legs, which left him with a normal-size torso but dwarf-size limbs. Shunned by his family, a freak to society, he felt more at home in the world of other outcasts—prostitutes, drunks, thieves, dancers, and actors. He settled in Montmartre, where he painted the life he lived, sketching the lowlife in the bars, cafés, dance halls, and brothels he frequented. He drank absinthe and hung out with Van Gogh. He carried a hollow cane filled with booze. When the Moulin Rouge nightclub opened, Henri was hired to do its posters. Every night, the artist put on his bowler hat and visited the Moulin Rouge to draw the crowds, the can-can dancers, and the backstage action. Toulouse-Lautrec died at age 36 of syphilis and alcoholism.

Toulouse-Lautrec's painting style captures Realist scenes with strong, curvaceous outlines. He worked quickly, creating sketches in paint that serve as snapshots of a golden era.

In ***Jane Avril Dancing*** (*Jane Avril Dansant*, 1891), he depicts the slim, graceful, elegant, and melancholy dancer, who stood out above the rabble. Her legs keep dancing while her mind is far away. Toulouse-Lautrec, the "artistocrat," might have identified with her noble face—sad and weary of the nightlife, but immersed in it.

• *Just past the last room in this section, ride the escalator down to level 2, an open-air mezzanine lined with statues. Make a circle around the mezzanine as you enjoy the work of Rodin, Claudel, and their contemporaries.*

LEVEL 2—FRENCH SCULPTURE

This section is frequently shuffled about. You should find most of these works close by, though some may be away for restoration.

Auguste Rodin (1840-1917)

Born of working-class roots and largely self-taught, Rodin combined classical solidity with Impressionist surfaces to become the greatest sculptor since Michelangelo. He labored in obscurity for decades, making knickknacks and doorknobs for a construction company. By age 40, he started to gain recognition.

• *As you go along, look for a Rodin statue of a man missing just about everything but his legs.*

Like his statue of **The Walking Man** (*L'Homme Qui Marche*, 1905), Rodin had one foot in the past and one stepping boldly into the future. This muscular, forcefully striding man could be a symbol of the Renaissance Man with his classical power. With no mouth or hands, he speaks with his body. Get close and look at the statue's surface. It's alive, rippling with frosting-like gouges. This rough, "unfinished" look reflects light like the rough Impressionist brushwork. And that makes the statue come to life, never quite at rest in the viewer's eye. Rodin's subject was always the human body, showing it in unusual poses that express inner emotion.

Another good example of Rodin's style is *St. John the Baptist* (*Saint Jean-Baptiste*, 1878), which captures the mystical visionary who was the forerunner of Christ. Rodin's inspiration was a shaggy peasant—looking for work as a model—whose bearing caught the artist's eye. Coarse and hairy, with both feet planted firmly in mid-stride, this sculpture challenged the traditional poses expected from a 19th-century artist. A sense of movement and spontaneity mattered more to Rodin than mimicking classical stances.

Imagine Rodin's work process. Rodin paid models to run, squat, leap, and spin around his studio however they wanted. When he saw an interesting pose, he'd yell, "Freeze!" (or "statue maker") and get out his sketchpad. Rodin worked quickly, using his powerful thumbs to make a small statue in clay, which he would then reproduce as a life-size clay statue that in turn was used as a mold for casting a plaster or bronze copy. Authorized copies of Rodin's work are now included in museums all over the world.

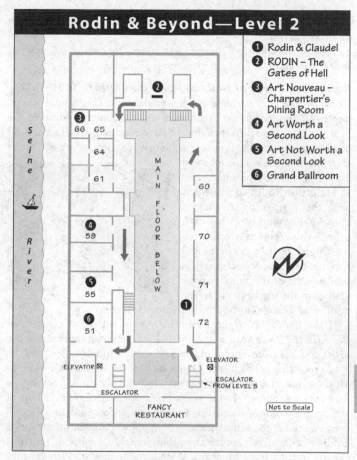

• *You should pass a few more works by Rodin before landing (toward the far end of the mezzanine) on a deeply bronzed sculpture with three figures.*

Camille Claudel (1864-1943)

Camille Claudel was Rodin's student, mistress, and muse. In *Maturity* (*L'Age Mur*, c. 1902)—a small bronze statue group of three

figures—Claudel may have portrayed their doomed love affair. A young girl desperately reaches out to an older man, who is led away reluctantly by an older woman. The center of the composition is the empty space left when their hands separate. In

real life, Rodin refused to leave his wife, and Claudel ended up in an insane asylum.

• *At the far end of the hall (hooking left, around the corner), you will run into a large gate cluttered with sculptural brilliance...*

Rodin, *The Gates of Hell (La Porte de l'Enfer),* 1880-1917

Rodin worked for decades on this model for a ceremonial "door" depicting the lost souls of Dante's hell. It contains some of his greatest hits—small statues that he later executed in full size. Find *The Thinker* squatting above the doorway, contemplating Man's

fate. *The Thinker* was meant to be Dante surveying the characters of Hell. But Rodin so identified with this pensive figure that he chose it to stand atop his own grave. This *Thinker* is only two feet high, but it was the model for the full-size work that has become one of the most famous statues in the world (you can see a full-size *Thinker* in the Rodin Museum garden).

The door's 186 figures eventually inspired larger versions of *The Kiss*, the *Three Shades*, and more. (You can read more about the artist and *The Gates of Hell* in the Rodin Museum Tour.)

From this perch in the Orsay, look down to the main floor at all the classical statues between you and the big clock, and realize how far we've come—not in years, but in stylistic changes. Many of the statues below—beautiful, smooth, balanced, and idealized—were created at the same time as Rodin's powerful, haunting works. Rodin's sculptures capture the groundbreaking spirit of much of the art in the Orsay Museum. With a stable base of 19th-century stone, he launched art into the 20th century.

• *While you've now seen the essential Orsay, you'll need to return to the other end of the gallery to leave. For a little artistic dessert, stay on this level and slalom down the other side of the mezzanine, popping into some entertaining last rooms.*

LEVEL 2—THE "OTHER" ORSAY

The beauty of the Orsay is that it combines all the art from 1848 to 1914, both modern and classical, in one building. The classical art, so popular in its day, was maligned and largely forgotten in the later 20th century. It's time for a reassessment. Is it as gaudy and gawd-awful as we've been led to believe? From our 21st-century perspective, let's take a look at the opulent *fin de siècle* French high society and its luxurious art.

• *At the start of the corridor, enter room 65. From here, Rooms 61–66 feature curvaceous Art Nouveau furniture.*

Art Nouveau

The Industrial Age brought factories, row houses, machines, train stations, geometrical precision—and ugliness. At the turn of the 20th century, some artists reacted against the unrelieved geometry of harsh, pragmatic, iron-and-steel Eiffel Tower art with a

"new art"—Art Nouveau. (Hmm. I think I had a driver's ed teacher by that name.)

Stand amid a reconstructed wood-paneled dining room (Room 66) designed by Alexandre Charpentier *(Boiserie de la Salle à Mangér)*. With its carved vines, leafy garlands, and tree-branch arches, it's one of the finest examples of Art Nouveau.

Like nature, which also abhors a straight line, Art Nouveau artists used the curves of flowers and vines as their pattern. They were convinced that "practical" didn't have to mean "ugly." They turned everyday household objects into art. Another well-known example of Art Nouveau is the sinuous wrought-ironwork of some of Paris' early Métro entrances—which were commissioned by banker Adrien Bénard, the same man who ordered this dining room for his home.

• *Return to the open-air mezzanine and turn right. Enter Room 59.*

Art Worth a Second Look

We've seen some great art. Now let's see some not-so-great art—at least, that's what modern critics tell us. This is realistic art with a subconscious kick. The centerpiece of Room 59 is Henri Martin's **Serenity** *(Sérénité,* 1899), a dream in the woods. Three nymphs with harps waft off through the trees to the right. These people are stoned on something. High above on the right, Jean Delville's **The School of Plato** *(L'Ecole de Platon,* 1898) could be subtitled "The Athens YMCA." A Christ-like Plato surrounded by adoring, half-naked nubile youths gives new meaning to the term "platonic relationship." Will the pendulum shift so that one day art like *The School of Plato* becomes the new, radical avant-garde style?

• *Continue down the mezzanine until you reach Room 55.*

Art Not Worth a Second Look

A director of the Orsay once said, "Certainly, we have bad paintings. But we have only the greatest bad paintings." And here they

ORSAY

are. On the left, Fernand Cormon's *Cain* (1880) depicts the world's first murderer, whose murder weapon is still in his belt as he's exiled with his family. Archaeologists had recently discovered a Neanderthal skull, so the artist makes Cain's family part of a prehistoric hunter-gatherer tribe. Opposite the entry, in Edouard Detaille's *The Dream* (*Le Rêve*, 1888), soldiers lie still, asleep without beds, while visions of Gatling guns dance in their heads. Behind that, in the next room, Léon Lhermitte, often called "the grandson of Courbet and Millet," depicts peasants getting their wages in his *Paying the Harvesters* (*La Paye des Moissonneurs*, 1882). The subtitle of the work could be, "Is this all there is to life?" (Or, "The Paycheck...After Deductions.")

• *Climb a few steps and continue along the mezzanine. Near the escalators, turn right and find the palatial Room 51, with mirrors and chandeliers, marked* Salle des Fêtes *(Grand Ballroom).*

Grand Ballroom (Salle des Fêtes)

This room was part of the hotel that once adjoined the Orsay train station. One of France's poshest nightspots, it was built in 1900, abandoned after 1939, condemned, and then restored to the elegance you see today. You can easily imagine gowned debutantes and white-gloved dandies waltzing the night away to the music of a chamber orchestra. Take in the interior decoration: raspberry marble-ripple ice-cream columns, pastel ceiling painting, gold work, mirrors, and leafy garlands of chandeliers. People it with the glitterati of Paris circa 1910.

Is this stuff beautiful or merely gaudy? Divine or decadent? Whatever you decide, it was all part of the marvelous world of the Orsay's century of art.

• *The exit is directly below. A good place to ponder it all is Le Restaurant, located near the escalators on level 2. It's pricey, but there's an affordable coffee-and-tea happy hour. After all this art, you deserve it. Or, for a good, fresh-air museum antidote, stroll the pedestrian-only riverside promenade* (Les Berges du Seine), *which starts below the Orsay and runs west to Pont de l'Alma, near the Eiffel Tower. There you can enjoy an Impressionist Parisian scene come to life.*

ORANGERIE MUSEUM TOUR

Musée de l'Orangerie

This Impressionist museum is as lovely as a water lily. Step out of the tree-lined, sun-dappled Impressionist painting that is the Tuileries Garden and into the Orangerie (oh-rahn-zhuh-ree), a little bijou of select works by Monet, Renoir, Matisse, Picasso, and others.

On the main floor you'll find the main attraction, Monet's *Water Lilies (Nymphéas)*, floating dreamily in oval rooms. The rooms were designed in the 1920s to display this art, following the artist's exacting specifications. But in the 1960s the museum added a floor above the *Water Lilies*, cutting them off from the daylight that was, after all, their inspiration and subject matter. In 2006 the upstairs collection was moved underground, and the upper floor was transformed into a tall skylight—drenching the *Water Lilies* in natural light.

In the underground gallery are select works of other Impressionist heavyweights well worth your time. The museum is small enough to enjoy in a short visit, but complete enough to show the bridge from Impressionism to Modernism. And it's all beautiful.

Orientation

Cost: €12.50 timed-entry ticket required (purchase online in advance), free for those under 18, free on the first Sun of the month, €18 combo-ticket with Orsay Museum, ask about combo-ticket with Monet's Garden and House at Giverny, covered by Museum Pass.

Hours: Wed-Mon 9:00-18:00, closed Tue.

Information: +33 1 44 77 80 07, www.musee-orangerie.fr.

Reserved Entry: The Orsay requires all visitors—including Museum Pass holders—to reserve a time slot for your visit. In quiet times, you might be able to get a reservation in person for the same day, but I'd err on the side of booking ahead.

When to Go: The museum is small and popular. It's most crowded on weekends and 14:00-18:00.

Getting There: It's in the Tuileries Garden near Place de la Concorde (Mo: Concorde) and a lovely 15-minute stroll from the Orsay Museum through the Tuileries.

Getting In: A security checkpoint causes lines, but there may be a shorter security line for Museum Pass holders.

Tours: €6 **guided tours** in English are offered a few times a week; ask for the current program. The €5 **audioguide** adds nothing beyond what's in this book on the *Water Lilies*, but it provides good detail about individual canvases in the Walter-Guillaume Collection.

Length of This Tour: Allow one hour. Temporary exhibitions often merit extra time. With less time, you could see (if not "experience") the two rooms of *Water Lilies* in a glance.

Starring: Claude Monet's *Water Lilies* and select works by the pioneers of modern painting.

Cuisine Art: Between the two floors, a cheery café with reasonable prices offers a welcome pause.

The Tour Begins

MONET'S *WATER LILIES*

• *Monet's* Water Lilies *float serenely in two pond-shaped rooms, straight ahead past the ticket takers. Examine them up close to see Monet's technique; stand back to take in the whole picture.*

Salle I

Like Beethoven going deaf, a nearly blind Claude Monet (1840-1926) wrote his final symphonies on a monumental scale. Even as he struggled with cataracts, he planned a series of huge six-foot-tall canvases of water lilies to hang in special rooms at the Orangerie.

These eight mammoth, curved panels immerse you

in Monet's garden. We're looking at the pond in his garden at Giverny—dotted with water lilies, surrounded by foliage, and dappled by the reflections of the sky, clouds, and trees on the surface. The water lilies (*nymphéas* in French) range from plain green lily pads to flowers of red, white, yellow, lavender, and various combos.

The effect is intentionally disorienting; the different canvases feature different parts of the pond from different angles, at different times of day, with no obvious chronological order. Monet mingles the pond's many elements and lets us sort it out.

• *Start with the long wall on your right (as you enter) and work counterclockwise.*

It's *Morning* on the pond at Giverny. The blue pond is the center of the composition, framed by the green, foliage-covered banks at either end. Lilies float in the foreground, and the pond stretches into the distance.

The sheer scale of the Orangerie project was daunting for an artist in his twilight years. This vast painting is made from four separate canvases stitched together and spans 6 feet 6 inches by 55 feet. Altogether, Monet painted 1,950 square feet of canvas to complete the *Water Lilies* series. Working at his home in Giverny, Monet built a special studio with skylights and wheeled easels to accommodate the canvases.

The panel at the far end, called *Green Reflections*, looks deep into the dark water. Green willow branches are reflected on the water in a vertical pattern; lily pads stretch horizontally.

Along the other long wall *(Clouds)*, green lilies float among lavender clouds reflected in blue water. Staring into Monet's pond, we see the intermingling of the four classical elements—earth (foliage), air (the sky), fire (sunlight), and water—the primordial soup of life.

The true subject of these works is the play of reflected light off the surface of the pond. Monet would work on several canvases at once, each dedicated to a different time of day. He'd move with the sun from one canvas to the next. Pan slowly around this hall. Watch the pond turn from predawn darkness (far end) to clear morning light *(Morning)* to lavender late afternoon *(Clouds)* to glorious sunset—in the west, where the sun actually does set.

In *Sunset* (near end), the surface of the pond is stained a bright yellow. Get close and see how Monet worked. Starting from the gray of the blank canvas (lower right), he'd lay down big, thick brushstrokes of a single color, weaving them in a (mostly) horizontal and vertical pattern to create a dense mesh of foliage. Over this, he'd add more color for the dramatic highlights, until (in the center of the yellow) he got a dense paste of piled-up paint. Up close, it's a mess—but back up, and the colors begin to

resolve into a luminous scene. There are no clearly identifiable objects in this canvas—no lilies, no trees, no clouds, no actual sun—just pure reflected color.

• *Continue into Salle II, starting with the long wall on your right and working counterclockwise.*

Salle II

In this room, Monet frames the pond with pillar-like tree trunks and overhanging foliage. The compositions are a bit more symmetrical and the color schemes more muted, with blue and lavender and green-brown. Monet's paintings almost always deal with the foundation of life and unspoiled nature. This room begs you to stroll its banks, slowly ambling with the artist in a complete loop—perhaps while listening to Debussy.

In *Willows on a Clear Morning* (on the long wall to the right), we seem to be standing on the bank of the pond, looking out through overhanging trees at the water. The swirling branches and horizontal ripples on the pond suggest a gentle breeze.

The Two Willows (far end) frame a wide expanse of water dotted with lilies and the reflection of gray-pink clouds.

Stand close in front of *Morning Willows* (long left wall). Notice how a "brown" tree is a tangled Impressionist beard of purple, green, blue, and red. Each leaf is a long brushstroke, each lily pad a dozen smudges.

At the near end, *Reflections of Trees* is a dark mess of blue-purple paint brightened only by the lone rose lilies in the center. Each lily is made of many Impressionist brushstrokes—each brushstroke is itself a mix of red, white, and pink paints. Put a mental frame around a single lily, and it looks like an abstract canvas. Monet demonstrates both his mastery of color and his ability to render it with paint, applied generously and deftly. He wanted the vibrant colors to keep firing your synapses.

With this last canvas, darkness descends on the pond. The room's large, moody canvases, painted by an 80-year-old man in the twilight of his life, invite meditation.

For 12 years (1914-1926), Monet worked on these paintings obsessively. A successful eye operation in 1923 gave him new energy. Monet completed all the planned canvases, but he didn't live to see them installed here. In 1927, the year after his death, these rooms were completed and the canvases put in place. Some call this the first "art installation"—art displayed in a space specially designed for it in order to enhance the viewer's experience.

Monet's final work was more "modern" than Impressionist. Each canvas is fully saturated with color, the distant objects as bright as the close ones. Monet's mosaic of brushstrokes forms a colorful design that's beautiful even if you just look "at" the canvas, like wallpaper. He wanted his paintings to be realistic and three-dimensional, but with a pleasant, two-dimensional pattern. As the subjects become fuzzier, the colors and patterns predominate. Monet builds a bridge between Impressionism and modern, abstract art.

To see more of Monet's work, visit the Marmottan Museum, and to experience the place that inspired these water lilies, take a day trip to Giverny (see the Giverny & Auvers-sur-Oise chapter).
• *Descend the stairs to the lower floor. At the bottom of the stairs is a small room with information about the pioneering art collector Paul Guillaume, who funded and inspired many artists. This is a good place to read the sidebar about him and prepare to tour the...*

WALTER-GUILLAUME COLLECTION

These paintings—Impressionist, Fauvist, and Cubist—were amassed by the art dealer Paul Guillaume and inherited by his wife, Domenica Guillaume Walter. (You might see portraits of them as you tour their collection.) This power couple's collection is a snapshot of what was hot in the world of art, circa 1920. The once-revolutionary Impressionists had become completely old-school, though their paintings—now classics—commanded a fortune. The bohemian Fauvists and Cubists, who invented modern art atop Butte Montmartre (c. 1900-1915), had suddenly become the darlings of the art world. But they refused to be categorized, and their work in the 1920s branched out in dozens of new directions. Browse the rooms and watch the various "isms" unfold. (Note that though the displays change often, the place is small and you can easily find the artists covered in this tour, usually in the order I've listed them.)
• *Start with the long hallway.*

ORANGERIE

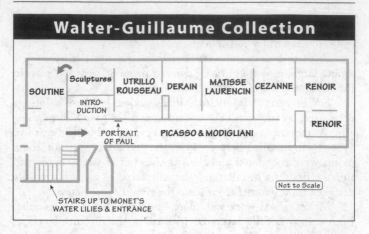

Walter-Guillaume Collection

SOUTINE | Sculptures | UTRILLO ROUSSEAU | DERAIN | MATISSE LAURENCIN | CEZANNE | RENOIR

INTRODUCTION

PORTRAIT OF PAUL | PICASSO & MODIGLIANI

RENOIR

Not to Scale

STAIRS UP TO MONET'S WATER LILIES & ENTRANCE

Introduction to the Collection

This hallway features a smattering of paintings by some of the era's greatest pioneers. You'll get a taste of Picasso's many styles, Modigliani's primitive heads, Derain's quirky still lifes, Matisse's "flatness," and Rousseau's charming childlike world.
• *You may see more of these artists later, but for now focus on the hallway's fine selection of work by two contrasting artists.*

Pablo Picasso (1881-1973)

Picasso is a shopping mall of 20th-century artistic styles. The Orangerie's collection alone traces his life through several periods: Rose (red-toned nudes with timeless, masklike faces), Blue (sad and tragic), Cubist (flat planes of interwoven perspectives), and Classical (massive, sculptural nudes—warm blow-up dolls with substance). If all roads lead to Paris, all art styles flowed through Picasso.

Amedeo Modigliani (1884-1920)

In his short, poverty-stricken, drug-addled life, Modigliani produced timeless-looking portraits of modern people. Born in Italy, Modigliani moved to Paris, where he hung around the fringes of the avant-garde crowd in the Montmartre. He gained a reputation for his alcoholic excesses and outrageous behavior.

Turning his back on the prevailing Fauvist/Cubist ambience of the times, Modigliani developed a unique style, influenced by primitive tribal masks. Modigliani died young, just as his work was gaining recognition.
• *At the end of the hall, turn left toward Room 1, with works by Renoir. As you enter each room you'll find a brief description of the artists whose works are shown there.*

ORANGERIE

Paul Guillaume (1891-1934)

For the first three decades of the 20th century, Paris was the center of the art world and the cradle of Modernism. At the center of Paris' art scene was Paul Guillaume. An art dealer, promoter of "modern" art, and friend of out-there artists, Guillaume rose from humble beginnings to become wealthy and famous.

In his early days, this self-made businessman struggled alongside struggling painters in Montmartre—Picasso, Modigliani, Derain, Laurencin, and many others. When the art market boomed in the 1920s (along with the stock market), he and his fellow bohemians became the toasts of high society. With his flamboyant wife, Domenica (also called Juliette), Guillaume hosted exotic parties featuring what we would now call "performance art" to shock and titillate the buying public.

Many of their artist friends honored Paul and Domenica by painting their portraits. In Modigliani's *Novo Pilota* (pictured above), young Paul strikes a pose as the dapper man-of-the-world he was soon to become. The title of the painting is Italian for "new helmsman," reflecting Paul's growing status as a champion of Modernism. Marie Laurencin's portrait captures the winsome beauty of Domenica, whose charm helped establish the nouveau riche couple in social circles. André Derain's and Kees van Dongen's portraits feature Paul and Domenica when they are older, more confident, and sophisticated.

The Orangerie displays Guillaume's personal collection of favorite paintings. After Paul's death, Domenica married Jean Walter and took her new husband's last name, which is why it's officially called the "Walter-Guillaume" collection.

Pierre-Auguste Renoir (1841-1919)

These pleasant works by Renoir provide a smooth transition from 19th-century Impressionism to 20th-century Modernism.

Renoir loved to paint *les femmes*—women and girls—nude and innocent, taking a bath or practicing the piano, all with rosy-red cheeks and a relaxed grace. We get a feel for the happy family life of middle-class Parisians (including Renoir's own family) during the belle époque—the beautiful age of the late 19th century. Renoir's warm, sunny colors (mostly red) are Impressionist, but he adds a classical touch with his clearer lines and, in the later nudes, the voluptuousness of classical statues and paintings. He seems to enjoy capturing the bourgeoisie, soft and elegant, enjoying their leisure pursuits.

• *The next artists may be featured in a different order, but in this small museum, they're not hard to find.*

Paul Cézanne (1839-1906)

These small canvases of simple subjects pushed modern artists to reinvent the rules of painting. The fruit of Cézanne's still lifes has an underlying geometry "built" from patches of color. In the shapes of nature, Cézanne saw spheres, cylinders, and cones. He was fond of saying, "First you must learn to paint these simple shapes. Then you will be able to do whatever you want."

There's no traditional shading to create the illusion of three dimensions, but this fruit bulges out like a cameo from the canvas. The fruit is clearly at eye level, yet it's also clearly placed on a table seen from above. Cézanne broke the rules, showing multiple perspectives at once. Picasso was fascinated with Cézanne's strange new world—which seems to give us a peek into the secret lives of fruits.

In his landscapes, Cézanne the Impressionist creates "brown" rocks out of red, orange, and purple, and "green" trees out of green, lime, and purple. Cézanne the proto-Cubist builds the rocks and trees with blocks of thick brushstrokes.

Henri Matisse (1869-1954)

After World War I, Matisse moved to the south of France. He abandoned his fierce Fauvist style and painted languid women in angular rooms with arabesque wallpaper. These paler tones evoke the sunny luxury of the Riviera. Traditional perspective is thrown out the occasional hotel window as the women and furnishings in the "foreground" blend with the wallpaper "background" to become part of the decor.

Marie Laurencin (1883-1956)

As the girlfriend of the poet and art critic Guillaume Apollinaire, Laurencin was right at the heart of the Montmartre circle when modern art was born. Her work—featuring women and cuddly animals intertwined in pink, blue, and gray tones—spreads a pastel sheen over this tumultuous time.

André Derain (1880-1954)

Along with his friend Matisse, Derain helped invent Fauvism. Then, in Montmartre, along with his friend Picasso, he helped forge Cubism. In the 1920s, this former wild beast *(fauve)* tamed his colors. He and Picasso rode the rising wave of Classicism that surfaced after the chaos of the war years. With sharp outlines and studied realism, Derain's still lifes portray nudes, harlequins, portraits, and landscapes—all in odd, angular poses.

Henri Rousseau (1844-1910)

Rousseau, a simple government worker, never traveled outside France. But in his artwork he created an exotic, dreamlike, completely unique world. A good example is his painting of a Parisian wedding set amid tropical trees (you might find this painting in the main hall). Figures are placed in a 3-D world, but the lines of perspective recede so steeply into the distance that everyone is in danger of sliding down the canvas. Without any feet, the subjects seem barely tethered to the earth. The way Rousseau put familiar images in bizarre settings influenced the Surrealists. The Orangerie has France's biggest collection of Rousseaus.

ORANGERIE

Maurice Utrillo (1883-1955)

The hard-drinking, streetwise, bohemian artist is known for his postcard views of Montmartre—whitewashed buildings under perennially cloudy skies. For more on Utrillo, see page 400.

• *Room 7 is often dedicated to the **African sculpture** Paul Guillaume brought to Paris. This "primitive" style—of stylized features, elongated heads and necks, and almond eyes—inspired painters of the period, including Picasso, Derain, and Modigliani.*

Chaim Soutine (1893-1943)

When his friend Modigliani died (and Modigliani's widow committed suicide), Soutine went into a tailspin of depression that drove him to paint. The sub-

jects are ordinary—landscapes, portraits, and a fine selection of your favorite cuts of meat—but the style is deformed and Expressionistic. It shows a warped world in a funhouse mirror, smeared onto the canvas with thick, lurid colors. The never-cheerful Soutine was known to destroy work that did not satisfy him. Stand and ponder why these made the cut.

Did I say that the Orangerie's collection was as beautiful as an Impressionist painting? Well, Soutine's misery is so complete, it's almost a thing of beauty.

• *You'll find a few rooms for temporary exhibits at the end, usually worth checking out.*

ORANGERIE

RUE CLER WALK

The Art of Parisian Living

A stroll down this street introduces you to a thriving, traditional Parisian neighborhood and offers insights into the local culture. And although Rue Cler is a wealthy district, it retains an everyday charm still found in most neighborhoods throughout the city. This charming dimension of Paris is slowly changing, however. With increasing affluence, mobility, and tourism, businesses that offer workaday practicalities are slowly morphing into upscale shops and cafés. But the Parisian love and appreciation of community persists, and it can be sampled even on touristy and affluent Rue Cler.

Shopping for groceries is the backbone of daily life here. Parisians shop nearly every day for three good reasons: Refrigerators are small (tiny kitchens), produce must be fresh, and it's an important social event. Shopping is a chance to hear about the butcher's vacation plans, see photos of the florist's new grandchild, relax over *un café*, and kiss the cheeks of friends (for proper kissing etiquette, see "Le French Kiss" sidebar, later).

Rue Cler—traffic-free since 1984—offers plenty of space for narrow stores and their patrons to spill out onto the street. It's an ideal environment for this ritual to survive and for you to explore. The street is lined with the essential shops—wine, cheese, chocolate, bread—as well as a bank and a post office. People from all walks of life live side by side: Before moving to the Elysée Palace (France's White House), French president Emmanuel Macron lived on the seventh floor at 15 Rue Cler, right above Slim, the night-shift receptionist at one of my favorite Rue Cler

RUE CLER

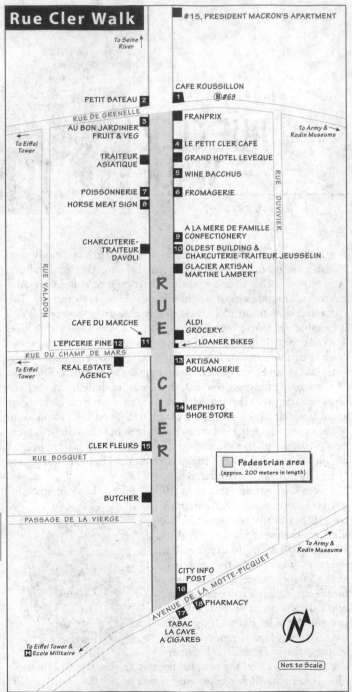

Rue Cler Walk

#15, PRESIDENT MACRON'S APARTMENT

To Seine River

To Eiffel Tower

CAFE ROUSSILLON

Ⓑ #69

PETIT BATEAU 2

1

RUE DE GRENELLE

3

FRANPRIX

To Army & Rodin Museums

AU BON JARDINIER FRUIT & VEG

4

LE PETIT CLER CAFE

TRAITEUR ASIATIQUE

GRAND HOTEL LEVEQUE

5

WINE BACCHUS

POISSONNERIE 7

6

FROMAGERIE

HORSE MEAT SIGN 8

RUE DUVIVIER

A LA MERE DE FAMILLE CONFECTIONERY

9

CHARCUTERIE-TRAITEUR DAVOLI

10

OLDEST BUILDING & CHARCUTERIE-TRAITEUR JEUSSELIN

GLACIER ARTISAN MARTINE LAMBERT

RUE VALADON

R U E   C L E R

CAFE DU MARCHE

ALDI GROCERY

L'EPICERIE FINE 12

11

LOANER BIKES

RUE DU CHAMP DE MARS

To Eiffel Tower

13

ARTISAN BOULANGERIE

REAL ESTATE AGENCY

14

MEPHISTO SHOE STORE

CLER FLEURS 15

RUE BOSQUET

Pedestrian area
(approx. 200 meters in length)

BUTCHER

PASSAGE DE LA VIERGE

To Army & Rodin Museums

CITY INFO POST

16

18 PHARMACY

17

TABAC LA CAVE A CIGARES

To Eiffel Tower & Ⓜ Ecole Militaire

AVENUE DE LA MOTTE-PICQUET

Not to Scale

hotels. And the shops of this community are run by people who've found their niche: boys who grew up on quiche and girls who know a good wine.

For those learning the fine art of living Parisian-style, Rue Cler provides an excellent classroom. And if you want to assemble the ultimate French picnic, there's no better place. The Rue Cler Walk is the only tour in this guidebook you should start while hungry. Remember that your ability to enthusiastically embrace the local etiquette of greeting people in French as you enter each shop (see below) will raise the "happy quotient" of your Rue Cler experience way up.

Orientation

Length of This Walk: Allow an hour to browse and café-hop along this short walk of two or three blocks.

When to Go: Visit Rue Cler when its markets are open and lively (Tue-Sat 8:30-13:00 & 15:00-19:30, Sun 8:30-12:00, dead Sun afternoon and Mon).

Getting There: Start your walk at the northern end of the pedestrian section of Rue Cler, at Rue de Grenelle (right by a bus #69 stop and a short walk from Mo: Ecole Militaire).

Tours: ∩ Download my Rue Cler Walk audio tour.

Shop Etiquette: Remember that these shops are busy serving regular customers; be careful not to get in the way. Be polite—say *"Bonjour, Madame/Monsieur"* as you enter and *"Bonne journée* (bohn zhoor-nay), *Madame/Monsieur"* when you leave. Buy something, but before making a purchase, watch the locals to see if self-service is allowed. Many shopkeepers prefer to serve you and don't want you to touch the goods. If you aren't sure of the protocol, ask, *"Je peux?"* (Can I?; zhuh puh). If you know what you want, point to your choice and say, *"S'il vous plaît"* (Please; see voo play). For extra credit, add, *"Je voudrais"* (I would like; zhuh voo-dray). And don't forget *"Merci beaucoup"* (Thank you very much; mehr-see boh-koo).

The Walk Begins

❶ Café Roussillon

Standing outside this traditional neighborhood bar/café, survey the neighborhood. In all four directions you'll see the same Baron Haussmann-designed buildings with their uniform height, balconies, and iconic slanted mansard roofs. With ground floors devoted to retail and upper floors housing people, there's a vitality here in the middle of a huge metropolis that you don't find in many American cities. Feel the community: people walking dogs, pushing carriages and dragging shopping carts, and tourists with their roller bags heading in and out. Electric scooters, quick-rent bikes, and motorbikes take up space previously dedicated to parked cars. Electric wires—buried underground—are nowhere to be seen. Paris is a city of neighborhoods. And this one's equipped with my favorite market street—a traffic-free mall serving this community—Rue Cler.

The **Café Roussillion,** with its traditional bar, is a neighborhood fixture. Cafés like this display a sign, required by French law, making it clear that drinks served at the bar are cheaper than drinks served at the tables. The blackboard lists wines sold by the glass, along with other drinks.

Cafés also post a decal on their door (for example, *Edenred restaurant ticket*) reminding local workers they accept lunch coupons. In France, an employee lunch-subsidy program is an expected perk. Thanks to strong tax incentives designed to keep the café culture vital, employers issue coupons or credits for each day an employee works in a month, good for a half-price lunchtime *plat du jour* (daily special). Sack lunches are rare, since a good lunch is sacred...and subsidized.

• *If you're shopping for designer baby clothes, you'll find them across the street at...*

❷ Petit Bateau

The French spend at least as much on their babies as they do on their dogs—dolling them up with designer jammies. This store is one in a popular chain. Little children around here are really sophisticated. (They even speak French.) And they just aren't comfortable unless they're making a fashion statement (such as underwear with sailor stripes).

In the last generation, an aging and shrinking population was a serious problem for Europe's wealthier nations. But France now has one of Europe's biggest baby populations—the French average two children per family, compared to 1.6 for the rest of Europe. Babies are trendy today, and the government rewards parents with big tax incentives for their first two children—and then doubles the incentives after that. Since childcare is subsidized and public school starts at age three, most new mothers get back into the workforce quickly.

Making babies is good business—and revered. Notice how locals give pregnant women the royal treatment: They get priority seating on subways and buses, and they go straight to the front of any line—no waiting on those swollen feet. And the French love to ogle babies. The community celebrates every new addition.

• *Cross Rue de Grenelle to find...*

❸ Au Bon Jardinier ("The Good Gardener") Fruits and Vegetables

Each morning, fresh produce is trucked in from farm fields to Paris' huge Rungis market—Europe's largest, near Orly Airport—and then dispatched to mer-

chants with FedEx-like speed and precision. Good luck finding a shopping bag—locals bring their own two-wheeled carts or reusable bags. The earth-friendly French also resist excessive packaging.

Notice what's local and what's not during your visit. Look at the price of those melons. What's the country of origin? (It must be posted by law.) If they're out of season, they come from Guadeloupe. Many people buy only local products (sticking with produce labeled "Fr" for France). Parisians—who know they eat best by being tuned in to the seasons—shop with their noses. Try it. Smell the cheap foreign strawberries. One sniff of the torpedo-shaped French ones *(gariguettes),* and you know which is better. Locals call those from Belgium "plastic strawberries"—red on the outside, white on the inside. Find the herbs in the back. Is today's delivery in?

The **Franprix** across the street is a small outpost of a nationwide supermarket chain. Opposite Grand Hôtel Lévêque is a *traiteur asiatique.* Fast Asian food-to-go is popular in Paris. These shops—about as common as bakeries—have had an impact on traditional Parisian eating habits.

• *Between the Franprix and Grand Hôtel Lévêque is...*

❹ Le Petit Cler

This small café, a fine choice for a drink or bite with a view, used to be a *tabac* (tobacco shop). It's a good example of how this one working-class market street is becoming increasingly upscale. Not so long ago, only one place on the entire street offered outdoor tables. Then others joined in, each displacing a more humble shop that addressed neighborhood needs. Now some locals regret that these shops are being lost to trendy café crowds.

• *Just past Grand Hôtel Lévêque is...*

❺ Wine Bacchus

Shoppers often visit the neighborhood wine shop last, after they've assembled their meal and are ready to pick the appropriate wine. Wines are classified by region. Most "Parisians" (born elsewhere) have an affinity for the wines of their home region. You can travel

throughout France by taking a spin tour of wines on the shelves. You'll see a locker for the most expensive wines, one small section for foreign wines, and a shelf for craft beers. Many are Belgian beers, but French labels are becoming more common as the French embrace craft brewing. Notice the prices: Most wines are €20 or less, and several sell for under €6. You can get a good bottle for €12. Wines of the month are stacked in the center and are usually great deals. The helpful clerk is a counselor who works with your menu and budget to help you select just the right wine. They can pop a bottle of white wine into "Le Chiller" and have it cooled for you in three minutes—and also equip you with cups for a picnic.

• *Next door, smell the...*

❻ *Fromagerie*

A long, narrow, canopied cheese table brings the *fromagerie* into the street. Wedges, cylinders, balls, and miniature hockey pucks are all powdered white, gray, and burnt marshmallow—it's a festival of mold. The street cart and front window feature both cow *(vache)* and goat *(chèvre)* cheeses. Locals know the shape indicates the region of origin (for example, a pyramid shape indicates a cheese from the Loire). And this is important. Regions create the *terroir* (physical and magical union of sun, soil, and generations of farmer love) that gives the production—whether wine or cheese—its personality. *Oh là là* means you're impressed. If you like cheese, show greater excitement with more *là*s. *Oh là là là là*. A Parisian friend once held the stinkiest glob close to her nose, took an orgasmic breath, and exhaled, "Yes, it smells like zee feet of angels." Go ahead...inhale.

Step inside, say "*bonjour*," and browse through more than 200 types of French cheese. A *fromagerie* is lab-coat serious but friendly. Also known as a *crémerie* or a "BOF" (for *beurre, oeuf,* and *fromage*), this is where people shop for butter, eggs, and cheese. (In fact, notice the circa-1950 photo posted to the right as you step in, showing this very shop when it was named simply "butter and eggs.") Just like wines, quality cheeses need to be aged in the

cool, humid environment of a *cave* (cellar). Under the careful watch of an *affineur* (the "finisher"), some cheeses will rest a few weeks, others for months. Like produce, cheeses are seasonal, as the milk produced by cows or goats changes flavor according to the animal's varied diet. Ask what's in season.

In the back room, the shop keeps *les meules*—big, 170-pound wheels of cheese, made from 250 gallons of milk. The "hard" cheeses are cut from these. Don't eat the skin of these big ones... they're rolled on the floor. But the skin on most smaller cheeses— the Brie, the Camembert—is part of the taste. "It completes the package," says my local friend.

If buying soft cheese, tell the shop when you're planning to eat it—they'll squeeze the cheese to make sure it'll reach *la maturité parfaite* on the day you want to consume it. One of your authors' favorites is Epoisses, from Burgundy.

If you order a set *menu* at dinner tonight, you can take the cheese course just before or instead of dessert. On a good cheese plate you have a hard cheese (perhaps a Comté, similar to a white cheddar), a softer cheese (maybe Brie or Camembert), a bleu cheese, and a goat cheese—ideally from different regions. Because it's strongest, the goat cheese is usually eaten last.

• *Across the street, find the fish shop.*

❼ *Poissonnerie*

Fresh fish is brought into Paris daily from ports on the English Channel, 110 miles away. In fact, fish here is likely fresher than in many towns closer to the sea, because Paris is a commercial hub (from here, it's shipped to outlying towns). Anything wiggling? This *poissonnerie*, like all such shops, was upgraded to meet Europe-wide hygiene standards. Because fishermen don't fish on Sunday and freshness is not optional, this shop is closed on Monday.

• *Next door, under the awning (get close to see), is a particularly tempting Rue Cler storefront.*

❽ No More Horse Meat

The mosaics and glass set over the doorway advertise horse meat: *Boucherie Chevaline*. While you'll no longer find horse meat here, the classy old storefront survives. Created in the 1930s and signed by the artist, it's a work of art fit for a museum— but it belongs right here, and that's where it will stay.

• *A few steps farther, across the street, is...*

❾ A la Mère de Famille Confectionery

This shop has been in the neighborhood for 30 years. The owner sells modern treats but has always kept the traditional candies, too.

"The old ladies, they want the same sweets that made them so happy 80 years ago," she says. You can buy chocolate by the piece (about €1 each). You're welcome to assemble a small assortment.

Until a few years ago, the chocolate was dipped and decorated right on the premises. As was the tradition in Rue Cler shops, the merchants resided and produced in the back and sold in the front.

• *Next door is the neighborhood's...*

❿ Oldest Building and Charcuterie-Traiteur Jeusselin

Rue Cler's oldest building is at #37—the one with the two garret windows on the roof. It's from the early 1800s, when this street was part of a village near Paris and lined with structures like this. Over the years, Paris engulfed these surrounding villages—and now the street is a mishmash of architectural styles.

Occupying the ground floor of this house is Charcuterie-Traiteur Jeusselin. *Traiteurs* (people who "treat" food) sell mouthwatering deli food to go. Because Parisian kitchens are so small, these gourmet delis are handy, even for those who cook. Home chefs can concentrate on creating the main course and then buy beautifully prepared side dishes to complete a fine dinner.

Charcuteries by definition are pork butchers, specializing in sausage, pâté, and ham. The charcuterie business is fiercely competitive in France, with countless cooking contests allowing owners to test their products and show off their skills. Jeusselin proudly displays its hard-earned diplomas on its back walls (right side) and hard-won awards on the right side of the storefront. Even with such accolades, many charcuteries have had to add *traiteur* services to survive. They're now selling prepared dishes, pastries, and wines to-go.

The photogenic Italian *charcuterie-traiteur* **Davoli** sits right across Rue Cler. Each day these two places go *tête à tête*, cooking up *plats du jour*.

Both charcuteries put out their best stuff just before lunch and dinner. If you want a roasted chicken off the spit, pick one up—cooked and hot—at 11:00 or at 17:00, when Parisians buy provisions for that day's meals. Note the system: Order, take your ticket to the cashier to pay, and return with the receipt to pick up your food.

• *The ice cream shop next door to Jeusselin,* **Glacier Artisan Martine Lambert,** *serves what many locals consider Paris' best ice cream. A few paces from here you'll find...*

⓫ Café du Marché and More

Café du Marché, on the corner, is *the* place to sit and enjoy the action (see listing in Eating in Paris, on page 438). It's Rue Cler's

living room, where locals gather before heading home, many staying for a relaxed and affordable dinner. The owner has priced his menu so that residents can afford to dine out on a regular basis, and it works—many patrons eat here five days a week.

For a reasonable meal, grab a chair and check the chalk menu listing the *plat du jour*. Notice how the no-indoor-smoking laws have made outdoor seating a huge hit.

Across Rue Cler, the sterile **Aldi grocery store** sells at discount prices. Because storage space is so limited in Parisian apartments, bulk purchases (à la Costco) are unlikely to become a big deal here. The latest shopping trend is to stock up on nonperishables online, pick up produce three times a week, and buy fresh bread daily. Compare this storefront with the elegance of the other shops on this street. Its *moderne* exterior suggests some corruption around the building permit. Normally, any proposed building modification on Rue Cler must undergo a rigorous design review before the owner obtains the required permit.

City Hall is enthusiastic about making the town bike-friendly. Notice the **loaner bikes** parked in the Vélib' rack. There are many of these self-service stands around town (for more on using this system, see www.velib-metropole.fr). The system is intended to let people take short one-way rides by bike.

• *From Café du Marché, hook right and side-trip a couple of doors down Rue du Champ de Mars to visit...*

⓬ L'Epicerie Fine

A fine-foods boutique like this stands out because of its gentle owners, Pascal and Nathalie. Their mission in life is to explain to travelers, in fluent English, what the French

RUE CLER

Le French Kiss *(Faire la Bise)*

You can't miss the cheek pecking in Paris. It's contagious—and (even after the pandemic) it's how Parisians greet each other. Here's the skinny.

You won't see any American-style hugging in Paris; that's far too aggressive for the French. What you will see between acquaintances is a public display of proffered cheeks and puckered lips when saying hello and goodbye. Observe. The lips don't actually touch the cheek—only the cheeks touch, and a gentle kiss noise is made (except when parents kiss children). You usually start by going left (so the right cheeks almost touch), then alternate to the right. The number of times varies with the region or circumstances—two, three, or four kisses. Different regions kiss a different number of times. Parisians *faire la bise* in social settings but rarely in the workplace. When being introduced for the first time (at a dinner party, for example), women kiss women, men kiss women, but men shake hands with other men. If you haven't seen someone in a long while, Parisians often double the standard two kisses into four.

How many kisses are appropriate for an American? If it happens to you, my recommendation is to go for two with confidence, and then—hover and wait.

fuss over food is all about. They'll tempt you with fine gourmet treats, Berthillon ice cream, and generous tastes of caramel, balsamic vinegar, and French and Italian olive oils. Their salted caramels from Normandy and small jars of mustards and jams make good souvenirs.

Across the street is a **real estate agency** advertising condos and apartments for rent or sale. The touch screen in the window gives the details: the arrondissement (neighborhood, indicated by the number after "Paris" in the address), whether it's an apartment for rent *(location)* or a condo for sale *(vente)*, how many rooms *(pieces*—includes living and family rooms), square meters (25 square meters is about the size of a spacious hotel room), and the monthly rent or sales price.

• *Return to Rue Cler. The neighborhood bakery on the corner is often marked by a line of people waiting to pick up their daily baguette.*

⓭ Artisan Boulangerie

Since the French Revolution, the government has regulated the cost of a basic baguette (meaning "wand" or "stick" of bread). By law, it must weigh 250 grams and consist of only four ingredients: flour, yeast, salt, and water. Parisians specify their preferences when they place a *boulangerie* order—some like their baguette well done, and others prefer it more doughy. More than one trip a day to the bakery is *normale* in Paris, as a good baguette can become stale in a matter of hours. To keep it fresh, wrap it in a cloth, never a plastic bag.

Locals debate the merits of Paris' many *boulangeries*, often remaining loyal to their local bread-baker. *Boulangeries* must make their bread on the premises (otherwise, they can't be called a *boulangerie*). Most hotels won't serve breakfast until the corner bakery opens, to avoid having to set out yesterday's bread and croissants for their guests. Each spring, the city hosts a competition for the Best Baguette of Paris. The top prize? A cash award of €4,000 and the honor of providing the French president with baguettes for the coming year. This annual contest is the equivalent of Michelin's star system for bakeries.

It's said that a baker cannot be good at both bread and pastry—at cooking school, they generally major in one or the other. A *Boulangerie* diploma covers bread and *viennoiserie*, which includes all the breakfast items (croissants, *pain au chocolat*, and so on), and these bakers usually do *tartes* and anything with *choux* pastry (éclairs, for example). If you get a *Pâtisserie* diploma, your forte is pastries like *macarons* and fancy creamy cakes and chocolate creations. You can usually tell whether a *boulanger* or *pâtissier* runs a place by what a shop has more of—and what's selling best.

At Artisan Boulangerie, the baker has bucked the trend, demonstrating equal skill at the two specialties. But Rue Cler regulars worry that his new stand selling food to-go will distract him from what he does best—making top-quality bread and delicious pastries. And the new top-quality Ladurée pastry shop next door may draw some of his clients away.

• *A bit farther along is...*

⓮ Mephisto Shoe Store

Shoe stores are almost as popular as bakeries in this city of footwear-loving fashionistas. (French-made Mephistos are cheaper here than in the US.) You may see the locals checking out your "foreign" shoes. In a city where many people don't have cars, good shoes matter. The average Parisian's daily life is active: walking to the Métro, to lunch, to the shops after work, and then home (probably up several flights of stairs). No need for the gym with this routine. (Hence, gyms here are rare, expensive, and not well maintained.)

• *Across the street is...*

⑮ Cler Fleurs and Butcher Shop

Almost all Parisians who reside in the city center live in apartments or condos. Even the biggest, most luxury-laden city home shares walls with neighbors and has no yard. A lucky few may have access to a courtyard, but almost no one has a private garden. Parisians spend small fortunes bringing nature into their homes with plants and fresh flower arrangements. Notice the flower boxes on balconies—you work with what you have. When visiting friends in Paris, it's *de rigueur* to give a gift of flowers, and it's good form to have them delivered before you show up. Avoid chrysanthemums, as they are reserved for funerals.

Pop into the **butcher shop** a few doors down for a graphic peek at the meat Parisians are eating. Check out the chalkboard listing nine cuts of beef *(boeuf)*, three kinds of veal *(veau)*, four cuts of pork *(porc)*, and three cuts of lamb *(agneau)*. This meat cutter replaced a longtime butcher who recently retired (and is putting a fright into locals). Traditional butchery is struggling to survive in France, as the younger generation no longer considers it a "desirable" career option, but it continues on Rue Cler.

• *Walk on to the end of Rue Cler, where it hits a bigger street flooded with cars and buses.*

⑯ City Info Post

An electronic signpost (10 feet up) directs residents to websites for local information—transportation changes, surveys, employment opportunities, community events, and so on. Notice the big glass recycling bin nearby and the see-through garbage sacks. In the 1990s, Paris suffered a rash of trash-can bombings. Bad guys hid rigged camp-stove canisters in metal garbage cans, which shredded into deadly "shrapnel" when they exploded. City authorities solved this by replacing metal cans with translucent bags.

• *Across the busy Avenue de la Motte-Picquet is a* tabac.

⑰ Tabac La Cave à Cigares

Just as the US has liquor stores licensed to sell booze, the only place for people over 18 to buy tobacco legally in France is at a *tabac* (tah-bah) counter. Tobacco counters like this one are a much-appreciated fixture of each neighborhood, offering lots of services (and an insight into the local culture). Even nonsmokers enjoy perusing the wares at a *tabac*. Notice how European laws require a bold warning sign on cigarettes, with graphic, often grotesque photos—about half the size of the package—proclaiming, bluntly, *fumer tue* (smoking kills).

Tabacs serve their neighborhoods as a kind of government cash desk. All sell stamps and some sell public-transit tickets. Like back home, the LOTO is a big deal—and a lucrative way for the government to tax poor and less-educated people.

American smokers may not be able to resist the temptation to pick up a *petit* Habana cigar—your chance to buy a fine Cuban stogie.

• *Appropriately, next door you'll find a...*

⑱ Pharmacy

In France, as in much of Europe, pharmacists are the first point of contact for people who are ill. They make the first diagnosis and have the authority to prescribe certain drugs (and more recently, Covid tests and vaccines). If it's out of their league, they'll recommend a doctor. Pharmacies are also the only place to get many basic medical items, such as aspirin and simple reading glasses.

Inside, you'll notice locals handing over a green ID the size of a credit card, with an embedded chip and a photo. This is the essential *Carte Vitale,* the French health insurance card. The national health-care system, *Sécurité Sociale,* pays about 75 percent of pharmacy, doctor, and hospital bills. Private employer-related insurance, a *Mutuelle,* covers a varying amount of the rest. Filling a prescription is often completely covered. The last time the World Health Organization ranked health-care systems by country, France came out on top. The French are deservedly proud of their nationalized health care. But budget shortfalls are forcing the government to cut back on parts of France's social safety net. If there's a strike during your trip, it likely has to do with the erosion of such benefits.

You may notice "sexy" ads in pharmacies, as well as more public displays of affection among Parisian couples than you're accustomed to. The French are less inhibited about sex than Americans. In France, sex is approached from a practical perspective. Back in the 1990s, when France's president, François Mitterrand, was the focus of a sex scandal (similar to the one that embroiled Bill Clinton), his infamous response to the prying press was simply, *"Et alors?"* (So what?). The French generally agreed. They like to say, "If he's good behind his desk, that's what matters."

• *Step back onto the sidewalk and consider this.*

Walking down Rue Cler offers a window into how Paris charmingly combines a vibrant present with an ever-present past. A city of more than two million people—with all the complexity and challenges that brings—is organized in a way that maintains the refined culture that defines 21st-century France. History

RUE CLER

is all around you: Walk two blocks in one direction, down Avenue de la Motte-Picquet, and you'll be on a former military parade grounds leading to the Eiffel Tower, built to celebrate the centennial of the great revolution that ended the concept of  divine monarchs. Walk two blocks the other way, and under a glittering dome, you'll find the tomb of Napoleon, the emperor who centralized the French government in ways that endure to this day.

And all around you, the modern world fits into the 19th-century parameters laid out by Haussmann: Cars give way to buses, bikes, and pedestrians; modern buildings are folded into the eight-story limits still enforced by the city government; and residences sit above ground-floor shops and restaurants, ensuring high population density to keep things vibrant day and night. Rue Cler is just one in a vast collection of neighborhoods that together make up Paris—a city as vital today as it has been for centuries.

• *Your walk is done. I'm headed back to the bakery. If you bought a picnic along this walk, here are two good places to enjoy it: Leaving Rue Cler, turn left on Avenue de la Motte-Picquet for the Army Museum (find the small park after crossing Boulevard de la Tour Maubourg). Or, turn right to reach the Champ de Mars park (and the Eiffel Tower). Or if you're ready to move on, the Ecole Militaire Métro stop is just down Avenue de la Motte-Picquet to the right.*

EIFFEL TOWER TOUR

La Tour Eiffel

It's crowded, expensive, and there are probably better views in Paris, but visiting this 1,000-foot-tall ornament is unforgettable—and well worth the trouble. Visitors to Paris may find *Mona Lisa* to be less than expected, but the Eiffel Tower rarely disappoints, even in an era of skyscrapers. This is a once-in-a-lifetime, I've-been-there experience. Making the eye-popping ascent and ear-popping descent gives you membership into the exclusive society of the quarter of a billion other humans who have made the Eiffel Tower the most visited monument in the modern world.

Orientation

Cost: €27 to ride two elevators all the way to the top (third) level, €17.50 to ride to the first or second level, €11 to climb the stairs to the first or second level, €21 to take the stairs and then elevator to the summit—must purchase summit elevator before entering tower, 50 percent cheaper for those under 25, 75 percent cheaper for those under 12, not covered by Museum Pass.

Hours: Daily mid-June-Aug 9:00-24:45, Sept-mid-June 9:30-23:45, last ascent to top by elevator at 22:30 and to lower levels at 23:00 all year (stairs same except Sept-mid-June last ascent 18:30). The top level can close temporarily in windy weather or, more commonly, when it reaches capacity. If you've purchased a ticket to the top, you will be allowed to go unless the weather is dangerous.

Information: www.toureiffel.paris.

Advance Tickets Recommended: If you plan to ascend by elevator, it's strongly advised to book a reservation online (any ticket that includes the stairs can only be purchased on-site).

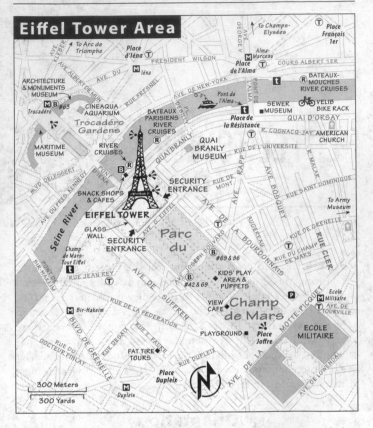

Eiffel Tower Area

Booking online allows you to reserve an entry time and skip the (usually long) ticket-buying line at no extra cost (though all must wait in line at security check).

Online ticket sales open up 60 days before any given date (at 8:30 Paris time)—and can quickly sell out (especially for April-Sept). Be sure of your date and time, as reservations are nonrefundable. If no slots are available, try buying a "Lift entrance ticket with access to 2nd floor"—the view from the second floor is arguably better anyway. Or, try the website again about a week before your visit—last-minute spots sometimes open up. To go all the way to the top, select "Lift entrance ticket with access to the summit."

You can print your tickets (follow the specifications carefully) or download e-tickets to your phone. Note that email or text confirmations alone will not get you in; you must have the printed or electronic ticket showing the bar code.

Buying Tickets On-Site: On occasion it's possible to just drop by, buy a ticket, and go directly up the tower. But you're much more likely to find yourself in horrible lines. Crowds over-whelm this place much of the year, with one- to two-hour waits (unless it's rainy, when lines evaporate). Weekends and holidays are worst.

If you don't have a reservation, arrive at least 30 minutes before the tower opens to pass security (security opens 30 minutes before the tower),  then immediately get in line to buy a ticket. Going much later in the day is the next-best bet (after 19:00 May-Aug, after 17:00 off-season, after 16:00 in winter as it gets dark by 17:00).

Once in line, estimate about 20 minutes for every 100 yards.

When you buy tickets on-site, all members of your party must be with you. To get reduced fares for kids, bring ID.

More Options for Avoiding Lines: You can bypass some lines with a reservation at either of the tower's view restaurants or for a concert (see below for details). Or you can buy a "Skip the Line" tour (almost right up to the last minute) through Fat Tire Tours (see page 49).

When to Go: For the best of all worlds, arrive with enough light to see the views, then stay as it gets dark to see the lights. At the top of the hour, a five-minute display features thousands of sparkling lights (best viewed from Place du Trocadéro or the grassy park below).

Concerts on the Eiffel Tower: Concerts (mostly classical) take place throughout the year on the Eiffel Tower's first floor in the Salon Gustave Eiffel (about €75, includes priority access ticket to first floor, www.classictic.com/en/special/eiffel-tower).

Getting There: The tower is about a 10-minute walk from the Métro (Bir-Hakeim or Trocadéro stops) or suburban train (RER/Train-C Champ de Mars-Tour Eiffel stop). The Ecole Militaire Métro stop in the Rue Cler area is 20 minutes away. Buses #42, #69, and #86 stop nearby on Avenue Joseph Bouvard in the Champ de Mars park.

Getting In: For security, the perimeter of the tower is surrounded by glass walls. So, while it's free to enter the area directly under the tower, to do so you must pass through an airport-like **security check** (allow 30 minutes or more at busy times). Entry points are at the southeast and southwest corners of the tower, just off Avenue Gustave-Eiffel; see the map on page 236.

Once through security, you enter the vast area under the

Eating at or near the Eiffel Tower

The tower has two classy restaurants that offer great views: 58 Tour Eiffel (on the first level) and Le Jules Verne (on the second level). Making a reservation at either one lets you skip the initial elevator line—your reservation includes a ride to the restaurant level. But you can't skip security lines and you can't ascend more than 15-30 minutes prior to your reservation time (though you can linger afterward). Get details online when you book. Last-minute reservations for both restaurants may be available from their info kiosk at the tower's base, between the north and east pillars.

$$$$ 58 Tour Eiffel, reopening in 2022 after a renovation, offers breakfast, lunch, dinner, and a lounge bar for drinks and a light menu. The dining room is reserved for more serious eating (though lunches are more casual). Reserve long in advance, especially if you want a view (+33 1 72 76 18 46, www.restaurants-toureiffel.com). No jeans or tennis shoes, please, at dinner.

The more expensive **$$$$ Le Jules Verne** restaurant has one Michelin star and a higher viewpoint from its second-level perch (lunch *menus* start at about €150, dinner *menus* start at about €200, daily 12:00-13:00 & 19:00-21:00). In summer, reserve weeks in advance for dinner; off-season or lunch anytime is easier. This is a dressy place—no shorts or overly casual sportswear (+33 1 45 55 61 44, www.lejulesverne-paris.com).

Other Options

The tower's base offers not much more than sandwich stands. The first and second levels have small sandwich-and-pizza cafés. The first floor occasionally has temporary "pop-up" restaurants—open only for a season—that enliven the cuisine scene. At the very top of the tower, a champagne bar serves glasses of bubbly.

Rue Cler, with many options, is a 20-minute walk away (see the Eating in Paris chapter). Avenue de la Bourdonnais, a block east of the tower, has a few eateries and sandwich shops. Snack shops and cafés on the river by the cruise boats offer cheap sandwiches and full meals with tower views. Moored to the embankment, **Le Bal de la Marine** is an old-fashioned boat with great seating in and out and reasonably priced drinks (daily, Port de Suffren, www.baldelamarine.com). **$$ Café Jacques,** in the garden at the nearby Quai Branly Museum, is a good but relatively pricey choice (see page 79).

Your tastiest option may be to assemble a picnic beforehand from any of several handy shops near Métro stop Ecole Militaire and picnic in the Champ de Mars park (on the side grassy areas or on benches along the central grass; the middle stretch may be off-limits).

EIFFEL TOWER

tower (where the view straight up the underbelly of the tower is very cool). This is where you'll line up for an elevator (or buy tickets if you haven't already).

If you have a reservation, arrive at the tower at least 30 minutes before your entry time to pass security. Once you're through, elevator entrances are at three of the tower's four pillars (though not all may be open for your visit). Look for an entrance with green signs showing *Visiteurs avec Reservation* (Visitors with Reservation), where attendants scan your ticket and put you on the first available elevator.

Without an elevator reservation, after passing security, go directly to the yellow-bannered ticket booth (follow signs for *Individuels* or *Visiteurs sans Tickets*). Avoid lines selling tickets only for *Groupes*. If two entrances are marked *Visiteurs sans Tickets,* pick the shortest line. Once you get your ticket, find the line with your time slot indicated. For more tips, see "Buying Tickets On-Site," earlier.

Stair walkers buy their tickets directly at the south pillar, which is for stair access only.

Length of This Tour: If you have reservations and crowds are light, the quickest you could get to the top and back (with minimal sightseeing) would be 90 minutes. Otherwise, budget three to four hours to wait in line, get to the top, and sightsee your way back down. With limited time or money, skip "the summit" (the views from the second level are actually better).

Pickpockets: Beware. Street thieves plunder awestruck visitors gawking below the tower. And tourists in crowded elevators are like fish in a barrel for predatory pickpockets. *En garde.* A police station is at the Jules Verne pillar.

Security Check: Bags larger than 19" × 8" × 12" are not allowed, but there is no baggage check. All bags are subject to a security search. No knives, glass bottles, or cans are permitted.

Services: The Eiffel Tower information office is at the west pillar. Free WCs are at the base of the tower, behind the east pillar. Inside the tower itself, WCs are on all levels, but they're small, with long lines.

Best Views of the Tower: The best place to view the tower is from Place du Trocadéro to the north. It's a 15-minute walk across the river to the top of the viewpoint; it's a happening scene at night, and especially fun for kids. Consider arriving at the Trocadéro Métro stop for the view, then walking toward the tower. Another delightful viewpoint is from the Champ de Mars park to the south. The pedestrian bridge a few blocks upriver near the Quai Branly Museum also offers terrific tower views.

Starring: All of Paris...and beyond.

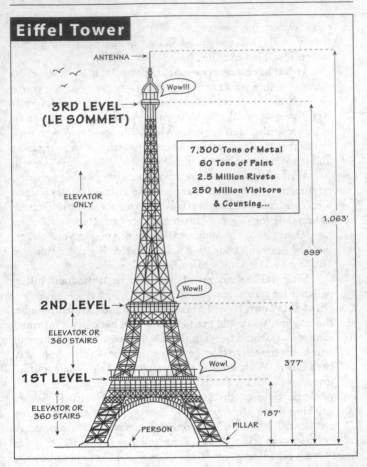

Eiffel Tower

ANTENNA →

Wow!!!

3RD LEVEL (LE SOMMET) →

7,300 Tons of Metal
60 Tons of Paint
2.5 Million Rivets
250 Million Visitors
& Counting...

ELEVATOR ONLY

1,063'

899'

Wow!!

2ND LEVEL →

ELEVATOR OR 360 STAIRS

377'

1ST LEVEL →

Wow!

ELEVATOR OR 360 STAIRS

187'

PERSON →   PILLAR

OVERVIEW

There are three observation platforms, at roughly 200, 400, and 900 feet. Although being on the windy top of the Eiffel Tower is a thrill you'll never forget, the view is better from the second level, where you can actually see Paris' monuments. The first level also has nice views, plus more tourist-oriented sights and a concert hall. All three levels have some displays, WCs, souvenir stores, and a few other services.

For the hardy, stairs lead from the ground level up to the first and second levels—and rarely have a long line. It's 360 stairs to the first level and another 360 to the second. The staircase is enclosed with a wire

EIFFEL TOWER

cage, so you can't fall, but those with vertigo issues may still find them dizzying.

If you want to see the entire tower, from top to bottom, then see it...from top to bottom. There isn't a single elevator straight to the top *(le sommet)*. To get there, you'll first ride an elevator (or hike up the stairs) to the second level. (Some elevators stop on the first level, but don't get off—it's more efficient to see the first level on the way down). Once on the second level, immediately line up for the next elevator, to the top. (Look for the shortest line; there are several elevators and feeder queues.) Enjoy the views from the "summit," then ride back down to the second level. Frolic there for a while, and when you're ready, head to the first level via the stairs (no line and can take as little as five minutes) or take the elevator down. Explore the shops and exhibits on the first level. To leave, you can line up for the elevator, but it's quickest and most memorable to take the stairs back down to earth.

The Tour Begins

Gaze up at the tower towering above you, and don't even think about what would happen if someone dropped a coin from the top.

Exterior

Delicate and graceful when seen from afar, the Eiffel Tower is massive—even a bit scary—close up. You don't appreciate its size until you walk toward it; like a mountain, it seems so close but takes forever to reach.

The tower, including its antenna, stands 1,063 feet tall, or slightly higher than the 77-story Chrysler Building in New York. Its four support pillars straddle an area of 3.5 acres. Despite the tower's 7,300 tons of metal and 60 tons of paint, it is so well engineered that it weighs no more per square inch at its base than a linebacker on tiptoes.

Once the world's tallest structure, it's now eclipsed by a number of towers (Tokyo Skytree, 2,080 feet, for one), radio antennae (KVLY-TV mast, North Dakota, 2,063 feet), and skyscrapers (Burj Khalifa in Dubai, UAE, 2,717 feet). France's sleek Le Viaduc de Millau, a 1.5-mile-long suspension bridge completed in late 2004, also has a taller tower (1,125 feet). The consortium that built the bridge included the same company that erected the Eiffel Tower.

The long green lawn stretching south of the tower is the Champ de Mars, originally the training ground for troops and students of the nearby military school (Ecole Militaire) and now a park. On the north side, across the Seine, is the curved palace colonnade framing a square called the Trocadéro.

Building the Tower

As you ascend through the metal beams, imagine being a worker, perched high above nothing, riveting this thing together. It was a massive project, and it took all the ingenuity of the Industrial Age—including mass production, cutting-edge technology, and capitalist funding.

The foundation was the biggest obstacle. The soil, especially along the river, was too muddy to support big pillars. Gustave Eiffel drew on his bridge-building experience, where support piers needed to be constructed underwater. He sank heavy, bottomless compartments (caissons) into the wet soil. These were watertight and injected with breathable air, so workers could dig out the mud beneath them, allowing the caisson to sink farther. When the workers were done, the hole was filled in with cement 20 feet thick and capped with stone. The massive iron pillars were sunk into the ground at an angle, anchored in the subterranean stone.

The tower went up like an 18,000-piece erector set, made of 15-foot iron beams held together with 2.5 million rivets. The pieces were mass-produced in factories in the suburbs and brought in on wagons. For two years, 300 workers assembled the pieces, the tower rising as they went. First, they used wooden scaffolding to support the lower (angled) sections, until the pillars came togeth-

History

The first visitor to the Paris World's Fair in 1889 walked beneath the "arch" formed by the newly built Eiffel Tower and entered the fairgrounds. This event celebrated both the centennial of the French Revolution and France's position as a global superpower. Bridge builder Gustave Eiffel (1832-1923) won the contest to build the fair's centerpiece by beating out rival proposals such as a giant guillotine.

Eiffel deserved to have the tower named for him. He did much more than design it. He oversaw its entire construction, personally financed it, and was legally on the hook if the project floundered. His factory produced the iron beams, and his workers built it, using cranes and apparatus designed by

er and the tower could support itself. Then the iron beams were lifted up with steam-powered cranes, including some on tracks

(creeper cranes) that inched up the pillars as the tower progressed. There, daring workers dangled from rope ladders, balanced on beams, and tightrope-walked their way across them as they put the pieces in place. The workers then hammered in red-hot rivets made on-site by blacksmiths. As the rivets cooled, they solidified the structure.

After a mere year and a half, the tower surpassed what had been the tallest structure in the world—the Washington Monument (555 feet), which had taken 36 years to build.

The tower was painted a rusty red. Since then, it's sported several colors, including mustard and the current brown-gray. It is repainted every seven years (it takes 25 full-time painters 18 months to apply 60 tons of paint by hand—no spraying allowed).

Two years, two months, and five days after construction began, the tower was done. On May 15, 1889, a red, white, and blue beacon was lit on the top, the World's Fair began, and the tower carried its first astounded visitor to the top.

Eiffel. Facing a deadline for the exposition, he brought in the project on time and under budget.

The tower was nothing but a showpiece, with no functional purpose except to demonstrate to the world that France had the

wealth, knowledge, and can-do spirit to erect a structure far taller than anything the world had ever seen. The original plan was to dismantle the tower as quickly as it was built after the celebration ended, but it was kept by popular demand.

To a generation hooked on technology, the tower was the marvel of the age, a symbol of progress and human ingenuity. Not all were so impressed, however; many found it a monstrosity. The writer Guy de Maupassant (1850-1893) routinely ate lunch in the tower just so he wouldn't have to look at it.

In subsequent years, the tower has come to serve many functions: as a radio transmitter (1909-present), a cosmic-ray observatory (1910), a billboard (spelling "Citroën" in lights, 1925-1934), a broadcaster of Nazi TV programs (1940-1944), a fireworks launch pad (numerous times), and a framework for dazzling lighting displays, including the current arrangement, designed in 2000 for the celebration of the millennium.

• *To reach the top, ride the elevator or walk (720 stairs) to the second level. From there, get in line for the next elevator and continue to the top. Pop out 900 feet above the ground. (Note: You'll likely hear noisy alarms jolting the atmosphere. These go off when too many crowd into the elevator.)*

Third Level *(Le Sommet)*

You'll find wind and grand, sweeping views on the tiny top level. The city lies before you (pick out sights with the help of the panoramic maps). On a good day, you can see for 40 miles. Do a 360-degree tour of Paris.

Looking west *(ouest):* The Seine runs east to west (though at this point it's flowing more southwest). At the far end of the skinny "island" in the river, find the tiny copy of the Statue of Liberty, looking 3,633 miles away to her big sister in New York. Gustave Eiffel, a man of many talents, also designed the internal supports of New York's Statue of Liberty, which was cast in copper by fellow Frenchman Frederic Bartholdi (1886).

Looking north *(nord):* At your feet is the curved arcade of the Trocadéro, itself the site of a World's Fair in 1878. Beyond that is the vast, forested expanse of the Bois de Boulogne, the three-square-mile park that hosts joggers and *boules* players by day and prostitutes by night. That angular glassy structure rising from the center of the green expanse is the Louis Vuitton Foundation modern art museum and cultural center, designed by Frank Gehry and opened in 2014.

The track with bleachers (on the left end of the park) is Paris' horseracing track, the Hippodrome de Longchamp. In the far distance are the skyscrapers of La Défense. Find the Arc de Triomphe to the right of the Trocadéro. The lone skyscraper between the Arc and the Trocadéro is the Palais des Congrès, a complex that hosts international conferences, trade shows, and major concerts.

Looking east *(est):* At your feet are the Seine and its many bridges, including the Pont Alexandre, with its four golden statues.

Looking farther upstream, find the Orsay Museum, the Louvre, Pont Neuf, and the twin towers of Notre-Dame. On the Right Bank (which is to your left), find the Grand Palais (with its huge iron-and-glass roof), next to the Pont Alexandre. Beyond the Grand Palais is the bullet-shaped dome of Sacré-Cœur, atop Butte Montmartre.

Looking south *(sud):* In a line, find the Champ de Mars, the Ecole Militaire, the Y-shaped UNESCO building, and the 689-foot Montparnasse Tower skyscraper. To the left is the golden dome of Les Invalides marking Napoleon's tomb, and beyond that, just past the green Luxembourg Garden, is the state-capitol-shaped dome of the Panthéon.

The tippy top: Ascend another short staircase to the open-air top. Look up at all the satellite dishes and communications equipment (and around to find the tiny WC). You'll see the small apartment given to Gustave Eiffel, who's now represented by a mannequin (he's the one with the beard).

The mannequins re-create the moment during the 1889 World's Fair when the American Thomas Edison paid a visit to his fellow techie, Gustave (and Gustave's daughter Claire), presenting them with his new invention, a phonograph. (Then they cranked it up and blasted The Who's "I Can See for Miles.") Feeling proud you made it this high? You can celebrate your accomplishment with a glass of champagne from the bar.

• *Ride the elevator down to the...*

Second Level

The second level (400 feet) has the best views because you're closer to the sights, and the monuments are more recognizable. (For a review of this view, refer to the descriptions given above.) The second level has souvenir shops, WCs, and a small stand-up café.

The world-class Le Jules Verne restaurant is on this level, but you won't see it; access is by a private elevator. The head chef is

Up and Down

The tower—which was designed from the start to accommodate hordes of visitors—has always had elevators. Today's elevators are modern replacements. Back in the late 19th century, elevator technology was so new that this was the one job that Gustave Eiffel subcontracted to other experts (including an American company). They needed a special design to accommodate the angle of the tower's pillars. Today's elevators make about 100 round-trip journeys a day.

There are 1,665 stairs to the top level, though tourists can only climb 720 of them, up as far as the second level. During a race in 1905, a gentleman climbed from the ground to the second level—elevation gain nearly 400 feet—in 3 minutes, 12 seconds.

currently Frédéric Anton, one of the most revered chefs in France today. One would hope his brand of haute cuisine matches the 400-foot haute of the restaurant.

• *Catch the elevator. (There are two different departure lines, so choose the one with the shorter wait.) Or take 360 steps down to the...*

First Level

The first level (200 feet) has more great views, all well described by the tower's panoramic displays. There's really not much here: a

small concert hall, a restaurant, and a public hall with a café, shop, and little theater. Pop-up restaurants and kiosks appear with every season—even a little playground for kids. In winter, part of the first level is often set up to host an ice-skating rink.

The highlight is the breathtaking, vertigo-inducing, selfie-inspiring **glass floor.** Venture onto it and experience what it's like to stand atop an 18-story building and look straight down. Then look up at the massive structure around you. Check out your fellow visitors—the crowds may make the place a total zoo, but everyone's still thrilled.

The Salon Gustave Eiffel is a private reception hall that hosts occasional concerts.

Explore the various exhibits (which change often). A continuously running film (in the glass-walled Ferrié Pavilion) shows a  montage of the tower's construction, paint job, place in pop culture, and guts and glory. As you wander the first floor, you may find exhibits on the tower's past, jobs there, other creations by Monsieur Eiffel, or the tower's famous visitors—from Adolph Hitler to Katy Perry. You might learn how the sun warms the tower's metal, causing the top to expand and lean about five inches away from the sun, or how the tower oscillates slightly in the wind. Because of its lacy design, even the strongest of winds can't blow the tower down, but only cause it to sway a few inches. In fact, Eiffel designed the tower primarily with wind resistance in mind, wanting a structure seemingly "molded by the action of the wind itself."

• *To return to the bottom, take either the elevator or the stairs (five minutes, 360 steps). The stairs are generally much quicker.*

Back on the Ground

Welcome back to earth. After you've climbed the tower, you come to appreciate it even more from a distance. For a final look, stroll  across the river to Place du Trocadéro or to the end of the Champ de Mars and look back for great views. However impressive it may be by day, the tower is an awesome thing to behold at twilight, when it becomes engorged with light, and virile Paris lies back and lets night be on top. When darkness fully envelops the city, the tower seems to climax with a spectacular light show at the top of each hour...for five glorious minutes.

• *Near the tower, you can catch a boat for a Seine cruise (see page 48), start my Bus #69 Sightseeing Tour, or rent a bike and cruise the car-free riverside promenade, which starts on the south side of the river near here and stretches all the way to Place de la Bastille (see map on page 68). The Trocadéro viewpoint, which looks "right there," is a good 15-minute walk away. Also nearby are the Quai Branly Museum and the Rue Cler area. The Army Museum/Napoleon's Tomb and the Rodin Museum are each about a 25-minute walk from here.*

EIFFEL TOWER

RODIN MUSEUM TOUR

Musée Rodin

Auguste Rodin (1840-1917) was a modern Michelangelo, sculpting human figures on an epic scale, revealing through their bodies his deepest thoughts and feelings. Like many of Michelangelo's unfinished works, Rodin's statues rise from the raw stone around them, driven by the life force. With missing limbs and scarred skin, these are prefab classics, making ugliness noble. Rodin's people are always moving restlessly. Even the famous *Thinker* is moving; while he's plopped down solidly, his mind is a million miles away.

The museum presents a full range of Rodin's work, housed in a historic mansion and its gardens where the artist once lived and worked.

Orientation

Cost: €13, free for those under 18, free on the first Sun of the month Oct-March, €24 combo-ticket with Orsay Museum, both museum and gardens covered by Museum Pass. Your ticket or Museum Pass also covers any special exhibits.

Lines are rarely a problem here, but if you have a Museum Pass or a ticket purchased online (€1 fee), you can bypass both the line for buying tickets and the one for entering the museum building. Everyone must pass through a (sometimes slow) security check.

Hours: Tue-Sun 10:00-18:30, closed Mon; Oct-March garden closes at dusk.

RODIN

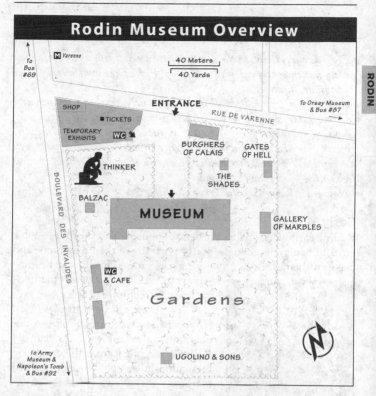

Rodin Museum Overview

Ⓜ *Varenne*

To Bus #69

40 Meters
40 Yards

ENTRANCE

RUE DE VARENNE

To Orsay Museum & Bus #87

SHOP

■ TICKETS

TEMPORARY EXHIBITS

WC

THINKER

BALZAC

BOULEVARD DES INVALIDES

BURGHERS OF CALAIS

GATES OF HELL

THE SHADES

MUSEUM

GALLERY OF MARBLES

WC & CAFE

Gardens

To Army Museum & Napoleon's Tomb & Bus #92

UGOLINO & SONS

Information: +33 1 44 18 61 10, www.musee-rodin.fr.

When to Go: The museum is busiest 11:00-13:00, on weekends, and on rainy days (when the building is packed and the gardens are unpleasant). Note that if you are tight on time and money, several good statues by Rodin can be seen at the Orsay.

Getting There: It's at 77 Rue de Varenne, near the Army Museum and Napoleon's Tomb (Mo: Varenne). Bus #69 stops nearby on Rue de Grenelle or Rue St. Dominique (depending on direction). Buses #82 and #92 get you within a 10-minute walk.

Tours: A €6 audioguide covers the museum and gardens and is helpful to fully appreciate the art.

Length of This Tour: Allow one hour.

Baggage Check: Even a fairly small bag must be checked, unless you tuck it under your arm like a purse.

Cuisine Art: A peaceful **$ self-service cafeteria** is in the gardens behind the museum. Picnics are not allowed in the gardens. For better options, you'll find many recommended cafés and restaurants in the **Rue Cler area** (a 15-minute walk; see the Eating in Paris chapter).

The Tour Begins

• *Enter and buy tickets in the modern entrance hall. There's a bookstore, a gallery for temporary exhibits, and WCs. Pick up the museum map (and audioguide, if interested).*

Exit the ticket hall, walk across the courtyard of the gardens, and enter the mansion (where you'll check your bag). You'll follow a one-way route over two floors (elevator available), circling each clockwise, ground floor first and then upstairs. My tour can help guide you through the museum's general layout, but be aware that the collection changes frequently—just go with the flow.

• *Now enter Room 1, which generally displays...*

Early Work

Rodin's early works match the belle époque style of the time—noble busts of bourgeois citizens, pretty portraits of their daughters, and classical themes. Born of working-class roots, Rodin taught him-

self art by sketching statues at the Louvre and then sculpting copies.

The Man with the Broken Nose (*L'Homme au Nez Cassé*, 1865)—a deliberately ugly work—was 23-year-old Rodin's first break from the norm. He meticulously sculpted this deformed man (one of the few models the struggling sculptor could afford), but then the clay statue froze in his unheated studio, and the back of the head fell off. Rodin loved it! Art critics hated it. Rodin persevered. (Note: The museum rotates the display of two different versions—the broken-headed one and a repaired version that Rodin made later and critics accepted.)

You may also see portraits and busts of Rodin's future wife, Rose Beuret, the woman who would suffer with him through obscurity and celebrity.

• *Continue to Room 2.*

Rodin the Employee

To feed his family, Rodin cranked out small-scale works—portraits, ornamental vases, nymphs, and knickknacks to decorate buildings—with his boss' name on them (the more established sculptor Albert Carrier-Belleuse). Still, the series of mother-and-childs

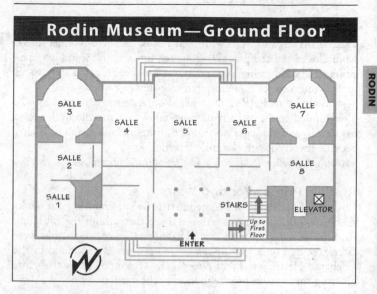

Rodin Museum—Ground Floor

SALLE 3

SALLE 4

SALLE 5

SALLE 6

SALLE 7

SALLE 2

SALLE 8

SALLE 1

STAIRS

Up to First Floor

ELEVATOR

ENTER

RODIN

he was hired to do (perhaps depicting Rose and baby Auguste?) allowed him to experiment on a small scale with the intertwined twosomes he'd perfect later in his career.

Rodin's work brought in enough money for him to visit Italy, where he was inspired by the boldness, monumental scale, restless figures, and "unfinished" look of Michelangelo's sculptures. Rapidly approaching middle age, Rodin was ready to rock.

• *In Room 3, Rodin finds his...*

First Success

Rodin moved to Brussels, where his first major work, *The Age of Bronze* (*L'Âge d'Airain*, 1877), brought controversy and the fame that surrounds it. This nude youth, perhaps inspired by Michelan-

gelo's *Dying Slave* (in the Louvre—see page 177), awakens to a new world. It was so lifelike that Rodin was accused of not sculpting it himself but simply casting it directly from a live body. The boy's raised left arm looks like it should be leaning on a spear, but it's just that missing element that makes the pose more tenuous and interesting.

The art establishment still snubbed Rodin as an outsider, and no wonder. *Saint John the Baptist* (1878)—though now acknowledged as a classic—was savaged by the critics for its awkward, flat-footed pose. His ultra-intense *The Call of Arms* (*La Défense*, 1912-1918) screams, "Off with their heads!" at the top of her lungs. Rodin loved twisted poses, fragmented figures, and weird juxtapositions. He was forging a style that was unique. He was a slave to his muses, and some of them inspired monsters.

Little by little, Rodin gathered an entourage around him of like-minded souls: wealthy patrons, fellow artists who understood his vision, and students who adored him...including one he'd later become involved with, Camille Claudel.

• *Rooms 4-8 generally display a variety of statues from...*

Rodin's Prime Working Years

Rodin and his stable of talented artists began cranking out works that have become classics. As you'll see throughout the museum, Rodin often started with small-scale versions of works that were later executed on a grand scale. (This process is explained in the sidebars.) He tinkered with *The Thinker* (Room 5) for years before creating the massive bronze version in the gardens (which we'll see later).

In the center of Room 5, a passionate woman twines around a solid man for their first, spontaneous kiss. Looking at their bodies, we can almost read the thoughts, words, and movements that led up to this meeting of lips. *The Kiss* (*Le Baiser*, 1888-1889) was the first Rodin work the public loved. Rodin came to despise it, thinking it simple and sentimental.

Find the opening in Room 5 to the museum's entrance area and peer left to find *The Hand of God* (*La Main de Dieu*, 1896). This work shapes Adam and Eve from the mud of the earth to which they will return. Rodin worked in "mud," using his hands to model clay figures, which were then reproduced in marble or bronze, usually by his assistants. You'll be able to inspect this masterpiece from every angle when you pass by it as you approach the stairs to the second floor. Rodin first worked on the front view, then checked the back and side profiles, then filled in the in-between.

• *Now enter Room 6.*

Rodin excelled in creating ensembles. As he worked on small-scale studies for the grim execution scene known as *The Burghers of Calais* (a small white plaster model in a glass case is on display here, the full-sized bronze version stands in the gardens), he needed to capture not only each man's individual expression but also how his body language conversed with the other members of the group.

RODIN

Rodin's Creative Process

The beauty of the Rodin Museum is that it shows so many works in progress. Rodin loved the creative process and the unfinished look.

Rodin worked with many materials—he chiseled marble (though not often), modeled clay, cast bronze, worked plaster, painted on canvas, and sketched on paper. He often created different versions of the same subject in different media.

The first flash of inspiration for a huge statue might be a single line sketched on notepaper. Rodin wanted nude models in his studio at all times—walking, dancing, squatting—in case they struck an interesting pose. Rodin thought of sculpture as simply "drawing in all dimensions."

Next, he might re-create a figure as a small-scale statue in plaster. The museum displays a number of these plaster "sketches," which you can compare with the final large-scale versions. Rodin employed and mentored many artists who executed these designs on a larger scale. Rodin rarely worked on marble statues (though the museum often displays newsreel footage of him doing exactly that). For that robust work, he hired others.

Rodin's figures struggle to come into existence. They are dancers stretching, posing, and leaping. Legendary lovers kiss and intertwine in yin-yang bliss. Embracing couples seem to emerge from the stone just long enough to love.

Rodin was fascinated by the theory of evolution—not Darwin's version of the survival of the fittest, but the ideas of Frenchman Jean-Baptiste Lamarck. Rodin's figures survive not by the good fortune of random mutation (Darwin) but by virtue of their own striving (Lamarck). They are driven by the life force, a restless energy that animates and shapes dead matter. Rodin must have felt that force even as a child, when he first squeezed soft clay and saw a worm emerge.

Rodin left many works "unfinished," reminding us that all creation is a difficult process of dragging a form out of chaos.

• *Move on to Room 7.*

Rodin's Women

What did Rodin think of women? There are many different images from which you can draw your own conclusions.

He loved sculpting women, either alone or as part of an intertwined couple. *Danaïd* (1889) buries her head in the marble over

RODIN

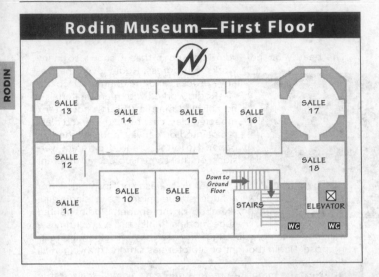

Rodin Museum—First Floor

SALLE 13 | SALLE 14 | SALLE 15 | SALLE 16 | SALLE 17

SALLE 12 | SALLE 18

SALLE 11 | SALLE 10 | SALLE 9

Down to Ground Floor → STAIRS

ELEVATOR

WC WC

her meaningless fate. *Eve* (1881) buries her head in shame, hiding her nakedness. But she can't hide the consequences—she's pregnant.

As Rodin became famous, wealthy, and respected, society ladies all wanted him to do their portraits. You may see a sculpture of his last mistress (*La Duchesse de Choiseul*, usually in Room 7 or 8), an American who lived with him here in this mansion. Rodin purposely left in the metal base points (used in the sculpting process), placing them suggestively.

Throughout the museum are studies of the female body in its different forms—crouching, soaring, dying, open, closed, wrinkled, intertwined.

• *Continue your visit upstairs in Room 9. You'll browse through a series of rooms with works that give a glimpse into...*

Rodin's Friends

Rodin started hanging out with Paris' intellectuals, artists, and glitterati as one of their own. As you explore these upstairs rooms, you may see statues and portrait busts of celebrities he knew personally. Remember, Rodin lived and worked in this mansion, renting rooms alongside Henri Matisse, the poet Rainer Maria Rilke (Rodin's secretary), and the dancer Isadora Duncan.

Rodin was especially fascinated with trying to capture the perfect portraits of his two famous writer friends, Victor Hugo and the controversial French novelist Honoré de Balzac (Room 9). With Balzac, Rodin's feverish attempts ranged from a pot-bellied Bacchus to a headless nude cradling an erection. In a moment of inspiration, Rodin threw a plaster-soaked robe over a nude form and watched it dry. This became the inspiration for the definitive version—proud and turning his nose up at his critics. (This version is displayed in the gardens, near *The Thinker;* other casts stand in the Orsay Museum and on a street median in Montparnasse.) When the Balzac statue was unveiled, the crowd booed, a fitting tribute to both the defiant novelist and the bold man who sculpted him.

• *As you survey these rooms, notice the sculptures of clasping and tilting hands (possibly the hands of Rodin and Rose Beuret, Room 10), and a series of busts of Rose (Room 11). Then, enter Room 12.*

The paintings in this gallery are by fellow artists Rodin either knew or admired, such as Vincent van Gogh, Claude Monet, and Pierre-Auguste Renoir. Rodin enjoyed discussions with Monet and other artists and incorporated their ideas into his work. Rodin is often considered an Impressionist because he captured spontaneous "impressions" of figures and created rough surfaces that catch reflected light.

• *When you reach Room #15 (on the mansion's back side), enjoy the nice views overlooking the gardens. On the back wall is a large painting of Rodin in his studio. The next room (#16) is dedicated to...*

Camille Claudel

You'll find several works by Camille Claudel, mostly in the style of her master. The 44-year-old Rodin, inspired by 18-year-old Camille's beauty and spirit, took her as his pupil, muse, colleague, and lover, and often used her as a model. (See several versions of her head.) We can follow the arc of their relationship in the exhibits.

As his student, "Mademoiselle C" learned from Rodin, doing portrait busts in his lumpy, molded-clay style. Her bronze bust of Rodin shows the steely-eyed sculptor with strong frontal and side profiles, barely emerging from the materials they both worked with.

Soon they were lovers. *The Waltz (La Valse)* captures the spinning exuberance the two must have felt as they embarked together on a new life. The couple twirls in a delicate balance.

But Rodin was devoted as well to his lifelong companion, Rose. Claudel's *Maturity* (*L'Age Mûr*, 1895-1907, also in Orsay Museum) shows the breakup. A young woman on her knees begs the man not to leave her, as he's reluctantly led away by an older woman. The statue may literally depict a scene from real life, in which a naked, fragile Claudel begged Rodin not to return to his wife. In the larger sense, it may also be a metaphor for the cruel passage of time, as Youth tries to save Maturity from the clutches of Old Age.

RODIN

The Bronze Casting Process

Rodin made his bronze statues not by hammering sheets of metal but by using the classic "lost wax" technique. He'd start by shaping the figure from wet plaster. This sculptural model was covered with a form-fitting mold. By pouring molten bronze into the narrow space between the model and the mold around it, letting it cool, and removing the mold—*voilà!*—Rodin had a hollow bronze statue ready to be polished and varnished.

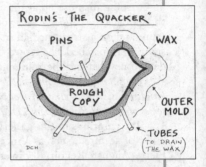

There were actually a number of additional steps (involving two different molds) before the bronze was poured. Rodin was intimately involved in every step—sanding down the clay model, coating it with wax, and touching up the waxy skin to add crucial surface details. Once the final mold was ready, Rodin's employees fitted it with ventilation tubes and poured in the molten bronze. The wax melted away—the "lost wax" technique—and the bronze cooled and hardened in its place, thus forming the final bronze statue.

Using a mold, Rodin could produce multiple copies, which is why there are many authorized bronze versions of Rodin's masterpieces all over the world.

Rodin did leave Claudel. Talented in her own right but tormented by grief and jealousy, she became increasingly unstable and spent her final years in an institution. Claudel's *The Wave* (*La Vague,* 1900), carved in green onyx in a very un-Rodin style, shows tiny, helpless women huddling together as a tsunami is about to engulf them.

• *Finally, step into the last few rooms.*

Final Years: Looking Back, Looking Forward

By the end of Rodin's long and productive life, he had become as famous as his works. He was viewed as a modern master of the most classic of art forms—sculpture, a tradition that stretched back to ancient times. At the same time, he was always looking ahead, restlessly forging new forms of expression.

Rodin took classical Greek motifs—myths and nymphs—and used them to create something completely new. He loved the broken look of Greek ruins and created his own ready-made fragments. He expanded the age-old repertoire of "acceptable" poses by studying the fluid movements of dancers. He loved the off-balance, unposed pose (which the invention of the camera also helped to capture).

The tall bronze *Walking Man* (*L'Homme Qui Marche*, 1900-1907), in Room 17, depicts the bold spirit of the turn-of-the-last-century era. Armless and headless, he plants his back foot forcefully, as though he's about to stride, while his front foot has already stepped. Rodin captures two poses at once—of a man who has one foot in the classical past, one in the modernist future.

• *The visit continues outside in the gardens. There you can see the finished, large-scale "studies" you may have seen inside the museum.*

THE GARDENS

Rodin loved the overgrown gardens that surrounded his home, and he loved placing his creations amid the flourishing greenery. These, his greatest works, show Rodin at his most expansive. The epic human figures are enhanced, not dwarfed, by the nature surrounding them.

• *Leaving the house, you've got four more stops: one to the left and three on the right. Beyond these stops is a big, breezy garden ornamented with many more statues, a cafeteria, and a WC. First head left to...*

The Thinker (Le Penseur), 1906

Leaning slightly forward, tense and compact, every muscle working toward producing that one great thought, Man contemplates his fate. No constipation jokes, please.

This is not an intellectual but a linebacker who's realizing there's more to life than frat parties. It's the first man evolving beyond his animal nature to think the first thought. It's anyone who's ever worked hard to reinvent himself or to make something new or better. Said Rodin: "It is a statue of myself."

There are 29 other authorized

copies of this statue, one of the most famous in the world. *The Thinker* was to have been the centerpiece of a massive project that Rodin wrestled with for decades—a doorway encrusted with characters from Dante's *Inferno*. It's our next stop, *The Gates of Hell.*

• *Follow* The Thinker's *gaze across the gardens. Standing before a tall, white backdrop is a big, dark door...*

The Gates of Hell
(La Porte de l'Enfer), 1880-1917

These doors (never meant to actually open) were never finished for a museum that was never built. But the vision of Dante's trip into hell gave Rodin a chance to explore the

dark side of human experience. "Abandon all hope ye who enter here," was hell's motto. The three Shades at the top of the door point down—that's where we're going. Beneath the Shades, pondering the whole scene from above, is Dante as the Thinker. Below him, the figures emerge from the darkness just long enough to tell their sad tale of depravity. There are Paolo and Francesca (in the center of the right door), who were driven into the illicit love affair that brought them here. Ugolino (left door, just below center) crouches in prison over his kids. This poor soul was so driven by hunger that he ate the corpses of his own children. On all fours like an animal, he is the dark side of natural selection. Finally, find what some say is Rodin himself (at the very bottom, inside the right doorjamb, where it just starts to jut out), crouching humbly.

You'll find some of these figures writ large in the gardens. *The Thinker* and *The Shades* (c. 1889) are behind you, and *Ugolino* (1901-1904) dines in the fountain at the far end.

It's appropriate that *The Gates*—Rodin's "cathedral"—remained unfinished. He was always a restless artist for whom the process of discovery was as important as the finished product. Studies for *The Gates* are scattered throughout the museum, and they constitute some of Rodin's masterpieces.

• *To the left of* The Gates of Hell, *along the street near where you entered, are...*

The Burghers of Calais (Bourgeois de Calais), 1889

The six city fathers trudge to their execution, and we can read in their faces and poses what their last thoughts are. They mill about, dazed, as each one deals with the decision he's made to sacrifice himself for his city.

Rodin depicts the actual event from 1347, when, in order to save their people, Calais' city fathers surrendered the keys of the city—and their lives to the king of England. Rodin portrays them, not in some glorious pose drenched in pomp and allegory, but as a simple example of men sacrificing their lives together. As the men head to the gallows, with ropes already around their necks, each body shows a distinct emotion, ranging from courage to despair.

Circle the work counterclockwise. The man carrying the key to the city tightens his lips in determination. The bearded man is weighed down with grief. Another buries his head in his hands. One turns, seeking reassurance from his friend, who turns away and gestures helplessly. The final key-bearer (in back) raises his hand to his head.

Each is alone in his thoughts, but they're united by their mutual sacrifice, by the base they stand on, and by their weighty robes—gravity is already dragging them down to their graves.

Pity the poor souls; view the statue from various angles (you can't ever see all the faces at once); then thank King Edward III, who, at the last second, pardoned them.

• *To the right of* The Gates of Hell *is a glassed-in building, the...*

Gallery of Marbles

Unfinished, these statues show human features emerging from the rough stone. Imagine Rodin in his studio, working to give them life.

Victor Hugo (at the far-right end of the gallery), the great champion of progress and author of *Les Misérables* and *The Hunchback of Notre-Dame,* leans back like Michelangelo's nude *Adam,* waiting for the spark of creation. He tenses his face and cups his ear, straining to hear the call from the blurry Muse above him. Once inspired, he can bring the idea to life (just as Rodin did) with the strength of his powerful arms. It's been said that all of Rodin's work shows the struggle of mind over matter, of brute creatures emerging from the mud and evolving into a species of thinkers.

ARMY MUSEUM & NAPOLEON'S TOMB TOUR

Musée de l'Armée

If you're considering trying to conquer Europe to become its absolute dictator, come here before gathering your army. Hitler did, but still went out and made the same mistakes as his role model. (Hint: Don't invade Russia.) Napoleon's tomb rests beneath the golden dome of Les Invalides church.

In addition to the tomb, the complex of Les Invalides—a former veterans' hospital built by Louis XIV—has various military collections, together called the Army Museum. You'll see medieval armor, Napoleon's horse stuffed and mounted, Louis XIV-era uniforms and weapons, and much more. The best part is the section dedicated to the two world wars, especially World War II. Visiting the different sections, you can watch the art of war unfold from stone axes to Axis powers.

Orientation

Cost: €14, covered by Museum Pass (show it at the entrance to each sight or exhibit), admission includes Napoleon's Tomb and all museum collections within the Invalides complex. Special exhibits and evening concerts are extra. Children are free, but you must line up to get them a ticket. The sight is also free for military personnel in uniform.

Hours: Daily 10:00-18:00; Napoleon's Tomb stays open Tue until 21:00.

Information: +33 1 44 42 38 77, www.musee-armee.fr.

Getting There: The museum and tomb are at Hôtel des Invalides, with its hard-to-miss golden dome (129 Rue de Grenelle). Ride the **Métro** (Mo: La Tour Maubourg, Varenne, or Invalides), or take a **bus**: #69 from the Marais and Rue Cler area or #63 from the St. Germain-des-Prés area (buses #82 and #92 also serve the sight). The museum is a 10-minute **walk** from Rue Cler. There are two entrances: one from the Grand Esplanade des Invalides, and the other from behind the gold dome on Avenue de Tourville.

Visitor Information: A helpful, free map/guide is available at the ticket office. Excellent English information is posted in most exhibits. Paired with the self-guided tour in this chapter, that should be sufficient info for most.

Tours: If you want even more background, a fine €5 multimedia guide covers the whole complex.

Length of This Tour: Allow 2-4 hours depending on your appetite for all things Napoleon and war.

Concerts: The museum hosts classical music concerts throughout the year. For schedules see the museum website.

Eating: The cafeteria is reasonable (outdoor tables available), and the museum gardens are picnic-perfect. Rue Cler eateries are a 10 minute walk away, as is the riverside promenade along the Seine, with many eating options.

Nearby: You'll likely see the French playing *boules* on the esplanade (as you face Les Invalides from the riverside, look for the dirt area to the upper right; for the rules of *boules*, see page 407).

Starring: Napoleon's Tomb, exhibits on World Wars I & II, memorabilia of Napoleon (including his stuffed horse).

OVERVIEW

The Army Museum and Napoleon's Tomb are in the Invalides complex (or should I say "Napoleon complex"?). Various exhibits are scattered around the large complex. Consult your free Army Museum map for the whole list and their locations. Your ticket covers them all—just flash your ticket or Museum Pass at each entrance.

Pick your favorite war. With limited time, visit only ▲▲▲ **Napoleon's Tomb** and the excellent ▲▲▲ **World War I and World War II** exhibits. Next on my list would be the exhibit ▲▲ **From Louis XIV to Napoleon I (1643-1814),** featuring swords and muskets, key battles of the Revolution, and memorabilia of Napoleon. If you still have energy, browse the ▲ **Charles de Gaulle Exhibit,** which honors France's WWII hero, or **Arms and Armor,** a vast collection of medieval suits of armor, pikes, swords, and cannons. Though there are other exhibits to see here, this chapter covers only the top sights in order of importance.

The Tour Begins

• *You can enter the Invalides complex from either the north or south side (ticket offices are at both entrances). Start at Napoleon's Tomb—underneath the golden dome, with its entrance on the south side (farthest from the Seine).*

NAPOLEON'S TOMB

Enter the church, gaze up at the dome, then lean over the railing and bow to the emperor lying inside the scrolled, red porphyry **tomb** (see photo). If the lid were opened, you'd find an oak coffin inside, holding another ebony coffin, housing two lead ones, then mahogany, then tinplate... until finally, you'd find Napoleon himself, staring up, with his head closest to the door. When his body was exhumed from the original grave and transported here (1840), it was still perfectly preserved, even after 19 years in the ground.

Born of humble Italian heritage on the French-owned isle of Corsica, Napoleon Bonaparte (1769-1821) went to school at Paris' Ecole Militaire, quickly rising through the ranks amid the chaos of the Revolution. The charismatic "Little Corporal" won fans by fighting for democracy at home and abroad. In 1799, he assumed power and, within five short years, conquered most of Europe. The great champion of the Revolution had become a dictator, declaring himself emperor of a new Rome.

Napoleon's red tomb on its green base stands 15 feet high in the center of a marble floor, circled by a mosaic crown of laurels and exalted by a glorious dome above.

Now, panning around the **chapel,** you'll find tombs of Napoleon's family. Despots are quick to make loyal family members part of their inner circle. After conquering Europe, he installed his big brother, Joseph, as king of Spain (turn around to see Joseph's black-and-white marble tomb in the alcove to the left of the door); his little brother, Jerome, became king of the German kingdom of Westphalia (tucked into the chapel to the right of the door); and his baby boy, Napoleon II (downstairs), sat in diapers on the throne of Rome.

In other **alcoves,** you'll find more dead war heroes, including Marshal Ferdinand Foch, the commander in chief of the multinational Allied forces in World War I, his tomb lit with otherworldly blue light. To the right of Foch lies Maréchal Vauban, Louis XIV's great military engineer, who designed the fortifications of more

ARMY MUSEUM

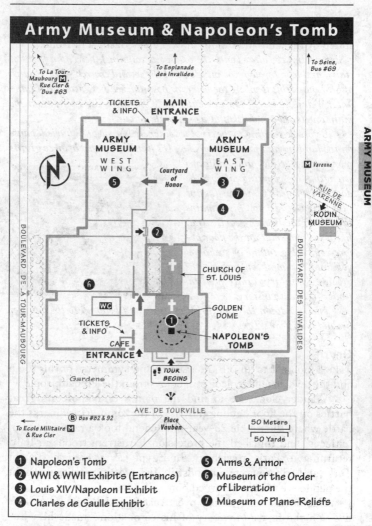

Army Museum & Napoleon's Tomb

To La Tour-Maubourg Ⓜ, Rue Cler & Bus #63

To Esplanade des Invalides

To Seine, Bus #69

TICKETS & INFO

MAIN ENTRANCE

ARMY MUSEUM
WEST WING
❺

Courtyard of Honor

ARMY MUSEUM
EAST WING
❸
❼

❹

Ⓜ Varenne

RUE DE VARENNE

RODIN MUSEUM

BOULEVARD DE LA TOUR-MAUBOURG

❷

CHURCH OF ST. LOUIS

❻

WC

GOLDEN DOME

❶

NAPOLEON'S TOMB

TICKETS & INFO

CAFÉ

ENTRANCE ↑

BOULEVARD DES INVALIDES

Gardens

TOUR BEGINS

AVE. DE TOURVILLE

← Ⓑ Bus #82 & 92

To École Militaire Ⓜ & Rue Cler

Place Vauban

50 Meters

50 Yards

❶ Napoleon's Tomb
❷ WWI & WWII Exhibits (Entrance)
❸ Louis XIV/Napoleon I Exhibit
❹ Charles de Gaulle Exhibit
❺ Arms & Armor
❻ Museum of the Order of Liberation
❼ Museum of Plans-Reliefs

than 100 French cities. Vauban's sarcophagus shows him reflecting on his work with his engineer's tools, flanked by figures of war and science. These heroes, plus many painted saints, make this a kind of French Valhalla.

Before moving on, consider the design of the church itself—find the model of this complex under glass in front of the altar. It's actually a double church—one for the king and one for his soldiers—built long before Napoleon under Louis XIV in the 17th century. You're standing in the **"dome chapel,"** decorated to the glory of Louis XIV and intended for royalty before it became the tomb of Napoleon. The original altar was destroyed in the Revolution. What you see today dates from the mid-1800s, and was inspired by the altar and canopy at St. Peter's Basilica in Rome.

• *Step behind the altar (with the corkscrew columns), descend a flight of stairs, and look through the windows at the* **second church***—the Church of St. Louis. This is where the veterans hospitalized here attended (mandatory) daily Mass. (You can enter the Church of St. Louis from the main courtyard—a quick and worthwhile detour.)*

Before descending to the crypt level where Napoleon is buried, pause on the landing and face the doorway. It's flanked by two **bronze giants** representing civic and military strength. The writing above the door is Napoleon's "desire" (as the inscription reads) for his remains to be with the French people. And, like a welcome mat on the floor before you, a big inlaid N welcomes you into the tomb of perhaps the greatest military and political leader in French history.

Now go down the final flight of stairs and belly up to the banister around Napoleon's Tomb.

Crypt

Take a moment to absorb the majesty and symmetry of this tomb and the reverence Napoleon still enjoys from the French people.

Wander clockwise to find the names of **Napoleon's great battles** on the floor circling the base of the tomb. *Rivoli* marks the battle where the rookie 26-year-old general took a ragtag band of "citizens" and thrashed the professional Austrian troops in Italy, returning to Paris a celebrity. In Egypt *(Pyramides)*, he fought Turks and tribesmen to a standstill. The exotic expedition caught the public eye, and he returned home a legend.

Napoleon's huge victory over Austria and Russia at Austerlitz—on the first anniversary of his coronation—made him Europe's top dog. At the head of the million-man Great Army *(La Grande Armée)*, he made a three-month blitz attack through Germany and Austria. As a military commander, he was daring, relying on top-notch generals and a mobile force of independent armies. His personal magnetism on the battlefield was said to be worth 10,000 additional men.

Pause to gaze at the grand **statue of Napoleon** the emperor in the alcove at the head of the tomb—royal scepter and orb of earth in his hands. By 1804, all of Europe was at his feet. He held an elaborate ceremony in Notre-Dame, where he proclaimed his wife, Josephine, empress, and himself—the 35-year-old son of humble immigrants—emperor. The laurel wreath, the robes, and the Roman eagles proclaim him the equal of the Caesars. The floor at the statue's feet marks the grave of his son, Napoleon II (*Roi de Rome*, 1811-1832).

Circling the tomb on the crypt walls are **relief panels** showing Napoleon's constructive side. Dressed in toga and laurel leaves, he dispenses justice, charity, and pork-barrel projects to an awed populace.

• *In the first panel to the right of the statue...*

He establishes an **Imperial University** to educate naked boys throughout *"tout l'empire."* The roll of great scholars links modern France with those of the past: Plutarch, Homer, Plato, and Aristotle.

Three panels later, his various building projects (canals, roads, and so on) are celebrated with a list and his quotation, "Everywhere he passed, he left durable benefits" *("Partout où mon regne à passé...").*

Hail Napoleon. Then, at his peak, came his most tragic errors.

• *Turn around and look down to Moscowa (the Battle of Moscow—marked beneath his tomb).*

Napoleon invaded Russia with 600,000 men and returned to Paris with 60,000 frostbitten survivors. Two years later, the Russians marched into Paris, and Napoleon's days were numbered. After a brief **exile** on the isle of Elba, he skipped parole, sailed to France, bared his breast, and said, "Strike me down or follow me!" For 100 days, they followed him, finally into Belgium, where the British and the Prussians hammered the French at the Battle of Waterloo (conspicuously absent on the floor's décor—for more on this battle, see "From Louis XIV to Napoleon I," near the end of this chapter).

Exiled again by a war tribunal, he spent his last years in a crude shack on the small South Atlantic island of St. Helena. When Napoleon died, he was initially buried in a simple grave. The epitaph was never finished because the French and British wrangled over what to call the hero/tyrant. The stone simply read, "Here lies..."

• *To get to the Courtyard of Honor and the various military collections, exit Napoleon's Tomb the same way you entered, make a U-turn right, and march past the cafeteria and ticket hall. Continue to the end of the hallway. Just before the courtyard, on the right, stairs lead up to the*

Napoleon Bonaparte (1769-1821)

Born to Italian parents on the French-ruled isle of Corsica, Napoleon attended French schools, although he spoke the language with an Italian accent to the end of his days. He graduated from Paris' Ecole Militaire, where he trained in the latest high-tech artillery. His military career took an unexpected turn when the Revolution erupted (1789), and he chose to return to Corsica to fight royalist oppression.

In 1793, as commander of artillery, Napoleon besieged Toulon, forcing the royalists to surrender and earning his first great victory. He later defended the Revolutionary government from royalist mobs in Paris by firing a "whiff of grapeshot" into the crowd (1795). Such daring military exploits and personal charisma earned him promotions and the nickname "the Little Corporal"—not for his height (he was an average 5'7") but as a term of endearment from the rank and file. When he married the classy socialite Josephine Beauharnais, Napoleon became a true celebrity. In 1798, having conquered Italy and Egypt, Napoleon returned to Paris, where the weak government declared him First Consul—ostensibly as the champion of democracy, but in fact he was a virtual dictator over much of Europe. He was 29 years old.

During the next 15 years, Napoleon solidified his reign with military victories over Europe's kings—  now allied against France. Under his rule, France sealed the Louisiana Purchase with America, and legal scholars drew up the Code of Napoleon, a system of laws still used by many European governments today. In 1804, his power peaked when he crowned himself emperor in a ceremony in Notre-Dame blessed by the pope. The Revolutionary general was now, paradoxically, part of Europe's royalty. Needing an heir to the throne, he divorced barren Josephine and married an Austrian duchess, Marie Louise, who bore him the boy known to historians as the "King of Rome."

In 1812, Napoleon decided to invade Russia, and the horrendous losses from that failed venture drained his power. Many of Europe's conquered nations saw their chance to pig-pile on France, toppling Napoleon and sending him to exile on the isle of Elba (1814). Napoleon escaped long enough to raise an army for a final hundred-day campaign before finally being defeated by British and Prussian forces at the Battle of Waterloo (1815). Guilty of war crimes, he was sentenced to exile on the remote South Atlantic island of St. Helena, where he talked to his dog, studied a little English, penned his memoirs, spoke his final word—"Josephine"—and died.

World War I and World War II exhibits. Go upstairs, following blue banners reading Les Deux Guerres Mondiales, 1871-1945. *The museum is laid out so you first see the coverage of World War I, though some may choose to pass through this section quickly to reach the more substantial WWII section.*

WORLD WAR I

World War I (1914-1918) introduced modern technology to the age-old business of war. Tanks, chemical weapons, monstrous cannons, rapid communication, and airplanes made their debut, collaborating to kill nearly 10 million people in just four years. In addition, the war ultimately seemed senseless: It started with little provocation, raged on with few decisive battles, and ended

with nothing resolved, a situation that sowed the seeds of World War II.

A quick walk-through of this 20-room exhibit leads you chronologically through World War I's causes, battles, and outcome, giving you the essential background for the next world war. There's good English information, but the displays are lackluster and low-tech: Move along quickly and don't burn out before getting to the World War II wing.

The War Begins

Room 1: The first room bears a thought-provoking name: "Honour to the Unfortunate Bravery." **Paintings** of dead and wounded soldiers from the Franco-Prussian War make it clear that World War I actually "began" in 1871, when Germany thrashed France. Suddenly, a recently united Germany was the new bully in Europe.

Rooms 2-3, France Rebounds: Snapping back from its loss, France began rearming itself, with spiffy new uniforms and weapons like the American-invented Gatling gun (early machine gun).

The French replaced the humiliation of defeat with a proud and extreme nationalism. Fanatical patriots hounded a (Jewish) officer named Alfred Dreyfus (**display** at the far left end) on trumped-up treason charges (1890s).

Rooms 4-6, Colonial Expansion: Europe's nations were in a race for wealth and power, jostling to acquire lucrative colonies in Africa and Asia (**uniforms**). In a climate of mutual distrust, nations allied with their neighbors, vowing to protect each other if war ever erupted. In Room 6, a **map of Europe** in 1914 shows the division: France, Britain, and Russia (the Allies) teamed up against Germany, Austria-Hungary, and Italy (the Central Powers). Europe was ready to explode, but the spark that would set it off had nothing to do with Germany or France.

Room 7, Assassination and War Begins: Bang. On June 28, 1914, an Austrian archduke was shot to death (see **video**). One by one, Europe's nations were dragged into the regional dispute by their webs of alliances. The Great War had begun.

Room 8, The Battle of the Marne: German forces swarmed into France, hoping for a quick knockout blow. Germany brought

its big guns (photo and miniature model of **Big Bertha**). The **projection map** shows how the armies tried to outflank each other along a 200-mile battlefront. As the Germans (purple-gray arrows) zeroed in on Paris, the French (blue arrows) and British ("BEF") scrambled to send 6,000 crucial reinforcements, shuttled to the front lines in 670 Parisian taxis (one is displayed nearby). The German tide was stemmed, and the two sides faced off, expecting to duke it out and get this war over quickly. It didn't work out that way.

• *The war continues upstairs.*

World at War

Rooms 9-10, The War in the Trenches: By 1915, the two sides reached a stalemate, and they settled in to a long war of attrition—French and Britons on one side, Germans on the other. The battle line, known as the Western Front, snaked 450 miles across Europe from the North Sea to the Alps. For protection against flying bullets, the soldiers dug **trenches** *(tranchées)*, which soon became home—24 hours a day, 7 days a week—for millions of men.

Life in the trenches was awful—cold,

La guerre des tranchées

rainy, muddy, disease-ridden—and, most of all, boring. Every so often, generals waved their swords and ordered their men "over the top" and into "no-man's-land." Armed with rifles and bayonets, they advanced into a hail of machine gun fire. The "victorious" side often won only a few hundred yards of meaningless territory that was lost the next day after still more deaths. During the 10-month Battle of Verdun, France had about 400,000 casualties.

The war pitted 19th-century values of honor, bravery, and chivalry against **20th-century weapons:** grenades, machine guns, tanks, and poison gas. To shoot over the tops of trenches while staying hidden, they even invented crooked and periscope-style rifles.

Rooms 11-13, "World" War/Colonial Empires in the War (labeled *1917* in floor): Besides the Western Front, the war extended elsewhere, including the colonies, where many "natives" (see their **uniforms**) joined the armies of their "mother" countries. On the Eastern Front, Russia and Germany wore each other down. (Finally, the Russian people had had enough; they overthrew their czar, brought the troops home, and fomented a revolution that put communists in power.)

• *Down a short hallway, enter Room 14.*

War Ends

Room 14, The Allies: By 1917, the Allied forces were beginning to outstrip the Central Powers, thanks to help from around the world.

When Uncle Sam said, "I Want You," five million Americans answered the call to go "Over There" (in the words of a popular song) and fight the Germans. The Yanks were not an enormous military factor, but their very presence signaled that the Allies seemed destined to prevail.

Room 15, Armistice (labeled *1918* in floor): In spite of a desperate last offensive by Generals Ludendorff and Hindenburg, the Germans were doomed. Under the command of French marshal Ferdinand Foch, the Allies undertook a series of offensives that would prove decisive. At the 11th hour of the 11th day of the 11th month (November 11, 1918), the guns fell silent. Allied Europeans celebrated the Armistice with victory parades (see the newsreel footage of the **Arc de Triomphe parade**)...and then began assessing the damage.

Room 16, Costly Victory: After four years of battle, the war had left 9.5 million dead and 21 million wounded (see plaster casts of disfigured faces). A generation was lost, and France never fully recovered its "superpower" status.

Rooms 17-19, From 1918 to 1938: The Treaty of Versailles (1919), signed in the Hall of Mirrors, officially ended the war. A map shows how it radically redrew **Europe's borders.** Germany was punished severely, leaving it crushed, humiliated, stripped of crucial land, and saddled with demoralizing war debts. Marshal Foch prophetically said of the Treaty: "This is not a peace. It is an armistice for 20 years."

France, one of the "victors," was drained, trying to hang on to its prosperity and its colonial empire. By the 1930s—swamped by the Great Depression and a stagnant military **(dummy on horseback)**—France was reeling, unprepared for the onslaught of a re-tooled Germany seeking revenge.

A **photo of Adolf Hitler** presages the awful events that came next.

• *World War II is covered directly across the hall, in the rooms marked 1939-1942. Good WCs are nearby.*

WORLD WAR II

World War II was the most destructive of earth's struggles. In this exhibit, the war unfolds in photos, displays, and newsreels, with special emphasis on the French contribution. (You may not have realized that it was Charles de Gaulle who won the war for us.) The museum takes you from Germany's quick domination (third floor), to the Allies turning the tide (second floor), to the final surrender (first floor).

Be ready—displays come in rapid succession and flow into each other without obvious walls or dividers (look for room numbers in red on wall posters and find your way with the display labels). Ideally, read this tour before your visit as an overview of the vast, complex, and horrific global spectacle known as World War II.

Third Floor: Axis Aggression, 1939-1941
The Phony War (La Drôle de Guerre) and
the Defeat of 1940 (Le Defaite de 1940)

On September 1, 1939, Germany, under Adolf Hitler, invaded Poland, starting World War II. But in a sense the war had really begun in 1918, when the "war to end all wars" ground to a halt, leaving 9.5 million dead, Germany defeated, and France devastated (if victorious). For the next two decades, Hitler fed off German resentment over the Treaty of Versailles, which humiliated and ruined Germany.

After Hitler's move into Poland, France and Britain mobi-

lized. For the next six months, the two sides faced off, with neither actually doing battle—a tense time known to historians as the
"Phony War" *(Drôle de Guerre).*

Then, in spring of 1940 came the Blitzkrieg ("lightning war"),
and Germany's better-trained and better-equipped soldiers and
tanks (see turret) swept
west through Belgium.
France was immediately
overwhelmed, and Brit-
ish troops barely escaped
across the English Chan-
nel from Dunkirk. With-
in a month, Nazis were
goose-stepping down the
Champs-Elysées.

• *A few paces farther along you see a large photo of...*

Charles de Gaulle (L'Appel du 18 Juin)

Just like that, virtually all of Europe was dominated by fascists.
During those darkest days, as France fell and Nazism spread

across the Continent,
one Frenchman—an ob-
scure military man named
Charles de Gaulle—re-
fused to admit defeat. This
20th-century John of Arc
had an unshakable be-
lief in his mission to save
France. De Gaulle (1890-
1970) was born into a liter-
ate, upper-class family, raised in military academies, and became a
WWI hero and POW. But when World War II broke out, he was
still only a minor officer with limited political experience, who was
virtually unknown to the French public.

After the invasion, de Gaulle escaped to London. From there
he made inspiring speeches over the radio, beginning with a famous address broadcast on June 18, 1940. He slowly convinced
a small audience of French expatriates that victory was still possible.

France After the Armistice
(La France Après l'Armistice)

After France's surrender, Germany ruled northern France, including Paris—see the **photo of Hitler as a tourist** at the Eiffel Tower.
Hitler made a three-hour blitz tour of the city, including a stop
at Napoleon's Tomb. Afterward he said, "It was the dream of my

life to be permitted to see Paris. I cannot say how happy I am to have that dream fulfilled today."

The Nazis allowed the French to administer the south and the colonies (North Africa). This puppet government, centered in the city of Vichy, was right-wing and traditional, bowing to Hitler's demands as he looted France's raw materials and manpower for the war machine. (In the movie *Casablanca*, set in Vichy-controlled Morocco, French officials follow Nazi orders while French citizens defiantly sing "The Marseillaise.")

The Battle of Britain
(La Solitude et la Bataille d'Angleterre)

Facing a "New Dark Age" in Europe, British prime minister Winston Churchill pledged, "We will fight on the beaches...We will fight in the hills. We will never surrender."

In June 1940, Germany mobilized to invade Britain across the English Channel. From June to September, they paved the way, sending bombers—up to 1,500 planes a day—to destroy military and industrial sites. When Britain wouldn't budge, Hitler concentrated on London and civilian targets. This was "The Blitz" of the winter of 1940, which killed 30,000 and left parts of London in ruins. But Britain hung on, armed with newfangled radar, speedy Spitfires, and an iron will.

They also had the Germans' secret "Enigma" code. The **Enigma machine** (in display case), with its set of revolving drums, allowed German commanders to scramble orders in a complex code that could be broadcast securely to their troops. The British (with crucial help from Poland) captured a machine, broke the code, then monitored German airwaves. (An Enigma machine co-starred with actor Benedict Cumberbatch, who played code-breaking mathematician Alan Turing, in the movie *The Imitation Game*.) For the rest of the war, Britain had advance knowledge of many

top-secret plans, but occasionally let Germany's plans succeed—sacrificing its own people—to avoid suspicion.

By spring of 1941, Hitler had given up any hope of invading the Isle of Britain. Churchill said of his people: "This was their finest hour."

Germany Invades the Soviet Union
(L'Allemagne Envahit l'Union Soviétique)

Perhaps hoping to one-up Napoleon, Hitler sent his state-of-the-art tanks speeding toward Moscow in June 1941 (betraying his former ally Joseph Stalin). By winter, the advance had stalled at the gates of Moscow and was bogged down by bad weather and Soviet stubbornness.

The Third Reich had reached its peak. Soon, Hitler would have to fight a two-front war. The French Renault **tank** (displayed)

was downright puny compared with the big, fast, high-caliber German Panzers. This war was often a battle of factories, to see who could produce the latest technology fastest and in the greatest numbers. And what nation might have those factories...?

• *In the corner is a glass case with a model of an aircraft carrier, announcing that...*

The United States Joins the War
(Les Etats-Unis Dans la Guerre)

On December 7, 1941, "a date which will live in infamy" (as US president Franklin D. Roosevelt put it), Japanese planes made a sneak attack on the US base at **Pearl Harbor,** Hawaii, and destroyed the pride of the Pacific fleet in two hours.

The US quickly entered the fray against Japan and her ally, Germany. In two short years, America had gone from isolationist observer to supplier of Britain's arms to full-blown war ally against fascism. The US now faced a two-front war—in Europe against Hitler, and in Asia against Japan's imperialist conquest of China, Southeast Asia, and the South Pacific.

America's first victory came when Japan tried a sneak attack on the US base at Midway Island (June 3, 1942). This time—thanks to the Allies who had cracked the Japanese code—America had the aircraft carrier **USS *Enterprise*** (see model) and two of her buddies lying in wait. In five minutes, three of Japan's carriers (with valuable planes) were mortally wounded, their major attack force was sunk, and Japan and the US were dead even, settling in for a long war of attrition.

Though slow to start, the US eventually had an army 16 million strong, 80,000 planes, the latest technology, $250 million a day, unlimited raw materials, and a population of Rosie the Riveters fighting for freedom to a boogie-woogie beat.

• Continue downstairs to the second floor.

Second Floor: The Tide Turns, 1942-1944

In 1942, the Continent was black with fascism, and Japan was secure on a distant island. The Allies had to chip away on the fringes.

Battle of the Atlantic (La Bataille de l'Atlantique)

German U-boats (short for *Unterseeboot,* meaning submarine) and battleships such as the *Bismarck* patrolled Europe's perimeter,

where they laid spiky mines to try to keep America from aiding Britain. (Until long-range transport planes were produced near war's end, virtually all military transport was by ship.) The Allies traveled in convoys with air cover, used sonar and radar, and dropped depth charges, but for years they endured the loss of up to 60 ships per month.

El-Alamein, Stalingrad, and Guadalcanal

Three crucial battles in the autumn of 1942 put the first chink in the fascist armor. Off the northeast coast of Australia, 10,000 US Marines (see **kneeling soldier** in glass case #14D) took an airstrip on Guadalcanal, while 30,000 Japanese held the rest of the tiny, isolated island. For the next six months, the two armies were marooned together, duking it out in thick jungles and malaria-infested swamps while their countries struggled to reinforce or rescue them. By February 1943, America had won and gained a crucial launch pad for bombing raids.

A world away, German tanks under General Erwin Rommel rolled across the vast deserts of North Africa. In October 1942, a well-equipped, well-planned offensive by British general Bernard ("Monty") Montgomery attacked at El-Alamein, Egypt, with 300 tanks. (See **British tank soldier** with headphones, #14F.) Monty drove "the Desert Fox" west into Tunisia for the first real Allied victory against the Nazi *Wehrmacht* war machine.

In 1942, the Allies began long-range bombing of German-held territory, including saturation bombing of civilians. It was global war and total war.

Then came Stalingrad. In August 1942, Germany attacked the Soviet city, an industrial center and gateway to the Caucasus oil fields. By October, the Germans had battled their way into the city center and were fighting house-to-house, but their supplies were running low, the Soviets wouldn't give up, and winter was coming. The snow fell, their tanks had no fuel, and relief efforts failed. Hitler ordered them to fight on through the bitter cold. On the worst days, thousands of men died. (By comparison, the US lost a total of 58,000 in Vietnam over 11 years.) Finally, on January 31, 1943, the Germans surrendered, against Hitler's orders. The six-month totals for the Battle of Stalingrad? Eight hundred thousand German and other Axis soldiers dead, 1.1 million Soviets dead. The Russian campaign put hard miles on the German war machine.

Landing in North Africa (Le Débarquement Américain en Afrique du Nord)

A **photo** shows Winston Churchill, US president Franklin D. Roosevelt, and France's Charles de Gaulle meeting to plan an indirect attack on Hitler by invading Vichy-controlled Morocco and Algeria. On November 8, 1942, 100,000 Americans and British—under the joint command of an unknown, low-key problem-solver named General Dwight ("Ike") Eisenhower—  landed on three separate beaches (including Casablanca). More than 120,000 Vichy French soldiers, ordered by their superiors to defend the fascist cause, confronted the Allies and...gave up. (Nearby, find displays of some standard-issue **weapons:** Springfield rifle, Colt 45 pistol, Thompson submachine gun, hand grenade.)

The Allies moved east, but bad weather, inexperience, and the powerful Afrika Korps under Rommel stopped them in Tunisia. But with flamboyant General George S. ("Old Blood-and-Guts") Patton punching from the west, and Monty pushing from the south, they captured the port town of Tunis on May 7, 1943. The Allies now had a base from which to retake Europe.

The French Resistance (L'Unification de la Résistance)

Inside occupied France, ordinary heroes fought the Nazis—the underground Resistance. **Jean Moulin** (see photo), de Gaulle's assistant, secretly parachuted into France and organized these scattered heroes into a unified effort.

Various **displays** show the Resistance's efforts. Bakers hid radios within loaves of bread to secretly contact London. Barmaids passed along tips from tipsy Nazis. Communists in black berets cut telephone lines. Farmers hid downed airmen in haystacks. Housewives spread news from the front with their gossip. Printers countered Nazi propaganda with pamphlets.

In 1943, Moulin was arrested by the Gestapo (Nazi secret police) and died. But Free France now had a (secret) government again, rallied around de Gaulle, and was ready to take over when liberation came.

Fans of Jean Moulin and the stirring Resistance story can explore it in greater depth at the Museum of Liberation and Jean Moulin, which opened in 2019 at Place Denfert-Rochereau (near the Catacombs, closed Mon, www.museeliberation-leclerc-moulin. paris.fr).

• *Meanwhile, on the Eastern Front...*

The Red Army (L'Armée Rouge)
Monty, Patton, and Ike certainly were heroes, but the war was won on the Eastern Front by Soviet grunts, who slowly bled Germany dry. **Maps** show the shifting border of the Eastern Front.

• *Bypass a couple of rooms, to...*

The Italian Campaign (La Campagne d'Italie)
On July 10, 1943, the assault on Hitler's European fortress began. More than 150,000 Americans and British sailed from Tunis and landed on the south shore of Sicily. (See **maps** and **video clips** of the campaigns.) Speedy Patton and methodical Monty began a "horse race" to take the city of Messina (the US won the friendly competition by a few hours). They met little resistance from 300,000 Italian soldiers, and were actually cheered as liberators. Mussolini was arrested by his own people, and Italy surrendered. Hitler quickly poured 50,000 German troops into Italy, reinstalled Mussolini, and ordered Italy to fight on.

In early September, the Allies landed on the beaches of southern Italy. Finally, after four long years of war, free men set foot on the European continent. Lieutenant General Mark Clark led the slow, bloody push north to liberate Rome.

In January 1944, the Germans dug in between Rome and Naples at **Monte Cassino,** a rocky hill topped by the monastery of St. Benedict (see the large photo showing the obliterated abbey). Thousands died as the Allies tried inching up the hillside. In frustration, the Allies air-bombed the historic monastery to smithereens, killing many noncombatants...but no Germans, who dug in deeper. After four months of vicious, sometimes hand-to-hand combat by the Allies (Americans, Brits, Free French, Poles, Italian partisans, Indians, etc.), a band of Poles stormed the monastery, and the German back was broken.

Meanwhile, 50,000 Allies had landed near Rome at Anzio and held the narrow beachhead for months against massive German attacks. Finally the Allied troops broke out and joined the assault on the capital. Without a single bomb threatening its historic treasures, Rome fell on June 4, 1944.

• *Room 23 (with benches) shows a film on...*

D-Day (Jour-J)

Three million Allies and six million tons of *matériel* were massed in England in preparation for the biggest fleet-led invasion in history—across the Channel to France, then eastward to Berlin. The Germans, hunkered down in northern France, knew an invasion was imminent, but the Allies kept the details top secret. On the night of June 5, 150,000 soldiers boarded ships and planes without knowing where they were headed until they were under way. Each one carried a note from General Eisenhower: "The tide has turned. The free men of the world are marching together to victory."

At 6:30 a.m. on June 6, 1944, Americans spilled out of troop transports into the cold waters off a beach in Normandy, code-named Omaha (see the black-and-white newsreel projection). The weather was bad, seas were rough, and the prep bombing had failed. The soldiers, many seeing their first action, were dazed and confused. Nazi machine guns pinned them against the sea. Slowly, they crawled up the beach on their stomachs. A thousand died. The survivors held on until the next wave of transports arrived.

All day long, Allied confusion did battle with German indecision; the Nazis never really counterattacked, thinking D-Day was just a ruse, instead of the main invasion. By day's end, the Allies had taken several beaches along the Normandy coast and begun building artificial harbors, providing a tiny port-of-entry for the reconquest of Europe. The stage was set for a quick and easy end to the war. Right.

• *Go downstairs to the...*

First Floor: The War Ends, 1944-1945
Battle of Normandy and Landing in Provence (Le Débarquement de Provence)

Through June, the Allies (mostly Americans) secured Normandy by taking bigger ports (Cherbourg and Caen) and amassing troops and supplies for the assault on Germany. In July they broke out and sped eastward across France, with Patton's tanks covering up to 40 miles a day. They had "Jerry" on the run.

On France's Mediterranean coast, American troops under General Alexander Patch landed near Cannes (see the big photo of the sky filled with **parachutes**), took Marseille, and headed north to meet up with General Patton. A tiny theater shows happy liberation scenes as France is freed city by city.

Les Maquis

French Resistance guerrilla fighters helped reconquer France from behind the lines. (Don't miss the **folding motorcycle** in its parachute case.) The liberation of Paris was started by a Resistance attack on a German garrison.

Liberation of Paris (La Libération de Paris)

As the Allies marched on Paris, Hitler ordered his officers to torch the city—but they sanely disobeyed and prepared to surrender. A video shows the exhilaration of August 26, 1944, as General Charles de Gaulle walked ramrod-straight down the Champs-Elysées, followed by Free French troops and US GIs passing out chocolate and Camels. Two million Parisians went crazy.

Toward Berlin (Vers Berlin)

The quick advance from the west through France, Belgium, and Luxembourg bogged down at the German border in autumn of 1944. Patton outstripped his supply lines, an airborne and ground invasion of Holland (the Battle of Arnhem) was disastrous, and bad weather grounded planes and slowed tanks.

On December 16, the Allies met a deadly surprise. An enormous, well-equipped, energetic German army appeared from nowhere, punched a "bulge" deep into Allied territory through Belgium and Luxembourg, and demanded surrender. General Anthony McAuliffe sent a one-word response—"Nuts!"—and the momentum shifted. The Battle of the Bulge was Germany's last great offensive.

The Germans retreated across the Rhine River, blowing up bridges behind them. But one bridge, at Remagen, was captured by the Americans and stood just long enough for GIs to cross and establish themselves on the east shore of the Rhine. Soon US tanks were speeding down the autobahns and Patton could wire the good news back to Ike: "General, I have just pissed in the Rhine."

Soviet soldiers did the dirty work of taking fortified Berlin by launching a final offensive in January 1945, and surrounding the city in April. German citizens fled west to surrender to the more-benevolent Americans and Brits. Hitler, defiant to the end, hunkered in his underground bunker. (See photo of **ruined Berlin**.)

On April 28, 1945, Mussolini and his girlfriend were killed and hung by their heels in Milan. Two days later, Adolf Hitler and his new bride, Eva Braun, avoided similar humiliation by committing suicide (pistol in mouth and poison), and having their bodies burned beyond recognition. Germany formally surrendered on May 8, 1945.

• *To the left, in the adjoining room, don't miss the exhibits on...*

Concentration Camps (Les Camps de Concentration)

Lest anyone mourn Hitler or doubt this war's purpose, gaze at photos from Germany's concentration camps. Some camps held political enemies and prisoners of war, including two million French. Others were expressly built to exterminate people considered "genetically inferior" to the "Aryan master race"—particularly Jews, Gypsies, homosexuals, and the mentally ill.

War of the Pacific (Les Batailles du Pacific)

Often treated as an afterthought, the final campaign against Japan was a massive American effort, costing many lives but saving millions of others from Japanese domination.

Japan was an island bunker surrounded by a vast ring of fortified Pacific islands. America's strategy was to take one island at a time, "island-hopping" until close enough for B-29 Superfortress bombers to attack Japan itself. The battlefield spread across thousands of miles. In a new form of warfare, ships carrying planes led the attack and prepared tiny islands (such as Iwo Jima) for troops to land on and build airfields. While General Douglas MacArthur island-hopped south to retake the Philippines ("I have returned!"), others pushed north toward Japan.

On March 9, Tokyo was firebombed, and 90,000 were killed. Japan was losing, but a land invasion would cost hundreds of thousands of lives. The Japanese had a reputation for choosing death over the shame of surrender—they even sent bomb-laden "kamikaze" planes on suicide missions.

America unleashed its secret weapon, an atomic bomb (originally suggested by German-turned-American Albert Einstein). On August 6, a B-29 dropped one (named **"Little Boy,"** see the replica dangling overhead) on the city of Hiroshima and instantly vaporized 100,000 people and four square miles.  Three days later, a second bomb fell on Nagasaki. The next day, Emperor Hirohito unofficially surrendered. The long war was over, and US sailors returned home to kiss their girlfriends in public places.

The Closing Chapter (Actes de Conclusion)

The death toll for World War II, tallied from September 1939 to August 1945, totaled 80 million soldiers and civilians. The Soviet Union lost 26 million, China 13 million, France 580,000, and the US 340,000. The Nazi criminals who started the war and perpetrated war crimes were tried and sentenced in an international court—the first of its kind—held in Nürnberg, Germany.

World War II changed the world, with the US emerging as the dominant political, military, and economic superpower. Europe was split in two. The western half recovered, with American aid. The eastern half remained under Soviet occupation. For 45 years, the US and the Soviet Union would compete—without ever actually doing battle—in a "Cold War" of espionage, propaganda, and weapons production that stretched from Korea to Cuba, from Vietnam to the moon.

• *Exit through the shop and turn left. The next exhibit is located on the east side of the large Courtyard of Honor (where Napoleon honored his troops, Dreyfus had his sword broken, and de Gaulle once kissed Churchill). Follow "From Louis XIV to Napoleon III" signs. Start upstairs on the second floor.*

FROM LOUIS XIV TO NAPOLEON I, 1643-1814

This display traces the evolution of uniforms and weapons through France's glory days, with the emphasis on Napoleon Bonaparte. As you circle the second floor, the exhibit unfolds chronologically in four parts: the Ancien Régime (Louis XIV, XV, and XVI), the Revolution, the First Empire (Napoleon), and the post-Waterloo world. Many (but not all) exhibits have some English information.

This museum is best for browsing, but I've highlighted a handful of the (many) exhibits to get you started. Room numbers are posted on doorjambs.

Hall 1: Ancien Régime (Louis XIV, XV, and XVI)

Louis XIV unified the army as he unified the country, creating the first modern nation-state with a military force. You'll see many glass cases of ❶ **weapons.** Gunpowder was quickly turning swords, pikes, and lances to pistols, muskets, and bayonets. Uniforms became more uniform, and everyone got a standard-issue flintlock.

At the end of the hall, a display case has some amazingly big and ❷ **odd-shaped rifles.** Nearby, there's a **video** on weapons, and a projection screen show-

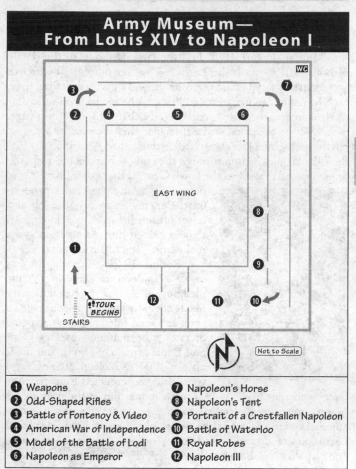

Army Museum—
From Louis XIV to Napoleon I

EAST WING

WC

TOUR BEGINS

STAIRS

Not to Scale

1 Weapons
2 Odd-Shaped Rifles
3 Battle of Fontenoy & Video
4 American War of Independence
5 Model of the Battle of Lodi
6 Napoleon as Emperor

7 Napoleon's Horse
8 Napoleon's Tent
9 Portrait of a Crestfallen Napoleon
10 Battle of Waterloo
11 Royal Robes
12 Napoleon III

ing a reenactment of the **3** **Battle of Fontenoy** (in present-day Belgium) in 1745. Put on headphones and watch how the French established their superiority on the Continent.

• *Turn the corner and enter...*

Hall 2: Révolution

Room 13 features the **4** **American War of Independence.** You'll see the sword *(épée)* of the French aristocrat Marquis de La Fayette, who—full of revolutionary fervor—sailed to America, where he took a bullet in the leg and fought alongside George Washington.

After France underwent its own Revolution, the king's Royal Army became the people's National Guard, protecting their fledgling democracy from Europe's monarchies while spreading revolutionary ideas by conquest.

Midway down Hall 2, find the large ❺ **model of the Battle of Lodi** in 1796 (push the English-language button). The French and Austrians faced off on opposite sides of a northern Italian river, each trying to capture a crucial bridge. The model shows the dramatic moment when the French cavalry charged across the bridge, overpowering the exhausted Austrians. They were led by a young, relatively obscure officer who had distinguished himself on the battlefield and quickly risen through the ranks—Napoleon Bonaparte. Stories spread that it was the brash General Bonaparte himself who

personally sighted the French cannons on the enemy—normally the job of a lesser officer. It turned the tide of battle and earned him a reputation and a nickname, "The Little Corporal."

Rooms 19-21 chronicle the era of ❻ **Napoleon as emperor.** While pledging allegiance to Revolutionary ideals of democracy, Napoleon staged a coup and soon ruled France as a virtual dictator. The museum displays General Bonaparte's hat, sword, and medals. In 1804, Napoleon donned royal robes and was crowned Emperor. The famous portrait by J. A. D. Ingres shows him at the peak of his power, stretching his right arm to supernatural lengths. The ceremonial collar and medal he wears in the painting are displayed nearby, as are an eagle standard and Napoleon's elaborate saddle.

Continue to the end of Hall 2 to find ❼ **Napoleon's beloved Arabian horse.** Le Vizir weathered many a campaign with Napoleon, grew old with him in exile, and now stands stuffed and proud.

Hall 3: The Reign of Napoleon

Ambitious Napoleon plunged France into draining wars against all of Europe. In Room 29 (midway down the hall), you'll find ❽ **Napoleon's tent** and bivouac equipment: a bed with mosquito netting, a director's chair, his overcoat, and a table where you can imagine his generals hunched over as they made battle plans.

Napoleon's plans to dominate Europe ended with disastrous losses when he attempted to invade Russia. The rest of Europe

ganged up on France, and in 1814 Napoleon was forced to abdicate. At the end of the hall, find Room 35 with a ❾ **portrait of a crestfallen Napoleon,** now replaced by King Louis XVIII (whose bust stands opposite). Napoleon spent a year in exile on the isle of Elba. In March of 1815, he escaped, returned to France, rallied the army, and prepared for one last hurrah.

ARMY MUSEUM

• *Turning the corner into Hall 4, you run right into what Napoleon did—Waterloo.*

Hall 4: Waterloo and the First Restoration

Study the projection screen that maps the course of the history-changing ❿ **Battle of Waterloo,** fought on the outskirts of Brussels, June 15-19, 1815.

On June 18, 72,000 French (the blue squares) faced off against the allied armies of 68,000 British-Dutch under Wellington (red and yellow) and 45,000 Prussians under Blücher (purple). Napoleon's only hope was to keep the two armies apart and defeat them individually.

First, Napoleon's Marshal Ney advances on the British-Dutch, commanded by the Prince of Orange. Then the French attack the Prussians on the right. They rout the Prussians, driving them north. Napoleon's strategy is working. Now he prepares to finish Wellington off.

On the morning of June 18, Wellington hunkers down atop a ridge at Waterloo. Napoleon advances, and they face off. Nothing happens. Napoleon decides to wait two hours to attack, to let the field dry—some say it was his fatal mistake. Finally, Napoleon attacks from the left flank. Next he punches hard on the right. Wellington pushes them back. Meanwhile, the Prussians are advancing from the right, so Napoleon sends General Mouton to check it out. Napoleon realizes he must act quickly or have to fight both armies at once. He sends General Ney into the thick of Wellington's forces. Fierce fighting ensues. Ney is forced to retreat. The Prussians advance from the right. It's a two-front battle. Caught in a pincer, Napoleon has no choice but to send in his elite troops, the Imperial Guard, who have never been defeated. The British surprise the Guard in a cornfield, and Wellington swoops down from the ridge, routing the French. By nightfall, the British and Prussian armies have come together, 12,000 men have died, and Napoleon's reign of glory is over.

Napoleon was sent into exile on St. Helena. Once the most powerful man in the world, Napoleon spent his final years as a lonely outcast suffering from ulcers, dressed in his nightcap and slippers, and playing chess, not war.

The French monarchy was restored, and King Louis XVIII donned the ⓫ **royal robes.**

• *Continuing on and crossing a hall, you should run right into a portrait of* ⓬ *Napoleon III, the emperor of France in the 1850s and the nephew of the great Napoleon Bonaparte...but that's a whole other story, and this area might be reorganized by the time of your visit. Our tour here is done.*

THE REST OF THE ARMY MUSEUM

• *Your ticket is good for all the exhibits and museums in the complex (consult your free museum map). If you still have an appetite for French military history, take the stairs down directly to the impressive...*

Charles de Gaulle Exhibit

This engaging memorial one floor below ground level brings France's history of war into the modern age. The exhibit leads you through the life of the greatest figure in 20th-century French history. A 25-minute documentary runs twice per hour. You can use the free audioguide, or just circle clockwise and let the big photos and video images tell de Gaulle's life story:

It starts in 1890 with childhood photos and posters capturing the 19th-century French world that shaped him. During World War I, de Gaulle fought bravely at Verdun. In the 1920s, as a "soldier-writer," he rose through the ranks ghostwriting for the war hero Marshal Petain. As fascism rose in the 1930s, de Gaulle encouraged France to modernize its armies.

When World War II broke out in 1939 and France capitulated, de Gaulle refused to collaborate with the Nazis and went into exile. He became the head of "La France Libre"—the small unoccupied territories of French people around the world. He was instrumental in France's liberation in 1944 and led the parade down the Champs-Elysées.

After helping to defeat Hitler, de Gaulle turned to politics. He led the nation for a decade (1958-69) as its president. But in 1968, student protests and worker strikes eventually toppled him. Today, he's honored as something much more than just an airport.

• *Back on the west side of the Courtyard of Honor is the exhibit called...*

Arms and Armor

Here you'll discover every size, shape, and style of body armor and swords. The collection's highlight (to the right down the hall after

you enter) is the suit of armor of France's great Renaissance king, François I, decorated with *fleur-de-lis*. He sits astride his horse, fitted out in matching armor. Connoisseurs of medieval armor, cannons, swords, pikes, crossbows, and early guns will love

this collection of weapons from the 13th to 17th centuries; others can browse a few rooms and move on.

More Sights

If you still haven't had enough of dummies in uniforms and endless glass cases of muskets, there's more. The **Museum of the Order of Liberation** honors heroes of the WWII Resistance. The **Museum of Plans-Reliefs** (on the top floor of the east wing) exhibits the 18th-century models of France's cities (1:1600 scale) that strategists used to thwart enemy attacks. Survey Antibes and ponder which hillside you'd use to launch an attack. Finally, you can end your visit in the pristine **Church of St. Louis**—the perfect place to remember all the fallen soldiers.

BUS #69 SIGHTSEEING TOUR

From the Eiffel Tower to Père Lachaise Cemetery

Why pay €35 for a tour company to give you an overview of Paris when city bus #69 can do it for the cost of a Métro ride? Get on the bus and settle in for a trip through some of the city's most interesting neighborhoods. Or use this tour as a handy way to lace together many of Paris' most important sightseeing districts. On this ride

from the Eiffel Tower to Père Lachaise Cemetery, you'll learn how great Paris' bus system is—and you'll wonder why you've been tunneling by Métro under this gorgeous city. And if you're staying in the Marais, Ile St. Louis, or Rue Cler neighborhoods, line #69 is a useful route for just getting around town. The end-of-the-line stop is right by the start of my Père Lachaise Cemetery Tour.

The bus often goes faster than you can read. It's best to look through this chapter and peruse the map ahead of time, then ride with an eye out for the various sights described here.

Orientation

Length of This Tour: Allow one hour. With limited time, get off at Bastille, with good Métro connections.

When to Go: You can board daily until 22:30 (last departure from Eiffel Tower stop). It's best to avoid weekday rush hours (8:00-9:30 & 17:30-19:30) and hot days (no air-conditioning). Sundays are quietest, and it's easy to get a window seat. Evening bus rides are pretty from fall through spring (roughly Sept-April), when it gets dark early enough to see the floodlit monuments before the bus stops running—though some of the finer points are harder to see in the dark (and you'll need a light to read by).

Getting There: Eastbound line #69 leaves from the Eiffel Tower on Avenue Joseph Bouvard (the street that becomes Rue St. Dominique as it crosses the Champ de Mars, two blocks from the tower through the park—for a more detailed view, see the map on page 408). Board at one of the first few stops to secure a view seat. The first stop is at the southwestern end of the avenue; the second stop is at the eastern end (just before Avenue de la Bourdonnais). Stops are located and clearly posted about every three blocks along the route. To see all the stop names, check the official *Plan de Lignes* at www.ratp.fr (click "Timetables" if viewing in English, then "Bus," then enter line number "69" in the box, then click on "Hours PDF" to see the route diagram). The map on page 42 shows part of the bus #69 route.

Bus Tips: You must use a Navigo card or pass, which can be purchased at staffed Métro stations and most *tabacs* (or loaded to your phone on the RATP app). Board through the front door, then validate your Navigo card in the machine behind the driver.

If it's hot, you can usually open the upper part of the window. Push the red button to request a stop. Exit through the rear door. Buses run every 10-15 minutes except in the late evening. The time until the next bus is usually displayed at the bus stop.

Tours: Many sights along this route are covered in more detail elsewhere in the book. Many have self-guided tours and some have audio tours. 📖 See the Eiffel Tower Tour, Orsay Museum Tour, Louvre Museum Tour, Left Bank Walk, Historic Paris Walk, Marais Walk, and Père Lachaise Cemetery Tour chapters. You can also 🎧 download my free Historic Paris Walk, Orsay Museum, Louvre Museum, and Père Lachaise Cemetery audio tours.

OVERVIEW

Handy line #69 crosses the city east-west, running between the Eiffel Tower and Père Lachaise Cemetery. In between, it passes close to these great monuments and neighborhoods: Ecole Militaire; Rue Cler; Les Invalides (Army Museum and Napoleon's Tomb); the Rodin, Orsay, and Louvre museums; Ile de la Cité (Notre Dame and Sainte-Chapelle); Ile St. Louis; Hôtel de Ville; Pompidou Center; Marais; and Bastille.

This tour is best done in the direction it's written (east from the Eiffel Tower to Père Lachaise Cemetery)—in the other direction, one-way streets change the route. It's still a scenic ride if going

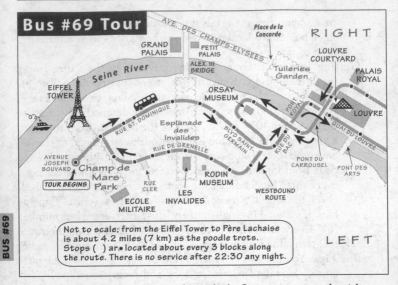

Bus #69 Tour

AVE. DES CHAMPS-ELYSÉES

RIGHT

Place de la Concorde

GRAND PALAIS

PETIT PALAIS

ALEX. III BRIDGE

Tuileries Garden

LOUVRE COURTYARD

PALAIS ROYAL

Seine River

EIFFEL TOWER

ORSAY MUSEUM

PONT ROYAL

LOUVRE

RUE ST. DOMINIQUE

Esplanade des Invalides

BLVD SAINT-GERMAIN

RUE DU BAC

QUAI DU LOUVRE

AVENUE JOSEPH BOUVARD

RUE DE GRENELLE

RODIN MUSEUM

PONT DU CARROUSEL

PONT DES ARTS

Champ de Mars Park

RUE CLER

TOUR BEGINS

ECOLE MILITAIRE

LES INVALIDES

WESTBOUND ROUTE

LEFT

Not to scale; from the Eiffel Tower to Père Lachaise is about 4.2 miles (7 km) as the poodle trots. Stops ( ) are located about every 3 blocks along the route. There is no service after 22:30 any night.

westbound—riders get to pass through the Louvre courtyard, with its stunning pyramid aglow after dark.

Grab a window seat—either side toward the back is good (rear seats are higher). If you get on at one of the first stops, you're likely to secure a good seat. Follow your progress by reading the stop names on the bus display or on the bus shelters you pass.

Many find the Bastille a good ending point (where you can begin this book's walking tour of the Marais). This ride also ties in well after a visit to the Eiffel Tower or on your way to visiting Père Lachaise Cemetery. OK—let's roll.

The Tour Begins

Champ de Mars and the Eiffel Tower

Your tour begins below this 1,000-foot, reddish-brown hood ornament. The park surrounding you is called the Champ de Mars (named for the god of war). It served as a parade ground for the

military school, Ecole Militaire, which seals the park at the right end. Napoleon Bonaparte is the school's most famous graduate.

In 1889, the Champ de Mars was covered with a massive temporary structure to house exhibitions of all sorts; it was a celebration of the Centennial World's Fair (the 100th anniversary of the French Revolution), the same event for which the

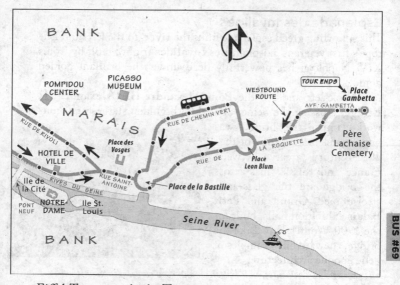

Eiffel Tower was built. The apartments surrounding the park are among the most exclusive in Paris.

The grass that runs down the center of the park becomes a playground at night, when much of Paris seems to descend on it (if it's not fenced off to give the grass a fighting chance). Picnics here are a delight, and warm evenings reveal Paris' multicultural population. Dogs and kids romp as soccer balls fly past, all within the glow of the Eiffel Tower.

• *Leaving the Champ de Mars, the bus slices through the 7th arrondissement along its primary shopping street.*

Rue St. Dominique

Paris functions as a city of hundreds of small neighborhoods. This area was once the village of Grenelle (before it was consumed by Paris). Many locals feel little need to leave the area, and neighbors trust each other. The dry cleaner knows that if customers forget to bring their wallet, they'll return to pay another time. If the plumber can only come during work hours, locals can leave their apartment keys with the nearest shop owner.

This neighborhood has long been an attraction for Americans. The American Library is a block to the left after crossing Avenue de la Bourdonnais, the American University of Paris is on the far left as you cross Avenue Bosquet, the American Church sits on the river farther to the left, and the American Cathedral is just across the river, on the Right Bank.

• *After crossing Boulevard de la Tour Maubourg, you'll enter the open world of Esplanade des Invalides.*

Esplanade des Invalides

This sprawling green esplanade links the **river** (to the left) and Europe's first veterans' hospital, **Les Invalides** (right), built by Louis XIV. Napoleon lies powerfully dead under the brilliant golden dome.

Look left and see the **Pont Alexandre III (Alexander III Bridge)** crossing the Seine. Spiked with golden statues and iron-work lamps, the bridge was built to celebrate a turn-of-the-20th-century treaty between France and Russia. Just across the bridge are the glass-and-steel-domed **Grand** and **Petit Palais** exhibition halls, built for the 1900 World's Fair. Like the bridge, they are fine examples of belle époque architecture.

• *Leaving Les Invalides, you'll reenter narrow streets lined with...*

Government Buildings

Many of France's most important ministries occupy these flag-bearing, golden-hued buildings with police guarding doorways, heavily barred windows, and people in suits speaking in hushed tones. The sprawling **Ministry of Defense** (on your left) was originally the mansion of Napoleon's mother.

• *After the Bellechasse stop, you'll emerge from the government area onto the broad, stylish, and leafy...*

Boulevard St. Germain

Colorful home-decorating stores and fine Haussmann-era architecture mark this upper-crust neighborhood. The boulevard is famous for its cafés frequented by existentialists Simone de Beauvoir, Albert Camus, and Jean-Paul Sartre.

But we turn left onto **Rue du Bac,** with its art galleries, antique shops, and smart clothing boutiques. The **Orsay Museum** is just a few blocks to the left at the Pont Royal bus stop.

• *Next, you'll cross the river (with a view of the Orsay Museum behind on the left) and enter the Right Bank.*

Tuileries Garden and Louvre Museum

The lovely Tuileries Garden (Jardin des Tuileries), well worth a stroll, lies ahead and to the left after you cross the Seine. This was once the royal garden of the Louvre palace, which is just ahead and to the right.

The bus turns right on the Right Bank and begins to travel the entire length of the looooong Grand Gallery of the **Louvre.** Once the biggest building in the world, the Louvre's 12 miles of galleries house some of the world's greatest works of art. The medallions on the facade show the initials of each king who made his small contribution to building the massive Louvre. Notice the **bus lane** you're in, separated from the slow-moving traffic by a low curb. Bicyclists have the right to use these lanes as well, making vast parts of Paris bike-friendly.

A few bridges ahead is the view-perfect pedestrian bridge **Pont des Arts.** Get off here if you'd like to take my self-guided Left Bank Walk. That curved **building with a dome** on the other side is where the Académie Française has met since the 1600s to compose the official French dictionary and defend the French language from corrupting influences (like English). Some 2,000 barges line the river below you.

The **riverside promenade** below, but out of view, was until recently an express lane carrying over 20,000 cars per day. Now it accommodates strolling Parisians and bike riders (see my recommended bike route on page 67).

Lining the sidewalk on the right are the green metal stalls of *bouquinistes*—independent booksellers who have plied this trade along the Seine for centuries.

• *As you roll past the end of the long Louvre building, on the right is the tree-lined tip of the narrow island called the...*

Ile de la Cité

Paris began here more than 2,000 years ago. The bridge you'll pass is the **Pont Neuf,** or "new bridge," though it's now Paris' oldest (1600).

To your left, you'll pass quirky **plant shops and pet stalls**. On the right, across the river, are the round towers (wearing pointy black cones) of the **Conciergerie,** where Marie-Antoinette was imprisoned during the French Revolution, awaiting the guillotine. Behind the Conciergerie is the slender spire of **Sainte-Chapelle,** with the most beautiful stained glass in Paris.

Farther ahead, on the right, you'll see the tops of the twin towers of **Notre-Dame Cathedral.** The huge crane hovering above it will be visible for many years as the roof structure is rebuilt. (Châtelet is the best stop if you'd like to tour the cathedral.)

Back to the left, the grand **Hôtel de Ville** (Paris' City Hall) stands proudly behind playful fountains. Each of the 20 arrondissements (governmental areas) in Paris has its own City Hall, and this one is the big daddy of them all. It's beautifully lit after dark all year.

• *The bus turns left—away from the river. It angles past St. Gervais Church—one of the first churches built on the Right Bank—and into the Marais neighborhood.*

Le Marais

This is jumbled, medieval Paris at its finest. On your left, a couple of blocks past St. Gervais near #13 (before the Jouy stop), stand

some of the oldest houses in Paris—tall, skinny, and half-timbered. The Marais has been a swamp, an aristocratic district, and a bohemian hangout. Today, classy stone mansions sit alongside trendy bars, fashion boutiques, and top-notch museums—the Picasso Museum, Carnavalet, Victor Hugo's House, Jewish Art and History Museum, and Pompidou Center.

The narrow street merges into the boulevard **Rue St. Antoine,** the main street of Paris in medieval times. On the right, at #103, are the dome and red door of the small-but-grand **Church of St. Paul and St. Louis**—the only Jesuit church in Paris and the church where Victor Hugo prayed.

If you want to explore the charming Marais—stretching to the left of Rue St. Antoine—get off at the Bastille-Rue St. Antoine stop (after the Birague stop). You could do my Marais Walk, visit La Coulée Verte Promenade-Park (see page 117), or get a bite to eat (see the Eating in Paris chapter).

• *Rue St. Antoine leads straight into Place de la Bastille, a vast round intersection with a giant pillar in the center.*

Place de la Bastille

This now-empty square is where the fortress-turned-prison called the Bastille once stood. For centuries, it was used to defend the

city—mostly from its own people, becoming a symbol of royal tyranny. On July 14, 1789, angry Parisians swarmed the Bastille, released its prisoners, and kicked off the French Revolution. (The building was destroyed.) Since then, the French have celebrated Bastille Day every July 14 as en-

thusiastically as Americans commemorate July 4. The column in the middle of the square honors France's ongoing struggle for democracy.

As you cross the square (usually a traffic mess—admire your driver's patience and agility), you'll pass over the covered **Canal St. Martin,** which runs under your feet from the Seine to northern Paris. Those red awnings lining the long boulevard to the left provide shade for vendors at one of Paris' best outdoor markets, the Marché Bastille (see page 507). Next you'll curve in front of the reflecting-glass **Opéra Bastille,** today's primary theater for the national opera company. Place de la Bastille (and surrounding streets) has become a trendy place for cafés and nightlife.

• *Leaving Place de la Bastille, the bus angles left up...*

Rue de la Roquette

This street gives a glimpse of the quirky, less-touristy Bastille neighborhood—an intriguing mix of galleries, wholesale clothing shops, seedy bars, and trendy eateries. The first street to the right is **Rue de Lappe,** one of the wildest nightspots in Paris, with a dizzying array of wacky bistros, bars, and dance halls.

The bus continues straight for about 10 minutes. As you go, notice how the cool cafés and chic boutiques give way to traditional businesses, though in Paris, you're never more than a short walk from a café.

• *The bus eventually turns left onto Boulevard de Ménilmontant (which locals happily associate with a famous Maurice Chevalier tune). From here, the bus travels alongside the wall of Père Lachaise Cemetery (on your right). Get off at **Place Gambetta** to visit the cemetery. As you exit the bus into the square, you'll see its centerpiece—the grandiose City Hall for the 20th arrondissement. To reach Père Lachaise Cemetery from here, follow Avenue du Père Lachaise for 100 yards, past inviting cafés and flower shops selling cyclamen, heather, and chrysanthemums—the standard flowers for funerals and memorials—to the gate of the cemetery. Our bus tour is over. What better place for your final stop?*

Père Lachaise Cemetery

This renowned cemetery is the final resting place of many famous Parisians, as well as artists, writers, and musicians from around the world who found a home in the City of Light. The cemetery is located far from the center of old Paris because it's relatively new—founded in 1804 by Napoleon to accommodate the city's expansion. Follow my Père Lachaise Cemetery Tour to find the graves of greats such as Frédéric Chopin, Oscar Wilde, Gertrude Stein, Edith Piaf, and Jim Morrison.

BUS #69

MARMOTTAN MUSEUM TOUR

Musée Marmottan Monet

The Marmottan has the best collection of works by the master Impressionist Claude Monet. In this mansion on the southwest fringe of urban Paris, you can walk through Monet's life, from black-and-white sketches to colorful open-air paintings to the canvas that gave Impressionism its name. The museum's highlights are scenes of his garden at Giverny, including larger-than-life water lilies. The Marmottan also features a world-class collection of works by Impressionist painter Berthe Morisot.

Paul Marmottan (1856-1932) lived here amid his collection of exquisite 19th-century furniture and paintings. He donated his home and possessions to a private trust (which is why your Museum Pass isn't valid here). After Marmottan's death, the more daring art of Monet and others was added. The combination of the mansion, the furnishings, the Impressionist and Empire paintings, and the many Monet masterpieces makes the Marmottan an aesthetic pleasure.

Orientation

Cost: €12, not covered by Museum Pass; €21.50 combo-ticket with Monet's garden and house at Giverny.

Hours: Tue-Sun 10:00-18:00, Thu until 21:00, closed Mon.

Information: +33 1 44 96 50 33, www.marmottan.fr.

Avoiding Lines: Advance tickets can be purchased at FNAC stores or on the Marmottan's website for special exhibits, which are frequent. Without a reservation, arrive close to opening time to minimize crowds.

Getting There: It's in Paris' west end at 2 Rue Louis-Boilly.

By Métro: Take Métro line 9 to La Muette. Exit via *sortie* 1. It's a six-block, 10-minute walk: Cross Chaussée de la

Muette street, turn left, and walk toward a major intersection (you'll see a brick building called La Gare—formerly a train station). Follow Chaussée de la Muette to a second intersection, where you'll continue straight onto a tree-lined pedestrian lane, Avenue Ranelagh. Walk through the peaceful park to the museum at the far end.

By RER Train (handy from Rue Cler): Catch RER/Train-C from Austerlitz, St-Michel, Orsay, Invalides, or Pont de l'Alma (board any train called NORA or GOTA), get off at the Boulainvilliers stop, and follow signs to *sortie Boulainvilliers*. Turn right up Rue Boulainvilliers, then turn left down Chaussée de la Muette, and follow the directions above to reach the museum. When returning to your hotel on RER/Train-C, make sure your stop is listed on the monitor: You don't want to end up in Versailles.

By Bus: Handy east-west bus #63 gets you kinda close, but requires a walk of about 600 yards. Get off at the Octave Feuillet stop on Avenue Henri Martin, cross Avenue Henri Martin, and follow the tree-lined street to the right that curves around to the museum.

Tours: The €4 audioguide, while overkill for some, supplements my tour well and includes coverage of temporary exhibits. Small information displays are in many rooms.

Length of This Tour: Allow one hour.

Services: There are two WCs, one on the second floor (usually with lines) and one downstairs by the Monet collection (bigger and quieter).

Cuisine Art: Cafés, *boulangeries,* and bistros are 10 minutes away around the La Muette Métro stop (Rue Mozart has good choices).

Nearby: The kid-friendly park in front of the museum is terrific for families with small kids. Parents can take turns visting the museum.

Make the most of the long trip here by combining a visit to the Marmottan with Trocadéro-area sights, a short Métro or bus ride away (see page 75).

Starring: Claude Monet, including *Impression: Sunrise* (shown at the top of this chapter); paintings of cathedrals, train stations, and beaches; scenes from Giverny; and water lilies.

OVERVIEW

The 19th-century Marmottan mansion, formerly a hunting lodge, has three pleasant, manageable floors, all worth perusing. (You might be free to see them in any order or, depending on crowd flow, be directed along a prescribed route.) The ground floor has several rooms of Paul Marmottan's period furnishings and notable paintings by French artists. Temporary exhibits are usually displayed in a gallery on this floor. Upstairs is the permanent collection, featuring illuminated manuscripts and works by Monet's fellow Impressionists—Edgar Degas, Camille Pissarro, Paul Gauguin, Pierre-Auguste Renoir, Edouard Manet, and especially Berthe Morisot. Monet's works—the core of the collection—are in the basement.

Because the museum rotates its large collection of paintings, this chapter is not designed as a room-by-room tour. Use it as a general background on Monet's life and some of the paintings you're likely to encounter. Read it once before you go, then let the museum surprise you.

The Tour Begins

• *You'll enter the museum on the ground floor. Pass through the temporary exhibition gallery (consider taking time to enjoy these works now) to reach the stairs leading down to the basement level. Descending the stairs, you're immediately plunged into the colorful and messy world of Claude Monet.*

CLAUDE MONET (1840-1926)

In this one long room, you'll find some 50 paintings by Monet spanning his lifetime. They're generally (and very roughly) arranged in chronological order—from Monet's youthful discovery of Impressionism, to his mature "series" paintings, to his last great water lilies from Giverny.

Claude Monet was the leading light of the Impressionist movement that revolutionized painting in the 1870s. Fiercely independent and dedicated to his craft, Monet gave courage to Renoir and other like-minded artists, who were facing harsh criticism. Let's survey Monet's long life:

Born in Paris in 1840, Monet grew up in seaside Le Havre as the son of a grocer and began his art career sketching caricatures of townspeople. He realized he had a gift for quickly capturing an overall impression with a few simple strokes. Monet defied his family, insisted he was an artist, and sketched the world around him—beaches, boats, and small-town life. Fellow artist Eugène Boudin encouraged Monet to don a scarf, set up his easel outdoors, and paint the scene exactly as he saw it. Today, we say, "Well, duh!" But "open-air" painting was unorthodox for artists of the day, who

MARMOTTAN

Monet's Family

You'll likely see portraits of Monet's wife and children. Monet's first wife, Camille, died in 1879, leaving Monet to raise 12-year-old Jean and babe-in-arms Michel. (Michel would grow up to inherit the family home and many of the paintings that ended up here.) But Monet was also involved with Alice Hoschede, who had recently been abandoned by her husband. Alice moved in with her six kids and took care of the dying Camille, and the two families made a Brady Bunch-style merger. Baby Michel became bosom buddies with Alice's baby, Jean-Pierre, while teenage Jean Monet and stepsister Blanche fell in love and later married.

were trained to study their subjects thoroughly in the perfect lighting of a controlled studio setting.

At 19, Monet went to Paris but refused to enroll in the official art schools. His letters to friends make it clear he was broke and paying the price for his bohemian lifestyle.

In 1867—the same year the Salon rejected his work—he and his partner Camille had their first child, Jean. They moved to the countryside of Argenteuil, where he developed his open-air, Impressionist style. *Impression: Sunrise* was his landmark work at the breakthrough 1874 Impressionist Exhibition. He went on to paint several series of scenes, such as *Gare Saint-Lazare,* at different times of day. His career was gaining steam.

After the birth of their second son, Michel, Camille's health declined, and she later died. Monet traveled a lot, painting landscapes *(Bordighera)*, people *(Portrait de Poly)*, and more series, including the famous Cathedral of Rouen. In 1890, he settled down at his farmhouse in Giverny and married Alice Hoschede. He traveled less, but visited London to paint the Halls of Parliament. Mostly, he painted his own water lilies and flowers in an increasingly messy style. He died in 1926 a famous man.

1870s: PURE IMPRESSIONISM

While living at Argenteuil, Monet and Camille played host to Renoir, Edouard Manet, Alfred Sisley, and other painters. Monet led them on open-air painting safaris to the countryside. Inspired by the realism of Manet, they painted everyday things—landscapes, seascapes, street scenes, ladies with parasols, family picnics—in bright, basic colors.

They began perfecting the distinct Impressionist style—painting nature as a mosaic of short brushstrokes of different colors placed side by side, suggesting shimmering light.

First, Monet simplified. A lady's dress might be composed of

MARMOTTAN

MARMOTTAN

just a few thick strokes of paint (as in his early work *On the Beach at Trouville*, 1870-1871). Monet gradually broke things down into even smaller "pixels"—small dots of different shades. If you back up from a Monet canvas, the pigments blend into one (for example, red plus green plus yellow equals a brown boat).

Still, they never fully resolve, creating the effect of shimmering light. Monet limited his palette to a few bright basics—cobalt blue, white, yellow, two shades of red, and emerald green abound. But no black—even shadows are a combination of bright colors.

Monet's constant quest was to faithfully reproduce nature in blobs of paint. His eye was a camera lens set at a very slow shutter speed to admit maximum light. Then he "developed" the impression made on his retina with an oil-based solution.

In search of new light and new scenes, Monet traveled throughout France and Europe, painting landscapes in all kinds of weather. Picture Monet at work, hiking to a remote spot—carrying an easel, several canvases, brushes (large-size), a palette, tubes of paint (an invention that made open-air painting practical), food and drink, a folding chair, and an umbrella (and this was before the invention of backpacks)—and wearing his trademark hat, with a cigarette on his lip. He weathered the elements, occasionally putting himself in danger by clambering on cliffs to get the scenes he wanted.

The key was to work fast, before the weather changed and the light shifted, completely changing the colors. Monet worked "wet-in-wet," applying new paint before the first layer dried, mixing colors on the canvas, and piling them up into a thick paste.

• *Monet's most famous "impression" was the one that gave the movement its name.*

Impression: Sunrise (Impression Soleil Levant), 1873

This is the painting that started the revolution—a simple, serene view of boats bobbing under an orange sun. At the first public showing by Monet, Renoir, Degas, and others in Paris in 1874, critics howled at this work and ridiculed the title. "Wallpaper," one called it. The sloppy brushstrokes and ordinary subject looked like a study, not a

finished work. The style was dubbed "Impressionist"—an accurate name.

The misty harbor scene obviously made an "impression" on Monet, who faithfully rendered the fleeting moment in quick strokes of paint. The waves are simple horizontal brushstrokes. The sun's reflection on the water is a few thick, bold strokes of orange tipped with white. They zigzag down the canvas the way a reflection shifts on moving water.

1890s: SERIES

Monet's claim to fame became a series of paintings of a single scene, captured at different times of day under different light. He first explored the idea with one of Paris' train stations, Gare St. Lazare, in the 1870s. Soon, he conceived paintings to be shown as a group, giving a time-lapse view of a single subject.

In Rouen, he rented several rooms offering different angles overlooking the Rouen Cathedral. He worked on up to 14 different canvases at a time, shuffling the right one onto the easel as the sun moved across the sky. The cathedral is made of brown stone, but at sunset it becomes gold and pink with blue shadows, softened by thick smudges of paint. The true subject is not the cathedral but the full spectrum of light that bounces off it.

He did another series in London. Turning his hotel room into a studio, Monet—working on nearly a hundred canvases si-multaneously—painted the changing light on the River Thames. He caught the reflection of the Houses of Parliament on the river's surface, stretching and bending with the current. London's famous fog epitomized Monet's favorite subject—the atmo-

sphere that distorts distant objects. That filtering haze gives even different-colored objects a similar tone, resulting in a more harmonious picture. When the light was just right and the atmosphere glowed, the moment of "instantaneity" had arrived, and Monet worked like a madman.

Monet started many of his canvases in the open air and then painstakingly perfected them later in the studio. He composed his scenes with great care—clear horizon lines give a strong horizontal axis, while diagonal lines (of trees or shorelines) create solid triangles.

These series—of London, the cathedral, haystacks, poplars, and mornings on the Seine—were very popular. Monet, poverty-stricken until his mid-40s, was slowly becoming famous, first in America, then London, and finally in France. He soon took up residence in what would be his home for the rest of his life: Giverny.

PAINTINGS OF GIVERNY (1883-1926)
Rose Trellises (L'Allée des Rosiers) and The Japanese Bridge (Le Pont Japonais)

In 1883, Monet's brood settled into a farmhouse in Giverny (50 miles west of Paris). Financially stable and domestically blissful, he turned Giverny into a garden paradise and painted nature without the long commute.

In 1890, Monet started work on his Japanese garden, inspired by tranquil scenes from the Japanese prints he collected. He divert-

ed a river to form a pond, planted willows and bamboo on the shores, filled the pond with water lilies, then crossed it with this wooden footbridge. As years passed, the bridge became overgrown with wisteria. Compare several versions. He painted the bridge at different times of day and year, exploring different color schemes.

Monet uses the bridge as the symmetrical center of simple, pleasing designs. The water is drawn with horizontal brushstrokes that get shorter as you move up the canvas (farther away), creating the illusion of distance. The horizontal water contrasts with the vertical willows, while the bridge "bridges" the sides of the square canvas and laces the scene together.

In 1912, Monet began to go blind. Cataracts distorted his perception of depth and color and sent him into a tailspin of despair. The (angry?) red paintings date from this period.

Early Water Lilies, Nymphéas, c. 1900

As his vision slowly failed, Monet concentrated on painting close-ups of the surface of the pond and its water lilies—red, white, yel-

low, and lavender. Some lilies are just a few broad strokes on a bare canvas (a study); others are piles of paint formed with overlapping colors.

But more than the lilies, the paintings focus on the changing reflections on the surface of the pond. Pan slowly around the room and watch the pond go from predawn to bright sunlight to twilight.

Early lily paintings show the shoreline as a reference point. But increasingly, Monet crops the scene ever closer, until there is no shoreline, no horizon, no sense of what's up or down. Stepping back from the canvas, you see the lilies just hang there on the museum wall, suspended in space. The surface of the pond and the surface of the canvas are one. Modern abstract art—a colored design on a flat surface—is just around the corner.

• *The climax of the visit is a round room (with benches), where you can immerse yourself in the...*

NYMPHEAS AND LARGE-SCALE CANVASES
Later Water Lilies, *Nymphéas,* 1915-1926

In the midst of the chaos of World War I, Monet began a series of large-scale paintings of water lilies. They were installed at the Or-angerie Museum. Here at the Marmottan are small-er-scale studies for that se-ries. But the sheer size of these studies is impressive.

MARMOTTAN

Get close—Monet did—and analyze how he composed these works. Some lilies are patches of thick paint circled by a squiggly "caricature" of a lily pad. Monet simplifies in a way that Henri Matisse and Pablo Picasso would envy. You can see that the simple smudge of paint that composes the flower is actually a complex mix of different colors. But to get these colors to fully resolve in your eye, you'd have to back up all the way to Giverny.

When Monet died in 1926, he was a celebrity. Starting with meticulous line drawings, he had evolved into an open-air realist, then Impressionist color analyst, then serial painter, and finally master of reflections. In the latter half of his life, Monet's world shrank—from the broad vistas of the world traveler to the tranquility of his home, family, and garden. But his artistic vision expanded as he painted smaller details on bigger canvases and helped invent modern abstract art.

• *After seeing Monet, continue upstairs through the gift shop and visit the rest of the Marmottan; it's worth browsing. I'd head to the first floor up for the eclectic permanent collection and finish off with furnished rooms on the ground floor.*

Berthe Morisot (1841-1895)

The Marmottan's large collection of Berthe Morisot's work cements her reputation as one of Impressionism's Founding Mothers. Born into a cultured, supportive family, she found early success painting landscapes (in the open air) in the proto-Impressionist style of her mentor, Camille Corot. Still in her 20s, Morisot exhibited to good reviews at the official Salon for seven straight years.

Meanwhile, she'd met Edouard Manet, married his big brother, and experimented with the Impressionist style. She threw away her black paint and replaced it with a brighter palette. In 1874, she joined the Impressionist gang, exhibiting her work at the same "Salon des Refusés" where Monet's *Impression: Sunrise* had caused a minor revolution.

Her paintings focus mainly on women, either in gardens or in peaceful, domestic situations. Her subjects were landscapes, friends (such as Manet), and family (her daughter, Julie). She had a keen eye for ladies' fashions (*At the Ball*, 1875). Like Manet's, Morisot's brand of Impressionism was always naturalistic and understated. She avoided the gritty urban scenes of Degas, the pointillistic color theory of Seurat, and the proto-abstract work of Monet. But like Renoir, she loved painting small-scale domestic scenes of her rosy-cheeked daughter and niece picking cherries or frolicking in the gardens. The tranquil Marmottan mansion is the perfect setting for the peaceful world of Morisot.

REST OF THE MUSEUM

The ground floor and permanent collection show off Paul Marmottan's eclectic tastes. Upstairs, in the **permanent collection,** look for Napoleon's bed and a portrait of him at 30, having just been appointed consul. You'll see works that look famous—statues by Canova and scenes of Venice by Canaletto—but most are by their students. A darkened room displays the Marmottan's excellent medieval collection: illuminated manuscripts (that is, colorfully illustrated books), musical scores, stained glass, and miniature paintings of saints and Bible scenes.

The highlight of the permanent collection is an ever-changing display of works by Monet's fellow Impressionists—Degas, Pissarro, Gauguin, Renoir—who were also his colleagues and friends. Special attention is often given to Berthe Morisot (see sidebar).

On the **ground floor** are Marmottan's furnishings, which tended toward the Empire style: high-polished mahogany with upholstery featuring classical motifs like laurel wreaths and torches and brass highlights. Chairs have arched backs, armrests, and tapered legs. The paintings are also from this period, when the French bourgeoisie reigned supreme. You'll see an embroidered portrait of Napoleon, and portraits of ladies wearing tiaras and gentlemen in high-collared suits painted in the seamless-brushstroke style that Monet rebelled against. Be sure to peruse the *salle à manger* (dining room) to gaze at works by Pierre-Auguste Renoir, Paul Gauguin, Gustave Caillebotte, and Marc Chagall.

• *You've reached the end of the tour. From here, if you need a taxi, you'll find a stand at the La Muette Métro stop. Across from the museum, bus #32 takes you to stops at Trocadéro and along the Champs-Elysées near the Grand Palais.*

Or, if you're up for a post-museum stroll, it's a pleasant one-hour walk (without stops) from here to the Eiffel Tower along Rue de Passy, one of Paris' most pleasant (and upscale) shopping streets. To reach Rue de Passy, head east up Chaussée de la Muette, past the La Muette Métro stop—follow that tower. After Rue de Passy ends, you could continue straight—on Boulevard Delessert—all the way to the Eiffel Tower.

MARMOTTAN

LEFT BANK WALK

From the Seine to Luxembourg Garden

The Left Bank is as much an attitude as it is an actual neighborhood. But this walk—from the Seine to St. Germain-des-Prés to Luxembourg Garden—captures some of the artistic, intellectual, and countercultural spirit long associated with the south side of the river.

We'll pass through an upscale area of art galleries, home-furnishing boutiques, antique dealers, bookstores, small restaurants, classic cafés, evening hot spots, and the former homes of writers, painters, and composers. Though trendy for a long time now, the area still has the offbeat funkiness that has always defined the Rive Gauche. (*Gauche,* meaning "left," has come to imply social incorrectness, like giving a handshake with the wrong—left—hand.)

Use this walk as a series of historical markers as you explore the Left Bank of today. The walk leads you through a fascinating neighborhood and dovetails perfectly with a shopping stroll (see "Sèvres-Babylone to St. Sulpice" on page 496) or downtime at Luxembourg Garden (where this walk ends). It also works well following a visit to the Louvre or after the Historic Paris Walk, and it's ideal for connoisseurs of contemporary art.

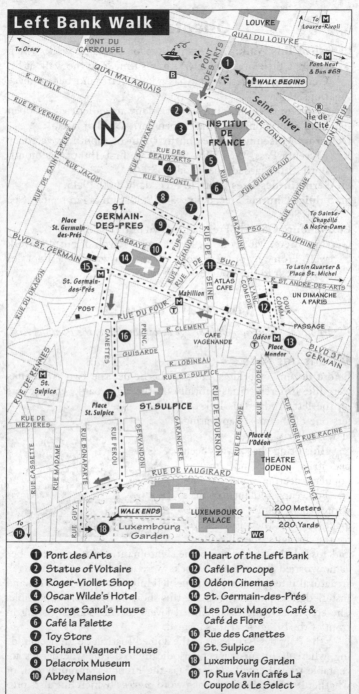

Left Bank Walk

1 Pont des Arts
2 Statue of Voltaire
3 Roger-Viollet Shop
4 Oscar Wilde's Hotel
5 George Sand's House
6 Café la Palette
7 Toy Store
8 Richard Wagner's House
9 Delacroix Museum
10 Abbey Mansion

11 Heart of the Left Bank
12 Café le Procope
13 Odéon Cinemas
14 St. Germain-des-Prés
15 Les Deux Magots Café & Café de Flore
16 Rue des Canettes
17 St. Sulpice
18 Luxembourg Garden
19 To Rue Vavin Cafés La Coupole & Le Select

Orientation

Length of This Walk: Allow two hours for the whole walk, which covers a little over a mile. With less time, end the walk at St. Germain-des-Prés, which has good Métro and bus connections.

When to Go: Evenings are pleasant. Many art galleries don't open until afternoon, but remain open until 19:00 or later.

Delacroix Museum: €7, free on first Sun of month, covered by Museum Pass, Wed-Mon 9:30-17:30, first Thu of the month until 21:00, closed Tue, good WC.

St. Germain-des-Prés Church: Free, daily 8:00-19:45.

St. Sulpice Church: Free, daily 7:30-19:30, Sun organ recitals (see page 86).

Luxembourg Garden: Free, daily dawn until dusk.

Getting There: Mo: Pont Neuf or Louvre-Rivoli or bus #69 work well. From any of these stops, make your way to the Pont des Arts, next to the Louvre.

The Walk Begins

• *Start on the pedestrian-only bridge across the Seine, the Pont des Arts.*

LEFT BANK

❶ Pont des Arts

Before dozens of bridges crossed the Seine, the two riverbanks were like different cities—royalty on the right bank, commoners on the left. Today this link offers one of the most captivating views in Paris.

This bridge has always been pedestrian only...and long a popular meeting point for lovers. For years, romantic couples wrote their names on a padlock, "locked" their love forever to the bridge's metal railings, and tossed the key in the Seine. Unromantic city engineers became worried that the heavy locks were jeopardizing the bridge's structural integrity (a whole panel fell into the Seine in 2015) and installed glass panels that make this show of devotion impossible. The city is advising disappointed lovers to take selfies kissing in front of the bridge's railings instead.

The Pont des Arts leads to the domed Institut de France building, where 40 linguists meet periodically to decide whether it's acceptable to call email *"le mail"* (as the French commonly do), or whether it should be the French word *courriel* (which linguists prefer). The Académie Française, dedicated to halting the erosion of French culture, is wary of new French terms with strangely foreign sounds—like *le week-end*, *le marketing*, *le fast-food*, and *c'est cool*.

Besides the Académie Française, the Institut houses several other Académies, such as the Académie des Beaux-Arts, which is dedicated to subjects appropriate for the Left Bank, such as music and painting.

• *Leave the bridge and cross the busy street. Angle toward the right side of the Institut de France and walk through the passageway between #25 and #27. Once on the other side of the Institut, you should be met by a statue in a street-corner garden (unless it's still removed for cleaning).*

❷ Statue of Voltaire

"Jesus committed suicide." The mischievous philosopher Voltaire could scandalize a party with a wicked comment like that, delivered with an enigmatic smile and a twinkle in his eye (meaning if Christ is truly God, he could have prevented his crucifixion). Voltaire—a commoner more sophisticated than the royalty who lived across the river—introduces us to the Left Bank.

Born François-Marie Arouet (1694-1778), he took up "Voltaire" as his one-word pen name. Although Voltaire mingled with aristocrats, he was constantly in trouble for questioning the ruling class and for fueling ideas that would soon spark a revolution. He did 11 months in the Bastille prison, then spent 40 years in virtual exile from his beloved Paris. Returning as an old man, he got a hero's welcome so surprising it killed him.

• *From here we'll head south down Rue de Seine to Boulevard St. Germain, making a few detours along the way. The first stop is a charcoal-colored storefront at 6 Rue de Seine.*

❸ Roger-Viollet

Look in the windows at black-and-white photos of Paris' storied past. The display changes often, but you might see a half-built Eiffel Tower, glitterati of yesteryear (Colette, Simone de Beauvoir,

Wilde in the Left Bank

Oscar Wilde (1854-1900), the Irish playwright with the flamboyant clothes and outrageous wit, died in a Left Bank hotel on November 30, 1900 (don't blame the current owners).

Just five years earlier, he'd been at his peak. He had several plays running simultaneously in London's West End and had returned to London triumphant from a lecture tour through America. Then news of his love affair with a lord leaked out, causing a scandal, and he was sentenced to two years in prison for "gross indecency." Wilde's wife abandoned him, refusing to let him see their children again.

After his prison term, a poor and broken Wilde was exiled to Paris, where he succumbed to an ear infection and died in a (then) shabby hotel room. Among his last words in the rundown place were: "Either this wallpaper goes, or I do."

Wilde is buried in Paris (□ see the Père Lachaise Cemetery Tour chapter).

Jean Cocteau), Hitler in Paris, and so on. Many more photos are tucked away inside the binders lining the walls, labeled alphabetically. This humble shop is the funky origin of a worldwide press agency (similar to Getty Images) dealing in historic photographs. The family of photographer Henri Roger expanded his photographs into an archive of millions of photos, chronicling Paris' changes through the years. After his death in 1985, they bequeathed the business and the collections to the city of Paris. You can shop inside (Mon-Sat 11:00-19:00, closed Sun) or order photos on their website (www.parisenimages.fr).

• *Continue down Rue de Seine, which cuts through a neighborhood of art galleries and upscale shops selling lamps, sconces, vases, bowls, and statues for people who turn their living rooms into art.*

At the first intersection, a half-block detour to the right leads to ❹ *Oscar Wilde's hotel (#13), where he died in 1900. The sight itself is hardly worth the walk there, but the story of how Wilde ended up here is fascinating (see the sidebar).*

Continuing along Rue de Seine, a plaque at #31 marks...

OSCAR WILDE
Poète et Dramaturge
NÉ A DUBLIN
LE 15 OCTOBRE 1856
EST MORT DANS CETTE MAISON
LE 30 NOVEMBRE 1900

❺ George Sand's House

In 1831 George Sand (1804-1876) left her husband and two children and moved into this apartment, determined to become a writer. During the year she lived here, she wrote articles for *Le Figaro* while turning her real-life experiences with men into a sensational novel, *Indiana,* which made her a celebrity and allowed her to afford a better apartment.

George Sand is known for her novels, her cross-dressing (men's suits, slicked-down hair, cigars—and trading in her married name, Amantine-Lucile-Aurore Dudevant, for a man's name), and for her complex love affair with a sensitive pianist from Poland, Frédéric Chopin.

• *At 43 Rue de Seine is...*

❻ Café la Palette

Though less famous than more historic cafés, this is a "real" one, where a *café crème,* beer, or glass of wine at an outdoor table is not outrageous. It's one café where I prefer sitting inside—the 100-year-old, tobacco-stained wood paneling and faded Art Nouveau decor lend an ambience of Left Bank cool. Toulouse-Lautrec would have liked it here. Have something to drink at the bar, admire

your surroundings, and snoop about the place—notice the artist palettes above the bar. Nothing seems to have changed since it was built in 1903, except the modern espresso machine (open daily).

• *At the fork, veer right down small Rue de l'Echaudé. Four doors up, at 6 Rue de l'Echaudé, is a...*

❼ Toy Store *(Jouets)*

French and American kids share many of the same toys and storybook characters: Babar the Elephant, Maisy Mouse, Tintin, the Smurfs, Madeline, Asterix, and the Little Prince. This store features figurines of these and other whimsical folk.

In *The Little Prince* (1943), written by Antoine de Saint-Exupéry, a pilot crashes in the Sahara, where a mysterious little prince takes him to various planets, teaching him about life from a child's wise perspective.

In his actual life, "Saint-Ex" (1900-1944) was indeed a daring aviator who had survived wrecks in the Sahara. After France fell to the Nazis, he fled to America, where he wrote and published *The Little Prince.* He returned to Europe, then disappeared while flying a spy mission for the Allies. Lost for six decades, his plane was finally found off the coast of Marseille. The cause of the crash remains a mystery, part of a legend as enduring in France as Amelia Earhart's is in the US.

LEFT BANK

• At the intersection with Rue Jacob, a half-block detour to the right leads to #14.

❽ Richard Wagner's House

Having survived a storm at sea on the way here, the young German composer (1813-1883) spent the gray winter of 1841-1842 in Paris in this building writing *The Flying Dutchman,* an opera about a ghost ship. It was the restless young man's lowest point of poverty. Six months later, a German company staged his first opera *(Rienzi),* plucking him from obscurity and leading to a production of *The Flying Dutchman* that launched his career.

Now the premises are occupied by a trendy boutique.

• Backtrack a few steps along Rue Jacob, then turn right and walk south on Rue de Furstenberg to a tiny, pleasant, tree-bordered square. At #6 is the...

❾ Delacroix Museum

The painter Eugène Delacroix (1798-1863) lived here on this peaceful square. Today, his home is a bite-sized museum with paintings and memorabilia. It's a delightful detour for his fans, skippable for most, and free with the Museum Pass (good WC, see listing on page 87).

Delacroix lived a full and successful life. An ambassador's son, he studied at the Beaux-Arts (which we saw earlier) and exhibited at the Salon. His *Liberty Leading the People* (1831) was an instant classic, a symbol of French democracy. Trips to North Africa added exotic Muslim elements to his palette. He hobnobbed with aristocrats and bohemians like George Sand and Frédéric Chopin (both of whom he painted). He painted large-scale murals for the Louvre, Hôtel de Ville, and Luxembourg Palace. In 1857, nearing 60 and in failing health, Delacroix moved in here. He was seeking a quiet home/studio where he could concentrate on his final great works for the Church of St. Sulpice (which we'll see later).

• Continue uphill as Rue de Furstenberg runs directly into...

❿ Abbey Mansion

This building (1586) was the administrative center for the vast complex of monks gathered around the nearby church of St. Germain-des-Prés. Today, it's a Catholic school.

• Facing the Abbey Mansion, turn left on Rue de l'Abbaye and start working your way east. Along the way is a wine shop, at 6 Rue de Bourbon-Le-Château, called **La Dernière Goutte**—*"The Last Drop." They*

Art Galleries

You'll see many arts-oriented shops in this vibrant neighborhood. There are fine-art galleries selling paintings and statues, art-supply stores, antique dealers, and chic boutiques for the latest in interior design.

Paris' art scene thrives. In the 20th century, the city attracted many of the foreigners who pioneered modern art (such as Picasso, Chagall, and Modigliani). Artists here still get respect not always given to artists in the States ("So you're an artist, huh? And what's your real job?"). Paris remains a clearinghouse of creative ideas...and fine art is big business, too. Lots of money passes through this city. Oil-rich sultans come here looking for trendy new works to hang over their sofas back home. Museum curators from America troll these Left Bank streets, taking notes on what's hot. Many travelers come here to enjoy the finer things in life. If they come across something they love, they pull out their plastic and make it their own. You could do the same. Paris is one city in the world where art supply does not necessarily outstrip art demand.

You're welcome to window shop or enter the galleries. Remember the niceties of shopping in Paris. Always say, *"Bonjour, Madame"* (or *Monsieur*) when entering, and *"Au revoir, Madame"* (or *Monsieur*) when leaving. *"Je regarde"* means "I'm just looking." *"Je voudrais acheter"* means "I would like to buy." Most clerks speak sufficient English and are happy to help or to let you browse. If you stroll neighborhoods in the evening, you're likely to pass what looks like a cocktail party spilling out of an art gallery. These "art openings," called *vernissages,* are sometimes private, though usually open to the public (even Americans). Be bold and join the party if you come across one.

welcome both connoisseurs and yokels for an unsnooty look at France's viniculture (tastings and classes listed on chalkboard; Tue-Sat 11:00-20:00, Mon from 15:30, closed midday Mon-Fri). At the T-intersection with Rue de Buci, turn left. You've arrived at what is, arguably, the geographical (if not spiritual)...

⓫ Heart of the Left Bank

Explore. Rue de Buci *(bew-see)* is perennially busy hosting *pâtis-series* and a produce market by day and bars by night. Mixing earthiness and elegance, it's a quintessential Left Bank scene. Continue east through the café cauldron of Rue de Buci, which crosses a busy five-corner intersection and becomes

Rue St. André-des-Arts. Notice the tall wood beams that pierce the roof of the **Atlas Café** while keeping the wall behind upright, and the fake-flower-festooned café opposite. That's so "Left Bank."

• *Cross Rue de l'Ancienne Comédie and soon turn right into the covered passageway called Cour du Commerce St. André. Stroll a half-block down this colorful alleyway, past shops and enticing eateries. On your right, you'll pass the back door of...*

⑫ Café le Procope

Founded in 1686, Le Procope is one of France's oldest continuously operating restaurants, and was one of Europe's first places to sample an exotic new stimulant—coffee—recently imported from the Muslim culture.

In the 1700s, Le Procope caffeinated the Revolution. Voltaire reportedly drank 30 cups a day, fueling his intellectual passion. Benjamin Franklin recounted war stories about America's Revolution. Robespierre, Danton, and Marat plotted coups over cups of double-short soy mochaccinos. And a young lieutenant named Napoleon Bonaparte ran up a tab he never paid. See portraits of some of the café's most famous regulars in the windows.

Located midway between university students, royalty, and the counterculture Comédie Française, Le Procope attracted literary types who loved the free newspapers, writing paper, and quill pens. Today, the one-time coffeehouse is a full-service restaurant (affordable if mediocre *menus,* open daily). If you're interested in a meal ($$) surrounded by memorabilia-plastered walls (and tourists), enter through the red-draped opening.

• *Continue down the cobbled lane until it spills out onto Boulevard St. Germain at an intersection (and Métro stop) called Odéon.*

⑬ Odéon Cinemas

When night falls, the neon signs buzz to life, and Paris' many lovers of film converge here for the latest releases at several multiplexes in the area.

• *Cross Rue de l'Ancienne Comédie to the right. Looking south up Rue de l'Odéon as you cross, notice the classical columns and pyramidal roofline of the* **Théâtre de l'Odéon,** *the descendant of the original Comédie Française (now housed in the Palais Royal). Continue walking west along busy Boulevard St. Germain for six blocks, passing* **Café Vagenande** *(famous for its plush Art Nouveau interior) and other fashionable, noisy* *cafés with outdoor terraces. You'll reach (on your right) the large stone church and square of...*

⑭ St. Germain-des-Prés

Paris' oldest church, dating from the 11th century (the square bell tower is original), stands on a site where a Christian church has stood since the fall of

Rome. (The first church was destroyed by Vikings in the 885-886 siege.) The restored interior is still painted in the medieval manner. The church is Romanesque, with round—not pointed—arches over the aisles of the nave.

The square outside is one of Paris' great gathering spots on warm evenings. The church is often lit up and open late.

• *On Place St. Germain-des-Prés, you'll find two venerable cafés—once meccas of creative coffee drinking, today just filled with tourists and milking their fabled past.*

⑮ Les Deux Magots Café and Café de Flore

Since opening in 1885, "The Two Chinamen Café" (wooden statues inside) has taken over from Le Procope as the café of ideas.

From Oscar Wilde's Aestheticism (1900) to Picasso's Cubism (1910s) to Hemingway's spare prose (1920s) to Sartre's Existentialism (with Simone de Beauvoir and Albert Camus, 1940s and '50s) to rock singer Jim Morrison (early 1970s), worldwide movements have been born in the simple atmosphere of these two cafés. Café de Flore, once frequented by Picasso, is more hip, but Deux Magots is more inviting (for details, see the Eating in Paris chapter). Across the street is Brasserie Lipp, a classic brasserie where Hemingway wrote much of *A Farewell to Arms*.

• *From the Church of St. Germain-des-Prés, cross Boulevard St. Germain and head a block south on Rue Bonaparte (walking past BNP Paribas bank). Jog left on Rue du Four, then right on...*

⑯ Rue des Canettes

Small, mid-priced restaurants, bars, and comfortable brewpubs make the streets in this area a popular nightspot for Parisians. **Chez Georges/Comptoir des Canettes** (at #11) is the last outpost of funkiness (and how!) in an increasingly gentrified neighborhood. Georges stays up very late, so you won't find much action here until the afternoon.

• *Continue south on Rue des Canettes to the church of...*

⓲ St. Sulpice

The impressive Neoclassical arcaded facade, with two round, half-finished towers, is modeled on St. Paul's in London. It has a re-markable organ and offers Sun-day-morning recitals. The lone café on the square in front (Café de la Mairie) is always lively and perfectly located for a break.

Inside, circle the church counterclockwise, making a few stops. In the first chapel on the right, find **Delacroix's three murals** (on the chapel's ceil-ing and walls) of fighting angels, completed during his final years while he was fighting a lengthy illness. They sum up his long career, from Renaissance/Baroque roots to furious Romanticism to proto-Impressionism.

The most famous is the agitated *Jacob Wrestling the Angel*. The two grapple in a leafy wood that echoes the wrestlers' rippling energy. Jacob fights the angel to a standstill, bringing him a well-earned blessing for his or-deal. Figures to the right of the tree roots include the shepherd Laban and his daughter Rachel (Jacob's future wife). Get close and notice the thick brushwork that influenced the next gen-eration of Impressionists—each leaf is a single brushstroke, often smudging two different colors in a single stroke. The "black" of the piled clothes in the foreground—notice the French flag among them—is built from rough strokes of purple, green, and white. (Too much glare? Take a couple of steps to the right to view it.)

On the opposite wall, *Heliodorus Chased from the Temple* has the smooth, seamless brushwork of Delacroix's prime. After Syrian Heliodorus has killed the king and launched a coup, he has entered the sacred Jewish Temple in Jerusalem trying to steal the treasure. Angry angels launch themselves at him, sending him sprawling.

The vibrant, clashing colors, swirling composition, and over-the-top subject are trademark Delacroix Romanticism. On the ceiling, *The Archangel Michael* drives demons from heaven.

Walking up the right side of the church, pause at the **fourth chapel,** with a statue of Joan of Arc and wall plaques listing hundreds upon hundreds of names. These are France's WWI dead—from this congregation alone.

In the chapel at the far end of the church, behind the altar, ponder the cryptic symbolism of Mary and Child lit by a sunburst, standing on an orb, and trampling a snake, while a stone cloud tumbles down to a sacrificial lamb.

Continue around the church. On the wall of the north transept is an Egyptian-style obelisk used as a **gnomon,** or part of a

sundial. At Christmas Mass, the sun shines into the church through a tiny hole—it's opposite the obelisk, high up on the south wall (in the upper-right window pane). The sunbeam strikes a mark on the obelisk that indicates the winter solstice. Then, week by week, the sunbeam moves down the obelisk and across the bronze rod in the floor, until, at midsummer, the sun lights up the area near the altar. (For a while, this corner of the church was busy with fans of *The Da Vinci Code*.)

In the final chapel before the exit, you should see on display a copy of the **Shroud of Turin** (the original is in Turin, Italy). This famed burial cloth is purported to have wrapped the body of Christ, who left it with a mysterious, holy stain of his image.

• Back out on Place St. Sulpice, take note that several interesting shopping streets branch off from here. (See the "Sèvres-Babylone to St. Sulpice" boutique stroll in the Shopping in Paris chapter.)

To complete this walk, turn left out of the church and continue south on Rue Henry de Jouvenel, which soon turns into Rue Férou and takes

you directly to Luxembourg Garden. You'll pass a **wall inscribed with a quotation** from one of France's most famous poems, "Le Bateau Ivre," by Arthur Rimbaud (1854-1891). He describes the feeling of drifting along aimlessly, like a drunken boat: "Comme je descendais... *As I floated down calm rivers, I could no longer feel the control of my handlers..."*

Drift along to Luxembourg Garden, at the Musée du Luxembourg (an art exhibition space), and circle to the right around the fence until you find an open entrance.

⑱ Luxembourg Garden

Paris' most interesting and enjoyable garden/park/recreational area, le Jardin du Luxembourg is a great place to watch Parisians at rest and play. This 60-acre garden, dotted with fountains and statues, is the property of the French Senate, which meets here in Luxembourg Palace. Al-though it seems like something out of a movie, it's a fact that France's secret service *(Générale de la Sécurité Extérieure)* is "se-cretly" headquartered beneath Luxembourg Garden. (Don't tell anyone.)

The palace was created in 1615 by Marie de Médici. Recent-ly widowed (by Henry IV) and homesick for Florence, she built the palace as a re-creation of her girlhood home, the Pitti Palace. When her son grew to be Louis XIII, he drove his mother from the palace, exiling her to Germany.

Luxembourg Garden has special rules governing its use (for ex-ample, where cards can be played, where dogs can be walked, where joggers can run, and when and where music can be played). The radi-ant flower beds are completely changed three times a year, and the boxed trees are brought out of the *orangerie* in May. In the southwest corner of the gardens, you can see beehives that have been here since 1872. Honey is made here for the *orangerie*. Close by, check out the apple and pear conservatory, with more than 600 varieties of fruit trees.

Children enjoy the rentable toy sailboats and other kid activi-ties. You'll find marionette shows several times weekly (Les Gui-gnols, like Punch and Judy; for times, see page 478). Pony rides are available from April through October. (And meanwhile, the French CIA keeps plotting.)

Challenge the card and chess players to a game (near the tennis courts) or find a free chair

near the main pond and take a well-deserved break, here at the end of our walk.

• *Nearby: The grand Neoclassical-domed Panthéon, now a mausoleum housing the tombs of great French notables, is three blocks away and worth touring (see listing on page 88). The historic cafés of Montparnasse—**⑲ La Coupole** and **Le Select**—are a few blocks from the southwest-corner exit of the park (down Rue Vavin, listed under "Les Grands Cafés de Paris" in the Eating in Paris chapter). Luxembourg Garden is ringed with Métro stops (all a 10-minute walk away).*

CLUNY MUSEUM TOUR

Musée National du Moyen Age

The National Museum of the Middle Ages doesn't sound quite so boring as I sink deeper into middle age myself. Aside from the solemn religious art, there's some surprisingly lively stuff here.

Paris emerged on the world stage in the Middle Ages, the time between ancient Rome and the Renaissance. Europe was awakening from a thousand-year slumber. Trade was booming, people actually owned chairs, and the Renaissance was moving in like a warm front from Italy.

Orientation

Cost: €12, free first Sun of the month, covered by Museum Pass.

Hours: Tue-Sun 9:30-18:15, first and third Thu of the month until 21:00, closed Mon, last entry 45 minutes before closing.

Information: +33 1 53 73 78 00, www.musee-moyenage.fr.

Expect Changes: The museum has been closed for a major renovation but should reopen by the time you visit. This tour reflects the collection before the museum's closure, but the highlights should still be on display upon its reopening.

Getting There: The museum, a five-minute walk from Ile de la Cité, is a block above the intersection of Boulevards St. Germain and St. Michel, at 6 Place Paul Painlevé (Mo: Cluny La Sorbonne, St-Michel, or Odéon; bus #63 from Rue Cler and #86 or #87 from the Marais).

Length of This Tour: You can see the highlights—the Roman Bath and the *Lady and the Unicorn* tapestries—in less than an hour, but definitely allow browsing time for this underrated museum.

Baggage Check: Required and free for bags larger than a purse.

Cuisine Art: Just a few blocks away, the charming Place de la

Sorbonne has several good cafés (see page 458; walk up Boulevard St. Michel toward the Panthéon). The peaceful square facing the museum entry has flowers, children playing, and plenty of picnic benches. To eat or drink with a smashing view of the Panthéon, walk a few blocks farther and find **Le Soufflot** (16 Rue Soufflot).

The Tour Begins

This chapter is less a room-by-room tour and more a chronological overview of the highlights.
• *First up is the biggest, oldest, and most venerable part of the museum—the 2,000-year-old...*

Roman Bath

This echoing cavern was a Roman *frigidarium*. Pretty cool. The museum is located on the site of a Roman bathhouse, which was in the center of town during the Roman years. The sunken area you see in the alcove was exactly what it looks like: a swimming pool. After hot baths and exercise in adjoining rooms, ordinary Romans would take a cold dip there, then relax cheek to cheek with such notables as Emperor Julian the Apostate (see his statue), who lived next door. As the empire decayed in the fourth century, Julian avoided the corrupt city of Rome and made Paris a northern power base.

The 40-foot-high ceiling is the largest surviving Roman vault in France, and it took the French another 1,000 years to improve on that crisscross-arch technology. The sheer size of this room—constructed in AD 200, when Rome was at its peak—gives an idea of the epic scale on which the Romans built. It inspired Europeans to greatness during the less civilized Middle Ages.
• *Among the ruins that littered medieval Paris after the fall of Rome was the...*

Roman Pillar of the Boatmen

Four fragments remain of the Pillar of the Boatmen *(Le Pilier des Nautes)*, which decorated the ancient Roman temple to Jupiter that stood where Notre-Dame is today. These fragments, probably the oldest man-made objects you'll see from Paris, once fit together to support a 20-foot-high altar to the king of the gods in the Roman temple. Take a closer look at three of these:

One fragment (the *pierre de la dédicace*, or dedication stone) is inscribed "TIB. CAESARE," announcing that the altar was built under Emperor Tiberius (AD 14-37; he reigned during the time of Jesus Christ) and was paid for by the Parisian boatmen's union (see them holding their shields).

CLUNY

Another fragment (the *Pierre aux quatre divinités*) depicts the horned Celtic god Cernunnos, who is also known as the Stag Lord and god of the hunt. The eclectic Romans allowed this local "druid" god to support the shrine of Jupiter in league with their own Vulcan, who hammers, and Castor and Pollux, who pet their horses.

The fragment labeled *Bloc dit "de Jupiter"* shows Jupiter in his royal robes leaning on a spear, as well as the god Vulcan hammering in his fiery forge.

• *The museum leads you from the fall of Rome (AD 476) to France's next chapter, beginning with the reign of the Frankish king Clovis I, the father of modern France.*

Early Medieval Artifacts

The museum's exquisite collection of objects from c. 500-1000 makes it clear that Roman art and learning lived on even after the empire's fall. Columns and capitals evoke the Roman-esque grandeur of early Christian churches. Statues of the Virgin Mary, decorative flourishes from church buildings, and exquisitely carved miniature altarpieces in ivory reveal Roman style and artistic techniques.

• *Throughout your visit, you'll see stunning examples of...*

Stained Glass

At a time when life could be harsh and brutal, stained glass gave people a glimpse of the glories of heaven. The panels displayed

here once adorned some of Paris' most venerable churches, such as St. Denis (the world's first truly Gothic church) and the glorious Sainte-Chapelle. Some are rare 800-year-old originals that were removed during renovations and replaced. They give us a window into the magical, supernatural, miraculous—and often violent—medieval mind.

High Middle Ages

Around the year 1200, Parisians were emerging from the Dark Ages. They'd survived their Y1K crisis, trade was booming, a university was founded (today's Sorbonne), and Paris was becoming a major European capital. The High Middle Ages produced art that was less about grim crucifixions and more a celebration of the beauty of the world. You'll see surprisingly joyful tapestries, golden altarpieces, statues with a budding realism, and inviting Madonnas with smiles and sashaying hips. One ivory box (c. 1300), finely carved from an elephant tusk, gives a look at the age of courtly love, with ladies shooting flowers as arrows and a tournament shown as a battle for love.

Stone Heads from Notre-Dame

The Cluny has some treasured artifacts from the High Middle Ages' most famous cathedral—Notre-Dame. Twenty-one stone
heads (sculpted 1220-1230), depicting the biblical kings of Judah, once sat atop statues decorating the front of the cathedral. In 1793 an angry mob of revolutionaries, mistaking the kings of Judah for the kings of France, abused and decapitated
the statues. (Today's heads on the Notre-Dame statues are reconstructions.) Someone gathered up the heads and buried them in his backyard near the present-day Opéra Garnier. There they slept for two centuries, unknown and noseless, until 1977, when someone accidentally unearthed them and brought them to an astounded world. Their stoic expressions accept what fate, time, and liberals have done to them.

A statue of Adam is also from Notre-Dame. It will be another 200 years before naked Adam, scrawny and flaccid, can step out from behind that bush.

• *As Europeans rediscovered the beauty of the world around them, a new sensuality crept into their artwork. A marvelous celebration of the senses—and the high point of the Cluny's collection—is the late medieval masterpiece known as the...*

Lady and the Unicorn Tapestries

Designed by an unknown (but probably French) artist before 1500, these six tapestries were woven in Belgium from wool and silk. Loaded with symbols—some serious, some playful—they have been interpreted in many ways, but, in short, the series deals with each of the five senses.

In medieval lore, unicorns were enigmatic, solitary creatures, so wild that only virgins could entice and tame them. In secular society, they symbolized how a feral man was drawn to his lady love. Religiously, the unicorn was a symbol of Christ—radiant, pure, and somewhat remote—who is made accessible to humankind by the Virgin Mary. These tapestries likely draw inspiration from all these traditions.

• *Moving clockwise around the room...*

Touch: This is the most basic and dangerous of the senses. The scene is set in the wild: monkeys, a leopard, and exotic birds. A blond lady "strokes the unicorn's horn"—if you know what I mean—and the lion gets the double entendre. Medieval Europeans were exploring the wonders of love and the pleasures of sex.

Taste: The lady takes candy from a servant's dish to feed it to her parakeet. A unicorn—a species extinct since the Age of Reason—and a lion look on. At the lady's feet, a monkey also tastes something, while the little white dog behind her wishes he had some. This was the dawn of the Age of Discovery, when overseas explorers spiced up Europe's bland gruel with new fruits, herbs, and spices.

The lion (symbol of knighthood?) and unicorn (symbol of "bourgeois nobility," purity, or fertility?) wave flags with the coat of arms of the family that commissioned the tapestries—three silver crescents in a band of blue.

Smell: The lady picks flowers and weaves them into a sweet-smelling wreath. On a bench behind, the monkey apes her. The flowers, trees, and animals are exotic and varied. Each detail is exquisite alone, but if you step back they blend together into pleasing patterns.

Hearing: Wearing a stunning dress, the lady plays sweet music on an organ, which soothes the savage beasts around her. The pattern and folds of the tablecloth are lovely. Humans and their fellow creatures (cats, dogs, and rabbits) live in harmony in an enchanted blue garden filled with flowers, all set in a red background.

Sight: The unicorn cuddles up and looks at himself in the lady's mirror, pleased with what he sees. The lion turns away and snickers. As the Renaissance dawns, vanity is a less than deadly sin.

Admire the great artistic skill in some of the detail work, such as the necklace and the patterns in the lady's dress. This tapestry had quality control in all its stages: the drawing of the scene, its enlargement and transfer to a cartoon, and the weaving. Still, the design itself is crude by Renaissance 3-D standards. The fox and rabbits, supposedly in the distance, simply float overhead, as big as the animals at the lady's feet.

Tapestry #6: The most talked-about tapestry gets its name from the words on our lady's tent: *A Mon Seul Désir* (To My Sole Desire). What is her only desire? Is it jewelry, as she grabs a necklace from the jewel box? Or is she putting the necklace away and renouncing material things in order to follow her only desire?

Our lady has tried all things sensual and is now prepared to follow the one true impulse. Is it God? Love? Her friends the unicorn and lion open the tent doors. Flickering flames cover the tent. Perhaps she's stepping out from the tent. Or is she going in to meet the object of her desire? Human sensuality is awakening, an old dark age is ending, and the Renaissance is emerging.

The Rest of the Cluny

Allow time to explore more of this wide-ranging museum. You'll find medallions, more tapestries, medieval altarpieces, old books, swords and guns, and even a narwhal tusk—in medieval times, these were sold as unicorn horns. Ah, the joys of the Middle Ages.

• *When you're ready, leave the Middle Ages and return to your modern, fast-paced life...*

CHAMPS-ELYSEES WALK

*From the Arc de Triomphe to
Place de la Concorde*

Don't leave Paris without a stroll along Avenue des Champs-Elysées
(shahnz ay-lee-zay). This is Paris at its most Parisian: monumental sidewalks, stylish shops, elegant cafés, glimmering showrooms,
and proud Parisians on parade. The whole world seems to gather
here to strut along the boulevard. It's a great walk by day, and even
better at night, allowing you to tap into the city's global scene. On
the first Sunday of the month, it's delightfully traffic-free.

Orientation

Length of This Walk: This two-mile, slightly downhill walk takes
three hours (including a one-hour visit to the Arc de Triomphe). Métro stops are located every few blocks along the
Champs-Elysées. With less time, end the walk at Rond-Point
(Mo: FDR).

Getting There: To reach the Arc de Triomphe at Place Charles de
Gaulle, take the Métro to Charles de Gaulle-Etoile. Following *Sortie #1* and *Champs-Elysées/Arc de Triomphe* signs, which
deposit you right at the entry to the pedestrian tunnel under
all the traffic to the arch itself. From Rue Cler and the Montparnasse area, bus #92 works best (see the map on page 327 for
stop locations).

Arc de Triomphe: Free to view exterior; 284 steps to rooftop—€13,
timed-entry tickets available online, free for those under age
18, free on first Sun of month Nov-March, covered by Museum Pass; daily 10:00-23:00, Oct-March until 22:30, last entry
45 minutes before closing, www.paris-arc-de-triomphe.fr.
With a timed-entry ticket or the Museum Pass, you'll bypass
the slow underground ticket line (pass holders do not need to
reserve a time slot).

Eating near the Champs-Elysées

Good eating options on the Champs-Elysées are slim. Most sit-down restaurants have lazy service, mediocre food, and inflated prices. Instead, try the lovely café at the **Petit Palais** near the end of this walk, or one of these places:

$$ Comptoir de L'Arc, a block from the Arc toward the Eiffel Tower, is a bustling place dishing out good *plats du jour* to locals, with side-Arc views from its terrace tables just below the tourist flow (Mon-Fri 7:00 until late, closed Sat-Sun, 73 Avenue Marceau, +33 1 47 20 72 04).

$ La Brioche Dorée and **$ Boulangerie Paul** sit side-by-side smack on the Champs-Elysées, each offering great Champs-side tables and good sandwiches and salads (about halfway along this walk at #82). Dorée has WCs, air-conditioning, and extra seating upstairs. A second Dorée is at #144, much closer to the Arc de Triomphe.

You can tour the base of the Arc sans ticket and line, but you need one for the climb to the top (in a line you can't avoid). The elevator is only for people with disabilities and runs only to the museum level, not to the top, which requires a 47-step climb (though if you or your partner feel unable to make the climb it's worth asking). The Arc is quieter first thing and after 17:00—come for sunset.

Grand Palais: This exhibition venue is closed for renovation until at least 2024.

Petit Palais: Free, Tue-Sun 10:00-18:00, Fri until 21:00 for special exhibits (fee), closed Mon, good café.

Services: A small, often-crowded WC is near the top of the Arc de Triomphe. You'll find others at the Arcades des Champs-Elysées, Petit Palais (no lines), Tuileries Garden (end of the walk), and at most bigger stores along the route.

Starring: Grand boulevards, grander shops, and grandiose monuments.

The Walk Begins

❶ Arc de Triomphe

• *Start at the top of the Champs-Elysées and view the Arc from the right side of the boulevard before crossing to it. There's just one pedestrian tunnel (near the Métro entrance, to the right of the Arc as you face it).*

Exterior

Construction of the 165-foot-high arch began in 1809 to honor Napoleon's soldiers, who, despite being vastly outnumbered by the

1. Arc de Triomphe
2. Champs-Elysées View
3. Rue de Tilsitt & Qatar Embassy
4. McDonald's
5. Petit Bateau, Lido
6. Louis Vuitton
7. Fouquet's & Ladurée
8. Thomas Jefferson Plaque
9. Arcades Mall, Sephora, Guerlain
10. Renault
11. International Shops
12. Rond-Point
13. De Gaulle Statue
14. Grand & Petit Palais
15. Place de la Concorde
16. Hôtel Crillon
17. Pont de la Concorde

Eateries

A. Comptoir de L'Arc
B. Boulangerie Paul & La Brioche Dorée
C. La Brioche Dorée
D. Petit Palais Café

Austrians, scored a remarkable victory at the Battle of Austerlitz.

Patterned after the ceremonial arches of ancient Roman conquerors (but more than twice the size), it celebrates Napoleon as emperor of a "New Rome." On the arch's massive left pillar, a relief sculpture shows a toga-clad Napoleon posing confidently, while an awestruck Paris—crowned by her city walls—kneels at his imperial feet. Napoleon died before the Arc's completion, but it was finished in time for his 1840 funeral procession to pass underneath, carrying his remains (19 years dead) from exile in St. Helena to Paris.

On the right pillar is the Arc's most famous relief, *La Marseillaise* (*Le Départ des Volontaires de 1792*), by François Rude). Lady

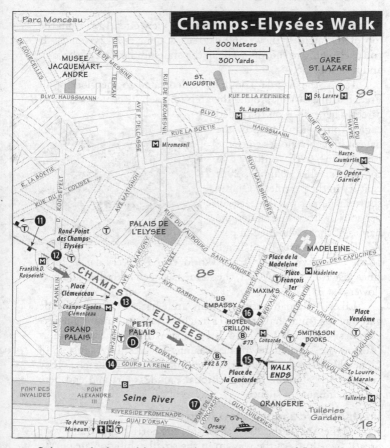

Champs-Elysées Walk

Parc Monceau

MUSÉE JACQUEMART-ANDRE

GARE ST. LAZARE

300 Meters

300 Yards

DE COURCELLES

AVE DE MESSINE

RUE DE TEHRAN

ST. AUGUSTIN

RUE DE LA PEPINIERE

St. Lazare

9e

BLVD. HAUSSMANN

AVE P. DELCASSE

RUE DE MIROMESNIL

BLVD

St. Augustin

RUE DE ROME

RUE DU HAVRE

RUE LA BOETIE

HAUSSMANN

Havre-Caumartin

R. LA BOETIE

Miromesnil

BLVD MALESHERBES

lo Opéra Garnier

RUE DU COLISEE

RUE DU FAUBOURG SAINT-HONORE

11

Rond-Point des Champs-Elysées

PALAIS DE L'ELYSEE

MADELEINE

Place de la Madeleine

BLVD. DES CAPUCINES

12

CHAMPS

AVE DE MARIGNY

8e

Place François 1er

Madeleine

Franklin D. Roosevelt

Place Clémenceau

AVE. GABRIEL

RUE BOISSY D'ANGLAS

MAXIM'S

RUE ST FLORENTIN

Place Vendôme

13

ELYSEES

US EMBASSY

RUE ROYALE

Champs-Elysées Clémenceau

W. CHURCHILL

PETIT PALAIS

16

HOTEL CRILLON

Concorde

SMITH&SON BOOKS

RUE DE CASTIGLIONE

GRAND PALAIS

#73

RUE DE RIVOLI

To Louvre & Marais

AVE EDWARD TUCK

B #42 & 73

15

WALK ENDS

14

COURS LA REINE

Place de la Concorde

Tuileries M

B

PONT DES INVALIDES

PONT ALEXANDRE III

ORANGERIE

Tuileries Garden

Seine River

RIVERSIDE PROMENADE

QUAI D'ORSAY

17

QUAI TUILERIES

1e

To Army Museum

Invalides

To Orsay

Liberty—looking like an ugly reincarnation of Joan of Arc—screams, "Freedom is this way!" and points the direction with a sword. The soldiers beneath her are tired, naked, and stumbling, but she rallies them to carry on the fight against oppression.

• *Now approach the Arc. Take the underground pedestrian walkway—don't try to cross the roundabout in all the traffic, as there are no crosswalks.*

It's worthwhile to explore the base of the arch even if you don't climb it. There's no cost to wander around. After crossing through the tunnel, you'll find the ticket booth (you can skip if you have a ticket or Museum Pass, or are not climbing the tower). Before leaving the tunnel, notice the long photo on the wall showing the nighttime view circa 1995 from the top of the arch. It shows 360 degrees: Count the 12 avenues. If you're climbing to the top, walk up the stairs to the base of the arch and find the line.

Today, the Arc de Triomphe is dedicated to the glory of all French armies. Walk around the arch to reach its center and stand directly beneath it on the faded eagle. You're surrounded by the lists of French victories since the Revolution—19th century on the arch's taller columns, 20th century in the pavement. On the shorter columns you'll see lists of generals (with a line under the names of those who died in battle). Find the flower-lined Tomb

of the Unknown Soldier (from World War I). Every day at 18:30 since just after World War I, the flame has been rekindled and new flowers set in place.

Like its Roman ancestors, this arch has served as a parade gateway for triumphal armies (French or foe) and important ceremonies. From 1940 to 1944, a large swastika flew from here as Nazis goose-stepped down the Champs-Elysées. In August 1944 General Charles de Gaulle led Allied troops under this arch as they celebrated liberation. Today, national parades start and end here with one minute of silence.

Inside the Arc and the View from the Top

Ascend the Arc via the 284 steps inside the north pillar. Catch your breath two-thirds of the way up in the small exhibition area (WC also on this mezzanine level). It hosts ho-hum exhibits about the arch and, of course, there's a gift shop.

From the top you have an eye-popping view of *tout Paris*. You're gazing at the home of 11 million people in greater Paris. (The city center has about 2.3 million residents and covers 40 square miles—a quarter the size of Denver.) With the highest density of any city in Europe, twice that of New York City, Paris has a powerful vibrancy day and night.

Looking East down the Champs-Elysées: Scan the cityscape of downtown Paris. That lonely hill in the distance a bit to the left is Montmartre, topped by the white dome of Sacré-Cœur; until 1860, this hill town was a separate city. Panning right, find the bulky

Opéra Garnier's pitched roof rising above other buildings, the blue top of the modern Pompidou Center, and the Louvre and Tuileries Garden capping the east end of the Champs-Elysées. Let your eyes move right to see the distant twin towers of Notre-Dame, the dome of the Panthéon breaking the horizon, a block of small skyscrapers on a hill (the Quartier d'Italie, which is outside the city center), and the golden dome of Les Invalides. Near Les Invalides, find the lonely-looking Montparnasse Tower, standing like the box the Eiffel Tower came in; in the early 1970s, it served as a wake-up call to city planners that they needed to preserve building height restrictions and strengthen urban design standards.

Aside from the Montparnasse Tower, notice the symmetry of this massive traffic hub. Each corner building surrounding the arch is part of an elegant grand scheme. The beauty of Paris—basically a flat basin with a river running through it—is man-made. There's a harmonious relationship between the width of its grand boulevards and the standard height and design of the buildings. If you continue panning right and then look closer, you'll spot several small, golden onion domes crowning a vast new Russian Orthodox cathedral and spiritual center.

Looking West: Cross the arch and look to the west. In the distance, the huge, white, rectangular Grande Arche de la Défense, standing amid skyscrapers, is the final piece of a grand city axis—from the Louvre, up the Champs-Elysées to the Arc de Triomphe, and continuing on to a forest of skyscrapers at La Défense, three miles away. Former French president François Mitterrand  had the Grande Arche built as a centerpiece of this mini-Manhattan. Notice the contrast between the skyscrapers of La Défense and the more uniform heights of the buildings closer to the Arc de Triomphe.

Below you, the wide boulevard lined with grass and trees angling to your left is Avenue Foch (named after the WWI hero), which ends at the huge Bois de Boulogne park. Avenue Foch is the best address to have in Paris. Nicknamed the "Avenue of Millionaires," it was home to the last shah of Iran and Aristotle Onassis. Today many fabulously rich Arabs call it home. To the left of La Défense (in the Bois de Boulogne) are the glassy "sails" of the Louis Vuitton Foundation. This wavy building, another of Frank Gehry's wild creations, offers contemporary art exhibits. The skyscraper to the right between you and La Défense is the Hôtel Hyatt Regency

CHAMPS-ELYSÉES

Paris Etoile, which delivers a fine view from its bar (described on page 100).

The Etoile: Gaze down at what appears to be a chaotic traffic mess. The 12 boulevards that radiate from the Arc de Triomphe (forming an *étoile,* star) were part of Baron Haussmann's master plan for Paris: the creation of a series of major boulevards intersecting at diagonals, with monuments (such as the Arc de Triomphe) as centerpieces of those intersections (see sidebar on page 106). Haussmann's plan did not anticipate the automobile—obvious when you watch the traffic scene below. But see how smoothly it functions. Cars entering the circle have the right of way (the only roundabout in France with this rule); those in the circle must yield. Still, there are plenty of accidents, many caused by tourists oblivious to the rules. Tired of disputes, insurance companies split the fault and damages of any Arc de Triomphe accident 50/50. The trick is to make a parabola—get to the center ASAP, and then begin working your way out two avenues before you want to exit.

• *We'll start our stroll down the Champs-Elysées at the Charles de Gaulle-Etoile Métro stop, on the north (sunnier) side of the street where the tunnel deposits you. Look straight down the Champs-Elysées toward Tuileries Garden at the far end.*

❷ Champs-Elysées

You're at the top of one of the world's grandest and most celebrated streets, home to big business, celebrity cafés, glitzy nightclubs, high-fashion shopping, and international people-watching. People gather here to celebrate Bastille Day (July 14), World Cup triumphs, the finale of the Tour de France (see sidebar later in the chapter), and the ends of wars.

In 1667, Louis XIV opened the first section of the street as a short extension of the Tuileries Garden. This year is considered the birth of Paris as a grand city. The Champs-Elysées soon became *the* place to cruise in your carriage. (It still is today; traffic can be gridlocked even at midnight.) One hundred years later, the café scene arrived. From the 1920s until the 1960s, this boulevard was pure elegance; Parisians actually dressed up to come here. It was mainly residences, rich hotels, and cafés. Then, in 1963, the government pumped up the neighborhood's commercial metabolism by bringing in suburban trains to give commuters easy access, and *pfft*—there went the neighborhood. Today's visitors can expect security checks inside any store on this famous avenue.

• *Start your descent, pausing at the first tiny street you cross, Rue de Tilsitt. This street is part of a "shadow ring road"—an option for drivers who'd like to avoid the chaos of the Arc—complete with stoplights.*

❸ Rue de Tilsitt and Qatar Embassy

A few steps down Rue de Tilsitt is a building housing the Qatar Embassy (stand as far back as you can to take it in). It's one of the few survivors of a dozen uniformly U-shaped buildings from Haussmann's original 1853 grand design.

Back on the main drag, look across to the other side of the Champs-Elysées at the big, gray, concrete-and-glass "Publicis" building. Ugh. In the 1960s, venerable old buildings (similar to the Qatar Embassy building) were leveled to make way for new commercial operations like Publicis. Then, in 1985, a law prohibited the demolition of the old building fronts that gave the boulevard a uniform grace. Today, many modern businesses hide behind preserved facades.

Most of this tour is a stroll down the left side, which—because it gets more sun and therefore lots more pedestrians—earns landlords double the rent.

The *nouveau* Champs-Elysées, revitalized in 1994, has newer benches and lamps, broader sidewalks, all-underground parking, and a fleet of green-suited workers who drive motorized street cleaners. Blink away the modern elements, and it's not hard to imagine the boulevard pre-1963, with only the finest structures lining both sides all the way to the palace gardens.

❹ McDonald's

A hundred yards farther down on the left (at #140), the arrival of McDonald's in the 1970s was a shock to the boulevard...and to the country. At first it
was allowed to have only
white arches painted on
the window. Today, dining
chez MacDo has become
typically Parisian. France
has more than a thou-
sand McDonald's, and the
Champs-Elysées branch is
considered the most prof-
itable one in the world.

A Big Mac here, at a sidewalk table, buys good people-watching. Notice how many of the happy clients are French and how efficient the big screens are for managing the onslaught of orders. The popularity of *le fast-food* in Paris is a sign that life has changed, and that the era of two-hour lunches is passé. The most commonly

Le Tour de France

On one day every July, the Champs-Elysées is the focus of the world's sports fans, when it serves as the finish line of the Tour de France bicycle race. (While the overall winner is decided by the time they arrive in Paris, the last stage—which includes 10 laps on this boulevard—is one last chance for bikers to take home a yellow jersey.)

For three weeks, French sporting life comes to a standstill as the Tour de France whizzes across the nation's landscape and TV screens, pushing the world's top cyclists to their physical extremes and fans to the edges of their seats. What began in 1903 as a six-day publicity stunt for a cycling newspaper—in the era of wood-framed bikes and wine-and-cigarette breaks—has since grown into the sport's most prestigious race: a grueling 21-day, 2,000-mile test of strength and stamina, fueled by cutting-edge equipment and training regimens.

The route changes each year, but always finishes on the Champs-Elysées. The riders cycle slowly into Paris from its outskirts, savoring the views. Then, as they approach the city center, the race begins in earnest. Up and down the Champs-Elysées they go, making several laps. Thousands of spectators line the street, cheering them on. Finally, the cyclists speed down the boulevard one last time and cross  the finish line, spilling into Place de la Concorde. The winner takes a slow victory lap, followed by the *peloton* (the pack), to acknowledge the crowd and then stops at a makeshift podium at the base of the street. There he's declared champion and raises his fists in salute, exalted by the dramatic backdrop of the Arc de Triomphe.

The long race is divided into daily stages, during which riders

ordered dish in French restaurants is now—by far and away—the hamburger (both as fast food and as a trendy gourmet dish). The French must now compete in a global world, and if that means adopting a more American lifestyle, *c'est la vie.*

❺ Glitz: Lido and Petit Bateau

In the 19th century, this was a district for horse stables; today, it's the district of garages, limo companies, and fancy car dealerships.

At #116 is the famous **Lido,** Paris' largest cabaret (and a multiplex cinema). For 75 years, the Lido has staged glitzy Vegas-style shows featuring sequined dancers, cabaret singers, and vaudeville

compete both as individuals and as members of their nine-man team. While the Tour produces only one overall winner, cycling is very much a team sport, and each member is critical (the loss of any rider along the way generally dooms a team's chances).

Minimizing air resistance is key to strategy, and riders spend most of each stage "drafting" behind *domestiques* ("servants," usually young riders paying their dues), who take turns pedaling in front. The team's constant maneuvering is a matter of choreographed precision, aimed at minimizing fatigue...and the chance of a collision. At the end of each stage, fans breathlessly watch for that critical moment when the lead riders break away for the final sprint. Meanwhile, the team tries to jockey its way to the best position within the peloton while plotting how best to tap its members' varied talents over the course of the race.

Specialists ride to bolster their team and to compete for their own distinctions: Climbers, usually smaller racers, battle to wear the *maillot à pois rouges* (red-polka-dot jersey), awarded to the "King of the Mountains." Bigger riders are usually sprinters, who vie for the *maillot vert* (green jersey). Time trialists help lower the team's aggregate time by excelling at individual races, where they must maintain high speeds over a long distance. The team's star is its captain, usually a solid "all-rounder." He's going for the famous *maillot jaune* (yellow jersey), worn by whoever holds the overall lead in the "general classification" standings at the end of each stage. A complex point system helps determine who has the lowest cumulative time—and, ultimately, who gets the €1.5 million prize, and recognition as the world's greatest cyclist.

If you catch the Tour in person, you'll experience the excitement firsthand and hear the loud whoosh of passing cyclists—but they're gone in a blink (viewing is best—and most crowded—on uphill slopes; for dates and details, see www.letour.fr). Any time of year, you imagine the Tour's final stretch here on the nation's grandest avenue, where cheering crowds cram the sidewalks, their necks craned for a glimpse of the yellow jersey.

acts. You can step into the lobby, and see a video advertising the show (from €75 for a seat, €145-330 for dinner and the show). Moviegoing on the Champs-Elysées provides another kind of fun, with theaters showing the very latest releases. Find the posted movie schedule and check if there are films you recognize, then look for the showings *(séances)*. "VOST" *(version originale sous-titrée)* next to the time indicates the film will be shown in its original language with French subtitles; "VF" stands for *version française*.

Two doors farther down is **Petit Bateau**. The store's presence on the Champs-Elysées is proof of the success of the government's efforts to encourage couples to have more babies. With generous financial rewards for each child, France's birthrate is well above the rest of Europe's.

• *Next, cross the boulevard (a few steps uphill), pausing at the center to enjoy the view and energy. Look back at the Arc de Triomphe, its rooftop bristling with tourists. Notice the variety of architecture along this street—old and elegant, new, and new-behind-old-facades. Notice too how the broad sidewalks and now the bike lanes constrict traffic even more. (They say city politics here is divided as much by those who own cars and those who don't as by left and right.) Continue to the big and proud Louis Vuitton store.*

❻ Louis Vuitton

The flagship store of this famous producer of leather bags may be the largest single-brand luxury store in the world. Step inside. The store provides enough salespeople to treat each customer royally— if there's a line, it means shoppers have overwhelmed the place. If you need clothing and shoes to put in your fancy new bag, head upstairs.

• *Continue downhill. Cross Avenue George V and find Fouquet's, a Paris institution. The white spire you see down Avenue George V is the American Cathedral.*

❼ Café Culture: Fouquet's and Ladurée

Fouquet's café-restaurant (#99), under the red awning, is *the* place to enjoy a slow (if pricey) coffee on the Champs-Elysées. Opened in 1899 as a coachman's bistro, Fouquet's gained fame as the hangout of France's WWI biplane fighter pilots—those who weren't shot down by Germany's infamous "Red Baron." It also served as James Joyce's dining room.

Since the early 1900s, Fouquet's has been a favorite of French celebrities. The golden plaques at the entrance honor winners of France's Oscar-like film awards, the Césars. There are plaques for Gérard Depardieu, Catherine Deneuve, Yves Montand, Roman Polanski, Juliette Binoche, and several famous Americans (but not Jerry Lewis). More recent winners are shown on the floor just inside. Every February, after the Césars are handed out at a nearby theater, France's biggest movie stars descend on Fouquet's. Here they emerge from their limos for the night's grandest red-carpet event as they make their way inside for the official gala dinner.

The hushed interior is at once classy and intimidating—and also a grand experience...if you dare. Enter and be guided to a table, inside or out, where you can splurge for a €6 espresso. Or, to say "I'm just looking" in French, say *"Je regarde"*—zhuh ruh-gard (though fluent English is spoken). The outdoor setting is more relaxed, but everyone still looks rich and famous to me.

Once threatened with foreign purchase and eventual destruction, Fouquet's was spared that fate when the government declared it a historic monument. The upscale café was vandalized in March 2019 by anti-government "yellow vest" protestors, who saw it as a symbol of France's elite. It was restored and back in business within six months.

Ladurée (two blocks downhill at #75) is a classic 19th-century tea salon/restaurant/*pâtisserie*. Nonpatrons can discreetly wander

around the place, though photos are not allowed. A coffee here is *très élégant* and reasonable (I prefer the tables upstairs). The bakery sells traditional *macarons* and cute little cakes to go. The rear café-bar feels otherworldly bizarre.

• *Cross back to the lively (north) side of the street.* Macaron-*lovers swoon at Pierre Hermé. Others turn left and go about 20 yards uphill (to #92) where a wall plaque marks the* ❽ *place Thomas Jefferson lived while serving as minister to France (1785-1789). He replaced popular Benjamin Franklin but quickly made his own mark, extolling the virtues of America's Revolution to a country approaching its own. Back downhill, find two good-value lunch options: Boulangerie Paul and La Brioche Dorée (see the sidebar at the beginning of this chapter).*

❾ French Shopping: Arcades Mall, Sephora, Guerlain

Stroll into the **Arcades des Champs-Elysées** mall at #76. With its fancy lamps, mosaic floors, glass skylight, and classical columns,

it captures faint echoes of the *années folles*—the "crazy years," as the Roaring '20s were called in France. Architecture buffs can observe how the flowery Art Nouveau of the 1910s became the simpler, more geometric Art Deco of the 1920s. The Starbucks may seem out of place here, but the ambience is great.

Next door, at #74, the Galerie du Claridge building sports an old facade. You'd never guess that its ironwork awning, balconies, *putti*, and sculpted fantasy faces disguise an otherwise new building. One of the current tenants is FNAC, a French version of Best Buy.

For a noisy and fragrant commercial carnival of perfumes, and a chance to sense the French passion for cosmetics, take your nose sightseeing at #72 and glide down the ramp of the largest **Sephora** in France. Grab a disposable white strip from a lovely clerk, spritz it with a sample, and sniff. In the main showroom, women's perfumes line the right wall and men's line the left—organized alphabetically by company, from Armani to Versace.

While Sephora seems to be going all out to attract the general public, the venerable **Guerlain** perfume shop sits next door and shows off a dash of the Champs-Elysées' old gold-leaf elegance. Notice the 1914 details. Climb upstairs. It's *très* French. If Sephora is a mosh-pit for your nose, Guerlain is a harem.

At the intersection with Rue la Boëtie, the English-speaking **pharmacy** is open until midnight (entrance around the corner).

Car buffs should detour across the boulevard and park themselves at the sleek café (with great Champs-Elysées views) in the ❿ **Renault** store (open noon-midnight). Though the exhibits change regularly, there's always something hot to entertain car buffs.

⓫ International Shopping

Back on earth, a block or so farther down on the north side, the Disney and Adidas stores are reminders of global economics: The French may live in a world of their own, but they love these places as much as Americans do.

⓬ Rond-Point

At the Rond-Point des Champs-Elysées, the shopping ends and the park begins. This round, leafy traffic circle is often colorful, lined with flowers or seasonal decorations (thousands of pumpkins at Halloween, hundreds of decorated trees at Christmas). Avenue Montaigne, jutting off to the right, is lined by the most exclusive shops in town—the kinds of places where you need to make an appointment to buy a dress.

• *If you're pooped, Rond-Point's Métro stop is a good place to cut this walk short. Otherwise, continue downhill on the right side. Arc around*

Rond-Point and stroll for about 200 yards farther downhill. The square at Place Clemenceau and Avenue de Marigny features a high-pedestaled ⓑ statue of Charles de Gaulle—ramrod-straight and striding purposefully, as he did the day Paris was liberated in 1944. One long block up Avenue de Marigny to the north is the well-secured Elysée Palace— the official residence of the French president. But our walk takes us south to the...

⓮ Grand and Petit Palais

From the statue of de Gaulle, a grand boulevard (Avenue Winston Churchill) passes through the site of the 1900 World's Fair, leading between the glass- and steel-domed Grand and Petit Palais exhibition halls and across the river over the ornate bridge called Pont Alexandre III. (You can view these sights from the statue, if you don't feel like walking down to the bridge.) Imagine pavilions like the two you see today lining this street all the way to the golden dome of Les Invalides—examples of the "can-do" spirit that ran rampant in Europe at the dawn of the 20th century.

Today, the huge Grand Palais (on the right side, under renovation until at least 2024) houses impressive temporary exhibits.

The smaller Petit Palais (left side) has a pleasing permanent collection of lesser paintings by Courbet, Monet, Pissarro, Cézanne, and other 19th-century masters. It's free to enter and has a garden café that's worth a quick detour (fine WCs with no lines). For more on these museums, see page 99.

Looking to the Seine, notice the exquisite Pont Alexandre III, spiked with golden statues and ironwork lamps, which was built to celebrate a turn-of-the-20th-century treaty between France and Russia. The grand and gilded dome in the distance marks Les Invalides, built by Louis XIV as a veterans' hospital for his battle-weary troops (covered in the Army Museum and Napoleon's Tomb Tour). The esplanade leading up to Les Invalides—possibly the largest patch of accessible grass in the city—gives soccer balls and Frisbees a warm Paris welcome.

• *From the de Gaulle statue it's a straight shot down the rest of the*

Champs-Elysées to the finish line. (Speaking of finish lines, this stretch is where the Tour de France reaches its annual climax—see sidebar.) The plane trees that you'll see—a kind of sycamore with peeling bark—thrive even in big-city pollution. They're a legacy of Napoleon III—president/ emperor from 1849 to 1870—who had 600,000 trees planted to green up the city. Your final destination is the 21-acre Place de la Concorde. View it from the obelisk in the center.

⑮ Place de la Concorde

During the Revolution, this was the Place de la Révolution. The guillotine sat on this square, and many of the 2,780 people who were beheaded during the Revolution lost their bodies here during the Reign of Terror. A bronze plaque in the ground in front of the obelisk memorializes the place where Louis XVI, Marie-Antoinette, Georges Danton, Charlotte Corday, and Maximilien de Robespierre, among about 1,200 others, were made "a foot shorter on top." Three people worked the guillotine: One managed the blade, one held the blood bucket, and one caught the head, raising it high to the roaring crowd. (In 1981, France abolished the death penalty—one of many preconditions for membership in today's European Union.)

The 3,300-year-old, 72-foot, 220-ton, red granite, hieroglyph-inscribed **obelisk of Luxor** now forms the centerpiece of Place de la Concorde. Here—on the spot where Louis XVI was beheaded—his brother (Charles X) erected this obelisk to honor those who'd been executed. (Charles became king when the monarchy was restored after Napoleon.) The obelisk was carted here from Egypt in the 1830s. The gold pictures on the pedes-

tal tell the story of the obelisk's incredible two-year journey: pulled down from the entrance to Ramses II's Temple of Amon in Luxor; encased in wood; loaded onto a boat built to navigate both shallow rivers and open seas; floated down the Nile, across the Mediterranean, along the Atlantic coast, and up the Seine; and unloaded here, where it was reerected in 1836. Its glittering gold-leaf cap is a recent addition (1998), replacing the original, which was stolen 2,500 years ago.

Looking up the Champs-Elysées, the obelisk forms a center point along a line that locals call the "royal perspective." You can hang a lot of history along this straight line (Louvre-obelisk-Arc de Triomphe-Grande Arche de la Défense). The Louvre symbolizes the old regime (the divine right of kings). The obelisk and Place de la Concorde symbolize the people's Revolution (cutting off the king's head). The Arc de Triomphe calls to mind the triumph of nationalism (victorious armies carrying national flags under the arch). And the huge modern arch in the distance, surrounded by the headquarters of multinational corporations, heralds a future in which business entities are more powerful than nations.

• *Our walk is over. From here the closest Métro stop is Concorde (entrance hides in the northeast corner of the square, away from the river on the Tuileries Garden side); buses #42 and #73 stop in the square and run up the Champs-Elysées (#42 continues to the Eiffel Tower). Taxis congregate outside Hôtel Crillon. But if you're not quite ready to go, Paris has more to offer...*

Near Place de la Concorde

The beautiful Tuileries Garden (with a public WC just inside on the right) is just through the iron gates. Pull up a chair next to a pond or at one of the cafés in the garden. From the garden you can access the Orangerie Museum and, at the other end, the Louvre (this book includes tours of both museums).

On the north side of Place de la Concorde, ⓰ **Hôtel Crillon** is one of Paris' most exclusive hotels. Of the twin buildings

that guard the entrance to Rue Royale (which leads to the Greek-style Church of the Madeleine), it's the one on the left. This hotel is so fancy that one of its belle époque rooms is displayed in New York's Metropolitan Museum of Art. Eleven years before Louis XVI lost his head on Place de la Concorde, he met with Benjamin Franklin in this hotel to sign a treaty recognizing the US as an independent country. You can enter the hotel and enjoy a pricey hot or cold drink in the elegant salon or way-classy bar. Today's low-profile, heavily fortified **US Embassy and Consulate** is located next to the hotel.

Nearby, those of a certain generation may want to seek out **Maxim's** restaurant (3 Rue Royale), once the world's most glamorous bistro (c. 1900-1970) and a nightspot frequented by everyone from British royalty to Jackie O. Today, its famed carved-wood, Art Nouveau exterior and high prices remain intact, but it's become a generic link in a chain franchise. Farther north up Rue Royale is a fancy shopping area near Place de la Madeleine (see the Shopping in Paris chapter).

South of Place de la Concorde is the ⓱ **Pont de la Concorde,** the bridge that leads to the many-columned building where the **French National Assembly** (similar to the US Congress) meets. The Pont de la Concorde, built of stones from the Bastille prison (which was demolished by the Revolution in 1789), symbolizes the *concorde* (harmony) that can come from chaos—

through good government. The bridge arcs over a freeway underpass that was converted to a pedestrian-only promenade in 2014 and is well worth a stroll.

Stand midbridge and gaze upriver (east). The Orangerie hides behind the trees at 10 o'clock, and the tall building with the skinny chimneys at 11 o'clock is the architectural caboose of the sprawling Louvre palace. The thin spire of Sainte-Chapelle is dead center at 12 o'clock, with the twin towers of Notre-Dame to its right. The Orsay Museum is closer on the right, connected with the Tuileries Garden by a sleek pedestrian bridge (the next bridge upriver) or by the riverside promenade on the Left Bank. Paris awaits.

MARAIS WALK

From Place Bastille to the Pompidou Center

This walk introduces you to one of Paris' most intriguing quarters, the Marais. Naturally, when in Paris you want to see the big sights—but to experience the city, you also need to visit a vital neighborhood. The Marais fits the bill, with trendy boutiques and art galleries, with-it cafés, narrow streets, leafy squares, Jewish bakeries, aristocratic mansions, and fun nightlife—and it's filled with real Parisians. It's the perfect setting to appreciate the flair of this great city.

The walk mixes history with glimpses of daily life in the Marais. Follow this suggested route for a start, then explore. If at any point you want to wander into a store or savor a *café crème*, by all means, you have permission to press pause.

Orientation

Length of This Walk: Allow about 2 hours for this level, two-mile walk. Add an additional hour for each museum you decide to visit along the way.

When to Go: The Marais is liveliest on Sundays when many streets are off limits to cars (and shops are open, unlike in other neighborhoods). Monday mornings are sleepy. On Saturdays, Jewish businesses may close, but the area still hops.

Victor Hugo's House: Free, fee for optional special exhibits, Tue-Sun 10:00-18:00, closed Mon, 6 Place des Vosges.

Carnavalet Museum: Free, Tue-Sun 10:00-18:00, closed Mon, 16 Rue des Francs Bourgeois.

Jewish Art and History Museum: €10, covered by Museum Pass, free on first Sat of month Oct-June; Tue-Fri 11:00-18:00, Sat-Sun from 10:00, open later during special exhibits—Wed until

21:00 and Sat-Sun until 19:00, closed Mon year-round, last entry 45 minutes before closing, 71 Rue du Temple.

Holocaust Memorial: Free, Sun-Fri 10:00-18:00, Thu until 22:00, closed Sat and certain Jewish holidays.

Pompidou Center: €14, free on first Sun of month; Museum Pass covers permanent collection, sixth-floor view, and occasional special exhibits; permanent collection open Wed-Mon 11:00-21:00, closed Tue.

Tours: Paris Walks offers excellent guided tours of this area (see page 49).

Starring: The grand Place des Vosges, the Jewish Quarter, several museums, and the boutiques and trendy lifestyle of today's Marais.

The Walk Begins

• *Start at the west end of Place de la Bastille. Bus #69 stops on Rue St. Antoine, a half-block to the west. From the Bastille Métro, exit following signs to* Place de la Bastille/Place des Vosges. *Ascend onto a vast, noisy traffic circle dominated by the bronze Colonne de Juillet (July Column). The figure atop the column is, like you, headed west. Lean against the Métro railing in front of the Banque de France.*

❶ Place de la Bastille

The famous Bastille fortress once stood on this square. All that remains today is a faint cobblestone outline of the fortress' round turrets traced in the pavement on Rue St. Antoine (30 yards before it hits the square). Though virtually nothing remains, it was on this spot that history turned.

It's July 1789, and the spirit of revolution is stirring in the streets of Paris. The king's troops have evacuated the city center, withdrawing to their sole stronghold, a castle-like structure guarding the east edge of the city—the Bastille. The Bastille was also a prison (which even held the infamous Marquis de Sade in 1789) and was seen as the very symbol of royal oppression. On July 14, the people of Paris gathered here at the Bastille's main gate and demanded the troops surrender. When negotiations failed, they stormed the prison and released its seven prisoners. For good measure, they decorated their pikes with the heads of a few bigwigs. This triumph of citizens over royalty ignited all of France and inspired the Revolution. Over

Bastille Day in France

Bastille Day—July 14, the symbolic kickoff date of the French Revolution—became the French national holiday in 1880. Traditionally, Parisians celebrate at Place de la Bastille starting at 20:00 on July 13, but the best parties are on the numerous smaller squares, where firefighter units sponsor dances. At 10:00 on the morning of the 14th, a grand military parade fills the Champs-Elysées. Then, at 22:30, there's a fireworks display at the Eiffel Tower (arrive at Champ de Mars park by 20:00 to get a seat on the grass). *Vive la France!*

the next few months, the Parisians demolished the stone prison brick by brick.

Though the fortress is long gone, Place de la Bastille has remained a sacred spot for freedom lovers ever since. The July Column—with its gilded statue of Liberty elegantly carrying the torch of freedom into the future—is a symbol of France's long struggle to establish democracy. It was built to commemorate the revolution of 1830, when the conservative King Charles X—who forgot all about the Revolution of the previous generation—needed to be tossed out. The mid-19th century was a time of social unrest throughout Europe; the square drew worker rallies, and at times, the streets of Paris were barricaded by the working class, as dramatized in *Les Misérables*.

Today the square remains a popular spot for demonstrations, and the Bastille is remembered every July 14 on France's independence day—Bastille Day (see sidebar).

Across the square, the southeast corner is dominated (some say overwhelmed) by the flashy, curved, glassy gray facade of the Opéra Bastille. In a symbolic attempt to bring high culture to the masses, former French president François Mitterrand chose this location for the building that would become Paris' main opera venue, edging out the city's earlier "palace of the rich," the  Garnier-designed opera house. Designed by Uruguayan-Canadian architect Carlos Ott, the grand Opéra Bastille—one of the largest theaters in the world, with nine stages—was opened with fanfare by Mitterrand on the 200th Bastille Day, July 14, 1989. Tickets are subsidized to encourage the unwashed masses to attend, though

Marais Walk

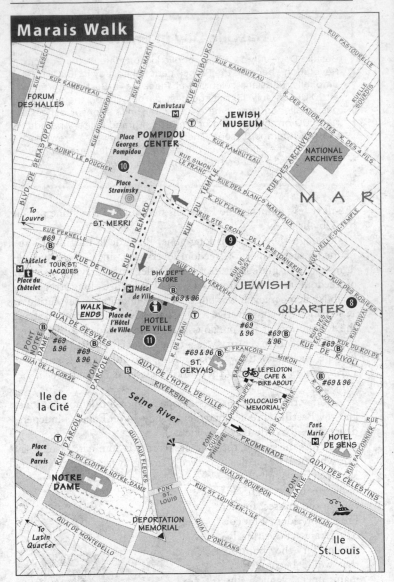

how much high culture they have actually enjoyed here is a subject of debate. (For opera ticket info, see page 513.)

• *Now turn your back on Place de la Bastille and head west down Rue St. Antoine about four blocks into the Marais.*

❷ Rue St. Antoine

From Paris' earliest days, this has been one of its grandest boulevards, part of the east-west axis from Place de la Concorde to the

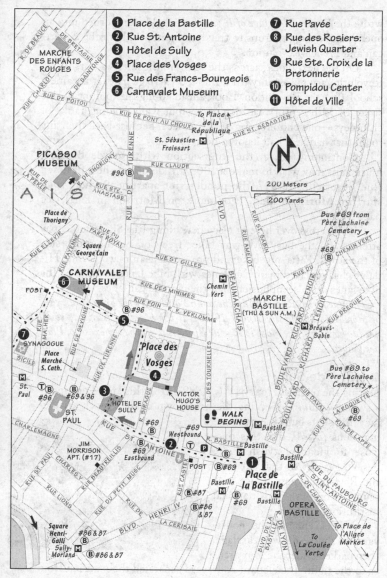

1. Place de la Bastille
2. Rue St. Antoine
3. Hôtel de Sully
4. Place des Vosges
5. Rue des Francs-Bourgeois
6. Carnavalet Museum
7. Rue Pavée
8. Rue des Rosiers: Jewish Quarter
9. Rue Ste. Croix de la Bretonnerie
10. Pompidou Center
11. Hôtel de Ville

eastern gate, Porte St. Antoine. The street was broadened in the mid-1800s as part of the civic renovation plan by Baron Georges-Eugène Haussmann (see sidebar on page 106). Today, it's an ordinary street with a typical mix of workaday shops: banks, clothing stores, produce stands, restaurants.

Just past the first block, a **statue of Beaumarchais** (1732-1799) introduces you to the aristocratic-but-bohemian spirit of the Marais. Beaumarchais, who lived near here, made watches for Louis XV, wrote the bawdy *Marriage of Figaro* (which Mozart turned into an opera), and smuggled guns to freedom fighters in both the American and French Revolutions.

On the next block, across the street to the left, is a stately pre-Revolutionary **mansion** with a fine red carriage gate. It became a school after the Revolution. Look ahead, along the roofline of this street of 19th-century facades with stout walls holding ranks of chimneys—one chimney for each fireplace, because back then any room that had heat had its own hearth.

Continuing on, at the intersection with Rue de Birague, music fans may wish to make a 100-yard detour to the left, down Rue Beautreillis to #17, the nondescript apartment **where rock star Jim Morrison died.** (For more on Morrison in Paris, see page 379.)

If you cross over here or elsewhere along Rue St. Antoine, pay attention to the busy two-way bike "freeway" on the south side of the street. Paris' pro-bike and pro-pedestrian mayor, Anne Hidalgo, has replaced many car lanes with bike lanes like these. The bike lanes often seem busier than the parallel car lanes.

• *Continue down Rue St. Antoine to #62 and enter the grand courtyard of Hôtel de Sully (daily 10:00-19:00). If the building is closed, you'll need to backtrack one block to Rue de Birague to reach the next stop, Place des Vosges.*

❸ Hôtel de Sully

During the reign of Henry IV (r. 1589-1610), this area—originally a swamp *(marais)*—became the hometown of the French aristoc-racy. Big shots built their private mansions *(hôtels)*, like this one, close to Henry's stylish Place des Vosges. *Hôtels* that survived the Revolution now house museums, libraries, and national institutions.

Nobles entered the courtyard by horse-drawn carriage, then parked under the four arches to the right. The elegant courtyard separated the mansion from the noisy and very public street. Look up at statues of Autumn (carrying grapes from the harvest), Winter (a feeble old man), and the four elements.

Enter the building between the sphinxes into a passageway and admire the sumptuous ceiling in the bookstore. Continue into the back courtyard, where noisy Paris takes a back seat. Enjoy the oak tree, manicured hedges, vine-covered walls, birdsong, and the back side of the mansion with its warm stone and statues. Use the bit of Gothic window tracery (on the right) for a fun framed photo of your travel partner as a haloed Madonna. At the far end, the French doors are part of a former *orangerie*, or greenhouse, for homegrown fruits and vegetables throughout winter; these days it warms office workers. Ostentatious as mansions like this might seem, they were often the second residences of a fabulously wealthy noble. Owners of such mansions were members of pre-Revolutionary France's one percent, whose primary residences were much grander châteaux in the countryside.

• *Continue through the small door at the far-right corner of the back courtyard, and pop out into one of Paris' finest squares.*

❹ Place des Vosges

Walk to the center, where Louis XIII, on horseback, gestures, "Look at this wonderful square my dad built." He's surrounded

by locals enjoying their community park. You'll see children frolicking in the sandbox, lovers warming benches, and pigeons guarding their fountains while trees shade this escape from the glare of the big city (you can refill your water bottle in the center of the square, behind Louis).

Study the architecture: nine pavilions (houses) per side. The two highest—at the front and back—were for the king and queen (but were never used). Warm red brickwork—some real, some fake—is topped with sloped slate roofs, chimneys, and another quaint relic of a bygone era: TV antennas. Beneath the arcades are cafés, art galleries, and restaurants—it's an atmospheric place for lunch or dinner (for recommendations, see the Marais section of the Eating chapter).

Henry IV built this centerpiece of the Marais in 1605 and called it "Place Royale." As he'd hoped, it turned the Marais into Paris' most exclusive neighborhood. Just like Versailles 80 years later, this was a magnet for the rich and powerful of France. The square served as a model for civic planners across Europe. With the Revolution, the aristocratic splendor of this quarter passed. To encourage the country to pay its taxes, Napoleon promised naming rights to the district that paid first—the Vosges region (near Germany).

The insightful writer **Victor Hugo** lived at #6 from 1832 to 1848. (It's at the southeast corner of the square, marked by the French flag.) This was when he wrote much of his most important work, including his biggest hit, *Les Misérables*. Inside this free museum you can wander through eight plush rooms, take in a fine view of the square, and enjoy a charming garden café and good WCs (see "Victor Hugo's House" on page 118).

Sample the flashy art galleries ringing the square (the best ones are behind Louis). Ponder a daring new piece for that blank wall at home and take a peek into the courtyard of the Hôtel le Pavillon de la Reine (#28) for a glimpse into refined living—my hotel doesn't look like this. Or consider a pleasant break at one of the recommended eateries on the square.

• *Exit the square at the northwest (far left) corner. Head west on…*

❺ Rue des Francs-Bourgeois

From the Marais of yesteryear, immediately enter the lively neighborhood of today. Stroll down a block full of cafés and eclectic

clothing boutiques with the latest fashions. A few doorways (including #8 and #13) lead into courtyards with more shops. Even this "main" street through the neighborhood is narrow and more fit for pedestrians than cars.

In the 19th century, the aristocrats moved elsewhere. The Marais became a working-class quarter, filled with gritty shops, artisans, immigrants, and a Jewish community. Haussmann's modernization plan put the Marais in line for the wrecking ball. But then the march of "progress" was halted by one tiny little event—World War I—and the Marais was spared. It limped along as a dirty, working-class zone until the 1960s, when it was transformed and gentrified.

Across the street from the Carnavalet Museum (described next), on the corner, is the storefront of a long-gone *boulangerie-pâtisserie*. Its facade is protected and so it survives, even though baked goods are no longer sold here.

• *The entrance to the museum is at the intersection of Rue des Francs-Bourgeois and Rue de Sevigné.*

MARAIS

❻ Carnavalet Museum

Housed inside a Marais mansion, this museum features the history of Paris, particularly the Revolution years. The bloody events of July 14, 1789, come to life in paintings and displays, including a model of the Bastille carved out of one of its bricks. The mansion itself provides the best possible look at the elegance of the neighborhood back when Place des Vosges was Place Royale. Walking past the mansion, notice the original Carnavalet entrance and the elaborate iron gate through which carriages would enter. For more on the museum, see page 112.

• *Continue west a half-block down Rue des Francs-Bourgeois to the post office. Modern-art fans can check out the nearby* **Picasso Museum**, *with temporary exhibits featuring a range of styles and media from the artist's long life (see page 114).*
Turn left onto...

❼ Rue Pavée

In a few steps, at #24, you'll pass the 16th-century Paris Historical Library (Bibliothèque Historique de la Ville de Paris). Step into
the courtyard of this rare Renaissance mansion to see its unstained-glass windows and clean classical motifs. From the street, notice the corner lookout—designed so guards could see from which direction angry peasants were coming.

Continue down Rue Pavée, keeping to the right, until you come to the intersection with Rue des Rosiers. Before we turn right on Rue des Rosiers, consider two little side-trips: A half-block straight ahead leads to the Agoudas Hakehilos **synagogue** (at #10)
with its striking (and filthy) Art Nouveau facade (c. 1913, closed to public). It was designed by Hector Guimard, the same architect who designed Paris' Art Nouveau Métro stations. A half-block to the left, along Rue des Rosiers, is the recommended Le Loir dans la Théière (at #3). With tasty baked goods and hot drinks, this place provides the perfect excuse for a break.

• *From Rue Pavée, turn right onto Rue des Rosiers, which runs straight for three blocks through Paris' Jewish Quarter.*

❽ Rue des Rosiers: Jewish Quarter

This street—the heart of the Jewish Quarter (and named for the roses that once lined the city wall)—has become the epicenter of Marais trendiness and fashion, with chic clothing boutiques and stylish cafés.

Once the largest in Western Europe, Paris' Jewish Quarter,

Eateries Along This Walk

Bring your appetite along, because I've peppered this walk with pleasant places to stop for a break. Some are best for a sit-down meal, and others for a quick coffee, crêpe, or snack. Find these spots on the map in this chapter. Many are described in more detail in the Eating in Paris chapter, where you'll find still more options.

$$$ La Place Royale: Traditional, well-priced cuisine on Place des Vosges, with outdoor seating (see page 446).

$ Café Hugo: Great for drinks or standard café fare on Place des Vosges (see page 447).

$$ Le Loir dans la Théière: A cozy, welcoming teahouse for lunch or dessert on Rue des Rosiers (see page 452).

$ Falafel Row: Eat in or take away from several joints serving good falafel along Rue des Rosiers between Rue des Ecouffes and Rue Vieille du Temple (see page 453).

$ Florence Kahn Yiddish bakery: Tiny takeaway shop for boutique baked goods and sandwiches (Wed-Sun 10:00-19:00, closed Mon-Tue, 24 Rue des Ecouffes, +33 6 09 66 52).

while greatly reduced in size, still reflects its colorful past. Notice the sign above #4, which says *Hamam* (Turkish bath). Although still bearing the sign of an old public bath, it now showcases trendy clothing. Next door, at #4 bis, the Ecole de Travail (trade school) has a plaque on the wall (left of the door) remembering the headmaster, staff, and students who were arrested here during World War II and killed at Auschwitz.

The size of the Jewish population here has fluctuated. It expanded in the 19th century when Jews arrived from Eastern Europe, escaping pogroms (surprise attacks on villages). The numbers swelled during the 1930s as Jews fled Nazi Germany. After France came under Nazi control, 75 percent of the Jews here were forcibly deported to concentration camps, where many were killed (for more information, visit the nearby Holocaust Memorial—see below). Most recently, Algerian exiles, both Jewish and Muslim, have settled in—living together peacefully here in Paris. (Nevertheless, much of the street has granite blocks on the sidewalk—an attempt to keep out any terrorists' cars.)

The district's traditional stores are being squeezed out by the

$ Sacha Finkelsztajn: Another Yiddish bakery/deli with Polish and Russian cuisine, same price to sit or take away (Wed-Sun 10:00-19:00, closed Mon-Tue, 27 Rue des Rosiers, +33 1 42 72 78 91).

$$ Chez Marianne: Neighborhood fixture for inexpensive Jewish cuisine (at the corner of Rue des Rosiers and Rue des Hospitalières-St.-Gervais; see page 452).

$$$ Mariage Frères: Luxurious tea extravaganza just off Rue Ste. Croix de la Bretonnerie (daily 10:30-19:30, serving tea from 12:00, 30 Rue du Bourg Tibourg, +33 1 42 72 28 11).

$ Dame Tartine and **$ Crêperie Beaubourg:** Two casual, inexpensive joints for salads, toasted sandwiches, and crêpes alongside Pompidou Center's Stravinsky fountain. Beaubourg offers a good €10 lunch special (Tartine daily 9:00-23:30, +33 1 77 18 88 59; Beaubourg daily 11:30-23:00, +33 1 42 77 63 62).

$ BHV Department Store fifth-floor cafeteria: Nice views and good-value cafeteria food (by Hôtel de Ville at the corner of Rue du Temple and Rue de la Verrerie; see page 453).

upscale needs of modern Paris. Case in point: The yellow-tiled shop at the intersection of Rue des Rosiers and Rue Ferdinand Duval once thrived as the venerable Jewish deli Jo Goldenberg. A plaque marks a 1982 terrorist bombing that occurred at this spot.

The intersection of Rue des Rosiers and Rue des Ecouffes marks the heart of the small neighborhood that Jews call the *Pletzl* ("little square"). Lively Rue des Ecouffes, named for a bird of prey, is a derogatory nod to the moneychangers' shops that once lined this lane. The next two blocks along Rue des Rosiers feature kosher *(cascher)* restaurants and fast-food places selling falafel, *shawarma, kefta,* and other Mediterranean dishes. Art galleries exhibit Jewish-themed works, and store windows post flyers for community events. You'll likely see Jewish men in yarmulkes, a few bearded Orthodox Jews, and Hasidic Jews with black coats and hats, beards, and sidelocks.

Lunch Break: This is a good place to stop. You'll be tempted by kosher pizza and plenty of cheap fast-food joints selling falafel "to go" *(emporter).* Choose from any of the many joints that line the street (for suggestions, see

the sidebar). For a breath of fresh air, step into the very Parisian Jardin des Rosiers, a half-block before the L'As du Falafel eatery, at 10 Rue des Rosiers.

• *Rue des Rosiers dead-ends at Rue Vieille du Temple. Turn left on Rue Vieille du Temple, then take your first right onto Rue Ste. Croix de la Bretonnerie and prepare for a little cultural whiplash (from Jewish culture to gay culture).*

Side Trip to the Holocaust Memorial: Consider a five-block detour to visit the memorial (for details, see the listing on page 65). To get there, head south on Rue Vieille du Temple, cross Rue de Rivoli, and make your second left onto the traffic-free passageway named Allée des Justes. It's at 17 Rue Geoffroy l'Asnier.

❾ Rue Ste. Croix de la Bretonnerie

Gay Paree's openly gay main drag is lined with cafés, lively shops, and crowded bars at night. Check out Le Point Virgule theater to see what form of edgy musical comedy is showing tonight (the name means "The Semicolon"; most productions of up-and-coming humorists are in French). A short detour left on Rue du Bourg Tibourg leads to the luxurious tea extravaganza of Mariage Frères (#30).

Farther ahead at Rue du Temple, consider detouring a few blocks to the right to the Jewish Art and History Museum (see listing on page 115). On the way, you'll pass a dance school wonderfully situated in a 17th-century courtyard above the Café de la Gare theater (41 Rue du Temple).

• *Continue west on Rue Ste. Croix (which turns into Rue St. Merri). Up ahead you'll see the colorful pipes of the Pompidou Center. Cross Rue du Renard and enter the Pompidou's colorful world of fountains, restaurants, and street performers.*

❿ Pompidou Center

Survey this popular spot from the top of the sloping square. Tubular escalators lead to the museum and a great view.

The Pompidou Center subscribes with gusto to the 20th-century architectural axiom "form follows function." To get a more spacious and functional interior, the guts of this exoskeletal building are draped on the outside and color-coded: vibrant red for people lifts, cool blue for air ducts, eco-green for plumbing, don't-touch-it yellow for electrical stuff, and white for the structure's bones. (Compare the Pompidou Center to another exoskeletal building, Notre-Dame.) ▢ See the Pompidou Center Tour chapter for details on visiting the museum.

Enjoy the adjacent fountain, an homage to Igor Stravinsky. Jean Tinguely and Niki de Saint-Phalle designed it as a tribute

to the composer: Every sculpture within the fountain represents one of his hard-to-hum scores. For low-stress meals or an atmospheric spot for a drink, try the lighthearted Dame Tartine (or the *crêperie* next door), which overlooks the fountains and serves good, inexpensive food.

• *Double back to Rue du Renard, turn right, and stroll past Paris' ugliest (modern) building on the left. Walk toward the river until you find...*

⓫ Hôtel de Ville

Looking more like a grand château than a public building, Paris' City Hall stands proud. This spot has been the center of city government since 1357. Each of Paris' 20 arrondissements has its own City Hall and mayor, but this one is the big daddy of them all.

The Renaissance-style building (built 1533-1628 and reconstructed after a 19th-century fire) displays hundreds of statues of famous Parisians on its facade. Peek from behind the iron fences through the doorways to see elaborate spiral stairways, which are reminiscent of Château de Chambord in the Loire. Playful fountains energize the big, lively square in front.

This spacious stage has seen much of Paris' history. On July 14, 1789, Revolutionaries rallied here on their way to the Bastille. In 1870, it was home to the radical Paris Commune. During World War II, General Charles de Gaulle appeared at the windows to proclaim Paris' liberation from the Nazis. And in 1950, Robert Doisneau snapped a famous black-and-white photo of a kissing couple, with Hôtel de Ville as a romantic backdrop.

Today, it's the seat of the mayor of Paris, who has one of the most powerful positions in France. In the 1990s, Jacques Chirac used the mayoralty as a stepping stone to another powerful position—president of France.

The square in front is a gathering place for Parisians. Demonstrators assemble here to speak their minds. Crowds cheer during big soccer games shown on huge TV screens. In summer, the square hosts sand volleyball courts; in winter, a big ice-skating rink. There's often a children's carousel, or *manège*. Now a Paris institution, carousels were first introduced by Henri IV in 1605—the same year Place des Vosges was built. Year-round, the place is always beautifully lit after dark.

After our walk through the Marais, one of the city's oldest neighborhoods, it's appropriate to end up here, at the governmental heart of Paris.

• *The tour's over. The Hôtel de Ville Métro stop is right here. If you need information, Paris' **main TI** is in the Hôtel de Ville (enter from the north side of the building at 29 Rue de Rivoli).*

POMPIDOU CENTER TOUR

Centre Pompidou

The Pompidou Center contains what is possibly Europe's best collection of 20th-century art. After the super-serious Louvre and Orsay museums, finish things off with this artistic kick in the pants. You won't find classical beauty here—no dreamy Madonnas-and-children—just a stimulating, offbeat, and, if you like, instructive walk through nearly every art style of the wild-and-crazy last century.

The Pompidou's "permanent" collection...isn't. But while the paintings (and other pieces) change amid regular renovations (expect some room closures), the museum generally keeps the artists and various styles in a set order. That's why, rather than a painting-by-painting description, this chapter is more a general overview of the major trends of 20th-century art in the sequence you'll likely see them as you visit the rooms. I've put the emphasis on artists you're most likely to find on display. See the classics—Picasso, Matisse, etc.—but be sure to leave time to browse the thought-provoking and fun art of more recent artists.

Orientation

Cost: €14, €11 for youth 18-25, free for kids 17 and under, €5 for escalator to sixth-floor view (but no museum entry). The regular ticket gets you into everything—both the permanent collection (the Musée National d'Art Moderne) and the special exhibits that make this place so edgy. The museum is free on the first Sunday of the month.

Using the Museum Pass here provides access to the permanent collection, the sixth-floor view, and some special exhibits.

Buy tickets on the ground floor. If lines are long, use the red ticket machines (credit cards only).

Hours: Permanent collection open Wed-Mon 11:00-21:00, closed Tue, ticket counters close at 20:00; rest of the building open until 22:00 (Thu until 23:00).

Information: +33 1 44 78 12 33, www.centrepompidou.fr.

Renovation: The museum is scheduled to close in late 2024 for a multiyear facelift.

When to Go: Crowds (mainly for special exhibits) are worst from 11:00-12:00 and on weekends. It's least crowded after 17:00.

Getting There: Take the Métro to Rambuteau or Hôtel de Ville. Bus #69 from the Marais and Rue Cler also stops a few blocks away at Hôtel de Ville. The wild, color-coded exterior of the museum makes it about as hard to locate as the Eiffel Tower.

Visitor Information: There's a helpful info desk in the lobby. The Espace de Médiation on the fifth floor is the museum's main information office. Note that Parisians call the complex the "Centre Beaubourg" (sahn-truh boh-boor), but official publications call it the "Centre Pompidou." The free Centre Pompidou app covers both the permanent collection and special exhibits.

Length of This Tour: Allow one hour.

Services: Baggage check is free and required for bags bigger than a large purse. The terrific museum store on the main floor has zany gift ideas.

Cuisine Art: For a quick bite, there's a sandwich-and-coffee **café** on the mezzanine (nice interior views). For a stylish splurge with a grand and gourmet view (or an affordable drink), consider the **$$$ Georges Restaurant** on the sixth floor, with €20-30 lunch plates and €30-40 dinner plates (Wed-Mon 12:00-23:30, closed Tue, formal service, amazing seating inside and out, +33  1 44 78 47 99). You can picnic with the students on the museum's stony, sloping front yard (**Monop'** grocery store facing the museum at #135, plenty of takeout places nearby). And for a casual sit-down €14 lunch across from the kid action at the crazy Stravinsky fountain, head to the big square on the museum's river side for **$ Dame Tartine** (tartines or French pizzas) and **$ Crêperie Beaubourg** (sweet and savory crêpes).

Nearby: The studio of sculptor **Constantin Brancusi** (see page 364) is housed in the gray concrete bunker in front of the

Pompidou and is free to visit. Brancusi (1876-1957) often hosted Paris' artistic glitterati in his humble studio, where he served home-cooked dishes of his native Romania. After Brancusi's death, the Pompidou Center had the studio reconstructed here. See the unique space and some of his revolutionary work (Wed-Mon 14:00-18:00, closed Tue, same contact info as Pompidou).

Starring: Matisse, Picasso, Chagall, Dalí, Warhol, and contemporary art.

OVERVIEW

That slight tremor you may feel comes from Italy, where Michelangelo has been spinning in his grave ever since 1977, when the Pompidou Center first disgusted Paris. Still, it's an appropriate modern temple for the controversial art it houses.

The building itself is "exoskeletal" (like Notre-Dame, or a crab), with its functional parts—the pipes, heating ducts, and escalator—on the outside and the meaty art inside. It's the epitome of modern architecture, where form follows function.

Inside you'll find this general scheme (but confirm as you enter—galleries move around): ground floor—all services; basement—photography exhibits and always free; floors 1 and 6—temporary exhibits; floors 4 and 5—the museum (what you're likely here for). The museum starts on floor 5 with a one-way route, with the collection displayed in chronological order. It's that easy.

This chapter covers the Musée National d'Art Moderne: Collection Permanente (labeled simply *Musée* on signs), which is on the fourth and fifth floors. Generally, art from 1905 to 1980 is on the fifth floor (the core of this chapter), while the fourth floor contains more recent art. Use the museum's floor plans (posted on the wall) to find specific artists. The museum is bigger than you think—and you're smart to focus on a limited number of artists. Don't hesitate to ask, *"Où est Kandinsky?"*

The following text is not a "tour" of the museum per se—it's a chronological overview of modern art—but it does tend to follow the museum's general layout.

The Tour Begins

• Buy your ticket on the ground floor, then head up to the galleries. The series of escalators are in a long glass tube that rises diagonally to the top.

Behold the city! The city that, in the early 1900s, was the most cultured place on earth and the cradle of modern art. Survey famous buildings peeking above the commotion of roofs like mountain peaks breaking the urban cloudscape. You could go all the way to the top to the pricey view restaurant, but the best view is actually from a terrace within the permanent collection.

• The permanent collection entrance is either on the fourth or fifth floor (it varies). Enter and show your ticket. Make several spins and click your heels. Toto, we're not in Kansas anymore.

FIFTH FLOOR
Modern Art from 1905 to 1980

AD 1900: A new century dawns. War is a thing of the past. Science will wipe out poverty and disease. Rational Man is poised for a new era of peace and prosperity...

Right. This cozy Victorian dream was soon shattered by two world wars and rapid technological change. Nietzsche murdered God. Freud washed ashore on the beach of a vast new continent inside each of us. Einstein made everything merely "relative." Even the fundamental building blocks of the universe, atoms, were behaving erratically.

The 20th century—accelerated by technology and fragmented by war—was exciting and chaotic, and the art reflects the turbulence of that century of change.

Paris in the early 1900s was the cradle of modern art. For the previous 300 years (1600-1900), Paris had been the capital of the wealthiest, most civilized nation on earth. Europe's major artists—most of whom spoke French—flocked to Paris, knowing that if you could make it there, you'd make it anywhere.

The groundwork of modern art was first laid by the Impressionists and Post-Impressionists in the late 1800s. They pioneered the notion that the painted surface—of thick, colorful brushstrokes—was as inherently interesting as the subject itself. You can almost see the evolution: Monet's blurry *Water Lilies* canvases are patterns of color similar to a purely abstract canvas. Van Gogh would build a figure out of brushstrokes of different colors, Cezanne would turn those brushstrokes into patches of paint, then Picasso sharpened those patches into "cubes," which he would later shatter beyond recognition.

As you tour the Pompidou, remember that most of the artists, including foreigners, spent their formative years in Paris. In the 1910s, funky Montmartre was the mecca of Modernism—the era of Picasso, Braque, and Matisse. In the 1920s, the center shifted to the grand cafés of Montparnasse, where painters mingled with American expats such as Ernest Hemingway and Gertrude Stein. During World War II, it was Jean-Paul Sartre's Existentialist scene around St. Germain-des-Prés. After World War II, the global art focus moved to New York, but by the late 20th century, Paris had reemerged as a cultural touchstone for the world of modern art.

• *Start your visit with...*

Post-Impressionism to Fauvism

The Fauves ("wild beasts") were artists inspired by African and Oceanic masks and voodoo dolls; they tried to inject a bit of the jungle into bored French society. The result? Modern art that looked primitive: long, masklike faces with almond eyes; bright, clashing colors; simple figures; and "flat," two-dimensional scenes.

Henri Matisse, 1869-1954

Matisse's colorful "wallpaper" works are not realistic. A man is a few black lines and blocks of paint. The colors are unnaturally bright. There's no illusion of the distance and 3-D that were so important to Renaissance Italians. The "distant" landscape is as bright as any close-up, and the slanted lines meant to suggest depth are crudely done.

Traditionally, the canvas was like a window you looked "through" to see a slice of the real world stretching off into the distance. Now, a camera could do that better. With Matisse, you look "at" the canvas, like wallpaper. *Voilà!* What was a crudely drawn scene now becomes a sophisticated and decorative pattern of colors and shapes.

Though fully "modern," Matisse built on 19th-century art—the bright colors of Vincent van Gogh, the primitive figures of Paul

POMPIDOU

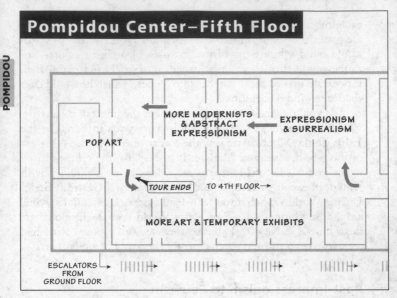

Pompidou Center—Fifth Floor

POP ART

MORE MODERNISTS & ABSTRACT EXPRESSIONISM

EXPRESSIONISM & SURREALISM

TOUR ENDS

TO 4TH FLOOR →

MORE ART & TEMPORARY EXHIBITS

ESCALATORS FROM GROUND FLOOR

Gauguin, the colorful designs of Japanese prints, and the Impressionist patches of paint that blend together only at a distance.

Cubism and Beyond

I throw a rock at a glass statue, shatter it, pick up the pieces, and glue them onto a canvas. I'm a Cubist.

Pablo Picasso, 1881-1973, and Georges Braque, 1882-1963

Born in Spain, Picasso moved to Paris as a young man, settling into a studio (Le Bateau-Lavoir) in Montmartre (see page 401). He worked with next-door neighbor Georges Braque in poverty so dire they often didn't know where their next bottle of wine was coming from. They corrected each other's paintings (it's hard to tell whose is whose without the titles), and they shared ideas, meals, and girlfriends while inventing a whole new way to look at the world.

They show the world through a kaleidoscope of brown and gray. The subjects are somewhat recognizable (with the help of the titles), but they are broken into geometric shards (let's call them "cubes," though there are many different shapes), then pieced back together.

Cubism gives us several different angles of the subject at once—say, a woman seen from the front and side angles simultaneously, resulting in two eyes on the same side of the nose. This involves showing three dimensions, plus Einstein's new fourth dimension, the time it takes to walk around the subject to see other angles. Newfangled motion pictures could capture this moving

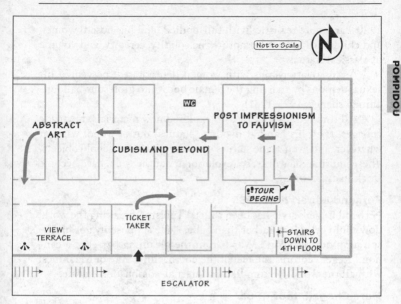

4-D world, but how to do it on a 2-D canvas? The Cubist "solution" is a kind of Mercator projection, where the round world is sliced up like an orange peel and then laid as flat as possible.

Notice how the "cubes" often overlap. A single cube might contain both an arm (in the foreground) and the window behind (in the background), both painted the same color. The foreground and the background are woven together so that the subject dissolves into a pattern.

Picasso's Synthetic Cubism and Other Periods

If the Cubists were as smart as Einstein, why couldn't they draw a picture to save their lives? Picasso was one modern artist who could draw exception-ally well (see his partly finished *Harlequin*). But he constantly explored and adapted his style to new trends, and so became the most famous painter of the century. Scattered throughout the museum are works from the many periods of Picasso's life.

Picasso soon began to use more colorful "cubes" (1912-1915). Eventually, he used curved shapes to build the subject, rather than the straight-line shards of early Cubism.

Picasso married and had children. Works from this period (the

1920s) are more realistic, with full-bodied (and big-nosed) women and children. He tries to capture the solidity, serenity, and volume of classical statues.

As his relationships with women deteriorated, he vented his sexual demons by twisting the female body into grotesque balloon-animal shapes (1925-1931).

All through his life, Picasso explored new materials. He made collages, tried his hand at making "statues" out of wood, wire, or whatever, and even made statues out of everyday household objects. These multimedia works, so revolutionary at the time, have become stock-in-trade today.

Fernand Léger, 1881-1955

Fernand Léger's style has been called "Tubism," breaking the world down into cylinders, rather than cubes. (He supposedly got his inspiration during World War I from the gleaming barrel of a cannon.) Léger captures the feel of the encroaching Age of Machines, with all the world looking like an internal-combustion engine.

Marc Chagall, 1887-1985

At age 22, Marc Chagall arrived in Paris with the wide-eyed wonder of a country boy. Lovers are weightless with bliss. Animals smile and wink at us. Musicians, poets, peas-ants, and dreamers ignore gravity, tumbling in slow-motion circles high above the rooftops. The colors are deep, dark, and earthy—a pool of mystery with figures bleeding through below the surface. (Chagall claimed his early poverty forced him to paint over used canvases, inspiring the overlapping images.)

Chagall's very personal style fuses many influences. He was raised in a small Belarus village, which explains his "naive" outlook and fiddler-on-the-roof motifs. His simple figures are like Russian Orthodox icons, and his Jewish roots produced Old Testament themes. Stylistically, he's thoroughly modern—Cubist shards, bright Fauve colors, and Primitive simplification. This otherworldly style was a natural for religious works, and so his murals and stained glass, which feature both Jewish and Christian motifs, decorate buildings around the world—including the ceiling of Paris' Opéra Garnier.

Abstract Art

Abstract art simplifies. A man becomes a stick figure. A squiggle is a wave. A streak of red expresses anger. Arches make you want a cheeseburger. These are universal symbols that everyone from a caveman to a banker understands. Abstract artists capture the essence of reality in a few lines and colors, and they capture things even a camera can't—emotions, abstract concepts, musical rhythms, and spiritual states of mind. Again, with abstract art, you don't look *through* the canvas to see the visual world, but *at* it to read the symbolism of lines, shapes, and colors.

Wassily Kandinsky, 1866-1944

The bright colors, bent lines, and lack of symmetry tell us that Kandinsky's world was passionate and intense.

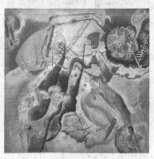

Notice titles like *Improvisation* and *Composition*. Kandinsky was inspired by music, an art form that's also "abstract," though it still packs a punch. Like a jazz musician improvising a new pattern of notes from a set scale, Kandinsky plays with new patterns of related colors as he looks for just the right combination. Using lines and color, Kandinsky translates the unseen reality into a new medium...like lightning crackling over the radio. Go, man, go.

Piet Mondrian, 1872-1944

Like a blueprint for Modernism, Mondrian's T-square style boils painting down to its basic building blocks (black lines, white canvas) and the three primary colors (red, yellow, and blue), all arranged in orderly patterns.

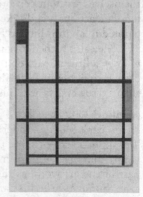

(When you come right down to it, that's all painting ever has been. A schematic drawing of, say, the *Mona Lisa* shows that it's less about a woman than about the triangles and rectangles of which she's composed.)

Mondrian started out painting realistic landscapes of the orderly fields in his native Netherlands. Increasingly, he simplified them into horizontal and vertical patterns. For Mondrian, who was heavy into Eastern mysticism, "up vs. down" and "left vs. right" were the perfect metaphors for life's dualities: "good vs. evil," "body vs. spirit," "man vs. woman." The canvas is a bird's-eye view of Mondrian's personal landscape.

Constantin Brancusi, 1876-1957

Brancusi's curved, shiny statues reduce objects to their essence. A bird is a single stylized wing, the one feature that sets it apart from other animals. He rounds off to the closest geometrical form, so a woman's head becomes a perfect oval on a cubic pedestal.

Humans love symmetry (maybe because our own bodies are roughly symmetrical) and find geometric shapes restful, even worthy of meditation. Brancusi follows the instinct for order that has driven art from earliest times, from circular Stonehenge and Egyptian pyramids, to Greek columns and Roman arches, to Renaissance symmetry and the Native American "medicine wheel."

To see a good selection of Brancusi's work, visit his studio just outside the Pompidou.

Paul Klee, 1879-1940

Paul Klee's small and playful canvases are deceptively simple, containing shapes so basic they can be read as universal symbols. Klee thought a wavy line, for example, would always suggest motion, whereas a stick figure would always mean a human—like the psychiatrist Carl Jung's universal dreams and symbols manifesting the "collective unconscious."

Klee saw these universals in the art of children, who express themselves without censoring or cluttering things up with learning. His art has a childlike playfulness and features simple figures painted in an uninhibited frame of mind.

Klee also turned to nature. The same forces that cause the wave to draw a line of foam on the beach can cause a meditative artist to draw a squiggly line of paint on a canvas. The result is a universal shape. True artists don't just paint nature, they become Nature.

Applied Arts

If you can't handle modern art, sit on it! (Actually, please don't.) The applied arts—chairs, tables, lamps, and vases—are as much a part of the art world as the fine arts. (Some say the first art object was the pot.) As machines became as talented as humans, artists embraced new technology and mass production to bring beauty to the masses. Look especially for examples by the in-

fluential designers Gerrit Rietveld (1888-1964) and Alvar Aalto (1898-1976).

Expressionism and Surrealism

This period could be called "World War I—The Death of Values." Ankle-deep in mud, a soldier shivers in a trench, waiting to be ordered "over the top." He'll have to run through barbed wire, over fallen comrades, and into a hail of machine-gun fire, only to capture a few hundred yards of meaningless territory that will be lost the next day. This soldier was not thinking about art.

World War I left nine million dead. (During the war, France lost more men in the Battle of Verdun than America lost in the entire Vietnam War.) The war also killed the optimism and faith in mankind that had guided Europe since the Renaissance. Now, rationality just meant schemes, technology meant machines of death, and morality meant giving your life for an empty cause.

Expressionism

Cynicism and decadence settled over postwar Europe, and artists such as Ernst Ludwig Kirchner, Max Beckmann, George Grosz, Chaïm Soutine, Otto Dix, and Oskar Kokoschka recorded it. They "expressed" their disgust by showing a distorted reality that emphasized the ugly. Using the lurid colors and simplified figures of the Fauves, they slapped paint on in thick brushstrokes and depicted a hypocritical, hard-edged, dog-eat-dog world that had lost its bearings. The people have a haunted look in their eyes—the fixed stare of corpses and those who have to bury them.

Dada

When people could grieve no longer, they turned to grief's giddy twin: laughter. The war made all old values, including art, a joke. The Dada movement, choosing a purposely childish name, made art that was intentionally outrageous: a moustache on the *Mona Lisa*, a shovel hung on a wall, or a modern version of a Renaissance "fountain"—a urinal (by either Marcel Duchamp, or I. P. Freeley, 1917). It was a dig at all the pompous prewar artistic theories based on the noble intellect of Rational Women and Men. While the experts ranted on, Dadaists sat in the back of the class and made cultural fart noises.

Hey, I love this stuff. My mind says it's sophomoric, but my heart belongs to Dada.

Surrealism

Greek statues with sunglasses, a man as a spinning top, shoes becoming feet, and black ants as musical notes...Surrealism. The world was moving fast, and Surrealist artists such as Salvador Dalí, Max Ernst, and René Magritte caught the jumble of images. The artist scatters seemingly unrelated items on the canvas, which leaves us to trace the links in a kind of connect-the-dots without numbers. If it comes together, the synergy of unrelated things can be pretty startling. But even if the juxtaposed images don't ultimately connect, the artist has made you think, rerouting your thoughts through new neural paths. If you don't "get" it...you got it.

Complicating the modern world was Freud's discovery of the "unconscious" mind that thinks dirty thoughts while we sleep. Many a Surrealist canvas is an uncensored, stream-of-consciousness "landscape" of these deep urges, revealed in the bizarre images of dreams.

In dreams, sometimes one object can be two things at once: "I dreamt that you walked in with a cat...no, wait, maybe you *were* the cat...no..." Surrealists paint opposites like these and let them speak for themselves.

Salvador Dalí, 1904-1989

Salvador Dalí could draw exceptionally well. He painted "unreal" scenes with photographic realism, thus making us believe they

could really happen. Seeing familiar objects in an unfamiliar setting—like a grand piano adorned with disembodied heads of Lenin—creates an air of mystery, the feeling that anything can happen. That's both exciting and unsettling. Dalí's images—crucifixes, political and religious figures, naked bodies—pack an emotional punch. Take one mixed bag of reality, jumble in a blender, and serve on a canvas...Surrealism.

Abstract Surrealists

Abstract artists such as Joan Miró, Alexander Calder, and Jean Arp described their subconscious urges using color and shapes alone, like Rorschach inkblots in reverse.

The thin-line scrawl of Miró's work is like the doodling of a three-year-old. You'll recognize crudely drawn birds, stars, animals, and strange cell-like creatures with whiskers ("Biological Cubism"). Miró was trying to express the most basic of human emotions using the most basic of techniques.

Calder's mobiles hang like Mirós in the sky, waiting for a gust of wind to bring them to life.

And talk about a primal image! Arp builds human beings out of amoeba-like shapes.

More Modernists
Georges Rouault, 1871-1958
Young Georges Rouault was apprenticed to a maker of stained-glass windows. Enough said?

His paintings have the same thick, glowing colors, heavy black outlines, simple subjects, and (mostly) religious themes. The style is modern, but the mood is medieval, solemn, and melancholy. Rouault captures the tragic spirit of those people—clowns, prostitutes, and sons of God—who have been made outcasts by society.

Decorative Art
Most 20th-century paintings are a mix of the real world ("representation") and the colorful patterns of "abstract" art. Artists purposely distort camera-eye reality to make the resulting canvas more decorative. So, Picasso flattens a woman into a pattern of colored shapes, Pierre Bonnard makes a man from a shimmer of golden paint, and Balthus turns a boudoir scene into colorful wallpaper.

Patterns and Textures
Increasingly, you'll have to focus your eyes to look *at* the canvases, not *through* them, especially in art by Jean Dubuffet, Lucio Fontana, and Karel Appel.

Enjoy the lines and colors, but also a new element: texture. Some works have very thick paint piled on—you can see the brushstroke clearly. Some have substances besides paint applied to the canvas, such as Dubuffet's brown, earthy rectangles of real dirt and organic waste. Fontana punctures the canvas so that the fabric itself (and the hole) becomes the subject. Artists show their skill by mastering new materials. The canvas is a tray, serving up a delightful array of different substances with interesting colors, patterns, shapes, and textures.

Alberto Giacometti, 1901-1966
Giacometti's skinny statues have the emaciated, haunted, and faceless look of concentration camp survivors. The simplicity of the figures may be "primitive," but these aren't stately, sturdy, Easter Island heads. Here, man is weak in the face of technology and the winds of history.

Abstract Expressionism
America emerged from World War II as the globe's superpower. With Europe in ruins, New York replaced Paris as the art capital of the world. The trend was toward bigger canvases, abstract designs, and experimentation with new materials and techniques. It was

called "Abstract Expressionism"—expressing emotions and ideas using color and form alone.

Jackson Pollock, 1912-1956

"Jack the Dripper" attacks convention with a can of paint, dripping and splashing a dense web onto the canvas. Picture Pollock in his studio, as he jives to the hi-fi, bounces off the walls, and throws paint in a moment of enlightenment. Of course, the artist loses some control this way—control over the paint flying in midair and over himself, now in an ecstatic trance. Painting becomes a whole-body activity, a "dance" between the artist and his materials.

The act of creating is what's important, not the final product. The canvas is only a record of that moment of ecstasy.

Barnett Newman, 1905-1970, and
Robert Rauschenberg, 1925-2008

All those huge, sparse canvases with just a few lines or colors—what reality are they trying to show?

In the modern world, we find ourselves insignificant specks in a vast and indifferent universe. Every morning each of us must confront that big, blank, existentialist canvas and decide how we're going to make our mark on it. Like, wow.

Another influence was the simplicity of Japanese landscape painting. A Zen master studies and meditates for years to achieve the state of mind in which he can draw one pure line. These canvases, again, are only a record of that state of enlightenment. (What is the sound of one brush painting?)

On more familiar ground, postwar painters were following in the footsteps of artists such as Mondrian, Klee, and Kandinsky (whose work they must have considered "busy"). The geometrical forms here reflect the same search for order, but these artists painted to the 5/4 asymmetry of Dave Brubeck's jazz classic, "Take Five."

Pop Art

America's postwar wealth made the consumer king. Pop Art is created from the "pop"-ular objects of that throwaway society—a soup can, a car fender, mannequins, tacky plastic statues, movie icons, advertising posters.

Is this art? Are all these mass-produced objects beautiful? Or crap? If they're not art, why do we work so hard to acquire them? Pop Art, like Dada, questions our society's values.

Andy Warhol, 1928-1987

Warhol (who coined the idea of everyone having "15 minutes of fame" and became a pop star himself) concentrated on another mass-produced phenomenon: celebrities. He took publicity photos of famous people and repeated them. The repetition—like the constant bombardment we get from repeated images on television—cheapens even the most beautiful things.

Pop Art makes you reassess what "beauty" really is. Take something out of Sears and hang it in a museum and you have to think about it in a wholly different way.

• *Exit down the stairs by the ticket-takers on the fifth floor (the escalator does not connect to the fourth floor) and browse your way back toward the entrance. Our tour ends here, but there's more contemporary art on the fourth floor.*

FOURTH FLOOR
Contemporary Art from 1980 to the Present

The "modern" world is history. Picasso and his ilk are now gathering dust and boring art students everywhere. Minimalist painting and abstract sculpture are old school. Enter the "postmodern" world, as seen through the eyes of current artists.

You'll see fewer traditional canvases or sculptures. Artists have traded paintbrushes for blowtorches (Miró said he was out to "murder" painting), and blowtorches for computer mice. Mixed-media work is the norm, combining painting, sculpture, photography, video/film, digital graphics and computer programming, new resins, plastics, industrial techniques, and lighting and sound systems.

The Pompidou groups the work of these artists under somewhat arbitrary labels—the artist as documentarian, as an archivist of events, or as a producer of commercial goods. Don't worry about trying to understand these cryptic conceptual labels. Browse the floor and enjoy some of the following trends:

Installations: An entire room is given to an artist to prepare. Like entering an art funhouse, you walk in without quite knowing what to expect. (I'm always thinking, "Is this safe?") Using the latest technology, the artist engages all your senses by controlling the lights, sounds, and sometimes even the smells.

Digital Media: Holograms replace material objects, and elaborate computer programming creates a fantastic multimedia display.

Assemblages: Artists raid Dumpsters, recycling junk into the building blocks for larger "assemblages." Each piece is intended to be interesting and tell its own story, and so is the whole sculpture. Weird, useless Rube Goldberg machines make fun of technology.

Natural Objects: A rock in an urban setting is inherently interesting.

The Occasional Canvas: This comes as a familiar relief. Artists of the New Realism labor over painstaking, hyper-realistic canvases to re-create the glossy look of a photo or video image.

Interaction: Some exhibits require your participation, whether you push a button to get the contraption going, touch something, or just walk around the room. In some cases the viewer "does" art, rather than just staring at it. If art is really meant to change, it has to move you—literally.

Deconstruction: Late-20th-century artists critiqued (or "deconstructed") society by examining our underlying assumptions. One way to do it is to take a familiar object (say, a crucifix) out of its normal context (a church) and place it in a new setting (a jar of urine). Video and film can deconstruct something by playing it over and over, ad nauseam. Words printed on a canvas force you to compare the meaning with the visual meaning of the painting. Ad copy painted on canvas deconstructs itself.

Conceptual Art: The *concept* of which object to pair with another to produce maximum effect is the key. (Crucifix + urine = million-dollar masterpiece.)

Postmodernism: Artists shamelessly recycled older styles and motifs to create new combinations: Greek columns paired with Gothic arches, Christmas lights, and a hip-hop soundtrack.

Performance Art: This is a kind of mixed-media of live performance. Many artists—who in another day would have painted canvases—have turned to music, dance, theater, and performance art. This art form is often interactive, by dropping the illusion of a performance and encouraging audience participation. When you finish with the Pompidou Center, go outside for some of the street theater.

Playful Art: Children love the art being produced today. If it doesn't put a smile on your face, well, then you must be a jaded grump like me, who's seen the same repetitious s#%t passed off as "daring" since Warhol stole it from Duchamp. I mean, it's *so* 20th century.

PÈRE LACHAISE CEMETERY TOUR

Cimetière du Père Lachaise

Enclosed by a massive wall and lined with 5,000 trees, the peaceful, car-free lanes and dirt paths of Père Lachaise cemetery encourage parklike meandering. Named for Father *(Père)* La Chaise, whose job was listening to Louis XIV's sins, the cemetery is relatively new, having opened in 1804 to accommodate Paris' expansion. Today, this 100-acre city of the dead (pop. 70,000) still accepts new residents, but real estate prices are sky high (a 21-square-foot plot costs more than €14,000). Père Lachaise has become a kind of national cemetery—like a Westminster Abbey of honored dead. French people come here to remember their history, mourn over national tragedies, and find inspiration from the past.

This walk takes you on a one-way tour through the cemetery. Start from the convenient Métro/bus stops at Place Gambetta, connect a handful of graves from some of this necropolis' best-known residents, and take a last bow at either the Père Lachaise or Philippe Auguste Métro stops, or a nearby bus #69 stop.

Orientation

Cost: Free.

Hours: Mon-Fri 8:00-18:00, Sat from 8:30, Sun from 9:00, closes at 17:30 in winter.

Getting There: Take bus #69 eastbound to Place Gambetta (see the Bus #69 Sightseeing Tour chapter) or ride the Métro to the Gambetta stop (not to the Père Lachaise stop), exit at Gambetta Métro, and take *sortie* #3 (Père Lachaise exit). From Place Gambetta, it's a two-block walk up Avenue du Père Lachaise to the cemetery.

Information: Maps are sold only at florists right across from the Porte Gambetta entrance (€2). An unofficial website, www.

PÈRE LACHAISE

pere-lachaise.com, has a searchable map (cemetery info: +33 1 55 25 82 10).

Length of This Tour: Allow 1.5 hours for this walk and another 30 minutes for your own detours. Bring good walking shoes for the rough, cobbled streets.

Tours: ∩ Download my Père Lachaise Cemetery audio tour.

Services: WCs are at the start of this tour, just inside the Porte Gambetta entrance to the right (BYO toilet paper), and at the end of this tour, to the left just before you exit Porte Principale.

Eating: You'll pass several cafés between Place Gambetta and the cemetery. After the tour, you can walk down Rue de la Roquette to a gaggle of lively, affordable cafés on the right side of the street, near the return stop for bus #69.

Starring: Oscar Wilde, Edith Piaf, Gertrude Stein, Molière, Jim Morrison, Frédéric Chopin, Colette, and Rossini.

OVERVIEW

From the Porte Gambetta entrance, we'll walk roughly southwest (mostly downhill) through the cemetery. At the end of the tour, we'll exit Porte Principale onto Boulevard de Ménilmontant, near the Père Lachaise and Philippe Auguste Métro entrances and another bus #69 stop. You could follow the tour in the other direction, but it's not recommended—it's confusing, and almost completely uphill.

This cemetery is big, with thousands of graves and tombs crammed every which way, and only a few pedestrian pathways to help you navigate. Pay close attention to this chapter's directions, refer to the map in this chapter, and follow street signs posted at intersections. The more detailed map available from florists near the entrance can also help guide you. Be patient, and ask passersby for graves you can't locate. You may be tempted to stray off my route to find graves on your own, but beware—it's very easy to get lost, and they'll bury you where they find you.

The Tour Begins

• *Entering the cemetery at the Porte Gambetta entrance, walk straight up Avenue des Combattants Etrangers past world war memorials dedicated to foreigners who fought for France: Armenians, Poles, Italians, and Russians. Cross Avenue Transversale No. 3, pass the first building, and look left to the...*

❶ Columbarium/Crematorium

Marked by a dome with a gilded flame and working chimneys on top, the columbarium sits in a courtyard surrounded by about 1,300 niches—small cubicles for cremated remains, often decorated with real or artificial flowers.

Beneath the courtyard (steps leading underground) are about 12,000 smaller niches, including one for Maria Callas (1923-1977), an American-born opera diva known for her versatility, flair for drama, and affair with Aristotle Onassis (niche #16258, on the immediate left, 20 yards down aisle J).

• *Turn around and walk back to the intersection with Avenue Transversale No. 3 and turn right. As you walk, notice how families built small chapels for several generations of loved ones to share. Turn left on Avenue Carette, and walk half a block to the block-of-stone tomb (on the left) with heavy-winged angels trying to fly.*

❷ Oscar Wilde (1854-1900)

The writer and martyr to homosexuality is mourned by "outcast men" (as the inscription says) and by wearers of heavy lipstick, who

used to cover the tomb and the angels' emasculated privates with kisses. (Now the tomb is behind glass, which has not stopped committed kissers.) Despite Wilde's notoriety, an inscription says, "He died fortified by the Sacraments of the Church."

There's a short résumé scratched (in English) into the back side of the tomb. For more on Wilde and his death in Paris, see the sidebar on page 308.

> *"Alas, I am dying beyond my means."*
>
> —Oscar Wilde

• *Continue along Avenue Carette and turn right (southeast) down Avenue Circulaire. In about 100 yards you'll pass monuments to national* **airline tragedies** *on your left (Sharm el-Sheikh, a 2004 crash in Egypt killing 135 people—mostly French tourists; crashes in Venezuela, including one in 2005 that took the lives of 152 French citizens; and a flight that blew up over Niger, killing 54 French, in 1989). Almost two blocks*

PÈRE LACHAISE

PÈRE LACHAISE

Tour
1 Columbarium/Crematorium
2 Oscar Wilde
3 Gertrude Stein
4 Mur des Fédérés
5 Edith Piaf
6 Bernard Verlhac
7 Molière
8 Jim Morrison
9 Frédéric Chopin
10 Baron Haussmann
11 Gioacchino Rossini
12 Colette

Others Elsewhere
Ⓐ Jacques-Louis David
Ⓑ Théodore Géricault
Ⓒ Eugène Delacroix
Ⓓ J. A. D. Ingres
Ⓔ Georges Seurat
Ⓕ Amadeo Modigliani
Ⓖ Marcel Proust
Ⓗ Sarah Bernhardt
Ⓘ Yves Montand & Simone Signoret
Ⓙ Héloïse & Abélard
Ⓚ Gilbert Morard

down, you'll reach Gertrude Stein's unadorned, easy-to-miss grave (it's the grave covered with pebbles, on the right, immediately before a beige-yellow stone structure—if you reach Avenue Pacthod, you've passed it by about 30 yards).

❸ Gertrude Stein (1874-1946)

While traveling through Europe, the twentysomething American dropped out of med school and moved to Paris, her home for the

rest of her life. She shared an apartment at 27 Rue de Fleurus (a couple of blocks west of Luxembourg Garden) with her brother Leo and, later, with her life partner, Alice B. Toklas (who's also buried here, see gravestone's flipside). Every Saturday night, Paris' brightest artistic lights converged *chez vingt-sept* (at 27) for dinner and intellectual stimulation. Picasso painted her portrait, Hemingway sought her approval, and Virgil Thompson set her words to music.

America discovered "Gerty" in 1933 when her memoirs, the slyly titled *Autobiography of Alice B. Toklas,* hit the best-seller list. After 30 years away, she returned to the United States for a triumphant lecture tour. Her writing is less well known than her persona, except for the oft-quoted, "A rose is a rose is a rose."

Stein's last words: When asked, "What is the answer?" she replied, "What is the question?"

• *Ponder Stein's tomb again and again and again, and continue southeast on Avenue Circulaire to where it curves to the right. Emaciated statues remember victims of the concentration camps and Nazi resistance heroes. Pebbles on the tombstones represent Jewish prayers. About 50 yards past Avenue Pacthod, veer left off the cobbled lane where you see the green Avenue Circulaire street sign to find the wall marked* Aux Morts de la Commune.

❹ Mur des Fédérés

The "Communards' Wall" marks the place where the quixotic Paris Commune came to a violent end.

In 1870, Prussia invaded France, and the country quickly collapsed and surrendered—all except the city of Paris. For six months, through a bitter winter, the Prussians laid siege to the city. Defiant Paris held out, even opposing the French government, which had fled to Versailles and was collaborating with the Germans. Parisians formed an opposition government that was revolutionary and socialist, called the Paris Commune.

The Versailles government sent French soldiers to retake Paris. In May of 1871, they breached the west walls and swept eastward. French soldiers fought French citizens, and tens of thousands died during a bloody week of street fighting (La Semaine Sanglante). The remaining resisters holed up inside the walls of Père Lachaise and made an Alamo-type last stand before they were finally overcome.

At dawn on May 28, 1871, the 147 Communards were lined up against this wall and shot by French soldiers. They were buried in a mass grave where they fell. With them the Paris Commune died, and the city entered five years of martial law.

• *Return up five steps to the road, continue to the next (unmarked) street, Avenue Transversale No. 3, and (at the Mauthausen Memorial on the right corner) turn right. A half-block uphill, Edith Piaf's grave is on the right. It's one grave off the street, behind a white tombstone with a small gray cross (Salvador family). Confusingly, Piaf's tombstone is labeled*

Gassion. *Edith Gassion-Piaf rests among many graves. Hers is often adorned with photos, fresh flowers, and love notes.*

❺ Edith Piaf (1915-1963)

A child of the Parisian streets, Piaf was raised in her grandma's bordello and her father's traveling circus troupe. The teenager sang for spare change in Paris' streets, where a nightclub owner discovered her. Waif-like and dressed in black, she sang in a warbling voice under the name "La Môme Piaf" (The Little Sparrow). She became the toast of pre-WWII Paris society.

Her offstage love life was busy and often messy, including a teenage pregnancy (her daughter is buried along with her, in a grave marked *Marcelle Dupont, 1933-1935*), a murdered husband, and a heartbreaking affair with co-star Yves Montand.

With her strong but trembling voice, she buoyed French spirits under the German occupation, and her most famous song, "La Vie en Rose" (The Rosy Life) captured the joy of postwar Paris. In her personal life she struggled with alcohol, painkillers, and poor health, while onstage she sang, *"Non, je ne regrette rien"* ("No, I don't regret anything").

• *From Edith Piaf's grave, continue uphill, cross Avenue Pacthod, and turn left on the next street, Avenue Greffulhe. Follow Greffulhe straight for roughly 80 yards until you reach a shiny black grave on the left, just beyond a grave with a slender cylindrical statue on it (10 yards before crossing Avenue Transversale No. 2).*

❻ Bernard Verlhac (pseudonym Tignous, 1957-2015)

A cartoonist for the French satirical magazine *Charlie Hebdo*, Tignous was one of 12 people assassinated by terrorists at the magazine's office in January 2015. *Charlie Hebdo* had long attracted controversy and episodes of violence due to its inflammatory cartoons of the Prophet Muhammad. The magazine's editor-in-chief, Stéphane Charbonnier, who also was killed in the attack, once said about their work: "We have to carry on until Islam has been rendered as banal as Catholicism."

As Paris has suffered other terrorist attacks since the Charlie Hebdo massacre, Verlhac's tomb has become a rallying point for mourners of those other tragedies as well. Visitors here remember the slogan of solidarity that was expressed around the world: *"Je suis Charlie."*

• *Continue up Avenue Greffulhe (even when it narrows) until it dead-ends at Avenue Transversale No. 1. Cross the street and venture down a dirt section that veers slightly to the right, then make a hard right onto another dirt lane named Chemin Molière et La Fontaine. Molière lies 30 yards down, on the right side of the street, just beyond the highest point of this lane.*

❼ Molière (1622-1673)

In 1804, the great comic playwright was the first to be reburied in Père Lachaise, a publicity stunt that gave instant prestige to the new cemetery.

Born in Paris, Molière was not of noble blood, but as the son of the king's furniture supervisor, he had connections. The 21-year-old Molière joined a troupe of strolling players who ranked very low on the social scale, touring the provinces. Twelve long years later, they returned to Paris to perform before Louis XIV. Molière, by now an accomplished comic actor, cracked the king up. He was instantly famous—writing, directing, and often starring in his own works. He satirized rich nobles, hypocritical priests, and quack doctors, creating enemies in high places.

On February 17, 1673, an aging Molière went on stage in the title role of his latest comedy, *The Imaginary Invalid*. Though sick, he insisted he had to go on, concerned for all the little people. His role was of a hypochondriac who coughs to get sympathy. The deathly ill Molière effectively faked coughing fits...which soon turned to real convulsions. The unaware crowd roared with laughter while his fellow players fretted in the wings.

In the final scene, Molière's character becomes a doctor himself in a mock swearing-in ceremony. The ultimate trouper, Molière finished his final line—*"Juro"* ("I accept")—and collapsed while coughing blood. The audience laughed hysterically. He died shortly thereafter.

Irony upon irony for the master of satire: Molière—a sick man whose doctors thought he was a hypochondriac—dies playing a well man who is a hypochondriac, succumbing onstage while the audience cheers. Molière lies next to his friend and fellow writer, La Fontaine (1621-1695), who wrote a popular version of Aesop's Fables.

"We die only once, and for such a long time."

—Molière

• *Continue downhill on Chemin Molière et La Fontaine (which becomes the cobbled Chemin du Bassin, bending right and ever downhill) to where it ends. Turn left (on Avenue de la Chapelle, going steeper downhill). Twenty steps down, on the left, find the train-engraved headstone of* **ⓚ** *Gilbert Morard, father of the Paris Métro. Continue to the Rond Point roundabout intersection.*

Cross Carrefour Rond Point and continue straight (opposite where you entered). This puts you going downhill on a street that's probably unmarked (though the official name is Chemin de la Bédoyère). Just a few steps along, turn right onto Chemin Lauriston. Keep to the left at the fork (now on Chemin de Lesseps) and look for the temple about 10 yards on the right with three wreaths. Jim Morrison lies just behind, often watched over by a personal security guard. You can't miss the commotion.

⑧ Jim Morrison (1943-1971)

Perhaps the most visited tomb in the cemetery belongs to this American rock star—lead singer for The Doors, named for the "Doors of Perception" they aimed to open. An iconic, funky bust of the rocker was stolen by fans and replaced with a more toned-down headstone. Even so, Morrison's faithful still gather here at all hours. The headstone's Greek inscription reads: "To the spirit (or demon) within." Graffiti-ing nearby tombs, fans write: "You still Light My Fire" (referring to Jim's biggest hit), "Ring my bell at the Dead Rock Star Hotel," and "Mister Mojo Risin'" (referring to the legend that Jim faked his death and still lives today).

When Morrison arrived in Paris in the winter of 1971, he was famous, notorious for his erotic onstage antics, and a burned-out alcoholic. Paris was to be his chance to leave celebrity behind, get healthy, and get serious as a writer.

Living under an assumed name in a nondescript sublet apartment near Place de la Bastille, he spent his days as a carefree artist. He scribbled in notebooks at Café de Flore and Les Deux Magots (in the Left Bank), watched the sun set from the steps of Sacré-Cœur, visited Baudelaire's house, and jammed with street musicians. He drank a lot, took other drugs, gained weight, and his health declined.

In the wee hours of July 3, he died in his bathtub at age 27, officially of a heart attack, but likely from an overdose. (Any police investigation was thwarted by Morrison's social circle of heroin users, leading to wild rumors surrounding his death.)

Jim's friends approached Père Lachaise Cemetery about burying the famous rock star there, in accordance with his wishes. The director refused to admit him, until they mentioned that Jim was a writer. "A writer?" he said, and found a spot.

"This is the end, my only friend, the end."

—Jim Morrison

• *Return to Rond Point. The statue in the center remembers Casimir Pèrier: President of France in 1894 for only six months—shortest of any French president—he still got a big monument. Casimir is looking directly through a forest of tombstones at the tomb of Frédéric Chopin, about 50 yards away. To get there, you'll need to tip-toe through the tombstones.*

Leave the roundabout near the Mallet Family tomb. Go straight ahead about a dozen steps (carefully past three or four tombs) and turn left when you reach a cobbled lane. Follow the lane downhill for 20 yards, then take your first right on another small cobbled lane. This leads to a white tomb (50 yards on the right) with a statue of a woman with her head bowed in mourning—the tomb of...

❾ Frédéric Chopin (1810-1849)

Fresh-cut flowers and geraniums on the gravestone speak of the emotional staying power of Chopin's music, which still connects souls across the centuries. A muse sorrows atop the tomb, and a carved relief of Chopin in profile captures the delicate features of this sensitive artist.

The 21-year-old Polish pianist arrived in Paris, fell in love with the city, and never returned to his homeland (which was occupied by an increasingly oppressive Russia). In Paris, he could finally shake off the "child prodigy" label and performance schedule he'd lived with since age seven. Cursed with stage fright ("I don't like concerts. The crowds scare me, their breath chokes me, I'm paralyzed by their stares...") and with too light a touch for big venues, Chopin preferred playing at private parties for Paris' elite. They were wowed by his technique; his ability to make a piano sing; and his melodic, soul-stirring compositions. Soon he was recognized as a pianist, composer, and teacher and even idolized as a brooding genius. He ran in aristocratic circles with fellow artists, such as pianist Franz Liszt, painter Delacroix, novelists Victor Hugo and Balzac, and composer Rossini. (All but Liszt and Hugo lie in Père Lachaise.)

Chopin composed nearly 200 pieces, almost all for piano, in many different styles—from lively Polish dances to the Bach-like counterpoint of his *Preludes* to the moody, romantic *Nocturnes*.

In 1837, the quiet, refined, dreamy-eyed genius met the scandalous, assertive, stormy novelist George Sand (see page 308 of the Left Bank Walk chapter). Sand was swept away by Chopin's music and artistic nature. She pursued him, and sparks flew. Though the romance faded quickly, they continued living together for nearly a decade in an increasingly bitter love-hate relationship. When Chopin developed tuberculosis, Sand nursed him for years (Chopin complained she was killing him). Sand finally left, Chopin was devastated, and he died two years later at age 39. At the funeral, they played perhaps Chopin's most famous piece, the *Funeral March* (it's that 11-note dirge that everyone knows). The grave contains Chopin's body, but his heart lies in Warsaw, embedded in a church column.

> *"The earth is suffocating. Swear to make them cut me open, so that I won't he buried alive."*

—Chopin, on his deathbed

• *Facing Chopin, walk left, uphill about 100 yards, until the lane dead ends at Avenue Laterale du Sud. Trespass straight ahead over three gravesites to the next lane and head left, downhill. About 20 steps after that lane hits the road, on the right is...*

❿ Baron Georges-Eugène Haussmann (1809-1891) / Famille Haussmann

Squint through the green door. Love him or hate him, Baron Haussmann made the Paris we see today. In the 1860s, Paris was a construction zone, with civil servant Haussmann overseeing the city's modernization. Narrow medieval lanes were widened and straightened into broad, traffic-carrying boulevards. Historic buildings were torn down. Sewers, bridges, and water systems were repaired. Haussmann rammed the Boulevard St. Michel through the formerly quaint Latin Quarter (as part of Emperor Napoleon III's plan to prevent revolutionaries from barricading narrow streets). The Opéra Garnier, Bois de Boulogne park, and avenues  radiating from the Arc de Triomphe were all part of Haussmann's grand scheme, which touched 60 percent of the city. How did he finance it all? That's what the next government wanted to know when they canned him.

Other Notable Residents

Though not along our walking tour, the following folks can be found on our map, as well as the maps for sale from vendors.

Ⓐ Jacques-Louis David (1748-1825), Section 56
The Neoclassical painter David chronicled the heroic Revolution and the Napoleonic Era. See his *Coronation of Emperor Napoleon* in the Louvre (page 174).

Ⓑ Théodore Géricault (1791-1824), Section 12
Géricault was the master of painting extreme situations (ship-wrecks, battles) and extreme emotions (noble sacrifice, courage, agony, insanity) with Romantic realism. See his *Raft of the Medusa* in the Louvre (page 176).

Ⓒ Eugène Delacroix (1798-1863), Section 49
For more on this Romantic painter, see his *Liberty Leading the People* in the Louvre (page 177) or visit the Delacroix Museum (page 87).

Ⓓ Jean-August-Dominique Ingres (1780-1867), Section 23
Often considered the anti-Delacroix, Ingres painted placid por-traits and bathing nudes, using curved outlines and smooth-sur-faced paint. Despite his deliberate distortions (as in his beauti-fully deformed *La Grande Odalisque* in the Louvre, page 175), he was hailed as the champion of traditional Neoclassical balance against the furious Romantic style (see *The Source* in the Orsay, page 190).

Ⓔ Georges Seurat (1859-1891), Section 66
Georges spent Sunday afternoons in the park with his easel, cap-turing shimmering light with tiny dots of different-colored paint.

Ⓕ Amadeo Modigliani (1884-1920), Section 96, near Edith Piaf
Poor, tubercular, and strung out on drugs and alcohol in Paris, this young Italian painter forged a distinctive style. His portraits and nudes have African masklike faces and elongated necks and arms.

Ⓖ Marcel Proust (1871-1922), Section 85
Some who make it through the seven volumes and 3,000 pages of Proust's autobiographical novel, *Remembrance of Things Past,* close the book and cry, "Brilliant!" Others get lost in the mean-dering, stream-of-consciousness style, and forget that the whole "Remembrance" began with the taste of a *madeleine* (a type of cookie) that triggered a flashback to Proust's childhood, as relived over the last 10 years of his life, during which he labored alone in his apartment on Boulevard Haussmann—midway between the Arc de Triomphe and Gare de l'Est—penning his life story with reflections on Time (as we experience it, not as we measure it on the clock) and Memory...in long sentences.

Ⓗ Sarah Bernhardt (1844-1923), Section 44
The greatest actress of her generation, she conquered Paris and the world. Charismatic Sarah made a triumphant tour of America

and Europe (1880-1881), starring in *La Dame aux Camélias*. No one could die onstage like Sarah, and in the final scene—when her character succumbs to tuberculosis—she had cowboys and railroad workers sniffling in the audience. Of her hundred-plus stage roles and many silent films, her most memorable one may have been playing...Hamlet (1899). Offstage, her numerous affairs and passionate, capricious personality set a standard for future divas.

❶ Yves Montand (1921-1991) and Simone Signoret (1921-1985), Section 44

Yves Montand was a film actor and nightclub singer with blue-collar roots, left-wing politics, and a social conscience. Montand's career was boosted by his lover, Edith Piaf, when they appeared together at the Moulin Rouge during World War II. Yves went on to stardom throughout the world (except in America, thanks partly to a 1960 flop film with Marilyn Monroe, *Let's Make Love*). In 1951, he married actress Simone Signoret, whose on-screen persona was the long-suffering lover. They remain together still, despite rumors of Yves' womanizing. After their deaths, their eternal love was tested in 1998, when Yves' body was exhumed to take a DNA sample for a paternity suit. (It wasn't him.)

❶ Héloïse (c. 1101-1164) and Abélard (1079-1142), Section 7

The oldest residents in Père Lachaise have a timeless story. Inde-

pendent scholar Peter Abélard shocked and titillated 12th century Paris with his reasoned critique of Church doctrine. He set up a Left Bank school that would become the University of Paris, bringing bright minds from all over Europe, including Héloïse, niece of the powerful canon of Notre-Dame. Abélard was hired to give private instruction to Héloïse. Their intense intellectual intercourse quickly flared into physical passion and a spiritual bond. They fled Paris and married in secret, and a year later Héloïse gave birth to a son (named Astrolabe). News got out and, in the middle of the night, thugs went to Abélard's bedroom and castrated him.

Disgraced, he retired to a monastery and she to a convent, but they remained intimately connected by the postal service. (The dog at Abélard's feet symbolizes their fidelity.) Abélard, who was on trial for heresy when he died, bounced back with some of his most critical writings, using logic to analyze Church pronouncements—a practice that flowered into the "scholasticism" accepted by the Church a century later. The canopy tomb we see today (1817) is made out of stones from both Héloïse's convent and Abélard's monastery.

• *Four doors downhill from Haussmann is Rossini.*

⓫ Gioacchino Rossini (1792-1868)

Dut. Dutta-dut. Dutta dut dut dut dut dut dut dut, dut dut dut dut dut dut dut dut...

The composer of the *William Tell Overture* (a.k.a. the *Lone Ranger* theme) was Italian, but he moved to Paris (1823) to bring his popular comic operas to France. Extremely prolific, he could crank out a three-hour opera in weeks, including the highly successful *Barber of Seville* (based on a play by Pierre Beaumarchais, who is also buried in Père Lachaise). When *Guillaume Tell* debuted (1829), Rossini, age 37, was at the peak of his career as an opera composer.

Then he stopped. For the next four decades, he never again wrote an opera and scarcely composed anything else. He moved back to Italy, went through a stretch of bad health, and then returned to Paris, where his health and spirits revived. He even wrote a little music in his old age. Rossini's impressive little sepulcher is empty, as his remains were moved to Florence.

• *Downhill ahead, on Avenue Principale, is the gate to the land of the living. But we have one more stop. Take a few steps downhill, then turn right at the corner and find the second gravesite. Here lies Colette.*

⓬ Colette (1873-1954)

France's most honored female writer led an unconventional life—thrice married and often linked romantically with other women—

and wrote about it in semi-autobiographical novels. Her first fame came from a series of novels about naughty teenage Claudine's misadventures. In her 30s, Colette went on to a career as a music hall performer, scandalizing Paris by showing her breasts. Her late novel, *Gigi* (1945)—about a teenage girl groomed to be a professional mistress, who blossoms into independence—became a musical film starring Leslie Caron and Maurice Chevalier (1958). Thank heaven for little girls!

> "*The only misplaced curiosity is trying to find out here, on this side, what lies beyond the grave.*"
>
> —Colette

Thank God You Can Leave

To leave the cemetery, continue downhill on Avenue Principale and exit onto Boulevard de Ménilmontant (WCs on the left before leaving). The Père Lachaise Métro stop is two long blocks to the right and the closer Philippe Auguste Métro stop is one block to the left. To find the return stop for bus #69 heading west to downtown, cross Boulevard de Ménilmontant and walk downhill on the right side of Rue de la Roquette; the stop is a few blocks down, on the right-hand side. Go in peace.

MONTMARTRE WALK

From Sacré-Cœur to the Moulin Rouge

Stroll along the hilltop of Butte Montmartre amid traces of the many people who've lived here over the years—monks stomping grapes (1200s), farmers grinding grain in windmills (1600s), dust-coated gypsum miners (1700s), Parisian liberals (1800s), Modernist painters (1900s), and all the struggling artists, poets, dreamers, and drunkards who came here for cheap rent, untaxed booze, rustic landscapes, and cabaret nightlife. In the jazzy 1920s, the neighborhood became the haunt of American GIs and expat African Americans (who experienced less discrimination here than in the US at that time). Today it's a youthful neighborhood in transition—slightly seedy, *très* trendy, and ever-more touristy.

Many tourists make the almost obligatory trek to the top of Paris' Butte Montmartre, eat an overpriced crêpe, marvel at the view—and miss out on the neighborhood's charm and history. Both are uncovered in this stroll. We'll ascend to the gleaming Sacré-Cœur Basilica, wander through the hilltop village, browse affordable art, ogle the Moulin Rouge nightclub, and catch echoes of those who once partied to a bohemian rhapsody during the belle époque.

Orientation

Length of This Walk: Allow at least two hours for this two-mile uphill/downhill walk.

When to Go: To minimize crowds at Sacré-Cœur, come on a

weekday or by 9:30 on a weekend. Sunny weekends are the busiest—especially Sunday, when Montmartre becomes a pedestrian-only zone and most shops stay open. If crowds don't get you down, come for the sunset and stay for dinner. This walk is best under clear skies, when views are sensational.

Getting There: This walk begins at Place des Abbesses (Mo: Abbesses). Other nearby stops include Anvers and Pigalle. (Expect some seediness around Anvers and Pigalle, and avoid the sketchy Métro station Barbès Rochechouart completely.)

From Place des Abbesses we'll walk a few level blocks and then take the funicular (one-minute ride, Métro passes valid) to the base of Sacré-Cœur. A taxi from the Seine or the Bastille to Sacré-Cœur costs about €20 (€25 at night).

Scam Alert: At Sacré-Cœur and in the areas around the Pigalle and Anvers Métro stations, beware of pickpockets, smartphone snatchings, the shell game, and the "found ring" and "friendship bracelet" scams (for more on scams, see page 32).

Tourist Information: A small TI may be open near the base of the funicular at 7 Rue Drevet (Tue-Sat 10:00-13:00 & 14:00-17:00, closed Sun-Mon).

Sacré-Cœur: Church—free, daily 6:30-22:30; dome—€7, not covered by Museum Pass, daily 10:00-18:00, June-Sept until 20:00, Jan-Feb until 17:00; modest dress required.

Church of St. Pierre-de-Montmartre: Free, Tue-Fri 9:00-12:00 & 15:00-18:00, Sat 9:00-19:00, Sun until 18:00, closed Mon.

Dalí Museum (Dalí Paris): €13, not covered by Museum Pass, daily 10:00-18:30, may stay open later July-Aug, audioguide-€3, 11 Rue Poulbot, +33 1 42 64 40 10, www.daliparis.com.

Montmartre Museum: €14, includes good 45-minute audioguide, not covered by Museum Pass, Wed-Mon 10:00-18:00, closed Tue, last entry 45 minutes before closing, 12 Rue Cortot.

Services: Pay WCs may be open outside of Sacré-Cœur, down the stairs to the left as you leave the church (daily 10:00-18:15). Others are in the Square Suzanne Buisson park (north of #14 on this tour); the Montmartre Museum (best); at the souvenir shop at the top of the funicular; and any cafés you patronize.

Eating: The starting point, Place des Abbesses, has some great spots for morning coffee and croissants. You'll find peaceful, picnic-ready benches all along this walk as well as a patch of grass in the park on the back side of the basilica. Good sandwiches are available from the award-winning bakeries along Rue des Abbesses, which also features several picnic-friendly cheese, wine, and fruit stalls and a fine selection of cafés. See page 463 for more restaurant and café recommendations.

Neighborhood Shopping Street: Appealing Rue des Martyrs runs for six blocks below Place Pigalle and feels a world apart from Montmartre. Featuring eye-popping bakeries, trendy cafés, and delicious food shops, it ends at a handy Métro station (see the Rue des Martyrs boutique stroll in the Shopping in Paris chapter).

Starring: Cityscape views, Sacré-Cœur, postcard scenes brought to life, a charming market street, and boring buildings where interesting people once lived.

The Walk Begins

• *From the Abbesses Métro stop, take the elevator up and surface through one of the original Art Nouveau "Métropolitain" entrances.*

❶ Place des Abbesses

Our tour starts in the heart of today's Montmartre. While the neighborhood center has shifted from the top of the hill to here, the

bohemian vibe lives on. Place des Abbesses and its surrounding streets are lively with cafés, bars, and rustic charm. Young Parisian hipsters (called *bobos*, or bourgeois bohemians) flock to Montmartre—as their forebears did—for cheaper rents, less urban noise, a lively arts community, and plenty of nightlife.

Named for an abbey that it once abutted, this perfectly Parisian square revolves around its carousel with just enough benches to meet demand. It's bordered by a small park, strollable lanes, and an unusual brick church (St-Jean de Montmartre, completed in 1904). This was the first building in Paris to use reinforced concrete and steel in this manner, which allowed for much faster and cheaper construction (worth a quick look inside). Romantics should wander into the small park to find the *Mur des je t'aime* (the "I Love You Wall"), a tiled area along the park's wall with "I love you" written artfully in about a hundred different languages.

The main drag, Rue des Abbesses, is lined with shops, bakeries, *pâtisseries*, and restaurants (great for breakfast and lunch). You could explore the street now, but our walk will also return to this street later.

• *Leave Place des Abbesses, heading east on Rue Yvonne le Tac (passing right by La Poste). You'll pass a few cafés. At the end of the block, **Le Progrès** has great café ambience. Veer slightly left onto Rue Tardieu and walk a block to the park below Sacré-Cœur. To get up the hill, you can either climb those 200 steps or take the funicular. At the top, find a good viewing spot on the steps of the church.*

❷ Sacré-Cœur Basilica and View

From Paris' highest natural point (430 feet), the City of Light fans out at your feet. Pan from left to right. The long triangular roof on your left is the Gare du Nord train station. The blue-and-red Pompidou Center is straight ahead, and the skyscrapers in the distance define the south ern limit of Paris. Next is the domed Panthéon, atop Paris' other (and far smaller) butte. Then, standing

solo to the right, comes the modern Montparnasse Tower, and finally (if you're in position to see this far to the right), the golden dome of Les Invalides. The grassy park below was once dotted with openings to gypsum mines, the source of the white "plaster of Paris" that plastered Paris' buildings for centuries.

Now turn and face the church. The Sacré-Cœur (Sacred Heart) Basilica's exterior, with its onion domes and bleached-bone pallor, looks ancient, but it was finished only a century ago by Parisians humiliated by German invaders. Roman Catholics built it as a kind of penance for how the surrounding neighborhood sowed rebelliousness and division. Many French people were disgusted that in 1871 their government actually shot its own citizens, the Communards, who held out here on Montmartre after the French leadership surrendered to the Prussians (the Communards' monument is in Père Lachaise Cemetery—read about their story on page 376).

The five-domed, Roman-Byzantine-looking basilica took 44 years to build (1875-1919). It stands on a foundation of 83 pillars sunk 130 feet deep, necessary because the ground beneath was honeycombed with gypsum mines. The exterior is laced with gypsum, which whitens with age.

• *Join the security line to get inside.*

MONTMARTRE

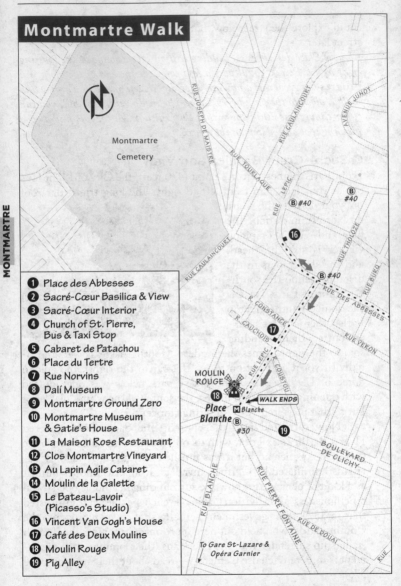

Montmartre Walk

1. Place des Abbesses
2. Sacré-Cœur Basilica & View
3. Sacré-Cœur Interior
4. Church of St. Pierre, Bus & Taxi Stop
5. Cabaret de Patachou
6. Place du Tertre
7. Rue Norvins
8. Dalí Museum
9. Montmartre Ground Zero
10. Montmartre Museum & Satie's House
11. La Maison Rose Restaurant
12. Clos Montmartre Vineyard
13. Au Lapin Agile Cabaret
14. Moulin de la Galette
15. Le Bateau-Lavoir (Picasso's Studio)
16. Vincent Van Gogh's House
17. Café des Deux Moulins
18. Moulin Rouge
19. Pig Alley

❸ Sacré-Cœur Interior

Crowd flow permitting, pause (sit in a pew) near the entrance and take in the nave.

ⒶView of the Nave: In the impressive mosaic high above the altar, a 60-foot-tall Christ exposes his sacred heart, burning with love and compassion for humanity. Joining him are a dove representing the Holy Spirit and God the Father high above. Christ is

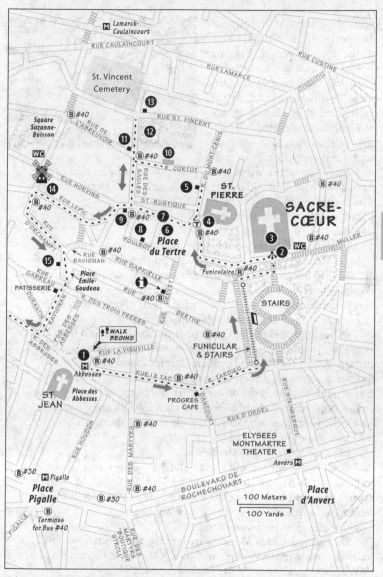

flanked by biblical figures on the left (including St. Peter, kneeling) and French figures on the right (a kneeling Joan of Arc in her trademark armor). If you get closer, you'll see other French figures: clergymen (who offer a model of this church to the Lord), government leaders (in business suits), and French saints, including St. Bernard (above, with his famous dog), and Louis IX, the king known as Saint Louis (with the crown of thorns). Remember, the church was built by a French populace recently humbled by a devastating war. At the base of the mosaic is the National Vow of the French people begging God's forgiveness: *"Sacritissimo Cordi Jesu Gallia poenitens et devota..."*—which means, "To the Sacred Heart of Jesus, we are penitent and devoted." Right now, in this church, at least one person is praying for Christ to be

understanding of the world's sins—part of a tradition that's been carried out here, day and night, 24/7, since Sacré-Cœur's completion a century ago.

• *Start shuffling clockwise around the church. Near the entrance, find the white...*

❸ Statue of St. Thérèse: Follow Thérèse's gaze to a pillar with a plaque ("L'an 1944..."). The plaque's map shows where, on April 21, 1944, 13 bombs fell on Montmartre in an Allied air raid during World War II—all in a line, all near the church—killing no one. This fueled local devotion to the Sacred Heart and to this church.

• *Continue up the side aisle to the apse, and find a...*

❹ Scale Model of the Church: It shows the church from the long side (you'd enter at left). This early-version model doesn't accurately reflect the finished product, but it's close. You see its central dome surrounded by smaller domes and the tower. The "Byzantine" style is clear in the onion domes and in the heavy horseshoe arches atop slender columns. The church is built of large rectangular blocks (just look around you), with no attempt to plaster over the cracks/lines in between.

• *Continue along, looking to the right at...*

❺ Colorful Mosaics of the 14 Stations of the Cross (about 10 feet high with Roman numerals): At #7, pause to rub **St. Peter's bronze foot** and look up to the heavens. After #14, you'll meet a solid silver statue of Christ with his sacred heart.

• *Continue your circuit around the church.*

❻ Stained-Glass Windows: Because the church's original stained-glass windows were broken by the concussive force of WWII bombs, all of the glass you see is post-1945.

• *As you approach the entrance you'll walk straight toward three stained-glass windows dedicated in 1947 to...*

❼ Joan of Arc (Jeanne d'Arc, 1412-1431): See the teenage girl as she hears the voice of the Archangel Michael (right panel, at bottom) and later (above on the same panel) as she takes up the Archangel's sword. Next, she kneels to take communion (central panel, bottom), then kneels before the bishop to tell him she's been sent by God to rally France's soldiers and save Orléans from

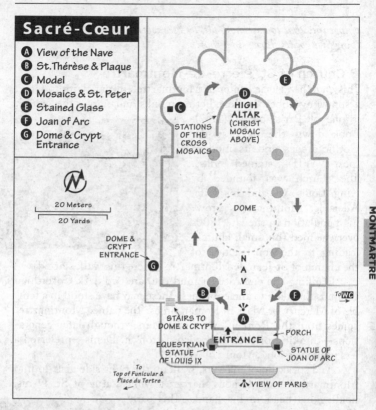

Sacré-Cœur

- **A** View of the Nave
- **B** St. Thérèse & Plaque
- **C** Model
- **D** Mosaics & St. Peter
- **E** Stained Glass
- **F** Joan of Arc
- **G** Dome & Crypt Entrance

20 Meters
20 Yards

DOME & CRYPT ENTRANCE

STATIONS OF THE CROSS MOSAICS

HIGH ALTAR (CHRIST MOSAIC ABOVE)

DOME

NAVE

STAIRS TO DOME & CRYPT

EQUESTRIAN STATUE OF LOUIS IX

ENTRANCE

PORCH

STATUE OF JOAN OF ARC

To WC

To Top of Funicular & Place du Tertre

VIEW OF PARIS

MONTMARTRE

English invaders (central panel, top). However, Burgundian forces allied with England arrest her, and she's burned at the stake as a heretic (left panel), dying with her eyes fixed on a crucifix and chanting, "Jesus, Jesus, Jesus..."

• *Exit the church. A public WC is to your left (when open), down 50 steps. To your right is the entrance to the church's...*

G Dome and Crypt: For an unobstructed panoramic view of Paris, climb 260 feet (292 steps) up the tight, claustrophobic, spiral stairs to the top of the dome—especially worthwhile if you have kids with excess energy. The crypt is just a big, empty basement.

• *Leaving the church, turn right and walk west along the ridge, following tree-lined Rue Azaïs. Turn right at the first street (Rue St. Eleuthère) and walk uphill a block to the Church of St. Pierre-de-Montmartre (at top on right). The small square in front of the church has a bus stop for little electric bus #40 that winds through the neighborhood to and from Place des Abbesses.*

You're in the heart of Montmartre, by Place du Tertre. A sign for the Cabaret de la Bohème reminds visitors that in the late 19th and early 20th centuries, this was the world capital of bohemian life. But before we *plunge into that tourist mosh pit, let's see where this whole Montmartre thing first got its start—in a church.*

❹ Church of St. Pierre-de-Montmartre

This church was the center of Montmartre's initial claim to fame, a sprawling abbey of Benedictine monks and nuns. The church is one of Paris' oldest (1147). Look down the nave at the Gothic arches and its modern (post-WWII) stained glass. The church was founded by King Louis VI and his wife, Adelaide. Montmartre's growing population in the late 1800s overwhelmed this small church, leading to the construction of

the church of St-Jean de Montmartre (where this walk started).

Flanking the entrance (behind you) are two dark Corinthian columns that date to ancient times. These may have stood in a temple of Mercury or Mars in Roman times. The name "Montmartre" comes from the Roman "Mount of Mars," though later generations—thinking of their beheaded patron St. Denis—preferred a less pagan version, "Mount of Martyrs."

And speaking of martyrs, walk up the right-side aisle to find Montmartre's most famous martyr: a white statue of St. Denis, holding his head in his hands. This early Christian bishop was sentenced to death by the Romans for spreading Christianity. As they marched him up to the top of Montmartre to be executed, the Roman soldiers got tired and just beheaded him near here. But Denis popped right up, picked up his head, and carried on another three miles north before he finally died.

To the right of Denis, the statue of "Notre Dame de Montmartre" marks a modern miracle—how the Virgin spared the neighborhood from the WWII bombs of April 21, 1944.

Before leaving, rub St. Peter's toe (again), look up, and ask for *déliverance* from the tourist mobs outside.

• *Now step back outside. Before entering the crowded Place du Tertre, get a quick taste of the area by making a short detour to the right down Rue du Mont-Cenis. These days it's lined with cafés and shops. But back in the day, #13 Rue du Mont-Cenis was the...*

❺ Cabaret de Patachou

This building (20 yards down a long entryway, now a pleasant art gallery—with serious art rather than touristy posters—run by friendly Julien and Sophie Roussard) is where singer Edith Piaf (1915-1963) once trilled "La Vie en Rose" to an intimate crowd of 80 diners. (Notice the historic photos just before the door.) Piaf—a destitute teenager who sang for pocket change in the streets of pre-WWII Paris—was discovered by a nightclub owner and became a star. Her singing inspired the people of Nazi-occupied Paris. In the heady days after the war, she sang about the joyous, rosy life in the city. For more on this warbling-voiced singer, see page 377.

• Head back uphill to the always-lively square, and stand on its cusp for the best perspective of...

❻ Place du Tertre: Bohemian Montmartre

Lined with cafés, shaded by acacia trees, and filled with artists, hucksters, and tourists, the scene mixes charm and kitsch in ever-changing proportions. Place du Tertre has been the town square of the small village of Montmartre since medieval times. (*Tertre* means "stepped lanes" in French.)

In 1800, a wall separated Paris from this hilltop village. To enter Paris you had to pass tollbooths that taxed anything for sale. Montmartre was a mining community where the wine flowed cheap (tax-free) and easy. Life here was a working-class festival of cafés, bistros, and dance halls. Painters came here for the ruddy charm, the light, and the low rents. In 1860, Montmartre was annexed into the growing city of Paris. The "bohemian" ambience survived, and it attracted sophisticated Parisians ready to get down and dirty in the belle époque of cancan. The La Mère Catherine restaurant is often called the first bistro—this is where Russian soldiers first coined the word by saying, "I'm thirsty, bring my drink *bistro!*" (meaning "right away").

The square's artists, who at times outnumber the tourists, are the great-great-grandkids of the Renoirs, Van Goghs, and Picassos who once roamed here—poor, carefree, seeking inspiration, and occasionally cursing a world too selfish to bankroll their dreams.

• Plunge headlong into the square—filled with tourists paying €50 for a 20-minute portrait (more for color)— meet an artist, sip an espresso, then continue west along the main drag, called...

MONTMARTRE

The Birth of the Counterculture

Montmartre of the late 19th century was a creative hive of non-conformist painters, writers, musicians, thinkers, and hard-to-classify eccentrics. They challenged society's norms, practically inventing the notion of a "counterculture," and paved the way to modernism.

The first wave of artists was the Impressionists, who came to paint the windmills *(moulins),* rustic cottages, and vine-covered stone walls. In 1871, Montmartre was a hotbed of revolution and resistance, quixotically defying the French government after it capitulated to Germany in the Franco-Prussian War. When the Moulin Rouge nightclub opened in 1889 with its racy cancan girls, sleepy Montmartre became the go-to place for edgy nightlife. It attracted artists of every stripe, who boldly championed new theories they were convinced would remake the world. There were Symbolists, Naturalists, Incoherents, Decadents, and "Les Nabis"—Hebrew for "prophets."

The gathering place for all these people was the cabaret. Here, the mix of food, drink (such as powerful absinthe), music, shadow plays, dancing, vaudeville, and circus acts created a heady atmosphere where great ideas were launched. Van Gogh came here to drink, and Toulouse-Lautrec sketched the dancers and prostitutes.

The bohemian spirit lasted into the next generation. Picasso arrived here in 1900, where he pioneered Cubism in his hillside studio and attended cabaret shows at Au Lapin Agile. The painter Utrillo captured Montmartre's otherworldly beauty, and the composer Erik Satie wrote his eccentric, stripped-down piano pieces.

In the 1920s Jazz Age, the cabaret scene shifted downhill a bit, but the party raged on, with the torch carried by jazz-loving African American expats. With World War II, Montmartre fell into disrepair, but the glories of bohemian Montmartre live on in the minds of romantics.

Montmartre helped birth the modern world. No wonder. Nonconformists could escape the shackles of their conventional Parisian upbringing, find freedom on Montmartre's 430-foot summit, and literally look down on the bourgeois world.

❼ Rue Norvins

Montmartre's oldest and main street is still the primary commercial artery, serving the current trade—tourism.

• *If you're a devotee of Dalí, a detour left on Rue Poulbot will lead you to the...*

❽ Dalí Museum (Dalí Paris)

This beautifully lit black gallery offers a walk through more than

300 statues, etchings, and drawings by the master of Surrealism. The Spaniard found fame in Paris in the 1920s and '30s. He lived in Montmartre for a while, hung with the Surrealist crowd in Montparnasse, and shocked the world with his dreamscape paintings and experimental films.

• *Return to Rue Norvins and continue west a dozen steps to the picturesque intersection with Rue des Saules. You've arrived at...*

❾ Montmartre Ground Zero

We're leaving most tourists behind and entering the residential part of Montmartre. Pause to survey the colorful jumble of classic storefronts, cafés, and
charm. Walk to the golden souvenir shop on the left (#12)—formerly a venerable old *boulangerie* that dated from 1900. This spot was a favorite place for the artist Maurice Utrillo to paint (see sidebar, later). From here, look back up

Rue Norvins to the dome of Sacré-Cœur rising above the rooftops—a classic scene Utrillo famously captured. Cross to the front of La Bonne Franquette restaurant and look right up Rue Saint-Rustique for another Utrillo scene.

• *Let's lose the tourists completely. Follow Rue des Saules downhill (north) onto the back side of Montmartre. Enjoy the "Van Gogh in Paris" info panels along the way. A block downhill, turn right on Rue Cortot to reach the...*

❿ Montmartre Museum and Satie's House

In what is now the Montmartre Museum (at #12), Pierre-Auguste Renoir once lived while painting his
best-known work, *Bal du Moulin de la Galette*. Every day he'd lug the four-foot-by-six-foot canvas from here to the other side of the butte to paint in the open air the famous windmill ballroom, which we'll see later.

A few years later, Utrillo lived and painted here with his mom, Suzanne Valadon. In 1893, she carried on a torrid six-month relationship with the lonely, eccentric man who lived two doors up at #6—composer Erik Satie, who wrote *Trois Gymnopédies* and was eking out a living playing piano in Montmartre nightclubs.

The Montmartre Museum offers the best look at the artistic Golden Age of this neighborhood (1870-1910)—and has the best public WCs on the hill. The museum's collection of paintings, posters, old photos, music, and memorabilia is split between two creaky 17th-century manor houses separated by a sweet little garden. An eight-minute film narrated by an actress playing Utrillo's mother, Suzanne Valadon, provides the perfect introduction to the world of the bohemian artists—Renoir, Picasso, Edith Piaf, Toulouse-Lautrec, and more—who lived on Montmartre before and after the construction of Sacré-Cœur.

Next, pass through the garden to find the first house's entry (before entering, continue to the end of the short stone path for great views over Montmartre's vineyard).

Inside, you'll learn about the butte's 2,000-year history and see photos of the gypsum quarries and flour-grinding windmills of the Industrial Age. Montmartre's cabaret years come to life here—there's the original *Lapin Agile* sign, the famous Chat Noir poster, and Toulouse-Lautrec's dashing portrait of red-scarved Aristide Bruant, the earthy singer, comedian, and club owner. You'll see more Toulouse-Lautrec posters and displays about the biggest and most famous cabaret of all: the cancan-kickers of the Moulin Rouge.

The second house holds temporary exhibits relevant to Montmartre (usually well worth a look), as well as the museum's highlight (hiding on the top floor): the tiny apartment and painting studio of Maurice Utrillo.

Before leaving, take a moment to reflect on this remarkable era by enjoying a coffee or lunch at the sun-dappled garden café. Rarely has so much artistic talent and creative energy been concentrated in one place at the same time.

• *Return to Rue des Saules and walk downhill to...*

⓫ La Maison Rose Restaurant

The restaurant, made famous by an Utrillo painting, was once frequented by Utrillo, Pablo Picasso, and Gertrude Stein. Today it serves reasonably good cuisine to nostalgic tourists.

• *Just downhill from the restaurant is Paris' last remaining vineyard.*

⓬ Clos Montmartre Vineyard

What originally drew artists to Montmartre was country charm like this. Ever since the 12th century, the monks and nuns of the large abbey have produced wine from here. With vineyards, wheat fields, windmills, animals, and a village tempo of life, it was the perfect escape from grimy Paris. In 1576, puritanical laws taxed wine in Paris, bringing budget-minded drinkers outside

the Paris city gates to Montmartre. Today's vineyard is off-limits to tourists except during the annual grape-harvest fest (first Sat in Oct, www.fetedesvendangesdemontmartre.com) when a thousand costumed locals bring back the boisterous old days. The vineyard's annual production of 300 liters is auctioned off at the fest to support local charities. Bottles sell for over €50 and are considered mediocre at best.

• *Continue downhill to the intersection with Rue St. Vincent, or save your energy by skipping the descent and reading about the next stop from where you are.*

⓭ Au Lapin Agile Cabaret

The poster above the door gives the place its name. A rabbit *(lapin)* makes an agile leap out of the pot while balancing the bottle of wine that he can now drink—rather than be cooked in. This was the village's hot spot. Artists and writers including Picasso, Renoir, Utrillo, Paul Verlaine, Aristide Bruant, and Amedeo Modigliani would gather for "performances" of serious poetry, dirty limericks, sing-alongs, parodies of the famous, or readings of anarchist manifestos. Once, to play a practical joke on the avant-garde art community, patrons tied a paintbrush to the tail of the owner's donkey and entered the resulting "abstract painting" in a show

at the Salon. Called *Sunset over the Adriatic*, it won critical acclaim and sold for a nice price.

The old Parisian personality of this cabaret survives, where several nights a week a series of performers takes a small, French-

Maurice Utrillo (1883-1955)

Born to a free-spirited single mom and raised by his grand-mother, Utrillo had his first alcohol detox treatment at age 18. Encouraged by his mother and doctors, he started painting as occupational therapy. That (plus guidance from his mother and, later, from his wife) allowed him to live productively into his 70s and become wealthy and famous despite occasional relapses into drinking and mental problems.

Utrillo grew up on Montmartre's streets. He fought, broke street lamps, and haunted the cafés and bars, paying for drinks with masterpieces. A very free spirit, he's said to have exposed himself to strangers on the street, yelling, "I paint with this!"

His simple scenes of streets, squares, and cafés in a vaguely Impressionist style became popular with commoners and scholars alike. He honed his style during his "white period" (c. 1909-1914), painting a thick paste of predominantly white tints—perfect for capturing Sacré-Cœur. In later years, after he moved out of Montmartre, he still painted the world he knew in his youth, using postcards and photographs as models. Utrillo's mom, Suzanne Valadon, was a former trapeze performer and artist's model who posed for Toulouse-Lautrec, slept with Renoir, studied under Degas, and went on to become a notable painter in her own right.

speaking audience on a wistful musical journey back to the good old days (for details, see page 512).

• *Backtrack uphill on Rue des Saules to "ground zero." Circle around the side of the golden souvenir shop and head downhill on Rue Lepic (the street that curves right). Staying on Rue Lepic, you come to a fine view of a windmill, the...*

⓮ Moulin de la Galette

Only two windmills *(moulins)* remain on a hill that was once dotted with 30 of them. Originally, they pressed monks' grapes and farm-ers' grain and crushed gypsum rocks into powdery plaster of Paris. When the gypsum mines closed (c. 1850) and the vine-yards sprouted apartments, the grounds around these windmills were turned into the ceremonial centerpiece of a popular outdoor dance hall. Renoir's *Bal du Moulin de la Galette* (in the Orsay—

see page 199) shows it in its heyday—a sunny Sunday afternoon in the acacia-shaded gardens with working-class people dancing, laughing, drinking, and eating the house crêpes, called galettes. Some call Renoir's version the quintessential Impressionist work and the painting that best captures—on a large canvas in bright colors—the joy of the Montmartre lifestyle. The namesake restaurant inside is well respected and worth considering.

• *Do an about-face, backtrack several steps, and turn right, heading downhill on narrow Rue d'Orchampt. Stop where it curves left and look right to see a memorial plaque to Dalida—a Madonna-like pop star Europeans still idolize. Continue along Rue d'Orchampt and turn right on Rue Ravignan. Next to the Timhotel, at 13 Place Emile-Goudeau, is another studio that Picasso lived in.*

⑮ Le Bateau-Lavoir (Picasso's Studio)

A humble facade marks the place where modern art was born. In this lowly abode (destroyed by fire in 1970 and rebuilt a few years later), as many as 10 artists lived and worked. Formerly a piano factory, it was converted into cheap housing and earned the nickname "the Laundry Boat" for its swaying, creaking, and crude facilities (sharing one water tap). It was "a weird, squalid place,"

wrote one resident, "filled with every kind of noise: arguing, singing, bedpans clattering, slamming doors, and suggestive moans coming from studio doors."

In 1904, a poor, unknown Spanish émigré named Pablo Picasso (1881-1973) moved in. He met dark-haired Fernande Olivier, his first real girlfriend, in Place Emile-Goudeau, the romantic square outside. She soon moved in, lifting him out of his melancholy Blue Period into his rosy Rose Period. *La belle Fernande* posed nude for him, inspiring a freer treatment of the female form.

In 1907, Picasso started on a major canvas. For nine months he produced hundreds of preparatory sketches, working long into the night. When he unveiled the work, even his friends were shocked. *Les Demoiselles d'Avignon* showed five nude women in a brothel (Fernande claimed they were all her), with primitive masklike faces and fragmented bodies. Picasso had invented Cubism.

For the next two years, he and his neighbors Georges Braque and Juan Gris revolutionized the art world. Sharing paints, ideas, and girlfriends, they made Montmartre "The Cubist Acropolis," attracting freethinking "Moderns" from all over the world to visit their studios—the artists Amedeo Modigliani, Marie Laurencin, and Henri Rousseau; the poet Guillaume Apollinaire; and the

American expatriate writer Gertrude Stein. By the time Picasso moved to better quarters (and dumped Fernande), he was famous. Still, Picasso would later say, "I know one day we'll return to Bateau-Lavoir. It was there that we were really happy—where they thought of us as painters, not strange animals."

• *Go a few steps downhill to the railing of Place Emile-Goudeau and marvel at Paris. While the rest of this tour is a lot of walking and thin on sights, it's a great chance to simply enjoy a vibrant Parisian neighborhood.*

Now, descend 10 steps and continue straight down Rue Ravignan. You'll pass an inviting café with fine terrace seating and views, and the Pâtisserie Gilles Marchal, selling top-end treats. Continue down Rue Ravignan to the T-intersection with Rue des Abbesses. (At this point, you could turn left to return to Place des Abbesses, where we started our walk—with several good lunch options.) To continue this walk, turn right on Rue des Abbesses. Continue a few blocks on this thriving neighborhood street, past bakeries, cheese shops, and tempting cafés. When you come to Rue Lepic, consider a short detour uphill on that street to #54, where you'll find...

⑯ Vincent van Gogh's House

Vincent van Gogh lived here with his brother Theo from 1886 to 1888, enjoying a grand city view from his third-floor window. In those two short years, Van Gogh transformed from a gloomy Dutch painter of brown and gray peasant scenes into an inspired visionary with wild ideas and Impressionist colors.

• *Retrace your steps down Rue Lepic to Rue des Abbesses and make a hard right at #36 (still Rue Lepic). Proceed downhill on Rue Lepic, now a lively market street. Take in the small shops and bustling ambience. Two blocks down, on the corner to your right (at #15), you'll find the pink...*

⑰ Café des Deux Moulins

For some time after it was featured in the quirky 2001 film *Amélie*, this café was a pilgrimage site for movie buffs worldwide (see the photo over the bar). Today it's just another funky place with unassuming ambience and reasonably priced food and drinks, frequented by the next generation of real-life Amélies who ignore the movie poster on the back wall (15 Rue Lepic, +33 1 42 54 90 50).

• *Continue downhill on Rue Lepic to Place Blanche. On busy Place Blanche is the...*

⑱ Moulin Rouge

Oh là là. The new Eiffel Tower at the 1889 World's Fair was nothing compared to the sight of pretty cancan girls kicking their legs at the newly opened "Red Windmill." The nightclub seemed to

sum up the belle époque—
the age of elegance, opulence, sophistication, and
worldliness. The big draw
was amateur night, when
working-class girls in risqué dresses danced "Le
Quadrille" (dubbed "can-
can" by a Brit). Wealthy
Parisians slummed it by
coming here.

On most nights you'd see a small man in a sleek black coat,
checked pants, a green scarf, and a bowler hat peering through his
pince-nez glasses at the dancers and making sketches of them—
Henri de Toulouse-Lautrec. Perhaps he'd order an absinthe, the
dense green liqueur (evil ancestor of today's *pastis*) that was the
toxic muse for so many great (and so many forgotten) artists. Toulouse-Lautrec's sketches of dancers Jane Avril and Louise Weber,
known as La Goulue, hang in the Orsay (see reproductions in the
entryway).

After its initial splash, the Moulin Rouge survived as a venue
for all kinds of entertainment. In 1906, the novelist Colette kissed
her female lover onstage, and the homophobic authorities closed
the "Dream of Egypt" down. Yves Montand opened for Édith Piaf
(1944), and the two fell in love offstage. It has hosted such diverse
acts as Ginger Rogers, Dalida, and the Village People—together on
one bill (1979). Mikhail Baryshnikov leaped across its stage (1986).
And, the club celebrated its centennial (1989) with Ray Charles,
Tony Curtis, Ella Fitzgerald, and...a French favorite, Jerry Lewis.

Tonight they're showing...well, find out for yourself: Walk into
the open-air entryway or step into the lobby to mull over the photos, show options, and prices. Tickets start at about €150. Their
souvenir shop is back up Rue Lepic a few steps at #9.

• *Our tour is over. The Blanche Métro stop is here in Place Blanche.*
(Plaster of Paris from the gypsum found on this mount was loaded slop-
pily at Place Blanche...the white square.)

If you want more, you can stroll eastward down racy Boulevard
de Clichy (known as "Pig Alley"), where you'll find another Métro stop
(Pigalle) and the start of my Rue des Martyrs boutique stroll (see the
Shopping in Paris chapter).

⓳ Pig Alley

The stretch of the Boulevard de Clichy from Place Blanche to Place
Pigalle is the den mother of all iniquities. Remember, this was once
the border between Montmartre and Paris, where bistros had tax-
free status, wine was cheap, and prostitutes roamed freely. Today,

sex shops, peep shows, the Museum of Erotic Art, live sex shows, chatty pitchmen, and hot-dog stands line the busy boulevard. Dildos abound.

In the Roaring Twenties, this neighborhood at the base of the hill became a new center of cabaret nightlife. It was settled by African American jazz musicians and WWI veterans who didn't want to return to a segregated America. Black-owned nightclubs sprang up. There was Zelli's (located at 16 bis Rue Fontaine, a block southeast of the Moulin Rouge), where clarinetist-saxophonist Sidney Bechet played. A block away was the tiny Le Grand Duc (at Rue Fontaine and Rue Pigalle), where poet Langston Hughes bused tables. Next door was the most famous of all, Bricktop's (at #73 and then at 66 Rue Pigalle), owned by the vivacious redhead who hosted Cole Porter, Duke Ellington, Picasso, the Prince of Wales, F. Scott Fitzgerald, Josephine Baker, and many more. The area was "Harlem East," where rich and poor, black and white, came for a good time.

By World War II, the good times were becoming increasingly raunchy, and GIs nicknamed the Pigalle neighborhood "Pig Alley." Although today's government is cracking down on sex work, and the ladies of the night are being driven deeper into their red-velvet bars as the area gentrifies, very few think of the great French sculptor Pigalle when they hear the district's name. Bars lining the streets downhill from Place Pigalle (especially Rue Pigalle) are lively with prostitutes eager to share a drink with anyone passing by.

SLEEPING IN PARIS

Paris is a good hotel city. I've focused my recommendations on five safe, handy, and colorful neighborhoods: the village-like Rue Cler (near the Eiffel Tower); the artsy and trendy Marais (near Place de la Bastille); the historic island of Ile St. Louis (next door to Notre-Dame); the lively, Latin, and classy Luxembourg Garden neighborhood (on the Left Bank); and the less polished, less central, but less pricey Montmartre neighborhood. I recommend the best accommodations values in each, from €25 dorm beds to deluxe €500 doubles with all the comforts.

Before choosing a hotel, read the descriptions of the neighborhoods closely. Each offers different pros and cons: Your neighborhood is as important as your hotel for the success of your trip. For each neighborhood I also list helpful hints and a selection of restaurants and cafés (in the Eating in Paris chapter).

For lower rates or greater selection, look farther from the river (prices drop proportionately with distance from the Seine), but be prepared to spend more time on the Métro or the bus getting to sights.

I rank accommodations from **$** budget to **$$$$** splurge. The French use stars to rate hotels based on their amenities (indicated by asterisks in this book). For the best deal, contact hotels directly by phone or email. When you book direct, the owner avoids a commission and may be able to offer a discount. Book well in advance for peak season or if your trip coincides with a major holiday or festival (see the appendix). For some travelers, short-term, Airbnb-type rentals can be a good alternative; search for places in my recommended hotel neighborhoods. I also list a few bed-and-breakfast agencies and give suggestions for sleeping near Paris' airports. For more details on reservations, short-term rentals, and chain hotels in Paris, see the "Sleeping" section in the Practicalities chapter.

For accommodations in Versailles, Chartres, and Giverny, see those chapters. For Fontainebleau, see page 596; for Disneyland Paris, see page 484.

RUE CLER NEIGHBORHOOD
(7th arr., Mo: Ecole Militaire, La Tour Maubourg, Invalides)
Rue Cler, lined with open-air produce stands and cafés, is a safe, tidy, pedestrian street. It's so French that when I step out of my hotel in the morning, I feel like I must have been a poodle in a previous life. How such coziness lodged itself between the high-powered government district, the Eiffel Tower, and Les Invalides, I'll never know. This is a neighborhood of wide, tree-lined boulevards, stately apartment buildings, and lots of Americans. The American Church and Franco-American Center, American Library, American University, and many of my readers call this area home. Hotels here are a fair value, considering the elegance of the neighborhood. And for sightseeing, you're within walking distance of the Eiffel Tower, Army Museum, Quai Branly Museum, Seine River, Champs-Elysées, riverside promenade, and Orsay and Rodin museums.

Become a local at a Rue Cler café for breakfast, or join the afternoon crowd for *une bière pression* (a draft beer). On Rue Cler you can eat and browse your way through a street full of cafés, pastry shops, delis, cheese shops, and colorful outdoor produce stalls. Afternoon *boules* (outdoor bowling) on the Esplanade des Invalides or in the Champ de Mars park is a relaxing spectator sport (look for the dirt areas in the southwest corners of each; see "The Rules of *Boules*" sidebar, later). The manicured gardens behind the golden dome of the Army Museum are free, peaceful, and filled with flowers (at southwest corner of grounds, closes about 19:00), and the riverside promenade along the Seine is a fine place to walk, run, bike, or just sit and watch the river of people stroll by.

Though hardly a happening nightlife spot, Rue Cler offers many low-impact after-dark activities. Take an evening stroll above or along the river through the parkway between Pont de l'Alma and Pont des Invalides. For an after-dinner cruise on the Seine,

The Rules of *Boules*

The game of *boules*—also called *pétanque*—is the horseshoes of France. Invented here in the early 1900s, it's a social yet serious sport and endlessly entertaining to watch—even more so if you understand the rules.

The game is played with heavy metal balls and a small wooden target ball called a *cochonnet* (piglet). Whoever gets  his *boule* closest to the *cochonnet* is awarded points. Teams commonly have specialist players: a *pointeur* and a *tireur*. The *pointeur*'s goal is to lob his balls as close to the target as he can. The *tireur*'s job is to blast away opponents' *boules*.

In teams of two, each player gets three *boules*. The starting team traces a small circle in the dirt (in which players must stand when launching their *boules*) and tosses the *cochonnet* about 30 feet to establish the target. The *boule* must be thrown underhand and can be rolled, launched sky-high, or rocketed at its target. The first *pointeur* shoots, then the opposing *pointeur* shoots until his *boule* gets closer. Once the second team lands a *boule* nearer the *cochonnet*, the first team goes again. If the other team's *boule* is very near the *cochonnet*, the *tireur* will likely attempt to knock it away.

Once all *boules* have been launched, the tally is taken. The team with a *boule* closest to the *cochonnet* wins the round, and they receive a point for each *boule* closer to the target than their opponents' nearest *boule*. The first team to get to 13 points wins. A regulation *boules* field is 10 feet by 43 feet, but the game is played everywhere—just scratch a throwing circle in the sand, toss the *cochonnet*, and you're off.

it's a 20-minute walk to the river and the Bateaux-Mouches. For a post-dinner cruise on foot, saunter into the Champ de Mars park to admire the glowing Eiffel Tower. For more ideas on nightlife activities here, see page 446.

The **American Church and Franco-American Center** is the community center for many Americans living in Paris. It hosts interdenominational worship services every Sunday (traditional service at 11:00; contemporary service at 14:00), and free Sunday concerts (generally Sept-June at 17:00—but not every week and not in Dec, 65 Quai d'Orsay, Mo: Invalides, +33 1 40 62 05 00, www.acparis.org).

Open-Air Markets and Shopping: The **Marché de Saxe** is

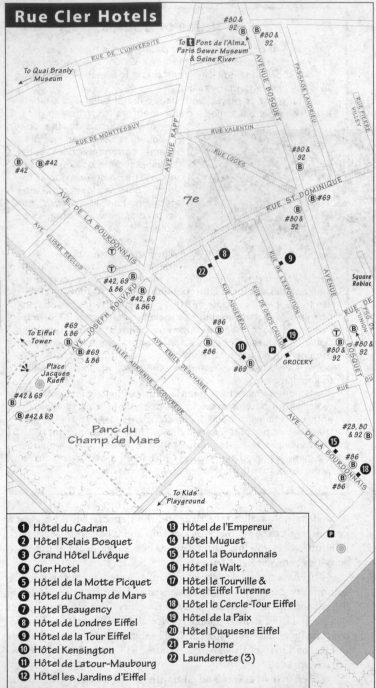

Rue Cler Hotels

1 Hôtel du Cadran
2 Hôtel Relais Bosquet
3 Grand Hôtel Lévêque
4 Cler Hotel
5 Hôtel de la Motte Picquet
6 Hôtel du Champ de Mars
7 Hôtel Beaugency
8 Hôtel de Londres Eiffel
9 Hôtel de la Tour Eiffel
10 Hôtel Kensington
11 Hôtel de Latour-Maubourg
12 Hôtel les Jardins d'Eiffel
13 Hôtel de l'Empereur
14 Hôtel Muguet
15 Hôtel la Bourdonnais
16 Hôtel le Walt
17 Hôtel le Tourville & Hôtel Eiffel Turenne
18 Hôtel le Cercle-Tour Eiffel
19 Hôtel de la Paix
20 Hôtel Duquesne Eiffel
21 Paris Home
22 Launderette (3)

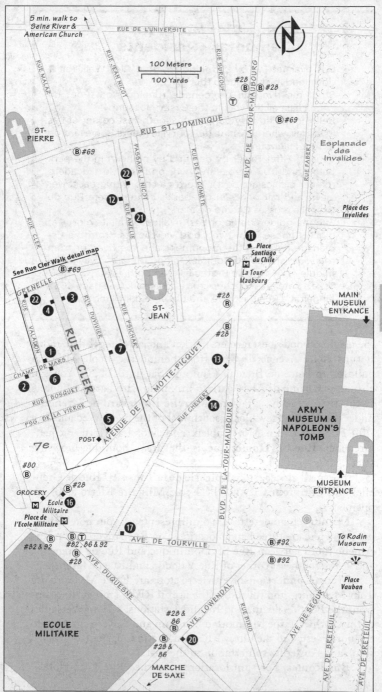

5 min. walk to
Seine River &
American Church

RUE DE L'UNIVERSITE

N

RUE MALAR

RUE JEAN NICOT

RUE SURCOUF

BLVD. DE LA-TOUR-MAUBOURG

100 Meters
100 Yards

B #28   #28

T

ST-
PIERRE

B #69

RUE ST. DOMINIQUE

B #69

RUE FABERT

Esplanade
des
Invalides

PASSAGE J. NICOT

RUE DE LA COMETE

22

Place des
Invalides

RUE CLER

12

RUE AMELIE

21

11
Place
Santiago
du Chile

T

M

La Tour-
Maubourg

MAIN
MUSEUM
ENTRANCE

See Rue Cler Walk detail map

B #69

GRENELLE

22   3

RUE DUVIVIER

RUE PSICHARI

ST-
JEAN

#28
B

RUE VALADON

4

1

RUE DE MARS

7

AVENUE DE LA MOTTE-PICQUET

#28
B

13

CHAMP DE MARS

6

RUE BOSQUET

RUE CHEVERT

14

2

PSG. DE LA VIERGE

5

ARMY
MUSEUM &
NAPOLEON'S
TOMB

7e

POST   AVENUE DE LA MOTTE-PICQUET

#00
B

BLVD. DE LA-TOUR-MAUBOURG

MUSEUM
ENTRANCE

GROCERY

B #28

M   16

Ecole
Militaire

Place de
l'Ecole Militaire

M

17

AVE. DE TOURVILLE

B #92

To Rodin
Museum

B   T
#82 & 92   #82, 86 & 92

B
#28

AVE. DUQUESNE

B #92

Place
Vauban

AVE. LOWENDAL

RUE BIXIO

AVE. DE SEGUR

ECOLE
MILITAIRE

#28 &
86
B

20

AVE. DE BRETEUIL

B
#28 &
86

MARCHE
DE SAXE

SLEEPING

SLEEPING

Rue Cler Musts for Temporary Residents

- Get over jet lag by 📖 taking my Rue Cler Walk (or 🎧 download my free audio tour).
- Stroll the riverside promenade running from Pont de l'Alma east all the way to the Orsay Museum.
- Relax in the flowery park at the southwest corner of Les Invalides, where Avenue de Tourville meets Boulevard de la Tour Maubourg.
- See the Eiffel Tower by day and by night from the park below and from across the river on Place du Trocadéro (dinner picnics are best). There's a café with great tower views and fair prices in the park's center where Rue de Grenelle crosses Champ de Mars.
- See the golden dome of Les Invalides in all its glory—at night. Choose from two good viewpoints: from the Esplanade between the monument and the river, or from the south side of the complex, along the greenway in the middle of Avenue de Breteuil. I'd do both.
- Take a Bateaux-Mouches cruise after dark (see page 465).
- Linger at a Rue Cler café and observe daily life.

the neighborhood's best farmers market and lasts longer than most. It runs along Avenue de Saxe from behind the Ecole Militaire building to Place de Breteuil (Thu and Sat until 14:30). You can also cross Champ de Mars park to mix it up with bargain hunters at the twice-weekly, sprawling **Marché Boulevard de Grenelle,** under the Métro, a few blocks southwest of the park (Wed and Sun 7:00-12:30, between Mo: Dupleix and Mo: La Motte-Picquet-Grenelle). **Rue St. Dominique** is the area's boutique-browsing street.

The small grocery store **Epicerie de la Tour** (197 Rue de Grenelle) and **Carrefour City** (at the Ecole Militaire Métro stop) are open late.

Laundry: Launderettes are omnipresent; ask your hotel for the nearest. Here are three handy locations: on Rue Augereau, on Rue Amélie (both between Rue St. Dominique and Rue de Grenelle), and at the southeast corner of Rue Valadon and Rue de Grenelle.

Métro Connections: Key Métro stops are Ecole Militaire, La Tour Maubourg, and Invalides. The useful RER/Train-C line runs from the Pont de l'Alma and Invalides stations, serving Versailles to the southwest; the Marmottan Museum and Auvers-sur-Oise to the northwest; and the Orsay Museum, Latin Quarter (St. Michel stop), and Austerlitz train station to the east.

Bus Routes: For stop locations, see the "Rue Cler Hotels" map.

Line #69 runs east along Rue St. Dominique and serves Les Invalides, Orsay, Louvre, Marais, and Père Lachaise Cemetery (see Bus #69 Sightseeing Tour chapter).

Line #63 runs along the river (Quai d'Orsay), passing near the Orsay Museum, and serves the Latin Quarter along Boulevard St. Germain to the east (ending at Gare de Lyon), and Trocadéro and areas near the Marmottan Museum to the west.

Line #92 runs along Avenue Bosquet, north to the Champs-Elysées and Arc de Triomphe (faster than the Métro) and south near the Army and Rodin museums to the Montparnasse Tower and Gare Montparnasse.

Line #86 runs eastbound from the Eiffel Tower on Avenue Joseph Bouvard, then along Avenue de la Bourdonnais to St. Sulpice (and the Sèvres-Babylone shopping area), and along Boulevards St. Germain and Henry IV to the Marais, the Bastille, and east to the Bois de Vincennes.

Line #80 runs on Avenue Bosquet, crosses the Champs-Elysées, stops near the Jacquemart-André Museum, and serves Gare St. Lazare.

Line #28 runs on Boulevard de la Tour Maubourg and serves Gare St. Lazare to the north and Gare Montparnasse to the south.

Line #42 runs from Avenue Joseph Bouvard in the Champ de Mars park, crosses the Champs-Elysées at the Rond-Point, then heads to Place de la Concorde, Place de la Madeleine, Opéra Garnier, and finally to Gare St. Lazare—a slow ride to the train station but less tiring than the Métro if you're carrying suitcases.

Taxi: You'll find taxi stands just off Place L'Ecole Militaire and near the intersection of Avenue Bosquet and Rue de Grenelle.

In the Heart of Rue Cler

Many of my readers stay in the Rue Cler neighborhood. If you want to disappear into Paris, choose a hotel elsewhere. The following hotels are within Camembert-smelling distance of Rue Cler.

$$$$ Hôtel du Cadran,**** a well-placed *boule* toss from Rue Cler, is modern and *très* stylish, with a wine bar in its lobby and designer rooms. The hotel has rooms in two locations a block apart. The main hotel has 40 tight rooms, and their 12-room annex has larger rooms, though you'll sleep well in either (RS% includes big breakfast—use code "RICK," 10 Rue du Champ de Mars, +33 1 40 62 67 00, www.cadranhotel.com, resa@cadranhotel.com).

$$$ Hôtel Relais Bosquet*** is a fine hotel in an ideal location, with comfortable public spaces and well-configured rooms that are large by local standards and feature effective darkness blinds. The staff is politely formal (RS%—use code "RSDEAL," good but pricey breakfast buffet with eggs and sausage, 19 Rue du Champ de

Mars, +33 1 47 05 25 45, www.hotel-paris-bosquet.com, hotel@relaisbosquet.com).

$$$$ Grand Hôtel Lévêque,*** recently updated, has a terrific location on Rue Cler but high prices and little ambience (29 Rue Cler, +33 1 47 05 49 15, www.hotel-leveque.com, info@hotelleveque.com).

$$$ Cler Hotel*** is an eager-to-please boutique hotel with appealing decor, a small outdoor patio, and a killer location right on Rue Cler. Rooms are well designed; those fronting Rue Cler come with some early morning noise as shopkeepers begin their days (RS%, 24 bis Rue Cler, +33 1 45 00 18 06, www.clerhotel.com, contact@clerhotel.com).

$$$ Hôtel de la Motte Picquet,*** at the corner of Rue Cler and Avenue de la Motte-Picquet, is an intimate and modest little place with 16 compact yet comfortable-enough rooms. The terrific staff makes staying here a pleasure (RS%—use code "STEVE-SMITH," family rooms, good—and free—breakfast served in a minuscule breakfast room, easy bike rental, 30 Avenue de la Motte-Picquet, +33 1 47 05 09 57, www.hotelmottepicquetparis.com, book@hotelmottepicquetparis.com).

$$ Hôtel du Champ de Mars*** is a top choice, brilliantly located just 30 yards off Rue Cler. This plush little hotel has a small-town feel from top to bottom. The adorable rooms are snug but lovingly kept by hands-on owner Céline, and single rooms can work as tiny doubles. It's popular, so book well ahead (continental breakfast only, 7 Rue du Champ de Mars, +33 1 45 51 52 30, www.hotelduchampdemars.com, reservation@hotelduchampdemars.com).

$$ Hôtel Beaugency*** has 30 smallish rooms, most with double beds, and a lobby that you can stretch out in. It's a fair value on a quieter street a short block off Rue Cler (free breakfast for Rick Steves readers, 21 Rue Duvivier, +33 1 47 05 01 63, www.hotel-beaugency.com, infos@hotel-beaugency.com).

Closer to Rue St. Dominique (and the Seine)

$$$ Hôtel de Londres Eiffel**** is my closest listing to the Eiffel Tower and the Champ de Mars park, and a fine value. Here you get immaculate, warmly decorated rooms (several are connecting, for families), warm public spaces, and a terrific staff that can't do enough to help. It's a bit less convenient to the Métro but very handy to buses #69, #80, and #92, and to RER/Train-C: Pont de l'Alma (RS%, some Eiffel Tower view rooms, 1 Rue Augereau, +33 1 45 51 63 02, www.londres-eiffel.com, info@londres-eiffel.com, helpful Arnaud and Adrien).

$ Hôtel de la Tour Eiffel** is a solid budget value on a quiet street near several of my favorite restaurants. The rooms are simple but well designed, with air-conditioning (breakfast deal arranged with nearby café). The six sets of connecting rooms are ideal for families (RS%, 17 Rue de l'Exposition, +33 1 47 05 14 75, www. hotel-toureiffel.com, hte7@wanadoo.fr).

$ Hôtel Kensington** is a fair budget value close to the Eiffel Tower. It's an unpretentious place offering basic comfort (some partial Eiffel Tower views, no air-con but ceiling fans, 79 Avenue de la Bourdonnais, +33 1 47 05 74 00, www.hotel-eiffel-kensington. com, hotelkensignton@gmail.com).

Near La Tour Maubourg Métro Stop

These listings are within three blocks of the intersection of Avenue de la Motte-Picquet and Boulevard de la Tour Maubourg.

$$$$ Hôtel de Latour-Maubourg**** owns a peaceful manor-home setting with 17 plush, mostly large and wonderfully traditional rooms, a small patio, and free spa for clients (across from La Tour-Maubourg Métro station at 150 Rue de Grenelle, +33 1 47 05 16 16, www.latourmaubourg.com, info@latourmaubourg.com).

$$$ Hôtel les Jardins d'Eiffel*** is a big place on a quiet street, with impersonal service, a peaceful patio, and a lobby you can stretch out in. The 81 well-configured rooms—some with partial Eiffel Tower views, some with balconies—offer a bit more space and quiet than other hotels (parking garage, 8 Rue Amélie, +33 1 47 05 46 21, www.hoteljardinseiffel.com, reservations@ hoteljardinseiffel.com).

$$$ Hôtel de l'Empereur*** is red-velvet plush and delivers smashing views of Invalides from many of its fine rooms. All rooms have queen- or king-size beds, are well designed with hints of the emperor, and are large by Paris standards (some view rooms, family rooms, 2 Rue Chevert, +33 1 45 55 88 02, www.hotelempereurparis. com, contact@hotelempereur.com).

$$$ Hôtel Muguet*** is sharp, quiet, well located, and reasonable, with tastefully appointed rooms and a helpful staff (some view rooms, 11 Rue Chevert, +33 1 47 05 05 93, www.hotelparismuguet. com, contact@hotelparismuguet.com).

Near Ecole Militaire Métro Stop

These listings are a five-minute walk from Rue Cler, near the Ecole Militaire Métro stop or RER/Train-C: Pont de l'Alma (may be closed for renovation).

$$$ Inwood Hotels has three sister hotels in this neighborhood; all are ****, well located, and offer top comfort and professional service—for a price (be clear about cancellation policies before booking). Public spaces and rooms are polished. The first two offer Rick Steves readers free breakfast; use www.inwood-hotels.com for booking at all three. **Hôtel la Bourdonnais,** near the Champ de Mars park, is the largest of the three and closest to the Eiffel Tower (113 Avenue de la Bourdonnais, +33 1 47 05 45 42, labourdonnais@inwood-hotels.com). **Hôtel le Walt** has a sharp interior courtyard terrace (37 Avenue de la Motte-Picquet, +33 1 45 51 55 83, lewalt@inwood-hotels.com). **Hôtel le Tourville** is the most intimate and my favorite of this group (6 Avenue de Tourville, +33 1 47 05 62 62, letourville@inwood-hotels.com).

$$$ Hôtel Eiffel Turenne*** is a good choice with sharp, well-maintained rooms, a pleasing lounge, and a service-oriented staff (20 Avenue de Tourville, +33 1 47 05 99 92, www.hoteleiffelturenne.com, reservation@hoteleiffelturenne.com).

$$$ Hôtel le Cercle-Tour Eiffel,*** a few steps from Champ de Mars park and the Eiffel Tower, is well run with sharp public spaces, plush and bigger-than-average rooms with modern accents, and a very narrow elevator (free breakfast for Rick Steves readers who book direct, 117 Avenue de la Bourdonnais, +33 1 47 05 42 30, https://hotelcercleparis.com, contact@hotelcercleparis.com).

$$$ Hôtel de la Paix, run by the same folks as the previous hotel, is an intimate place buried on a quiet lane. It has tastefully designed rooms with tight but good bathrooms, and six true singles (free breakfast for Rick Steves readers who book direct, 18 Rue du Gros Caillou, +33 1 45 51 86 17, https://hotelparispaix.com, contact@hotelparispaix.com).

$$ Hôtel Duquesne Eiffel,*** a few blocks farther from the action, is handsome, hospitable, and reasonably priced. It features a welcoming lobby, a street-front terrace, comfortable rooms (some with terrific Eiffel Tower views), and connecting rooms that work well for families (RS%; big, hot breakfast—free for my readers; 23 Avenue Duquesne, +33 1 44 42 09 09, www.hotel-duquesne-eiffel-paris.com, hotel@hde.fr).

MARAIS

Those interested in a more central, diverse, and lively urban locale should make the Marais their Parisian home. Once a forgotten Parisian backwater, the Marais—which runs from the Pompidou Center east to the Bastille (a 15-minute walk)—is now one of Paris' most popular residential, tourist, and shopping areas. This is jumbled, medieval Paris at its finest, where stone mansions sit above trendy bars, antique shops, and smart boutiques. The streets are an intriguing parade of artists, students, tourists, immigrants, and baguette-munching babies in strollers. The Marais is also known as a hub of the Parisian gay and lesbian scene. This area is *sans* doubt livelier and edgier than the Rue Cler area.

In the Marais you have these sights close at hand: Carnavalet Museum, Victor Hugo's House, Jewish Art and History Museum, Pompidou Center, and Picasso Museum. You're also a manageable walk from Paris' two islands (Ile St. Louis and Ile de la Cité), home to Notre-Dame and Sainte-Chapelle. The Opéra Bastille, La Coulée Verte Promenade-Park, Place des Vosges (Paris' oldest square), the Jewish Quarter (Rue des Rosiers), the Latin Quarter, and nightlife-packed Rue de Lappe are also walkable. Strolling home (day or night) from Notre-Dame along Ile St. Louis is marvelous.

Most of my recommended hotels are located a few blocks north of the Marais' main east-west drag, Rue St. Antoine/Rue de Rivoli.

Tourist Information: The city's main TI is in the north side of the Hôtel de Ville (daily 10:00-18:00, 29 Rue de Rivoli).

Services: Most banks and other services are on Rue de Rivoli, which becomes Rue St. Antoine as it heads east.

Markets and Shopping: The Marais has three good open-air markets. These include the sprawling **Marché Bastille,** along Boulevard Richard Lenoir, on the north side of Place de la Bastille (Thu and Sun only, Mo: Bastille); the **Marché d'Aligre** on Place d'Aligre (closed Mon, Mo: Ledru-Rollin); and Paris' oldest covered market, the **Marché des Enfants Rouges,** at 39 Rue de Bretagne, a 10-minute walk north of Rue de Rivoli (closed Mon, Mo: Filles du Calvaire or Temple). For market details, see the Shopping in Paris chapter.

A **Monoprix** with a basement grocery is near the St-Paul Métro stop (Mon-Sat 9:00-21:00, Sun until 13:00, 71 Rue St. Antoine). To shop at a Parisian Sears, find the **BHV** department store next to Hôtel de Ville.

Laundry: Launderettes are scattered throughout the Marais; ask your hotelier for the nearest. Here are two that you can count on: on Impasse Guéménée (north of Rue St. Antoine) and on Rue du Petit Musc (south of Rue St. Antoine).

Métro Connections: Key Métro stops in the Marais are, from east to west: Bastille, St-Paul, and Hôtel de Ville (Sully-Morland, Pont Marie, and Rambuteau are also handy). Métro connections are excellent, with direct service to the Louvre, Champs-Elysées, Arc de Triomphe, and La Défense (all on line 1); the Rue Cler area, Place de la Madeleine, and Opéra Garnier/Galeries Lafayette (line 8 from Bastille stop); and four major train stations: Gare de Lyon, Gare du Nord, Gare de l'Est, and Gare d'Austerlitz (all accessible from Bastille stop).

Bus Routes: For stop locations, see the "Marais Hotels" map.

Line #69 on Rue St. Antoine takes you eastbound to Père Lachaise Cemetery and westbound to the Louvre, Orsay, and Rodin

SLEEPING

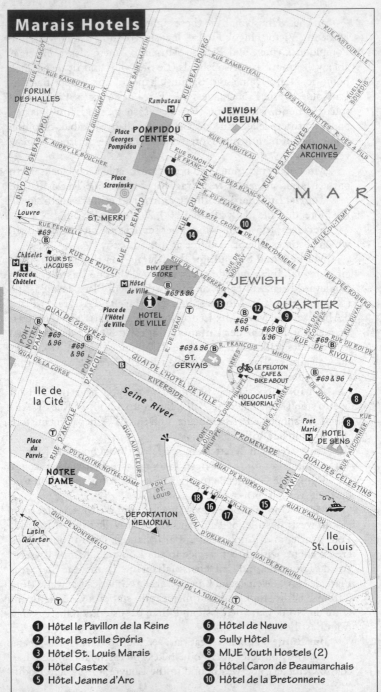

Marais Hotels

1 Hôtel le Pavillon de la Reine

2 Hôtel Bastille Spéria

3 Hôtel St. Louis Marais

4 Hôtel Castex

5 Hôtel Jeanne d'Arc

6 Hôtel de Neuve

7 Sully Hôtel

8 MIJE Youth Hostels (2)

9 Hôtel Caron de Beaumarchais

10 Hôtel de la Bretonnerie

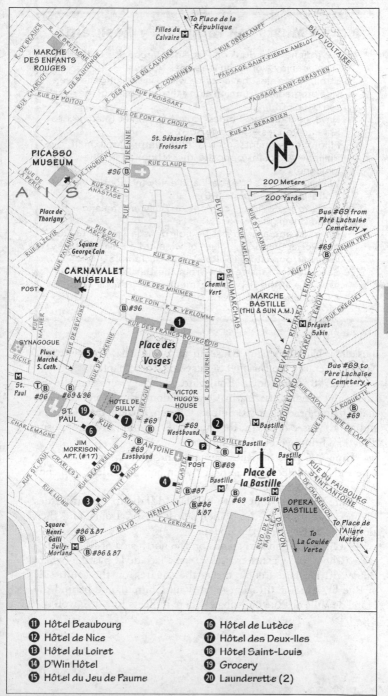

⑪	Hôtel Beaubourg	⑯	Hôtel de Lutèce
⑫	Hôtel de Nice	⑰	Hôtel des Deux-Iles
⑬	Hôtel du Loiret	⑱	Hôtel Saint-Louis
⑭	D'Win Hôtel	⑲	Grocery
⑮	Hôtel du Jeu de Paume	⑳	Launderette (2)

SLEEPING

SLEEPING

Marais Musts for Temporary Residents

- Have dinner or a drink on Place du Marché Ste. Catherine.
- Dine or enjoy a drink on Place des Vosges.
- Stroll, bike, or just have coffee with a view along the riverside promenade (running along the right bank of the river, see page 66).
- Have lunch at Paris' oldest covered market (Marché des Enfants Rouges—see page 506).
- Find the remnants of the 12th-century wall built by Philippe Auguste (opposite the school at 14 Rue Charlemagne).
- Walk Ile St. Louis after dark and enjoy the floodlit view of Notre-Dame (see page 516).
- Cross to Ile St. Louis on Pont de Sully and meander the island's riverside walkway.
- Have tea and a pastry at Le Loir dans la Théière (3 Rue des Rosiers) and/or a glass of wine at La Belle Hortense wine bar/bookstore (31 Rue Vieille du Temple).
- Savor the expansive view from the Bar Perchoir on the top floor of the BHV department store (opens at 20:15, expect long lines on warm days).

museums, plus the Army Museum and Rue Cler, ending at the Eiffel Tower (see the Bus #69 Sightseeing Tour chapter).

Line #87 runs down Boulevard Henri IV, crossing Ile St. Louis and serving the Latin Quarter along Boulevard St. Germain, before heading to St. Sulpice Church/Luxembourg Garden, ending at Musée d'Orsay. The same line, running in the opposite direction, brings you to Gare de Lyon.

Line #96 runs on Rues Turenne and Rivoli, serves Ile de la Cité and St. Sulpice Church (near Luxembourg Garden), and ends at Gare Montparnasse.

Line #67 runs from south of Place d'Italie to the Jardin des Plantes (just south of the Seine), across Ile St. Louis, and then along Rue de Rivoli, to the Louvre.

Taxi: You'll find taxi stands on the north side of Rue St. Antoine (where Rue Castex crosses it), on Place de la Bastille (where Boulevard Richard Lenoir meets the square), on the south side of Rue St. Antoine (in front of St. Paul Church), and behind the Hôtel de Ville on Rue du Lobau (where it meets Rue de Rivoli).

Near Place des Vosges
(3rd and 4th arr., Mo: Bastille, St-Paul, or Hôtel de Ville)

$$$$ Hôtel le Pavillon de la Reine,***** 15 steps off the beautiful Place des Vosges, merits its stars with top service and comfort and exquisite attention to detail, from its melt-in-your-couch lobby to its luxurious rooms (free access to spa and fitness room, parking, 28 Place des Vosges, +33 1 40 29 19 19, www.pavillon-de-la-reine.com, contact@pavillon-de-la-reine.com).

$$$ Hôtel Bastille Spéria*** is situated a short block off Place de la Bastille, offering business-type service and good comfort in a happening location. The 42 rooms have designer decor and are relatively spacious; rooms on the sixth floor have the most character (1 Rue de la Bastille, Mo: Bastille, +33 1 42 72 04 01, www.hotelsperia.com, info@hotelsperia.com).

$$$ Hôtel St. Louis Marais*** is an intimate and sharp little hotel that sits on a quiet street a few blocks from the river. The handsome rooms have character...and spacious bathrooms (1 Rue Charles V, Mo: Sully-Morland, +33 1 48 87 87 04, www.saintlouismarais.com, marais@saintlouis-hotels.com).

$$$ Hôtel Castex*** is a well-located place—on a quiet street near Place de la Bastille—with narrow and tile-floored rooms. Their system of connecting rooms allows families total privacy between two rooms, each with its own bathroom (free buffet breakfast for Rick Steves readers, just off Place de la Bastille and Rue St. Antoine at 5 Rue Castex, Mo: Bastille, +33 1 42 72 31 52, www.castexhotel.com, info@castexhotel.com).

$$ Hôtel Jeanne d'Arc*** is a lovely hotel that's ideally located for connoisseurs of the Marais who don't need air-conditioning. Here, artful decor meets stone walls and oak floors, rooms are thoughtfully appointed, and corner rooms are wonderfully bright in the City of Light. Rooms on the street can have some noise until the bars close (family rooms, some view rooms, 3 Rue de Jarente, Mo: St-Paul, +33 1 48 87 62 11, www.hoteljeannedarc.com, information@hoteljeannedarc.com).

$$ Hôtel de Neuve*** is a small, central, and dignified place with classical music in the lobby and high tea in the afternoon. Rooms are pleasant, quiet, and a good value in this pricey area. Twin rooms come with tub-showers and are a bit larger (behind the Monoprix at 14 Rue de Neuve, Mo: St-Paul, +33 1 44 59 28 50, www.hoteldeneuveparis.com, bonjour@hoteldeneuveparis.com).

$ Sully Hôtel,* right on Rue St. Antoine, is a basic, cheap place run by affable Monsieur Zeroual. The rooms are simple but updated and a good budget value. Two can spring for a triple for more room (family rooms, no elevator, no air-con, no breakfast, 48 Rue St. Antoine, Mo: St-Paul, +33 1 42 78 49 32, www.sullyhotelparis.com, sullyhotel@orange.fr).

¢ **MIJE Youth Hostels:** The Maison Internationale de la Jeunesse et des Etudiants (MIJE) runs two classy, old residences, ideal for budget travelers who are at least 18 years old or traveling with someone who is. Each is well maintained, with simple, clean, single-sex (unless your group takes a whole room) one- to four-bed rooms. The hostels are **MIJE Fourcy** (bigger and louder, dirt-cheap dinners available with a membership card, 6 Rue de Fourcy, just south of Rue de Rivoli) and **MIJE Fauconnier** (no elevator, 11 Rue du Fauconnier). Neither has double beds or air-conditioning. Both have private showers in every room—but bring your own towel or buy one there (includes breakfast, required membership-€3 extra/person, Wi-Fi in common areas only, rooms locked 12:00-15:00). They share the same contact information (+33 1 42 74 23 45, www.mije.com, info@mije.com) and Métro stop (St-Paul). Show up by noon or call to confirm a later arrival time.

Near the Pompidou Center
(4th arr., Mo: St-Paul, Hôtel de Ville, or Rambuteau)
These hotels are farther west, closer to the Pompidou Center than to Place de la Bastille.

$$$ Hôtel Caron de Beaumarchais*** transports you to the 18th century, with a small lobby that's cluttered with bits from an elegant old Marais house. If you want traditional French decor, stay here. Located on a busy street, it's well cared for and filled with character (12 Rue Vieille du Temple, +33 1 42 72 34 12, www.carondebeaumarchais.com, hotel@carondebeaumarchais.com).

$$ Hôtel de la Bretonnerie*** makes a fine Marais home. Located three blocks from the Hôtel de Ville, it has a warm, welcoming lobby and helpful staff. Its 30 good-value rooms are on the larger side with an antique, open-beam warmth (family rooms, free breakfast for Rick Steves readers who book direct, no air-con, between Rue Vieille du Temple and Rue des Archives at 22 Rue Ste. Croix de la Bretonnerie, +33 1 48 87 77 63, www.hotelparismaraisbretonnerie.com, hotel@bretonnerie.com).

$$ Hôtel Beaubourg*** is a top value on a small street in the shadow of the Pompidou Center. The place is surprisingly quiet, and the 28 plush and traditional rooms are well appointed (bigger doubles are worth the extra cost, 11 Rue Simon Le Franc, Mo: Rambuteau, +33 1 42 74 34 24, www.hotelbeaubourg.com, reservation@hotelbeaubourg.com).

$$ Hôtel de Nice,*** on the Marais' busy main drag, features a turquoise-and-fuchsia "Marie-Antoinette-does-tie-dye" decor. This character-filled place is littered with paintings and layered with carpets, and its 23 Old World rooms have thoughtful touches, though bathrooms are tight (reception on second floor, 42 bis

Rue de Rivoli, +33 1 42 78 55 29, www.hoteldenice.com, contact@
hoteldenice.com).

$$ Hôtel du Loiret*** has a basic lobby but rents sharp rooms
with tight bathrooms at good rates (no air-con, expect some noise,
8 Rue des Mauvais Garçons, +33 1 48 87 77 00, www.hotel-du-
loiret.fr, hotelduloiret@hotmail.com).

$$ D'Win Hôtel** is a solid budget value in the thick of the
Marais, with a helpful staff and 44 relatively spacious and quiet
rooms (family rooms, no air-con, no elevator, 20 Rue du Temple,
+33 1 44 54 05 05, www.dwinhotel.com, contact@dwinhotel.com).

ILE ST. LOUIS
(4th arr., Mo: Pont Marie)

The peaceful, residential character of this river-wrapped island,
with its brilliant location and homemade ice cream, has drawn
Americans for decades. There are no budget deals here—all the
hotels are three-star or more—though prices are respectable considering the level of comfort and wonderful location. The island's
village ambience and proximity to the Marais, Notre-Dame, and
the Latin Quarter make this area well worth considering. The following hotels are on the island's main drag, Rue St. Louis-en-l'Ile,
where I list several restaurants (see page 455 in the Eating in Paris
chapter). For nearby services, see the Marais neighborhood section;
for locations, see the "Marais Hotels" map, earlier in this chapter.
There are no Métro stops on Ile St. Louis; expect a 10-minute walk
to the closest station—Pont Marie—or a bit farther to Cité. Bus
#69 works well for Ile St. Louis residents.

$$$$ Hôtel du Jeu de Paume**** occupies a 17th-century tennis center. Its magnificent lobby and cozy public spaces make it a
fine splurge. Greet Lemon (luh-moe),
le chien, then take a spin in the glass
elevator for a half-timbered treehouse
experience. The 30 rooms are carefully
designed and tasteful, though not particularly spacious (you're paying for the
location and public areas). Most rooms
face a small garden courtyard; all are
pin-drop peaceful (apartments for 4-6
people, 54 Rue St. Louis-en-l'Ile, +33
1 43 26 14 18, www.jeudepaumehotel.
com, info@jeudepaumehotel.com).

The next two places share the
same hands-on owner and comfort.
$$$ Hôtel de Lutèce*** comes with a welcoming wood-paneled
lobby and a real fireplace (though fires are no longer allowed in
Paris). Rooms are traditional, warm, and fairly priced, and those

on lower floors have high ceilings. Most have wood-beam ceilings and good space for storage. Twin rooms are larger and the same price as doubles; most beds are doubles, and there are a few good triple rooms. Rooms with bathtubs are on the streetside, while those with showers are on the quieter courtyard (65 Rue St. Louis-en-l'Ile, +33 1 43 26 23 52, www.hoteldelutece.com, bonjour@ hoteldelutece.com).

$$$ Hôtel des Deux-Iles*** has a fun lobby and rents lovely rooms, with a few true singles. It's a bit cheaper than the Lutèce but otherwise hard to distinguish—you can't go wrong in either place (59 Rue St. Louis-en-l'Ile, +33 1 43 26 13 35, www. hoteldesdeuxiles.com, bonjour@hoteldesdeuxiles.com).

$$$ Hôtel Saint-Louis*** blends character with modern comforts. The sharp rooms come with cool stone floors and exposed beams. Rates are reasonable...for the location (some rooms with balcony, iPads available for guest use, 75 Rue St. Louis-en-l'Ile, +33 1 46 34 04 80, www.saintlouisenlisle.com, isle@saintlouis-hotels.com).

LUXEMBOURG GARDEN AREA

This neighborhood revolves around Paris' loveliest park and offers quick access to the city's best shopping streets and grandest café hopping. Hotels in this central area run the gamut from cheap sleeps to pricey boutique places. Sleeping in the Luxembourg area offers a true Left Bank experience without a hint of the commotion of the nearby Latin Quarter tourist ghetto. The Luxembourg Garden, Boulevard St. Germain, Cluny Museum, Place St. Sulpice, and Latin Quarter are all at your doorstep, and Place St. Michel is a 15-minute walk away. Here you get the best of both worlds: youthful Left Bank energy and the classic trappings that surround the monumental Panthéon and St. Sulpice Church.

Having the Luxembourg Garden as your backyard allows strolls through meticulously cared-for flowers, a great kids' play area (see the Paris with Children chapter), and a purifying escape from city traffic. Place St. Sulpice presents an elegant, pedestrian-friendly square and quick access to some of Paris' best boutiques (see the Shopping in Paris chapter). You're near several movie theaters (at Métro stop: Odéon), as well as lively cafés on Boulevard St. Germain, Rue de Buci, Rue des Canettes, Place de la Sorbonne, and Place de la Contrescarpe, all of which buzz with action until late.

It takes about 15 minutes to walk from one end of this neighborhood to the other. Most hotels are within a five-minute walk of Luxembourg Garden.

Services: The nearest **TI** is across the river at the Hôtel de Ville (daily 10:00-18:30, 29 Rue de Rivoli).

Markets: The colorful street market at the south end of Rue Mouffetard is a worthwhile 10-to-15-minute walk from these hotels (closed Mon, five blocks south of Place de la Contrescarpe, Mo: Place Monge, for details see the Shopping in Paris chapter).

Bookstore: San Francisco Book Company has a full selection of secondhand English-language books, including mine (17 Rue Monsieur le Prince). **Abbey Bookshop** is crammed with English-language books, many by Canadian authors (29 Rue de la Parcheminerie, Mo: Cluny La Sorbonne). For details on these bookstores, see page 34.

Métro Connections: Métro lines 10, 12, and 4 serve this area (10 connects to the Gare d'Austerlitz train station; 12 serves Gare St. Lazare, Gare Montparnasse, and the handy Concorde Métro station; and 4 runs to the Montparnasse, Est, and Nord train stations). Neighborhood stops are Cluny La Sorbonne, Mabillon, Odéon, Sèvres-Babylone, and St-Sulpice. RER/Train-B (Luxembourg station is handiest) provides direct service to Charles de Gaulle airport and Gare du Nord trains, and access to Orly airport via the Orlybus (transfer at Denfert-Rochereau) or via Orlyval trains (transfer at Antony RER/Train-B station).

Bus Routes: For stop locations, see the "Hotels near Luxembourg Garden" map.

Lines #86 and **#87** run eastbound through this area on or near Boulevard St. Germain, to the Marais (#87 continues to Gare de Lyon). Bus #87 runs westbound along the river (on Quai du Montebello) to the Orsay Museum; #86 runs westbound on Rue des Ecoles, stopping on Place St. Sulpice and continuing to the Eiffel Tower and Rue Cler area.

Line #63 provides a direct connection along Boulevard St. Germain west to the Rue Cler area (stops at Place St. Sulpice westbound), serving the Orsay and Marmottan museums along the way, and east to Gare de Lyon.

Line #96 stops at Place St. Sulpice southbound en route to Gare Montparnasse and runs north along Rue de Rennes and Boulevard St. Germain into the Marais.

Line #70 runs along Rue de Sèvres, connecting Sèvres-Babylone and St. Sulpice with the Pompidou Center and the Hôtel de Ville.

Near St. Sulpice Church

(6th arr., Mo: St-Sulpice, Rennes, Sèvres-Babylone, Mabillon, Odéon, or Saint-Germain-des-Prés; RER/Train-B: Luxembourg) These hotels are all within a block of St. Sulpice Church and two blocks from famous Boulevard St. Germain. This is nirvana for boutique-minded shoppers—and you'll pay extra for the location.

$$$$ Hôtel de l'Abbaye** is a lovely refuge just west of

Hotels near Luxembourg Garden

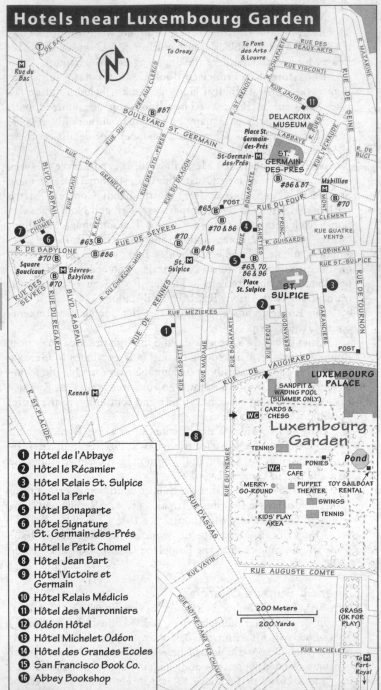

1. Hôtel de l'Abbaye
2. Hôtel le Récamier
3. Hôtel Relais St. Sulpice
4. Hôtel la Perle
5. Hôtel Bonaparte
6. Hôtel Signature St. Germain-des-Prés
7. Hôtel le Petit Chomel
8. Hôtel Jean Bart
9. Hôtel Victoire et Germain
10. Hôtel Relais Médicis
11. Hôtel des Marronniers
12. Odéon Hôtel
13. Hôtel Michelet Odéon
14. Hôtel des Grandes Ecoles
15. San Francisco Book Co.
16. Abbey Bookshop

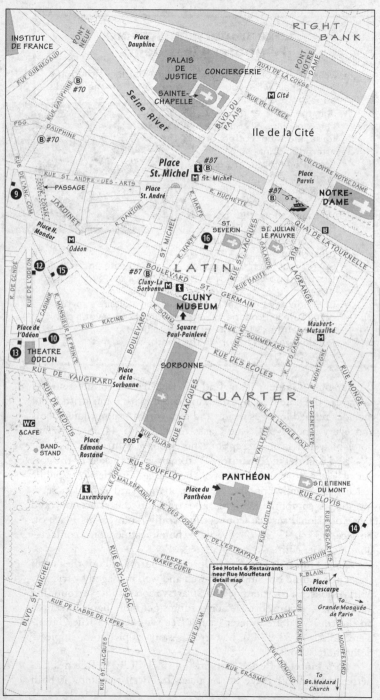

SLEEPING

Luxembourg Musts for Temporary Residents

- Pass oodles of time at Luxembourg Garden, sitting in a green chair with your feet propped up on the pond's edge.

- Join the locals at the only café on Place St. Sulpice for a morning coffee or afternoon drink.
- Stroll Rue Mouffetard day or night, and stop for a drink on delightful Place de la Contrescarpe.
- Window shop the boutiques between Sèvres-Babylone and St. Sulpice (described on page 496).
- Spend too much for a coffee at a grand café and watch the world go by (see "Les Grands Cafés de Paris," page 466).
- 📖 Follow my Left Bank Walk and find Voltaire's favorite café (Café le Procope, now a restaurant), or savor a drink at your author's favorite—Café la Palette.
- Ponder France's history in the Panthéon.

Luxembourg Garden; it's a find for well-heeled connoisseurs of this area. The hotel's four-star luxury comes with some attitude but includes refined lounges inside and out, with 44 sumptuous rooms and every amenity (10 Rue Cassette, +33 1 45 44 38 11, www. hotelabbayeparis.com, reception@hotelabbaye.com).

$$$$ Hôtel le Récamier,** romantically tucked in the corner of Place St. Sulpice, is a polished place with designer public spaces, elaborately appointed rooms, a courtyard tea salon serving guests complimentary tea and treats in the afternoon, and *très* professional service (connecting family rooms, 3 bis Place St. Sulpice, +33 1 43 26 04 89, www.hotelrecamier.com, contact@ hotelrecamier.com).

$$$ Hôtel Relais St. Sulpice,* burrowed on the small street just behind St. Sulpice Church and well managed by friendly Mirko, houses a cozy lounge and 26 artsy rooms, most surrounding a leafy glass atrium. Street-facing rooms get more light, but those on the courtyard are quieter (sauna free for guests, 3 Rue Garancière, +33 1 46 33 99 00, www.relais-saint-sulpice.com, sulpice@ designhotelst.com).

$$$ Hôtel la Perle* sits in the thick of lively Rue des Canettes, a block off Place St. Sulpice. This well-run hotel is built around a central bar and atrium and offers comfortable and traditional rooms, many with wood beams (14 Rue des Canettes, +33 1 43 29 10 10, www.hotellaperle.com, booking@hotellaperle.com).

$$ Hôtel Bonaparte*** is an unpretentious and welcoming place wedged between boutiques, a few steps from Place St. Sulpice. The hotel's decor is simple, rooms are spacious by Parisian standards, and the staff is very helpful (61 Rue Bonaparte, +33 1 43 26 97 37, www.hotelbonaparte.fr, reservation@hotelbonaparte.fr).

West of Luxembourg Garden
(6th and 7th arr., Mo: Sèvres-Babylone or St-Sulpice)
$$$ Hôtel Signature St. Germain-des-Prés,*** on a quiet street just steps from the trendy Sèvres-Babylone shopping area, feels as chic as its neighboring boutiques. The friendly staff takes great care of its guests with 26 colorful and tastefully decorated rooms, several with balconies. There are good rooms for families and some wonderfully large "prestige" rooms that can sleep three (RS%, 5 Rue Chomel, Mo: Sèvres-Babylone, +33 1 45 48 35 53, www.signature-saintgermain.com, info@signature-saintgermain.com).

$$$ Hôtel le Petit Chomel*** sits a few doors down, offering the same great location, good rates, and comfort, as well as warm public spaces, helpful staff, and decor with a country-French accent (RS%, 15 Rue Chomel, +33 1 45 48 55 52, www.lepetitchomel.com, info@lepetitchomel.com).

$ Hôtel Jean Bart*** feels like it's from another era—prices included. Run by smiling Madame Lechopier and her daughter Laureanne, it's a rare budget find in this neighborhood, one block from Luxembourg Garden. Beyond the dark lobby, you'll find 33 suitably comfortable rooms with creaking floors, some with tight bathrooms (includes breakfast, no air-con, 9 Rue Jean-Bart, +33 1 45 48 29 13, www.hoteljeanbart.com, hotel.jean.bart@gmail.com).

Near the Odéon Theater
(6th arr., Mo: Odéon, Cluny La Sorbonne, or Mabillon; RER/Train-B: Luxembourg)
The Hôtel Relais Médicis is between the Odéon Métro stop and Luxembourg Garden, and may have rooms when others don't.

$$$ Hôtel Victoire et Germain*** is a top choice a few steps off Boulevard St. Germain and Rue de Buci. Sleep here to be in the thickest of things. Rooms offer excellent comfort with Scandinavian accents under white beams (9 Rue Grégoire de Tours, +33 1 45 49 03 26, www.victoireetgermainhotel.com, reservation@victoireetgermainhotel.com).

$$$ Hôtel Relais Médicis*** is ideal if you've always wanted to live in a Monet painting. A glassy entry hides 17 rooms surrounding a fragrant little garden courtyard and fountain, giv-

SLEEPING

ing you a countryside break fit for a Medici in the heart of Paris. This delightful refuge is tastefully decorated and permeated with thoughtfulness (family rooms, faces the Odéon Theater at 5 Place de l'Odéon, +33 1 43 26 00 60, www.relaismedicis.com, reservation@relaismedicis.com).

$$$ Hôtel des Marronniers*** is wonderfully situated on a quiet street and delivers Old World charm with modern comfort. The atrium breakfast room, lovely garden courtyard, cozy lounges, and plush rooms make this worth booking well ahead (21 Rue Jacob, +33 1 43 25 30 60, www.hotel-marronniers.com, hotel-des-marronniers@orange.fr).

$$$ Odéon Hôtel*** welcomes guests with a large, linger-longer lobby-lounge. Dark hallways lead to Old World-style rooms with all the comforts (3 Rue de l'Odéon, + 33 1 43 25 90 76, www.odeonhotel.fr, odeon@odeonhotel.fr).

$$ Hôtel Michelet Odéon** sits in a corner of Place de l'Odéon with big windows overlooking the square. Rooms come with stylish colors but no frills and impersonal staff (family rooms, no air-con, 6 Place de l'Odéon, +33 1 53 10 05 60, www.hotelmicheletodeon.com, hotel@micheletodeon.com).

East of the Panthéon
(5th arr., Mo: Cardinal Lemoine or Place Monge ; RER/Train-B: Luxembourg)

$$$ Hôtel des Grandes Ecoles*** is idyllic. A private cobbled lane leads to three buildings that protect a flower-filled garden court-

yard, preserving a sense of tranquility rare in this city. Its 51 rooms are French-countryside pretty, reasonably spacious, and lovingly cared for. This romantic spot is deservedly popular; book ahead (no TVs, reserve ahead for pay parking, 75 Rue du Cardinal Lemoine, Mo: Cardinal Lemoine, +33 1 43 26 79 23, www.hoteldesgrandesecoles.com, contact@hoteldesgrandesecoles.fr).

Cheap Digs at the Bottom of Rue Mouffetard
(5th arr., Mo: Les Gobelins)

Southeast of the Panthéon is an appealing and unpretentious area whose bohemian soul is the Rue Mouffetard. Two thousand years ago, Rue Mouffetard was the principal Roman road south to Italy. Today, this small, meandering street has a split personality. The lower half thrives in the daytime as a pedestrian market street. The upper half sleeps during the day but comes alive after dark with

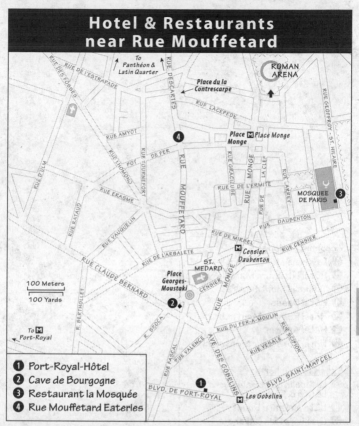

**Hotel & Restaurants
near Rue Mouffetard**

① Port-Royal-Hôtel
② Cave de Bourgogne
③ Restaurant la Mosquée
④ Rue Mouffetard Eateries

SLEEPING

a fun collection of restaurants and bars. A lively Saturday market sprawls along Boulevard Port Royal, just east of the Port Royal Métro stop.

$ Port-Royal-Hôtel, recently renovated, has only one star, but don't let that fool you. Its 46 rooms are polished top to bottom and have been well run by the same proud family for 80-plus years. You could eat off the floors of its spotless, modest, comfy rooms... but you won't find air-conditioning or a TV. Ask for a room away from the street (cheaper rooms with pay shower and WC down the hall, on busy Boulevard de Port-Royal at #8, Mo: Les Gobelins, +33 1 43 31 70 06, www.port-royal-hotel.fr, contact@port-royal-hotel.fr).

MONTMARTRE

Those interested in a more SoHo/Greenwich Village-type locale should consider making Montmartre their Parisian home. While the top of Montmartre's hill is terribly touristy, just below lies an

Hotels & Restaurants in Montmartre

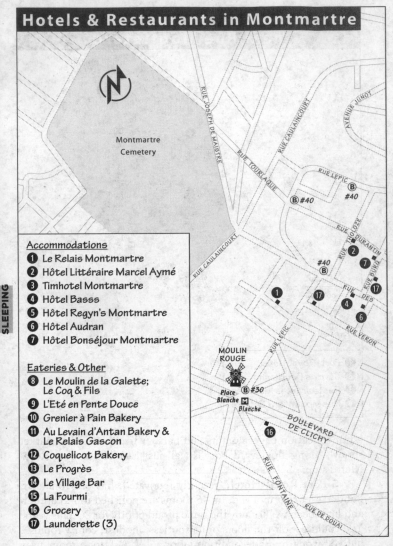

Accommodations

1 Le Relais Montmartre
2 Hôtel Littéraire Marcel Aymé
3 Timhotel Montmartre
4 Hôtel Basss
5 Hôtel Regyn's Montmartre
6 Hôtel Audran
7 Hôtel Bonséjour Montmartre

Eateries & Other

8 Le Moulin de la Galette;
Le Coq & Fils
9 L'Eté en Pente Douce
10 Grenier à Pain Bakery
11 Au Levain d'Antan Bakery &
Le Relais Gascon
12 Coquelicot Bakery
13 Le Progrès
14 Le Village Bar
15 La Fourmi
16 Grocery
17 Launderette (3)

overlooked workaday neighborhood happily living in the shadow of Sacré-Cœur.

Montmartre is a mix of young families, artists, and active seniors, and it is fast becoming popular with the *bobo* crowd (*bourgeois bohemian,* French for "hipster"). Travelers staying here trade a central location and level terrain for good deals on hotel rooms and a lively atmosphere, especially in the evenings, when café terraces thrive and tiny bars spill crowds onto the narrow streets. Expect some ups and downs here on Paris' lone hill.

Rue des Abbesses is the heart and soul of this area, starting at

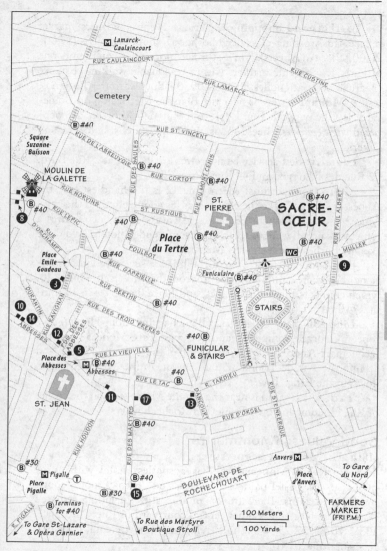

Place des Abbesses and stretching several blocks to Rue Lepic. Rue Lepic has good shops and services, but the lower you go the seedier it gets: Scammers and shady characters prowl the base of the hill after hours (along Boulevard Clichy and Boulevard Rochechouart, where you'll find what's left of Paris' red light district). For fun nightlife, stick to the narrow streets uphill from Rue des Abbesses around Rue Durantin and along Rue des Trois Frères. For restaurant suggestions, see the Eating in Paris chapter.

Services: Several ATMs are located along Rue des Abbesses and on Rue Lepic.

Markets and Shopping: A Friday evening farmers market reflects this working-class neighborhood's shopping needs (15:00-20:00, Place d'Anvers). On Saturday mornings, you'll find one of Paris' few organic markets within reasonable walking distance (Marché des Batignolles, 8:30-14:00, 34 Boulevard des Batignolles). A **Monoprix** store is near the Blanche Métro stop on Boulevard de Clichy. Both Rue Lepic and Rue des Abbesses are peppered with *épiceries*, cheese shops, wine shops, delis, butchers, and bakeries.

Laundry: Self-service launderettes are located at 2 Rue Burq, 92 Rue des Martyrs, and 44 Rue Veron.

Métro Connections: Métro line 12 is the handiest (use the Abbesses stop and take the elevator, as it's a long climb to the exit). Line 2 uses the Blanche, Pigalle, or Anvers stops but requires a four-block uphill walk to reach my recommended hotels. Avoid the sketchy Barbès Rochechouart Métro stop.

Bus Routes: At the base of the hill are several good bus options, but there's only one bus line on the hill itself—**bus #40,** which connects Pigalle, Abbesses, and Place du Tertre in 10 minutes (4/hour).

Line #30 picks up at Place Blanche (direction: Hôpital Européen Georges-Pompidou) and goes past Parc Monceau and the Jacquemart-André Museum, to the top of the Champs-Elysées and around the Arc de Triomphe roundabout, to the Trocadéro, then down to the Eiffel Tower.

Taxi: A taxi stand is near the Pigalle Métro stop on the corner of Rue Houdon and busy Boulevard Rochechouart.

Good Values in Montmartre
(18th arr., Mo: Abbesses or Anvers)

$$$ Le Relais Montmartre*** is a spotless hotel with cushy public spaces, pastel paint, fair prices, and 26 cozy rooms sporting floral curtains. There are lots of amenities, including a shared iPad, a fireplace, and a quiet central courtyard (6 Rue Constance, +33 1 70 64 25 25, www.hotel-relais-montmartre.com, contact@relaismontmartre.fr).

$$$ Hôtel Littéraire Marcel Aymé,*** a stylish and somewhat pricey hideaway a few blocks below the Moulin de la Galette, has smallish but well-designed rooms (16 Rue Tholozé, +33 1 42 55 05 06, www.hotel-litteraire-marcel-ayme.com, contact@hotel-litteraire-marcel-ayme.com).

$$ Timhotel Montmartre** sits above the others on a small leafy square, a short walk from the top of the hill and next to the famous (rebuilt) Bateau-Lavoir artists' hangout. Rooms are handsome, well maintained, and a fair value; those on the fourth and fifth floors have city views (11 Rue Ravignan, +33 1 42 55 74 79, www.timhotel.com, montmartre@timhotel.com).

$$ Hôtel Basss,*** right on Rue des Abbesses, offers snappy modern rooms with pastel colors and trendy furniture (57 Rue des Abbesses, +33 1 42 51 50 00, www.hotel-basss.com, contact@hotel-basss.com).

$ Hôtel Regyn's Montmartre** is welcoming and ideally located on the lively Abbesses square, with 22 clean, comfortable, and modest rooms with floral wallpaper. Those in the front come with pleasant views and noise from the square, and those on the fourth and fifth floors come with grand views to the Eiffel Tower (no air-con, great breakfast with ham, 18 Place des Abbesses, +33 1 42 54 45 21, www.regyns-montmartre.com, hotel.regynsmontmartre75@gmail.com).

$ Hôtel Audran, well situated a few stops off Rue des Abbesses, is a fair budget value with 39 simple, clean rooms. Some fourth- and fifth-floor rooms come with views (7 Rue Audran, +33 1 42 58 79 59, www.hotelaudran.com, contact@hotelaudran.com).

$ Hôtel Bonséjour Montmartre, run by eager Michel and his family, offers a mix of modern rooms and cheap basic rooms. The modern ones have private bathrooms and new beds; the far cheaper ones maintain the Old World tradition of shared facilities—one shower for every two rooms (RS%, no air-con, 11 Rue Burq, +33 1 42 54 22 53, www.hotel-bonsejour.com, hotel-bonsejour-montmartre@orange.fr).

AT OR NEAR PARIS' AIRPORTS
At Charles de Gaulle Airport

These three places are located a few minutes from the terminals (outside the T-3 RER/Train-B stop and on the CDGVAL airport shuttle train loop). All have restaurants. For locations, see the map on page 531.

$$$ Novotel*** is a step up from cookie-cutter airport hotels (+33 1 49 19 27 27, https://novotel.accor.com, h1014@accor.com).

$$ Hôtel Ibis CDG Airport** is huge and offers standard airport accommodations (+33 1 49 19 19 19, https://ibis.accor.com, h1404@accor.com). There are several IBIS airport hotels to choose from—you want IBIS Terminal 3.

$$ Holiday Inn Express** is also a good value and close (www.ihg.com, reception@hiexpariscdg.com).

Near Charles de Gaulle Airport, in Roissy

The small village of Roissy-en-France (you'll see signs just before the airport as you come from Paris) has better-value chain hotels with free airport-shuttle service (usually 4/hour, 15 minutes, look for *navettes hôtels* signs to reach these hotels). Most Roissy hotels list specials on their websites.

The following hotels are within walking distance of the town. **$$ Hôtel Ibis CDG Paris Nord 2**** is usually cheaper than the Ibis right at the airport (335 Rue de la Belle Étoile, +33 1 48 17 56 56, https://ibis.accor.com, h3299@accor.com). **$$ Hôtel Campanile Roissy***** is a decent place to sleep, and you can have a good dinner next door at Hôtel Golden Tulip (Allée des Vergers, +33 1 34 29 80 40, www.campanile-roissy.fr, roissy@campanile. fr). **$$$ Hôtel Golden Tulip Paris CDG***** has a fitness center, sauna, and good restaurant for the suburbs (11 Allée des Vergers, +33 1 34 29 00 00, www.goldentulipcdgvillepinte.com, info@ goldentulipcdgvillepinte.com). The cheapest option is **$ B&B Hôtel Roissy CDG,*** where many flight attendants stay (17 Allée des Vergers, +33 1 34 38 55 55 or +33 2 98 33 75 29, www.hotel-bb. com).

To avoid rush-hour traffic, drivers can consider sleeping north of Paris in either **Auvers-sur-Oise** (30 minutes west of airport) or in the pleasant medieval town of **Senlis** (15 minutes north of airport). **$$ Hôtel Ibis Senlis**** is a few minutes from town (72 Avenue du Général de Gaulle, +33 3 44 53 70 50, https://ibis.accor. com, h0709@accor.com).

Near Orly Airport

These two chain hotels are your best options near Orly. Both have free shuttles *(navettes)* to the terminals.

$$$ Hôtel Mercure Paris Orly*** provides high comfort for a price (+33 8 25 80 69 69, https://mercure.accor.com, h1246@ accor.com).

$$ Hôtel Ibis Orly Aéroport** is reasonable and basic (+33 1 56 70 50 60, https://ibis.accor.com, h1413@accor.com).

APARTMENT RENTALS

Consider this option if you're traveling as a family, in a group, or staying at least a few nights. Intrepid travelers around the world are accustomed to using Airbnb and VRBO when it comes to renting a vacation apartment. In Paris, you have many additional options among rental agencies, and I've found the following to be the most reliable. Their websites are good and essential to understanding your choices. Read the rental conditions very carefully.

Most of these agencies are middlemen, offering an ever-changing selection of private apartments for rent for a few days, a week, or longer. If staying a month or more, you may save money by renting directly from the apartment owners. Check the housing section in the ad-filled paper *France-USA Contacts* (www.fusac.fr).

For more information on renting apartments, see the "Sleeping" section in the Practicalities chapter.

These days, apartment rental in Paris is a controversial topic. Locals fear that vacation rentals are driving up the cost of rent overall because fewer apartments are available for long-term use (owners make more money on short-term vacation rentals). Hotels claim vacation rentals are unfair competition, as hotel owners pay taxes and meet rigorous safety and accessibility regulations that apartment owners can avoid.

If you choose to rent an apartment, please respect your neighbors. Minimize noise in entryways and in your apartment after hours. Pick an apartment in one of the neighborhoods I recommend for hotels and restaurants. Use the helpful suggestions in these chapters and become a temporary local.

Most apartments come with Wi-Fi and cable TV; some include free local and international phone calls, air-conditioning, and washers and dryers. Be clear on exactly what your apartment has before booking (air-conditioning in the summer is a godsend).

Rental Agencies

SLEEPING

Paris Perfect has offices in Paris with English-speaking staff who seek the "perfect apartment" for their clients and are selective about what they offer. Many units have Eiffel Tower views; most are air-conditioned and have washers and dryers (RS%, US toll-free +1 888 520 2087, www.parisperfect.com).

Cobblestone Paris Rentals is a small, North American-run outfit offering furnished rentals in central neighborhoods. Many have clothes-washing machines. Apartments come stocked with English-language DVDs about Paris, coffee, tea, cooking spices, basic bathroom amenities, and an English-speaking greeter who will give you the lay of the land (RS%—use code "RSPARIS"—plus two free river cruises, www.cobblestoneparis.com).

Home Rental Service has been in business for 20-some years and offers a big selection of apartments, boats, and bungalows throughout Paris at fair rates with no agency fees (120 Champs-Elysées, +33 1 42 25 65 40, www.homerental.fr).

Haven in Paris offers exactly that—well-appointed, stylish havens for travelers looking for a place to temporarily call home. Their fun blog, *Hip Paris,* is also worth checking out (US +1 617 395 4243, https://havenin.com).

Paris Home is a small outfit, with only two little studios and a one-bedroom unit, located on Rue Amélie in the heart of the Rue Cler area (see the "Rue Cler Hotels" map, earlier). Each has modern furnishings and laundry facilities. Friendly Slim, the owner, is the best part (no minimum stay, special rates for longer stays, payment by PayPal or cash only, free housekeeping service, mobile +33 6 19 03 17 55, www.parishome2000.com).

Paris for Rent, a San Francisco–based group, has been renting top-end apartments in Paris for more than a decade and offers a good selection throughout the city (US +1 866 4 FRANCE, www.parisforrent.com).

Adrian Leeds Group offers American-owned apartments for longer-term rental or sale and is ideal for travelers looking for all the comforts, conveniences, and amenities of home (US +1 415 779 5211, https://adrianleeds.com).

Cross-Pollinate is a reputable online booking agency representing B&Bs and apartments in a handful of European cities. Paris listings range from a small studio near the Bastille to a two-bedroom apartment in the Marais. Minimum stays vary from one to seven nights (www.cross-pollinate.com).

BED-AND-BREAKFASTS

Several agencies can help you go local by staying in a private home in Paris. While prices and quality range greatly, most rooms have a private bath and run from €85 to €150. Most owners won't take bookings for fewer than two nights. To limit stair climbing, ask whether the building has an elevator. Some agencies have a good selection, but there's no good way to check the quality of the rooms as I do with hotels (agencies work with an ever-changing list of owners—each with a few rooms at most). You are at the mercy of whatever information you get from the agency and its website. Buyer beware.

Alcôve & Agapes is the most-used B&B resource in Paris, offering a broad selection of addresses throughout the city. Their useful website helps you sort through the options with prices, information about the owners, and helpful photos (+33 6 99 44 75 75, www.bed-and-breakfast-in-paris.com).

EATING IN PARIS

The Parisian eating scene is kept at a rolling boil. Entire books (and lives) are dedicated to the subject. Paris is France's wine-and-cuisine melting pot. There is no "Parisian cuisine" to speak of (only French onion soup is truly Parisian), but it draws from the best of France. Paris could hold a gourmet Olympics and import nothing.

My restaurant recommendations are centered on the same great neighborhoods listed in the Sleeping in Paris chapter; you can come home exhausted after a busy day of sightseeing and find a good selection of eateries right around the corner. And evening is a fine time to explore any of these delightful neighborhoods, even if you're sleeping elsewhere. Serious eaters looking for even more suggestions should consult the always-appetizing www.parisbymouth. com, an eating-and-drinking guide to Paris.

To save piles of euros, consider a picnic. Tasty takeout dishes are available at charcuteries. Bakeries often have a selection of fresh sandwiches to-go and can generally heat them up on request. For a light lunch, these can feed often feed two for €5.

Or stop at a café for lunch. Cafés and brasseries are happy to serve a *plat du jour* (plate of the day, about €16-22) or a chef-like salad (about €16) day or night. Try eating your big meal at lunch, when many fine restaurants offer their dinnertime fixed-price *menus* at a reduced price.

Linger longer over dinner—restaurants expect you to enjoy a full meal. The current trend is to order only a main course (and maybe a first course), so many restaurants offer à la carte only. Others have set-price *menus* from about €26 to €40—good values if you want that much food. To maximize your experience, it's fun and fine to share. (You can even request a small extra plate.) In most cases, the few extra euros for the more expensive *menu* option open up a variety of better choices. Remember that a service charge is included in the prices (so little or no tipping is expected—see page 655 of the Practicalities chapter for advice).

Many restaurants close Sunday and/or Monday. Most open for dinner around 19:00, though some open at 18:30 and a few serve "nonstop" all day. Last seating is usually at about 22:00. Eat early with tourists or late with locals—restaurants that are popular with locals get crowded after 21:00.

If stymied because you arrived without a reservation, see if they have a few stools at the bar or counter. Waiters typically say "we're full" without offering this option, but dining with a view of the kitchen, with the locals who just dropped by for a drink, can add to the experience.

If a restaurant is open for lunch and doesn't serve continuously, the hours are generally 12:00-14:30 (last orders at about 13:30). If you want to eat in the late afternoon, when many restaurants are closed, pop in to a brasserie or café. At any eatery, before choosing a seat outside, remember that smokers love (and are welcome at) outdoor tables.

I rank eateries from **$** budget to **$$$$** splurge. For more advice on eating in Paris, including restaurant pricing; dining in Paris' restaurants, cafés, and brasseries; getting takeout and assembling a picnic; and a rundown of French cuisine, see the "Eating" section of the Practicalities chapter.

RUE CLER NEIGHBORHOOD

The Rue Cler neighborhood caters to its residents. Its eateries, while not destination places, have an intimate charm. I've provided a full range of choices—from cozy ma-and-pa diners to small and trendy boutique restaurants to classic, big, boisterous bistros.

On Rue Cler
(Mo: Ecole Militaire)

$ Café du Marché boasts the best seats on Rue Cler. The owner's philosophy: Brasserie on speed—crank out good-enough food at fair prices to appreciative locals and savvy tourists. It's high-energy, with young waiters who barely have time to smile...*très* Parisian.

This place works well if you don't mind average-quality cuisine and want to eat an inexpensive one-course meal among a commotion of people. The chalkboard lists your choices: good, hearty salads or more filling *plats du jour* (daily 11:00-23:00,

serves continuously, no reservations, often packed after 19:00, at the corner of Rue Cler and Rue du Champ de Mars, 38 Rue Cler, +33 1 47 05 51 27).

$ L'Eclair, a few doors down, is a bar-meets-bistro place with French bar food, a trendy vibe, and terrific seating amid the Rue Cler market action (daily until late, 32 Rue Cler, +33 1 44 18 09 04).

$ Le Petit Cler is an adorable and popular little bistro with long leather booths, a vintage interior, tight ranks of tiny and cramped tables—indoors and out—and simple, inexpensive *plats,* €10 omelets, and €9 soups. Eating (or just drinking) outside here with a view of the Rue Cler can be marvelous (daily, arrive early or call in advance; delicious *pots de crème* and good breakfasts as well; 29 Rue Cler, +33 1 45 50 17 50).

$$ Café Roussillon offers a rustic, pub-like ambience with food that works well for families. You'll find hearty hamburgers, salads, daily specials, and easygoing waiters (daily, serves nonstop from lunch until late, indoor seating only, corner

of Rue de Grenelle and Rue Cler, +33 1 45 51 47 53). While less charming than other spots, it's more likely to have a table available.

Close to Ecole Militaire
(Mo: Ecole Militaire)

$$ Le Septième Vin is a cozy and welcoming bistro. Hervé cooks while wife Stéphanie serves delicious traditional cuisine at good prices in a romantic and very Parisian setting (closed Sun, the *confit de canard* and *dorade* are memorable, 68 Avenue Bosquet, +33 1 45 51 15 97).

$$$ Le Florimond is fun for a special occasion in a warm setting. Locals come for classic French cuisine at fair prices. Friendly

Rue Cler Restaurants

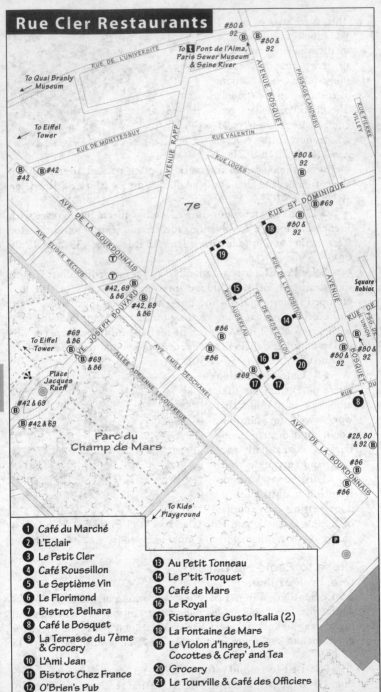

EATING

1 Café du Marché
2 L'Eclair
3 Le Petit Cler
4 Café Roussillon
5 Le Septième Vin
6 Le Florimond
7 Bistrot Belhara
8 Café le Bosquet
9 La Terrasse du 7ème
   & Grocery
10 L'Ami Jean
11 Bistrot Chez France
12 O'Brien's Pub

13 Au Petit Tonneau
14 Le P'tit Troquet
15 Café de Mars
16 Le Royal
17 Ristorante Gusto Italia (2)
18 La Fontaine de Mars
19 Le Violon d'Ingres, Les
   Cocottes & Crep' and Tea
20 Grocery
21 Le Tourville & Café des Officiers

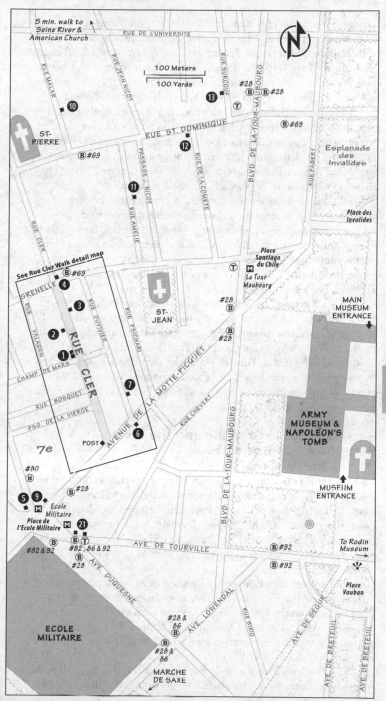

5 min. walk to
Seine River &
American Church

RUE DE L'UNIVERSITE

N

100 Meters

100 Yards

RUE MALAR

RUE JEAN NICOT

RUE SURCOUF

BLVD. DE LA-TOUR-MAUBOURG

RUE FABERT

⑩

Ⓑ #28

Ⓑ #28

⑬

Ⓣ

ST-
PIERRE

RUE ST. DOMINIQUE

Ⓑ #69

Esplanade
des
Invalides

Ⓑ #69

⑫

RUE DE LA COMETE

PASSAGE L'NICOT

⑪

RUE AMELIE

*Place des
Invalides*

RUE CLER

Place
Santiago
du Chile

Ⓣ

Ⓜ
La Tour
Maubourg

See Rue Cler Walk detail map

Ⓑ #69

GRENELLE

④

RUE

③

RUE DUVIVIER

RUE PSICHARI

#28

Ⓑ

MAIN
MUSEUM
ENTRANCE

②

RUE

RUE VALADON

①

ST-
JEAN

Ⓑ
#28

CHAMP DE MARS

CLER

RUE DE LA MOTTE-PICQUET

RUE BOSQUET

⑦

RUE CHEVERT

BLVD. DE LA-TOUR-MAUBOURG

ARMY
MUSEUM &
NAPOLEON'S
TOMB

PSG. DE LA VIERGE

7e

POST ◆

AVENUE DE

⑥

EATING

#80
Ⓑ

Ⓑ #28

MUSEUM
ENTRANCE

⑤ **⑨** ◆

Ⓜ Ecole
Militaire

Place de
l'Ecole Militaire

Ⓜ

㉑

Ⓑ Ⓣ

#82 & 92

#82, 86 & 92

AVE. DE TOURVILLE

Ⓑ #92

To Rodin
Museum

Ⓑ
#28

AVE. DUQUESNE

Ⓑ #92

Place
Vauban

ECOLE
MILITAIRE

#28 &
86
Ⓑ

AVE. LOWENDAL

RUE BIXIO

AVE. DE SEGUR

AVE. DE BRETEUIL

AVE. DE BRETEUIL

Ⓑ
#28 &
86

MARCHE
DE SAXE

Laurent, whose playful ties change daily, gracefully serves one small room of tables and loves to give suggestions. Pascal, his chef of more than 20 years, produces particularly tasty stuffed cabbage (that can feed two), lobster ravioli, and *confit de canard*. The house wine is excellent (closed Sat-Sun, reservations smart, 19 Avenue de la Motte-Picquet, +33 1 45 55 40 38, www.leflorimond.com).

$$$ Bistrot Belhara delivers a vintage French dining experience in an intimate space. Chef-owner Thierry cooks up a blend of inventive and classic dishes and offers a good-value *menu*. Earnest and helpful Frédéric runs the front of the house with a smile (closed Sun-Mon, reservations smart, a block off Rue Cler at 23 Rue Duvivier, +33 1 45 51 41 77, www.bistrotbelhara.com).

$$ Café le Bosquet is a contemporary Parisian brasserie facing a busy street where you'll dine for a decent price inside or outside on a broad sidewalk. Come here for standard café fare—salad, French onion soup, *steak-frites*, or a *plat du jour*. Lanky owner "Jeff" offers three-course meals and *plats* (serves nonstop, closed Sun, corner of Rue du Champ de Mars at 46 Avenue Bosquet, +33 1 45 51 38 13, www.bosquetparis.com).

$$ La Terrasse du 7ème is a sprawling, happening café with grand outdoor seating and a living room-like interior with comfy love seats. Located on a corner, it overlooks a busy intersection with a constant parade of people and traffic. Chairs face the street, as a meal here is like dinner theater—and the show is slice-of-life Paris (nonstop service—and parade of pedestrians—daily until 24:00; good *salades*, French onion soup, and foie gras; 2 Place de L'Ecole Militaire, +33 1 45 55 00 02).

Between Rue de Grenelle and the River, East of Avenue Bosquet

(Mo: La Tour-Maubourg)

$$$$ L'Ami Jean offers authentic Basque specialties in a snug-but-convivial Basque nationalist atmosphere. It's pricey, but portions are hearty and delicious. Parisians detour long distances to savor the gregarious chef's special cuisine and fun atmosphere. Reservations smart (closed Sat-Mon; €80 six-course dinner *menu*, more accessible lunch *menu* for €35; 27 Rue Malar, +33 1 47 05 86 89, www.lamijean.fr).

$$ Bistrot Chez France is a simple place lined with red-velvet booths where the focus is on food, not charming ambience. You must order from the two- or three-course *menu*. Sit back and trust Régis and Arnaud to manage your meal (closed Sun, good choices of classic French cuisine, well-priced and accessible wine options, 9 Rue Amelie, +33 1 40 67 96 54).

$$ O'Brien's Pub is a lively Parisian rendition of an Irish pub/sports bar, where young locals toss darts and order fine red wine

---

Make the Scene on the Seine for Dinner

A 15-minute walk from Rue Cler takes you to Pont Alexandre III and the wonderful riverside promenade along the Seine. Take a ramp near the bridge down to the traffic-free riverside promenade, where you'll find several great eating and drinking options. On a balmy evening this is a terrific—and *très* local—option. The **$ Faust Bar** cranks out drinks and clubby food to a young crowd (daily 12:00 until late, +33 1 44 18 60 60). **$$ Bistrot Alexandre III** is a notch above; you'll dine on a dressy boat, choosing from a fun menu with simple plates and fancy drinks (daily 12:00-24:00, +33 1 47 53 07 07). They have a fancier restaurant under the bridge. Adjacent to these are a couple of crêpe and sandwich bars that serve only in good weather.

---

with their hamburgers or plats (daily, good selection of beer on tap, 77 Rue St. Dominique, +33 1 45 51 75 87). Along with their pubby barroom they have appealing streetside seating.

$$$ Au Petit Tonneau is an endearing French bistro with original, time-warp decor, fleur-de-lis tiled floor, and carefully prepared food from a limited menu. Away from the Rue Cler tourist crush, this place is real, the cuisine is delicious, and the experience—mixing casual with classy—is what you came to France for (closed Mon off-season, good à la carte choices or three-course *menu* that changes with the season, well-priced wines, 20 Rue Surcouf, +33 1 47 05 09 01, charming owner Arlette at your service).

Between Rue de Grenelle and the River, West of Avenue Bosquet
(Mo: Ecole Militaire unless otherwise noted)
Some of these places line peaceful Rue de l'Exposition (a few blocks west of Rue Cler), allowing you to do a quick survey before sitting down.

$$ Le P'tit Troquet is a petite eatery taking you back to the Paris of the 1920s. Anna serves while hubby José cooks a tasty range of traditional choices. The homey charm of the tight and fragile little dining room makes this place a delight (dinner service from 18:30, closed Sun, reservations smart, €40 three-course dinner *menu*, 28 Rue de l'Exposition, +33 1 47 05 80 39, www.leptittroquet.fr).

$$ Café de Mars is a relaxed place where mellow Pierre features creative cuisine that draws from many countries—and half the menu is vegetarian. With its simple setting and fair prices, it feels more designed for neighbors than tourists. It's also comfort-

EATING

able for single diners thanks to its welcoming counter (closed Sun-Mon, 11 Rue Augereau, +33 1 45 50 10 90).

$ Le Royal is a tiny neighborhood fixture offering cheap and simple traditional dishes. This humble place, with prices and decor from another era, comes from an age when cafés sold firewood and served food as an afterthought (closed Sun, 212 Rue de Grenelle, +33 1 47 53 92 90).

Affordable Italian: $$ Ristorante Gusto Italia is fun, tight, and characteristic, serving classic dishes and pizza (daily, two locations—199 Rue de Grenelle and a less-appealing sister across the street, +33 1 45 55 00 43).

Rue St. Dominique Lineup
(Mo: Ecole Militaire or RER/Train-C: Pont de l'Alma)
A terrific string of restaurants gathers a few short blocks from the Eiffel Tower. Find the western end of Rue St. Dominique between Rue Augereau and Rue de l'Exposition for the restaurants below. Each is distinct, offering a different experience and price range. None is really cheap (except for the *crêperie*), but they're all a good value, delivering top-quality cuisine.

$$$ La Fontaine de Mars, a longtime favorite and neighborhood institution, is charmingly situated on a tiny, jumbled square with tables jammed together for the serious business of eating. Reserve in advance for a table on the ground floor or square, but pass on the upstairs room (daily, superb foie gras and desserts, 129 Rue St. Dominique, +33 1 47 05 46 44, www.fontainedemars.com).

$$$$ Le Violon d'Ingres has earned a Michelin star and makes for a good excuse to dress up and dine finely in Paris. Glass doors open onto a serious but accessible eating scene. Service is formal yet helpful (daily, reservations essential, order à la carte or consider their €150 seven-course tasting *menu*, €50 lunch *menu*, 135 Rue St. Dominique, +33 1 45 55 15 05, www.maisonconstant.com).

$$$ Les Cocottes attracts a crowd of in-the-know Parisians and tourists with its foodie energy and trendy-trad dishes served in *cocottes*—small cast-iron pots. There's good outside seating, or sit inside at one of the high tables or the long, inviting bar facing the kitchen action (daily, nonstop service from noon until late, 135 Rue St. Dominique, +33 1 45 50 10 28).

$ Crep' and Tea is a one-woman show with sweet-as-they-get Fatima serving a creative menu of homemade crêpes in her tidy, shoebox-size room with Tetris seating (daily, 139 Rue St. Dominique, +33 1 45 51 70 78).

Picnicking near Rue Cler
Picnics with floodlit views of the Eiffel Tower or along the riverside promenade are *très romantique*, and Rue Cler is a festival of food

Good Picnic Spots

Paris is picnic-friendly. Almost any park will do. Many have benches or grassy areas, though some lawns are off-limits—obey the signs. Parks generally close at dusk, so plan your sunset picnics carefully. Here are some especially scenic areas near major sights (for tips on assembling a picnic in Paris, see page 671).

Palais Royal: Escape to a peaceful courtyard full of relaxing locals across from the Louvre (Mo: Palais Royal-Musée du Louvre). The nearby Louvre courtyard surrounding the pyramid is less tranquil but very handy.

Place des Vosges: Relax in an exquisite grassy courtyard in the Marais, surrounded by royal buildings (Mo: Bastille). Its sandbox is a hit with local toddlers.

Square du Vert-Galant: For great river views, try this little triangular park on the west tip of Ile de la Cité. It's next to the statue of King Henry IV (Mo: Pont Neuf).

Pont des Arts: Munch from a bench on this pedestrian bridge over the Seine near the Louvre (Mo: Pont Neuf).

Riverside Promenades: The embankment areas along the Seine are ideal for picnics. All along the venerable river's stony promenade, you'll see locals spreading out their tablecloths as if sitting for a Monet painting.

Tuileries Garden: Have an Impressionist "Luncheon on the Grass" nestled between the Orsay and Orangerie museums (Mo: Tuileries).

Luxembourg Garden: The classic Paris picnic spot, with plenty of green metal chairs and benches, is this expansive Left Bank park (Mo: Odéon).

Les Invalides: Take a break from the Army Museum and Napoleon's Tomb in the gardens behind the complex (Mo: Varenne).

Champ de Mars: The long, grassy strip beneath the Eiffel Tower has breathtaking views of this Paris icon, but I prefer to grab a bench in the smaller, side park areas (Mo: Ecole Militaire).

EATING

just waiting to be celebrated. For an unforgettable picnic dinner, assemble it in no fewer than five shops on Rue Cler. For less character and more efficiency, there are several handy supermarkets with long hours. Carrefour City at the Ecole Militaire Métro is open 24/7 (yes, really, even in France!). You'll also find good grocery stores next to the recommended Hôtel la Bourdonnais (Avenue de la Bourdonnais) and Hôtel Relais Bosquet (Rue du Champ de Mars). A small, late-night grocery is at 197 Rue de Grenelle. If a picnic is too much work, delis (such as Traiteur Jeusselin at 37 Rue Cler, open until 19:00) sell fine hot meals to go.

Nightlife in Rue Cler

This sleepy neighborhood was not made for night owls—with a few notable exceptions. The focal point of before- and after-dinner posing occurs along the broad sidewalk at the intersection of Avenues de la Motte-Picquet and Tourville (Mo: Ecole Militaire). **Le Tourville** and **Café des Officiers** gather a sea of outward-facing seats for the important business of people-watching.

La Terrasse du 7ème, across the avenue, has a less pretentious clientele and is often busy until midnight (listed earlier). On Rue Cler, **Café du Marché** (listed earlier) attracts a Franco-American café crowd until at least midnight, though the younger-in-spirit **L'Eclair** cocktail café and bistro (listed earlier) rocks it until late. **Café Roussillon** has a French pubby atmosphere in its bar area at the corner of Rue de Grenelle and Rue Cler. **O'Brien's Pub** (also listed earlier) is a sports bar with dartboards and sports on the screens.

If it's a balmy evening, I'd hike down to the riverside and enjoy the bar scene under Pont Alexandre III, where several lively places serve drinks and fun until the wee hours (see the "Make the Scene on the Seine for Dinner" sidebar, earlier).

MARAIS

The trendy Marais is filled with diners enjoying fine food in colorful and atmospheric eateries. The scene—gay, fun, and creative—is competitive and changes all the time. I've listed an assortment of places—all handy to recommended hotels—that offer good food at decent prices, plus a memorable experience.

On Romantic Place des Vosges
(Mo: St-Paul or Bastille)

This square offers Old World Marais elegance, a handful of eateries, and an ideal picnic site until dusk, when the park closes. Strolling around the arcade after dark is more important than dining here—fanciful art galleries alternate with restaurants and cafés. Choose a restaurant that best fits your mood and budget; most have arcade seating and provide big space heaters to make outdoor dining during colder months an option. Also  consider just a drink on the square at Café Hugo.

$$ La Place Royale, offering a traditional menu and an exceptional location on the square—with comfortable seating inside or out—is good for a relaxed lunch or dinner. Come here for the setting and snag an outdoor table under the arches. The hearty cuisine is priced well and served nonstop all day, and Arnaud's lengthy wine list is reasonable. Splitting a large salad and ordering two main courses works well for two diners (daily, reserve ahead to dine outside under the arcade, lunch specials, 2 bis Place des Vosges, +33 1 42 78 58 16).

$ Café Hugo, named for the square's most famous resident, serves salads and basic café fare with a Parisian energy. The food's just OK, but the setting's terrific, with good seating under the arches (daily, 22 Place des Vosges, +33 1 42 72 64 04).

Near Place des Vosges
(Mo: Chemin Vert)

$$ Chez Janou, a Provençal bistro, tumbles out of its corner building and fills its broad sidewalk with happy eaters. Don't let the trendy, youthful crowd and the density of diners intimidate you: It's relaxed and charming, with helpful and patient service. The curbside tables are inviting, but I'd sit inside (with very tight seating) to immerse myself in the happy commotion. The style is French

Mediterranean, with an emphasis on vegetables (daily—book ahead or arrive when it opens at 19:00, 2 blocks beyond Place des Vosges at 2 Rue Roger Verlomme, +33 1 42 72 28 41, www.chezjanou.com). They serve 81 varieties of *pastis* (licorice-flavored liqueur, browse the list above the bar).

$$ Le Petit Marché, popular with tourists and locals, delivers a warm bistro experience inside and out with friendly service and a tasty cuisine that blends French classics with an Asian influence (smart to book a day ahead, daily, 9 Rue du Béarn, +33 1 42 72 06 67, www.lepetitmarche.eu).

Near Place de la Bastille
(Mo: Bastille or St-Paul)

$$ Brasserie Bofinger, an institution for over a century, specializes in seafood and traditional cuisine with Alsatian flair. You'll eat in a sprawling interior, surrounded by brisk, black-and-white-attired waiters. Come here for the one-of-a-kind ambience in the elaborately decorated ground-floor rooms, reminiscent of the Roaring Twenties. Reserve ahead to dine under the grand 1919 *coupole* (*sous le dôme;* "soo luh dohm") and avoid eating upstairs. If you've always wanted one of those pricey picturesque multitiered seafood platters, this is a good place, though the Alsatian dishes are far

EATING

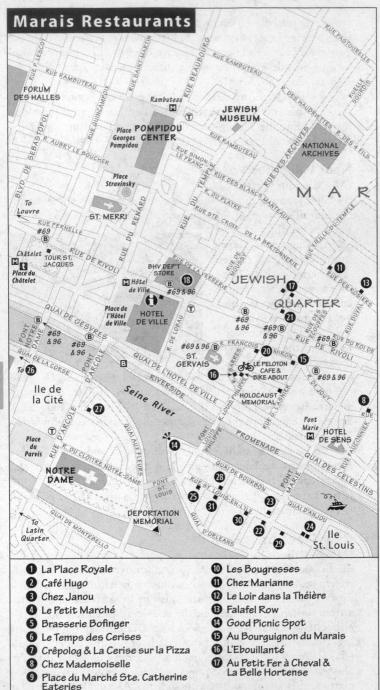

Marais Restaurants

1. La Place Royale
2. Café Hugo
3. Chez Janou
4. Le Petit Marché
5. Brasserie Bofinger
6. Le Temps des Cerises
7. Crêpolog & La Cerise sur la Pizza
8. Chez Mademoiselle
9. Place du Marché Ste. Catherine Eateries
10. Les Bougresses
11. Chez Marianne
12. Le Loir dans la Théière
13. Falafel Row
14. Good Picnic Spot
15. Au Bourguignon du Marais
16. L'Ebouillanté
17. Au Petit Fer à Cheval & La Belle Hortense

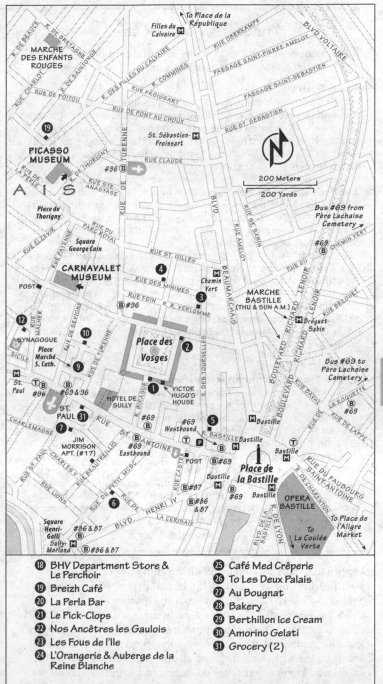

⑱ BHV Department Store & Le Perchoir
⑲ Breizh Café
⑳ La Perla Bar
㉑ Le Pick-Clops
㉒ Nos Ancêtres les Gaulois
㉓ Les Fous de l'Ile
㉔ L'Orangerie & Auberge de la Reine Blanche
㉕ Café Med Crêperie
㉖ To Les Deux Palais
㉗ Au Bougnat
㉘ Bakery
㉙ Berthillon Ice Cream
㉚ Amorino Gelati
㉛ Grocery (2)

The Paris Food Scene

To dig deeper into the food scene in Paris, consider a culinary walking tour or a class. These are just a few of the many available.

Food Tours

Some of my "Cooking Classes" listings also offer food tours.

Paris by Mouth offers well-respected yet casual small-group tours, with a maximum of seven foodies per group. Tours are organized by location, street market, or flavor and led by local food writers (€110/3 hours, includes tastings, www.parisbymouth.com, tasteparisbymouth@gmail.com).

Friendly Canadian Rosa Jackson designs personalized **Edible Paris** itineraries based on your interests. She and her colleagues also lead three-hour "food-guru" tours of Paris (unguided itineraries—€125-200, guided tours—€300 for 1-2 people, larger groups welcome, mobile +33 6 81 67 41 22, www.edible-paris. com, rosa@rosajackson.com).

Le Food Trip helps travelers create their own gourmet food tour by connecting them with local artisans and shopkeepers. Sign up online and get a Tasting Passport booklet with a good orientation to French foods, a map, and locations of shops where you'll be welcomed like a local. The pass includes a choice of 6-12 different products, from cassoulet to croissants to croque monsieurs and even Champagne (from €35, valid for 1 year, www.le-food-trip.com).

Cooking Classes

At **Les Secrets Gourmands de Noémie,** charming and knowledgeable Noémie shares her culinary secrets with hands-on fun. Classes are designed for French or English speakers and can be in both languages, depending on the participants (€85-140, possible add-on market tour, 92 Rue Nollet, Mo: La Fourche, mobile +33 6 64 17 93 32, www.lessecretsgourmandsdenoemie.com).

Cook'n with Class offers a range of convivial classes on breads, macarons, croissants, wine and cheese, and more—including market visits—with a maximum of six students. Tasting courses are offered as well (6-hour class—€200, multiday classes available, 6 Rue Baudelique, Mo: Jules Joffrin or Simplon, mobile +33 6 31 73 62 77, www.cooknwithclass.com/paris).

cheaper (open daily for lunch and dinner, fun kids' menu, 5 Rue de la Bastille, don't be confused by the lesser "Petite" Bofinger across the street, +33 1 42 72 87 82, www.bofingerparis.com).

$$ Le Temps des Cerises is a warm place with wads of character, a young and lively vibe, tight inside seating, and a couple of outdoor tables. (There are a few more upstairs that I'd avoid.) Come for a glass of wine at the small zinc bar, and stay for a very tasty dinner. Owner Ben takes good care of his guests and serves

La Cuisine Paris has a great variety of classes in English, reasonable prices, and a beautiful space in central Paris (€70-100, €165 for 4-hour class with market tour, also offers gourmet visit to Versailles, 80 Quai de l'Hôtel de Ville, +33 1 40 51 78 18, www.lacuisineparis.com).

REED is the creation of Catherine Reed, who also runs REED restaurant, a few blocks from Rue Cler. Classes are limited to eight students and focus on practical skills—basic techniques and classic French gastronomy (€155, Sun and Wed at 10:30, 11 Rue Amelie, +33 1 45 55 88 40).

For an upscale demonstration course, try **Le Cordon Bleu** (+33 1 53 68 22 50, www.lcbparis.com) or **Ritz Escoffier Ecole de Gastronomie** (+33 1 43 16 30 50, www.ritzparis.com).

Food and Wine Tasting

Many cooking outfits offer wine-tasting options, but **Ô Château** is decidedly wine-centric. Its team of sommeliers teach wine-tasting—in English—in the 18th-century residence of Madame de Pompadour. Their goal is to "take the snob out of wine" with informative but easygoing classes that teach the basics of French wine regions, the techniques of tasting, and how to read a French wine label. Classes include an introductory tasting with six wines and Champagne (€65, add €10 for a charcuterie plate). Register online using code "RS2023" for a 10 percent discount, or check the website for last-minute deals (tastings last about 2 hours, 12 people max, 68 Rue Jean-Jacques Rousseau, Mo: Louvre-Rivoli or Etienne Marcel, +33 1 44 73 97 80, www.o-chateau.com).

Le Cheese Geek delivers fun and informative cheese tastings. Using quizzes, charm, and sometimes blindfolds, owner Fabrice and his cheesemonger crew demystify a food the French take very seriously. They pair six seasonal cheeses with three beverages—not just wine but also cider, beer, liqueur, or juice, depending on the cheese (2-hour class—€70, 31 Rue Ste. Marthe, Mo: Belleville, mobile +33 7 82 03 50 03, www.lecheesegeek.com).

With **Eatwith,** you'll join a community of food and travel lovers seeking an insider's dining experience. Enjoy a meal with a Parisian family, a cooking class, a food tour, or a pop-up food event hosted by friendly locals (www.eatwith.com).

generous portions (daily, reasonable wine list, at the corner of Rue du Petit Musc and Rue de la Cerisaie, 31 Rue de la Cerisaie, +33 1 42 72 08 63).

$ Crêpes and Pizza: Two tiny budget finds are open daily and sit side by side where Rue St. Paul meets Rue Neuve St. Pierre. Both are open daily and have good but limited seating inside and out. **Crêpolog** dishes out a tasty range of appetizer, main course, and dessert crêpes using fresh batter, and offers a good three-course *menu* (Mo: St-Paul, +33 1 43 48 28 34). At **La Cerise sur la Pizza** ("Cherry on the Pizza"), Marko fires up Marseille-style pizza (eat there or take it to go, Mo: St-Paul, +33 1 42 78 15 59).

In the Heart of the Marais
(Mo: St-Paul)

$$$ **Chez Mademoiselle**'s eclectic decor and fun energy recall charming owner Alexia's previous career as a French *comédienne*. This local favorite comes with lots of noise, so it's best for a fun night out. Dine inside or at a sidewalk table. Ingredients are fresh and prepared simply. Let the easygoing staff share their enthusiasm for the seasonal dishes before you choose (daily from 19:30, good wine list, 16 Rue Charlemagne, +33 1 42 72 14 16).

$$ **On Place du Marché Ste. Catherine:** This small, romantic square, just off Rue St. Antoine, is cloaked in extremely Parisian, leafy-square ambience. It feels like the Latin Quarter but classier. On a balmy evening, it's a neighborhood favorite, with a handful of restaurants offering mediocre cuisine (you're here for the setting). It's also family-friendly: Most places serve French hamburgers, and kids can dance around the square while parents relax. Survey the square. You'll find several French bistros with similar features and menus. **Le Marché** is a good choice.

$$ **Les Bougresses,** just off the charming square, offers less romance but far more taste and a fine three-course *menu* for under €30. Stepping inside this cozy place, you feel like you've joined a food lovers' party with owners Mika and Constantin overseeing the fun (closed Mon, open from 18:30, inside seating only, 6 Rue de Jarente, +33 1 48 87 71 21).

In the Jewish Quarter, Rue des Rosiers
(Mo: St-Paul or Hôtel de Ville)

$$ **Chez Marianne** is a neighborhood fixture that serves tasty Jewish cuisine in a fun atmosphere with Parisian *élan*. Choose an indoor spot with a cluttered wine shop/deli feeling, or sit outside. You'll select from a list of hot and cold *zakouskis* (like Jewish tapas or mezes, about €4 each) to assemble your *plat*. It's Jewish "diaspora cuisine"—from Israel to Iberia to Poland. Vegetarians will find great options (long hours daily, takeaway falafel sandwiches, 2 Rue des Hospitalières St. Gervais—at the corner with Rue des Rosiers, +33 1 42 72 18 86).

$$ **Le Loir dans la Théière** ("The Dormouse in the Teapot"— think Alice in Wonderland) is a cozy, mellow teahouse offering a welcoming ambience for tired travelers (laptops and smartphones are not welcome). It's ideal for lunch but slammed on weekends. They offer a daily assortment of creatively filled quiches and bake an impressive array of homemade desserts that are proudly dis-

played in the dining room (daily 9:00-19:00 but only dessert-type items offered after 15:00, 3 Rue des Rosiers, +33 1 42 72 90 61).

$ Falafel Row is a series of inexpensive joints serving filling falafel sandwiches (and other Jewish dishes to go or to eat in) that line Rue des Rosiers between Rue des Ecouffes and Rue Vieille du Temple. Take a stroll along this short stretch to compare, then decide. Their takeout services draw a constant crowd (long hours most days, most are closed Fri evening and all day Sat).

Close to Hôtel de Ville
(Mo: Hôtel de Ville)

$$$ Au Bourguignon du Marais is a dressy wine bar/bistro for Burgundy lovers, where excellent wines (Burgundian only, available by the glass) blend

with a good selection of well-designed dishes and efficient service. The *œufs en meurette* are mouthwatering and the *bœuf bourguignon* could feed two. English-fluent Vincent runs the place with panache (daily, pleasing indoor and outdoor seating on a perfect Marais corner, 52 Rue François Miron, +33 1 48 87 15 40).

$ L'Ebouillanté is a breezy café, romantically situated near the river on a broad, cobbled pedestrian lane behind a church. With great outdoor seating on flimsy chairs and an artsy interior, it's good for an inexpensive and relaxing tea, snack, or lunch—or, when open, for dinner on a warm evening. Their *bricks*—paper-thin, Tunisian-inspired pancakes stuffed with what you would typically find in an omelet—come with a small salad (daily 12:00-21:30, closes earlier in winter, a block off the river at 6 Rue des Barres, +33 1 42 74 70 52).

$$ Au Petit Fer à Cheval, serving fairly priced, standard café fare, seems tailor-made for memories. The horseshoe-shaped zinc bar, which feels like a movie set, immerses you in the clatter of the scene. The tight dining room in the rear is Old World adorable—a tobacco-stained Cubist time warp. And the few outdoor tables offer classic café seating—street-theater perfect (daily, 30 Rue Vieille du Temple, +33 1 42 72 47 47).

$ BHV Department Store's fifth-floor cafeteria, La Kantine, provides nice views, good prices, and many main courses to choose from, with a salad bar, pizza by the slice, and pasta. It's family-easy (daily 11:00-19:00, hot food served until 16:00, open later Wed, at intersection of Rue du Temple and Rue de la Verrerie, one block from Hôtel de Ville).

Close to Rue de Bretagne
(Mo: Filles du Calvaire or Rambuteau)

$$ Breizh Café is worth the hike for some of the best Breton crêpes in Paris ("Breizh" means Brittany). This simple joint serves organic crêpes—both sweet and savory—and small rolls made for dipping in rich sauces and salted butter. They talk about cider like a sommelier would talk about wine. Try a sparkling cider, a Breton cola, or my favorite—*lait ribot,* a buttermilk-like drink (closed Mon, serves nonstop 11:30-late, reservations highly recommended, 109 Rue du Vieille du Temple, +33 1 42 72 13 77, https://commande. breizhcafe.com).

Picnicking in the Marais

Picnic at peaceful Place des Vosges (closes at dusk), Square George Caïn (near the Carnavalet Museum), or on the Ile St. Louis *quais*. Stretch your euros at the basement supermarket of the **Monoprix** department store (closed Sun, near Place des Vosges on Rue St. Antoine). You'll find a small **grocery** open until 23:00 on Ile St. Louis.

Nightlife in the Marais

Trendy cafés and bars—popular with gay men—cluster on Rue des Archives and Rue Ste. Croix de la Bretonnerie. There's also a line of bars and cafés providing front-row seats for the buff parade on Rue Vieille du Temple, a block north of Rue de Rivoli—the horseshoe-shaped **Au Petit Fer à Cheval** bar (see earlier) and the atmospheric **La Belle Hortense** bookstore/wine bar are the focal points of the action. Nearby, Rue des Rosiers bustles with youthful energy, but there are no cafés to observe from. **La Perla** dishes up imitation Tex-Mex and is stuffed with Parisian millennials in search of the perfect margarita (26 Rue François Myron, +33 1 42 77 59 40).

Le Pick-Clops bar-restaurant is a happy peanuts-and-lots-of-cocktails diner with bright neon, loud colors, and a garish local crowd. It's perfect for immersing yourself in today's Marais world—a little boisterous, a little edgy, fun-loving, and easygoing. Sit inside on old-fashioned diner stools or street-side to watch the constant Marais parade (daily 7:00-24:00, 16 Rue Vieille du Temple, +33 1 40 29 02 18). While it's mostly a drinking place, its fun, eclectic menu of French bar food (burgers, tartines, salads), all seasoned with a happy dollop of Marais character, is tempting.

Le Perchoir, a rooftop bar atop the BHV department store, owns the best Marais view over Paris, but expect pricey drinks and appetizers—and crowds, particularly in good weather (Mon-Sat

20:15 until late, Sun from 19:15, access is from a separate elevator at the BHV entrance, 37 Rue de la Verrerie).

More Options: The best scene for hard-core clubbers is the dizzying array of wacky eateries, bars, and dance halls on **Rue de Lappe.** Just east of the stately Place de la Bastille, it's one of the wildest nightspots in Paris and not for everyone.

The most enjoyable peaceful evening may be simply mentally donning your floppy "three musketeers" hat and slowly strolling **Place des Vosges,** window shopping the art galleries.

ILE ST. LOUIS
(Mo: Pont Marie)

This romantic and peaceful neighborhood merits a trip for dinner even if your hotel is elsewhere. Cruise the island's main street for a variety of options, and after dinner, sample Paris' favorite ice cream before strolling across to Ile de la Cité to see a floodlit Notre-Dame. These recommended spots—ranging from rowdy to petite, rustic to elegant—line the island's main drag, Rue St. Louis-en-l'Ile (for locations, see the "Marais Restaurants" map, earlier).

$$ Nos Ancêtres les Gaulois ("Our Ancestors the Gauls"), famous for its rowdy, medieval-cellar atmosphere, is made for hun-

gry warriors and wenches who like to swill hearty wine. For dinner they serve up rustic, all-you-can-eat fare with straw baskets of raw veggies and bundles of *saucisson* (cut whatever you like with your dagger), plates of pâté, a meat course, cheese, a dessert, and all the wine you can stomach for about €40. The food is perfectly edible; burping is encouraged. If you want to overeat, drink too much wine, be surrounded by tourists (mostly French), and holler at your friends while receiving smart-aleck buccaneer service, you're home. If you stay later, the atmosphere progresses from sloppy to frat party (daily, 39 Rue St. Louis-en-l'Ile, +33 1 46 33 66 07).

$$ Les Fous de l'Ile is a tasty, lighthearted mash-up of a collector's haunt, art gallery, and bistro. It's a fun place to eat bistro fare with gourmet touches for a good price (daily, 2- or 3-course *menus* or *plat du jour* only, 33 Rue des Deux Ponts, +33 1 43 25 76 67).

$$ L'Orangerie is an inviting, rustic yet elegant place with soft lighting, comfortable spacious seating, and a hushed ambience. The cuisine blends traditional with modern touches (closed Mon, 28 Rue St. Louis-en-l'Ile, +33 1 85 15 21 31).

Riverside Picnic for Impoverished Romantics

On sunny lunchtimes and balmy evenings, the *quai* on the Left Bank side of Ile St. Louis is lined with locals who have more class than money, spreading out tablecloths and even lighting candles for elegant picnics. And tourists can enjoy the same budget meal. A handy grocery store at #67 on the main drag (closed Tue) has tabbouleh and other simple, cheap takeaway dishes for your picnicking pleasure. The bakery at #80 serves quiche and pizza (open until 20:00) .

$ Auberge de la Reine Blanche—woodsy, cozy, and tight—welcomes diners willing to rub elbows with their neighbors. Earnest owner Michel offers basic French cuisine at reasonable prices. Along with like-mother-made-it comfort food, he serves good dinner salads (opens at 18:30, closed Mon, 30 Rue St. Louis-en-l'Ile, +33 1 85 15 21 30).

$ Café Med Crêperie, near the pedestrian bridge to Notre-Dame, is a tiny, cheery place with good-value salads, crêpes, pasta, and several meat dishes (daily, 77 Rue St. Louis-en-l'Ile, +33 1 43 29 73 17). Two less atmospheric *crêperies* are just across the street.

Ice Cream Dessert: Half the people strolling Ile St. Louis are licking an ice cream cone because this is the home of the famous *les glaces Berthillon* (now sold throughout Paris, though still made here on Ile St. Louis). The original **Berthillon** shop, at 31 Rue St. Louis-en-l'Ile, is marked by the line of salivating customers (closed Mon-Tue). For a less famous but still satisfying treat, the Italian gelato a block away at **Amorino Gelati** is giving Berthillon competition (daily until late, no line, bigger portions, easier to see what you want, and they offer small tastes—Berthillon doesn't need to, 47 Rue St. Louis-en-l'Ile, +33 1 44 07 48 08). Having a little of each is not a bad thing.

ILE DE LA CITÉ

These two eateries are near Notre-Dame and Sainte-Chapelle on Ile de la Cité.

$$ Les Deux Palais is a venerable old-school bistro with lamps, mirrors, vests, and ambience that takes you back to the 1870s. With professional service, decent prices, and a convenient location facing Sainte-Chapelle (across from the exit), it's handy for lunch or a drink while sightseeing (daily until 21:00, 3 Boulevard du Palais—see the map on page 124, +33 1 34 54 20 86).

$$ Au Bougnat delivers traditional cuisine at very fair prices with oodles of character. It's a short hop from Notre-Dame and where local cops and workers get sandwiches, coffee, and reasonably priced *menus* (daily, 26 Rue Chanoinesse, +33 1 43 54 50 74).

LUXEMBOURG GARDEN AREA

Sleeping in the Luxembourg neighborhood puts you near many appealing dining and after-hours options. Because my hotels cluster near St. Sulpice Church, the Panthéon, and Rue de Sèvres, I've focused my restaurant picks in the same areas. Restaurants around St. Sulpice tend to be boisterous, while those near the Panthéon and Rue de Sèvres are calmer. It's a short walk from one area to the other.

Restaurant Row Streets near St. Sulpice Church
(Mo: St-Sulpice or St-Germain-des-Près)

Rue des Canettes and **Rue Guisarde** teem with busy eateries offering a lively selection of low-brow cuisine at generally affordable prices. It's hard to recommend one over the next, but it's a fun neighborhood to browse—offering what many hope to find in the Latin Quarter (but don't).

Two Rue Guisarde places stand out from the rest for a good meal: **$$ Monte Verdi** serves dressy Italian cuisine with live piano music and is a fun change from traditional French dining. There are several rooms, each offering a different experience. One is romantic, with cushy seating and the piano close by (book ahead for this room); others offer a "barstools and friends" vibe or cozy seating under beams by a fireplace (closed Sun, 5 Rue Guisarde, +33 1 42 34 55 90, www.lemonteverdi.com). **$$$ Chez Fernand** is a solid choice for a great range of classic and beefy bistro fare, with long, tight rows of seating and red-checkered tablecloths. The volume goes up as you go deeper into the restaurant—a high-energy immersion in happy French dining (Tue-Sun 19:00-late, closed Mon, 13 Rue Guisarde, +33 1 43 54 61 47).

On Rue des Canettes you'll find a down-and-dirty bar, **Chez Georges,** with a dank cellar for a drink before or after dinner (#11). If you're feeling bohemian, you could play chess or talk philosophy over a dinner of cold cuts with wine here.

$$ Pizza Chic is an almost elegant pizza joint with a good vibe that's popular with locals. It's a family-friendly place serving delicious, wood-fired pizza (daily, 13 Rue de Mézières, +33 1 45 48 30 38).

A block north of Boulevard St. Germain (toward the river), **Rue de Buci** has a lineup of bars, cafés, and bistros targeted toward a young, trendy

EATING

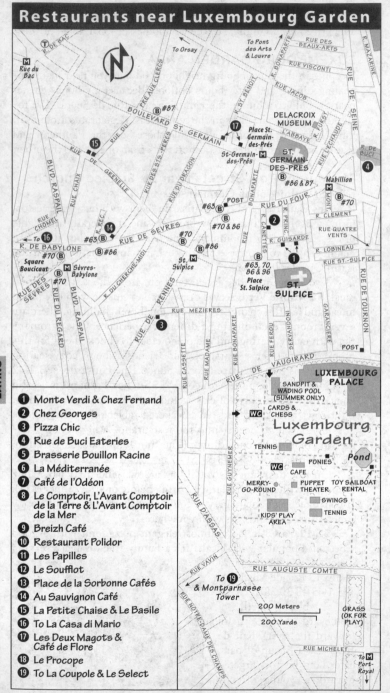

Restaurants near Luxembourg Garden

EATING

1. Monte Verdi & Chez Fernand
2. Chez Georges
3. Pizza Chic
4. Rue de Buci Eateries
5. Brasserie Bouillon Racine
6. La Méditerranée
7. Café de l'Odéon
8. Le Comptoir, L'Avant Comptoir de la Terre & L'Avant Comptoir de la Mer
9. Breizh Café
10. Restaurant Polidor
11. Les Papilles
12. Le Soufflot
13. Place de la Sorbonne Cafés
14. Au Sauvignon Café
15. La Petite Chaise & Le Basile
16. To La Casa di Mario
17. Les Deux Magots & Café de Flore
18. Le Procope
19. To La Coupole & Le Select

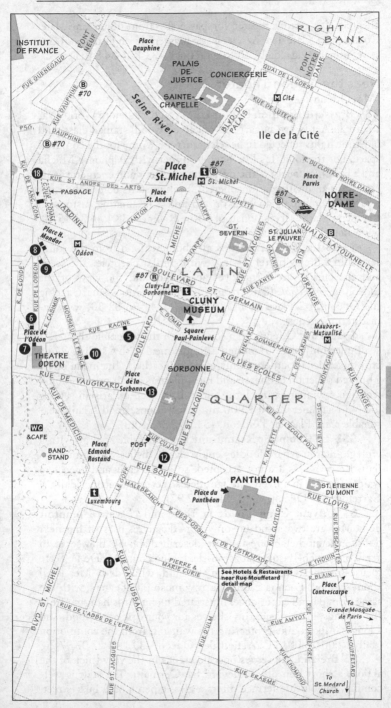

EATING

clientele. It's terrific theater for passersby from 18:00 until late. Consider **$$ Café de Paris,** a classic brasserie with hearty and creative dinner salads (daily, 10 Rue de Buci, +33 1 46 34 84 11).

Near the Odéon Theater
(Mo: Odéon)

$$$ Brasserie Bouillon Racine takes you back before World War I with an Art Nouveau carnival of carved wood, stained glass, and old-time lights reflected in beveled mirrors. Come for the convivial space, not the food. It's like having dinner with Alphonse Mucha and a bunch of tourists. The over-the-top decor and energetic waiters give it an inviting atmosphere. Check upstairs before choosing a table. There's Belgian beer on tap and a fascinating history on the menu (daily, serves nonstop, 3 Rue Racine, +33 1 44 32 15 60, www.bouillon-racine.com).

$$$$ La Méditerranée is all about seafood from the south served in a dressy pastel setting...with similar clientele. The scene and the cuisine are formal yet accessible, and the view of the Odéon is *formidable* (daily from 19:30, reservations smart, facing the Odéon at 2 Place de l'Odéon, +33 1 43 26 02 30, www.la-mediterranee.com).

$ Café de l'Odéon, on a square with the venerable theater, is a summer-only place to munch a simple meal with a stylish young crowd (service is outdoors-only in good weather). The menu offers a limited selection of cheese and meat platters at fair prices—you'll feel like a winner eating light but well in such a Parisian setting (daily in summer 12:00-23:00, no reservations, good salads, reasonable *plats,* Place de l'Odéon, +33 7 72 36 69 13).

$$$ Le Comptoir Restaurant is a venerable splurge with a vintage interior where foodies enjoy classic dishes with a modern flair. Reservations are not accepted, so arrive early and expect to wait for a table in a lively and jammed street-front setting (daily, 9 Carrefour de l'Odéon, +33 1 44 27 07 97).

$$ L'Avant Comptoir de la Terre and **L'Avant Comptoir de la Mer** are two stand-up-only hors d'oeuvres bars sitting next door to the mothership restaurant (described above). They serve an array of French-Basque tapas on sleek zinc counters. De la Terre focuses on meats and food from the land, while de la Mer is all about seafood. Each is a long, narrow mosh pit of eaters, with the same formula and experience: illustrated menu cards hanging from the ceilings, loud music, tiny shelves for your drink and food, and a long bar like a dike protecting the waitstaff from the commotion (daily 12:00-23:00, 3 Carrefour de l'Odéon, +33 1 44 27 07 97).

$$ Breizh Café serves upscale crêpes in the very thick of the action, a short hop off Boulevard St. Germain. The staff is welcoming, the outside terrace offers a classic perch on a busy street, and the interior has a stone-wall-and-oak-floor warmth. If tables are full, snag a spot at the bar (limited choices, daily, reservations smart, 1 Rue de l'Odéon, +33 1 42 49 34 73, www.breizhcafe.com).

$ Restaurant Polidor is the Parisian equivalent of a beloved neighborhood diner. A fixture here since 1845, it's much loved for its unpretentious quality cooking, lively old-Paris atmosphere, and fair value. Noisy, happy diners sit tightly at shared tables, savoring classic bourgeois *plats* from every corner of France. The drawers you see at the back on the left? They held napkins for regulars. The back room is quieter and less memorable (daily 12:00-14:30 & 19:00-23:00, reservations smart, 41 Rue Monsieur-le-Prince, +33 1 43 26 95 34, www.polidor.com).

Between the Panthéon and the Cluny Museum
(Mo: Cluny La Sorbonne or RER/Train-B: Luxembourg)

$$$ Les Papilles is worth the walk. You'll dine surrounded by bottles of wine in a warm, woody bistro and eat what's offered... and you won't complain. It's one *menu*, no choices, and no regrets. Select your wine from the shelf or ask for advice from the burly, rugby-playing owner, then relax and let the food arrive. Reserve ahead and make sure that you're OK with what he's cooking (closed Sun-Mon, 30 Rue Gay Lussac, +33 1 43 25 20 79, www.lespapillesparis.fr).

$$ Le Soufflot, named after the architect of the Panthéon, delivers dynamite views of the inspiring dome. Dine on café cuisine or just enjoy a drink (16 Rue Soufflot, +33 1 43 26 57 56).

Cafés on Place de la Sorbonne: Several cafés are on an appealing little square surrounding a gurgling fountain and facing Paris' legendary Sorbonne University—just a block from the Cluny Museum. **$$ Café de l'Ecritoire** is handy for a simple brasserie lunch with salads, *plats du jour*, and seating inside and out.

Near Sèvres-Babylone
(Mo: Sèvres-Babylone)

$$ Au Sauvignon Café is perfectly positioned for a good lunch or predinner drink and people-watching. The marvelous interior is vintage Paris, with wall-to-ceiling decor and a fine zinc bar (daily, 80 Rue des Saints-Pères, +33 1 45 48 49 02).

$$ La Petite Chaise, founded in 1680, is Paris' oldest restaurant (which alone justifies the trip here for me). Offering a good selection of generous, traditional dishes at reasonable prices, this friendly place appeals to those in search of a classic Parisian dining experience that won't break the bank. Dine in a smaller, characteristic room downstairs or the more elegant upstairs space (good three-course dinner *menu*, daily, 36 Rue de Grenelle, +33 1 42 22 13 35).

$$ La Casa di Mario offers delicious Italian cuisine served by friendly staff in a tight but adorable dining room where you'll get to know your neighbor (closed Sun-Mon, 132 Rue du Bac, +33 1 45 48 76 25).

$ Le Basile is full of young, loud, and happy eaters thrilled to have found a place where drinks are cheap and nothing on the menu costs more than €17 (open daily from 7:00, food served Mon-Fri 12:00-23:00, Sat-Sun closes at 19:00, 34 Rue de Grenelle, +33 1 42 22 59 46).

On or near Rue Mouffetard
(Mo: Censier Daubenton or Place Monge)
Several blocks behind the Panthéon, Rue Mouffetard is a conveyor belt of comparison-shopping eaters with wall-to-wall budget options (fondue, crêpes, Italian, falafel, and Greek). Come here to sift through the crowds and eat cheaply. This street stays up late and likes to party. For locations, see the map on page 429.

The **Rue Mouffetard eateries** gauntlet begins on top, at thriving Place de la Contrescarpe, and ends below where Rue Mouffetard stops at St. Médard Church. Both ends offer fun cafés where you can watch the action. The upper stretch is pedestrian and touristy; the bottom stretch is purely Parisian. Anywhere between is no-man's-land for consistent quality. Still, strolling with so many fun-seekers is enjoyable. A five-minute walk from Place de la Contrescarpe are the ruins of a Roman amphitheater, *Les arênes de Lutèce*, which make for a quiet picnic spot with local kids.

If you're undecided, my recommendations below are solid choices.

$$ Cave de Bourgogne, a local hangout, has reasonably priced café fare at the bottom of Rue Mouffetard. The outside has picture-perfect tables; the lively interior has heaps of character (daily, 144 Rue Mouffetard, +33 1 47 07 82 80).

$$ Restaurant la Mosquée transports diners to Morocco with its dazzling Arabic ambience and cuisine at fair prices. It's tucked into the back of the Grande Mosquée de Paris (see the Sights in Paris chapter) and serves tasty baked goods, teas, and even tastier meals—including several varieties of couscous and tagine (tea room daily 9:00-late, restaurant opens at 11:30, 39 Rue Geoffroy-Saint-Hilaire, +33 1 43 31 38 20).

MONTMARTRE

Montmartre can be hit or miss; the top of the hill is extremely touristy, with mindless mobs following guides to cancan shows. But if you walk a few blocks away, you'll find a quieter, more authentic meal at one of the places I've listed below. For locations, see the map on page 430.

Near Sacré-Cœur
(Mo: Abbesses or Anvers)

The steps in front of Sacré-Cœur are fun for a picnic with a view, though the spot is jammed with tourists. For a quieter setting, consider the park directly behind the church. Along the touristy main drag (near Place du Tertre and just off it), several piano bars serve mediocre crêpes and overpriced bistro fare but offer great people-watching. The options become less touristy and more tasty as you escape from the top of the hill.

$$$ **Le Moulin de la Galette** is a fine place to dine *chez* Renoir under the famous windmill. Along with the stylish decor, there's well-respected classic French cuisine (daily, 83 Rue Lepic, +33 1 46 06 84 77).

$$$ **Le Coq & Fils** venerates poultry. The proud chef serves Paris' best roast chicken, pigeon, or duck—slow cooked for three hours, then roasted and served with tasty fries and terrific desserts. Sharing a whole bird is best. No red meat or vegetarian options (daily, reservations smart, 98 Rue Lepic, +33 1 42 59 82 89, https://lecoq-fils.com).

$ **L'Eté en Pente Douce** is a good budget choice, hiding under some trees just downhill from the crowds on a classic neighborhood corner. It features cheery indoor and outdoor seating, cheap *plats du jour* and salads, vegetarian options, and good wines (daily, many steps below Sacré-Cœur to the left as you leave, 8 Rue Paul Albert, +33 1 42 64 02 67).

EATING

Near Place des Abbesses
(Mo: Abbesses unless otherwise noted)

Halfway down Montmartre's hill, residents pile into a long line-up of brasseries and cafés near Place des Abbesses. Locals tend to gravitate to the cafés on the north side of Rue des Abbesses, leaving the sunnier and pricier cafés on the south side to visitors. Come here for a lively, less touristy scene. Rue des Abbesses is good for café lounging and a picnic-gathering stroll with cheese shops, delis, wine stores, and bakeries. In fact, the bakers at **Grenier à Pain** (closed Tue-Wed, 38 Rue des Abbesses) and at **Au Levain d'Antan** (closed Sat-Sun, 6 Rue des Abbesses) have won an award for the best baguette in Paris.

$ Coquelicot is part bakery, part café, serving fine baked goods and simple, reasonably priced meals from an ideal setting either inside, upstairs, or outside (Tue-Sun until 20:00, closed Mon, 24 Rue des Abbesses, +33 1 46 06 18 77).

$$ Le Progrès is straight out of a movie, with a vintage wood-paneled interior and reasonably priced cuisine (daily, 7 Rue des Trois Frères, +33 1 42 64 07 37).

$$ Le Village is a dive bar turned trendy, serving tiny cups of espresso to garbage collectors in the morning and to mustached nonconformists in the afternoon. They have one or two warm *plats du jour* and several meat-and-cheese-plate combinations (daily 7:00-24:00, 36 Rue des Abbesses, +33 1 42 54 99 59).

$$ Le Relais Gascon is a pleasing bistro with a string of tables lining its front, a warm interior, and a focus on cuisine from France's southwest regions (daily, serves nonstop from noon until late, 6 Rue des Abbesses, +33 1 42 58 58 22).

$ La Fourmi, sitting at the bottom of the hill, is a raucous café/bar with lovable rough edges. Open all day, they offer coffee, croissants, and simple, affordable lunches. In the evening, the place is taken over by hilltop hipsters who come for the inexpensive beer and generous cheese plates (daily, 74 Rue des Martyrs, Mo: Anvers or Pigalle, +33 1 42 64 70 35, Eloise).

Nightlife on Montmartre: Place du Tertre buzzes with tourist activity after hours. Rue des Abbesses and Rue des Trois Frères attract a more local crowd with cafés, bars, and clubs in all shapes and sizes.

LUNCH AND DINNER CRUISES

The following companies offer **$$$$** lunch and dinner cruises (reservations required). Both offer multicourse meals and music in aircraft-carrier-size dining rooms with glass tops and good views. Ask ahead about proper attire—"smart dress" is required (no denim, shorts, or sport shoes). Earlier cruises (around 18:00) offer cheaper *menus* than later cruises; prices also vary with seating.

History of Cafés in Paris

The first café in the Western world was in Paris—established in 1686 at Le Procope (still a restaurant today; see listing). The French had just discovered coffee, and their robust economy was growing a population of pleasure seekers and thinkers looking for places to be seen, to exchange ideas, and to plot revolutions—both political and philosophical. And with the advent of theaters such as La Comédie Française, the necessary artsy, coffee-sipping crowds were born. By 1700, more than 300 cafés had opened their doors; at the time of the Revolution (1789), there were more than 1,800 cafés in Paris. Revolutionaries from Jean-Paul Marat and Napoleon to Salvador Dalí enjoyed the freethinking café spirit.

Café society took off in the early 1900s. Life was changing rapidly, with new technology and wars on a global scale. Many retreated to Parisian cafés to try to make sense of the confusion. Vladimir Lenin, Leon Trotsky, Igor Stravinsky, Ernest Hemingway, F. Scott Fitzgerald, James Joyce, Albert Einstein, Jean-Paul Sartre, Simone de Beauvoir, Gene Openshaw, and Albert Camus were devoted members of café society. Some practically lived at their favorite café, where they kept their business calendars, entertained friends, and ate every meal. Parisian apartments were small, walls were thin (still often the case), and heating (particularly during war times) was minimal, making the warmth of cafés all the harder to leave.

There are more than 12,000 cafés in Paris today, though their numbers are shrinking. They're still used for business meetings, encounter sessions, political discussions, and romantic interludes. Most Parisians are loyal to their favorites and know their waiter's children's names.

EATING

Bateaux Parisiens, considered the better of the two for dinner, features a lively atmosphere with a singer, band, and dance floor. There are several departures daily from Port de la Bourdonnais, just east of the bridge under the Eiffel Tower (Mo: Bir-Hakeim or RER/Train-C: Champ de Mars-Tour Eiffel, +33 1 76 64 14 45, www.bateauxparisiens.com). On board, the middle level is best. Pay the extra euros to get seats next to the windows—it's more romantic and private, with sensational views.

Bateaux-Mouches, started in 1949, delivers reasonable cuisine, with violin and piano music on its 20:30 trip. You can't miss its sparkling port on the north side of the river at Pont de l'Alma (RER/Train-C: Pont de l'Alma, +33 1 42 25 96 10, www.bateauxmouches.fr).

BUS RESTAURANTS

Dine to soft jazz as you glide along Paris' most famous boulevards and around its greatest monuments on an elegant double-decker bus restaurant. Dining is on the upper deck well above cars below, affording great views and glimpses into Parisian apartments. Buses are designed from scratch for this purpose with a kitchen, drink holders, big windows, toilets, and more. They move slowly, making drinking and dining a breeze. For about the same price as a dinner cruise on a boat, you can dine for about two hours as Paris passes outside your window. The four-course meal is very good (if not gourmet) and the setting is almost elegant. Two companies offer these tours: **Bus Toqué** (€65 for lunch, €90-110 for dinner, good wines, mobile +33 6 21 40 20 41, www.bustoque.fr) and **Bustronome** (+33 9 54 44 45 55, www.bustronome.com).

LES GRANDS CAFES DE PARIS

Here's a short list of grand (expensive) Parisian cafés, worth the detour only if you've got the time and money for such touristy elegance. Think of these cafés as monuments to another time, and learn why they still matter (see sidebar). For tips on enjoying Parisian cafés, review "Cafés and Brasseries" on page 676 of the Practicalities chapter; for locations, see the "Restaurants near Luxembourg Garden" map, earlier in this chapter. All are open daily.

On and near St. Germain-des-Prés
(Mo: St-Germain-des-Prés)

Where Boulevard St. Germain meets Rue Bonaparte (and nearby) you'll find several cafés.

$$$ Les Deux Magots offers prime outdoor seating and a warm interior. Once a favorite of Ernest Hemingway (in *The Sun Also Rises,* Jake met Brett here) and Jean-Paul Sartre (he and Simone de Beauvoir met here), today the café is filled with international tourists (6 Place St. Germain-des-Prés, +33 1 45 48 55 25).

$$$ Café de Flore, on the next block, feels more literary—wear your black turtleneck. Pablo Picasso was a regular at the time he painted *Guernica* (172 Boulevard St. Germain-des-Prés, +33 1 45 48 55 26).

$$ Le Procope, Paris' first and most famous café (1686), was a *café célèbre,* drawing notables such as Voltaire, Rousseau, Balzac, Zola, Robespierre, Hugo, and two Americans, Benjamin Franklin and Thomas Jefferson. The dining rooms are beautiful, but the cuisine is average (13 Rue de l'Ancienne Comédie, +33 1 40 46 79 00).

Near Luxembourg Garden
(Mo: Vavin)

An eclectic assortment of historic cafés gathers along the busy Boulevard du Montparnasse near its intersection with Boulevard Raspail. Combine these historic cafés with a visit to Luxembourg Garden, which lies just a few blocks away, down Rue Vavin (next to Le Select).

$$$ La Coupole, built in the 1920s, was decorated by aspiring artists (Léger, Brancusi, and Chagall, among others) in return for free meals. It still supports artists with regular showings on its vast walls. This cavernous café feels like a classy train station, with acres of seating, brass decor, and tuxedoed waiters by the dozen. The food is basic and the service impersonal, but you come for the crazy social scene (food served from 12:00 until the wee hours, come early to get better service, 102 Boulevard du Montparnasse, +33 1 43 20 14 20).

$$$ Le Select, more easygoing and traditional, was once popular with the more rebellious types—Leon Trotsky, Jean Cocteau, and Pablo Picasso loved it. It feels rather conformist today, with good outdoor seating and pleasant tables just inside the door—though the locals hang out at the bar farther inside (99 Boulevard du Montparnasse, across from La Coupole, +33 1 45 48 38 24).

At Gare de Lyon

$$$$ Le Train Bleu is a grandiose restaurant with a low-slung, leather-couch café-bar area built right into the train station for the Paris Exhibition of 1900 (which also saw the construction of the Pont Alexandre III and the Grand and Petit Palais). It's simply a grand-scale-everything experience, with over-the-top belle époque decor that speaks of another age, when going to  dinner was an event—a chance to see and be seen. Forty-one massive paintings of scenes along the old rail lines tempt diners to consider a getaway. Reserve ahead for dinner, or drop in for a drink before your train leaves (up the stairs opposite track L, Gare de Lyon, +33 1 43 43 09 06, www.le-train-bleu.com). To locate Gare de Lyon, see the "Paris Train Stations" map in the Paris Connections chapter.

PARIS WITH CHILDREN

Paris works well with children—smart parents enjoy the "fine art" of simply experiencing Paris' great neighborhoods, parks, and monuments while watching their kids revel in the City of Light. After enjoying the city's most family-friendly sights, your children may want to return to Paris before you do.

Trip Tips

PLAN AHEAD

Involve your kids in trip planning. Have them read about the places that you may include in your itinerary (even the hotels you're considering), and let them help with your decisions.

Where to Stay

- Choose hotels in a kid-friendly area near a park. The Rue Cler and Luxembourg neighborhoods are both good.
- If you're staying more than a few days, think about renting an apartment (for tips, see the "Sleeping" section in the Practicalities chapter).

What to Bring

- If traveling with infants, plan on bringing or buying a light stroller *(poussette)* for neighborhood walks and a child backpack *(porte bébé)* for riding the Métro. Strollers usually work fine on the bus (enter through buses' larger central doors, then park the stroller in the designated *poussette* area...if there's room), but they're tough in

Parenting French-Style

Famous for their topless tanning, French women are equally comfortable with public breastfeeding of their babies—no need for large scarves or "Hooter Hiders" here. Changing tables are nonexistent, so bring a roll-up changing mat and get comfortable changing your baby on your knees, on a bench, or wherever you find enough space.

French grandmothers take their role as community elders seriously and won't hesitate to recommend that you put more sunscreen on your child in the summer or add a layer of clothing if it's breezy.

Consider hiring a babysitter for a night or two—ask your hotelier or apartment rental agency for a babysitting recommendation, or look up babysitting agencies in Paris.

the Métro (miles of stairs). Many sights allow either strollers or backpacks, but usually not both (some museums that don't allow backpacks may provide strollers).

- Bring your own drawing supplies and English-language books; they're harder to find and pricey in Paris. If you run out, visit one of the English-language bookstores listed on page 34.

EATING

Try these tips to keep your kids content throughout the day.

What to Eat (and Drink)

- Kid-friendly foods that are commonly available and easy to order include crêpes (available at many takeout stands), *croque*

monsieurs (grilled ham-and-cheese sandwiches), and *tartines* (open-faced sandwiches). Common meaty choices include hamburgers, *saucisse* (skinny grilled sausages), or *steak haché* (a burger without the bun or toppings). Plain pasta is available at many cafés and some bistros (ask for *pâtes au beurre*). Carry a baguette to snack on.

- For breakfast, try a *pain au chocolat* (chocolate-filled pastry) or dip your baguette in a *chocolat chaud* (hot chocolate). Fruit, cereals, and yogurt are usually available.
- If your kids love peanut butter, bring it from home (hard to find in France) for food emergencies...or help them acquire a taste for Nutella (chocolate and hazelnut spread), available

everywhere. Look for organic *(bio)* stores, where you can find numerous nut butters and *Chocolade,* a less-sugary version of Nutella.

- For older kids, be aware that the drinking age is 18 in France. Your server may assume that your teen will have wine with you at dinner. Teens are also welcome in most bars and lounges (there's no 21-and-older section).

When and Where to Eat

- Eat dinner early, before the sophisticated Parisian crowd dines (aim for sitting down by 19:00 at restaurants, earlier at cafés and places that serve food continually).
- Skip romantic places. Look for cafés (or fast-food restaurants) where kids can move around without bothering others.
- Picnics work well. *Boulangeries* are good places to grab off-hour snacks when restaurants aren't serving. (For picnic tips, see the "Eating" section in the Practicalities chapter).

SIGHTSEEING

The key to a successful Paris family vacation is to slow down. Tackle one or two key sights each day, mix in a healthy dose of pure fun at a park or square, and take extended breaks when needed.

Planning Your Time

- Involve your children in the trip. Let them help choose daily activities, lead you through the Métro, and so on.
- Older kids and teens can help plan the details of a museum visit, such as what to see, how to get there, and ticketing details.
- To minimize unnecessary travel, try to match kid activities with areas where you'll be sightseeing (for example, the Louvre is near the kid-friendly Palais Royal's courtyards and Tuileries Garden). Additional kid-friendly sights are located within Paris' parks; see "Parks and Gardens," later.
- For information on children's activities, including shows, museums, and park events, look in *L'Officiel des Spectacles* magazine under "Jeunes" (see page 510).
- Limit museum visits to 45 minutes—period! Kids will tolerate a little culture if it's short and focused, with plenty of breaks (for *macarons,* crêpes, *glace, madeleines,* etc.). At the Eiffel Tower, that first level may be plenty.
- Since many schools let out early on Wednesdays, expect parks

and other children's sights to be busy on Wednesday afternoons, and expect more kid activities at those sights.

Successful Sightseeing

- Follow this book's crowd-beating tips. Buy Museum Passes, book sights ahead when possible, or buy skip-the-line tickets for adults (kids are usually free). Kids despise long lines even more than you do.
- Deputize your child to lead you on my self-guided walks and museum tours.
- Museum audioguides and apps are great for older children. For younger children, hit the gift shop first so they can buy postcards and have a scavenger hunt to find the pictured artwork. When boredom sets in, try "I spy" games or have them count how many babies or dogs they can spot in all the paintings in the room.
- Bring a sketchbook to a museum and encourage kids to select a painting or statue to draw. It's a great way for them to slow down and observe.
- Instead of hot, all-day sightseeing, mix in a nighttime stroll among the street performers on Paris' pedestrian-friendly streets. See "Night Walks" in the Entertainment in Paris chapter for ideas.
- Kids love climbing to the summit of things—domes, towers, and viewpoints.
- Take a bike tour with the family (see "Biking," later).

Making or Finding Quality Souvenirs

- Buy each of your children a trip journal, where they can record observations, thoughts, and memories. This journal could end up being your child's most cherished souvenir.
- For a group project, keep a family journal. Pack a small diary and a glue stick. While relaxing at a café over a *citron-pressé* (lemonade), take turns writing about the day's events and include mementos such as colorful ticket stubs from museums, postcards, or stalks of lavender.
- Let kids pick out some toys and books. Large department stores, such as Bon Marché, have a good selection of toys. Note that Legos are sometimes different in Europe than in the US, and the French have wonderful doll clothes with a much wider selection than typically found in the US. Kids like the French adventure comics Astérix and Tintin (both available in English, sold in bigger bookstores with English sections).
- Learn and play *boules*, a form of outdoor bowling (see the sidebar on page 407. The best thing we did on one trip was to buy our own set of *boules*. We'd play before dinner, side by side with real players at the neighborhood park. Buy your *boules de*

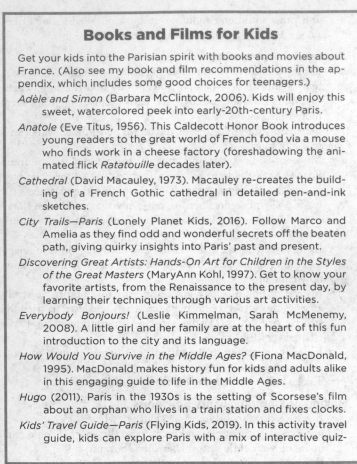

Books and Films for Kids

Get your kids into the Parisian spirit with books and movies about France. (Also see my book and film recommendations in the appendix, which includes some good choices for teenagers.)

Adèle and Simon (Barbara McClintock, 2006). Kids will enjoy this sweet, watercolored peek into early-20th-century Paris.

Anatole (Eve Titus, 1956). This Caldecott Honor Book introduces young readers to the great world of French food via a mouse who finds work in a cheese factory (foreshadowing the animated flick *Ratatouille* decades later).

Cathedral (David Macauley, 1973). Macauley re-creates the building of a French Gothic cathedral in detailed pen-and-ink sketches.

City Trails—Paris (Lonely Planet Kids, 2016). Follow Marco and Amelia as they find odd and wonderful secrets off the beaten path, giving quirky insights into Paris' past and present.

Discovering Great Artists: Hands-On Art for Children in the Styles of the Great Masters (MaryAnn Kohl, 1997). Get to know your favorite artists, from the Renaissance to the present day, by learning their techniques through various art activities.

Everybody Bonjours! (Leslie Kimmelman, Sarah McMenemy, 2008). A little girl and her family are at the heart of this fun introduction to the city and its language.

How Would You Survive in the Middle Ages? (Fiona MacDonald, 1995). MacDonald makes history fun for kids and adults alike in this engaging guide to life in the Middle Ages.

Hugo (2011). Paris in the 1930s is the setting of Scorsese's film about an orphan who lives in a train station and fixes clocks.

Kids' Travel Guide—Paris (Flying Kids, 2019). In this activity travel guide, kids can explore Paris with a mix of interactive quiz-

CHILDREN

pétanque at a Décathlon sports store (www.decathlon.fr). The *boules* make great (if weighty) souvenirs and also provide entertainment (and memories) once you're back home.

MONEY, SAFETY, AND STAYING CONNECTED

Before your trip gets underway, talk to your kids about safety and money.

- Give your child a money belt and an expanded allowance; you are on vacation, after all. Let your kids budget their funds by comparing and contrasting the dollar and euro.
- If you allow older kids to explore a museum or neighborhood on their own, be sure to establish a clear meeting time and place.
- Have a "what if" procedure in place in case something goes

zes, tips, and coloring pages alongside their personal tour guide, Leonardo.

Kiki and Coco in Paris (Nina Gruener, Stephanie Rausser, 2011). The story of a friendship between a young girl and her doll unfolds in a series of photographs, documenting their journey to Paris.

Madeline (Ludwig Bemelmans, 1939). Kids love the *Madeline* series, where "in an old house in Paris that was covered with vines, lived twelve little girls in two straight lines." It's also a live-action film from 1998.

Mission Paris: A Scavenger Hunt Adventure (Catherine Aragon, 2014). Young explorers will have hands-on fun completing missions while discovering the city.

The Mona Lisa Caper (Rick Jacobson, Laura Fernandez, 2005). This Louvre-heist adventure will engage the under-10 set.

Paris: Great Cities Through the Ages (Renzo Rossi, 2003). Kid historians will devour this fun introduction to the city and its history, told mainly through illustrations.

Ratatouille (2007). A rat becomes a chef at a fine Parisian restaurant in this Pixar film.

The Red Balloon (1956). In this classic film, a small boy chases his balloon through the streets of Paris, showing how beauty can be found even in the simplest toy.

This Is Paris (Miroslav Sasek, 1959). Kids of all ages will enjoy the whimsical impressions in Sasek's classic picture book.

A Walk in Paris (Salvatore Rubbino, 2014). The littlest travelers can prepare themselves for the City of Light by joining a girl and her grandfather on a stroll through Paris.

CHILDREN

wrong. If your child has a mobile phone, enable the "Find My Phone" feature in case you get separated. Give your kids your hotel's business card, your mobile phone number, and emergency taxi fare. Let them know to ask to use the phone at a hotel if they are lost. If they're using their mobile phone, show them how to make calls in France (see the "Staying Connected" section in the Practicalities chapter).

• Readily available Wi-Fi (at hotels, some cafés, and all Starbucks and McDonald's) makes bringing a mobile device worthwhile. Most parents find it worth the peace of mind to buy a supplemental messaging plan for the whole family. Adults can stay connected to teenagers while allowing them maximum independence, and teens can keep in touch with friends both old and new via apps such as FaceTime, WhatsApp, Facebook Messenger, Snapchat, Google Chat, or Skype.

Top Kids' Activities and Sights

ATTRACTIONS

Kids 17 and under are free at all sights where the Museum Pass is accepted, such as the Arc de Triomphe, Louvre, Orsay, and Versailles. Note that at some sights (such as the Army Museum), Museum Pass holders must wait in line to pick up their free children's tickets.

Eiffel Tower and Nearby

You could fill an entire kid-centric day here. Come early and ride the elevator up the tower before crowds appear, or ride it above the lights at night (🕮 see the Eiffel Tower Tour chapter). The **Champ de Mars** park stretches out from the tower's base, with picnic-perfect benches, sand pits, and other fun. Big toys are located at the nonriver end of the park (with your back to the tower, it's to the far right). Pony rides, puppet shows, and

pedal go-carts are in the center in the park (usually after 11:00 Wed, Sat-Sun, and on all summer days; after 15:00 otherwise, Mo: Ecole Militaire, RER/Train-C: Champ de Mars-Tour Eiffel, or bus #69). A view café with good prices sits at the center of the park next to these kid-friendly activities.

All ages enjoy the view from **Place du Trocadéro,** across the river from the Eiffel Tower, especially after dark (Mo: Trocadéro). The terrific **National Maritime Museum** (Musée National de la Marine) is docked at Trocadéro, with all things nautical, including wonderful ship models (closed until 2023). The **Cinéaqua** aquarium/cinema in the gardens below the Trocadéro boasts 10,000 fish in more than 40 tanks (minimal English posted, though staff stationed at various points can give info in English). There are regular shows (French only) and subtitled kids' movies, usually with a "sea creatures" theme (€17.50 for kids 12 and under, €25 for ages 13 and up, daily 10:00-19:00, 5 Avenue Albert de Mun, Mo: Trocadéro, +33 1 40 69 23 23, www.cineaqua.com).

Notre-Dame

Paris' famous Gothic cathedral will be closed for several years following the 2019 fire, though the reconstruction is fascinating to observe (best from the Left Bank side). 🕮 See the Historic Paris Walk chapter or 🎧 download my free audio tour.

Teens in Paris

All three of this book's co-authors have brought their children to Paris many times. Based on those experiences, here are some favorite activities for teens:

- As a general rule, plan for strolls on warm nights in festive areas (see "Night Walks" in the Entertainment in Paris chapter).
- Climb the Eiffel Tower and have a picnic in the park below.
- Enjoy the Eiffel Tower views and nutty tourist action from Place du Trocadéro, best at night.
- Stroll or pedal a rented bike along the car-free riverside promenades.
- Cruise the Champs-Elysées by day or—even better—at night (maybe take in a movie). Kids dig the glitz, the glam, and the car shops.
- Wander the Latin Quarter, with the immediate "Harry Potter" feel that many grew up with and love. Buy a used book (in English) at Shakespeare and Company. Comics and anime fans will find several shops on Rue Dante, a few blocks south of Notre-Dame.
- Check out the Catacombs, Père Lachaise Cemetery, and the Paris Sewer Museum—all creepy and way different.
- Linger at the Pompidou Center, which appeals to teens because it's *weird*.
- Wander the romantic hilltop of Montmartre and stop by the famous Moulin Rouge.
- Shop at the Sèvres-Babylone and Marais boutiques, and at Galeries Lafayette and Printemps department stores (the perfume sections alone justify the trip). Pause for a drink at Printemps' rooftop terrace.
- Tour the Orsay Museum's top floor of classic Impressionist paintings.
- Take a boat ride on the Seine at night—parents can relax while teens can snap photos of the passing sights.
- Ride the elevator up the Montparnasse Tower for fantastic views.
- Mix it up with Parisians at the summer fair in the Tuileries Garden, and ride the Paris Ferris Wheel (summers only).
- Rent a toy sailboat at the central pond at Luxembourg Garden.

The Paris Archaeological Crypt on the square in front of Notre-Dame is quick and interesting (covered by Museum Pass). Kids can push buttons to highlight remains of Roman Paris and leave with a better understanding of how different civilizations build on top of each other.

Teenagers love the traffic-free lanes of the Latin Quarter across the river.

Arc de Triomphe and the Champs-Elysées

This area is popular with teenagers, day and night. Mine couldn't get enough of it. Watch the crazy traffic rush around the Arc de Triomphe for endless entertainment, then stroll Avenue des Champs-Elysées with its car dealerships, Disney store, and the river of humanity that flows along its broad sidewalks. Take your teenager to see a movie on the Champs-Elysées ("VOST" next to the showtime means it's shown in the original language).

📖 See the Champs-Elysées Walk chapter.

Pompidou Center

Teens like the Pompidou Center for its crazy outdoor entertainers, throngs of young people, happening cafés, and fun fountains next

door (but it's dead on Tue, when the museum is closed). Inside, the temporary exhibits and gift shop on the main floor are visually impressive. The museum's wild collection of art (particularly the art installations) will make kids smile. The escalator to the top is a good ride with great views for all ages.

📖 See the Pompidou Center Tour chapter.

Paris Zoo (Le Parc Zoologique de Paris)

The Paris Zoo is spectacular, re-creating habitats from five continents for both beasts and visitors to enjoy. Visit the modern glass greenhouse and walk among colorful birds, jumping monkeys, and other furry tree dwellers. Combining time at the zoo with a picnic lunch (pick up elsewhere) in the Bois de Vincennes park (with paddleboats, pony rides, and chateau tours) is a delightful way to spend the day.

Cost and Hours: €15 for kids 3-11, €20 for ages 12 and up, free for ages 2 and under; Mon-Fri 9:30-18:00, Sat-Sun until 19:30, Nov-March 10:00-17:00 and closed Tue; tram line 3 or Mo: Porte Dorée or St-Mandé, then 15-minute walk—head toward the skyscraper-sized rock at edge of Bois de Vincennes; bus #46 or #86 brings you closer, +33 08 11 22 41 22, www.parczoologiquedeparis.fr.

Musée en Herbe

For budding artistes, a trip here is a must. This small art museum near the Louvre, designed with the youngest of art lovers in mind, offers contemporary art exhibits, a colorful bookstore, and workshops where kids can make their own art. Workshops are offered only in French—but the smiling, paint-covered kids don't seem to mind, and there are plenty of kind, English-speaking staff to help.

Cost and Hours: €7, free for kids under age 3, daily 10:00-19:00; €22-31 for one-hour workshops, price includes entry; offered daily July-Aug, Wed and Sat-Sun only during school year; parents must stay with kids ages 2.5-4.5 but can leave kids ages 5-12; book online, by phone, or stop by; 23 Rue de L'Arbre-Sec, Mo: Louvre-Rivoli, Pont Neuf, Les Halles, or Châtelet; +33 1 40 67 97 66, http://museeenherbe.com.

Versailles

This massive conglomeration of palaces, gardens, fountains, and forest can be brutal—or a good family getaway if well planned. Sundays, Tuesdays, and Saturdays are crazy busy, but the fountains are fun to experience. Strollers are allowed in the gardens, but not inside the palace (you'll have to check it). Rent a bike and let the kids go wild on park paths (bikes of all sizes are available, even toddler bikes with training wheels). Or explore the gardens in a rented golf cart—while pricey, it's great fun and extremely easy. (For liability reasons, the staff wants only parents to do the driving, but once away from the palace...) Or you can row row row a boat on the Grand Canal or attend an equestrian performance at Versailles' stables. The Domaine de Marie-Antoinette (opens at noon) has trails for scampering on, and her Hamlet has barnyard animals up close and personal.

See the Versailles chapter or download my free audio tour.

PARKS AND GARDENS

Paris' public parks are perhaps your single best source of kid-friendly fun. Besides providing an outlet for high-energy kids (and a chance for the whole family to take a sightseeing breather), Parisian parks host a variety of activities, many of them with a quintessentially French flair.

Marionette shows, called *guignols* (geen-yohl), can be interesting for children patient enough to sit still. Shows are in French but have fairly easy-to-follow plots and some internationally understood slapstick (look for them in bigger parks, such as Luxembourg Garden, and check *L'Officiel des Spectacles*, under "Marionettes," for times and places). The game of *boules* is played in most parks.

Temporary **amusement parks** come to life in public parks throughout the city; the Ferris wheel pops up in summer in the Tuileries Garden, and the rides in the Tuileries are the best—my daughter preferred them to Disneyland Paris.

You can rent **toy boats** to sail on a park's pond, or rent real **rowboats** at bigger parks, such as in Versailles' gardens (along the

Grand Canal) or in the huge Bois de Vincennes (Mo: Porte Dorée).
Bigger parks can be perfect for a relaxing **bike ride. Pony rides** are
offered on certain days in some parks, such as Luxembourg Garden
and the Bois de Boulogne; to learn when and where the ponies are
trotting, check www.animaponey.com/index.php/jardins-parisiens
or call +33 6 07 32 53 95.

Luxembourg Garden

This is my favorite place to mix kid business with pleasure. This
perfectly Parisian park has it all—from tennis courts to cafés—

as well as a big-toys play area
with imaginative slides, swings,
jungle gyms, rope towers, and
chess games (see "Luxembourg
Garden" map on page 317). To
find the big-toys play area, head
to the southwest corner (small
fee, entry good all day, many
parents watch from chairs outside the play area, open daily,
usually 10:00-19:00 in summer, until 16:00 in winter, pay WC
nearby). Kids also like the speedy merry-go-round (small fee), the
pony rides, and the toy sailboats for rent in the main pond (activities open daily in summer, otherwise Wed and Sat-Sun only). Near
the main building is a toddler wading pool (summer only) and sand
pit (both free). A **puppet theater** hosts *guignol* shows (in French),
located in the southwest corner of the park near the children's play
area (€7; shows year-round Sat-Sun at 10:30 or 11:00 and also
Sat-Sun and Wed at 15:30 or 16:30—times vary by season, 1-2
shows daily during school breaks and for most of July-Aug, check
schedule online; 45 minutes, no air-con, +33 1 43 26 46 47, www.
marionnettesduluxembourg.fr). The park has many shaded paths as
well as big, open areas perfect for kicking a ball. Kids can even play
in the grass opposite the palace (Mo: St-Sulpice, Odéon, or Notre-
Dame-des-Champs).

Tuileries Garden

This central park, located between the Louvre and Place de la Concorde, across the river from the Musée d'Orsay, comes in handy for
kid breaks. You'll find fun trampolines in the northwest corner of
the park near the Place de la Concorde Métro stop (about €3 for 7
minutes, ages 2-12 only, daily 11:00-19:00). Nearby is a play area
with rope towers and slides, and an old-fashioned merry-go-round.
The Tuileries Garden also hosts a summer fair with rides, games,
and a grand Ferris wheel.

Riverside Promenades

These one-time expressways-turned-riverfront parks—running from Pont de l'Alma (near the Eiffel Tower) to the Orsay Museum on the Left Bank, and from the Louvre to Place de la Bastille on the Right Bank—are a joy for families, with kid activities such as climbing walls, *pétanque* courts, and big chess sets, plus good eating options. It's also tailor-made for bike rides away from traffic (for details, see page 66).

Jardin des Plantes

These colorful gardens are lined with museums and draw gardeners, botanists, natural scientists, and troops of kids. Located on the Left Bank southeast of the Latin Quarter, the park is short on grass and English information but long on kid activities, including several play areas and some kid-friendly natural-science museums. There's also a zoo, but it has just a few animals in old cages. From the park entrance near the river on Place Valhubert, you'll find several museums lining the left side of the park (Mo: Gare d'Austerlitz, Censier-Daubenton, or Jussieu).

The sights are described in the order in which you'll pass them when coming from the riverside entrance. An information office is located in the small house at the riverside entrance to the park (www.jardindesplantesdeparis.fr).

At the **Galerie d'Anatomie Comparée et de Paléontologie**, kids gaze into the eyes of dinosaurs and huge animal skeletons. There are no English explanations, but they're not really needed (free for ages 25 and under, €10 for adults, not covered by Museum Pass, Wed-Mon 10:00-18:00, closed Tue, busiest on weekends, entrance faces river next to McDonald's, +33 1 40 79 56 01).

The **Ménagerie des Jardins des Plantes,** a modest little zoo on the park's opposite side, displays live animals—although the population here is old and a bit sleepy (€10 for kids 4-25, free for kids 3 and under, €13 for adults, daily 9:00-18:00, +33 1 40 79 37 94).

The **Galerie de Minéralogie** is made for fans of stuff that comes from the earth. Your kids may dig the collection of rocks, big crystals, and more, but there's nary a shard of English (€5 for ages 25 and under, €7 for adults, Wed-Mon 10:00-18:00, closed Tue, +33 1 40 79 56 01).

The **Grande Galerie de l'Evolution,** at the nonriver end of the park, is an impressive, *Night at the Museum* kind of place focused on the evolution of animals. With an open floor plan and high ceilings, it features giant whale skeletons, tons of dead bugs under glass, all sorts of taxidermied animals, and many other kid-cool exhibits. Pick up the map and look for the good English explanations inserted into wood benches throughout the gallery (free for ages 25 and

CHILDREN

under, €10 for adults, €13 with special exhibits, not covered by Museum Pass, book timed-entry ticket online in advance to ensure entry; open Wed-Mon 10:00-18:00, closed Tue, busiest on weekends and Wed; gift shop sells a helpful book about the collection in English, +33 1 40 79 30 00, www.mnhn.fr). You can pay extra to visit the **Galerie des Enfants du Muséum,** a fun series of exhibits within the Galerie de l'Evolution. It's stuffed with animal-centric interactive displays and activities designed for 6- to 12-year-olds, all in English. Consider booking a time slot online a few days ahead (€10 for ages 4-25, free for kids 3 and under, €13 for adults, same hours as Grande Galerie, last entry one hour before closing, +33 1 40 79 54 79, www.galeriedesenfants.fr).

Parc de la Villette

This vast area of modern parks and museums is designed to encourage all ages to interact with nature, art, and technology. It's Europe's largest science park, with outdoor concerts and movies, a playground great for summer visits, and grass you're allowed to run around on. The main attractions for kids are Europe's largest science museum (Cité des Sciences et de l'Industrie), a 360-degree movie theater (Planétarium), a real French submarine, acres of parks, play areas including the Garden of the Dragon (a huge steel dragon with a really long slide), a working canal, and working windmills (download English guide, 211 Avenue Jean Jaurès, Mo: Porte de la Villette, follow Corentin-Cariou or Porte de Pantin signs, +33 1 40 03 75 75, www.villette.com).

Cité des Sciences et de l'Industrie: For families, the best part of this big science-museum complex is **Cité des Enfants,** a fun place that's perfect for simultaneously teaching and exhausting your children. Kids can climb inside a living ant farm, operate a crane (safety vest and hard hat provided), create whirlpools in the water exhibit, step into a tornado, film themselves driving down the highway in front of a green screen, and much more. Tickets are sold for a specific 1.5-hour time slot, and for one of two sections of the museum: the area designed for ages 2-7, or the one designed for ages 5-12 (€9 for kids, €12 for adults; starting at 9:30, 11:30, 13:30, and 15:30—verify times on website; closed Mon, www.cite-sciences.fr). There is a good café with healthy options on the ground floor, an indoor picnic space, and a bookshop to keep you busy while you wait for your entrance time.

At the permanent **Expositions,** you can explore a real submarine, take a trip through the human body, see a 360-degree movie in the Planétarium, get immersed in the video game universe at E-Lab, and much more. This area is likely to appeal more to hard-core science fans and teenagers on the honor roll (€9 for ages 6-25, €3 for ages 5 and under, free for ages 2 and under, €12 for adults, deals if you combine with other sights/activities, Tue-Sat 10:00-18:00, Sun until 19:00, closed Mon, no specific entrance time required).

Jardin d'Acclimatation

This fun-filled park delivers a brilliant kids' day with multiple playgrounds, an apiary, a small zoo, and a spray park (€7 entry). You can buy separate tickets for the more elaborate rides and activities (€3 each, €26 day passes available). Kids can play independently while parents lounge on the comfy chairs, and there are good food options. Crowds grow in afternoons and on weekends (daily 11:00-18:00, Wed and Sat-Sun from 10:00, in the Bois de Boulogne, Mo: Les Sablons, then follow Rue de l'Orléans to the entrance, +33 1 40 67 90 85, www.jardindacclimatation.fr).

OTHER EXPERIENCES
Biking

Take your kids out for a bike ride (see page 67 for a suggested route). If the city's streets seem too intimidating, consider heading to one of the parks outside the city center—many of them are great for biking, and even offer rentals (such as the gardens of Versailles).

Bike About Tours has good information and rentals (baby seats, tandem attachments, kids' bikes). They also offer fun private family tours of Paris (see page 45 for prices and contact information).

Rollerblading

Sunday afternoons are fun for rollerblading with locals at your own pace, starting at the south side of Place de la Bastille at 14:30 (see page 53, www.rollers-coquillages.org; skate-rental shop nearby).

Riverboat Rides

A variety of companies offer one-hour Seine cruises on huge glass-domed boats. Or hop on a Batobus, a river bus connecting eight stops along the river: Eiffel Tower, Orsay Museum, St. Germain-des-Prés, Notre-Dame, Jardin des Plantes, Hôtel de Ville, the Louvre, and Pont Alexandre III—near the Champs-Elysées. Longer boat trips ply the tranquil waters of a peaceful canal between the Orsay and Bassin de la Villette (see page 48).

Bus and Car Tours

The hop-on, hop-off double-decker bus tours (see page 47) are a good way to begin your visit. Taking a nighttime tour in a convertible Deux Chevaux is a terrific way to end your trip (page 517).

Watery Fun

Paris has more than three dozen swimming pools. Ask your hotelier for the location of the nearest pool, or head for one of the places listed next. Note that boys and men are required to wear Speedo-style (tight) swimsuits at pools *(oh là là!)*, and most public pools require everyone to wear a swim cap (bring one with you, or find them at a Monoprix or Décathlon sporting-goods store).

Aquaboulevard: Paris' huge pool/waterslide/miniature golf complex is easy to reach and a complete escape from the museum scene. Indoor and outdoor pools with high-flying slides, waves, geysers, wakeboards, and whirlpool tubs draw kids of all ages. It's pricey (and steamy inside), but a good opportunity to see soaked Parisians at play (a day pass is €20 for kids 3-11, €35 for adults, cheaper rates for more than one visit, no children under 3, daily 9:00-23:00, English-speaking staff, keep spare change for lockers, men's swimsuits and swim caps are affordable at the Décathlon store right there, +33 1 40 60 10 00, www.aquaboulevard.fr). Ride the Métro to the end of line 8 (Balard stop), walk two blocks under the elevated freeway, veer left across the traffic circle, and find Aquaboulevard in a complex of theaters and shops.

Joséphine Baker Pool: Housed in a giant barge docked along the Seine, this state-of-the-art floating swimming pool (Piscine Joséphine Baker) boasts generous wood decks and views of the city that get even better (though the pool gets more crowded) on sunny days, when the retractable rooftop is opened up (€6.50 for first 2 hours, then €6.50/hour, less for kids and in winter, generally open Mon-Fri 7:00-8:30 & 13:00-20:00, Sat-Sun 11:00-19:00, opens earlier in summer, cabana-type cafés next door, near Gare d'Austerlitz at 8 Quai François Mauriac, Mo: Quai de la Gare or François Mitterrand, +33 1 56 61 96 50).

DISNEYLAND PARIS

Europe's Disneyland is a remake of California's, with most of the same rides and smiles with a Franco-international vibe. Here, Mickey Mouse speaks French, and you can buy wine with your lunch. My kids went ducky for it. It's fun to experience a European take on a very American creation.

The Disneyland Paris Resort is a sprawling complex housing two theme parks (Disneyland Paris and Walt Disney Studios), a

CHILDREN

few entertainment ven-
ues, and several hotels.
Opened in 1992, it was the
second Disney resort built
outside the US (Tokyo was
first). With upwards of 15
million visitors a year, it
is Europe's single leading
tourist destination.

Disneyland Paris: This park has cornered the fun market,
with classic rides and Disney characters. You'll find familiar favorites wrapped in French packaging, like Sleeping Beauty Castle (Le
Château de La Belle au Bois Dormant) and Pirates of the Carib-
bean *(Pirates des Caraïbes).*

Walt Disney Studios: This zone has a Hollywood focus
with animation, special effects, and movie magic "rides," featuring well-known movies and characters. A thrill-ride favorite is the
new Marvel Cinematic Universe (which allows guests to test their
courage alongside their favorite superheroes). Gentler attractions
include a re-creation of the parachute jump in *Toy Story* and a *Finding Nemo*-themed ride (Crush's Coaster) that whisks you through
the ocean current.

Getting There

Disneyland is easy to get to and may be worth a day—if Paris is
handier than Florida or California.

By Bus or Train from Downtown Paris: The slick 45-minute
RER/Train-A trip is the best way to get to Disneyland from Paris.
Take RER/Train-A to Marne-la-Vallée-Chessy (check the signs
over the platform to be sure Marne-la-Vallée-Chessy is served).
Catch it from one of these stations: Charles de Gaulle-Etoile,
Auber, Châtelet-Les Halles, or Gare de Lyon (at least 3/hour,
drops you 45 minutes later right in the park, about €10 each way).
The last train back to Paris leaves shortly after midnight. When
returning, remember to use the same RER/Train-A ticket for your
Métro connection in Paris.

You'll need to buy a Navigo Découverte pass or Navigo Easy
card covering Zones 1-5 (which covers your Paris Métro rides
for the day and the round-trip train to Disneyland (about €18 for
Zones 1-5 ticket).

Disneyland Express runs buses to Disneyland from several
stops in central Paris (including Opéra, Châtelet, Eiffel Tower,
and Gare du Nord). A single ticket combines transportation and
entrance to Disneyland (about €100 for ages 3-11, free for ages 2
and under, €115 for adults; several morning departures to choose

from and one return time of 20:00, book tickets online, www.
disneylandparis-express.com).

By Bus or Train from the Airport: Both of Paris' major airports (Charles de Gaulle and Orly) have direct shuttle buses to
Disneyland Paris. Fast TGV trains (also called "InOui") run from
Charles de Gaulle to near Disneyland. For details on these options,
see page 535 (for Charles de Gaulle) and 537 (for Orly).

By Car: Disneyland is about 40 minutes (20 miles) east of
Paris on the A-4 autoroute (direction Nancy/Metz, exit #14). Parking is about €30/day at the park.

Orientation to Disneyland

Cost: A variety of single and multiday tickets and packages (including transportation, lodging, and/or meals) are sold for
Disneyland Paris and/or Walt Disney Studios. Regular prices
are discounted about 25 percent Nov-March, and promotions
are offered occasionally (check their website).

Hours: Disneyland—daily 10:00-22:00, mid-May-Aug until
23:00, until 20:00 in winter, open later on weekends, hours
fluctuate with the seasons (check website for precise times.
Walt Disney Studios—daily 10:00-19:00).

Skipping Lines: The Premier Access system allows park-goers to
skip the lines for the most popular rides by paying a fee that
varies by date and attraction (see website for details). You'll
also save time by buying park tickets in advance (at airport
TIs, some Métro stations, or along the Champs-Elysées at the
Disney Store).

Avoiding Crowds: Saturday, Sunday, Wednesday, public holidays,
and any day in July and August are the most crowded. After
dinner, crowds tend to clear out.

Information: Disney brochures are in every Paris hotel. For more
info and to make reservations, call +33 1 60 30 60 53, or try
www.disneylandparis.com.

Eating with Mickey: Food is fun and not outrageously priced.
(Still, many smuggle in a picnic.)

Sleeping at Disneyland

Most are better off sleeping in the real world (i.e., Paris), though
with direct buses and freeways to both airports, Disneyland makes
a convenient first- or last-night stop. Seven different Disney-owned
hotels offer accommodations at or near the park in all price ranges.
Prices are impossible to pin down, as they vary by season and by the
package deal you choose (deals that include park entry are usually a
better value, with more in the **$$$$** range). To reserve any Disneyland hotel, call +33 1 60 30 60 53, or check www.disneylandparis.
com. The prices you'll be quoted include entry to the park. **Hotel**

Cheyenne** and **Hotel Santa Fe**** offer fair midrange values, with frequent shuttle service to the park (or a 20-minute walk). Another option is **Davy Crockett's Ranch Hotel,** but you'll need a car to stay there. The most expensive is the **Disneyland Hotel,**** right at the park entry, about three times the price of the Santa Fe. The **Vienna House Dream Castle Hotel**** is another higher-end choice, with nearly 400 rooms done up to look like a lavish 17th-century palace.

SHOPPING IN PARIS

Shopping in chic Paris is altogether tempting—even reluctant shoppers can find good reasons to indulge. Wandering among elegant boutiques provides a break from the heavy halls of the Louvre and, if you approach it right, a little cultural enlightenment.

If you need just souvenirs, visit a souvenir shop. A neighborhood supermarket is a good place to find that Parisian box of tea, jam, or cookies—perfect for tucking into your suitcase at the last minute. For more elaborate purchases, large department stores provide painless one-stop shopping in classy surroundings. Neighborhood boutiques offer the greatest reward at the highest risk. Clerks and prices can be intimidating, but the selection is more original and the experience is purely Parisian. If you leave your shopping for Sunday, when most stores are buttoned up tight, head for one of the department stores or snappy Marais boutiques listed below.

Even if you don't intend to buy anything, budget some time for window shopping, or, as the French call it, *faire du lèche-vitrines* ("window licking").

TIPS ON SHOPPING

Before you enter a Parisian store, remember the following points:

- In small stores, always say, *"Bonjour, Madame/Monsieur"* when entering. And remember to say, *"Au revoir, bonne journée, Madame/Monsieur"* when leaving.
- The customer is not always right. In fact, figure the clerk is doing you a favor by waiting on you.
- Except in department stores, it's not normal for the customer to handle clothing. Ask first before you pick up an item: *"Je peux?"* (zhuh puh), meaning, "Can I?"
- By law the price of items in a window display must be visible. It's often written on a slip of paper set on the floor or framed

Key Shopping Phrases

English	French
Just looking.	*Je regarde.* (zhuh ruh-gard)
How much is it?	*Combien?* (kohn-bee-an)
Too big/small/ expensive.	*Trop grand/petit/cher.* (troh grahn/puh-tee/shehr)
May I try it on?	*Je peux l'essayer?* (zhuh puh lay-say-yay)
Can I see more?	*Je peux en voir d'autres?* (zhuh puh ahn vwahr doh-truh)
I'd like this.	*Je voudrais ça.* (zhuh voo-dray sah)
On sale	*Solde* (sohld)
Discounted price	*Prix réduit* (pree ray-dwee)
Big discounts	*Prix choc* (pree shohk)

on the wall and gives a good indication of the shop's general price range.

- For clothing size comparisons between the US and France, see the appendix.
- Forget returns (and don't count on exchanges).
- Observe French shoppers. Then imitate.
- Saturday afternoons are *très* busy.
- Stores are generally closed on Sunday. Exceptions include the Galeries Lafayette store near the Opéra Garnier, the Carrousel du Louvre (underground shopping mall at the Louvre with a Printemps department store), and some shops near Sèvres-Babylone, along the Champs-Elysées, and in the Marais.
- Some small stores may not open until 14:00 on Mondays.
- Don't feel obliged to buy. If a shopkeeper offers assistance, just say, *"Je regarde, merci."*
- For information on VAT refunds and customs regulations, see page 655.

SOUVENIR SHOPS

Avoid souvenir carts in front of famous monuments, and instead look for souvenir shops. You can find cheaper gifts around the Pompidou Center, on the streets of Montmartre, and in some department stores. Those green riverfront stalls near Notre-Dame sell a variety of used books, old posters and postcards, magazines, refrigerator magnets, and other tourist paraphernalia in the most romantic setting. You'll find better deals at the souvenir shops that line Rue d'Arcole between Notre-Dame and Hôtel de Ville and on Rue de Rivoli, across from the Louvre. The cheapest souvenirs you'll see are sold by *vendeurs à la sauvette* (vendors on the fly), usually recent immigrants from Africa who find public spaces to roll out a tarp (illegally) that can morph into a handy bag when they need to vacate the premises *tout de suite*.

DEPARTMENT STORES (LES GRANDS MAGASINS)

Like cafés, department stores were invented here (surprisingly, not in America). These popular stores are often crowded and may seem overwhelming at first, but the ones listed here are accustomed to wide-eyed foreign shoppers and should have English-speaking staff. The stores are not just beautiful monuments; they also offer insights into how Parisians live. It's instructive to see what's in style, check out Parisians' current taste in clothes and furniture, and compare the selection with stores back home.

Parisian department stores begin with their showy perfume and purse sections, almost always central on the ground floor and worth a visit to see how much space is devoted to these luxuries. Helpful information desks are usually located at the main entrances near the perfume section (with floor plans in English). Stores generally have affordable restaurants (some with view terraces) and a good selection of fairly priced souvenirs and toys. Opening hours are customarily Monday through Saturday from 10:00 to 19:00 or 20:00. The major stores (like those listed here) are open shorter hours on Sundays, and all are jammed on Saturdays.

You'll find both Galeries Lafayette and Printemps stores in several neighborhoods. The most convenient and most elegant sit side by side behind the Opéra Garnier, complementing that monument's similar, classy ambience (Mo: Chaussée d'Antin-La Fayette, Havre-Caumartin, or Opéra). Both stores sprawl over multiple buildings and consume entire city blocks. The selection is huge, crowds can be huger (especially on summer Saturdays), and the prices are considered a tad high.

Galeries Lafayette is a must-see for its colorful ceiling, trad-chic ambience, and city views from the rooftop. To reach the store, circle around either side of the Opéra Garnier to the main building (of three) located right at the Chaussée d'Antin Métro stop, at 40 Boulevard Haussmann. Enter and work your way to the heart of the store, where you can gaze up at the main attraction: a dazzling, stained-glass belle époque dome hovering 150 feet overhead. Ride the escalator up. The first three floors up have bars or cafés with great views of the dome above and the shopping action below. (The café on

SHOPPING

the third floor has amazing view seats.) The fifth floor has unique children's toys, and the sixth floor has Paris souvenirs and a good-value cafeteria with views (the salad bar is a great deal). Finally, ascend to the seventh floor *(la terrasse)* for a grand, open-air rooftop view of *tout* Paris, starring the well-put-together backside of the Opéra Garnier. Fashion shows are open to the public once a week through the season (€14, 30 minutes, details at https://haussmann. galerieslafayette.com).

A block to the west past Galeries Lafayette *Hommes* (men's) store (Mo: Havre-Caumartin), **Printemps,** established in 1865

(30 years before Galeries Lafayette), has an impressive four-dome facade, best viewed from the opposite side of Boulevard Haussmann. The store spans two huge buildings. The one closest to Galeries Lafayette offers a must-see circular **$$** restaurant/tea-room under a sensational blue glass dome on the sixth floor. The second building houses an amazing assortment of eating options on the eighth floor and a panoramic view from its ninth-floor rooftop (ask: *la terrasse?*), which I find a bit better than that from Galeries Lafayette because it includes an unobstructed view of Montmartre. The rooftop comes with breezy and reasonable bar/café Perruche, with good interior and exterior seating.

Teens and twentysomethings will flip for the **Citadium** mall of shops (filling a third Printemps block) on Rue Caumartin, under the skyway.

Continue your shopping by walking from this area to Place de la Madeleine (see next).

BOUTIQUE STROLLS

Give yourself a vacation from sightseeing by sifting through window displays, pausing at corner cafés, and feeling the rhythm of neighborhood life. (Or have you been playing hooky and doing this already?) Though smaller shops are more intimate, sales clerks are still formal—so mind your manners. Three very different areas to lick some windows are described next: Place de la Madeleine to Place de l'Opéra, Sèvres-Babylone to St. Sulpice, and along Rue des Martyrs.

Most shops are closed on Sunday, which is the perfect day to head for the **Marais.** Many Marais shops remain open on Sunday (instead they close on Saturday), and most of the neighborhood is off-limits to cars. For eclectic, avant-garde boutiques, peruse the

SHOPPING

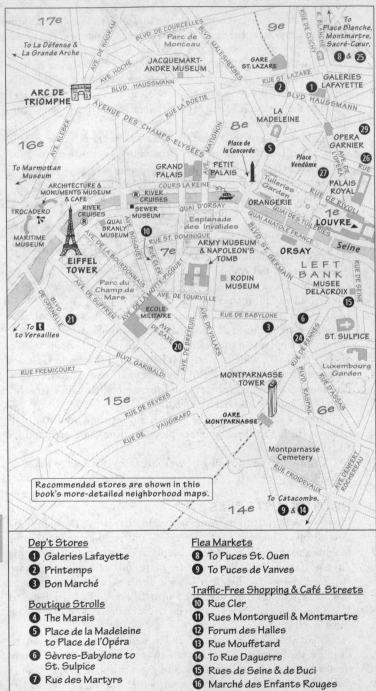

Recommended stores are shown in this book's more-detailed neighborhood maps.

Dep't Stores
1 Galeries Lafayette
2 Printemps
3 Bon Marché

Boutique Strolls
4 The Marais
5 Place de la Madeleine to Place de l'Opéra
6 Sèvres-Babylone to St. Sulpice
7 Rue des Martyrs

Flea Markets
8 To Puces St. Ouen
9 To Puces de Vanves

Traffic-Free Shopping & Café Streets
10 Rue Cler
11 Rues Montorgueil & Montmartre
12 Forum des Halles
13 Rue Mouffetard
14 To Rue Daguerre
15 Rues de Seine & de Buci
16 Marché des Enfants Rouges

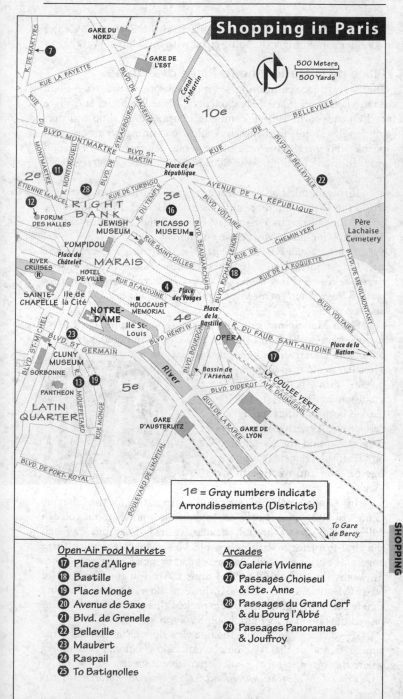

Shopping in Paris

1e = Gray numbers indicate
Arrondissements (Districts)

To Gare
de Bercy

Open-Air Food Markets

- ⑰ Place d'Aligre
- ⑱ Bastille
- ⑲ Place Monge
- ⑳ Avenue de Saxe
- ㉑ Blvd. de Grenelle
- ㉒ Belleville
- ㉓ Maubert
- ㉔ Raspail
- ㉕ To Batignolles

Arcades

- ㉖ Galerie Vivienne
- ㉗ Passages Choiseul
  & Ste. Anne
- ㉘ Passages du Grand Cerf
  & du Bourg l'Abbé
- ㉙ Passages Panoramas
  & Jouffroy

artsy shops between Place des Vosges and the Pompidou Center (consider combining a shopping stroll with my Marais Walk).

Place de la Madeleine to Place de l'Opéra

The ritzy streets connecting several high-priced squares—Place de la Madeleine, Place de la Concorde, Place Vendôme, and Place de l'Opéra—form a miracle mile of gourmet food shops, glittering jewelry stores, posh hotels, exclusive clothing boutiques, and people who spend more on clothes in one day than I do in a good year. This walk highlights the value Parisians place on outrageously priced products.

This walk takes about 1.5 hours (one hour if you skip the extension to Place Vendôme and Place de l'Opéra). Most stores are open Monday through Saturday from around 10:00 (or earlier) until 19:00 (or later). Most close on Sunday.

• *We'll start at Eglise de la Madeleine (Mo: Madeleine). From the Métro stop, look for* Sortie Eglise de la Madeleine *and start with the square's namesake church. From there, we'll work counterclockwise around the square. To get directly to the shopping, take* Sortie Place de la Madeleine *and skip to #2.*

❶ La Madeleine: Looking like a Roman temple with fifty-two 65-foot Corinthian columns, this church dominates the cen-

ter of the square. Designed as a secular temple to honor Napoleon's army, it didn't become a church until 1842; today it's used as both a church and a concert venue. Yes, this is a shopping stroll, and there's nothing on sale inside, but this church is free to enter and worth a quick look.

The facade is getting a face-lift in preparation for the Olympic Games of 2024, so it may be covered during your visit, but you can still go inside. Enter through the massive brass doors and approach the altar featuring a striking marble Mary Magdalene with three angels. The ceiling fresco celebrates great French Christians—from St. Louis (King Louis IX) to Jeanne d'Arc—in the company of Mary Magdalene and Christ in heaven above. During Chopin's funeral, in 1849, 3,000 mourners packed this church as musicians played the famous dirge of Chopin's *Funeral March*.

As you leave, appreciate the fine view down Rue Royale to the similar facade of the Assemblée Nationale (National Assembly), where the lower house of France's parliament meets.

• *Go around the church counterclockwise, enjoying the flower stalls and*

Place de la Madeleine Shopping Walk

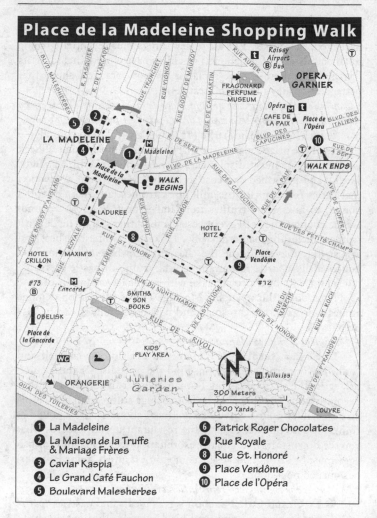

1 La Madeleine
2 La Maison de la Truffe & Mariage Frères
3 Caviar Kaspia
4 Le Grand Café Fauchon
5 Boulevard Malesherbes
6 Patrick Roger Chocolates
7 Rue Royale
8 Rue St. Honoré
9 Place Vendôme
10 Place de l'Opéra

shops. Head to the northeast corner (at #24). Before diving into shopping, consider this bit of history.

The neighborhood surrounding you was originally a suburb of medieval Paris, but by the time La Madeleine was completed in the mid-1800s, it had become Paris' most fashionable neighborhood. Glitzy belle époque Paris revolved around this square and its surrounding streets. Until just a few years ago, the whole square was a gourmet's fantasy, lined with Paris' most historic and tasty food shops. Perhaps the most famous of all was **Fauchon,** which anchored this corner of the square starting in 1886. This bastion of over-the-top edibles became famous around the world, catering to the refined tastes of the rich and famous. Fauchon was where you could find that perfect bottle of cognac for only €9,000 (flawlessly packaged, of course). But all pricey things must eventually come to an end. Many of Fauchon's franchises have closed, including its flagship store here—to be replaced by more practical shops that better serve today's Parisian lifestyle.

• *Continue counterclockwise around Place de la Madeleine. The western side of the church still hosts a row of delicacy shops. First, step inside tiny...*

❷ **La Maison de la Truffe** (#19): Get a whiff of the product—truffles, those prized, dank, and dirty cousins of mushrooms. Check out the tiny jars in the display case. Ponder how something so ugly, smelly, and deformed can cost so much. Choose from a selection that varies from run-of-the-mill black truffles (a bargain at €50 a pound) to rare white truffles from Italy—up to €3,000 a pound. At the counter they sell every possible food that can be made with truffles, including Sauterne wine. I like the truffle brushes, and at just €11, they might be the cheapest item here. The shop also houses a sharp little restaurant serving truffle dishes (e.g., truffle omelet for €30, or chocolate cake with truffle ice cream for €15).

Next door, the venerable **Mariage Frères** (#17) shop demonstrates how good tea can smell and how beautifully it can be displayed.

• *A few steps along, you'll find...*

❸ **Caviar Kaspia** (#17): Here you can add caviar, eel, and vodka to your truffle collection. Find the price list for these cured fish eggs. The sharper-tasting Iranian caviars run €50 for a tiny but decorative tin. The "finer" ones, from beluga sturgeon in the Caspian Sea, sell for up to €12,500 a kilo (that's about €5,700 a pound—think I'll pass on that today). The restaurant upstairs serves what you see downstairs—at equally exorbitant prices. Demand for fish eggs must be strong, because a competitor **(Café-Caviar Prunier)** has opened next door.

• *Next up is the the modern reinvention of Fauchon.*

❹ **Le Grand Café Fauchon** serves meals and pastries *(pâtisseries)* in its emblematic pink-and-black interior. The boutique has a good selection of wines, chocolates, and fine groceries. Good WCs hide in the basement.

• *Exit and veer right, past Fauchon's razzle-dazzle hotel, then cross to the island in the middle of...*

❺ **Boulevard Malesherbes:** Look to the right, down the boulevard. This kind of vista—of a grand boulevard anchored by a domed church (dedicated to St. Augustine)—is vintage Haussmann. (For more on the man who shaped modern-day Paris, see the sidebar on page 106.) When the street officially opened in 1863, it ushered in the golden age of this neighborhood.

• *Continue across Boulevard Malesherbes and veer left, passing an exclusive restaurant (Lucas Carton) and a stylish whiskey boutique, to find...*

SHOPPING

❻ **Patrick Roger Chocolates** (#3): This place is famous for its chocolates, and even more so for M. Roger's huge, whimsical, 100-pound chocolate sculptures.

• *Continue on, turning right down...*

❼ **Rue Royale:** Along this broad boulevard, we trade expensive food for expensive...stuff. There's Dior, Chanel, and Gucci. A half-block down Rue Royale, dip into the classy **Village Royale** shopping courtyard—an oasis of calm with its restful Le Village Café.

If you went a few hundred yards farther down Rue Royale—which we won't on this walk—you'd reach the once-famous restaurant Maxim's (at #3) and then spill into Place de la Concorde, with the still-famous Hôtel Crillon (see page 339). The US Embassy is located nearby, and this area has long been the haunt of America's wealthy, cosmopolitan jet set.

• *At Rue St. Honoré, turn left and cross Rue Royale, pausing in the middle for a great view both ways. Check out **Ladurée** (#16) for an out-of-this-world pastry break in the busy 19th-century tea salon, or to just pick up some world-famous macarons.*

If you've had enough, you're a few blocks from the Place de la Concorde Métro stop, the Tuileries Garden, and the Orangerie Museum. If you have more shopping in you, continue east down...

❽ **Rue St. Honoré:** The street is a three-block parade of chic boutiques—L'Oréal cosmetics, Jimmy Choo shoes, Valentino, Versace, and so on. Looking for a €1,000 handbag? This is your spot. (Or, maybe it's a good place to ponder the fact that about half of the seven billion people living on this planet are doing it on $2 a day.) The place has long been tied to fashion. Industry titans like Hermès, Givenchy, and Lancôme were launched a few blocks west of this stretch. You'll pass the domed Church of the Assumption, a former convent that now caters to Paris' Polish community.

• *Find the shortcut on the left at #362 or turn left on Rue de Castiglione to reach...*

❾ **Place Vendôme:** This octagonal square is *très* elegant—enclosed by symmetrical Mansart buildings around a 150-foot column. On the left side is the original Hôtel Ritz, opened in 1898. Since then, it's been one of the world's most fashionable hotels. It gives us our word "ritzy." Hemingway liberated its bar in World War II.

The square was created by Louis XIV during the 17th century as a setting for a statue of himself (then called Place Louis le Grand). One hundred and fifty years later, Louis XIV was replaced by a towering monument to Napoleon capped by a statue of the emperor himself. That column, designed in the style of Trajan's Column in Rome, was raised by Napoleon to commemorate his victory at the Battle of Austerlitz. The encircling bronze reliefs were made from cannons won in this and other battles. Look for images of the emperor directing battle with his distinctive hat as you scroll up the column. Elsewhere on the square is where Chopin died, at #12.

The square is also known for its upper-crust jewelry and designer stores—Van Cleef & Arpels, Dior, Chanel, Cartier, and others (if you have to ask how much...).

• *Leave Place Vendôme by continuing straight, up* **Rue de la Paix**—*strolling by still more jewelry, high-priced watches, and crystal—and enter...*

⑩ Place de l'Opéra: You're in the middle of Right Bank glamour. Here you'll find the Opéra
Garnier and the Fragonard Perfume Museum (described on pages 104 and 109). If you're shopping till you're dropping, the Galeries Lafayette and Printemps department stores (both described earlier) are located a few blocks up Rue Halévy. If you're exhausted from counting the zeroes on price tags, relax with a drink at venerable **Café de la Paix** across from the Opéra (daily, 12 Boulevard des Capucines). It's an appropriately elegant—and pricey—way to end this tour.

• *When you're ready to go, look for the convenient Opéra Métro stop.*

Sèvres-Babylone to St. Sulpice

This Left Bank shopping stroll runs from the Sèvres-Babylone Métro stop to St. Sulpice Church, near Luxembourg Garden and Boulevard St. Germain, finishing near the Odéon Métro stop. You'll sample smart clothing boutiques and clever window displays—and be tempted by tasty treats—while enjoying one of Paris' more attractive and boutique-filled neighborhoods. This shopping walk ties in well with the one in the Left Bank Walk chapter. Some stores on this walk are open Sunday afternoons, though the walk is better on other days.

Start at the Sèvres-Babylone Métro stop (take the Métro or bus #87). You'll find the
❶ Bon Marché behind a small park. The Bon Marché (means "inexpensive," but it's not) is Paris' oldest and most upscale department store. It opened in 1852, when fascination with iron and steel construction led to larger structures (like train stations, exhibition halls, and

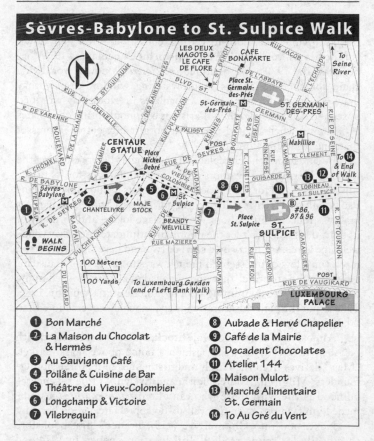

Sèvres-Babylone to St. Sulpice Walk

1. Bon Marché
2. La Maison du Chocolat & Hermès
3. Au Sauvignon Café
4. Poilâne & Cuisine de Bar
5. Théâtre du Vieux-Colombier
6. Longchamp & Victoire
7. Vilebrequin
8. Aubade & Hervé Chapelier
9. Café de la Mairie
10. Decadent Chocolates
11. Atelier 144
12. Maison Mulot
13. Marché Alimentaire St. Germain
14. To Au Gré du Vent

Eiffel Towers). The Bon Marché was the first large-scale store to offer fixed prices (no bargaining) and a vast selection of items under one glass roof, arranged in various "departments." This rocked the commercial world and forever changed the future of shopping. High-volume sales allowed low prices and created loyal customers—can you say "Costco"? But what began as a bargain store has evolved into one of Paris' most elegant shopping destinations.

Start your tour in the center, under the atrium with a high glass ceiling and crisscross elevators. Browse the purses and perfumes, then take the escalator up to higher floors for a better perspective. Find the less glamorous escalators in the corners of the store to bring you to the third floor, where you'll find a treasure trove of children's books, toys, and clothing. If you're hungry, there are trendy restaurants in the basement.

From the Bon Marché, walk through the small park, cross Boulevard Raspail, and start heading down Rue de Sèvres (along the right side). The imposing **Hôtel Lutetia** to your right was built for shoppers by the Bon Marché's owners; its dazzling facade is thanks to a multiyear floor-to-ceiling renovation. A few steps down Rue de Sèvres, you'll find ❷ **La Maison du Chocolat** at #19. What began in the 1970s as a boutique *chocolaterie* is now a worldwide chain for chocoholics. Its mouthwatering window display may draw you inside for handmade chocolates in exquisitely wrapped boxes and delicious *macarons*. Parisians commonly bring chocolates or *macarons* when invited over, and no gift box better impresses than one from this store.

Be sure to lick the chocolate off your fingers before entering the world of **Hermès** (a few doors down, at #17), famous for its pricey silk scarves—and for the former designer of its fashion house, Jean-Paul Gaultier. Hermès' 19th-century origin as a bridle and harness maker is reflected in its horse-and-carriage logo—and in many of its scarf designs. Don't let the doorman intimidate you: Everyone's welcome here. Ask to try on a scarf or two and have the salesperson teach you a few quintessential French ways to tie it. Then pause for a coffee in the airy café. This store, opened in 2011, is housed in the original Art Deco swimming pool of Hôtel Lutetia, built in 1935. Take a spin through this ultratrendy space, which covers more than 20,000 square feet.

Almost next door, find **Maje Stock,** a French outlet store with *prêt-à-porter* (ready-to-wear) fashion a notch above mass market. "Maje" derives from the family and first names of its three sibling-founders: Milgrom, André, Judith, and Evelyn. While this neighborhood is rife with those who can afford *haute-couture* (custom-made high fashion), even the well-to-do appreciate a good bargain.

Next, pop into **Chantelivre** (#13), France's first bookstore specifically for young readers. This location opened in 1974 and has everything from nursery-rhyme books to educational resources to coloring books to the much-beloved (by adults as well as young ones) *bandes-déssinées* (comic books or graphic novels). An illustrated French children's book is a charming souvenir for kids and a smart resource for savvy travelers wanting to learn the language.

Across the street at 10 Rue de Sèvres sits the marvelously old-school ❸ **Au Sauvignon Café** (open daily). It's well situated for watching the conveyor belt of smartly coiffed shoppers glide by. Check in for a hot or cold drink, and check out the zinc bar and picture-crazy interior.

Continue a block farther down Rue de Sèvres to Place Michel Debré, a six-way intersection. A wicked half-man, half-horse statue (ouch), the *Centaur,* stands guard. Designed by French sculptor César in 1985 to pay homage to his friend and mentor Pablo Picasso, it was originally intended for a more prominent square but was installed here after many deemed it too provocative because of its metallic genitalia. The face is of the sculptor himself.

From Place Michel Debré, boutique-lined streets fan out like spokes on a wheel. Each street merits a peek if shopping matters to you.

Make a short detour up Rue du Cherche-Midi (follow the horse's fanny). This street offers an ever-changing but always chic selection of shoe, purse, and clothing stores. Find Paris' most celebrated bread—beautiful round loaves with designer crust—at the low-key ❹ **Poilâne** at #8 (Mon-Sat 8:00-19:00, closed Sun). Look for samples. Parisians love getting their *punitions* (punishments—buttery shortbread cookies) here. Next door, the small **Cuisine de Bar** café is a *bar à pains* (bread bar) and serves open-faced sandwiches (tartines) and salads with Poilâne bread (Mon-Sat 8:30-17:00, Sun 9:30-15:30).

Now turn right down Rue du Vieux Colombier.

You'll pass the ❺ **Théâtre du Vieux-Colombier** (1913), one of three key venues for La Comédie Française, a historic state-run troupe. The theater has hosted a wide range of acts, from playwright Anton Chekov to poet T. S. Eliot to folk singer John Denver.

In the next two blocks, you'll pass many stores that specialize in just one or two items, but in a variety of colors and patterns. At ❻ **Longchamp** (#21), you can hunt for a stylish French handbag in any color, and **Victoire** (a few doors down) offers items for the rugged gentleman.

Cross busy Rue de Rennes— glancing to the right at the dreadful Montparnasse Tower in the distance. If you have a teenage girl in tow, take a short detour down Rue de Rennes to #71 and **Brandy Melville** (trendy and inexpensive clothes with a one-size-fits-all approach).

Others can continue down Rue du Vieux Colombier. Here you'll find more specialty boutiques. If the man or *petit-garçon* in your life needs a swimsuit, check out ❼ **Vilebrequin** (#5). There's ❽ **Aubade** (#4) for lingerie and **Hervé Chapelier** (#1) for travel totes and handbags.

Spill into Place St. Sulpice, with its big, twin-tower church. ❾ **Café de la Mairie** is a great spot to sip a *café crème*, admire the lovely square, and consider your next move. Sightseers can visit St. Sulpice Church or Luxembourg Garden (both described in the Sights in Paris chapter). You're also near several points along the route of my Left Bank Walk. Or you can head left on Rue Bonaparte two blocks to Boulevard St. Germain for more shopping and several *grands cafés* (described on page 466. If it's eating time, two good *crêperies* are a block down Rue des Canettes.

Our walk continues east, exiting the square (with the church on your right) along what is now called Rue St. Sulpice. Dueling chocolatiers occupy opposite ends of the block. ❿ **Patrick Roger**'s wild chocolate sculptures contrast mightily with **Chapon et la Chocolaterie** (#34), where master *chocolatier* Patrice Chapon roasts and processes his own cocoa beans to produce the shop's delicacies. Farther down, at ⓫ **Atelier 144,** you can admire the window display of extravagant and wildly expensive hats (23 Rue St. Sulpice).

Now turn left onto Rue de Seine. What's the best pastry shop in Paris? According to local shopkeepers, it's ⓬ **Maison Mulot**'s *pâtisserie* (closed Mon, 76 Rue de Seine). That's saying a lot. Ogle the window display and try his chocolate *macarons* and savory quiches—oh, baby. Pick up lunch to go and munch it at nearby Luxembourg Garden. If you're missing any other food supplies for the picnic, pop into ⓭ **Marché Alimentaire St. Germain** (a covered food market on the block behind Mulot featuring a Marks & Spencer grocery).

Cross Rue de Seine and walk to 10 Rue des Quatre Vents and find ⓮ **Au Gré du Vent,** a well-established consignment clothing and accessory shop, where you can rummage through the designer and even mass-market cast-offs of well-heeled neighborhood residents.

If you'd like more shopping options, you're in the heart of boutique shopping. If that's enough, catch the Métro at St-Germain, Odéon, or Mabillon to your next destination. As for me, stick a *fourchette* in me—I'm done.

Rue des Martyrs

As they race from museum to monument, visitors often miss the market streets and village-like charm that give Paris a warm and human vibrancy. Traffic-free Rue Cler is my favorite market street (covered in my Rue Cler Walk). But for a younger and more trendy, less-touristy market ambience that still serves village Paris, stroll down Rue des Martyrs. While cars are allowed on the street, it's still a pleasant shopping stroll.

This walk starts at the base of Montmartre's hill, a block from the Pigalle Métro stop, and glides downhill for six blocks, ending at the handy Métro station Notre-Dame-de-Lorette. Like any market street, it's generally quiet on Sunday from 12:00 on, all day Monday, and the rest of the week from about 13:00 to 15:00, when shops close for a break.

From the **Pigalle Métro** stop, head east a short distance along Boulevard de Clichy to the first street and turn right on Rue des Martyrs, passing a Carrefour supermarket. Peaceful and sophisticated, Rue des Martyrs makes a stark contrast with the Montmartre scrum; here you'll enter a calmer neighborhood with broader streets, richer buildings...and signs of the reality of raising a family in an urban setting.

Security is a concern. The school a block down on your right (find flags above the doorway) has fence barriers to keep possible car bombs at a distance. The carousel at the intersection is a reminder that families here live in tight quarters. Along with small children, they have small merry-go-rounds, small kitchens, tiny fridges, and minuscule cars. They shop daily for small amounts—which helps keep the neighborhood strong. Several side streets are *"voie privée"*—private lanes or high-rise, gated communities. Behind big carriage doors, lanes lead to peaceful inner courtyards serving clusters of apartments.

Slalom past baby strollers and cute dogs. Notice the variety of small shops. Goods spill out onto the sidewalk. People know their butcher and baker as if they lived in a village (in their opinion, they do). Locals willingly pay more in a shop that's not part of a chain, and *le fast food* is not cool.

Paris is one of the most densely populated cities in Europe, which makes the streets particularly vibrant. Look up and imagine how population density is great news for fishmongers, flower merchants, and bakers. In some areas, fishmongers and butchers are being replaced with Wi-Fi coffee shops and trendy deli-type restaurants, though a good bakery still seems in demand.

At #56, find one of Paris' countless **late-night grocery** stores. These are generally run by North African immigrants who are willing to work the night shift for the convenience of others. Beware: Produce with the highest prices is often priced by the half-kilo.

At #50, the **cheese-monger** has been serving the neighborhood ever since it actually had goats and cows grazing out back. Notice the marble shelves, old milk jugs, and small artisanal cheeses.

At #46, the English-owned **Rose Bakery** serves a young, affluent, and health-conscious crowd with top-quality organic and vegetarian breakfasts and lunches. The selection of mouth-watering foods at their takeout shop next door merits a look. Across the street in a gorgeous building, the baker **Delmontel** (at #39) proudly displays his "best baguette in Paris" award from 2007 and his fresh-baked temptations. The metal windmill sign above the store advertises the bakery's traditional approach. Another temptation lurks at **La Meringaie** (#35), where every week a new meringue fruit tart is created. **Maison Landemaine** (at #26) is yet another eye-popping bakery.

Continuing your stroll on Rue des Martyrs, you'll pass the

traditional butcher at #21. You know he's good because the ceiling hooks—where butchers once hung sides of beef—now display a red medallion that certifies the slaughtered cow's quality. Just as carrots come with greenery intact for the discerning shopper, here the chicken comes with its head on, the rabbit with his heart exposed, and the fish with eyes open. Freshness is expected.

Sebastian Gaudard's *pâtisserie* at #22 is worth popping in to see the typically French edible works of art. Bakers enjoy making special treats in sync with the season: Easter, Christmas, First Communion, and so on.

Nearby, at #20, the *tabac/café* copes with the smoking ban by putting out as many tables as will fit on the sidewalk—plus heaters if it's cold. Shops like this—once run by rural people from what was then France's poorest region, Auvergne—are now often managed by Chinese immigrants. Traditionally the corner café was the community's utility sales outlet—where you could pay parking tickets, pick up stamps and Métro tickets, and play the lottery. Despite the giant letters reading "*fumer tue*" (smoking kills), cigarettes sell well. Oh...and there's good coffee, too.

Down the street (at #9) sits an ultraspecialized food shop: **La Chambre aux Confitures,** displaying fruity creations like fine jewels that will forever change the way you think of jam (they're generous with samples).

The **"City" Carrefour** at #7 is a small version of a big supermarket chain. With long hours daily and more convenience, modern supermarkets are threatening many smaller shops. Across from Carrefour, browse the long line of produce. Note how price tags come with the place each item was grown. Two more butchers and a cheese shop later, you reach the neighborhood church (the Neoclassical **Notre-Dame-de-Lorette,** circa 1836) and the end of this street.

Our walk is over. The Métro station Notre-Dame-de-Lorette (line 12) awaits. Find the discreet entrance on the opposite (front) side of the church.

MARKETS
Flea Markets

Paris' sprawling flea markets (*marché aux puces;* mar-shay oh-pews; *puce* is French for "flea") started in the Middle Ages, when middlemen sold old, flea-infested clothes and discarded possessions of

SHOPPING

the wealthy at bargain prices to eager peasants, allowing buyers to rummage through piles of aristocratic garbage.

Puces St. Ouen: The Flea Market at Porte de Clignancourt

Puces St. Ouen (pews sant-oo-an), at Porte de Clignancourt, carries on the Parisian flea market tradition, but at a more elevated level—the fleas are gone, as are the bargain prices. But the selection is incredible at this mother of all flea markets. It's a sprawling complex of covered market halls and vendor-friendly streets, attracting interior designers and those who appreciate this ever-changing museum of household goods. More than 2,000 vendors sell everything from flamingos to faucets, but mostly intriguing antiques and vintage silver and art. Some find it claustrophobic; others find French *diamants*-in-the-rough and return happy (Sat 9:00-18:00, Sun 10:00-18:00, Mon 11:00-17:00, closed Tue-Fri, pretty dead the first 2 weeks of Aug, +33 1 58 61 22 90, www.marcheauxpuces-saintouen.com). There's a TI dead center in the market at 120 Rue des Rosiers. Wear your money belt; pickpockets and scam artists thrive at these wall-to-wall-shopper events.

Getting to Puces St. Ouen: Take Métro line 4 to the end of the line at Porte de Clignancourt, then carefully follow *Sortie, Marché aux Puces* signs and walk straight out of the Métro down Avenue de la Porte de Clignancourt toward the white overpass (should you exit at a different *Sortie,* cross the big square with your back to the lone red-brick building to find Avenue de la Porte de Clignancourt). Approaching the flea market, you'll pass blocks of tents hawking trinkets and cheap clothing. There are also street vendors selling knockoff designer bags, watches, fake Marlboro cigarettes, and more. Your destination is just beyond the elevated freeway. Cross under the freeway—leaving Paris and entering the suburb of St. Ouen—and turn left on Rue des Rosiers, the spine that links the many markets of St. Ouen (see map).

Bus #85 runs (slowly) from central Paris right into the St. Ouen market along Rue des Rosiers, letting you skip the scruffy stretch between the Métro station and the market. Catch it (direction: St-Ouen-Les Docks) from stops located near Hôtel de Ville or Montmartre. Catch it along the south side of Rue des Rosiers to return.

Visiting the Market: The area just outside the market complex shows off Paris' gritty, suburban underbelly (in Paris, the have-nots live in the burbs, while the haves want to be as central as they can get). No event brings together the melting-pot population of Paris better than this carnival-like market. Even if antiques, African objects, and junk jewelry aren't your thing, you may still find this market worth the trip. Pretend you just rented a big, empty apart-

Puces St. Ouen Flea Market

To Ⓜ Garibaldi

ST. OUEN

RUE J. FERRY
RUE GAMBETTA
RUE EUGÈNE LUMEAU
RUE MATHIEU
RUE LOUIS DAIN
R. M. PEEK
RUE P. CURIE
L'ENTREPOT
RUE DES ROSIERS
RUE MARIE CURIE
BIRON
RUE KLEBER
BONS ENFANTS
L'USINE
IMP. SIMON
PAUL BERT
CAMBO
RUE BIRON
RUE DE LA VILLA BIRON
LECUYER
R. DE LA GAÎTÉ
JULES VALLES
SERPETTE
RUE VOLTAIRE
RUE PLAISIR
RUE JULES VALLES
❷ ROSIERS
#85 Ⓑ
AVENUE MICHELET
RUE CHARLES SCHMIDT
RUE NEUVE
PIERRE CURIE
❶
Ⓑ #85
WC
WC
LE PASSAGE
RUE PAUL BERT
ⓘ
ANTICA
RUE LECUYER
WC
VERNAISON
DAUPHINE
MALIK
MALASSIS Ⓑ #85
WC
RUE JEAN-HENRI FABRE

ELEVATED FREEWAY (PERIPHERIQUE)

LE PLATEAU

100 Meters
100 Yards

❶ La Chope des Puces Bar
❷ Café Paul Bert

☐ MARKET STREETS
▨ COVERED MARKETS

AVENUE DE LA PORTE DE CLIGNANCOURT

To Ⓜ Porte de Clignancourt ↓

ment...and need to furnish it. Come for a reality check—away from the beautiful people and glorious monuments of Paris. If you're considering buying a large item, be aware that shipping is very expensive (the Camard company has the best reputation, +33 1 49 46 10 82).

The St. Ouen "market" is actually a well-organized collection of five markets, each with a different name and specializing in a particular angle on antiques, bric-a-brac, and junk. The markets feel safe and calm; they get downright peaceful the farther in you venture. Avoid the crowds along Avenue Jean-Henri Fabre, parallel to the freeway, and you'll do fine. You can bargain a bit (best deals are made with cash at the end of the day), though don't expect swinging deals here.

Space for this flea market was created in the 1800s, when the city wall was demolished (its path is now a freeway), leaving large tracts of land open. Eventually the vacuum was filled by street vendors, then antique dealers. The hodgepodge pattern of the market reflects its unplanned evolution. Strolling the stalls can feel more like touring a souk in North Africa—a place of narrow alleys packed with people and too much to see.

Explore the markets of Puces St. Ouen by walking down the "spine" of the market area, Rue des Rosiers—look for a map that tries to explain the general character of each (get it at shops or the TI branch at 120 Rue des Rosiers). Here's a brief rundown of the markets accessed from Rue des Rosiers: **Vernaison** is mostly small shops selling a mishmash of stuff from lace doilies to clock parts to coffee tables. **Dauphine** is a glass-roofed arcade with quiet, mostly eclectic furniture shops lining its interior-only lanes; you'll find vintage clothing upstairs. **Biron** and **Serpette** have classy antiques, and **Paul Bert** features open lanes of shops selling high-end designs for your home, with clean—and free—WCs.

Eating at Puces St. Ouen: Time your trip around lunch; there are many lively and reasonable cafés. Buried in Vernaison Market, **\$\$ La Chope des Puces** bar has a down-and-dirty, *très* local feel and is famous for its live concerts of Roma music on Saturday and Sunday afternoons (open 10:30-19:00, next to the TI at 122 Rue des Rosiers, +33 1 40 11 28 80). **\$\$ Café Paul Bert** is where locals come for a traditional brasserie meal and owns the best outside seating. The decor is wonderful, and the cuisine wins rave reviews (lunch only, closed Tue-Wed, in the heart of the Paul Bert Market at 20 Rue Paul Bert, +33 1 40 11 90 28).

Puces de Vanves

Comparatively tiny and civilized with sidewalk stalls and a more traditional flea-market feel, Puces de Vanves is preferred by many market connoisseurs (Sat-Sun 7:00-14:00, best to arrive before 13:00—when the best stalls close, closed Mon-Fri, Mo: Porte de Vanves).

Traffic-Free Shopping and Café Streets

Several traffic-free street markets overflow with flowers, produce, fish vendors, and butchers, illustrating how most Parisians shopped before there were supermarkets and department stores. Shops are open daily except Sunday afternoons, Monday, and lunchtime throughout the week (13:00 to 15:00 or 16:00). Browse these markets for picnics, or find a corner café from which to appreciate the scene.

Rue Cler—a wonderful place to sleep and dine as well as

shop—is like a refined street market, serving an upscale neighborhood near the Eiffel Tower (Mo: Ecole Militaire; for details, see the Rue Cler Walk chapter and the Sleeping in Paris and Eating in Paris chapters).

Rue Montorgueil and **Rue Montmartre** are thriving and locally popular café-lined streets that run parallel just north of Les Halles. Several traffic-free lanes cross these streets, creating a delightful area for pedestrians. Ten blocks from the Louvre and five blocks from the Pompidou Center, Rue Montorgueil (mohn-torgoy) is famous as the last vestige of the once-massive Les Halles market (just north of St. Eustache Church, Mo: Etienne Marcel). Once home to big warehouses and wholesale places to support the market, the area is now home to cafés and cute bistros. Among the few food shops are, most importantly, the irresistible creations at **Pâtissier Stohrer,** where the French expression for "window licking" must have started (51 Rue Montorgueil). Don't miss the nearby covered arcade, **Passage du Grand Cerf,** described later. Rues Montorgueil and Montmartre lead directly from the **Forum des Halles,** a huge modern shopping mall under a vast, yellow, eye-catching (and water-catching) glass-and-steel canopy; see page 72 for more information.

Rue Mouffetard, originally built by the Romans, is a happening market street by day and does double-duty as restaurant row at night (see page 462). Hiding several blocks behind the Panthéon, it starts at Place Contrescarpe and ends below at St. Médard Church (Mo: Censier Daubenton). The upper stretch is pedestrian and touristic; the bottom stretch is purely Parisian. Pause for a drink on picturesque Place Contrescarpe, then make your descent down this popular street.

Rue Daguerre, near the Catacombs and off Avenue du Général Leclerc, is the least touristy of the street markets listed here, mixing food shops with cafés along a traffic-free street (Mo: Denfert-Rochereau).

Rue de Seine and **Rue de Buci** combine to make a central, lively, and colorful market within easy reach of many sights (Mo: Odéon; see also "Les Grands Cafés de Paris," on page 466, and the Left Bank Walk chapter). This is a fine place to enjoy a late-afternoon drink and observe Parisian shoppers at work (also fun for dinner and late-night café action).

Rue des Martyrs, near Montmartre, makes Paris feel like a village. Consider exploring this lively (though not traffic-free) market scene as part of my Rue des Martyrs boutique stroll, earlier.

Marché des Enfants Rouges is a compact, covered market for the northern Marais neighborhood. It's also the oldest covered food market in Paris, built when Louis XIII ruled in 1615. It's named for an orphanage where the children wore red uniforms (the name means "Market of the Red Children"). Here you'll find everything under one roof: organic produce; stands offering wine tastings; fun, cheap, international lunch options—and wads of character (Tue-Sat 8:30-19:30, until 18:00 in winter, produce stands closed 13:00-15:00; Sun 9:00-14:00, closed Mon; a 15-minute walk north from the heart of the Marais at 39 Rue de Bretagne, Mo: Filles du Calvaire or Temple, see the East Paris color map at the back of this book). Find the man making *socca*—a chickpea-flour crêpe specialty from Nice—and consider lunch at any of the food stands.

Open-Air Food Markets

Every Paris neighborhood has a *marché volant* ("flying market"), where food stalls take over selected boulevards and squares for one to three mornings each week. Ever since the magnificent and massive food market at Les Halles was demolished in the 1970s, Parisians have had to rely on neighborhood markets  for their connection to the farmers and producers. Paris is peppered with thriving neighborhood markets selling everything from rich cheeses, fresh produce, and wines and liquors to bric-a-brac. These markets draw all Parisians; they're a melting pot of Europeans, North Africans, Portuguese, West Africans, and Asians. And what's best is that you'll often find a few casual stalls to eat at for a deal.

Marché d'Aligre, 10 blocks behind the Opéra Bastille down Rue de Faubourg St. Antoine, is a small open-air market where you'll encounter few tourists and find some of the cheapest produce in Paris. There's a small but atmospheric market hall, and a swap-meet-like square for trinket shopping and some tasty food stalls (Tue-Sat 9:00-13:30 & 16:00-19:30, Sun 9:00-13:30, closed Mon, Place d'Aligre, Mo: Ledru-Rollin). From Métro Ledru-Rollin, walk east (with your back to the Bastille column) and veer right at the second traffic light onto Rue Crozatier.

Marché Bastille is the best of the lot, with a vast selection of products extending more than a half-mile north of Place de la Bastille along Boulevard Richard Lenoir (Thu and Sun until 14:30, Mo: Bastille); consider combining either of these two markets with a stroll through La Coulée Verte Promenade-Park (see page 117) and my Marais Walk.

Marché Place Monge is small, with produce, clothing, and a few crafts (Wed, Fri, and Sun 7:00-14:30; near Rue Mouffetard, Mo: Monge).

Marché de Saxe, near the Eiffel Tower, is a thriving street market that runs along Avenue de Saxe from behind the Ecole Militaire building to Place de Breteuil (Thu and Sat until 15:00).

Marché Boulevard de Grenelle, a few blocks southwest of Champ de Mars park and the Rue Cler area, is packed with produce, nonperishable goods, and Parisians in search of a good value (Wed and Sun 7:00-14:30, between Dupleix and La Motte Pic-quet-Grenelle Métro stops).

Marché Belleville is big, favored by locals, and very untouristy (Tue and Fri until 14:30, Mo: Belleville).

Marché Maubert, in the Latin Quarter, is handy for those sleeping in the Luxembourg Garden and Ile St. Louis neighborhoods (Tue, Thu, and Sat 7:00-14:30, on Boulevard St. Germain and Place Maubert, Mo: Maubert Mutualité).

Marché Raspail, between Rue du Cherche-Midi and Rue de Rennes, is where the rich and famous shop for organic and high-end foods (Sun 9:00-14:00, traditional market Tue and Fri 7:30-14:30, Mo: Rennes).

Marché Biologique des Batignolles is Paris' largest organic market, located along Boulevard des Batignolles between Métro stations Place de Clichy and Rome (Sat 8:30-14:00). Saturdays are also big wedding days in Paris: Sneak up Rue des Batignolles to the neighborhood Hôtel de Ville (16 Rue des Batignolles), have a post-market coffee in a café across the street, and watch as the colorful wedding parties stream by.

ARCADED SHOPPING STREETS *(PASSAGES)*

More than 200 of these covered shopping streets once crisscrossed Paris, providing much-needed shelter from the rain. The first were built during the American Revolution, though the ones you'll see date from the 1800s. Today only a handful remain to remind us where shopping malls got their inspiration, although they now sell things you would be more likely to find in flea markets than at Macy's. Here's a short list to weave into your sightseeing plan. (They're found on the map in this chapter and on the East Paris color map at the back of this book.)

Galerie Vivienne, behind the Palais Royal off Rue des Petits-Champs and a few blocks from the Louvre (ideal to combine with a visit to the courtyards of Palais Royal), is the most refined and accessible of the *passages* (Mo: Pyramides, Bourse, or Palais Royal). Inside this classy arcade, you'll find a chic wine bar (**Legrand Filles et Fils,** +33 1 42 60 07 12), a tea salon, a funky café, and trendy dress shops.

Passage Choiseul and **Passage Ste. Anne,** four blocks west of Galerie Vivienne, are fine examples of most Parisian *passages*, selling used books, paper products, trinkets, and snacks (down Rue des Petits-Champs toward Avenue de l'Opéra, same Métro stops).

Passage du Grand Cerf and **Passage du Bourg l'Abbé,** near Les Halles, are two elegant arcades separated by Rue St. Denis and home to small offices, artsy galleries, fabric shops, and paint stores. Savor a drink at the atmospheric **Le Pas Sage Bar a Vins** at the eastern entry to the Passage du Grand Cerf. These *passages* combine well with a visit to the nearby Rue Montorgueil street market described earlier (a block from Rue Montorgueil up Rue Marie Stuart, Mo: Etienne Marcel).

Passage Panoramas and **Passage Jouffroy** are long galleries that connect with several other smaller *passages* to give you the best sense of the elaborate network of arcades that once existed (on both sides of Boulevard Montmartre, between Métro stops Grands Boulevards and Richelieu Drouot).

ENTERTAINMENT IN PARIS

Paris is brilliant after dark. Save energy from your day's sightseeing and experience the City of Light lit. Whether it's a concert at Sainte-Chapelle, a boat ride on the Seine, a walk in Montmartre, a hike up the Arc de Triomphe, or a late-night café, you'll see Paris at its best. Night walks in Paris are wonderful. Any of the self-guided walking tours in this book are terrific after dark. And our DIY taxi/Uber tour of floodlit Paris is a sure memory of a lifetime.

EVENT LISTINGS

The best single guide is the weekly *L'Officiel des Spectacles* (€1, comes out on Wed, www.offi.fr). For help deciphering the all-French listings, see www.colleensparis.com (hover over the "What's On" drop-down menu, then "How to Find What's On in Paris," and then "*L'Officiel des Spectacles* Translated"). The magazine offers a complete weekly listing of music, cinema, theater, opera, and other special events. The order of the contents changes periodically, but the basics described below are always there...somewhere.

"**Théâtre**" describes what's playing at all key theater venues. "**Cinéma**" takes up a third of the magazine. A code marks films as "Comédie," "Documentaire," "Drame," "Karaté," "Erotisme," and so on. The key mark for non-French speakers is "v.o.," for *version originale* (original-language version)—this means the movie hasn't been dubbed in French. Films are listed alphabetically, by neighborhood ("Salles Paris") and by genre. To find a showing near your hotel, simply look for a cinema in the same arrondissement (*banlieue* means the cinema is in the suburbs). Many cinemas offer discounts on Monday or Wednesday nights.

"**Concerts**" lists each day's performances, from jazz to classical to dance. This section also includes both opera houses if performances are scheduled. Some concerts are free (*entrée libre*).

The **"Enfants"** section covers children's activities, from musicals to treasure hunts. Look for "Spectacles" (events such as magic shows), "Marionettes" (puppet shows), and "Cirques" (circuses). These events usually are offered only in French, but they can be worthwhile even for non-French speakers.

"Expositions" lists the hours of Paris' many museums alphabetically and by type—Beaux-Arts, Contemporain, Photographie, Histoire, Sciences, etc. (*tlj* = daily, *sf* = except, *Ent* = entry price, *TR* = reduced price—usually for students and children). Also provided are hours and locations for gallery showings (big and small). Type "musées" in the search bar to find this info.

Online English Sources: If you want event information in English, the *Paris Voice* website has helpful reviews of Paris art shows, entertainment, and more (www.parisvoice.com). *Time Out*'s English website is another good resource, with listings for the city's most talked-about restaurants, reviews of concerts and stores, and ideas for how to enjoy Paris' nightlife and shopping on a budget (www.timeout.fr/paris/en).

MUSIC, FILM, AND THEATER
Jazz and Blues Clubs

With a lively mix of American, French, and international musicians, Paris has been an internationally acclaimed jazz capital since World War II. You'll pay €12-25 to enter a jazz club (may include one drink; if not, expect to pay €5-10 per drink; beer is cheapest). See *L'Officiel des Spectacles* under "Concerts" for listings, or, even better, the *Paris Voice* website. You can also check each club's website (all have English versions) or drop by the clubs to check out the calendars posted on their front doors. Music starts after 21:00 in most clubs. Some offer dinner concerts from about 20:30 on. Here are several good bets:

Caveau de la Huchette, a fun, characteristic old jazz/dance club, fills an ancient Latin Quarter cellar with live jazz and frenzied dancing every night (admission about €16, €12 for those under 25, drinks from €7, daily from 21:00, no reservations needed, buy tickets at the door, 5 Rue de la Huchette, Mo: St-Michel, +33 1 43 26 65 05, www.caveaudelahuchette.fr).

For a spot teeming with late-night activity and jazz, go to the two-block-long Rue des Lombards, at Boulevard Sébastopol, midway between the river and the Pompidou Center (Mo: Châtelet). **Au Duc des Lombards** is one of the most popular and respected jazz clubs in Paris, with concerts nightly in a great, plush, 110-seat theater-like setting (€25-55, buy online and arrive early for best seats, reasonable drink prices, shows usually at 19:30 and 21:30, 42 Rue des Lombards, +33 1 42 33 22 88, www.ducdeslombards. fr). **Le Sunside** is just a block away. The club offers two little stages (ground floor and downstairs): "Le Sunset" stage tends toward contemporary world jazz; "le Sunside" stage features more traditional and acoustic jazz (concerts €25-35, a few are free; 60 Rue des Lombards, +33 1 40 26 46 60, www.sunset-sunside.com).

For a less pricey—and less central—concert club, try **Utopia** in the Montparnasse area. From the outside it's a hole-in-the-wall, but inside it's filled with devoted fans of rock and folk blues. Though Utopia is officially a private club (and one that permits smoking), you can pay €3 to join for an evening, then pay a reasonable charge for the concert (usually €12 or less, concerts start about 22:00; 79 Rue de l'Ouest, Mo: Pernety, +33 1 43 22 79 66, www.utopia-cafeconcert.fr).

Old-Time Parisian Cabaret

Au Lapin Agile, a historic little cabaret on Montmartre, tries its best to maintain the atmosphere of the heady days when bohemians would gather here to enjoy wine, song, and sexy jokes. Today, you'll mix in with a few locals and many tourists (the Japanese love the place) for a drink and as many as 10 different performers—mostly singers with a piano. Performers range from sweet and innocent Amélie types to naughty Maurice Chevalier types. And though tourists are welcome, there's no accommodation for English speakers (except on their website), so non-French speakers will be lost. You sit at carved wooden tables in a dimly lit room, taste the traditional drink (a small brandy with cherries), and are immersed in an old-

time Parisian ambience. The soirée covers traditional French standards, love ballads, sea chanteys, and more (€35, €25 for those under 26, €5-9 drinks; Tue and Thu-Sat from 21:00; closed Mon, Wed, and Sun; best to reserve ahead, 22 Rue des Saules, +33 1 46 06 85 87, aulapinagile.fr).

Au Lapin Agile and the overrated and touristy **Moulin Rouge** nightclub are both described in more detail in the Montmartre Walk chapter.

Classical Concerts

For classical music on any night, consult *L'Officiel des Spectacles* magazine (check "Classique" under "Concerts" for listings), and look for posters at tourist-oriented churches. From March through November, these churches regularly host concerts: St. Sulpice, St. Germain-des-Prés, La Madeleine, St. Eustache, St. Julien-le-Pauvre, and Sainte-Chapelle.

Sainte-Chapelle: Enjoy the pleasure of hearing Mozart,

Bach, or Vivaldi, surrounded by 800 years of stained glass (unheated—bring a sweater). The acoustical quality is surprisingly good. There are usually two concerts per evening, at about 19:00 and 20:30; specify which one you want when you buy or reserve your ticket. Tickets run about €40-50, and the more you pay, the closer you sit, though there isn't a bad seat in the chapel. Seats are unassigned within each section, so arrive at least 30 minutes early to get through the security line and snare a good view.

You can book online, by phone, or at the box office. Several companies sell tickets online but easiest by far is to buy at www.fnactickets.com (search "Concerts Ste. Chapelle"). The small box office (with schedules and tickets) is to the left of the chapel entrance gate (8 Boulevard du Palais, Mo: Cité), or call +33 1 42 77 65 65 or mobile +33 6 67 30 65 65 for schedules and reservations. You can leave your message in English—just speak clearly and spell your name. Schedules and tickets are also available at www.euromusicproductions.fr.

Philharmonie de Paris: This dazzling, 2,400-seat concert hall is situated in the Parc de la Villette complex. It hosts world-class artists, from legends of rock and roll to string quartets to international opera stars. Tickets range from €10 to €150, depending on the artist and seats, and are usually hard to come by, so it's best to buy them in advance (221 Avenue Jean-Jaurès, Mo: Porte de Pantin, +33 1 44 84 44 84, www.philharmoniedeparis.fr).

Other Venues: Look for daytime concerts in parks, such as the Luxembourg Garden. Even the Galeries Lafayette department store offers concerts. Many of these concerts are free *(entrée libre)*, such as the Sunday atelier concert sponsored by the American Church (generally Sept-June at 17:00 but not every week and not in Dec, 65 Quai d'Orsay, Mo: Invalides, RER/Train-C: Pont de l'Alma, +33 1 40 62 05 00, www.acparis.org). The Army Museum offers inexpensive afternoon and evening classical music concerts all year round (for programs—in French only—see www.musee-armee.fr). There are also concerts at the Eiffel Tower (see page 237) and at the Louvre's auditorium on Wednesday and Friday evenings (www.louvre.fr/en/auditorium-louvre/music).

Opera

Paris is home to two well-respected opera venues. The **Opéra Bastille** is the massive modern opera house that dominates Place de la

Bastille. Come here for state-of-the-art special effects and modern interpretations of classic ballets and operas. In the spirit of this everyman's opera, unsold seats are available at a big discount to seniors and students 15 minutes before the show. Standing-room-only tickets for €15 are also sold for some performances (Mo: Bastille).

The **Opéra Garnier,** Paris' first opera house, hosts opera and ballet performances. Come here for grand belle époque decor (Mo: Opéra; generally no performances mid-July-mid-Sept). To get tickets for either opera house, it's easiest to reserve online at www.operadeparis.fr, or call +33 1 71 25 24 23 (office closed Sun). You can also buy tickets in person at their ticket offices (open Mon-Sat: Opéra Bastille 14:30-18:30, Opéra Garnier 11:30-18:30; both also open an hour before show; closed Sun).

Theater

The **Theatre in Paris** group enables Anglophones to enjoy selected Parisian theater productions by providing English-language ticketing and specially created programs with show synopses and theater insight. The company also arranges for English-language comedians, easy-to-read subtitles, and optimal seating at a variety of historic theaters. You'll get a personal welcome to the event from an English-speaking host (shows Tue-Sun, none on Mon, +33 1 85 08 66 89, schedule at www.theatreinparis.com).

Lost in Frenchlation screens French films with English subtitles; see the "Connecting with the Culture" sidebar on page 50.

Movies

The **Open-Air Cinema** at La Villette (Cinéma en Plein Air) is your chance to relax on the grass and see a movie under the stars with happy Parisians. Films, shown in their original language with French subtitles, start at dusk (free, chair rental €7, mid-July-Aug Wed-Sun, inside Parc de la Villette complex—enter through main entrance at Cité des Sciences et de l'Industrie, 30 Rue Corentin-Cariou, Mo: Porte de la Villette, www.villette.com).

EVENING SIGHTSEEING
Museum Visits

Various museums (Orsay, Pompidou, Marmottan, and possibly the Louvre) are open late on different evenings—called *visites nocturnes*—offering the opportunity for more relaxed, less crowded visits. See the sidebar on page 82 for details and other night-owl attractions.

Versailles Spectacles: An elaborate sound-and-light show (Les Grandes Eaux Nocturnes) takes place in the gardens at Versailles on some Saturday evenings in summer (see page 561).

Seine River Cruises

Several companies offer cruises after dark as well as dinner cruises on huge glass-domed boats (or open-air decks in summer) with departures along the Seine, including from the Eiffel Tower; see "Lunch and Dinner Cruises" in the Eating in Paris chapter.

NIGHT WALKS

Go for an evening walk to best appreciate the City of Light. Break for ice cream, pause at a café, and enjoy the sidewalk entertainers as you join the post-dinner Parisian parade. Use any of this book's self-guided walking tours as a blueprint. (They're worth doing twice—once by day with the self-guided tour information and again after dark to enjoy the lively people scene and beautiful lighting.) Consider the following suggestions; most are partial versions of this book's longer walking tours. Don't dilly-dally; lights at many major monuments are turned off at midnight.

▲▲▲Trocadéro and Eiffel Tower

This is one of Paris' most spectacular views at night. Take the Métro to the Trocadéro stop and join the party on Place du Trocadéro for a magnificent view of the glowing Eiffel Tower. It's a festival of hawkers, gawkers, drummers, and entertainers. Walk down the stairs, passing the fountains, then cross the river to the base of the tower, well worth the effort even if you don't go up.

From the Eiffel Tower you can stroll through the Champ de Mars park past tourists and romantic couples, and take the Métro home (Ecole Militaire stop, across Avenue de la Motte-Picquet from far southeast corner of park). Or there's a handy RER/Train-C stop (Champ de Mars-Tour Eiffel) two blocks west of the Eiffel Tower on the river.

▲▲Champs-Elysées and the Arc de Triomphe

The Avenue des Champs-Elysées (covered in the Champs-Elysées Walk chapter) is best after dark. Start at the Arc de Triomphe (open late), then stroll down Paris' glittering grand promenade. A right turn on Avenue George V leads to the Bateaux-Mouches river cruises. A movie on the Champs-Elysées is a fun experience (weekly listings in *L'Officiel des Spectacles* under "Cinéma"), and a drink or snack at Renault's futuristic bar/lounge is a kick (at #53).

ENTERTAINMENT

▲▲Ile St. Louis and Notre-Dame

Do a shortened version of the beautiful Historic Paris Walk after dinner, starting on the island of Ile St. Louis.

To reach Ile St. Louis directly, take the Métro (line 7) to the Pont Marie stop, then cross Pont Marie to Ile St. Louis. Turn right up charming Rue St. Louis-en-l'Ile, stopping for dinner—or at least a Berthillon ice cream (at #31) or Amorino Gelati (at #47). At the west end of Ile St. Louis, cross Pont St. Louis to Ile de la Cité, with a knockout view of Notre-Dame. Wander to the Left Bank on Quai de l'Archevêché, and drop down to the river for the best floodlit views. From May through September you'll find moored barges *(péniches)* that operate as bars. Although I wouldn't eat dinner on one of these barges, the atmosphere is great for a drink, often including live music on weekends (May-Sept only, daily until late, live music often Thu-Sun from 21:00). End your walk in front of Notre-Dame.

Dancing with the Stars

On warm summer evenings, some Parisian parks and riverfront *quais* are alive with dancing. Go to www.parisinfo.com and search on "dancing outdoors" to find out what's going on where. One good place to look is the Open-Air Sculpture Garden near Jardin des Plantes. Day or night, this skinny riverfront park dotted with modern art makes for a pleasant walk, but it's especially fun on balmy evenings in the summer, when you may encounter people dancing to rock, salsa, or whatever's in vogue. It's on the Left Bank across from Ile St. Louis, running between the Arab World Institute and Jardin des Plantes (free, music around 20:00, very weather dependent, Quai St. Bernard, Mo: Cardinal Lemoine plus an eight-minute walk on Rue Cardinal Lemoine toward the river).

Place de la Concorde, Place Vendôme, and Place de l'Opéra

These three squares tie together nicely for an elegant post-dinner walk (see page 491 in the Shopping in Paris chapter). Take the Métro to Place de la Concorde and cross to the obelisk for a terrific view of the Champs-Elysées and the beautifully lit, Greek-looking Assemblée Nationale building (to your left as you look up the Champs-Elysées). Then walk up Rue Royale toward La Madeleine, turn right on Rue St. Honoré, then left after several blocks on Rue Castiglione. Enjoy the sumptuous Place Vendôme, then exit at the opposite end and walk up Rue de la Paix to find Opéra Garnier, stunning at night. End your stroll with a pricey drink at one of Paris' grandest cafés (Café de la Paix), across from Opéra Garnier (the Opéra Métro stop is right there to take you home).

Marais

This artsy neighborhood is a hotbed for nightlife, full of cafés and tiny bars catering to locals and tourists alike. The action centers on Rue Vieille du Temple (Mo: St-Paul), which offers something for every taste and attracts all age groups and sexual persuasions. Look for the Au Petit Fer à Cheval bar and the bookstore/wine bar La Belle Hortense, and fan out from there. At the western edge of the Marais, you'll find good boy-meets-girl energy at bars along Rue des Lombards near where it crosses Boulevard de Sebastopol (Mo: Châtelet or Hôtel de Ville, see also "Jazz and Blues Clubs," earlier).

Place St. Germain-des-Prés and Odéon

These areas are close to each other and worth combining for evening fun. The church of St. Germain-des-Prés is usually open at night and beautifully lit, and Parisians sip drinks at two famous nearby cafés: Les Deux Magots and Café de Flore (see page 305; Mo: St-Germain-des-Prés). A few blocks toward St. Sulpice Church, night owls prowl along Rues des Canettes and Guisarde, and a few blocks toward the river, they do the same along Rue de Buci (for more on these streets, see page 457). The Odéon, a few blocks away, is home to several movie theaters and still more lively cafés.

AFTER-DARK TOURS ON WHEELS

Several companies offer evening tours of Paris. You can join a traditional, mass-produced bus tour or, for more money, take a vintage-car tour with a student guide. Do-it-yourselfers can save money by using Uber or a taxi for a private tour. All options are described next.

▲Deux Chevaux Car Tours

If rumbling around Paris and sticking your head out of the rolled-back top of a funky old 2CV car *à la* Inspector Clouseau sounds like your kind of fun, consider this. Two enterprising companies have assembled a veritable fleet of these "tin-can" cars for giving tours of Paris day and night: 4 Roues Sous 1 Parapluie (the better choice) and Paris Authentic. Night is best for the  tour; skip it in daylight. The informal student-drivers are not professional guides (you're paying for their driving services), though they speak some English. Appreciate the simplicity of the car. It's France's version of the VW "bug" and hasn't been made since 1985. Notice the bare-bones dashboard. Ask your guide to honk the horn, to run the silly little wipers, and to open and close the air vent—*c'est magnifique!*

They'll pick you up and drop you at your hotel or wherever you choose. **4 Roues Sous 1 Parapluie** ("4 wheels under 1 umbrella") offers several tours with candy-colored cars and drivers dressed in striped shirts and berets (for 2 people it's about €50/person for an hour; 10 percent tip appropriate if you enjoyed your ride, longer tours available, maximum 3 people/car, +33 1 58 59 27 82, mobile +33 6 67 32 26 68, www.4roues-sous-1parapluie.com, info@4roues-sous-1parapluie.com). **Paris Authentic** offers similar options and prices (www.parisauthentic.com, paris@parisauthentic.com).

▲Nighttime Bus Tours

The **Paris City Vision** Paris by Night tour connects all the great illuminated sights of Paris with a 100-minute bus ride in 12 languages. The double-decker buses have huge windows, but the most desirable front seats are sometimes reserved for customers who've bought tickets for the overrated Moulin Rouge. Left-side seats are better. Visibility is fine in the rain. You'll stampede on with a United Nations of tourists, get a set of headphones, dial up your language, and listen to a recorded spiel (which is interesting but includes an annoyingly bright TV screen and a pitch for other, more expensive excursions). Uninspired as it is, the ride provides an entertaining overview of the city at its floodlit and scenic best. Bring your city map to stay oriented as you go. You're always on the bus, but the driver slows for photos at viewpoints (€27, kids-€21, 1.75 hours, April-Oct at 22:00, Nov-March at 20:00, reserve one day in advance, ask about departure location when booking, arrive 30 minutes early to wait in line for best seats, +33 1 44 55 61 00, www.pariscityvision.com). Ask also about small-group minibus tours, which follow a similar route and pick up/drop off at your hotel (€78).

You can also take a night tour on a **TootBus** double-decker bus (€28, www.tootbus.com) or on a **Big Bus Paris** tour (€27, cheaper online, +33 1 53 95 39 53, www.bigbustours.com).

▲▲▲Floodlit Paris Driving Tour by Taxi or Uber

Seeing the City of Light floodlit is one of Europe's great travel experiences and a great finale to any day in Paris. With this suggested route, you can hire your own driver and have a glorious hour of illuminated Paris. Compared with a big-bus tour, it's cheaper than the cost of two seats, and you can jump out at many stops to get the best views and pictures. (On the other hand, you don't have the high vantage point and big windows of a bus.)

Tour Overview: This is a circular, one-hour route from Place du Châtelet (near Notre-Dame) to the Eiffel Tower along the Left Bank, then back along the Right Bank via the Champs-Elysées.

Start on Place du Châtelet (a taxi stand is on the northwest corner), at any convenient point along the route, or from your hotel. Suggested stops are in bold on the "Uber & Taxi Instructions" (see next; *"arrêt"* means "stop"), though you can make any stops you like. To make it more of a party, bring a bottle of red wine and some chocolate to enjoy each time you hop out (do not consume in the car).

Traffic can be sparse, and lights are shining between 22:00 and 24:00 every night. Sunday is the best night, as there's less traffic. Complete your tour by midnight, when lights are shut off at major monuments. Your other timing consideration: The Eiffel Tower twinkles for only the first five minutes of each hour after dark. If you start at Place du Châtelet at half past the hour, you should be right on time for the sparkles.

Taxi Versus Uber: Taxis and Uber cost roughly the same. Taxi drivers can be moody, but they have access to bus lanes, which is an advantage at the Louvre (see tour description later). Uber can cost about 20 percent less, with drivers who tend to be more fun and flexible. Taxis have a strict meter (figure €40/hour plus about €1/ kilometer; taxis start with €2.60 on the meter). This  suggested loop costs around €50 (more on Sun). If your driver was easy to work with, add a 10 percent tip; if not, tip just 5 percent. Drivers can take up to four people in a cab or regular sedan, though this is tight for decent sightseeing (with three, everyone gets a window).

The Route: Before you go, photocopy the instructions on the next page or rip the page out (but keep a copy of the route on hand so you can follow along).

Give the driver the instructions. Learn your driver's name and use it (no first names for taxi drivers; use *Monsieur* or *Madame*). Make sure the driver understands the plan—and enjoys the challenge. (If the cab picks you up where you're staying, your hotelier can also help explain your plan to the French-speaking driver.) Review with the driver exactly where you hope to stop before you start. Don't worry about the exact streets the driver takes (as there are necessary deviations); just stick to the overall hit list of stops. Ask the driver to go slowly (or go around again—see sidebar) when you want to enjoy a particular scene.

And you're on your way. Roll the windows down, and use your phone's flashlight to read this. Stop when you want (but remember

ENTERTAINMENT

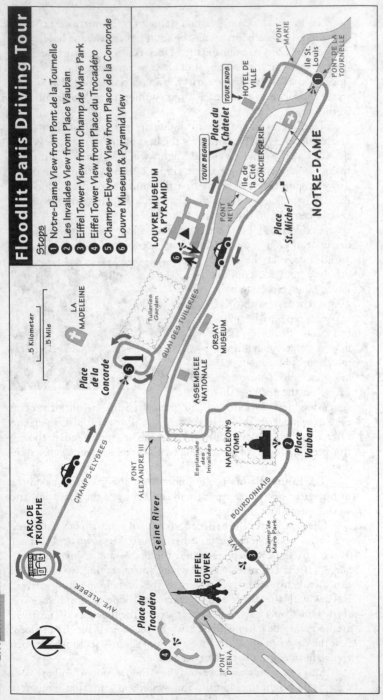

Floodlit Paris Driving Tour

Stops

1. Notre-Dame View from Pont de la Tournelle
2. Les Invalides View from Place Vauban
3. Eiffel Tower View from Champ de Mars Park
4. Eiffel Tower View from Place du Trocadéro
5. Champs-Elysées View from Place de la Concorde
6. Louvre Museum & Pyramid View

.5 Kilometer
.5 Mile

LA MADELEINE

Place de la Concorde

Tuileries Garden

QUAI DES TUILERIES

LOUVRE MUSEUM & PYRAMID

ORSAY MUSEUM

ASSEMBLEE NATIONALE

PONT NEUF

Ile de la Cité

CONCIERGERIE

Place du Châtelet

TOUR BEGINS

TOUR ENDS

HOTEL DE VILLE

Ile St. Louis

PONT MARIE

PONT DE LA TOURNELLE

Place St. Michel

NOTRE-DAME

Esplanade des Invalides

NAPOLEON'S TOMB

Place Vauban

PONT ALEXANDRE III

Seine River

BOURDONNAIS

AVE. BOURDONNAIS

Champ de Mars Park

EIFFEL TOWER

CHAMPS-ELYSEES

ARC DE TRIOMPHE

AVE. KLEBER

Place du Trocadéro

PONT D'IENA

Uber & Taxi Instructions

Bonjour, Monsieur/Madame. Nous voulons faire un circuit de Paris Illuminé d'une heure, avec quelques petits arrêts. Nous paierons le montant indiqué sur le compteur. Nous voudrions suivre la route suivante—combien cela va t-il coûter approximativement? Ça marche?

Greetings, Monsieur/Madame. We would like a tour of Paris at night for an hour, with a few short stops. We will pay the metered rate. We would like to take the following route—approximately how much will it cost? Can you do it?

1. Place du Châtelet
2. Hôtel de Ville
3. Pont Marie
4. **Pont de la Tournelle (arrêt)**
5. Quai de la Tournelle
6. Musée d'Orsay
7. Esplanade des Invalides
8. Invalides
9. **Place Vauban/Eglise du Dôme (arrêt)**
10. **Champ de Mars (Place Jacques Rueff—arrêt)**
11. Tour Eiffel
12. Pont d'Iena
13. **Place du Trocadéro (arrêt)**
14. Avenue Kléber
15. Arc de Triomphe (2 révolutions)
16. Champs-Elysées
17. **Place de la Concorde (1 ou 2 révolutions)**
18. Quai François Mitterrand
19. **Musée du Louvre/Place du Carrousel/Pyramide (arrêt)**
20. Quai du Louvre
21. Hôtel de Ville

Driver Lingo

Use these phrases to communicate with your driver.

English	French
What is your name?	*Quel est votre nom?* (kehl ay voh-truh noh<u>n</u>)
Drive slowly, please.	*Conduisez lentement, s'il vous plaît.* (kohn-dwee-zay lahn-tuh-ma<u>hn</u> see voo play)
Slower, please.	*Lentement, s'il vous plaît.* (lahn-tuh-ma<u>hn</u> see voo play)
Stop, please.	*Arrêtez, s'il vous plaît.* (ah-reh-tay see voo play)
Wait, please.	*Patientez, s'il vous plaît.* (pah-see-yahn-tay see voo play)
Go around again.	*Faites le tour encore.* (fet luh tour ahn-core)
I love Paris!	*J'adore Paris!* (zhah-dor pah-ree)

that the meter still runs when stopped). Some drivers might speak a little English; if not, learn and use the key words in the sidebar.

○ **Self-Guided Tour:** Start on Place du Châtelet, across the river from Ile de la Cité on the Right Bank. Drive east along the river to Hôtel de Ville, then continue along the Seine (the white stripe of light is a modern bridge connecting the two islands).

Cross the Ile St. Louis on Pont Marie. Stop on the next bridge—**Pont de la Tournelle**—just after the island, get out, and giggle with delight at the city and illuminated Notre-Dame. Then turn right along the Seine on Quai de la Tournelle, motoring scenically past Notre-Dame.

Drive west along the river, passing the long Louvre across the river—once the world's biggest building (across the river), then right past the Orsay Museum (on left). The Assemblée Nationale (National Assembly, on left) faces Place de la Concorde (on right). The ornate Pont Alexandre III comes next (on right).

Turn left down Esplanade des Invalides to the gilded dome of Les Invalides, marking Napoleon's Tomb. As you approach the grand building, watch the illusion of the fancy dome sinking behind the facade. Circle clockwise around Invalides for a close-up view. Get out at **Place Vauban** (behind the dome) and marvel at its symmetry.

Take Avenue de Tourville to Avenue de la Bourdonnais, which runs alongside the **Champ de Mars park** (former military training grounds that now serve as the Eiffel Tower's backyard). Turn left onto Avenue Joseph Bouvard, leading to a circle made to order for viewing the Eiffel Tower. Get out and gasp.

Pont d'Iéna leads from directly in front of the tower across the Seine to **Place du Trocadéro** for another grand Eiffel view (get out again and walk toward the tower to get the best photos and to enjoy the night scene here).

Avenue Kléber leads through one of Paris' ritziest neighborhoods to the Arc de Triomphe. Battle twice around the eternal flame marking the Tomb of the Unknown Soldier and Paris' craziest traffic circle: Ask for *"Deux révolutions, s'il vous plaît"* (duh ray-voh-loo-see-yohn see voo play). Notice the rules of the road: Get to the center ASAP, those entering have the right-of-way, and any accidents are no-fault (insurance companies split the costs down the middle). As you circle, notice the uniform boulevards reaching out like spokes from this hub. Try to find the huge and modern La Grande Arche in the distance opposite the Champs-Elysées.

When ready to continue, say the rhyme, "Champs-Elysées, *s'il vous plaît"* (shahnz ay-lee-zay see voo play). Glide down Europe's grandest boulevard—past fancy restaurants, car dealerships, and theaters—to the bold white obelisk marking the former site of the guillotine, **Place de la Concorde.**

Circle once (maybe twice) around Place de la Concorde, picking out all the famous landmarks near and far. Stop at the center to look up the Champs-Elysées. Then continue east (reminding your driver the next stop is "la Pyramide du Louvre") along the Seine on Quai des Tuileries (the two train-station clocks across the river mark the Orsay Museum) and sneak (via a taxi/bus-only lane if you're in a cab) into the courtyard of the **Louvre** for a close look at the magically glowing pyramid. Stop here.

Return to the riverfront along the Right Bank and pass the oldest bridge in Paris, Pont Neuf, and the impressive Conciergerie with its floodlit medieval turrets (this is where Marie-Antoinette was imprisoned during the Revolution). End your tour at the Hôtel de Ville, or ask your driver to take you back to your hotel (roughly €15 more).

Give your driver a hearty thank you: *"Merci, monsieur/madame/mon ami(e)! Bonne soirée!"*

ENTERTAINMENT

PARIS IN WINTER

The City of Light sparkles year-round, but Paris has a special appeal in winter. You'll find less expensive airfares, fewer crowds, and soft prices for hotel rooms and apartments (rent one for a week or more). Sure, the weather can be cold and rainy (average high in Dec is 44°F), but if you dress in layers, you'll keep warm and easily deal with temperature changes as you go from cold streets to heated museums and cafés.

Museums, restaurants, and stores stay open as usual; the concert and arts season is in full bloom; and Paris belongs to the Parisians. So go local, save money, and skip the crowds that confound peak-season travelers. There are worse ways to spend a wintry day than enjoying world-class art, architecture, and shopping, then lingering over a fine dinner at a cozy corner bistro in the evening. As Cole Porter put it: "I love Paris in the winter, when it drizzles."

Slow down and savor your favorite museums and monuments—spending one-on-one time with Mona and Venus is worth the extra sweater you want to pack. Attend a cooking demonstration, go to the opera or theater (good English language options; see the Entertainment in Paris chapter), take a short course in art or architecture, or dabble in a wine-tasting class (for more ideas, see the "Paris Food Scene" sidebar in the Eating in Paris chapter). Linger in cafés for a break from sightseeing or shopping and to warm up. Get on a first-name basis with the waiter at your corner café—just because you can now.

Easter marks the start of the tourist season, when locals find they need to make reservations for their favorite restaurants and can no longer find seats on the Métro.

This chapter reviews off-season highlights in Paris, but remember—your reward for traveling in winter is the joy of feeling part of a city, like you almost belong here. That's what you'll find on a trip to Paris from November to March.

NOVEMBER

From late October well into November, leaves tumble from Paris' trees, revealing magnificent building facades and turning parks into austere yet romantic places. Win-  ter also brings early sunsets and long evenings, ideal for floodlit neighborhood walks, boat rides, and taxi tours that allow you to view the City of Light at a reasonable hour.

Beginning one minute after midnight on the third Thursday of November and running through mid-December, Paris welcomes the arrival of the **Beaujolais Nouveau** with an enthusiasm uncharacteristic for such a coolly indifferent place. The fresh, fruity table wine is rushed from vineyards a bit north of Lyon directly to Paris, where wine bars and most cafés serve it happily, buzzing with news of the latest vintage. The first 24 hours are the most fun and raucous, and it's easy to join the party if you don't mind elbowing your way to the *comptoir* for *un verre*. Cafés and bistros continue the celebration for weeks, many offering special dishes with a glass of the Beaujolais Nouveau.

And speaking of wine, the annual *Salon des Vins des Vignerons Indépendents* (independent winemakers' trade show) is held in Paris on the last weekend of November at the Porte de Versailles exhibition center (Mo: Porte de Versailles, line 12). Here, anyone can sample fine wines from more than 1,000 different stands (small entry fee, ask your hotelier for details or check www.vigneron-independant.com/salons, French only).

DECEMBER

One of Europe's greatest treats is strolling down the glowing Champs-Elysées in win-  ter. From late November through early January, **holiday lights** adorn city streets, buildings, and monuments, and the Champs-Elysées beams with a dazzling display of lights on the trees that line the long boulevard. The city springs for 1,000 fresh-cut fir trees to put up and decorate around town, some of which ring the Rond-Point roundabout at the lower end of the Champs-Elysées. You should also find cheerful lighting displays on many traffic-free streets, including Rues Cler, Montorgueil, and Daguerre.

Parisians live to **window shop** (remember that *faire du lèche-vitrines* means "window licking"). Do some licking of your own along Boulevard Haussmann and view the storefront lights and wild window displays at the grand department stores such as Printemps and Galeries Lafayette. Here you can have your picture taken with Père Noël—France's slimmer version of Santa Claus, dressed in red trimmed with white fur. The seasonal displays in neighborhood boutiques around Sèvres-Babylone and in the Marais (among other areas) are more intimate and offer a good contrast to the shows of glitz around the department stores.

Several **ice-skating rinks** pop up in festive locations (even on the Eiffel Tower in some years). These locations are most reliable: Tuileries Garden, in front of the Forum des Halles, by the Galeries Lafayette (near the Opéra Garnier; look also for a small sled run), and along a portion of the Champs-Elysées. The rinks are free to use (you can rent skates, generally open late Nov-Jan from noon into the evening).

For the kids, there are **Christmas carousels** *(Manèges de Noël)* that whirl at various locations, including the biggies at Hôtel de Ville, the Eiffel Tower, and at the base of Sacré-Cœur in Montmartre. As soon as school lets out, parks come alive with pony rides, puppet shows, and other activities.

The dazzling château **Vaux-le-Vicomte,** an hour south of Paris, often reopens for Christmas with special holiday decorations (€20, weekends only Dec-early Jan 11:00-18:30; see the More Grand Châteaux chapter).

Christmas Season

With the arrival of St. Nicholas on December 6, the Christmas season kicks into gear. (Bear in mind, though, that Paris celebrates Christmas with only a fraction of the holiday cheer and commercialism that you'll find in the States.) In mid-December, **Christmas markets** pop up, particularly on the Left Bank (St. Sulpice and St. Germain-des-Prés), along the Champs-

Elysées, along the north side of the Tuileries Garden, and clustered around the Abbesses Métro stop in Montmartre.

Parisians pick up tiny and expensive Christmas trees for their homes at flower shops—if you rent an apartment, you could do the same. Check online or pick up the *L'Officiel des Spectacles* magazine (€1 at newsstands) to find popular and often free or inexpensive **Christmas concerts.**

Christmas Eve and Christmas Day

The big event is the Christmas Eve dinner, called **Le Réveillon**—"the awakening"—when Parisians stay awake late to celebrate the arrival of Jesus. Traditionally, they attend evening Mass, then meet with family and friends for a big feast. The meal begins

with (what else?) *escargots,* smoked salmon or oysters, and then foie gras. The main dish, similar to American Thanksgiving, is turkey, served with chestnuts and potatoes *(gratin dauphinois).*

This evening is normally celebrated at home and with family, though some Paris restaurants (and other businesses) stay open late to accommodate parties indulging in raw oysters, cheese, and the Yule Log *(Bûche de Noël)*—a log-shaped sponge cake iced with chocolate "bark." After dinner the kiddies leave their slippers next to the fireplace for Père Noël to fill with treats.

On Christmas Day, Paris is very sleepy—make arrangements ahead of time if you've got a plane to catch, and don't plan on visiting the Louvre (which is closed, along with most museums and businesses). Visitors looking for **religious services in English** will find no shortage of churches to attend—choose between the interdenominational American Church, American Cathedral, Unitarian Church, and St. George's Anglican Church (listed in the appendix). Some of these churches—especially the American Church—also offer Christmas concerts.

WINTER

Festive Foods

Winter is the season for the hunt, when you'll find game birds and venison on restaurant menus. Seventy percent of France's oysters are eaten in the month of December, most of them raw and on the half-shell. Look for busy shuckers outside big cafés, where most oysters are consumed. On street corners you'll hear shouts of *"Chaud les marrons!"* from vendors selling chestnuts roasting on coals. Chocolatiers and pastry shops everywhere do a bang-up business during the holiday

season, serving traditional treats such as Epiphany cakes (flaky marzipan cakes called *galette des rois*). Bakeries over-flow with these popular cakes starting January 6.

If you like gourmet food, take a spin around Place de la Madeleine, admire festive displays, and spring for a truffle om-elet at La Maison de la Truffe—after all, winter is truffle season (for locations, see the "Place de la Madeleine Shopping Walk" map on page 493). Just because it's cold doesn't mean that outdoor markets are quiet—*au contraire,* you'll find markets alive with shoppers and vendors no matter what the weather (on Place d'Aligre and along Avenue de Saxe, for example).

One of the great pleasures Paris offers is watching the city bustle while you linger at an outdoor table with *un café,* a *vin chaud* (hot wine), or, best, a hot chocolate (simply called *chocolat* and *très* popular in winter). Most cafés fire up the braziers and drape blankets over chairs to keep things toasty outside (though there is talk of banning outdoor heaters). And with strict smoking laws, café and restaurant interiors are wonderfully free of any trace of smoke.

JANUARY

All of Paris parties on New Year's Eve, and a table at a restaurant is next to impossible to land (book early or dine at a café). The holidays aren't over yet—Paris celebrates the arrival of the Three Kings on **Epiphany** (Jan 6) with as much fanfare as Christmas itself. Twinkling Christmas lights stay lit through most of the month.

The **after-Christmas sales** *(soldes)* are an even bigger post-holiday tradition, as locals jam boutiques and department stores looking for bargains. These sales, which last until mid-February, force stores to keep longer hours.

Parisians celebrate the **Chinese New Year** in a big way (usually falls near the end of January) with parades, decorations, and fanfare. Ask your hotelier or a TI for parade locations.

FEBRUARY AND MARCH

These are the quiet months, when Paris is most alone with itself. And although holiday decorations disappear, the City of Light is as beautiful and seductive as ever. Romantics enjoy Paris on Valentine's Day, of course, and there is no shortage of romantic places to linger in Paris.

Someday, visit Paris in winter and—for a few days—become a Parisian.

WINTER

PARIS CONNECTIONS

This chapter covers Paris' two main airports, one smaller airport, seven train stations, long-distance buses, parking tips for drivers, and how to reach the city from the cruise port at Le Havre.

Whether you're aiming to catch a train or plane, budget plenty of time to reach your departure point. Paris is a big, crowded city, and getting across town or from terminal to terminal on time is a goal you'll share with millions of others. Factor in traffic delays and walking time through huge stations and vast terminals. At the airport, expect healthy lines at check-in, baggage check, and security points. Always keep your luggage safely near you. Thieves prey on jet-lagged and confused tourists using public transportation.

By Plane

Here's a rundown of Paris' major airports and the best ways to get into the city from each. For more on flights within Europe, see the Practicalities chapter.

CHARLES DE GAULLE AIRPORT

Paris' main airport (code: CDG, www.charlesdegaulleairport. co.uk) has three terminals: T-1, T-2, and T-3. Most flights from the US use T-1 or T-2. Connect the three terminals on the free CDGVAL shuttle train (departs every 5 minutes, 24/7). Allow a full hour to travel between gates across terminals T-1, T-2, and T-3. All three terminals have access to ground transportation.

When leaving Paris, make sure you know which terminal you are departing from (if it's T-2, you'll also need to know which hall you're leaving from—they're labeled *A* through *F*). Plan to arrive at the airport three hours early for an overseas flight, and two hours for flights within Europe (particularly on budget airlines, which

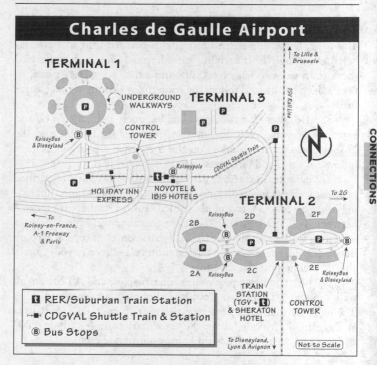

Charles de Gaulle Airport

TERMINAL 1

UNDERGROUND
WALKWAYS

TERMINAL 3

CONTROL
TOWER

RoissyBus
& Disneyland

To Lille &
Brussels

TGV Rail line

CDGVAL Shuttle Train

Roissypole

HOLIDAY INN
EXPRESS

NOVOTEL &
IBIS HOTELS

To
Roissy-en-France,
A-1 Freeway
& Paris

TERMINAL 2

To 2G

RoissyBus

2D   2F

2B

2A   RoissyBus   2C   2E   RoissyBus
& Disneyland

TRAIN
STATION
(TGV + 🚇)
& SHERATON
HOTEL

CONTROL
TOWER

To Disneyland,
Lyon & Avignon

🚇 RER/Suburban Train Station
▪ CDGVAL Shuttle Train & Station
Ⓑ Bus Stops

Not to Scale

can have especially long check-in lines). For airport and flight info,
visit www.parisaeroport.fr.

Services: Terminals 1 and 2 have Paris Tourisme information
desks, where you can get city maps, buy a Paris Museum Pass, and
get tickets for the RoissyBus or RER/Train-B to Paris—a terrific
time- and hassle-saver. Ticket machines at the two airport train
stations sell Navigo Découverte passes and five-zone Navigo Easy
cards, both of which cover the trip from the airport into Paris (for
details, see page 35; Navigo Easy cards may also be sold at Paris
Tourisme desks). You'll also find ATMs *(distributeurs),* free Wi-Fi,
shops, cafés, and bars. If you're returning home and want a VAT
refund, look for tax-refund centers in the check-in area.

Terminal 1 (T-1)

This three-floor circular terminal was closed in 2022 for a floor-to-
ceiling renovation and may not reopen until late 2023. If arriving
here, walk around the terminal to find the Paris Tourisme desk,
RoissyBus, Disneyland shuttle, car-rental counters, and taxis. (The
terminal's round shape can be confusing—if you feel like you're
going around in circles, you probably are.) The CDGVAL shuttle
train is on the first floor. Those departing from this terminal will
find the usual assortment of shops and eateries.

Terminal 2 (T-2)

This long, horseshoe-shaped terminal is divided into six halls, labeled *A* through *F*. If arriving here, be ready for long walks and short train rides to baggage claim and exits. It's a busy place, so take a deep breath and follow the sometimes skimpy signage carefully.

Shuttle buses *(navettes)* circulate between T-2 halls A, C, and F on the arrivals level. To find bus stops for RoissyBus, and the Disneyland shuttle—marked on the map on the previous page—follow *bus* signs and bus icons from exit *(sortie)* E-8.

T-2 has a **train station,** with RER trains into Paris (described later), as well as longer-distance trains to the rest of France (including high-speed TGV trains, also called "InOui" trains). It's located between T-2C/D and T-2E/F, below the Sheraton Hotel (prepare for a long walk to reach your train). Shuttle buses to several **airport hotels** leave from above the train station at T-2 (verify your hotel's shuttle pickup point in advance).

Car-rental offices, post offices, pharmacies, and ATMs are all well-signed. T-2 E/F has duty-free shopping arcades, and other T-2 halls have smaller duty-free shops. You can stash your bags at Baggage du Monde, above the train station in T-2 (daily 6:00-21:30, +33 1 48 16 02 15, www.bagagesdumonde.com).

Terminal 3 (T-3)

By far the smallest of the three terminals, T-3 serves mostly smaller, low-cost, and charter airlines. It's connected to the CDGVAL shuttle train and offers limited shops and food services. There is no Paris Toursime office nor car rental here, but a handy RER-B station and Roissybus bus stop are a 5-minute walk away at Roissypole. Blablabus and Flixbuses depart from here.

Getting Between Charles de Gaulle Airport and Paris

Buses, RER trains, airport vans, and taxis link the airport's terminals with central Paris. If you're traveling with two or more companions, carrying lots of baggage, or are just plain tired, taxis (or Uber) are well worth the extra cost, but keep in mind that they can be slow during weekday rush-hour traffic. Total travel time to your hotel should be around 1.5 hours by bus and Métro, one hour by train and Métro, and 50 minutes by taxi. At the airport, using buses and taxis requires shorter walks than the RER train. Transfers to Métro lines often involve stairs and long corridors. For more information, check the "Getting There" tab at www. charlesdegaulleairport.co.uk. For tips on reaching your hotel neighborhood from the various bus/train/van drop-off points, see the sidebar.

Public Transportation to Recommended Hotels

You have many options for traveling between Charles de Gaulle Airport and Paris; which alternative makes the most sense depends on where you're staying and your budget. Here are my tips for reaching recommended hotel neighborhoods.

Rue Cler Area: For hotels near the Ecole Militaire and La Tour Maubourg Métro stops, take the **RoissyBus** directly to the Opéra, then take Métro line 8 (direction: Balard). For hotels closer to the river take **RER/Train-B** from the airport, change at the St. Michel stop for RER/Train-C (direction: Versailles Château Rive Gauche or Pontoise), and get off at Invalides or Pont de l'Alma.

Marais: For hotels near Place des Vosges, take the **RoissyBus** to the Opéra Métro, then transfer to Métro line 8 (direction: Créteil Préfecture) and get off at Bastille. Or, take **RER/Train-B** from the airport to the Châtelet-Les Halles stop and transfer to Métro line 1 (direction: Château de Vincennes; long walk with some stairs in a huge station—it's the biggest subway station in the world), and get off at Hôtel de Ville, St. Paul, or Bastille.

Ile St. Louis: Take **RER/Train-B** to the St. Michel stop, follow signs for *Sortie Notre-Dame,* and walk 15 minutes to your hotel.

Luxembourg Garden: Ride **RER/Train-B** to the Luxembourg stop.

Montmartre: Take **RER/Train-B** to Gare du Nord, transfer to Métro line 4 (direction: Porte de Clignancourt) and ride three stops to Marcadet-Poissoniers, then transfer to line 12 (direction: Mairie d'Issy). Ride three or four stops and get off at Abbesses or Pigalle.

By Bus

RoissyBus: This bus drops you off at the Opéra Métro stop in central Paris (€15, runs 6:00-23:00, 3-4/hour, 50 minutes; buy ticket at airport Paris Tourisme desk, ticket machine, or on bus; www.ratp.fr). The RoissyBus arrives on Rue Scribe; to get to the Métro entrance or nearest taxi stand, turn left as you exit the bus and walk counterclockwise around the lavish Opéra building to its front. A taxi to any of my recommended hotels costs about €15 from here.

By RER Train

Paris' commuter RER/Train-B is the fastest public transit option for getting between the airport and the city center (€11.50, runs 5:00-24:00, 4/hour, about 35 minutes; you'll see "RER" on maps and signage). There are two RER-B train stations at CDG airport, a busy one at Terminal 2 and a quiet one near Terminal 3 (called

Roissypole). The two stations are connected to all terminals by frequent CDGVAL shuttle trains.

RER/Train-B runs directly to several central RER/Métro stations (including Gare du Nord, Châtelet-Les Halles, St. Michel, and Luxembourg); from there, you can hop the Métro to your destination. RER/Train-B is handy and cheap, but it can require walking with your luggage through big, crowded stations—especially at Châtelet-Les Halles, where a transfer to the Métro can take 10-15 minutes and may include stairs.

To reach RER/Train-B from any airport terminal, follow *Train* signs. (If you land at T-1, take the CDGVAL shuttle to T-3/Roissypole.) Paris Tourisme offices may sell five-zone Navigo Easy cards for the RER to Paris, or you can buy either the Navigo Easy card or Navigo Découverte pass from ticket machines at the station (labeled *Paris/Ile de France,* takes cash and American credit cards).

For step-by-step instructions on taking RER/Train-B into Paris, see www.parisbytrain.com (see the options under "Airport"). Beware of thieves on the train; wear your money belt and keep your bags close.

To return to the airport on RER/Train-B from central Paris, allow plenty of time to get to your departure gate (plan for a 15-minute Métro or bus ride to the closest RER/Train-B station, a 15-minute wait for your train, a 35-minute train ride, plus walking time through the stations and airport). Navigo Découverte passes and Navigo Easy passes (with the 5-zone add-on) are valid on RER/B to the airport. The standard 2-zone Navigo Easy passes are not. When you catch your train, make sure the sign over the platform shows *Aéroport Roissy-Charles de Gaulle* as a stop served. (The line splits, so not every RER/Train-B serves the airport.) If you're not clear, ask another rider, *"Air-o-por sharl duh gaul?"*

Other Options

These transportation options can be slow on weekday mornings due to rush-hour traffic.

Airport Van: Shuttle vans carry passengers to and from their hotels, with stops along the way to drop off and pick up other riders. Shuttles require you to book a precise pickup time in advance—even though you can't know if your flight will arrive on time. For that reason, they work best for trips *from* your hotel to the airport. Though not as fast as taxis, shuttle vans are a good value for single travelers and big families (about €30 for one person, per-person price decreases the more you have in your party; have hotelier book at least a day in advance). Several companies offer shuttle service; I usually just go with the one my hotel uses. For groups of three or four, take a taxi or Uber instead.

Taxi or Uber: Taxis charge a flat rate into Paris (€60 to the Left Bank, €55 to the Right Bank). Taxis can comfortably carry three people with bags, and are legally required to accept a fourth passenger (though they may not like it; beyond that, there's an extra passenger supplement). Larger parties can wait for a larger vehicle. Don't take an unauthorized taxi from cabbies greeting you on arrival. Official taxi stands are well signed.

For taxi trips from Paris to the airport, have your hotel arrange it. Specify that you want a real taxi *(un taxi normal)*, not a limo service that costs €20 more (and gives your hotel a kickback). For weekday-morning departures (7:00-10:00), reserve at least a day ahead (€7 reservation fee payable by credit card).

Uber offers Paris airport pickup and drop-off for the same rates as taxis, but since they can't use the bus-only lanes (normal taxis can), expect some added time. Charles de Gaulle does not have a designated ride-sharing pickup point, making Uber a more complicated option. You'll have to work out a meeting point with your driver.

Private Car Service: These professional car services work well from the airport because your driver meets you inside the terminal and waits if you're late: **Paris Webservices Private Car** (2 people/€90 one-way, €5-10/extra person up to 7, +33 1 45 56 91 67 or +33 9 52 06 02 59, www.pariswebservices.com). They also offer guided tours—see page 55. **Inter Service Prestige** is a reliable service with good rates (www.interserviceprestige.com, + 33 7 62 23 23 3).

Rental Car: Car-rental desks are well signed from the arrival halls. Be prepared for a maze of ramps as you drive away from the lot—get directions from the rental clerks when you do the paperwork. For information on driving and parking in Paris, see the end of this chapter.

When returning your car, allow ample time to reach the drop-off lots (at T-1 and T-2), especially if flying out of T-2. Check your rental company's exact drop-off location—there are several, and imperfect signage can make return lots confusing to find.

From Charles de Gaulle Airport to Disneyland Paris

The Magical Shuttle bus to Disneyland leaves from T-2 E/F, door 8 or T-1, door 34 (€23, €10 for children 11 and under, daily 7:00-18:00, later in summer, 45 minutes, see timetable at www. magicalshuttle.co.uk). TGV trains run to Disneyland from the airport in 10 minutes, but they leave only hourly and require a shuttle bus ride at the Disneyland end.

ORLY AIRPORT

This easy-to-navigate airport (code: ORY, www.airport-orly.com) feels small, but it has all the services you'd expect at a major airport: ATMs and currency exchange, car-rental desks, cafés, shops, post offices, and more. Orly is good for rental-car pickup and drop-off, as it's closer to Paris and easier to navigate than Charles de Gaulle Airport.

Orly has four terminals (1-4). At all terminals, arrivals are on the ground level (level 0) and departures are on level 1. You can connect the terminals with the free Orlyval shuttle train (well signed).

Services: Paris Tourisme desks are in the arrivals area (a good spot to buy the Paris Museum Pass and fares for public transit into Paris).

Getting Between Orly Airport and Paris

Shuttle buses *(navettes)*, RER trains, airport vans, and taxis connect Paris with Orly. Bus stops and taxis are centrally located at arrivals levels and are well signed.

By Bus or Tram: Bus bays are found in the Sud terminal outside exits L and G, and in the Ouest terminal outside exit D.

For the cheapest (but slow) access to central Paris (best for the Marais area), take **tram line 7** from outside the Terminal 4 (direction: Villejuif-Louis Aragon) to the Villejuif station to catch Métro line 7 (you'll need one fare for the tram and one for the Métro—buy a Navigo Easy card at the Paris Tourisme desk in the terminal, 4/hour, 45 minutes to Villejuif Métro station, then 15-minute Métro ride to the Marais).

By RER Train: The next two options take you to **RER/Train-B,** with access to the Luxembourg Garden area, Notre-Dame Cathedral, handy Métro line 1 at the Châtelet stop, Gare du Nord, and Charles de Gaulle Airport. You can use a Navigo Easy card (with an €8.50 Orlybus add-on) or Navigo Découverte pass for the Orlybus (and RER), but not the Orlyval shuttle train.

The **Orlybus** goes directly to the Denfert-Rochereau Métro and RER/Train-B stations (€9.50, 3/hour, 30 minutes). The pricier but more frequent—and more comfortable—**Orlyval shuttle train** takes you to the Antony RER/Train-B station (about €12, 6/hour, 40 minutes). The Orlyval train is well signed and leaves from the departure level. Once at the RER/Train-B station, take the train in direction: Mitry-Claye or Aéroport Charles de Gaulle to reach central Paris.

For access to Left Bank neighborhoods (including Rue Cler) via **RER/Train-C,** take the bus marked *Go C Paris* five minutes to the Pont de Rungis station (€2 shuttle only, €6.35 combo-ticket includes RER/Train-C), then catch RER/Train-C to St. Michel,

Musée d'Orsay, Invalides, or Pont de l'Alma (direction: Versailles Château Rive Gauche or Pontoise, 4/hour, 35 minutes).

By Airport Van: From Orly, figure about €25 for one person or €30 for two (less per person for larger groups and kids). For more on airport vans, see "Getting Between Charles de Gaulle and Paris," earlier.

By Taxi: Taxis wait outside baggage claim areas. Allow 30 minutes for a taxi ride into central Paris (fixed fare: €32 for Left Bank, €37 for Right Bank).

By Uber: Follow the signs to *Ground Transportation* and *Baggage Claim*, exit the terminal, and look for signs showing *Passenger Pickups* or *TNC/Rideshares*, then call or message your driver with your precise location (your terminal and the number of the closest exit door).

From Orly Airport to Disneyland Paris

The Magical Shuttle bus to Disneyland departs from the main bus bays (€23, €10 for kids under 12, runs hourly about 9:00-20:00, 45 minutes, www.magicalshuttle.co.uk).

BEAUVAIS AIRPORT

Budget airlines such as Ryanair use this small airport with two terminals (T-1 and T-2), offering dirt-cheap airfares but leaving you 50 miles north of Paris. Still, this airport has direct buses to Paris and is handy for travelers heading to Normandy or Belgium (car rental available). The airport is basic, waiting areas can be crowded, and services sparse (code: BVA, toll +33 8 92 68 20 66, www.aeroportparisbeauvais.com).

Getting Between Beauvais Airport and Paris

By Bus: Buses depart from a stop between the two terminals (€17 one-way, 2/hour, 1.5 hours to Paris, buy ticket online to save time, http://tickets.aeroportbeauvais.com). Buses arrive at Porte Maillot on the west edge of Paris (where you can connect to Métro line 1 and RER/Train-C); the closest taxi stand is next door at the Hôtel Hyatt Regency Paris Etoile. To return to Beauvais Airport from Porte Maillot, catch the bus in the parking lot at 22 Boulevard Pershing next to the Hyatt Regency.

By Train: You'll first connect from Beauvais Airport to the town's train station: Take the Hôtel/Aéroport Navette shuttle or local bus #6 (2-4/hour, 25 minutes). From here, trains connect Beauvais' city center and Paris' Gare du Nord (1-2/hour, 1.5 hours).

By Taxi: Cabs run from Beauvais Airport to the Beauvais train station or city center (€18), or to central Paris (allow €170 and 1.5 hours).

CONNECTING PARIS' AIRPORTS
Charles de Gaulle and Orly

RER/Train-B connects Charles de Gaulle and Orly but requires a transfer to the Orlyval train. It's faster than a taxi when there's traffic (€20, 5/hour, 1.5 hours). This line splits at both ends: Heading from Charles de Gaulle to Orly, take trains that serve the Antony stop (direction: St-Rémy-les-Chevreuse), then transfer to the Orlyval shuttle train; heading from Orly to Charles de Gaulle, take trains that end at the airport—Aéroport Charles de Gaulle-Roissy, not Mitry-Claye (use Navigo Découverte or Navigo Easy pass with 5-zone add-on).

Taxis take about one hour and are easiest, but pricey (about €100, book online for best rates, http://city-airport-taxis.com).

Charles de Gaulle (or Orly) and Beauvais

You can connect Charles de Gaulle or Orly to Beauvais via Gare du Nord, then by train to the town of Beauvais. From there, you can take a shuttle, local bus, or taxi to Beauvais Airport. From Charles de Gaulle, take **RER/Train-B** to Gare du Nord; from Orly, take the **Orlybus or Orlyval shuttle** train (described earlier, under "Orly Airport") to the RER train station to pick up RER/Train-B to Gare du Nord.

Taxis between Charles de Gaulle and Beauvais take one hour and cost about €120; from Orly, it's about a 1.5-hour taxi ride and about €150 (http://city-airport-taxis.com).

By Train

In this section, I provide an overview of Paris' major train stations and specialty train routes from Paris (including the Eurostar). For more details on train schedules, buying tickets, and using France's long-distance rail system, see the Practicalities chapter. It's also smart to comparison shop with bus services like BlaBlaBus and FlixBus, (see "Paris Bus Connections," later).

Paris is Europe's rail hub, with six major stations and one minor station, and trains heading in different directions:
- Gare du Nord (northbound trains)
- Gare Montparnasse (west- and southwest-bound trains)
- Gare de Lyon (southeast-bound trains)
- Gare de l'Est (eastbound trains)
- Gare St. Lazare (northwest-bound trains)
- Gare d'Austerlitz (southwest-bound trains)
- Gare de Bercy (smaller station with non-TGV trains mostly serving cities in Burgundy)

At any train station you can get schedule information, make

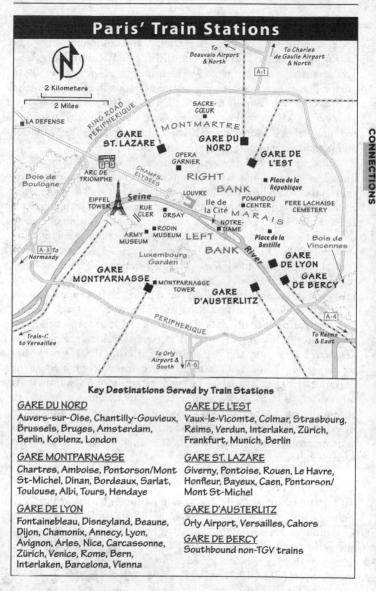

Paris' Train Stations

2 Kilometers

2 Miles

LA DEFENSE

RING ROAD PERIPHERIQUE

To Beauvais Airport & North

To Charles de Gaulle Airport & North

A-1

SACRE-CŒUR

MONTMARTRE

GARE ST. LAZARE

GARE DU NORD

GARE DE L'EST

OPERA GARNIER

Bois de Boulogne

ARC DE TRIOMPHE

CHAMPS-ELYSEES

RIGHT BANK

Place de la République

EIFFEL TOWER

Seine

LOUVRE

Ile de la Cité

POMPIDOU CENTER

PERE LACHAISE CEMETERY

RUE CLER

ORSAY

NOTRE-DAME

MARAIS

A-3 *To Normandy*

ARMY MUSEUM

RODIN MUSEUM

LEFT BANK

Place de la Bastille

River

Bois de Vincennes

Luxembourg Garden

GARE DE LYON

GARE MONTPARNASSE

MONTPARNASSE TOWER

GARE DE BERCY

GARE D'AUSTERLITZ

PERIPHERIQUE

A-4

Train-C to Versailles

To Orly Airport & South

A-6

To Reims & East

CONNECTIONS

Key Destinations Served by Train Stations

GARE DU NORD
Auvers-sur-Oise, Chantilly-Gouvieux, Brussels, Bruges, Amsterdam, Berlin, Koblenz, London

GARE MONTPARNASSE
Chartres, Amboise, Pontorson/Mont St-Michel, Dinan, Bordeaux, Sarlat, Toulouse, Albi, Tours, Hendaye

GARE DE LYON
Fontainebleau, Disneyland, Beaune, Dijon, Chamonix, Annecy, Lyon, Avignon, Arles, Nice, Carcassonne, Zürich, Venice, Rome, Bern, Interlaken, Barcelona, Vienna

GARE DE L'EST
Vaux-le-Vicomte, Colmar, Strasbourg, Reims, Verdun, Interlaken, Zürich, Frankfurt, Munich, Berlin

GARE ST. LAZARE
Giverny, Pontoise, Rouen, Le Havre, Honfleur, Bayeux, Caen, Pontorson/Mont St-Michel

GARE D'AUSTERLITZ
Orly Airport, Versailles, Cahors

GARE DE BERCY
Southbound non-TGV trains

reservations, and buy tickets for any destination. The main train stations all have free Wi-Fi, banks or currency exchanges, ATMs, train information desks, cafés, newsstands, and clever pickpockets (pay attention in ticket lines—keep your bag firmly gripped in front of you). Not all have baggage checks.

Each station offers two types of rail service: long distance to other cities, called Grandes Lignes (major lines, TGV—also called

"InOui"—or slower, TER trains that serve smaller destinations and generally don't require reservations); and commuter service to nearby areas, called Banlieue, Transilien, or RER train lines A-K. You also may see ticket windows identified as *Ile de France*. These are for Transilien trains serving destinations outside Paris in the Ile de France region (usually no more than an hour from Paris). When arriving by Métro, follow signs for *Grandes Lignes–SNCF* to find the main tracks. Métro and RER train lines A-K, as well as buses and taxis, are well marked at every station.

Budget plenty of time before your departure to factor in ticket lines and making your way through large, crowded stations. Paris train stations can be intimidating, but if you slow down, take a deep breath, and ask for help, you'll find them manageable and efficient. Bring a pad of paper and a pen for clear communication at ticket/info windows. It helps to write down the ticket you want. For instance: "28/05/23 Paris-Nord→Lyon dep. 18:30." All stations have a central information booth *(accueil)*; bigger stations have roving helpers, usually wearing red or blue vests. They're capable of answering rail questions more quickly than the staff at the information desks or ticket windows. I make a habit of confirming my track number and departure time with these helpers (all rail staff speak English).

Ticket sales are often split between trains leaving today *(Départs pour ce jour)* and departures for another day *(Départs pour un autre jour)*. You may need to use touch-screen computers at the entrance (English available) to get a ticket-window number. At all stations in Paris, you'll need to scan your ticket at turnstiles to access the tracks. Smaller stations continue to use the old system of validating your ticket in yellow machines near the platform or waiting area. Print-at-home tickets or etickets on your phone don't require validation.

GARE DU NORD

The granddaddy of Paris' train stations serves cities in northern France and international destinations north of Paris, including Copenhagen, Amsterdam, and the Eurostar to London, as well as two of the day trips described in this book (Chantilly and Auvers-sur-Oise).

From the Métro, follow *Gare du Nord* signs through a maze of escalators and mezzanines to reach the tracks at street level. Grandes Lignes (main line) trains depart from tracks 2-21 (tracks 20 and 21 are around the corner), Banlieue/Transilien lines and RER (H and K) leave from tracks 30-36 (signed *Réseau Ile-de-France*), and RER trains (B, D, E) are signed one floor below. Eurostar trains (to London via the Chunnel) check in on the second level, up the stairs near track 17. The lounge for Thalys trains (high-speed trains to Brussels and Amsterdam) is at 22 Rue de Dunkerque (outside to the left if facing the train station).

Services: Look for circulating information-helpers. A helpful TI kiosk (labeled *Paris Tourist Office*, Mon-Sat 9:00-17:00, closed Sun) opposite track 8 sells Paris Museum Passes and fast-pass *"coupe-file"* tickets (credit cards only). International and main-line ticket counters are opposite track 3. Tickets for other trains are sold at the windows past track 19 around the corner. Pay WCs are down the stairs across from track 10. Baggage check and rental cars are near track 3 and down the steps. Taxis are out the door past track 3. Steps down to the Métro are opposite tracks 10 and 19.

Key Destinations Served by Gare du Nord Grandes Lignes: **Auvers-sur-Oise** (hourly, 1.5 hours with transfer, one direct train April-Oct Sat-Sun only at about 9:30, 45 minutes, may not appear on rail websites except www.transilien.com, usually leaves from track 36), **Chantilly-Gouvieux** (look for destination "Creil" or "Compiègne," every 1-1.5 hours, fewer on weekends, 25 minutes, also served by slower RER/Train-D), **Brussels** by Thalys (at least hourly, 1.5 hours), **Bruges** (at least hourly, 3 hours, change in Brussels), **Amsterdam** by Thalys (8/day direct, more with transfer, 3.5 hours), **Berlin** (6/day, 8.5 hours, change in Cologne or Dortmund), **Koblenz** (6/day, 5 hours, change in Cologne, more from Gare de l'Est that don't cross Belgium), and **London** by Eurostar (1-2/hour, 2.5 hours).

By Banlieue/RER Lines: Chantilly-Gouvieux (3/hour, 50 minutes), **Charles de Gaulle Airport** (4/hour, 35 minutes, track 41-44), and **Pontoise** (2/hour, 50 minutes).

GARE MONTPARNASSE

This big, modern station covers three floors, serves lower Normandy and Brittany, and has TGV service to the Loire Valley and southwestern France, as well as suburban service to Chartres. Trains to Chartres usually depart from tracks 18-24.

Services: Most services are provided on the top level (second floor up, Hall 1), where all trains arrive and depart. Baggage check *(consignes)* and WCs are by track 24, and the ticket office *(billetterie)* is by track 1. Taxis are to the far right. Car-rental desks are also to the right, along track 24 and up the escalator to Hall 2 (except Hertz, which has offices outside the station at 45 Avenue du Maine and at 15 Rue du Commandant René Mouchotte).

City buses are out front, between the train station and the Montparnasse Tower (down the escalator through the glassy fa-

Key Transportation Phrases

French	English
accueil (ah-kuh-yeh)	information/assistance
niveau (nee-voh)	level
billets (bee-yay)	tickets
réservation (ray-zehr-vah-see-ohn)	reservation
départs (day-par)	departures
arrivées (ah-ree-vay)	arrivals
aller simple (ah-lay san-pluh)	one-way
aller-retour (ah-lay ruh-toor)	round-trip
côté fenêtre/couloir (koh-tay fuh-neh-truh/kool-wahr)	window/aisle seat
fenêtre isolée (fuh-neh-truh ee-zoh-lay)	single seat by window (first class only)
première classe (pruhm-yehr klahs)	first class
deuxième classe (duhz-yehm klahs)	second class
voyageurs munis de billets (voy-ah-zhur moo-nee duh bee-yay)	travelers with tickets
la porte du masque est obligatoire (lah pohrt dew mahsk eht oh-blee-gah-twahr)	wearing a mask is required

cade). Bus #96 is good for connecting to Marais and Luxembourg-area hotels, while #92 is ideal for Rue Cler hotels (both easier than the Métro).

Key Destinations Served by Gare Montparnasse: Chartres (14/day, 1 hour), **Amboise** (8/day in 1.5 hours with change in St-Pierre-des-Corps, requires TGV reservation; non-TGV trains leave from Gare d'Austerlitz), **Pontorson/Mont St-Michel** (2-3/day, 4 hours, via Rennes or Caen), **Dinan** (6/day, 3 hours, change in Rennes and Dol), **Bordeaux** (10/day, 2.5 hours), **Sarlat** (4/day, 5 hours, change in Bordeaux), **Toulouse** (6/day, 4.5 hours, more with change in Bordeaux), **Albi** (6/day, 6.5 hours, change in Montauban or Toulouse), **Tours** (8/day, 1 hour), and **Hendaye** (8/day, 5 hours, connect here to **San Sebastian** by local train).

French	English
navette (nah-veht)	shuttle bus
banlieue (bahn-lee-yuh)	suburban
quai (kay)	platform
accès aux quais (ahk-seh oh kay)	access to the platforms
voie (vwah)	track
à l'heure (ah lur)	on time
retard (ruh-tar)	delay
salle d'attente (sahl dah-tah<u>n</u>t)	waiting room
consignes (koh<u>n</u>-seen-yuh) (also *espaces bagages*)	baggage check (also *espaces bagages*)
consignes automatique (koh<u>n</u>-seen-yuh oh-toh-mah-teek)	storage lockers
Grandes Lignes (grah<u>n</u>d leen-yuh)	major domestic and international lines
Transilien (trahn-seel-ee-yehn)	suburban lines
RATP (ehr ah tay pay)	Paris' Métro and bus system
SNCF (S N say F)	France's countrywide train system
TGV (tay zhay vay)	high-speed lines (old term)
InOui (in-wee)	high-speed lines (new term)

GARE DE LYON

This huge, bewildering station offers TGV and regular service to southeastern France, Italy, Switzerland, and other international destinations. Frequent Banlieue trains serve Fontainebleau.

From the RER train or Métro, follow signs for *Grandes Lignes/ Gare de Lyon* to reach the street-level platforms (Grandes Lignes and Banlieue lines share the same tracks). Platforms are divided into two areas: Hall 1 (tracks A-N) and Hall 2 (tracks 5-23). Hall 3 is underground with more ticket offices, food services, and quieter waiting areas—but no trains.

Monitors indicate the hall number at least 30 minutes before the track number is posted, so you know in advance which hall your train leaves from. For Grandes Lignes, arrive at your track at least 20 minutes early to pass ticket control (your ticket or reservation will be scanned).

Taxi stands are well signed in front of, and underneath, the station.

Services: An interior corridor connecting Halls 1 and 2 (by track A) offers many services, including shops and ticket windows for Grandes Lignes. Hall 2 has the best services—including a train-information office, pharmacy, and a handy Monop grocery store. You'll find baggage check *(consignes)* in Hall 2 down the ramp, opposite track 17, and in Hall 1, downstairs by track M. Car rental is out the exit past track M (Hall 1). There's a Starbucks below Hall 2 with good Wi-Fi. Don't leave the station without at least taking a peek at the recommended Le Train Bleu Restaurant in Hall 1, up the stairs opposite tracks G-L (no elevator, see listing on page 467). Its pricey but atmospheric bar/lounge works well as a quiet waiting area—and there's free Wi-Fi. Slip into a leather chair and time travel back to another era.

Key Destinations Served by Gare de Lyon: Fontainebleau (nearly hourly, 45 minutes; depart from the Grandes Lignes level), **Disneyland** (RER/Train-A to Marne-la-Vallée-Chessy, at least 3/hour, 45 minutes), **Beaune** (roughly hourly at rush hour but few midday, 2.5 hours, most require change in Dijon; direct trains from Paris' Bercy station take an hour longer), **Dijon** (TGV trains only, roughly hourly, 1.5 hours; see Gare de Bercy for local trains), **Chamonix** (7/day, 7 hours, some change in Switzerland), **Annecy** (hourly, 4 hours, many with change in Lyon), **Lyon** (at least hourly, 2 hours), **Avignon** (10/day direct, 2.5 hours to Avignon TGV station; 10/day in 3.5 hours to Avignon Centre-Ville Station), **Arles** (11/day, 4 hours), **Nice** (hourly, 6 hours, may require change; night train available, 12 hours), **Carcassonne** (10/day, 5-6 hours, 1-2 changes), **Zürich** (4/day direct, 4 hours), **Venice** (7/day, 11 hours with 1-3 changes; 1 direct overnight—see "Specialty Trains from Paris," later), **Rome** (7/day, 12 hours, 1-3 changes), **Bern** (8/day with change in Basel, 4.5 hours), **Interlaken** (8/day with change in Basel, 6 hours, 8/day more from Gare de l'Est), **Barcelona** (2-4/day direct, 7 hours), and **Vienna** (3/week, 14 hours).

GARE DE L'EST

This two-floor station (with underground Métro and mini shopping mall) serves northeastern France and international destinations east of Paris. All trains depart at street level from tracks 1-30. Separate monitors show Ile de France and Grandes Lignes departures.

Services: A train-information and ticket office is opposite track 9. Most other services are on the floor below, opposite tracks 12-20 (baggage check, car rental, WC, small grocery store, and Métro access). Access to taxis and buses is in front of the station (exit with your back to the tracks).

Key Destinations Served by Gare de l'Est: Vaux-le-Vicomte (take train to Verneuil-l'Etang, direction: Provins, 1/hour, 30 minutes, and catch connecting bus from there, see the More Grand Chateaux chapter), **Colmar** (12/day by TGV, 2.5 hours, 3 direct, others change in Strasbourg), **Strasbourg** (hourly by TGV, under 2 hours), **Reims** Centre station (8/day by direct TGV, 45 minutes, more with transfer in Champagne-Ardenne, 75 minutes), **Verdun** (5/day direct to Meuse TGV station and shuttle bus, 2 hours; 3 hours with transfer), **Interlaken** (12/day, 6 hours, 1-2 changes, faster trains from Gare de Lyon), **Zürich** (12/day, 5-7 hours, 1-2 changes, faster direct trains from Gare de Lyon), **Frankfurt** (4 direct/day, 4 hours; more with change in Karlsruhe, 4.5 hours), **Munich** (1/day direct, 6/day with 1 change, 6 hours), and **Berlin** (6/day, 8.5 hours, 1 change; trains run via Germany, not Belgium).

GARE ST. LAZARE

This compact station serves upper Normandy, including Rouen and Giverny. All trains arrive and depart one floor above street level.

From the Métro, follow signs to *Grandes Lignes* to reach the tracks five floors up (escalators available). You'll pass through several levels of shops, including a good grocery shop, pharmacy, and more. On departure monitors, purple squares  are for tracks 1-11, green for tracks 12-21, and blue for tracks 22-27. Most Grandes Lignes to Normandy depart from tracks 22-27 (though a few depart from the Ile de France section). Ile de France trains depart from 1-16. The ticket and information office *(accueil)*, car rental, and WCs are near track 27. The Ile de France train information office is opposite track 6. Baggage check is available near the station at Annexx Lockers (6 Rue de Constantinople, www.lockers.fr). Taxis, the Métro, and buses are well signed.

Key Destinations Served by Gare St. Lazare: Giverny (train to Vernon, about hourly, 1 hour; then bus to Giverny, 2/hour, 15 minutes), **Pontoise** (1-2/hour, 40 minutes), **Rouen** (nearly hourly, 1.5 hours), **Le Havre** (hourly, 2.5 hours, some change in Rouen), **Honfleur** (13/day, 2-3.5 hours, via Lisieux, Deauville, or Le Havre, then bus), **Bayeux** (9/day, 2.5 hours, most change in Caen, some require a second change), **Caen** (14/day, 2.5 hours), and **Pontorson/Mont St-Michel** (4/day, 4-5.5 hours, via Caen; more trains from Gare Montparnasse).

GARE D'AUSTERLITZ

This small station currently provides non-TGV service to the Loire Valley and southwestern France (several tracks are being retrofitted to accommodate TGV trains). All tracks are at street level. The information booth and a comfortable waiting room are opposite track 17, and all ticket sales are in the riverside entry hall. Baggage check and WCs are at "Espaces Services," near track 1 (with pay showers that include towel and soap).

To get to the Métro and RER/Train-C, you must walk outside and along either side of the station. Car rental is across the river at Gare de Lyon (a level 10-minute walk—follow signs opposite track 1).

Key Destinations Served by Gare d'Austerlitz: Orly Airport (via RER/Train-C, 4/hour, 35 minutes), **Versailles** (via RER/Train-C, 4/hour, 35 minutes), and **Cahors** (4/day direct, 5 hours; slower trains with transfers and from Gare Montparnasse).

GARE DE BERCY

This smaller station mostly handles southbound non-TGV trains such as to **Dijon** (6/day, 3 hours), but some TGV trains also stop here in peak season (Mo: Bercy, one stop east of Gare de Lyon on line 14, exit the Bercy Métro station and it's across the street). Facilities are limited—just a WC and a sandwich-fare takeout café.

SPECIALTY TRAINS FROM PARIS
Low-Cost TGV Trains to Elsewhere in France

A TGV train called OuiGo (pronounced "we go") offers rock-bottom fares and no-frills service to select French cities also served by regular TGV trains. Departures are from TGV stations at Gare de Lyon, Gare Montparnasse, Gare de L'Est, Charles de Gaulle Airport, and near Disneyland at Marne-la-Vallée. From central Paris, most routes to western France depart from Montparnasse Vaugirard station in Hall 2, most east-bound service departs from Gare de l'Est, and most southbound service leaves from Gare de Lyon. You must print your ticket within four days of departure (or download it to your phone), arrive 30 minutes before departure, and activate your ticket. Rail passes are not accepted, and you can only bring one carry-on-size bag plus one handbag for free (children's tickets allow you to bring a stroller). Larger or extra luggage is €5/bag if you pay when you buy your ticket. If you show up without paying in advance, it's €20/bag on the train. There's no food service on the train (BYO), but children under age 12 pay only €8 for a seat. The website explains it all in easy-to-understand English (https://en.oui.sncf/en/ouigo).

To Brussels and Amsterdam by Thalys Train

The pricey highspeed Thalys train has the monopoly on the rail route between Paris and Brussels. Without a rail pass, for the Paris-Amsterdam train, you'll pay about €80-205 first class, €35-135 second class (compared to €38-50 by bus); for the Paris-Brussels train it's €65-140 first class, €30-100 second class (€20-30 by bus). Even with a rail pass, you need to pay for train reservations (first class-€25-30, includes a light meal; second class-€20-25). Book early for the best rates (discounted seats are limited, www.thalys.com).

Rail Routes

Eurostar · · · · ·
Thalys +++++
Channel Tunnel ·······

Not to Scale

Thalys also operates a slower, cheaper Paris-to-Brussels train called IZY (2-3/day, 2.5 hours, tickets from €10 for standing room to €29 full fare, rail passes not accepted, luggage limits, online only at www.izy.com). Thalys and IZY trains use Gare du Nord. For another cheap option, try FlixBus or BlaBlaBus (see "Paris Bus Connections," later).

To London by Eurostar Train

The Eurostar zips you from downtown Paris to downtown London at 190 mph in 2.5 hours (about hourly). The tunnel crossing is a 20-minute, silent, 100 mph nonevent. Your ears won't even pop.

Eurostar Tickets and Fares: A one-way ticket between London and Paris can vary widely in price; for instance, $60-275 (Standard class), $150-375 (Standard Premier), and $400 (Business Premier). Fares depend on how far ahead you reserve and whether you're eligible for discounts—available for children (under 12), youths (under 26), and adults booking months ahead or purchasing roundtrip. You can book tickets up to 4-6 months in advance. Tickets can be exchanged before the scheduled departure for a fee (about $55, may be waived for early exchanges) plus the cost of any price increase, but only Business Premier class allows a refund.

Buy tickets ahead at Ricksteves.com/rail or at Eurostar.com (French toll +33 1 70 70 60 88, €14 handling fee if you book by phone). In continental Europe you can buy Eurostar tickets at any major train station in any country or at any travel agency that handles train tickets (booking fee).

If you have a Eurail Global Pass, seat reservations are avail-

Building the Chunnel

The toughest obstacle to building a tunnel under the English Channel was overcome in 1986, when longtime rivals Britain and France reached an agreement to build it together. Britain began in Folkestone, France in Calais, planning a rendezvous in the middle.

By 1988, specially-made machines three football fields long were boring 26-foot-wide tubes under the ground. The dirt they hauled out became landfill in Britain and a hill in France. Crews crept forward 100 feet a day until June 1991, when French and English workers broke through and shook hands midway across the Channel—the tunnel was complete. Rail service began in 1994.

The Chunnel is 31 miles long—24 miles of it under water. It sits 130 feet below the seabed in a chalky layer of sediment. It's segmented into three separate tunnels—two for trains (one in each direction) and one for service and ventilation. The walls are concrete panels and rebar fixed to the rock around it. Sixteen-thousand-horsepower engines pull 850 tons of railcars and passengers at speeds up to 100 mph through the tunnel.

The ambitious project—the world's longest undersea tunnel—helped to show Europeans that cooperation between nations could benefit everyone.

able at Eurostar departure stations, Eurail.com, or by phone with Eurostar (generally harder to get at other train stations and travel agencies; $35 in Standard, $45 in Standard Premier, can sell out).

Taking the Eurostar: Eurostar trains depart from and arrive at Paris' Gare du Nord. Arrive early to go through security and passport control (must be completed at least 45 minutes before departure) and locate your departure gate (shown on a TV monitor). Times listed on tickets are local; Britain is one hour earlier than continental Europe. The currency-exchange booth here has rates about the same as you'll find on the other end. There's a reasonable restaurant before the first check-in point, but only a couple of tiny sandwich-and-coffee counters in the cramped waiting area.

Crossing the Channel Without Eurostar: For speed and affordability, look into cheap **flights.** The old-fashioned ways of crossing the Channel are cheaper than Eurostar (taking the **bus** is cheapest; see below)—but twice as complicated and slow. To go by **train and boat** to London, take the TGV train from Paris to Calais, taxi to the port, then catch a P&O ferry to Dover, England (hourly, 1.5 hours, www.poferries.com). From Dover's Priory Station, take a train to London's St. Pancras, Charing Cross, or Victoria Station (hourly, 1.5-2 hours).

By Bus, Car, or Cruise Ship

Below I've provided some information for travelers not arriving by plane or train.

PARIS BUS CONNECTIONS

Buses generally provide the cheapest—if less comfortable and more time-consuming—transportation between French cities, airports, and popular destinations (such as le Mont St. Michel).

For international connections, buses are often far cheaper but much slower than trains: For example, a Thalys train to Amsterdam from Paris takes 3 hours and costs about €135; a bus costs only €20 but takes 6 hours. The bus is also the cheapest way to cross the English Channel; book at least two days in advance for the best fares.

Eurolines is the old standby; two newcomers (BlaBlaBus and FlixBus) are cutting prices drastically, adding more destinations, and ramping up onboard comfort with easy-to-use apps, Wi-Fi, and snacks. These companies provide service from train stations and airports to places within France plus many international destinations. If the schedule works for you, it's a handy and cheap way to connect Paris airports with other French destinations (Blois, Rouen, and Caen, for example) and skip central Paris train stations.

BlaBlaBus has routes mostly within France but also serves some European cities (central Paris stop is at Gare de Bercy, Mo: Bercy, some trips leave from Orly and Charles de Gaulle airports, easy online booking, www.blablabus.com). German-run **FlixBus** connects key cities within France and throughout Europe, often from secondary airports and train stations (central Paris stop is near Gare de Bercy at 208 Quai de Bercy, handy eticket system and easy-to-use app, +33 1 76 36 04 12, www.flixbus.com). **Eurolines'** buses depart from several locations in Paris (www.eurolines.com).

DRIVING AND PARKING IN PARIS

Prepare for monumental traffic jams during rush hours and slow driving at any time in Paris. Speeds are limited to 30 kph (about 19 mph) on all Paris streets within the Périphérique (ring road) freeway. Remember that bus lanes (there are many) are off-limits to cars. There is some talk about limiting traffic in the city center and charging congestion fees; check with your rental company to determine whether this has been implemented and how to arrange for payment.

Street parking is generally free at night (20:00-9:00) and all day Sunday. To pay for streetside parking, use a credit card. Meters limit street parking to a maximum of two hours.

Underground garages are plentiful in Paris. You'll find them under Ecole Militaire, St. Sulpice Church, Les Invalides, the Bastille, and the Panthéon; all charge about €30-55/day (€50-80/3 days, about €10/day more after that, for locations see www.parisfranceparking.com). Some hotels offer parking for less—ask your hotelier.

For a longer stay, park at an airport (about €20/day) and take public transport or a taxi into the city. Orly is closer and easier for drivers to navigate than Charles de Gaulle.

BlaBlaCar is a popular long-distance ride-sharing service connecting drivers with riders, enabling travelers to share the cost of gas, tolls, and other expenses (www.blablacar.in). It's the cheapest way to get around France.

LE HAVRE CRUISE PORT

Though it's a landlocked city, Paris is a popular cruise destination. Ships visiting "Paris" actually call at the industrial city of Le Havre, France's second-biggest port (after Marseille), and the primary French port on the Atlantic.

Paris and Le Havre are connected by train (about 3 hours each way). To get from the port to the Le Havre train/bus station, you can ride a cruise-line shuttle bus or take a taxi. From there, trains leave about every 1-2 hours for the three-hour journey to Paris' St. Lazare station (fewer on weekends).

For port information, see Lehavre-etretat-tourisme.com.

DAY TRIPS FROM PARIS

Château de Versailles • More Grand Châteaux • Chartres • Giverny and Auvers-sur-Oise

Though there's plenty to see within Paris' ring road, quick and efficient public transportation expands your sightseeing horizons. The sights covered in this section are about 30 to 60 minutes from central Paris. Do them as day trips, or—for a more relaxed experience—stay overnight.

The granddaddy of them all is the palace of **Versailles,** 12 miles southwest of Paris. It was the residence of French kings and the cultural heartbeat of Europe for a century (that's right, 100 years). While Versailles is the grandest of the **Grand Châteaux,** fans of these big palaces have plenty of other options, including Vaux-le-Vicomte (the most beautiful), Fontainebleau (thriving town center), or Chantilly (best art). In **Chartres,** an hour southwest of Paris, one of Europe's greatest Gothic cathedrals soars above traffic-free lanes and people-friendly squares—and helps compensate for Notre-Dame's closure in Paris. Lovers of Impressionism and flowers

should make a pilgrimage to **Giverny** to see Claude Monet's garden, with its pond and lily pads still as picturesque as when he painted them. Fans of Vincent van Gogh can visit **Auvers-sur-Oise,** a modest little town that attracted many Impressionist painters, and where Van Gogh spent his final days gazing at crows over wheat fields.

Day Trips from Paris

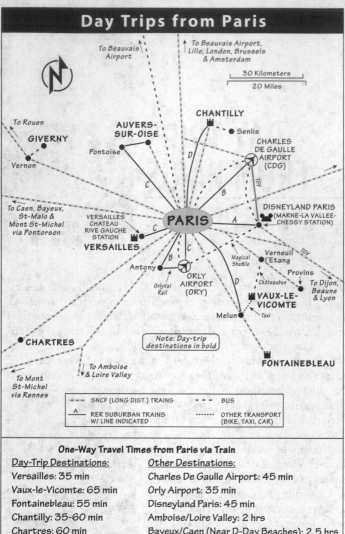

30 Kilometers
20 Miles

To Beauvais Airport

To Beauvais Airport, Lille, London, Brussels & Amsterdam

To Rouen

GIVERNY

Vernon

AUVERS-SUR-OISE

Pontoise

CHANTILLY

Senlis

CHARLES DE GAULLE AIRPORT (CDG)

D

B

TGV

To Caen, Bayeux, St-Malo & Mont St-Michel via Pontorson

VERSAILLES CHATEAU RIVE GAUCHE STATION

C

PARIS

A

DISNEYLAND PARIS (MARNE-LA VALLEE–CHESSY STATION)

C

VERSAILLES

B

Antony

C

Magical Shuttle

Verneuil l'Etang

TGV

OrlyVal Rail

ORLY AIRPORT (ORY)

D

Provins

Châteaubus

To Dijon, Beaune & Lyon

VAUX-LE-VICOMTE

Melun

Taxi

CHARTRES

Note: Day-trip destinations in bold

FONTAINEBLEAU

To Amboise & Loire Valley

To Mont St-Michel via Rennes

SNCF (LONG DIST.) TRAINS   BUS

A   RER SUBURBAN TRAINS
    W/ LINE INDICATED   OTHER TRANSPORT
                                  (BIKE, TAXI, CAR)

One-Way Travel Times from Paris via Train

Day-Trip Destinations:
Versailles: 35 min
Vaux-le-Vicomte: 65 min
Fontainebleau: 55 min
Chantilly: 35-60 min
Chartres: 60 min
Vernon (Giverny): 60 min
Auvers-sur-Oise: 45-90 min

Other Destinations:
Charles De Gaulle Airport: 45 min
Orly Airport: 35 min
Disneyland Paris: 45 min
Amboise/Loire Valley: 2 hrs
Bayeux/Caen (Near D-Day Beaches): 2.5 hrs

VERSAILLES

Château de Versailles

Every king's dream, Versailles (vehr-"sigh") was the residence of French monarchs and the cultural heartbeat of Europe for about 100 years—until the Revolution of 1789 changed all that. The Sun King (Louis XIV) created Versailles, spending freely from the public treasury to turn his dad's hunting lodge into a palace fit for the gods (among whom he counted himself). Louis XV and Louis XVI spent much of the 18th century gilding Louis XIV's lily. In 1837, about 50 years after the royal family was evicted by citizen-protesters, King Louis-Philippe (then a constitutional monarch rather than a divine one) opened the palace as a museum. Today you can visit parts of the huge palace and wander through acres of manicured gardens sprinkled with fountains and studded with statues. Europe's next-best palaces are just Versailles wannabes.

Worth ▲▲▲, Versailles offers three blockbuster sights. The main attraction is the palace itself, called the **Château.** Here you

walk through dozens of lavish, chandeliered rooms once inhabited by Louis XIV and his successors, starring the magnificent Hall of Mirrors. Next come the expansive **Gardens** behind the palace, a landscaped wonderland crossed with footpaths and dotted with statues and fountains. Finally, at the far end of the Gardens, is the pastoral area called the **Trianon Palaces and Domaine de Marie-Antoinette** (a.k.a. Trianon/Domaine), a vast walled enclosure designed for frolicking blue bloods and featur-

Kings and Queens and Guillotines

Versailles is the architectural embodiment of the *ancien régime,* when society was divided into rulers and the ruled, when you were born to be rich or to be poor. To some, Versailles is the pinnacle of civilization; to others, it's a sign of a civilization in decay. Either way, it remains one of Europe's most impressive sights.

Versailles was the residence of the king and the seat of France's government for a hundred years. Louis XIV (r. 1643-1715) moved from the Louvre, the previous royal residence, and built an elaborate palace in the forests and swamps of Versailles, 10 miles west of Paris. The reasons for the move were personal—Louis XIV loved the outdoors and disliked the sniping environs of stuffy Paris—but also political.

Louis XIV was creating the first modern, centralized state. At Versailles, he consolidated his government's scattered ministries so that he could personally control policy. More important, he obliged France's nobles to be in residence at Versailles. Living directly under Louis' control, the "domesticated" aristocracy couldn't interfere with the way he ran things.

With 18 million people united under one king (England had only 5.5 million), a booming economy, and a powerful military, France was Europe's number-one power and Versailles was its cultural heartbeat. Throughout Europe, when you said "the king," you meant the French king—Louis XIV. Every king wanted a palace like Versailles. Everyone learned French. French taste in clothes, hairstyles, table manners, theater, music, art, and kissing spread across the Continent. That cultural dominance continued, to some extent, right up to the 20th century.

Louis XIV

At the center of all this was Europe's greatest king. He was a true

ing several small palaces and Marie's Hamlet—perfect for getting away from the mobs at the Château.

Visiting Versailles can seem daunting because of its size and hordes of visitors. But if you follow my tips, a trip here during even the busiest times is manageable.

GETTING THERE

By Train: The town of Versailles is 35 minutes southwest of Paris. Take **RER/Train-C** from any of these stations: Gare d'Austerlitz, St. Michel, Musée d'Orsay, Invalides, Pont de l'Alma, or Champ

Renaissance Man, a century after the Renaissance: athletic, good-looking, a musician, dancer, horseman, statesman, patron of the arts, and lover. For all his grandeur, he was one of history's most polite and approachable kings, a good listener who could put even commoners at ease in his presence.

Louis XIV called himself the Sun King because he gave life and warmth to all he touched. He was also thought of as Apollo, the Greek god of the sun. Versailles became the personal temple of this god on earth, decorated with statues and symbols of Apollo, the sun, and Louis XIV himself. The classical themes throughout underlined the divine right of France's kings and queens to rule without limit.

Louis XIV was a hands-on king who personally ran affairs of state. All decisions were made by him. Nobles, who in other countries were the center of power, became virtual vassals dependent on Louis' generosity. For 70-some years he was the perfect embodiment of the absolute monarch. He summed it up best himself with his famous expression—*"L'état, c'est moi!"*: "The state, that's me!"

Another Louis or Two to Remember

Three kings lived in Versailles during its century of glory. Louis XIV built it and established French dominance. Louis XV, his great-grandson, carried on the tradition and policies, but without the Sun King's flair. During Louis XV's reign (1715-1774), France's power abroad was weakening, and there were rumblings of rebellion from within.

France's monarchy was crumbling, and the time was ripe for a strong leader to reestablish the old feudal order. They didn't get one. Instead, they got Louis XVI (r. 1774-1792), a shy, meek bookworm, the kind of guy who lost sleep over revolutionary graffiti... because it was misspelled. Louis XVI married a sweet girl from the Austrian royal family, Marie-Antoinette, and together they retreated into the idyllic gardens of Versailles while revolutionary fires smoldered. Each had their final day on Paris' Place de la Concorde, thanks to the brutally efficient guillotine.

de Mars. Use your Navigo Découverte pass, buy a four-zone all-day Easy pass, or, if paper tickets are still available, buy a round-trip Versailles Rive Gauche/Château ticket from a ticket machine or ticket window (about €7.20 round-trip, credit card or coins, 4/hour). Not all trains go to Versailles: Check the departure board, which will list the next train to "Versailles Rive Gauche/Château" and its track.

Board your train and relax. (It's a good time to read the "Kings and Queens and Guillotines" sidebar in this chapter for some background.) On all RER/Train-C Versailles-bound trains, Versailles Rive Gauche/Château is the final stop.

To reach the Château, follow the flow: Turn right out of the station, then left at the first boulevard, and walk 10 minutes.

Returning to Paris: To return to Paris from the Versailles Rive Gauche/Château train station, just hop on the next train—all trains departing this station zip back to the city, stopping at all stations along line C. The monitor above the turnstiles shows how many minutes until the next train leaves and from which track. And remember, your RER/Train-C ticket covers any connecting Métro ride once you're back downtown.

By Taxi: The 30-minute ride (without traffic) between Versailles and Paris costs about €65.

By Tour: Minivan tours will pick you up at your hotel and whisk you painlessly to the Château and back. Paris Webservices tours are excellent (around €120/person, RS%—see page 55 for details). Big-bus tour companies do Versailles day trips from Paris for around €30/person (transportation only) or about €90/person with guided tour and entry (get details at your hotel or www.pariscityvision.com).

By Car: Get on the *périphérique* freeway that circles Paris, and take the toll-free A-13 autoroute toward Rouen. Exit at Versailles, follow signs to *Versailles Château,* and avoid the hectic Garden lots by parking in the big pay lot at the foot of the Château on Place d'Armes (about €5/hour, €36/11 hours).

PLANNING YOUR TIME

Versailles merits a full sightseeing day. In general, allow 1.5 hours each for the Château, the Gardens (includes time for lunch), and the Trianon/Domaine. Add another two hours for round-trip transit, and you're looking at nearly an eight-hour day.

Versailles is all about crowd management; a well-planned visit can make or break your experience. Take this advice to heart. Versailles is much more enjoyable with a relaxed, unhurried approach. Here's what I'd do on a first visit to avoid the worst lines and crowds:

- Get an **individual ticket or Le Passeport** pass in advance and choose your Château entry time (see next). If you have a **Paris Museum Pass,** you have several options—see "Using the Paris Museum Pass," later.
- In high season, **avoid holidays, Sundays, Tuesdays, and Saturdays**—in that order—when crowds smother the palace interior. Thursdays and Fridays are best.

- Leave Paris by 8:00, **get in line before the palace opens** at 9:00, and follow my self-guided tour of the Château interior. Have lunch. Spend the afternoon touring the Gardens and the Trianon Palaces/Domaine de Marie-Antoinette. To shorten your visit, skip the Trianon/Domaine, which takes 1.5 hours to see, plus a 30-minute walk each way.

- An alternate plan is to **arrive later in the morning** and see the Trianon/Domaine first. Arrive at Versailles around 11:00 and go directly to the Trianon/Domaine to be there when it opens at noon: Either walk directly there through the Gardens (do not enter the Château or stand in any line for the Château) or catch the *petit train* tram (see the "Getting Around the Gardens" sidebar later in this chapter). Then work your way back through the Gardens to the Château, arriving after the crowds have died down (usually by 14:00, later on Sun).

- If you're a late riser, leave Paris around 12:30 and **start at the Château after the morning rush** and end at the Trianon/Domaine.

Orientation

Cost and Reservations: A timed-entry ticket is required to enter the Château. Reserve ahead (no fee) and book your entry time on the Versailles website. You can also purchase Versailles tickets at any Paris TI or at FNAC department stores (small fee). If you have a Paris Museum Pass, see "Using the Paris Museum Pass," later.

  Château: €18 (Château only) or €20 Le Passeport ticket (includes Trianon/Domaine; €27 on Garden Spectacle days), both tickets come with timed entry and audioguide to the Château. Free for kids 17 and under, and free on the first Sun of the month Nov-March.

  Trianon Palaces and Domaine de Marie-Antoinette: €12, covers all the buildings within this walled enclosure. Free for kids 17 and under, and free on the first Sun of the month Nov-March.

  Gardens: Free on weekdays April-Oct, except when there are events in the Gardens (likely on Tue and Fri-Sun in high season—see "Spectacles in the Gardens," later). The Gardens are free daily Nov-March. You can enter the Gardens directly from the passageway to the left of the main Château entrance (see the "Versailles Château" map).

Hours: The **Château** is open Tue-Sun 9:00-18:30, Nov-March until 17:30, closed Mon year-round.

  The **Trianon Palaces and Domaine de Marie-Antoinette** are open Tue-Sun 12:00-18:30, Nov-March until 17:30,

VERSAILLES

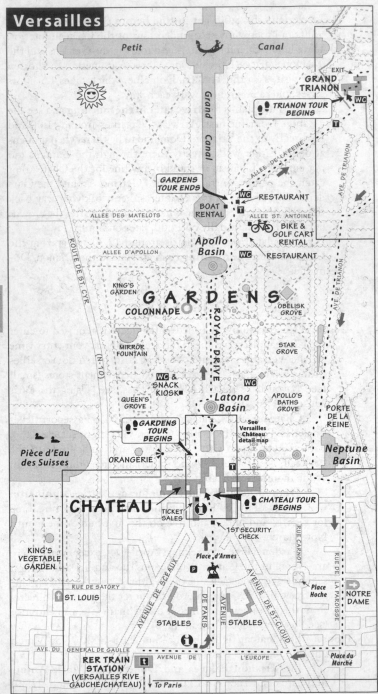

Versailles

Petit Canal

Grand Canal

GRAND TRIANON

EXIT

WC

TRIANON TOUR BEGINS

ALLEE DE LA REINE

AVE. DE TRIANON

GARDENS TOUR ENDS

WC

RESTAURANT

T

BOAT RENTAL

ALLEE DES MATELOTS

ALLEE ST. ANTOINE

BIKE & GOLF CART RENTAL

Apollo Basin

WC

RESTAURANT

ALLEE D'APOLLON

ROUTE DE ST. CYR (N-10)

KING'S GARDEN

G A R D E N S

COLONNADE

ROYAL DRIVE

OBELISK GROVE

AVE. DE TRIANON

MIRROR FOUNTAIN

STAR GROVE

QUEEN'S GROVE

WC & SNACK KIOSK

WC

Latona Basin

APOLLO'S BATHS GROVE

PORTE DE LA REINE

GARDENS TOUR BEGINS

See Versailles Château detail map

Neptune Basin

Pièce d'Eau des Suisses

ORANGERIE

T

CHATEAU

TICKET SALES

i

CHATEAU TOUR BEGINS

KING'S VEGETABLE GARDEN

1ST SECURITY CHECK

RUE CARNOT

RUE DE LA PAROISSE

RUE DE SATORY

Place d'Armes

P

Place Hoche

NOTRE DAME

ST. LOUIS

AVENUE DE SCEAUX

DE PARIS

AVENUE

AVENUE DE ST-CLOUD

STABLES

STABLES

i

Place du Marché

AVE. DU GENERAL DE GAULLE

AVENUE DE

L'EUROPE

RER TRAIN STATION (VERSAILLES RIVE GAUCHE/CHATEAU)

t

↓ To Paris

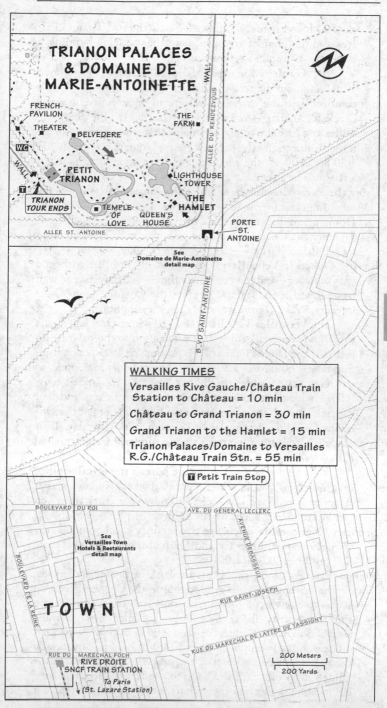

TRIANON PALACES & DOMAINE DE MARIE-ANTOINETTE

FRENCH PAVILION

THEATER

BELVEDERE

THE FARM

WC

WALL

ALLEE DU RENDEZVOUS

PETIT TRIANON

LIGHTHOUSE TOWER

T

TRIANON TOUR ENDS

TEMPLE OF LOVE

QUEEN'S HOUSE

THE HAMLET

PORTE ST. ANTOINE

ALLEE ST. ANTOINE

See Domaine de Marie-Antoinette detail map

B - VD SAINT-ANTOINE

WALKING TIMES

Versailles Rive Gauche/Château Train Station to Château = 10 min

Château to Grand Trianon = 30 min

Grand Trianon to the Hamlet = 15 min

Trianon Palaces/Domaine to Versailles R.G./Château Train Stn. = 55 min

T Petit Train Stop

BOULEVARD DU ROI

AVE. DU GENERAL LECLERC

See Versailles Town Hotels & Restaurants detail map

AVENUE DE BOSSEUX

BOULEVARD DE LA REINE

T O W N

RUE SAINT-JOSEPH

RUE DU MARECHAL DE LATTRE DE TASSIGNY

RUE DU MARECHAL FOCH
RIVE DROITE
SNCF TRAIN STATION

To Paris (St. Lazare Station)

200 Meters

200 Yards

VERSAILLES

closed Mon year-round (off-season only the two Trianon Palaces and the Hamlet are open, not other outlying buildings), last entry 45 minutes before closing.

The **Gardens** are open daily 8:00-20:30, Nov-March until 18:00, but may close earlier for special events.

Information: Use the excellent website to book your entry and check for updates—www.chateauversailles.fr. The free Versailles app includes interactive maps that work without an internet connection. The palace's general contact number is +33 1 30 83 78 00. At the Château, an information office is to the left as you face the palace.

Using the Paris Museum Pass: The Paris Museum Pass covers the most important parts of the complex (Château and Trianon/Domaine); it does not include the Gardens on Spectacle days. To enter the Château using the pass, you must book an entry time ("Palace Ticket"—free) on the Versailles website.

Buying Tickets in Versailles: If you arrive in Versailles without a pass or ticket—and reserved entry time—you may have to wait (sometimes hours or days) to enter the Château. If you have internet access, try the website, then these options:

The **Versailles TI** sells tickets (10 percent fee; you'll pass the TI on your walk from the train station to the palace—it's just past the fancy Hôtel at 2 bis Avenue de Paris, open Tue-Sun 8:30-19:00, Mon 9:30-18:00, shorter hours in winter).

Get Your Guide usually has space on its guided tours (€55—twice the price of booking your own tickets and tour yourself), which include entry to the Château but not the Domaine de Marie-Antoinette or Gardens if it's a fee day. Their office is across from the train station, under the stone arch at #10, www.getyourguide.co.uk).

Your last option is the busy **Château ticket-sales office** (to the left as you face the palace). Ticket windows accept American credit cards. Once you know your entry time, you can kill time by wandering the gardens.

Security Checkpoints: There are two security checkpoints: at the Château's courtyard entry and again at the Château entrance (longest lines 10:00-12:00).

Pickpockets: Assume pickpockets are working the tourist crowds.

Tours: The 1.5-hour English **guided tour** of the Château gives you access to a few extra rooms (the itinerary varies) and lets you skip the security line at the Château entrance (€10, generally at least 5 tours in English between 9:00 and 15:00 April-Oct; off-season likely only at 9:30 and 14:00). Book in advance on the palace website, or reserve immediately upon arrival at the guided-tours office (in the wing to the left of the Château—but location in flux; ask if you don't see it). Tours often sell out by 12:00 (and sometimes by 10:00), though more are usually available than indicated online.

A free and worthwhile **audioguide** to the Château is included in your admission. To avoid waiting at the audioguide desk, download the free "Palace of Versailles" **app** and listen to the audioguide on your phone (download in advance).

🎧 Download my free Versailles **audio tour.** (Note that my tour and the official audioguide complement each other—"A" students enjoy listening to both.)

Spectacles in the Gardens: The Gardens and fountains at Versailles come alive at selected times, offering a glimpse into Louis XIV's remarkable world. The Sun King had his engineers literally reroute a river to fuel his fountains and feed his plants. Even by today's standards, the fountains are impressive. Check the Versailles website for current hours and to find out what else might be happening during your visit.

The Gardens' fountains are in full squirt during a production called **Les Grandes Eaux Musicales,** with 55 fountains gushing for an hour in the morning and up to two hours in the afternoon; individual fountains run periodically throughout the day (the impressive Neptune fountain runs every 15 minutes); it's all accompanied by loud classical music (€9.50; April-Oct Sat-Sun 11:00-12:00 & 15:30-17:00, also Tue May-June 11:00-12:00 & 14:30-16:30. On varied weekdays April-Oct, you get the music but no fountains (called **Les Jardins Musicaux,** €8.50). For all garden events, check www.chateauversailles.fr. Pay or show proof of payment at the entrance to the Gardens.

And finally, on Saturday nights in summer, **Les Grandes Eaux Nocturnes** lets you meander past a thousand lights, illuminated groves, and shimmering pools while the fountains play to the sound of the Sun King's music. Your experience ends with a fireworks show over the largest fountain pool (€29, Sat early June-mid-Sept 20:30-23:00, fireworks at 22:50). On these nights, the Royal Serenade option lets you go into the palace with costumed characters (€42 combo-ticket).

Baggage Check: Free and located just after Château entry security. You must retrieve your items one hour before closing (maximum size is same as airlines allow for carry-on bags). Large bags and baby strollers are not allowed in the Château and the two Trianons (use a baby backpack).

Services: WCs are plentiful and well signed in the Château, but fewer and farther between in the Gardens.

Eating: Near the Château entry, the **$ Grand Café d'Orléans** offers good value self-service meals (sandwiches and small salads, great for picnicking in the Gardens). In the Gardens, you'll find several cafés and snack stands with fair prices. One is located near the Latona Fountain (less crowded) and others are in an atmospheric cluster at the Grand Canal (more crowds and more choices, including two restaurants).

Across from the train station, there's a McDonald's and a Starbucks (both with WCs and Wi-Fi). For more eating options in the town of Versailles, see the end of this chapter.

Starring: Luxurious palaces, endless gardens, Louis XIV, Marie-Antoinette, and the *ancien régime*.

The Tour Begins

On this self-guided tour, we'll see the Château (the State Apartments of the king as well as the Hall of Mirrors), the landscaped Gardens in the "backyard," and the Trianon Palaces and Domaine de Marie-Antoinette, located at the far end of the Gardens. If your time is limited or you don't enjoy walking, I give you permission to skip the Trianon/Domaine, which is a hefty 30-minute hike (each way) from the Château.

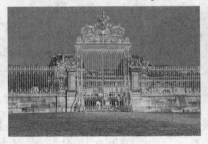

The Château

• *Stand in the huge courtyard and face the palace. The golden Royal Gate in the center of the courtyard—nearly 260 feet long and decorated with 100,000 gold leaves—is a replica of the original. The entrance to the Château is marked* Entrance A *(where the line usually is). Before entering (or while standing in line), take in the Château and the open-air courtyard on the other side of the golden Royal Gate.*

Original Château and Courtyard

The section of the palace with the clock is the original château, once a small hunting lodge where little Louis XIV spent his happiest boyhood years. Naturally, the Sun King's private bedroom (the three arched windows beneath the clock) faced the rising sun. The palace and grounds are laid out on an east-west axis.

Once king, Louis XIV expanded the lodge by attaching wings, creating the present

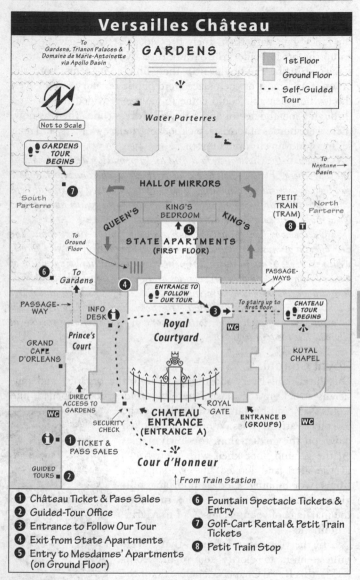

Versailles Château

GARDENS

To Gardens, Trianon Palaces & Domaine de Marie-Antoinette via Apollo Basin

- 1st Floor
- Ground Floor
- - - Self-Guided Tour

Not to Scale

Water Parterres

GARDENS TOUR BEGINS

❼

South Parterres

HALL OF MIRRORS

QUEEN'S   KING'S BEDROOM   KING'S

❺

STATE APARTMENTS (FIRST FLOOR)

To Ground Floor

To Gardens

❻

❹

ENTRANCE TO FOLLOW OUR TOUR

❸

To stairs up to first floor

CHATEAU TOUR BEGINS

PASSAGE-WAYS

PETIT TRAIN (TRAM)

❽ T

North Parterre

To Neptune Basin

PASSAGE-WAY

INFO DESK ⓘ

Prince's Court

Royal Courtyard

WC

ROYAL CHAPEL

GRAND CAFE D'ORLEANS

DIRECT ACCESS TO GARDENS

SECURITY CHECK

ROYAL GATE

CHATEAU ENTRANCE (ENTRANCE A)

ENTRANCE B (GROUPS)

WC

WC

ⓘ

❶ TICKET & PASS SALES

Cour d'Honneur

↑ From Train Station

GUIDED TOURS

❷

❶ Château Ticket & Pass Sales
❷ Guided-Tour Office
❸ Entrance to Follow Our Tour
❹ Exit from State Apartments
❺ Entry to Mesdames' Apartments (on Ground Floor)
❻ Fountain Spectacle Tickets & Entry
❼ Golf-Cart Rental & Petit Train Tickets
❽ Petit Train Stop

VERSAILLES

U-shape. Later, the long north and south wings were built. The total cost of the project has been estimated at half of France's entire GNP for one year.

Think how busy this courtyard must have been 300 years ago. As many as 5,000 nobles were here at any one time, each with an entourage. Riding in sedan-chair taxis, they'd buzz from games to parties to amorous rendezvous. Servants ran about delivering secret messages and roast legs of lamb. Horse-drawn carriages arrived at the fancy gate with their finely dressed passengers, having driven up the broad boulevard that ran directly from Paris (the horse stables still line the boulevard). Incredible as it seems, both the grounds and most of the palace were public territory, where even the lowliest peasants could come to gawk—provided they passed through a metal detector and followed a dress code. Then, as now, there were hordes of tourists, pickpockets, palace workers, and men selling wind-up children's toys.

• *As you enter the Château, you'll find an information desk (get a map) and bag check. Follow the crowds directly across the courtyard, where you'll go back inside. If you haven't already downloaded the official Versailles app, line up here for your free (and worth-the-wait) audioguide. Now make your way to the start of our tour.*

On the way, you'll pass through a dozen ground-floor rooms. The first offers a glimpse through a doorway at the impressive Royal Chapel, which we'll see again upstairs. The next rooms have interesting videos of palace history and models of Versailles at different stages of growth. The second floor has skippable paintings of Louis XIV, XV, XVI, and more. Climb the stairs and keep following the flow. You'll eventually reach a palatial golden-brown room, with a doorway that overlooks the Royal Chapel. Let the tour begin.

Royal Chapel

Dut-dutta-dah! Every morning at 10:00, the organist and musicians struck up the music, these big golden doors opened, and Louis XIV and his family stepped onto the balcony to attend Mass. While Louis looked down on the golden altar, the lowly nobles on the ground floor knelt with their backs to the altar and looked up—worshipping Louis worshipping God. Important religious ceremonies took place here, including the marriage of young Louis XVI to Marie-Antoinette.

In the vast pagan "temple" that is Versailles—built to glorify one man, Louis XIV—this Royal Chapel is a paltry tip of the hat to that "other" god...the Christian one. It's virtually the first, last, and only hint of Christianity you'll see in the entire complex. Versailles celebrates Man, not God, by raising Louis XIV to almost godlike status, the personification of all good human qualities. In a way, Versailles is the last great flowering of Renaissance humanism and a revival of the classical world.

• *Enter the next room, an even more sumptuous space with a fireplace and a colorful painting on the ceiling.*

Hercules Drawing Room

Pleasure ruled. The main suppers, balls, and receptions were held in this room. Picture elegant partygoers in fine silks, wigs, rouge, lipstick, and fake moles (and that's just the men) as they dance to the strains of a string quartet.

On the wall opposite the fireplace is an appropriate painting showing Christ in the middle of a Venetian party. The work—by Paolo Veronese, a gift from the Republic of Venice—was one of Louis XIV's favorites, so the king had the room decorated around it. Stand by the fireplace for the full effect: The room's columns, arches, and frieze match the height and style of Veronese's painted architecture, which makes the painting an extension of the room.

The ceiling painting, ringed by a balustrade, creates the effect of a sunroof opening up to heaven. Hercules (with his club) hurries up to heaven on a chariot, late for his wedding to the king of the gods' daughter. The scene echoes real life—Louis XIV built the room for his own daughter's wedding reception. The style is pure Baroque, a riot of 142 exuberant figures depicted at all angles by Louis' court painter, Charles Le Brun.

• *From here on it's a one-way tour—getting lost is not allowed. Follow the crowds into the small green room with a goddess in pink on the ceiling. The names of the rooms generally come from the paintings on the ceilings.*

THE KING'S WING
Salon of Abundance

If the party in the Hercules Room got too intense, you could always step in here for some refreshments. Silver trays were loaded with liqueurs, exotic stimulants (coffee), juice, chocolates, and, on really special occasions, three-bean salad.

The ceiling painting shows the cornucopia of riches poured down on invited guests.

Around the edges of the ceiling are painted versions of the king's actual treasures and royal dinnerware—golden bowls, urns, and gravy boats. The two black chests of drawers are from Louis' furniture collection (most of it was lost in the Revolution). They rest on heavy bases and are heavily ornamented—the so-called Louis XIV style.

Louis himself might be here. He was a gracious host who enjoyed letting his hair down at night. If he took a liking to you, he might sneak you through those doors there (in the middle of the wall) and into his own private study, or "cabinet of curiosities," where he'd show off his collection of dishes, medals, jewels, or...the *Mona Lisa,* which hung on his wall. Louis' favorite show-and-tell items are now in the Louvre.

The paintings on the walls are of Louis XIV's heirs. He reigned for more than 70 years and outlived three of them, finally leaving the crown to his pink-cheeked, five-year-old great-grandson, Louis XV (on the right).

Venus Room

Love ruled at Versailles. In this room, couples would cavort beneath the goddess of love floating on the ceiling. Venus sends down a canopy of flowery garlands to ensnare mortals in delicious amour. Another ceiling painting (above the statue, in a rectangular frame) symbolizes the marriage of Louis XIV and Marie-Thérèse, shown in their wedding-limo chariot.

Baroque artists loved to mix their media to fool the eye. Notice how in the paintings at both ends of the room, the painted columns match the real ones, extending this grand room into mythical courtyards.

Don't let the statue of a confident Louis XIV as a Roman emperor fool you. He started out as a poor little rich kid with a chip on his shoulder. His father died before Louis was old enough to rule, and, during the regency period, the French *parlements* treated little Louis and his mother like trash. They were virtual prisoners, humiliated in their home, the Royal Palace in Paris (today's Louvre).

There they eked by with bland meals, hand-me-down leotards, and pointed shoes. After Louis XIV attained power and wealth, he made Versailles a pleasure palace, with happy hours held in this room every evening. There was one topic you never discussed in Louis' presence: poverty. Maybe Versailles was his way of saying, "Living well is the best revenge."

Diana Room

Here in the billiards room, Louis and his men played on a table that stood in the center of the room, while ladies sat surrounding them on Persian-carpet cushions, and music wafted in from next door. Louis was a good pool player, a sore loser, and a king—thus, he rarely lost.

The famous bust of Louis by Giovanni Lorenzo Bernini (in the center) shows a handsome, dashing, 27-year-old playboy-king.

His gaze is steady amid his wind-blown cloak and hair. Young Louis loved life. He hunted animals by day (notice Diana the Huntress, with her bow, on the ceiling) and chased beautiful women at night.

Games were actually an important part of Louis' political strategy, known as "the domestication of the nobility." By distracting the nobles with the pleasures of courtly life, he was free to run the government his way. Billiards, dancing, and concerts were popular, but the biggest distraction was gambling, usually a card game similar to blackjack. Louis lent money to the losers, making them even more indebted to him. The good life was an addiction, and Louis kept the medicine cabinet well-stocked.

As you move into the next room, notice the fat walls that hid thin servants, who were to be at their master's constant call—but out of sight when not needed.

Mars Room

Also known as the Guard Room (as it was the room for Louis' Swiss bodyguards), this red room is decorated with a military flair. On the ceiling is Mars, the Greek god of war, in a chariot pulled by wolves. The bronze cupids in the corners are escalating from love arrows to heavier artillery. But it's not all war. Louis loved music and playing his guitar, and enjoyed concerts here in the Mars Room nearly every evening.

Out the window are sculpted gardens in the style of a traditional Italian villa—landscaped symmetrically, with trimmed hedges and cone-shaped trees lining walkways that lead to fountains.

As you wander, you'll notice that the palace feels bare (except for the wall-to-wall tourists), but remember that entire industries were created to decorate the place with carpets, mirrors, furniture, and tapestries. Most of the furniture we see today is not original, but is from the same period.

Mercury Room

Louis' life was a work of art, and Versailles was the display case. Everything he did was a public event designed to show his subjects

how it should be done. This room may have served as Louis' official (not actual) bedroom, where the Sun King would ritually rise each morning to warm his subjects.

From a canopied bed (like this 18th-century one), Louis would get up, dress, and take a seat for morning prayer. Meanwhile, the nobles would stand and watch, in awe of his piety, nobility, and clean socks. At breakfast, they murmured with delight as he deftly decapitated his boiled egg with a knife. And when Louis went to bed at night, the dukes and barons would fight over who got to hold the candle while he slipped into his royal jammies. Bedtime, wake-up, and meals were all public rituals.

Apollo Room

This was the grand throne room. Louis held court from a 10-foot-tall, silver-and-gold canopied throne on a raised platform placed in the center of the room (the platform is there, though not the throne). Even when the king was away, passing courtiers had to bow to the empty throne.

Everything in here reminds us that Louis XIV was not just any ruler, but the Sun King, who lit the whole world with his presence. On the ceiling, the sun god Apollo (representing Louis) drives his chariot, dragging the sun across the heavens to warm the four corners of the world (counterclockwise from above the exit door): 1) Europe, with a sword; 2) Asia, with a lion; 3) Africa, with an elephant; and 4) good ol' America, a Native American maiden with a crocodile. Notice the ceiling's beautifully gilded frame and *Goldfinger* maidens.

The famous portrait by Hyacinthe Rigaud over the fireplace gives a more human look at Louis XIV. He's shown in a dancer's pose, displaying the legs that made him one of the all-time dancing fools of kingery (see a photo of this portrait on page 567). At night, they often held parties in this room, actually dancing around the throne.

Louis XIV (who was 63 when this was painted) had more than 300 wigs like this one, and he changed them many times a day. This fashion first started when his hairline began to recede, then sprouted all over Europe, and even spread to the American colonies in the time of George Washington.

Louis XIV may have been treated like a god, but he was not an overly arrogant man. His subjects adored him because he was a symbol of everything a man could be, the fullest expression of the Renaissance Man. Compare the portrait of Louis XIV with the one across the room of his last successor, Louis XVI—same arrogant pose, but without the inner confidence to keep his head on his shoulders.

• *Continue into the final room of the King's Wing.*

War Room

"Louis Quatorze was addicted to wars," and the room depicts his victories—in marble, gilding, stucco, and paint. France's success made other countries jealous and nervous. At the base of the ceiling (in semicircular paintings), we see Germany (with the double eagle), Holland (with its ships), and Spain (with a red flag and roaring lion) ganging up on Louis XIV. But Lady France (center of ceiling), protected by the shield of Louis XIV, hurls thunderbolts down to defeat them. The relief on the wall shows Louis XIV on horseback, triumphing over his fallen enemies.

Versailles was good propaganda. It showed the rest of the world how rich and powerful France was. A visit to the Château and Gardens sent visitors reeling. And Louis XIV's greatest triumph may be the next room, the one that everybody wrote home about.

Hall of Mirrors

No one had ever seen anything like this hall when it was opened. Mirrors were still a great luxury at the time, and the number and size of these monsters was as-

tounding. The hall is nearly 250 feet long. There are 17 arched mirrors, matched by 17 windows letting in that breathtaking view of the Gardens. Lining the hall are 24 gilded candelabra, eight busts of Roman emperors, and eight classical-style statues (seven of them ancient).

The ceiling decoration chronicles Louis' military accomplishments, topped off by Louis himself in the central panel (with cupids playing cards at his divine feet) doing what he did best—triumphing. Originally, two huge carpets mirrored the action depicted on the ceiling.

Imagine this place lit by the flames of thousands of candles, filled with ambassadors, nobles, and guests dressed in silks and powdered wigs. At the far end of the room sits the king, on the canopied throne moved in temporarily from the Apollo Room. Servants glide by with silver trays of hors d'oeuvres, and an orchestra fuels the festivities. The mirrors reflect an age when beautiful people loved to look at themselves. It was no longer a sin to be proud of good looks and fine clothes, or to enjoy the good things in life: laughing, dancing, eating, drinking, flirting, and watching the sun set into the distant canal.

From the center of the hall you can fully appreciate the epic scale of Versailles. The huge palace (by architect Louis Le Vau), the fantasy interior (by Charles Le Brun), and the endless gardens (by André Le Nôtre) made Versailles *le* best. In 1871, after the Prussians defeated the French, Otto von Bismarck declared the establishment of the German Empire in this room. And in 1919, Germany and the Allies signed the Treaty of Versailles, ending World War I (and, some say, starting World War II) right here, in the Hall of Mirrors.

• *Backtrack a few stops to find the door that leads into the heart of the palace, to the...*

King's Bedroom and Council Rooms

Pass through a first large room to find Louis XIV's bedroom. It's elaborately decorated, and the decor changed with the season.

On the wall behind the impressive bed, a golden Lady France watched over her king as he slept. The balustrade separated the courtiers from the king. Though this was Louis' actual bedroom, it was also a somewhat public space where he received visitors.

The two rooms on either side of the bedroom—right next to where the king slept—were large halls for ambassadorial receptions and cabinet meetings.

Find an uncovered window and notice how this small room is at the exact center of the immense horseshoe-shaped building, overlooking the main courtyard and—naturally—facing the rising sun in the east. It symbolized the exact center of power in France. Imagine the humiliation on that day in 1789 when Louis' great-great-great-grandson, Louis XVI, was forced to stand here and acknowledge the angry crowds that filled the square demanding the end of the divine monarchy.

• *Return to the Hall of Mirrors, and continue to the end, being sure to enjoy views of the garden. Enter the...*

Peace Room

By the end of the Sun King's long life, he was tired of fighting. In this sequel to the War Room, peace is granted to Germany, Holland, and Spain as cupids play with the discarded cannons, and swords are transformed into violins. Louis XIV advised his great-grandson to "be a peaceful king."

The oval painting above the fireplace shows 19-year-old Louis XV bestowing an olive branch on Europe. Beside him is his Polish wife, Marie Leszczyńska, cradling their baby twin daughters. On Sundays the queen held chamber-music concerts here for family and friends (notice the gilded music motifs).

• *The Peace Room marks the beginning of the suite of rooms where France's queens lived, slept, ate, and entertained.*

THE QUEEN'S WING

The Queen's Wing is a mirror image of the King's Wing. The King's Wing was mostly ceremonial and used as a series of reception rooms; the Queen's Wing is more intimate.

• *Enter the first room of the Queen's Wing, with its canopied bed.*

Queen's Bedchamber

It was here that the queen rendezvoused with her husband. Two queens died here, and this is where 19 princes were born. The chandelier is where two of them were conceived. (Just kidding.) Royal babies were delivered in public to prove their blue-blood-edness.

True, Louis XIV was not the most faithful husband. There was no attempt to hide the fact that the Sun King warmed more than one bed, for he was above the rules of mere mortals. Adultery became acceptable—even fashionable—in court circles. The secret-looking door on the left side of the bed was for Louis' late-night liaisons—it led straight to his rooms.

Some of Louis XIV's mistresses became more famous and powerful than his rather quiet queen, but he was faithful to the show of marriage and had genuine affection for his wife. Louis XIV made a point of sleeping with the queen as often as possible, regardless of whose tiara he tickled earlier in the evening.

This room looks just like it did in the days of the last queen, Marie-Antoinette, who substantially redecorated the entire wing. That's her bust over the fireplace, and the double eagle of her native Austria in two of the corners. The big mahogany chest to the left of the bed held her jewels.

The large canopied bed is a reconstruction. The bed, chair, and wall coverings switched with the seasons. This was the cheery summer pattern.

Salon of the Nobles

Here, in this mint green room, the wife of Louis XV and her circle of friends met, under paintings by Boucher—popular with the queen for their pink-cheeked Rococo exuberance. Discussions ranged from politics to gossip, food to literature, fashion to philosophy. All three of Versailles' rulers considered themselves enlightened monarchs who promoted the arts and new ideas. Louis XIV laughed at the anti-authoritarian plays of Molière, and Louis XV gave free room and board here to the political radical Voltaire. Ironically, these discussions planted the seeds of liberal thought that would grow into the Revolution.

Queen's Antechamber

The royal family dined publicly in this room (also called the Grand Couvert), while servants and nobles fluttered around them, admired their table manners, and laughed at the king's jokes. A typical dinner consisted of four soups, two whole birds stuffed with truffles, mutton, ham slices, fruit, pastries, compotes, and preserves.

You may see a portrait of luxury-loving, "let-them-eat-cake" Marie-Antoinette, who became a symbol of decadence to the peasants. The portrait at the far end is a public-relations attempt to soften her image by showing her with three of her children.

Queen's Guard Room

On October 5, 1789, a mob of revolutionaries—perhaps appalled by their queen's taste in wallpaper—stormed the palace. They were fed up with the ruling class leading a life of luxury in the countryside while they were starving in the grimy streets of Paris.

The king and queen locked themselves in. Some of the revolutionaries gained access to this upper floor. They burst into this room where Marie-Antoinette was hiding, overcame her bodyguards, and dragged her off along with her husband. (Some claim that, as they carried her away, she sang, "Louis, Louis, oh-oh...we gotta go now.")

The enraged peasants then proceeded to ransack the place as revenge for the years of poverty and oppression they'd suffered. (The stripped palace was refurnished a decade later under Napoleon and eventually turned into a national museum.) Marie-Antoinette and Louis XVI were later taken to Place de la Concorde in Paris, where they knelt under the guillotine and were made a foot shorter at the top.

Did the king and queen deserve it? Were the revolutionaries destroying civilization or clearing the decks for a new and better one? Was Versailles a symbol of progress or decadence?

Coronation Room

No sooner did the French throw out a king than they got an emperor. The Revolution established democracy, but it was shaky in a country that wasn't used to it. In the midst of the confusion, the upstart general Napoleon Bonaparte took control and soon held dictatorial powers.

This room captures the glory of the Napoleonic years, when Bonaparte conquered most of Europe. In the huge canvas, we see him crowning himself emperor of a new, revived "Roman" Empire. (The original by Jacques-Louis David now hangs in the Louvre; this is a later but lesser-quality copy by the master himself.)

Turn and face the windows to see the portrait (between the windows on the right) of a dashing, young, charismatic Napoleon in 1796, when he was just a general in command of the Revolution's army in Italy. Above the young Napoleon is a portrait of Josephine—his wife and France's empress. Compare the young Napoleon with the adjacent portrait from 10 years later—looking less like a revolutionary and more like a Louis. Above the older Napoleon is a portrait of Empress Marie-Louise, his second wife.

In David's *Distribution of Eagles* (opposite the *Coronation*), the victorious general, in imperial garb, passes out emblems of victory to his loyal troops. In *The Battle of Aboukir* (opposite the window, see photo), Joachim Murat, Napoleon's general and brother-in-law, looks bored as he slashes through a tangle of dark-skinned warriors. His horse, though, has a look of, "What are we doing in this mob? Let's get out of here!" Let's.

• *This ends our tour of the Château. From here, head down the stairs, skipping the long gallery of famous French battles. Consider a break in the Salon de Thé Angelina, with a self-service sandwich bar, and an elegant sit-down restaurant featuring a decadent hot chocolate and the Mont Blanc—a chestnut-cream meringue with whipped cream.*

Continuing downstairs to the exit, you'll reach the audioguide-return desk, WCs, and checked bag pick-up.

Exit the palace (once you leave, you can't return without going through security again) and turn right into the Gardens (les Jardins), located behind the Château.

The Gardens

Louis XIV was a divine-right ruler. One way he proved it was by controlling nature like a god. These lavish grounds—elaborately planned, pruned, and decorated—showed everyone that Louis was in total command. Louis loved his gardens and, until his last days, presided over their care. He personally led VIPs through them and threw his biggest parties here. With their Greco-Roman themes and incomparable beauty, the Gardens further illustrated his immense power.

The Gardens are vast. For some, a stroll through the landscaped shrubs around the Château and quick view down the Royal Drive is plenty. But it's worth the 10-minute walk down the Royal Drive to the Apollo Basin and back (even if you don't continue further to the Trianon/Domaine). To trace the route of this tour, see the "Versailles" map earlier in this chapter.

• *Entering the Gardens, make your way into the king's spacious backyard. Angling right, you'll pass by artificial ponds, reclining river-god statues, and cookie-cutter patterns of shrubs and green cones. As you walk, consider that a thousand orange trees were once stored beneath your feet in greenhouses. On sunny days, they were wheeled out in their silver planters and scattered around the grounds. The warmth from the Sun King was so great that he could even grow orange trees in chilly France.*

You'll eventually reach the top step of a staircase overlooking the Gardens. Face away from the palace and take in the jaw-dropping...

View Down the Royal Drive

This, to me, is the most stunning spot in all of Versailles. With the palace behind you, it seems as if the grounds stretch out forever. Versailles was laid out along an eight-mile axis that included

the grounds, the palace, and the town of Versailles itself, one of the first instances of urban planning since Roman times and a model for future capitals, such as Washington, DC, and Brasilia.

Looking down the Royal Drive (also known as "The Green Carpet"), you see the round Apollo fountain in the distance. Just beyond that is the Grand Canal. The groves on either side of the Royal Drive were planted with trees from all over, laid out in an elaborate grid, and dotted with statues and fountains. Of the original 1,500 fountains, 300 remain.

Looking back at the palace, you can see the Hall of Mirrors—it's the middle story, with the arched windows.

• *Stroll down the steps to get a good look at the frogs and lizards that fill the round...*

Getting Around the Gardens

On Foot: It's a 45- to 60-minute walk from the palace, down to the Grand Canal, past the two Trianon palaces, to the Hamlet at the far end of Domaine de Marie-Antoinette. Allow more time if you stop along the way. After the slow Château shuffle, stretching your legs out here feels pretty good.

By Bike: There's a bike-rental station by the Grand Canal. A bike won't save you that much time (you can't take it inside the grounds of the Trianon/Domaine; park it nearby while you tour inside). Instead, simply enjoy pedaling around the greatest royal park in all of Europe (about €9/hour or €20/half-day, a bit more for electric bikes, kid-size bikes and tandems available, daily 10:00-18:30).

By *Petit Train*: The slow-moving tram leaves from behind the Château (see map on page 563) and makes a one-way loop, stopping at the Grand Trianon and Petit Trianon (entry points to Domaine de Marie-Antoinette), then the Grand Canal before returning to the Château (€8.5 round-trip, €4.60 one-way, free for kids 10 and under, 2-4/hour, Tue-Sun 11:30-19:00, Mon 11:00-17:00, shorter hours in winter). The round-trip ticket allows you to hop off at one stop and back on at the next, following the one-way loop (€4 audioguide available)

By Golf Cart: These make for a fun drive through the Gardens, complete with music and a relaxing commentary. But you can't go wherever you want—the cart shuts off automatically if you diverge from the prescribed route. You can't drive it in the Trianon/Domaine, but you can park it outside the entrance while you sightsee inside. Be warned: There are steep late fees. To go out to the Hamlet, sightsee quickly, and get back within your allotted hour, rent a cart at the Grand Canal and put the pedal to the metal (€38/hour, €9/15 minutes after that, 4-person limit per cart, rental stations by the canal and behind the Château—near the Gardens entrance). You must return your cart to the place you started.

Latona Basin

Everything in the garden has a symbolic meaning. The theme of Versailles is Apollo, the god of the sun, associated with Louis XIV. This round fountain tells the story of the birth of Apollo and his sister, Diana. On top of the fountain are Apollo and Diana as little kids with their mother, Latona (they're facing toward the Apollo fountain). Latona, an unwed mother, was

insulted by the local peasants. She called on the king of the gods, Zeus (the children's father), to avenge the insult. Zeus swooped down and turned all the peasants into the frogs and lizards that ring the fountain.

• *As you walk down past the basin toward the Royal Drive, you'll pass by "ancient" statues done by 17th-century French sculptors. You'll see statues of gods, nymphs, mythological heroes, allegories of the seasons, and huge Roman-style vases. A cheap snack kiosk and WCs are close by. Find the Colonnade, hidden in the woods on the left side of the Royal Drive, about three-fourths of the way to the Apollo Basin (you'll spot it off the main path through an opening).*

Colonnade

Versailles had no prestigious ancient ruins, so the king built his own. This prefab Roman ruin is a 100-foot circle of 64 red-marble columns supporting pure white arches. The arches are decorated with cherubs playing harps. In the center stands a statue of

Pluto (Greek god of the Underworld) carrying off Proserpine while her mom gets trampled. Surrounding the whole thing are small birdbath fountains (imagine them all spouting water). Nobles would picnic in the shade to the tunes of a string quartet and pretend that they were the enlightened citizens of the ancient world.

Apollo Basin

The fountains of Versailles were once its most famous attraction, a marvel of both art and engineering. This one was the centerpiece, showing the sun god—Louis XIV—in his sunny chariot as he starts his journey across

the sky. The horses are half-submerged, giving the impression, when the fountains play, of the sun rising out of the mists of dawn. Apollo's entourage includes dolphins leading the way and Tritons blowing their conch shells.

Most of the fountains were turned on only when the king walked by, but this one played constantly for the benefit of those watching from the palace. Look into the water to see the substantial pipes that feed this powerful fountain.

All the fountains are gravity-powered. They work on the same principle as blocking a hose with your finger to make it squirt. Underground streams (pumped into Versailles by Seine River pressure) feed into smaller pipes at the fountains, which shoot the water high into the air.

Looking back at the palace from here, realize that the distance you just walked is only a fraction of this vast complex of buildings, gardens, and waterways. Be glad you don't have to mow the lawn.

Grand Canal

Why visit Venice when you can just build your own? In an era before virtual reality, this was the next best thing to an actual trip. Couples in gondolas would pole along the waters accompanied by barges with orchestras playing *"O Sole Mio."* The canal is actually cross-shaped; you're looking at the longest part, one mile from end to end. Of course, this, too, is a man-made body of water with no function other than to please. Originally, authentic gondoliers, imported with their boats from Venice, lived in a little settlement next to the canal.

These days, the Grand Canal hosts eateries, rental boats, bike and golf-cart rentals, and a *petit train* tram stop (see the "Getting Around the Gardens" sidebar, earlier).

• *Next stop, the Trianon Palaces and Domaine de Marie-Antoinette, a walled-off part of the Gardens accessible only with a ticket. To get to our tour's starting point at the Grand Trianon, veer right past the second Grand Canal restaurant (see the "Versailles" map, earlier), and follow the dirt path along a looooong, tree-lined strip of lawn that leads uphill 500 yards to the Grand Trianon (a 15-minute walk). It's possible to take a bike, golf cart, or* petit train *as far as the Grand Trianon entry, but you'll need to walk inside.*

Trianon Palaces and Domaine de Marie-Antoinette

Versailles began as an escape from the pressures of kingship. But in a short time, the Château became as busy as Paris ever was. Louis XIV needed an escape from his escape, so he built a smaller palace out in the boonies. Later, his successors retreated still farther from the Château and French political life, ignoring the real world that

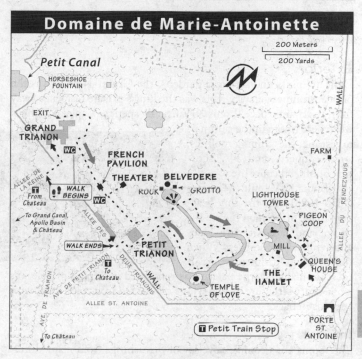

Domaine de Marie-Antoinette

Petit Canal

HORSESHOE FOUNTAIN

200 Meters
200 Yards

EXIT

GRAND TRIANON

WC

FRENCH PAVILION

THEATER   BELVEDERE

ROCK   GROTTO

FARM

LIGHTHOUSE TOWER

PIGEON COOP

ALLEE DE LA REINE

WALK BEGINS

WC

From Chateau

To Grand Canal, Apollo Basin & Château

ALLEE DES

WALK ENDS

PETIT TRIANON

DEUX TRIANONS

To Chateau

MILL

QUEEN'S HOUSE

THE HAMLET

TEMPLE OF LOVE

AVE. DE TRIANON

AVE. DE PETIT TRIANON

WALL

ALLEE ST. ANTOINE

To Château

PORTE ST. ANTOINE

ALLEE DU RENDEZVOUS

WALL

Petit Train Stop

VERSAILLES

was crumbling all around them. They expanded the Trianon area, building a fantasy world of palaces, ponds, pavilions, and pleasure gardens—the enclosure called Marie-Antoinette's Domaine.

If you're monitoring your time and energy, note that it's a 1.5-hour commitment to see the whole Trianon/Domaine, plus a 30-minute walk back to the Château and a 10-minute walk from there to the Versailles Rive Gauche/Château train station.

• *You can enter/exit at only three spots: near the palace known as the Grand Trianon (where we'll enter), near the Petit Trianon palace, or way around back on the far side of the Hamlet.*

GRAND TRIANON

• *Enter the Grand Trianon and pass through its security checkpoint. Pick up the free palace brochure and follow the simple one-way route through the rooms (basic English information posted in most rooms). Read your flier as you follow this tour to get the most out of your visit (some rooms may be closed).*

Exterior

Delicate, pink, and set amid gardens, the Grand Trianon was the perfect summer getaway. This was the king's private residence away from the main palace. Louis XIV usually spent a couple of nights a week here (more in the summer) to escape the sniping politics, strict etiquette, and 24/7 scrutiny of official court life.

Louis XIV built the palace (1670-1688) near the tiny peasant village of Trianon (hence the name) and faced it with blue-and-white ceramic tiles. When those began disintegrating almost immediately, the palace was renovated with pink marble. It's a one-story structure of two wings connected by a colonnade, with gardens in back.

Interior

The rooms are a complex overlay of furnishings from many different kings, dauphins, and nobles who lived here over the centuries. Louis XIV alone had three different bedrooms. Concentrate on the illustrious time of Louis XIV (1688-1715) and Napoleon Bonaparte (1810-1814). Use your map (which has room numbers on it) to find these highlights.

• *From the gift shop, pass down a long hall to the **Boudoir of the Empress (Room 1)** and the...*

Mirrors Salon (Room 2): This spacious living room has the original white walls and mirrors of Louis XIV, and the Empire-style furniture of Napoleon (unornamented, high-polished wood, with classical motifs). Napoleon inhabited the Grand Trianon with his second wife, Empress Marie-Louise, and his mother—the women in the left wing, the emperor in the right.

Bedroom of the Empress (Room 3): This spacious red-and-white room is best known as being Louis XIV's bedroom. Louis built the Grand Trianon as home for his chief mistress, while his wife lived in the Château. Imagine waking up in this big bed with your lover, throwing back the curtain, and looking out the windows at the gardens. These light, airy, many-windowed rooms were cheery even when skies were gray, a strong contrast to the heavy-metal decor in the mother Château. The adjoining room (divided by classical columns) was the dressing room.

• *Pass through Rooms 4 and 5, and exit into the open-air* **colonnade** *(Peristyle) that connects the two wings. Originally, this pink-columned passageway had windows, an enormously expensive luxury that allowed visitors to enjoy the gardens even in bad weather. Entering the right wing of the palace, you walk across the impressive red-white-*

black marble floor of the **Round Salon** *(Room 6), and detour right (if open) to find the...*

Emperor's Family Drawing Room (Room 7): This room had many different uses over the years: a theater for Louis XIV, a game room for Louis XV, and Napoleon's family room. After Napoleon was defeated and France's royalty returned, King Louis-Philippe I lived here. In Room 8, admire the impressive canopied bed.

• *Backtrack to the Round Salon and continue on through a series of rooms, passing through Louis-Philippe's billiards room, until you reach a room decorated in green malachite.*

Malachite Room (Room 11): This was Napoleon's living room, and his library was next door. You'll see the impressive green basin, vases, and candelabras made of Russian malachite given to Napoleon by Czar Alexander I. Another czar, Peter the Great, who

lodged in the Grand Trianon in 1717 and then returned home, was inspired to build the Peterhof—a similarly lavish summer palace near St. Petersburg known as the "Russian Versailles."

• *Next, amble through the elegant* **Cotelle Gallery,** *with works that show the gardens in the 17th century, then exit into the* **gardens.** *Look back. The facade of pink, yellow, and white is a welcome contrast to the imposing Baroque facade of the main palace. The landscaping is similar to the Château—cone-shaped trees, ponds, and hedges—but everything is mini-*

sized. *The flower gardens were changed daily for the king's pleasure—for new color combinations and new "nasal cocktails."*

VERSAILLES

DOMAINE DE MARIE-ANTOINETTE

• *Our next stop is the French Pavilion. To get there from the Grand Trianon gardens, walk clockwise around the perimeter of the Grand Trianon. Make it a tight, 180-degree loop, hugging the palace on your right, and follow signs to the* Petit Trianon. *A path leads across a footbridge. Directly ahead, you'll see the...*

French Pavilion

This small, cream-colored building (generally closed) with rooms fanning out from the center was one more step away from the modern world. Inside is a circular room with four small adjoining rooms. With its red-white-gold decor, flower-draped chandelier, and starburst floor, it's a small jewel of interior design. Big French doors let in a cool breeze. Here Marie-Antoinette spent summer evenings with family and a few friends, listen-

ing to music or playing parlor games. She and her friends explored all avenues of *la douceur de vivre*, the sweetness of living.

• *Up ahead is the large, cube-shaped Petit Trianon palace. Head toward the Petit Trianon, but midway there, turn left, where you can peek into...*

Marie-Antoinette's Theater

Marie-Antoinette adored the theater and was an aspiring performer herself. In this intimate playhouse, far from the rude in-

trusions of the real world, the queen and her friends acted out plays. The soft blue decor, gold trim, and upholstered walls and benches give the theater a dollhouse feel. Though small, it has everything you'd find in a major opera house: stage, orchestra pit, balconies, a painted backdrop setting a peasant scene, ornate gold ceiling, and raked seating for 100.

• *Continue to the Petit Trianon, through the oh-so-bucolic gardens. If you'd like to cut this tour short, you could skip ahead and visit the Petit Trianon now. Otherwise, turn left and follow paths uphill to a pond graced with a tiny palace.*

Belvedere, Rock, and Grotto

The octagonal Belvedere palace is as much windows as it is walls. When the doors were open, it could serve as a gazebo for musicians,

serenading nobles in this man-made alpine setting. The interior has a marble-mosaic floor and walls decorated with birds and delicate, Pompeii-esque garlands. To the left of the Belvedere is the "Rock," a fake mountain that pours water into the pond. To the right of the Belvedere (you'll have to find it) is the secret Grotto.

• *Facing the Belvedere, turn right (east), following the pond's meandering stream. Continue gamboling along the paths. In the distance you'll spy a complex of buildings, with a round, fanciful tower and a smattering of rustic, half-timbered buildings. Head there to find the Hansel-and-Gretel-like...*

Hamlet

Marie-Antoinette longed for the simple life of a peasant—not the hard labor of real peasants, who sweated and starved around her,

but the fairy-tale world of simple country pleasures. She built this complex of 12 thatched-roof buildings fronting a lake as her own private "Normand" village.

The main building is the Queen's House—actually two buildings con-

nected by a wooden skywalk. It's the only one without a thatched roof. Like any typical peasant farmhouse, it had a billiard room, library, elegant dining hall, and two living rooms.

This was an actual working farm with a dairy (walk past the lighthouse tower), a water mill, a pigeon coop (in a thatched cottage called Le Colombier), and domestic animals. Beyond the lighthouse tower (La Tour de Marlborough—departure point for boat trips on the pond), you'll see where the queen's servants kept cows, goats, chickens, and ducks. The harvest was served at Marie-Antoinette's table. Marie-Antoinette didn't do much work herself, but she "supervised," dressed in a plain, white muslin dress and a straw hat. Though the royal family is long gone, kid-pleasing animals still inhabit the farm, and beaucoup fat fish swim languid circles in the pond.

• *Head back toward the Petit Trianon. Along the way (in about five minutes), you'll see the white dome of the...*

Temple of Love

A circle of 12 marble Corinthian columns supports a dome, decorating a path where lovers could stroll. Underneath there's a statue of Cupid making a bow (to shoot arrows of love) out of the club of Hercules. It's a delightful monument to a society where the rich could afford that ultimate luxury, romantic love.

• *And, finally, you'll reach the...*

Petit Trianon

This gray, cubical building from the 1760s is a masterpiece of Neo-classical architecture, built by the same architect (Ange-Jacques Gabriel) who created the Opera House in the main palace. It has four distinct facades, each a perfect and harmonious combination of Greek-style columns, windows, and railings. Walk around it and find your favorite.

Louis XV built the Petit Trianon as a place to rendezvous with his mistress Madame de Pompadour. He later gave it to his next mistress, Countess du Barry. After the crown passed to Louis XVI, it became the principal residence of Marie-Antoinette, who was uncomfortable with the court intrigue in the big Château. As you tour the Petit Trianon, you'll see portraits and historical traces of this intriguing cast of characters.

Ground Floor (Rooms 1-8): Breeze through these less interesting rooms, seeing the pantry (with the Sevres china dinnerware of these royals) and Louis XV's big billiard table (a reconstruction). Then head upstairs.

Antechamber (Room 9): This otherwise bare room has a portrait of the palace's most famous resident—Marie-Antoinette, holding a rose.

Grand Dining Room (Room 10): Imagine a meal here, enjoying all the bounties of the season. The four big paintings depict the four seasons, and the various pleasures each offers. On the mantle is a bust of Marie-Antoinette.

Small Dining Room (Room 11): See portraits of Louis XV in a red military coat (left) and his mistress, Madame de Pompadour (right). Madame de Pompadour was the cultural heartbeat of Versailles, a patron of the arts and the progressive ideas of the Enlightenment.

Salon de Compagnie (Room 12): The red-and-white-upholstered music room has a number of period instruments, including a harp and harpsichord.

Queen's Bedroom (Room 13): Here you see Marie-Antoinette's pastel-mint bedroom much as it appeared back in 1788. It has her small bed (though this is a reconstruction) with a flowery canopy and matching Tootsie Roll pillows and drapes. Next door is her dressing room. Notice the ingenious sliding mirrors. She could slide them in place to block the windows (to dress discreetly), or slide them away (for great views of the gardens).

As you exit, don't miss the ultimate luxury—her small **bathroom** with a state-of-the-art hole in a wooden plank.

Marie-Antoinette made the Petit Trianon her home base. On the lawn outside, she installed a carousel. Despite her bad reputation with the public, Marie-Antoinette was a sweet girl from Vienna who never quite fit in with the fast, sophisticated crowd at Versailles. At the Petit Trianon, she could get away and re-create the charming home life that she remembered from her childhood. Here she played, while in the cafés of faraway Paris, revolutionaries plotted the end of the *ancien régime*.

• *Our tour is over. Here are your options for getting back:* The main **Château** *is a 30-minute walk straight out the exit to the southeast (plus another 10 minutes to reach the train station). Or you can ride the petit train from here back to the Château. It leaves from just outside the wall at the Petit Trianon. For a slightly shorter walk back to the train station by way of* **downtown Versailles,** *follow the "Versailles" map earlier in this chapter.*

Town of Versailles

The town of Versailles offers a classic, small French town experience that doesn't feel touristy—and it's a good overnight stop, especially for drivers. Park in the palace's main lot on Place d'Armes while looking for a hotel, or leave your car there overnight (see "Versailles" map for location).

The pleasant town center—around Place du Marché Notre-

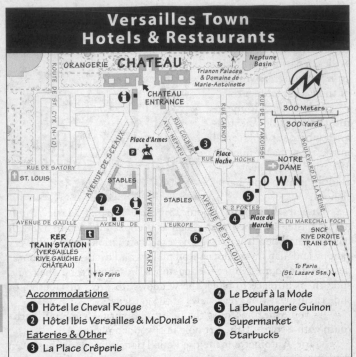

Versailles Town Hotels & Restaurants

Accommodations
1. Hôtel le Cheval Rouge
2. Hôtel Ibis Versailles & McDonald's

Eateries & Other
3. La Place Crêperie
4. Le Bœuf à la Mode
5. La Boulangerie Guinon
6. Supermarket
7. Starbucks

Dame—hosts a thriving open market defined by four L-shaped halls. The two halls closest to the palace (Carré à la Marée and Carré aux Herbes, Tue-Sat 7:30-13:00 & 15:30-19:00, Sun 7:30-13:00, closed Mon) are worth a wander. The square itself hosts regular markets (food market Sun, Tue, and Fri mornings until 13:30; clothing market all day Wed-Thu and Sat). Nearby streets have a variety of reasonably priced restaurants, cafés, and shops.

Tourist Information: The TI is near the Rive Gauche/Château train station (2 bis Avenue de Paris, open Tue-Sun 8:30-19:00, Mon 9:30-18:00, shorter hours in winter, +33 1 39 24 88 88, www.versailles-tourisme.com).

SLEEPING IN VERSAILLES

$ Hôtel le Cheval Rouge,*** built in 1676 as Louis XIV's stables, now boards tourists. Tucked into a corner of Place du Marché, this modest hotel has a big courtyard with cheap pay parking and sufficiently comfortable rooms at good rates. Superior rooms are well worth the slightly higher price (40 rooms, no air-con, 18 Rue André Chénier, +33 1 39 50 03 03, www.chevalrougeversailles.fr, chevalrouge@sfr.fr).

$ Hôtel Ibis Versailles,* across from the Rive Gauche/ Château station, offers a good weekend value and modern comfort, with 85 air-conditioned rooms (good buffet breakfast open to public and served daily until 10:00; pay parking, 4 Avenue du Général de Gaulle, +33 1 39 53 03 30, www.ibishotel.com, h1409@ accor.com).

EATING IN VERSAILLES

In the Versailles town center, the best choices are along traffic-free Rue de Satory (veer right as you leave the Château) or on the lively **Place du Marché** (a 15-minute walk from the Château; veer left as you leave), with a supermarket nearby. This market square is lined with colorful and inexpensive eateries with good seating inside and out. Troll the various options or try one of these:

$$ La Place Crêperie, located just off the Place d'Armes by the Château, serves good crêpes (decent lunch menu, 17 Rue Colbert, +33 1 85 15 22 80).

$$ Le Bœuf à la Mode is the place in Versailles to enjoy traditional French cuisine (meat is their *forté*) in a warm setting (upstairs seating is best, daily, Place du Marché, +33 1 39 50 31 99).

$ La Boulangerie Guinon has mouthwatering sandwiches, salads, quiches, and more (Tue-Sat until 20:00, Sun until 13:30, closed Mon, 60 Rue de la Paroisse).

Breakfast: The **Hôtel Ibis Versailles,** across from the train station to the right, offers a good buffet breakfast daily until 10:00. It's great for early birds who want to fuel up before sightseeing. Starbucks may appeal to others (across from the station to the left).

Supermarket: A big **Monoprix** is centrally located between the Versailles Rive Gauche/Château train station and Place du Marché Notre-Dame (entrances from Avenue de l'Europe and at 5 Rue Georges Clemenceau, Mon-Sat 8:30-19:50, closed Sun).

MORE GRAND CHATEAUX

Vaux-le-Vicomte • Fontainebleau • Chantilly

The region around Paris (called the Ile de France) is studded with sumptuous palaces. The city's booming elite class made this the heartland of European château-building in the 16th and 17th centuries. Most of these châteaux were lavish hunting lodges—getaways from the big city. The only things they defended were aristocratic egos.

If you're planning to visit just one palace in all of Europe, it should be Versailles (see previous chapter). But unlike heavily touristed Versailles, the three châteaux recommended here are quiet (at least on weekdays), letting you enjoy their original pastoral ambience. Consider visiting at least one; they are each very different.

▲▲▲Vaux-le-Vicomte
For sheer beauty and intimacy (open daily, closed Nov-March); see next page.

▲▲Fontainebleau
For its history, fine interior, and pleasant city (closed Tue, covered by Paris Museum Pass); see page 593.

▲Chantilly
For its beautiful setting and fine collection of paintings (open daily, closed Tue Nov-March, covered by Paris Museum Pass); see page 597.

Transit Passes: Travelers with a **Navigo Découverte Pass** can use it to travel to Fontainebleau and Vaux-le-Vicomte, but not to Chantilly. Without this pass, day-trippers to Vaux-le-Vicomte or Fontainebleau should purchase a **Navigo Easy** five-zone day pass, which covers a day of travel in the greater Paris region (€18, buy at any Métro station). This single-day pass covers Métro rides to and from the train station and round-trip train fare (for Fontainebleau, it also includes the bus to and from the château), saving you about €9 total (see page 35 for more on these passes).

Travelers heading to Chantilly must buy train tickets for this trip (see later in this chapter).

Vaux-le-Vicomte

Versailles may be most travelers' first choice for its sheer historic importance, but Vaux-le-Vicomte (voh luh vee-komt) is just flat-out ravishing. With a harmony of architecture, interior decor, and garden design that you won't find anywhere else, it gets my vote for one of the most beautiful châteaux in all of France.

Compared with Versailles, it's also more intimate, better furnished, and comes with a fraction of the crowds. Though getting to Vaux-le-Vicomte requires more effort, it's an absolute joy to tour. Located in a huge forest, with magnificent gardens and no urban sprawl in sight, Vaux-le-Vicomte gives me more than a twinge of palace envy.

GETTING THERE

By Train via Verneuil-l'Etang: Ideally, leave Paris from Gare de l'Est before 12:00, traveling to Verneuil-l'Etang (on Transilien line P, direction: Provins). Buying a Navigo Découverte or Easy card saves time and money (explained earlier, under "Transit Passes"). Otherwise, buy a round-trip ticket at the white ticket machines. Trains generally depart Paris from tracks 13-22 (€18 round-trip, hourly at :46 past the hour, 30 minutes; return trains depart Verneuil-l'Etang's track 2 at :32 past the hour). A train schedule is available on the château's website.

Outside the station at Verneuil-l'Etang, a Châteaubus shuttle, timed to train arrivals, takes you to Vaux-le-Vicomte (€10 round-trip, cash only, pay driver, daily April-early Nov plus Sat evenings May-Sept). Return shuttles leave the château at 12:05, 13:05, 15:05, and 18:05, with additional Saturday departures at 16:05, 19:05, and 22:05. A 23:30 shuttle (€25) takes you all the way back to Paris' Gare de Lyon after candlelit events.

By Train via Melun: Using a Navigo pass you can take

Combining Vaux-le-Vicomte and Fontainebleau

These two châteaux can be combined into a full, though manageable, day trip by car, taxi, excursion bus, or train from Paris (except on Tue, when Fontainebleau is closed). Fontainebleau is 12 minutes by train from Melun or a 25-minute drive from Vaux-le-Vicomte (about €50 by taxi). Without a car, the City Vision excursion is the most economical solution, as you'd spend just as much visiting both châteaux by train and taxi. If you want to sleep out here, check out my recommended hotels in Fontainebleau (listed on page 596).

RER/Train-D to **Melun** from Gare de Lyon, Gare du Nord, or Châtelet-Les Halles (direction: Melun, 3/hour, 50 minutes). Faster Banlieue/Transilien R trains to Melun leave from Gare de Lyon (nearly hourly, 30 minutes; direction: Montereau, Montargis, or Laroche-Migennes; Melun is the first stop). The last return train from Melun to Paris departs at about 23:45.

From Melun's scruffy train station, taxis make the 15-minute drive to Vaux-le-Vicomte (about €22 one-way Mon-Sat, €30 evenings and Sun, taxi +33 1 64 52 51 50). Ask a staffer at the château to call a cab for your return, or schedule a pickup time with your driver. Seek others with whom you can split the fare.

By Excursion Bus: The City Vision tour company offers a handy excursion bus that combines Vaux-le-Vicomte and Fontainebleau, making this day trip a breeze (from €105, includes châteaux entry; runs April-Oct a few days a week, check website, +33 1 44 55 60 00, www.pariscityvision.com).

By Car: From Paris, take the A-6 autoroute toward Lyon, then follow signs to Melun. In Melun, follow signs to Meaux, then Vaux-le-Vicomte.

ORIENTATION TO VAUX-LE-VICOMTE

Cost: €17—smart to book ahead, €11 for kids 17 and under, €20 for candlelit visits (described below); ticket includes entire château, gardens, carriage museum, and audioguide; family deals available, not covered by Paris Museum Pass.

Hours: Daily 11:00-19:00 except on candlelit visit days (described below), when the château opens at 14:00 and closes at 24:00 (Sat in mid-May-Sept plus Fri in July-Aug); last entry 1.5 hours before closing.

The château is generally closed in winter (Nov-March) but often reopens, with special decorations, during the holidays (€20, weekends only Dec-early Jan 11:00-18:30).

Information: +33 1 64 14 41 90, www.vaux-le-vicomte.com.

Tours: The excellent audioguide is included. Guided tours are also available, though most are in French only (check website).

Services: Parking is easy and free. The gift shop has fine palace guidebooks. Outside the shop are a WC and the **$ L'Ecureuil** ("The Squirrel") cafeteria, with a limited but reasonably priced selection (daily 10:00-18:00, until 22:30 during candlelit visits). The leafy **$$$ Les Charmilles** restaurant serves dinner only during candlelit visits (see next). Picnics are welcome in designated areas before you enter the grounds or on the very far end of the gardens. A variety of additional activities is possible for a price, including period costume rentals.

Candlelit Visits: On Fridays and Saturdays in high season, the château opens and closes later for candlelit visits (see "Hours," above). Two thousand candles illuminate the palace, and piped-in classical music and impressive fountains provide ambience. These *visites aux chandelles* re-create a party thrown in Louis XIV's honor in 1661. Note that the gardens are hard to see by candlelight (although it doesn't get truly dark until around 22:00 from late May through July). Buses provide service to and from Verneuil-l'Etang's train station for these events (see "Getting There," earlier). Fancy dinners are available in the Les Charmilles garden restaurant (€65 *menus*, reservations required—book online).

BACKGROUND

When Vaux-le-Vicomte and Versailles were built, France was slowly heading toward a revolution. Of its 18 million people, 200,000 were clergy ("those who pray"), 150,000 were nobles (those who fight or "carry a sword"), and the rest (17.6 million) were the Third Estate ("those who work"). Of course, there was no democracy—just one king and his ministers who ran the show. Somewhat like modern bankers and financiers, these people controlled the workings of the economy, amassing almost unfathomable wealth.

One of them was Nicolas Fouquet, France's finance minister during the reign of Louis XIV, in the 17th century. Vaux-le-Vicomte was his home. A brilliant collaboration between three masters—architect Louis Le Vau, artist Charles Le Brun, and landscape designer André Le Nôtre (who pioneered the French formal

GRAND CHATEAUX

garden)—this château was the architectural inspiration for Versailles and set the standard for European palaces to come. In fact, after several visits to the château during its construction, a very young Louis XIV found himself impressed that one man could create such magnificence. He was also curious how one man (other than himself) could pay for it. So Louis had the overly ambitious Fouquet arrested, hired his talented trio, and proceeded to have his bigger and costlier (but not necessarily more splendid) palace of Versailles built.

Monsieur Fouquet's arrest features prominently in the third Musketeer book by Alexandre Dumas (and at least two versions of *The Man in the Iron Mask* were filmed here). From the prison cell where he died, Fouquet wrote longingly of his lost home, "This was the estate I regarded as my principal seat and where I intended to leave some traces of the status I had enjoyed."

If the château feels a bit quirky in the way it's run today, remember it's not national property. It's private. The château has been in the same family for five generations and was opened to the public in 1968 by Patrice de Vogüé, who still lives on the grounds (but not in the château).

VISITING THE CHATEAU

Start your tour in the stables, at the fine **Museum of Carriages** *(Musée des Equipages),* where you can gallop through two long halls lined with elegant carriages from a time when horses were a big part of daily life. The exhibit begins with a reminder that when the château was built, France had 2.5 million horses (more than 100 horses per thousand people). Today France has 300,000 horses (just five per thousand people). While these stables are worth a look, there is no English info other than the entrance and exit signs.

Next, stroll like a wide-eyed peasant across the **stone bridge** that spans the ornamental moat facing the palace. Take some time to survey the grand design and admire the symmetry and elegance of the grounds, the outbuildings, and the palace itself. The gardens stretch far beyond the palace, but their main axis runs straight through the center of the château.

Enter the **palace** (pick up the included audioguide here). As you wander through Fouquet's dream home, you'll understand Louis XIV's envy. Versailles was a simple hunting lodge when this was built. Most of the paintings and furniture you'll see here are not original—Louis confiscated what he liked for Versailles.

The one-way route first takes you through lavish rooms, then gives you the option of climbing upstairs to a simple attic for an exhibition on carpentry and a peek at the wood structure of the building. Next you can climb 80 steps between the inner and outer **domes** (claustrophobic for some) to a small terrace at the very top, where you can look out to the magnificent grounds—the first French formal gardens (€3, pay at château entry, kids must be taller than four feet, five inches).

Continue through the last rooms on the tour route—these are among the best and are explained with concise histories on the walls. Next, make your way to the **lower levels** of the château to see where the servants and cooks shared their meals. You'll see the servants' dining room and the castle's kitchen, then pass by a cell re-creating the imprisonment of the "Man with the Iron Mask" from the film for which the château was used as the backdrop.

Exit and stand on the palace's back steps to survey André Le Nôtre's first claim to fame. This **garden** was the cutting edge of sculpted French gardens. The designer integrated ponds, shrubbery, and trees in a style that would be copied in palaces all over Europe. Consider the long 30-minute walk (one-way) to the viewpoint atop the grassy hill far in the distance. Rentable golf carts are worth the fee to make the trip easier (€20/45 minutes, 4 passengers maximum, ID and deposit required).

Fontainebleau

When it comes to showing the sweep of French history, the Château of Fontainebleau is unrivaled among French palaces. But don't expect Versailles-like unity here. It's a gangly and confusing series of wings that has grown with centuries of kings. Still, rooms are lavishly furnished and well explained in English.

Its core was built by François I in 1528 over medieval foundations. While Vaux-le-Vicomte and Versailles are French-designed, Fontainebleau was built a century earlier by an Italian. Inspired by his travels through Renaissance Italy, François I hired Italian artists to build his palaces. He even encouraged one artist—Leonardo da Vinci—to abandon his native Italy and settle in France for the last three years of his life.

It seems every king, queen, and emperor since has loved this place—Louis XIII was born here, Louis XV got married here, and Napoleon III was baptized here. And many years later, General George Patton set up headquarters here on his way to Berlin.

Above all, Fontainebleau has more Napoleon Bonaparte connections than any other palace in France. It was here that the pope met Napoleon before the general's 1804 coronation as emperor. And it was from the château's famous horseshoe-shaped staircase that Napoleon gave his stirring abdication speech, trading his rule of France for exile to Elba in 1814.

Tourist Information: Fontainebleau's TI is located in the city center in the pedestrian-only Place de la République. It has hiking and biking maps, information on where to rent bikes fit for the forest trails, and posted train/bus schedules (Mon-Sat 10:00-18:00, Sun 10:00-13:00 & 14:00-17:30, Nov-March closed Sun afternoon, 4 Place de la République, +33 1 60 74 99 99, www.fontainebleau-tourisme.com).

GETTING THERE

By Train: For a day trip to Fontainebleau, use a Navigo Découverte or Easy card)—see details at the start of this chapter.

From Gare de Lyon, catch a train to Fontainebleau-Avon station (nearly hourly, 45 minutes, direction: Montereau, Montargis, or Laroche-Migennes). Trains leave from the Grandes Lignes tracks, typically in Hall 1, but finding the right train can be tricky in huge Gare de Lyon. Arrive at your track at least 20 minutes early to pass ticket control (your ticket or reservation will be scanned). Check return times before leaving Paris, as there can be big gaps.

From Fontainebleau-Avon station, take a bus or taxi to reach the château. Bus line 1 (direction: Les Lilas/Château) leaves from the bus stall marked *#1-Château* and makes the 20-minute trip to the Château stop (4/hour, €2 if purchased on board, Paris Métro passes valid, included with Navigo Découverte pass—validate on-board, fewer buses on Sun). To return to the station, board bus #1 (direction: Avon Gare). Confirm when you board the bus by asking, *"Bonjour, ce bus va à la gare?"* (seh bews vah ah lah gar?).

A taxi from the train station to the château costs under €10 and is worth the convenience (taxis are scarce on Sun and after 19:00, taxi +33 6 07 30 13 09).

By Car: Follow signs to *Centre*, then *Château*. Several lots are close by, including Parking du Château next to the Hôtel Londres and Parking du Marché near the TI. To reach Vaux-le-Vicomte from Fontainebleau (about 20 minutes), follow signs to Melun.

ORIENTATION TO FONTAINEBLEAU

Cost: €13, free for kids 17 and under, free first Sun of the month except July-Aug, €9 last hour of the day, covered by Paris Museum Pass. It's smart to buy a timed-entry ticket online in advance in high season. If you don't have an eticket or Museum Pass and there's a line, try the ticket machine in the main entrance, just past security (US credit cards should work).

Hours: Wed-Mon 9:30-18:00, Oct-March until 17:00, closed Tue year-round, last entry 45 minutes before closing. The ballroom often closes one hour before château, and the Papal Apartment is sometimes closed 11:30-14:30.

Information: +33 1 60 71 50 70, www.chateaudefontainebleau.fr.

Tours: The worthwhile videoguide costs €4.

Services: Free lockers are available to store your bags.

VISITING THE CHATEAU

The château's complex floor plan can seem overwhelming, but visitors follow a one-way route when touring the place—don't struggle to understand the overall design. Find the entry (inside the main gate on the right), and follow along through the Napoleon I Museum, special exhibit, and royal apartments.

The **Napoleon I Museum** is fascinating. The first room to the left features grand portraits of Emperor Napoleon and his first wife, Empress Josephine (painted by Gérard after their coronation). Other rooms—each drenched in the Empire style—are dedicated to Napoleon at war (with his battle coat, tent, and camp gear); his second wife, Empress Marie Louise (whom he married for her Habsburg heritage, which Napoleon hoped would color his Corsican blood blue); and to their son, the "King of Rome," Napoleon II (who lived in exile after his dad's defeat and died of tuberculosis at 21).

The hallway is lined with busts and **portraits** of the sprawling imperial family Napoleon created—relatives he put on various thrones across his empire. Looking at the final painting, which depicts Napoleon with symbols of the legal system he gave France, the "Code Napoléon," it's fascinating to consider the mix of idealism, charisma, and megalomania of this leader. This revolutionary hero came out of a movement that killed off the Old Regime—only to create a new Old Regime.

After a swing through the portrait gallery, you'll enter the **royal apartments.** The highlights are many. The Papal Apartment was renovated by Napoleon to house Pope Pius VII. The stunning Renaissance hall of François I, which dates from 1528, inspired other royal galleries, including the Hall of Mirrors at Versailles. The opulent ballroom *(salle de bal)* comes with piped-in music and has garden views that evoke royal *fêtes.* Napoleon's throne room is the only French *salle du trône* that survives

(sidebar) GRAND CHATEAUX

with its original furniture. You'll also see the emperor's bathroom, bed, and very important-looking desk.

The palace is slathered in royal and imperial symbolism, and its walls are hung with exquisite tapestries. As you walk its halls, track the artistic shift in style, from Renaissance to Rococo—whose whimsy infuriated the revolutionary mobs—to the more sober, postrevolutionary Neoclassical.

After touring the palace, the **gardens**—designed in the 17th century by landscape architect André Le Nôtre—are worth a stroll.

TOWN OF FONTAINEBLEAU

The town itself has a helpful TI (described earlier), a few hotels, and lots of eating options. The English bookstore **ReelBooks,** at 9 Rue de Ferrare, has a good collection of new, used, and children's books. If you stop in, say hi to Sue (Tue-Sat 11:00-19:00, open some Sun, closed Mon, +33 1 64 22 85 85).

Sleeping: $$$ Hôtel de Londres*** is run by avid golfer Philippe, who rents 16 immaculate rooms, some with views of the château, all with air-conditioning. He also loans out free golf clubs—one of France's most famous golf courses is close by (no elevator, 1 Place du Général de Gaulle, +33 1 64 22 20 21, www.hoteldelondres.com, hdelondres1850@aol.com).

$$ Hôtel Ibis Château de Fontainebleau,** a five-minute walk from the château, is central, clean, and easy (18 Rue Ferrare, +33 1 64 23 45 25, www.ibishotel.com, h1028@accor.com).

Eating: Scads of restaurants, and shops perfect for picking up picnic fare, are in the town center. To reach the center, turn right out of the château courtyard and walk down Rue Denecourt. An appealing collection of pedestrian lanes begins after Place Napoléon Bonaparte. Rue des Sablons is a market street bustling with cheese shops, bakeries, fruit stands, and butchers roasting chickens. Rue Montebello is restaurant row; you'll find quieter places along the lanes off Rue de la Corne.

$$ Le Bistrot, a top option with tasty, traditional cooking in a cozy atmosphere, has a loyal local clientele and friendly staff (open daily, lunch only on Sun, 9 Rue Montebello, +33 1 64 22 87 84).

$ Le Ferrare makes a decent lunch spot for working locals, with good prices and classic fare (closed Sun, 23 Rue de France, +33 1 60 72 37 04).

$$ Le Grand Café sits prettily on the main square in front of the garden entrance to the château, serving convenient brasserie dishes (daily, 33 Place Napoléon Bonaparte, +33 1 64 22 20 32).

Chantilly

Chantilly (shahn-tee-yee), 30 minutes north of Paris, floats serene-ly on a reflecting pond. This extravagant hunting palace delivers

a peaceful château set-ting, great art, and formal (read: no flowers) French gardens, but you won't get a feel for authentic château life here. The rooms are 19th-century re-creations, as the place was pretty much razed during the Revolution. And while the famous cream's invention is often attributed to this château, the sweet white stuff predates the palace by a long shot (though it gained a certain status in the 17th century thanks to the château's chef).

Tourist Information: The TI is located in Chantilly's town center, a few blocks before the château-like stables (Grandes Ecuries) when coming from the train station (Wed-Sat 9:30-12:30 & 14:00-17:30, Sun until 17:00, closed Mon-Tue, 73 Rue du Conné-table, +33 3 44 67 37 37, www.chantilly-tourisme.com).

GETTING THERE

Taking a train to Chantilly is a breeze, but the last 1.5 miles from the station to the château is tricky unless you spring for a cab (wise idea at least one way) or enjoy a good walk. Leave from Paris' Gare du Nord for Chantilly-Gouvieux (on the Creil and Compiègne lines, Grandes Lignes). RER/Train-D serves Chantilly, but service is twice as fast on the Grandes Lignes main lines and the same price. Main line trains and RER trains each run about every 1.5 hours (check schedules at http://reiseauskunft.bahn.de—TER is the faster train). You can also ask at the Gare du Nord information desk for the next departure (fewer on weekends, 25 minutes by TER train, 50 minutes by RER/Train-D, €9 one-way).

Upon arrival in Chantilly, confirm return times to Paris as there are service gaps in the afternoon.

Getting from the Station to the Château: It's a level, easy-to-follow, 30-minute **walk** to the château (remember that you'll also be walking a lot once there). Walk straight out of the train station and cross the big road that separates the town from the woods, turn left, and follow *Château* signs. The first grand building you see after about 20 minutes is not the château but the elaborate stables (the château gate is another five minutes on foot). To return to the station on foot, follow the sign from the horse stables and walk the broad path with the racetrack off to your left. You'll enter the main drag in Chantilly where you'll turn left (and find cafés, etc.) to the station. Don't hesitate to ask, *"La gare?"*

The no-brainer station-to-château trip is by **taxi** (€10 one-way, Central Taxis, +33 9 74 56 53 81, www.central-taxis-senlis.com; minivans available if you call ahead). The ticket office at the château will call a cab for your return.

The free city **DUC bus** runs infrequently (75 yards to the left as you leave the train station) to the château, and usually is not well timed with train arrivals (no buses on Sun). It's easier to return to the station by bus; the schedule is posted at the stop across from the château entry (check return times before you enter the château).

ORIENTATION TO CHANTILLY

Cost: The basic Domaine ticket is €17 (€13.50 for kids ages 7-17, kids under 7 free), covered by Paris Museum Pass. The basic ticket covers the château, gardens, horse museum (Musée du Cheval), stables (Grandes Ecuries), and dressage horse demonstration (when available). To visit the gardens only, buy the Billet Parc (€8). Or for €30, see it all (including Spectacle Equestre horse show; see below).

Hours: Daily 10:00-18:00, Nov-March Wed-Mon 10:30-17:00, closed Tue; last entry one hour before closing.

Information: +33 3 44 27 31 80, www.domainedechantilly.com.

Tours: A free official app in English is available.

WCs: You'll find WCs at the horse stables and at the entry to the château.

Horse Shows: Horse enthusiasts can buy a €22 ticket for just the horse museum, stables, dressage demonstration (check website for times), and the fancy Spectacle Equestre horse show. These well-choreographed, one-hour performances take place mid-April-June and mid-Sept-Oct on Thu and Sun at 14:30 (show dates and times on website).

VISITING THE CHATEAU

The château dates from the 1500s and, like so many in the Loire Valley, its aristocratic history is tied to France's most popular sport at the time, hunting. That explains the focus on horses.

Chantilly has a turbulent history. Because of the social upheaval in France during the Revolution of 1848, the château's owner, Prince de Condé, fled to England. Twenty years later, when blue blood was safe again in France, he returned to his château with a fabulous collection of art (800 paintings, including three Raphaels) and priceless books. He turned his palace into the museum you see today and willed it to France on the condition that it would be maintained as he left it and the collections would never be loaned to any other museum.

Lacking the grandiose interiors of other châteaux, Chantilly lays its claim to fame with its art collection. The château was destroyed during the French Revolution—today's palace is a fanciful 19th-century-style reconstruction. The château that you can tour today is divided into three parts: apartments, art gallery, and library.

The château's lovely waterfront setting is a highlight, though its remarkable art collection is the main draw. Start with the **main gallery,** through the lavish dining room immediately to the right as you enter the château. The art is scattered among many smaller rooms that branch off the main gallery (tour it counterclockwise). Read the handheld translations and wall-posted explanations. Gallery highlights include paintings by Raphael, Poussin, Ingres, Van Dyck, Géricault, and Delacroix (Raphael's tiny works are in the Santuario room out the left side of the main gallery).

Tour the **library** and other gold-leafed rooms after the art galleries, each well described in English. Of the 13,000 books in the prince's library, the most exquisite is the brilliantly illuminated *Book of Hours* by Jean Fouquet (c. 1460). You'll exit from the lower level through the book shop and graphite art collection (good Delacroix works here).

Gardens: Immediately behind the château, you'll see geometric and austere gardens. Find the water ponds behind the château and walk down to them. Turn right along the canal following signs for 10 minutes to *le Hameau,* where you'll find a sweet little garden café (limited menu features pricey desserts served with real Chantilly cream, open April-Oct). This little hamlet of three

half-timbered, thatched-roofed homes was the prototype for the more famous *hameau* at Versailles. While the homes are peasant-simple on the outside, they are lavishly decorated within: The prince had certain needs when he played peasant.

Stables: The prince believed he'd be reincarnated as a horse, so he built an opulent horse château—now a museum/training center (it's the huge building to the right as you look out from the château—allow five minutes to walk there from the château; those walking from the station will pass it on the way). I imagine that such a sumptuous structure devoted solely to horses did not go over well with locals in prerevolutionary France.

Today's **horse museum** boards horses and boasts 15 well-presented rooms that tell the story of how horses evolved to become essential in human life. The museum is beautifully done, with excellent English explanations and videos, carved wooden horses from carousels, paintings, and examples of riding gear. You might see riders training in the rinks or theater where the shows take place; some demonstrations are more elaborate. To get the most from a visit, plan your time to see a demonstration (times on website).

TOWN OF CHANTILLY

There's a small grocery shop and a café across from the station. You'll also find many cafés and restaurants in Chantilly town. A lively outdoor **market** runs on Saturday and Wednesday mornings until 12:30 on appealing Place Omer Vallon (10-minute walk from the château).

CHARTRES

Chartres, about 50 miles southwest of Paris, gives travelers a pleasant break in a lively, midsize town with a thriving, pedestrian-friendly old center. But the big reason to come to Chartres (shar-truh) is to see its famous cathedral—arguably Europe's best example of pure Gothic. And with the interior of Paris' Notre-Dame Cathedral off-limits, the cathedral at Chartres is your best chance to experience a glorious Gothic church as a day trip from Paris.

Chartres' old church burned to the ground on June 10, 1194. Some of the children who watched its destruction were actually around to help rebuild the cathedral and attend its dedication Mass in 1260. That's astonishing, considering that other Gothic cathedrals, such as Paris' Notre-Dame, took literally centuries to build. Having been built so quickly, the cathedral has a unity of architecture, statuary, and stained glass that captures the spirit of the Age of Faith like no other church.

While overshadowed by its cathedral, the town of Chartres also merits exploration. Discover the picnic-perfect park behind the cathedral, check out the colorful pedestrian zone, and wander the quiet alleys and peaceful lanes down to and along the small river.

PLANNING YOUR TIME

Chartres is an easy day trip from Paris (even if you leave Paris in the afternoon and return later in the evening). But with its statues glowing in the setting sun—and with hotels and restaurants much less expensive than those in the capital—Chartres also makes a worthwhile overnight stop. If you'll be here at night, don't miss the dazzling light show—Chartres en Lumières—when dozens of Chartres' most historic buildings are colorfully illuminated, adding to the town's after-hours appeal (early April-mid-Oct; details at TI). Chartres' historic center is quiet Sunday and Monday, when most shops are closed.

Chartres is a one-hour ride from Paris' Gare Montparnasse (14/day, about €16 one-way; see the Paris Connections chapter for Gare Montparnasse details). Jot down return times to Paris before you exit the Chartres train station (last train generally departs Chartres around 21:30; verify for your day of travel).

Upon arrival in Chartres, head for the cathedral. Allow an hour to savor the church on your own as you follow my self-guided tour. Try to make the cathedral tour at noon, led by Anne-Marie Woods (details later). Take another hour or two to wander the appealing old city, following my Chartres Walk. On Saturday and Wednesday mornings, a small outdoor market sets up a few short blocks from the cathedral on Place Billard.

Orientation to Chartres

Tourist Information: The TI is in the historic Maison du Saumon building (Mon-Sat 10:00-18:00, Sun until 17:00, closes earlier Nov-March, 8 Rue de la Poissonnerie, +33 2 37 18 26 26, www.chartres-tourisme.com). It offers specifics on cathedral tours and also rents audioguides for the old town (€5.50, €8.50/double set, about 2 hours). The narration offers little more information than my self-guided Chartres Walk but is relaxing and easy to follow. Skip the Chartres Pass sold here.

The TI has a small map that shows the floodlit Chartres en Lumières sites, and information on the *petit train* you can take to see them all (check the website or ask at the TI for details).

Arrival in Chartres: Exiting Chartres' **train** station, you'll see the spires of the cathedral dominating the town. It's a 10-minute walk up Avenue Jehan de Beauce to the cathedral. The free minibus, called the Filibus, runs to near the cathedral (line: Relais des Portes, 3/hour, Mon-Sat 8:30-19:00), or you can take a taxi for about €7.

If arriving **by car,** you'll have fine views of the cathedral and city as you approach from the A-11 autoroute. Pay underground parking is on Place des Epars and Place Châtelet, both a short walk from the cathedral. Free parking is available in the lower medieval town (Parking Trois Détours), a 15-minute uphill walk to the cathedral following my Chartres Walk.

Helpful Hints: A **launderette** is a few blocks from the cathedral (by the TI) at 16a Place de la Poissonnerie (daily 7:00-21:00). If you need to call a **taxi,** try +33 2 37 36 00 00.

Sights in Chartres

CHARTRES CATHEDRAL

The church, worth ▲▲▲, is (at least) the fourth one on this spot dedicated to Mary, the mother of Jesus, who has been venerated here for some 1,700 years.  There's even speculation that the pagan Romans dedicated a temple here to a mother-goddess. In earliest times, Mary was honored next to a natural spring of healing waters (not visible today).

In 876, the church acquired the torn veil (or birthing gown) supposedly worn by Mary when she gave birth to Jesus. The 2,000-year-old veil (now on display) became the focus of worship at the church. By the 11th century, the cult of saints was strong. And Mary, considered the "Queen of All Saints," was hugely popular. God was enigmatic and scary, but Mary was maternal and accessible, providing a handy go-between for Christians and their Creator. Chartres, a small town of 10,000 with a prized relic, found itself in the big time on the pilgrim circuit.

When the fire of 1194 incinerated the old church, the veil was feared lost. Lo and behold, several days later, townspeople found it miraculously unharmed in the crypt (beneath today's choir). Whether the veil's survival was a miracle or a marketing ploy, the people of Chartres were so stoked, they worked like madmen to erect this grand cathedral in which to display it. Thinkers and scholars gathered here, making the small town with its big-city church a leading center of learning in the Middle Ages (until the focus shifted to Paris' university).

By the way, the church is officially called the Cathédrale Notre-Dame de Chartres. Many travelers think that "Notre-Dame" is in Paris. That's true. But more than a hundred churches dedicated to Mary—"Notre-Dames"—are scattered around France, and Chartres Cathedral is one of them.

Cost and Hours: Free, daily 8:30-19:30, July-Aug until 22:00 on Tue, Fri, and Sun. Mass usually Mon-Sat at 11:45 (in crypt), daily at 18:15, Sun also at 9:00 (Gregorian) and 11:00. Confirm times by phone or online, +33 2 37 21 59 08, www.cathedrale-chartres.org (click "Cathedral," then "Celebrations," then "Masses").

Tours: A now-beloved English scholar who moved here about 60 years ago when he was 24, **Malcolm Miller** has dedicated his

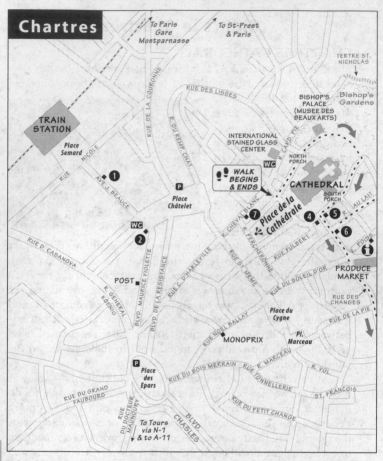

life to studying this cathedral and sharing its wonder through his guided lecture tours. While he has retired now, his very capable American understudy, **Anne-Marie Woods,** leads 1.25-hour tours, worthwhile even if you've taken my self-guided tour. No reservation is needed; just show up with cash (€12, €5 for students, includes headphones that allow her to speak softly, Easter–mid-Oct Tue-Sat at 12:00; no tours last half of Aug or on religious holidays, +33 2 37 21 75 02, annemariechartres@gmail.com). Tours begin just inside the church at the *Visites de la Cathédrale* sign. Consult this sign for changes or cancellations..

Malcolm still offers private tours (millerchartres@aol.com). Miller's guidebook provides a detailed look at Chartres' windows, sculpture, and history (sold at cathedral).

You can rent a **videoguide** to the right as you enter the cathedral, a good way to get a closer look at the window details (€7, 70

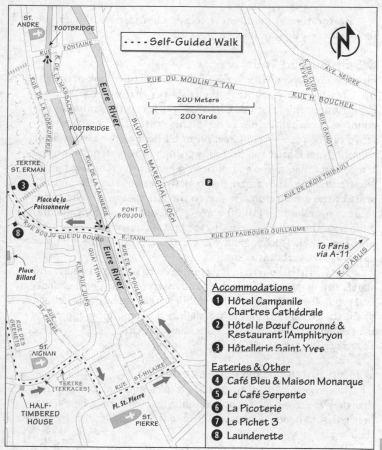

- - - - Self-Guided Walk

200 Meters
200 Yards

Accommodations

1. Hôtel Campanile Chartres Cathédrale
2. Hôtel le Bœuf Couronné & Restaurant l'Amphitryon
3. Hôtellerie Saint-Yves

Eateries & Other

4. Café Bleu & Maison Monarque
5. Le Café Serpente
6. La Picoterie
7. Le Pichet 3
8. Launderette

CHARTRES

minutes). **Binoculars** are a big help for studying the cathedral art (rent at souvenir shops around the cathedral).

Tower Climb: €6 to climb the 200 steps to the rooftop with a French-only guided tour; daily May-Aug at 11:00, 14:30, and 16:00, Sept-April at 11:00 and 15:00; call ahead at +33 2 37 21 22 07 as this may change due to renovations.

Crypt: Beneath the cathedral are extensive remnants of earlier churches, a modern copy of the old wooden Mary-and-baby statue, an amazing 2,000-year-old well, and frescoes from the 12th and 13th centuries.

The only way to see the crypt is on a tour. Anne-Marie Woods' tour (see above) includes the crypt and helps bring it to life, but I'd avoid the more frequent 30-minute tours in French with English handout (€4, 5/day late June-mid-Sept, fewer Sun and off-season, book at cathedral gift shop, +33 2 37 21 75 02).

Restoration: A multiyear restoration is underway, though you should see few signs of it when you visit.

❯ Self-Guided Tour

Historian Malcolm Miller calls Chartres a picture book of the entire Christian story, told through its statues, stained glass, and architecture. In this "Book of Chartres," the text is the sculpture and windows, and its binding is the architecture. The complete narrative can be read—from Creation to Christ's birth (north side of church), from Christ and his followers up to the present (south entrance), and then to the end of time, when Christ returns as judge (west entrance). The remarkable cohesiveness of the text and the unity of the architecture are due to the fact that nearly the entire church was rebuilt in just 30 years (a blink of an eye for cathedral building). The cathedral contains the best and most intact library of medieval religious iconography in existence. Most of the windows date from the early 13th century.

The Christian universe is a complex web of heaven and earth, angels and demons, and prophets and martyrs. Much of the medieval symbolism is obscure today. While it's easy to be overwhelmed by the thousands of things to see, make a point to simply appreciate the perfect harmony of this Gothic masterpiece.

• *Start outside, taking in the...*

❶ Main Entrance (West Facade)

Chartres' soaring (if mismatched) steeples announce to pilgrims that they've arrived. For centuries, pilgrims have come here to see holy relics, to honor "Our Lady," and to feed their souls.

The facade is about the only survivor of the intense, lead-melting fire that incinerated the rest of the church in 1194. The church we see today was rebuilt behind this c. 1150 facade in a single generation (1194-1260).

Compare the **towers.** The right (south) tower, with a Romanesque stone steeple, survived the fire. The left (north) tower lost its wooden steeple in the fire. In the 1500s, it was topped with the flamboyant Gothic steeple we see today.

The emaciated column-like statues flanking the three **west doors** are pillars of the faith. These kings of Judah, prophets, and Old Testament big shots foretold the coming of Christ. With solemn gestures and faces, they patiently endure the wait.

What they predicted came to pass. History's pivotal event is

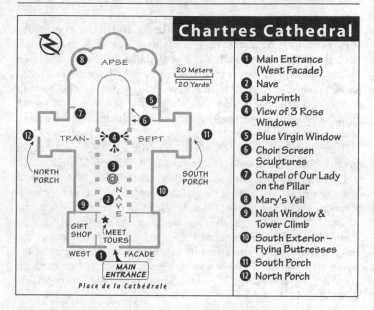

Chartres Cathedral

① **Main Entrance (West Facade)**
② **Nave**
③ **Labyrinth**
④ **View of 3 Rose Windows**
⑤ **Blue Virgin Window**
⑥ *Choir Screen Sculptures*
⑦ *Chapel of Our Lady on the Pillar*
⑧ *Mary's Veil*
⑨ *Noah Window & Tower Climb*
⑩ *South Exterior – Flying Buttresses*
⑪ *South Porch*
⑫ *North Porch*

APSE
20 Meters
20 Yards
TRAN- SEPT
NORTH PORCH
SOUTH PORCH
NAVE
GIFT SHOP
MEET TOURS
WEST FACADE
MAIN ENTRANCE
Place de la Cathédrale

shown above the **right door,** where Mary (seated) produces Baby Jesus from her loins. This Mary-and-baby sculpture is a 12th-century stone version of an even older wooden statue that burned in 1793. Centuries of pilgrims have visited Chartres to see Mary's statue, gaze at her veil, and ponder the mystery of how God in heaven became man on earth, as He passed through immaculate Mary like sunlight through stained glass.

Over the **central door** is Christ in majesty, surrounded by animals symbolizing Matthew, Mark, Luke, and John. Over the **left door,** Christ ascends into heaven after his death and resurrection.

• *Enter the church (from a side entrance if the main one is closed) and wait for your pupils to enlarge.*

❷ Nave

The place is huge—the nave is 427 feet long, 20 feet wide, and 120 feet high. Notice the height of the entrance doors compared to the tourists...the doors are 24 feet tall!

The long, tall central nave is lined with 12 pillars, which support pointed, crisscrossed arches that lace together the heavy stone vaulting. The pillars themselves are supported by flying buttresses on the

CHARTRES

outside of the church (which we'll see later). This skeleton structure was the miracle of Gothic design, making it possible to build tall cathedrals with ribbed walls and lots of stained-glass windows (see the big saints in the upper stories of the nave). Chartres has 28,000 square feet of stained glass. The nave—the widest Gothic nave in France—is flanked by raised side aisles. This design was for crowd flow, so pilgrims could circle the church without disturbing worshippers.

Try to picture the church in the Middle Ages—painted in greens, browns, and golds (like colorful St. Aignan Church in the old town, described later in my self-guided walk). It was packed with pilgrims, and was a rough cross between a hostel, a soup kitchen, and a flea market. The floor of the nave slopes in to the center, for easy drainage when hosing down the dirty pilgrims who camped here. Looking around the church, you'll see stones at the base of the columns smoothed by centuries of tired pilgrim butts. With all the hubbub in the general nave, the choir (screened-off central zone around the high altar) provided a holy place with a more sacred atmosphere.

Taking it all in from the nave, notice that, as was typical in medieval churches, the windows on the darker north side feature Old Testament themes—awaiting the light of Christ's arrival. And the windows on the brighter south side are New Testament. Regardless of which direction they face, the highest windows—way up in the clerestory—are dark from decades of candle soot. As the ongoing cleaning job proceeds, more of the interior will be bright and sparkling like the apse (area behind the front altar).

• *On the floor, midway up the nave, find the...*

❸ Labyrinth

The broad, round labyrinth inlaid in black marble on the floor is a spiritual journey. Labyrinths like this were common in medieval churches. Pilgrims enter from the west rim, by foot or on their knees, and wind around, meditating, on a metaphorical journey to Jerusalem. About 900 feet later, they hope to meet God in the middle. (The chairs are removed on Fridays between 10:00 and 17:00 from Lent to November 1.) To let your fingers do the walking, you'll find a small model of the maze just outside the gift shop, where the tours begin.

• *Walk up the nave to where the transept crosses. As you face the altar and gleaming choir, north is to the left.*

❹ Rose Windows

The three big, round "rose" (circular) windows over the north, south, and west entrances receive sunlight at different times of day. All three are predominantly blue and red, but each has different "petals," and each tells a different part of the Christian story in a kaleidoscope of fragmented images.

Stained glass was created to teach Bible stories to the illiterate medieval masses...who apparently owned state-of-the-art binoculars. The windows were used in many ways—to tell stories, to allow parents to teach children simple lessons, to help theologians explain complex lessons, to enable worshippers to focus on images as they meditated or prayed...and, of course, to light a dark church in a colorful and decorative way.

The brilliantly restored **north rose window** charts history from the distant past up to the birth of Jesus. On the outer rim, a ring of semicircles, ancient prophets foretell Christ's coming. Then (circling inward) there's a ring of red squares with kings who are Jesus' direct ancestors. Still closer, circles with white doves and winged angels zero in on the central event of history—Mary, the heart of the flower, with her newborn baby, Jesus.

This window was donated by Blanche of Castile, mother of the future King Louis IX (who would build Paris' stained-glass masterpiece of a church, Sainte-Chapelle) Blanche's heraldry frames the lower edge of the window: yellow fleur-de-lis on a blue background (for France) and gold castles on a red background (for her home kingdom of Castile).

The **south rose window,** with a similar overall design, tells how the Old Testament prophecies were fulfilled. Christ sits in the center (dressed in blue, with a red background), setting in motion radiating rings of angels, beasts, and instrument-playing apocalyptic elders who labor to bring history to its close. The five lancet windows below show Mary flanked by four Old Testament prophets (Jeremiah, Isaiah, Ezekiel, and Daniel) lifting New Testament writers (Luke, Matthew, John, and Mark) on their shoulders. (In the first window on the left, see white-robed Luke riding piggyback on dark-robed Jeremiah.) These demonstrated how the ancients prepared the way for Christ—and how the New Testament evangelists had a broader perspective from their lofty perches.

In the center of the **west rose window,** a dark Christ rings in history's final Day of Judgment. Around him, winged angels blow their trumpets and the dead rise, face judgment, and are sent to hell or raised to eternal bliss. The frilly edge of this glorious "rose" is flecked with tiny clover-shaped dewdrops.

• *Now walk around the altar to the right (south) side and find the window with a big, blue Mary (second one from the right).*

The Chartres Generation—the 1200s

From king to bishop and knight to pawn, French society was devoted to the Christian faith. It inspired knights to undertake the formidable Crusades, artists to re-create the divine in statues and stained glass, and architects to build skyscraping cathedrals filled with the mystic light of heaven. They aimed for a Golden Age, blending faith and reason. But misguided faith often outstripped reason, resulting in very un-Christian intolerance and violence.

c. 1194: The old cathedral burns down.

1200: The University of Paris is founded, using human reason to analyze Christian faith. Borrowing from the pagan Greek philosopher Aristotle, scholars described the Christian universe as a series of concentric rings spinning around the earth in geometrical perfection.

1202: The pope calls on all true Christians to rescue the Holy Land from Muslim "infidels" in the Fourth Crusade (1202-1204). This crusade ends disastrously in the sacking of Christian Constantinople.

1206: Chartres' cornerstone is laid. The style is *opus francigenum* ("French-style work")—what we now call Gothic. Chartres is just one of several great cathedrals under construction in Europe.

1207: Francis of Assisi, a rebellious Italian youth, undergoes a conversion to a life of Christian poverty and love. His open spirit inspires many followers, including France's King Louis IX (a generation later).

1209: France's King Philip Augustus, based in Paris, invades southern France and massacres fellow Christians (members of the Cathar sect) as heretics.

CHARTRES

❺ Blue Virgin Window

Mary, dressed in blue on a rich red background, cradles Jesus, while the dove of the Holy Spirit descends on her. This very old window (mid-12th century) was the central window behind the altar of the church that burned in 1194. It survived and was reinserted into this frame in the new church around 1230. Mary's glowing dress is an example of the famed "Chartres blue," a sumptuous color made by mixing cobalt oxide into the glass (before cheaper materials were introduced). The Blue Virgin was one of the most popular stops for pilgrims—especially pregnant ones—of the cult of the Virgin-about-to-give-birth. Devotees prayed, carried stones to repair the church, and donated to the

1212: Thousands of boys and girls idealistically join the Children's Crusade to save the Holy Land. Most die in transit or are sold into slavery.

1220: The external structure of Chartres Cathedral is nearly finished. Work begins on the statues and stained glass.

1226: Eleven-year-old Louis IX is crowned as *rex et sacerdos,* "king and priest," beginning a 45-year Golden Age combining church and state. His mother, Blanche of Castile (granddaughter of Eleanor of Aquitaine), serves as his regent during his minority and is his lifelong mentor.

1230: Most of Chartres' stained glass is completed.

1244: At age 30, Louis IX falls sick and, while in a coma, sees a vision that changes his life. His personal integrity helps unify the nation. He reforms the judicial system along Christian lines, helping the poor.

1245: The last Albigensian heretics are burned at Montségur, in a crusade ordered by Louis IX and his mother, Blanche.

1248: Louis IX personally leads the Seventh Crusade by walking barefoot from Paris to the port of departure. During the fighting, he is captured and ransomed. He later returns home a changed man. Humbled, he adopts the poverty of the Franciscan brotherhood. His devotion earns him the title of St. Louis.

1260: Chartres Cathedral is dedicated. The church is the physical embodiment of the Age of Faith, with architecture as mathematically perfect as God's Creation, sculpture serving as sermons in stone, and stained glass lit by the light of God.

church coffers; Mary rewarded them with peace of mind, easy births, and occasional miracles.

Below Mary (bottom panel), see **Christ being tempted** by a red-faced, horned, smirking devil.

The **Zodiac Window** (two windows to the left) shows the 12 signs of the zodiac (in the right half of the window; read from the bottom up—Pisces, Aries, Gemini in the central cloverleaf, Taurus, Cockroach, Leo, Virgo, etc.). On the left side are the corresponding months (February warming himself by a fire, April gathering flowers, and so on).

• *Now turn around and look behind you.*

❻ Choir Screen: Life of Mary

The choir (enclosed area around the altar where church officials sat) is the heart *(coeur)* of the church. A stone screen rings it with **41 statue groups** illustrating Mary's life. Although the Bible says

Surviving the Centuries

Chartres contains the world's largest collection of medieval stained glass, with more than 150 early-13th-century windows, about 80 percent with the original glass. Through the centuries, much of the rest of France's stained glass was destroyed by various ideologues: Protestant puritans who disapproved of papist imagery (they would never think of it as art), revolutionaries who turned churches into "temples of reason" (or stables), Baroque artists who preferred clear windows and lots of light, and the bombs of World War II.

Chartres was spared many (but not all) of these ravages. During World War II, in anticipation of Nazi destruction, the citizens removed all the windows (burying them in cellars in southwest France) and piled sandbags to protect the statues. Today, Chartres survives as Europe's best-preserved medieval cathedral.

little about the mother of Jesus, legend and lore fleshed out her life. Take some time to learn about the Lady this church is dedicated to.

Scene #1 (south side) shows Mary's dad hearing the news that Mary is on the way. In #4, Mary is born, and maidens bathe the new baby. In #6, Mary marries Joseph (sculpted with the features of King François I). In scene #7, an angel announces to Mary that she'll be the mother of the Messiah, and (#10) she gives birth to Jesus in a manger. In #12, the Three Kings—looking like the three musketeers—arrive. In #14, Herod orders all babies slaughtered, but Mary's son survives to begin his mission.

Next come episodes from the life of Jesus. On the other side of the choir screen, in #27, Jesus is crucified and, in #28, lies lifeless in his mother's arms. Scene #34 depicts the Ascension, as Jesus takes off, Cape Canaveral-style, while his awestruck followers look up at the bottoms of his rocketing feet. In #39, Mary has died and is raised by angels into heaven, where (#40) she's crowned Queen of Heaven by the Father, Son, and Holy Ghost.

The **plain windows** surrounding the choir date from the 1770s, when the dark mystery of medieval stained glass was replaced by the open light of the French Enlightenment. The plain windows and the choir are some of the only "new" features. Most of the 13th-century church has remained intact, despite style changes, revolutionary vandals, and war bombs.

• *Do an about-face and find the chapel with Mary on a pillar.*

❼ Chapel of Our Lady on the Pillar

A 16th-century statue of Mary and baby—draped in cloth, crowned and sceptered—sits on a 13th-century column in a wonderful carved-wood alcove. This is today's pilgrimage center, built to keep visitors from clogging up the altar area. Modern pilgrims (including lots of new moms pushing strollers) honor the Virgin by leaving flowers, lighting candles, and kissing the column.

• *Double back a bit around the ambulatory, heading toward the back of the church. In the next chapel you encounter (Chapel of the Sacred Heart of Mary), you'll find a gold frame holding a fragment of Mary's venerated veil. These days it's kept—for its safety and preservation—out of the light and behind bulletproof glass.*

❽ Mary's Veil

This veil (or tunic) was supposedly worn by Mary when she gave birth to Jesus. It became the main object of adoration for the cult of the Virgin. The great King of the Franks, Charlemagne (742-814), received the veil as a present from Byzantine Empress Irene. Charlemagne's grandson gave the veil to Chartres in 876. In 911, with the city surrounded by Vikings, the bishop hoisted the veil like a battle flag and waved it at the invaders. It scared the bejeezus out of them, and the town was saved.

In the frenzy surrounding the fire of 1194, the veil mysteriously disappeared, only to reappear three days later (recalling the Resurrection). This was interpreted by church officials and the townsfolk as a sign from Mary that she wanted a new church, and thus the building began. Recent tests confirm that the material itself, and the weaving technique used to make the cloth, date to the first century AD, lending support to claims of the relic's authenticity.

• *Return to the west end and find the last window on the right (near the tower entrance).*

❾ Noah Window and Tower Climb

Read Chartres' windows in the medieval style: from bottom to top. In the bottom diamond, God tells Noah he'll destroy the earth.

Next, Noah hefts an ax to build an ark, while his son hauls wood (diamond #2). Two by two, he loads horses (cloverleaf, above left), purple elephants (cloverleaf, right), and other animals. The psychedelic ark sets sail (diamond #3). Waves cover the earth and drown the wicked (two cloverleafs). The ark survives (diamond #4), and Noah releases a dove. Finally, up near the top (diamond #7), a rainbow (symbolizing God's promise never to bring another flood) arches overhead, God drapes himself over it, and Noah and his family give thanks.

Chartres was a trading center, and its merchant brotherhoods donated money to make 42 of the windows. For 800 years, these panes have publicly thanked their sponsors. In the bottom left is a man making a wheel. More workers are to the right. The panels announce that "these windows are brought to you by..." the wheel-, ax-, and barrelmaking guilds.

• *To climb the north tower, you'll need to join a tour (see "Tower Climb," earlier). Exit the church through the main entrance or the door in the south transept to view its south side.*

❿ South Exterior: Flying Buttresses

Six flying buttresses (the arches that stick out from the upper walls) push against six pillars lining the nave inside, helping to hold up

the heavy stone ceiling and sloped, lead-over-wood roof. The ceiling and roof push down onto the pillars, of course, but also outward (north and south) because of that miracle of Gothic architecture: the pointed arch. The flying buttresses push back, channeling the stress outward to the six vertical buttresses, then down to the ground. The result is a tall cathedral held up by slender pillars buttressed from the outside, allowing the walls to be opened up for stained glass.

The church is built from large blocks of limestone. Peasants trod in hamster-wheel contraptions to raise these blocks into place—a testament to their great faith.

GOD = LIGHT

You can try to examine the details, but a better way to experience the mystery of Chartres is just to sit and stare at these enormous panels as they float in the dark of empty space like holograms or space stations or the Queen of Heaven's crown jewels. Ponder the medieval concept that God is light.

To the Chartres generation, the church was a metaphor for how God brings his creation to life, like the way light animates stained glass. They were heavy into mysticism, feeling a oneness with all creation in a moment of enlightenment. The Gospel of John (as well as a writer known to historians as the Pseudo-Dionysus) was their favorite. Here are select verses from John 1:1-12 (loosely translated):

In the beginning was The Word.
Jesus was the light of the human race.
The light shines in the darkness
 and the darkness cannot resist it.
It was the real light coming into the world,
 the light that enlightens everyone.
He was in the world, but the world did not recognize Him.
But to those who did, He gave the power
 to become the children of God.

⓫ South Porch

The three doorways of the south entrance show the world from Christ's time to the present, as Christianity triumphs over persecution.

Center Door, Christ and Apostles: Standing between the double doors, **Jesus** holds a book and raises his arm in blessing. He's a simple, itinerant, bareheaded, barefoot rabbi, but underneath his feet, he tramples symbols of evil: the dragon and lion. Christ's face is among the most noble of all Gothic sculpture.

Christ is surrounded by his **apostles,** who spread the good news to a hostile world. **Peter** (to the left as you face Jesus), with curly hair and beard, holds the keys to the kingdom of heaven. **Paul** (to the right of Jesus) fingers the sword of his martyrdom and contemplates the inevitable loss of his head. In fact, all of these apostles were killed or persecuted, and their faces are humble, with sad eyes. But their message prevailed, and under their feet they crush the squirming rulers who once persecuted them.

The final triumph comes above the door in the **Last Judgment.** Christ sits in judgment, raising his hands, while Mary and John beg him to take it easy on poor humankind. Beneath Christ the souls are judged—the righteous on our left, and the wicked on our right, who are thrown into the fiery jaws of hell. Farther to the right (above the statues of Paul and the apostles), horny demons subject wicked women to an eternity of sexual harassment.

Left Door, Martyrs: Eight martyrs flank the left door. **St. Lawrence** (second from left) cradles the grill (it looks like a book) on which he was barbecued alive. His last brave words to the Romans were: "You can turn me over—I'm done on this side." **St. George** (far right on right flank) wears the knightly uniform of the 1200s, when Chartres was built and King Louis IX was crusading. Depicted beneath the martyrs are gruesome **methods of torture,** such as George stretched on the wheel. Many of these techniques were actually used in the 1200s by Christians against heretics, Muslims, Jews, and Christian Cathars.

• *Reach the north side by circling around the back end of the church. As you walk, enjoy the peaceful park, fine views over the town, and the church's architecture. Ponder the exoskeletal nature of Gothic design and the ability of medieval faith to mobilize the masses.*

⑫ North Porch

In the "Book of Chartres," the north porch is chapter one, from the Creation up to the coming of Christ.

Look between the double doors to see **Baby Mary** (headless), in the arms of her mother, Anne, marking the end of the Old Testament world and the start of the New.

History begins in the tiny details in the concentric arches over the doorway. **God creates Adam** (at the peak of the outermost arch, just to the left of the keystone) by cradling his head in his lap like a child.

Next, look at the statues that flank the doors. **Melchizedek** (farthest to the left of Mary and Anne), with the cap of a king and the cup of Communion, is the biblical model of the *rex et sacerdos* (king-priest), the title bestowed on King Louis IX.

Abraham (next to Melchizedek) holds his son by the throat and raises a knife to slit him for sacrifice. Just then, he hears something and turns his head up to see God's angel, who stops the bloodshed. The drama of this frozen moment anticipates Renaissance naturalism by 200 years.

John the Baptist (fourth to the right from Mary/Anne), the

last Old Testament prophet, who prepared the way for Jesus, holds a lamb,
the symbol of Christ. John is skinny
from his diet of locusts and honey. His
body and beard twist and flicker like
a flame.

All these prophets, with their
beards turning down the corners of
their mouths, have the sad, wise look
of having been around since the beginning of time and having seen it all—
from Creation to Christ to Apocalypse.
Over the door is the culmination of all
this history: **Christ on his throne,**
joined by Mary, the Queen of Heaven. These sculptures are some
of the last work done on the church, completing the church's stone-
and-glass sermon.

Imagine all this painted and covered with gold leaf in preparation for the dedication ceremonies in 1260, when the Chartres
generation could finally stand back and watch as their great-grand-
children, carrying candles, entered the cathedral.

CHARTRES WALK

Chartres' old town bustles with activity (except Sun and Mon) and
merits exploration. You can rent an audioguide from the TI, or better, just wander (follow the
route shown on the "Char-
tres" map).

In medieval times,
Chartres was actually two
towns—the pilgrims' town
around the cathedral, and
the industrial town along
the river, which was pow-
ered by watermills. This
self-guided walk takes you on a 45-minute loop around the cathedral, through the old pilgrims' town, down along the once-indus-
trial riverbank, and back up to the cathedral.

• *Begin at the square in front of the church.*

Cathedral Close: Around the cathedral was a town within
the town. Essentially a precinct run by the church, it was called the
"close" of Notre-Dame *(cloître Notre-Dame)*. Looking at the square
in front of the church, imagine a walled-in cathedral town with
nine gates. It was busy, with a hospital, a school (Chartres was a
leading center of education in the 12th century), a bishop's palace,
markets, fairs, and lots of shops—many of them tucked up against

the church between its huge buttresses. Chartres was on the medieval map because of the cathedral and its relic. The town was all about the church. For example, in the medieval mind, the foundation of truth was the number three—the Trinity. Nine (three times three) was also a good number. Chartres consisted of three entities—the town, the close, and the church. And each was sure to have nine gates or doors.

About 20 paces in front of the cathedral's main door, a modern plaque in the pavement points pilgrims to Santiago de Compostela in northwest Spain, home of the tomb of St. James (notice the pilgrim with his walking stick and the stylized scallop shell symbolizing the various routes from all over Europe converging on Santiago). For a thousand years, the faithful have trekked from Paris to Chartres and on to Santiago, a thousand miles away. And for centuries, pilgrims have stoked the economy of Chartres.

• *Circle the cathedral clockwise, passing a fine 24-hour clock as you round the corner, and then find the striking carvings of the north porch (described earlier). Head under a stately 18th-century wrought-iron gate to the...*

Bishop's Palace and Grounds: The bishop essentially ruled from here until the French Revolution secularized the country. This fine building has housed King Henry IV (here for his coronation), Napoleon, and—since 1939—the city's Museum of Fine Arts (Musée des Beaux Arts). An ivy-covered arcade, running from near the church to the palace, is all that remains of a covered passageway designed to make the bishop's commute  more pleasant. Stand close to the banister as you survey the lower levels of the bishop's terraced gardens and enjoy a view of the lower town. From here, you can see why this point has been a strategic choice since ancient times. Beyond the gardens nestles the lower town, which was centered not on the church but on the river, which powered the local industry.

• *From the bishop's garden, continue circling around the cathedral until you reach its south porch (described earlier). Turn left onto...*

Rue des Changes: This "street of the money changers" runs south from the cathedral. The layout, street names, and building facades of this historic district all date back to a time when businesses catered to the needs of pilgrims rather than tourists. At Rue de la Poissonnerie (where fish were sold), side-trip half a block left, to a fine old half-timbered building called **Maison du Saumon** (House of Salmon). It dates from about 1500, and as you might guess from the wood carvings, it faced the former fish market.

Today it's Chartres' TI. Find the carving of the entangled sow (one floor up, right side) designed to remind medieval people to focus on what they are meant to do on this earth.

Back on Rue des Changes, a few more paces brings you to the sky-blue open-air **produce market** on Place Billard (open Sat and Wed until 13:00). Char-tres' castle stood here until 1802, when it was demol-ished with revolutionary gusto to make way for the market.

• *From here, Rue des Changes turns into Rue des Grenets. For a detour into a bigger-than-you-thought pedestrian zone of shops, colorful lanes, and café-dappled squares, turn right up Rue de la Pie to Place Marceau (the hub of this network) and Rue Noël Ballay (the main shopping drag). Return to Rue des Grenets and continue walking away from the cathedral.*

Rue des Grenets: Farther down the street is the **Church of St. Aignan.** Squat, crumbling, and lopsided, this is the oldest of Chartres' parish churches. Remember: Locals didn't worship in the great cathedral (that was for visitors—like us); they worshipped in the town's simple parish churches. This one is built upon the tomb of a fourth-century bishop of Chartres (his statue stands in front of the choir). Its interior, dating from about 1625, shows how colorful a stone church could be. The vibrant colors, lavish decoration, and vaulted wood ceiling are astonishing given the plain exterior. The wood ceiling reminds us that even stone churches can catch fire, a poignant lesson relearned in 2019 at Notre-Dame Cathedral in Paris.

Continue down Rue des Grenets to a tall, skinny **half-tim-bered house.** As the population grew, so did the fire hazard, and the town required half-timbered buildings to be plastered over for safety. Today, the town government—interested in pumping up the touristic charm—pays folks to peel away the plaster and re-expose those timbers. You can see that this building is one of the oldest—the tilting lintel and the asymmetrical windows are dead giveaways.

Turn left at the house and drop down the *tertre,* a series of **stair-step terraces** that link the upper and lower towns. The well-worn stone benches along the way evoke a day when washerwomen, laden with freshly washed laundry, rested as they climbed the hill after a trip to the river.

• *At the bottom, turn right on Rue St. Pierre, then find the **Church of St. Pierre** (great photo-op of flying buttresses and a delicate yet decrepit in-*

CHARTRES

*terior). Follow Pont St. Hilaire a block below the church, and—bam!—
Eure at the river.*

The Eure River: This is another photogenic spot, with old
buildings, humpback bridges, and cathedral steeples in the distance. As in nearly any industri-
al town back then, waterwheels
provided power. The river was
once lined with busy mills and
warehouses. The worst polluters
were kept downstream (dyers,
tanners, slaughterhouses). The
names of the riverside lanes
evoke those times: Rue du Massacre, Rue de la Tannerie, and
Rue de la Foulerie (named for a process of cleaning wool).

When the industry moved out to make room for Chartres'
growing population, laundry places replaced the old mills. These
were two-story structures—the wash cycle downstairs at the river,
then the dry cycle upstairs, where vents allowed the wind to blow
through. You can still see some of the mechanisms designed to
accommodate periodic changes in the river level. The last riverside
laundry closed in the 1960s.

• *Turn left on Rue de la Foulerie and follow the river back toward the
cathedral. The bridge at Rue du Bourg was once the town's main bridge.
Cross it and climb uphill—you'll see Queen Bertha's Staircase (Escalier
de la Reine Berthe), a one-of-a-kind half-timbered spiral staircase. Soon
after, turn left up the stairs, and in a few blocks arrive back at the cathedral. From here, consider stopping by the...*

International Stained Glass Center (Centre International
du Vitrail): This low-key center on the north side of the cathedral
is worth a visit to learn about the techniques behind the mystery
of this fragile but enduring art (€7, daily 14:00-17:45, 5 Rue du
Cardinal Pie, 50 yards from cathedral, +33 2 37 21 65 72, www.
centre-vitrail.org).

Here you'll gaze into the eyes of original stained-glass windows from the 12th to the 17th century. The windows you see
were gathered from several par-
ish churches around Chartres
that were destroyed during the
French Revolution. You'll also
see several windows from the
nearby churches of St. Aignan
and St. Pierre (both described
earlier). Finish your visit in the
12th-century vaulted wine cel-

CHARTRES

lar to enjoy contemporary windows made using modern techniques.

Panels describe the displays, many of which are original windows. Ask at the entrance about the 25-minute video in English describing the process of blown glass and the 10-minute French-only video explaining how it is turned into stained glass (easy to follow for non-French speakers). The center also offers five-day classes; call ahead or email for topics and dates.

Sleeping in Chartres

$$ Hôtel Campanile Chartres Cathédrale,*** a block up from the train station, is central and comfortable. Don't let the facade fool you—the 58 rooms are modern and sharp. Several rooms connect—good for families—and many have partial cathedral views (buffet breakfast extra; elevator, air-con, handy and safe pay parking, 6 Avenue Jehan de Beauce, +33 2 37 21 78 00, www.campanile-chartres-centre-gare-cathedrale.fr, chartres.centre@campanile.fr).

$ Hôtel le Bœuf Couronné*** is more like a vintage two-star hotel, with 17 colorful, good-value rooms and a handy location halfway between the station and cathedral (buffet breakfast extra, elevator, no air-con, good restaurant with views of the cathedral, reserve ahead for pay parking, 15 Place Châtelet, +33 2 37 18 06 06, www.leboeufcouronne.com, resa@leboeufcouronne.fr).

$ Hôtellerie Saint Yves, which hangs on the hillside just behind the cathedral, delivers well-priced simplicity with 50 spic-and-span rooms in a renovated monastery with meditative garden areas. Single rooms have no view; ask for a double room with views of the lower town (small bathrooms, good breakfast extra, 3 Rue des Acacias, +33 2 37 88 37 40, www.maison-st-yves.com, reception@saintyves.net).

Eating in Chartres

Dining out in Chartres is a good deal—particularly if you've come from Paris. Troll the places basking in cathedral views, and if it's warm, find a terrace table (several possibilities). Then finish your evening cathedral-side, sipping a hot or cold drink at Le Serpente.

$$ Café Bleu offers a great view terrace and an appealing interior. It serves classic French fare at acceptable prices (closed Tue, 1 Cloître Notre-Dame, +33 2 37 36 59 60).

$$ Le Café Serpente saddles up next door to the cathedral, with terrific view tables and an adorable collector's interior. The cuisine is basic bistro fare and fairly priced. Simple dishes and to-go food are available all day from the room at the back (daily, 2 Cloître Notre-Dame, +33 2 37 21 68 81).

$ La Picoterie efficiently serves up inexpensive fare such as omelets, crêpes, and salads in its cozy dining room (daily, 36 Rue des Changes, +33 2 37 36 14 54).

$$ Le Pichet 3 is run by endearing Marie-Sylvie and Xavier. This local-products shop and snug bistro make a fun stop. Sit on the quiet terrace or peruse the artsy inside. Laura—the daughter—serves a tasty *assiette végétarienne* and a good selection of *plats*. Try the local specialty, *la poule au pot,* and the rabbit with plums (Thu-Sun lunch and dinner, Mon lunch only, closed Tue-Wed, 19 Rue du Cheval Blanc, +33 2 37 21 08 35).

$$ Restaurant l'Amphitryon at the recommended Hôtel le Bœuf Couronné is the place to go in Chartres for a traditional French dinner, served with class (daily from 19:00, see "Sleeping in Chartres," earlier).

$ Maison Monarque offers decadent pastries and light dishes until 20:00 with a cathedral view (closed Mon, 49 Rue des Changes, +33 2 34 40 04 00).

GIVERNY & AUVERS-SUR-OISE

Paris is the unofficial capital of Impressionism, its museums speckled with sun-dappled paintings. But hard core Impressionist fans will want to do what the Impressionist painters did: Don a scarf and beret, and escape to the countryside.

At Giverny and Auvers-sur-Oise, follow in the footsteps of Monet, Van Gogh, Pissarro, Cézanne, and others. See the landscapes and small-town life that inspired these great masters. Little has changed over time: You'll be surrounded by pastoral scenes that still look like an Impressionist painting come to life.

At Giverny, you can visit Monet's home and flower-filled garden. (Be warned: the gardens are pretty, but they're bursting with tourists, so time your visit carefully.) Auvers-sur-Oise is a quieter village, with Van Gogh's grave, recognizable settings of several of the artist's paintings, and a multimedia museum on Impressionism. Both places are about an hour's journey from Paris and accessible by public transportation.

Giverny

Claude Monet's gardens at Giverny are like his paintings—brightly colored patches that are messy but balanced. Flowers were his brushstrokes, a bit untamed and slapdash, but part of a carefully composed design. Monet spent his last (and most creative) years cultivating his garden and his art at Giverny (zhee-vayr-nee), the spiritual home of Impressionism (1883-1926). Visiting the Marmottan and/or the Orangerie museums in Paris before your visit here, or at least reading the chapters on those museums, heightens your appreciation of these gardens.

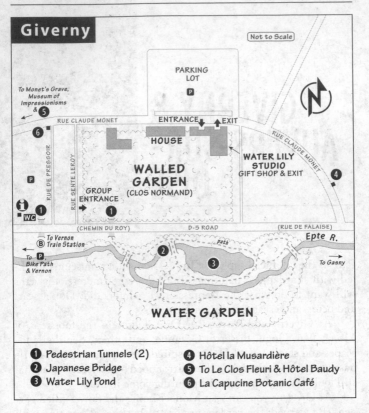

Giverny

Not to Scale

PARKING LOT
P

To Monet's Grave,
Museum of
Impressionisms
& ⑤

⑥

RUE CLAUDE MONET

ENTRANCE   EXIT

HOUSE

RUE CLAUDE MONET

WATER LILY
STUDIO
GIFT SHOP & EXIT

WALLED
GARDEN
(CLOS NORMAND)

RUE DE PRESSOIR

RUE SENTE LEROY

GROUP
ENTRANCE

①

④

P

i
WC   ①

(CHEMIN DU ROY)   D-5 ROAD   (RUE DE FALAISE)

To Vernon
Ⓑ Train Station

②

Path

Epte R.

To
Bike Path
& Vernon   P

③

To Gasny

WATER GARDEN

① Pedestrian Tunnels (2)
② Japanese Bridge
③ Water Lily Pond
④ Hôtel la Musardière
⑤ To Le Clos Fleuri & Hôtel Baudy
⑥ La Capucine Botanic Café

In 1883, middle-aged Claude Monet, his wife Alice, and their eight children from two families settled into this farmhouse, 50 miles northwest of Paris (for more on Monet's family, see sidebar on page 297). Monet, already a famous artist and happiest at home, would spend 40 years in Giverny, traveling less with each passing year. He built a pastoral paradise complete with a Japanese garden and a pond full of floating lilies.

In 1912, Monet—the greatest visionary, literally, of his generation—began to go blind with cataracts. To compensate, he used larger canvases and painted fewer details. The true subject of these later works is not really the famous water lilies but the changing reflections on the pond's surface—of the blue sky, white clouds, and green trees that line the shore.

GIVERNY & AUVERS

GETTING TO GIVERNY

Minivan and big bus tours take groups to Giverny. The trip is also doable in a half-day by car or public transportation by train with a connection by bus, taxi, bike, or hike. This website gives a clear explanation of your options: Giverny.org/transpor.

By Tour: Minivan tours will pick you up at your hotel and whisk you painlessly there and back. Paris Webservices tours are excellent, with informative drivers and ample time to savor the experience (figure $95-120/person for groups of 4 or more; see contact info on page 55). Big bus tour companies do a Giverny day trip from Paris for around €80 (5 hours, includes entry, get details at your hotel or www.pariscityvision.com).

By Car: From Paris' *périphérique* ring road, follow A-13 toward Rouen, exit at *Sortie 14* to Vernon, and follow *Centre Ville* signs, then signs to *Giverny*. You can park right at Monet's house or at one of several nearby lots. Romantics can take the scenic route from the same exit by following tiny D-201 over the river and through the woods.

By Train: This option is less expensive than a tour and puts you in charge of your own time (allow about 6 hours round-trip). Take the Rouen-bound train from Paris Gare St. Lazare Station to Vernon, about four miles from Giverny (normally leaves from tracks 20-25, 1 hour, about €30 round-trip). The train that leaves Paris at around 8:15 is ideal, with departures about hourly after that. Before boarding, use an information desk in Gare St. Lazare to get return times from Vernon to Paris.

Getting from Vernon's Train Station to Giverny: From the Vernon station to Monet's garden, you have four options: bus, taxi, bike, or hike. The Vernon-Giverny **bus** generally departs every 2 hours for the 15-minute run to Giverny (9:15-17:15, €10 round-trip, pay driver). A bus-and-train timetable is available at the bus stops, on the bus, and online (www.giverny.org/transpor)—note return times. To reach the bus stop, across from the L'Arrivée de Giverny café, walk through the station and keep straight. Don't dally in the station—the bus may leave soon after your train arrives.

Returning to the station, the bus leaves Giverny from the same stop where it drops you off (near the pedestrian underpass—see map; TI and good WCs on the north side of the underpass). Return buses generally run hourly in the morning and afternoon (every two hours midday, at :25 after the hour, last departure about 19:10, confirm times by checking schedule upon arrival). Get to the stop at least 15 minutes early to ensure a space. If you miss the return bus and can't wait for the next one, ask any approachable service personnel to call a taxi.

Taxis wait in front of the station in Vernon (allow €20 one-way for up to 3 people). Try Damien Taxi at mobile +33 6 03 30 85 47 or +33 2 77 02 94 97 (for other taxis call +33 6 77 49 32 90 or +33 6 50 12 21 22).

Another option is to rent a **bike** at L'Arrivée de Giverny café (opposite the station, closed Mon, +33 2 32 21 16 01) and take a 30-minute ride along a well-signed, paved bike path *(piste cyclable)* that runs from near Vernon along an abandoned railroad right-of-way.

Hikers can go on **foot** to Giverny (4 level miles, about 1.5 hours one way) following the bike path and take a bus or taxi back.

Extension to Rouen: Consider combining your morning Giverny visit with an afternoon excursion to nearby Rouen—together they make an efficient and memorable day trip from Paris. Note that Rouen's museums are closed on Tuesdays. From Vernon (the halfway point between Rouen and Paris), it's about 40 minutes by train to Rouen; the return trip from Rouen back to Paris takes 70-90 minutes. Plan to arrive at Monet's garden when it opens (at 9:30) so you can be back to the Vernon train station by 13:00. You'll land in Rouen by 14:00 and have just enough time to see Rouen's cathedral and surrounding medieval quarter. In Rouen, the TI is a 15-minute walk from the station and offers an audioguide walking tour (or, better yet, get your hands on the Rouen section from the Normandy chapter of my *Rick Steves France* guidebook). If you leave Rouen around 18:00, you'll pull into Paris about 19:15, having spent a wonderful day sampling rural and urban Normandy.

Orientation to Giverny

Giverny is a tiny village about four miles from the town of Vernon. All of Giverny's sights and shops string along Rue Claude Monet, which runs in front of Monet's house. The **TI** is located by the WCs in the parking lot near the road to Vernon (see map, daily April-Sept, closed off-season, 80 Rue Claude Monet, +33 2 32 64 45 01).

Sights in Giverny

▲MONET'S GARDEN AND HOUSE

All kinds of people flock to Giverny. Gardeners admire the earth-moving landscaping and layout, botanists find interesting new plants, art lovers can see paintings they've long admired come to life, and romantics can glue themselves to a bench surrounded by water lily views. Fans enjoy wandering through the house where Monet spent half his life and seeing the rowboat he puttered around in, as well as the henhouse where his family got the eggs for their morning omelets.

There are two gardens, split by a busy road, plus the house, which displays Monet's prized collection of Japanese prints. The gardens are always flowering with something; they're at their most colorful April through July.

Cost and Hours: €11, not covered by Paris Museum Pass, €19 combo-ticket with nearby Museum of Impressionisms, ask about combo-tickets with Paris' Orangerie or Marmottan Museum; daily April-Oct 9:30-18:00, closed Nov-late March; +33 2 32 51 90 31, http://fondation-monet.com.

Crowd-Beating Tips: Though lines may be long and tour groups may trample the flowers, true fans still find magic in the gar-

dens. Minimize crowds by arriving a little before 9:30, when it opens, or come after 16:00 and stay until it closes. The busiest months are May and June. Sunday mornings are busiest in any season when cruise groups arrive in force.

Advance ticket and combo-ticket holders skip the ticket-buying line and use the nifty group entrance, a huge advantage in high season (see map). You can buy advance tickets online or at any FNAC store in Paris (www.fnactickets.com), or at the TI in Vernon. Alternately, buy combo-tickets with either the Orangerie or Marmottan Museum in Paris, or the Museum of Impressionisms here.

Visiting the House and Gardens

There are two parts to the gardens: the Walled Garden (next to the house) and the Water Garden (across the road). Most visitors use the main entry and start in the Walled Garden (Clos Normand). Those able to use the group entrance should start with the Water Garden and end with the Walled Garden and house.

Walled Garden: Smell the pretty scene. Monet cleared this land of pine trees and laid out symmetrical beds, split down the

middle by a "grand alley" covered with iron trellises of climbing roses. He did his own landscaping, installing flowerbeds of lilies, irises, and clematis. The arched arbors leading to the home's entry form a natural tunnel that guides your eye down the path—

an effect exploited in his *Rose Trellis* paintings (on display in Paris at the Marmottan Museum). In his carefree manner, Monet throws

An Impressionist's Garden

Impressionism was a revolutionary movement and all the rage in European art in the 1880s. Artists abandoned realism in favor of a wispy style that captured light, glimmers, feelings, and impressions. Committed to conveying subtle atmospheric effects, the Impressionists captured nature as a mosaic of short brushstrokes of different colors placed side by side, suggesting shimmering light. And there is no better nature for an Impressionist ready to paint than Monet's delightful mix of weeping willows, luminous clouds, delicate bridges, reflecting ponds...and lush water lilies.

together hollyhocks, daisies, and poppies. The color scheme of each flowerbed contributes to the look of the whole garden.

Water Garden: In the southwest corner of the Walled Garden (near the group entrance), you'll find a pedestrian tunnel that leads under the road to a garden with Monet's famous pond and lilies. Follow the meandering path to the Japanese bridge, under weeping willows, over the pond filled with water lilies, and past countless scenes that leave artists aching for an easel. Find a bench and stop for a while. Monet landscaped like he painted—he built an Impressionist pattern of blocks of color. After he planted the gardens, he painted them, from every angle, at every time of day, in all kinds of weather. Assisted by his favorite stepdaughter, Blanche (also a painter, who married Monet's son Jean, from an earlier marriage), he worked on several canvases at once, moving with the sun from one to the next. In a series of canvases, you can watch the sunlight sweep over the gardens from early dawn to twilight.

House: End your visit with a wander through Monet's charming, I-could-retire-here home, with period furnishings, Japanese prints, old photos, and rooms filled with copies of his and other artists' paintings. The gift shop at the exit is the actual sky-lighted studio where Monet painted his masterpiece water-lily series (displayed at the Orangerie Museum in Paris). Many visitors spend more time in this tempting gift shop than in the gardens themselves.

NEARBY SIGHTS
Village of Giverny
The village is a sight in itself, with flowery lanes home to a few souvenir shops, art galleries, and cafés. Cars are not allowed to enter the center of the village.

Museum of Impressionisms (Musée des Impressionnismes)
This bright, modern museum, dedicated to the history of Impressionism and its legacy, houses temporary exhibits of Impressionist art. Check its website for current shows or just drop in. Meander through its colorful, picnic-friendly gardens for more color.

Cost and Hours: €9, €19 combo-ticket with Monet's Garden and House, free first Sun of month; open April-Nov 6 daily 10:00-18:00, Nov 7-Dec Fri-Sun only, closed Jan-March and for 10 days in mid-July to change exhibitions; audioguide-€4; to reach the museum, turn left after leaving Monet's place and walk 200 yards; +33 2 32 51 94 00, www.mdig.fr.

Claude Monet's Grave
Monet's grave is a 15-minute walk from his door. Turn left out of his house and walk down Rue Claude Monet, pass the Museum of Impressionisms and the Hôtel Baudy, and find it in the backyard of the white church Monet attended (Eglise Sainte-Radegonde). Look for flowers, with a cross above. The inscription says: *Here lies our beloved Claude Monet, born 14 November 1840, died 5 December 1926; missed by all.*

Vernon Town
If you have extra time at Vernon's train station, take a five-minute walk into town and sample the peaceful village. From the station, pass Café de l'Arrivée on your left, follow the street as it curves left, and keep straight. You'll find a smattering of half-timbered Norman homes near Hôtel de Ville (remember, you're in Normandy), several good cafés and shops, and the town's towering Gothic church.

Sleeping and Eating in Giverny

Sleeping: $$ Hôtel la Musardière*** is nestled in the village of Giverny two blocks from Monet's home (exit right when you leave Monet's) with 10 comfortable rooms and a fine **$$ restaurant** serving beautifully presented dishes in a smart dining room—or better, on the sun-dappled terrace (123 Rue Claude Monet, tel. 02 32 21 03 18, www.lamusardiere.fr, hotelmusardieregiverny@wanadoo.fr).

$ Le Clos Fleuri is a family-friendly B&B with three spacious and very comfortable rooms, each with a king-size bed and a private terrace facing the grassy garden. The rooms also share handy cooking facilities. It's a 15-minute walk from Monet's place and is run by charming, English-speaking Danielle (with Australian heritage), who serves up a good included breakfast (cash only, 5 Rue de la Dîme, +33 2 32 21 36 51, www.giverny-leclosfleuri.fr, leclosfleuri27@gmail.com).

Eating: You'll find various snack places just outside the entrance to Monet's home. Your best lunch option is a block to the left at **$ La Capucine**'s self-serve restaurant. Eat tasty, cheap soups, salads, and quiches at a table in the warm interior or the welcoming garden (Wed-Sun 12:00-18:00, closed Mon-Tue).

Rose-colored **$$ Hôtel Baudy,** once a hangout for American Impressionists, offers an appropriately pretty setting for lunch or dinner. The décor looks as though it has not changed since painters hung their brushes here (outdoor tables in front, good-value *menus*, popular with tour groups at lunch, daily, 5-minute walk past Museum of Impressionisms at 81 Rue Claude Monet, +33 2 32 21 10 03). Don't miss a stroll through the artsy gardens behind the restaurant.

For finer dining, consider the restaurant at **Hôtel la Musardière,** listed earlier.

Auvers-sur-Oise

This small town draws Van Gogh pilgrims and those in search of a green escape from the city. Auvers-sur-Oise (oh-vehr soor wahz) is a peaceful place on a bend of the lazy Oise River, northwest of Paris. A manageable day trip by car, it takes patience by train. Here you'll get an intimate glimpse into life (and death) during the Impressionist era. Walkers enjoy stretching their legs between the sights in this countryside setting.

Auvers was a magnet for artists in the late 1800s. Charles-François Daubigny, Jean-Baptiste-Camille Corot, Camille Pissarro, and Paul Cézanne all adored this rural retreat (they were also unknowns then). But Auvers is best known as the village where Vincent van Gogh committed suicide.

GIVERNY & AUVERS

He moved here from southern France to be near his brother Theo (who lived in Paris). Vincent had talked his way out of the asylum in St-Rémy-de-Provence with assurances that he would be under good care from an understanding doctor and avid painter, Auvers resident Paul Gachet. Fans of the 2017 movie *Loving Vincent*, about Van Gogh's final days, will find a trip to Auvers-sur-Oise a moving experience. Watching the movie before you visit makes this trip more meaningful.

Today, this modest little town opens its doors to visitors with a handful of sights and walking trails leading to scenes painted by

various artists (some with copies of the paintings posted). Most sights are closed Mondays (some are also closed Tue) and from November to Easter. Several less-essential sights are also closed in the morning. Auvers makes a convenient first or last overnight stop for drivers using Charles de Gaulle airport, as it avoids traffic hassles (Auvers is about 20 miles from the airport). Allow a good half-day to appreciate the package of sights offered in little Auvers-sur-Oise.

GETTING TO AUVERS-SUR-OISE

The TI's website offers a clear overview of your transportation options in English (www.tourisme-auverssuroise.fr).

By Train: Main-line trains direct to Auvers-sur-Oise run on weekends and holidays from Gare du Nord (one round-trip per day April-mid-Oct, 45 minutes, departs at about 9:35, returns at about 18:30). This is your surest bet for a stress-free trip, but it leaves you there all day. Because several sights don't open until the afternoon, consider arriving later by RER train (see below) and take the main-line train back. The station in Auvers-sur-Oise is unmanned on weekends, so use the ticket machines or buy round-trip tickets in Paris, and confirm the return schedule in advance.

Frequent RER trains get you there daily but take 75-90 minutes each way and require a transfer. Take RER/Train-C to Pontoise (2/hour, 1 hour to Pontoise, catch in Paris at St. Michel,

Vincent van Gogh

In the dead of winter in 1888, 35-year-old Vincent van Gogh left big-city Paris for the town of Arles in Provence, hoping to jump-start his floundering career and personal life. Coming from the gray skies and flat lands of the north, Vincent was bowled over by everything Provençal—the sun, bright colors, rugged landscape, and raw people. For two years, he painted furiously, creating a new masterpiece every few days.

The son of disinterested parents, Vincent never found the social skills necessary to sustain close friendships. Lonely Vincent—who dreamed of making Arles a magnet for fellow artists—persuaded Paul Gauguin to join him there. At first, the two got along well, but within a few months, their relationship deteriorated. Gauguin left Arles, leaving Vincent deeply depressed. The local paper reported what happened next: "At 11:30 p.m., Vincent Vaugogh (sic), painter from Holland, appeared at the brothel at no. 1, asked for Rachel, and gave her his cut-off earlobe, saying, 'Treasure this precious object.' Then he vanished." Vincent woke up the next morning at home with his head wrapped in a bloody towel and his earlobe missing.

The bipolar genius (a modern diagnosis) admitted himself to the St. Paul Monastery and Hospital in St-Rémy-de-Provence in the spring of 1889. He spent a year in the hospital, thriving in the care of nurturing doctors and nuns. Painting was part of Vincent's therapy, so they gave him a studio to work in, and he produced more than 100 paintings. Alcohol-free and institutionalized, he did some of his wildest work. With thick, swirling brushstrokes and surreal colors, he made his placid surroundings throb with restless energy.

In the spring of 1890, Vincent left St-Rémy and traveled to Auvers-sur-Oise to enter the care of Dr. Paul Gachet, whom he hoped could help stabilize his mental condition. Gachet advised the artist to throw himself into his work as a remedy for his illness, which he did—Vincent spent the last 70 days of his life in this little town, knocking out a masterpiece each day.

On July 27, Vincent shot himself by his easel in the famous Auvers wheat field, dying of his injuries two days later.

Musée d'Orsay, Invalides, or Pont de l'Alma stops). Pontoise is the end of the line, where it's easy to transfer to Auvers (the route is covered by the Navigo Découverte pass or five-zone Navigo Easy card). Ask at any RER/Train-C station for the best connection or check www.ratp.fr for RER lines. Service from Pontoise back to Paris is frequent, with trains to Gare du Nord, Gare St. Lazare, and points along the RER/Train-C route.

To get from Pontoise to Auvers, a 10-minute ride away, you have three options. Take the **train** (direction: Creil, hourly, before leaving Auvers' train station, get return times to Pontoise—posted on signs). **Bus #9507** stops right outside the Pontoise train station, and in Auvers stops are below the TI and below the château (runs hourly, look for the posted schedule—you're at Chemin de la Gare in Pontoise, and you want the Marie stop in Auvers). Or you can go by **taxi** (around €15; for a bit more money, the same taxi can pick you up in Auvers for the return; see "Helpful Hints," later).

    By Car, Taxi, or Tour: Auvers is about 45 minutes northwest of Paris. Take the A-15 autoroute to A-115, follow Beauvais and exit at Auvers-sur-Oise. Allow €100 by taxi one-way. Tour companies combine Auvers-sur-Oise with Giverny for about €270 per person.

Orientation to Auvers-sur-Oise

Tourist Information: The TI is well-signed in the small Parc Van Gogh (from the train station, it's about a block to the left toward town). The TI has Wi-Fi and good information on all sights, as well as bus and train schedules (generally open Tue-Sun 9:30-12:30 & 14:00-18:00, closed Mon year-round, +33 1 30 36 71 81, www.tourisme-auverssuroise.fr). Pick up the helpful town map that shows all of the Van Gogh sights. You can also take advantage of the good WCs behind the TI.

    Helpful Hints: There's a handy **supermarket** and **bakery** on your way into town from the station. For a **taxi** in Auvers, call +33 6 05 07 94 20 or +33 1 30 74 45 45, or in Pontoise +33 1 30 30 45 45.

Sights in Auvers-sur-Oise

The best way to spend a few hours in Auvers is to wander the village lanes and nearby paths connecting the sights that interest you. I've described the sights below in the order that works best to visit them. Doing the entire loop would take 45 minutes with no stops. Orange signs identify sight locations.

• *Start by climbing the path behind the TI, then veer right, joining the small road that leads to the...*

Church at Auvers
(Notre-Dame d'Auvers)

This small church at the edge of town was built in the 1100s, is beautifully lit inside, and was made famous by Van Gogh's paintings (interior open daily 9:30-19:00).

GIVERNY & AUVERS

In a letter to his sister Wilhelmina, Vincent wrote: "I have a larger picture of the village church—an effect in which the building appears to be violet-hued against a sky of simple deep blue color, pure cobalt; the stained-glass windows appear as ultramarine blotches, the roof is violet and partly orange. In the foreground some green plants in bloom, and sand with the pink flow of sunshine in it."

• *From here, follow signs for* Tombes de Théo et Vincent *up the small street behind the church and walk about 300 yards to the simple cemetery.*

Vincent's Grave

Vincent and his caring brother are buried side by side against the cemetery's upper wall about halfway down (look for the ivy). No

one can be sure why Vincent ended his life at 37, but standing at his grave, you can feel the weight of the tragedy and only imagine the paintings he might have created. You can thank Japanese travelers if you spot gray dust on the ivy that covers Vincent's and Theo's graves: Vincent is wildly popular among the Japanese, some of whom ask to have their ashes spread over his grave. Vincent lies in a coffin made by the same carpenter who built his picture frames.

• *Leave the cemetery and follow the dirt path that bisects a broad wheat field, following signs to* Château via Sente du Montier, *and find...*

Wheatfield with Crows

Find the copy of Vincent's famous painting and stop there. Vincent shot himself in this field and died two days later in his bedroom at the Auberge Ravoux (described later). His brother was at his side. *Wheatfield with Crows,* painted in this very field in 1890, was one of his very last paintings.

• *Continue on to the woods on the far side of the field and drop down to a street. Turn left when you reach the "T," and pass...*

La Maison-Atelier de Daubigny

This well-preserved home/studio once belonged to Charles-François Daubigny, who created the artist colony that Auvers became in the 1880s.

Cost and Hours: €6, Thu-Fri 10:00-12:00 & 14:00-18:30, Sat-Sun 10:30-12:30 & 14:00-18:30, closed Mon-Wed and Nov-March, tel. 01 30 36 60 60.

• *Past the Maison-Atelier de Daubigny, veer right at signs to the château. You'll soon pass...*

Musée de l'Absinthe

This small, one-of-a-kind tribute features the highly alcoholic, herb-based beverage popular among artists and writers (including Van Gogh) in the late 1800s. Considered dangerously addictive, absinthe was banned in 1915. Another anise-flavored drink—*pastis*—took its place; it tasted similar but was less toxic. Then, in 2011, absinthe was again declared legal in France. The museum has only minimal English information, but the staff make a good effort to explain the displays.

Cost and Hours: €5, Sat-Sun 13:30-18:00, July-Aug likely also Wed-Fri 13:30-18:00, closed mid-Oct-mid-April, last entry one hour before closing, bottled absinthe for sale.

• *From here it's a straight, 300-yard shot to...*

▲Château d'Auvers

This château has been transformed into a multimedia re-creation of life during the Impressionist years, using state-of-the-art technology to immerse visitors into this lively era. The "show" is changed every few years but always features an immersive experience with impressive displays and sounds designed to transport you to another time. The château has a fine café with outdoor seating in the summer.

Cost and Hours: €12, family rates, not covered by Paris Museum Pass; Tue-Sun 10:00-18:00, Oct-March until 17:00, closed Mon; +33 1 34 48 48 48, www.chateau-auvers.fr.

• *A healthy walk beyond the château, Van Gogh fans can visit the restored home of Dr. Gachet (well signed), but I'd skip it and be satisfied with the description below.*

Maison du Docteur Gachet

It was at Camille Pissarro's suggestion that Dr. Gachet agreed to see Van Gogh, who made an immediate connection with the doctor—"I have found a friend in Dr. Gachet...and something of a new brother, since we are so similar both mentally and physically." In addition to being Vincent's personal physician in Auvers, Dr. Gachet was an avid painter and adored entertaining famous artists such as Cézanne, Monet, Renoir, and Pissarro. He inherited all of Van Gogh's works from his time in Auvers (those you see at the Orsay Museum were donated by Dr. Gachet's family). Dr. Gachet is buried at Père Lachaise cemetery in Paris.

The small home is furnished as it was when Vincent lived in

Auvers, with bits of memorabilia. The "wild" garden has medicinal plants that the homeopath Dr. Gachet cultivated and used to treat Van Gogh, but there are no English descriptions.

Cost and Hours: Free, Wed-Sun 10:30-18:30, closed Mon-Tue and Nov-March, 78 Rue du Dr. Gachet.

• *Follow the main road leading down from the château to return to the TI and find...*

Auberge Ravoux

Vincent lived and died in an attic room of this rustic inn (also called "Maison de Van Gogh"). His modest room has been re-created to look exactly as it did during his short time here, though his few furnishings were burned by church officials shortly after his death (suicide was considered a sin and not tolerated). Start with the 12-minute slideshow (English subtitles) and read the large information displays in the courtyard that explain Vincent's tragic life. Guides escort groups up the steps to Van Gogh's room and give some commentary in English (allow 30 minutes total for this sight).

Cost and Hours: €6, Wed-Sun 10:30-18:30, closed Mon-Tue and Nov-early March.

• *Food connoisseurs can enjoy a tasty lunch in the Auberge Ravoux's perfectly preserved restaurant (described later). Nearby, you could visit...*

Musée Daubigny

This skippable museum houses a small collection of works by Charles-François Daubigny and other artists who came to work with him. Daubigny was a big supporter of the Impressionist movement (€5, Tue-Fri 14:00-17:30, Sat-Sun 10:30-12:30 & 14:00-18:00, closed Mon, Rue de la Sansonne).

Eating in Auvers

The most atmospheric place to eat in Auvers is **$$$ Auberge Ravoux,** unchanged (except for its prices) since 1876, when painters would meet here over a good meal. It's wise to make a reservation for lunch on weekends (closed Mon-Tue, on Place de la Mairie, +33 1 30 36 60 60, www.maisondevangogh.fr).

Auvers also has grocery stores, cafés, *crêperies,* restaurants, and bakeries with sandwiches, all within blocks of the TI.

FRANCE: PAST & PRESENT

French History

CELTS AND ROMANS (52 BC-AD 500)

Julius Caesar conquered the Parisii, turning Paris from a tribal fishing village into a European city. The mix of Latin (southern) and Celtic (northern) cultures, with Paris right in the middle, defined the French character.

Sights

- Cluny Museum (Roman baths)
- Louvre (Roman antiquities)
- Paris Archaeological Crypt (in front of Notre-Dame)

DARK AGES (500-1000)

Roman Paris fell to German pirates known as the Franks (hence "France"), and later to the Vikings (a.k.a. Norsemen, which became "Normans"). During this turbulent time, Paris was just another island-state ("Ile de France") in the midst of many warring kingdoms. The lone bright spot was the reign of Charlemagne (AD 768-814), who briefly united the Franks, giving a glimpse of the modern nation-state of France.

Sights

- Cluny Museum (artifacts)
- Statue of Charlemagne (in front of Notre-Dame)

BORDER WARS WITH ENGLAND (1066-1500)

In 1066, the Norman duke William the Conqueror invaded and conquered England. This united England, Normandy, and much of what is today western France; sparked centuries of border wars; and

Paris Almanac

Population: Paris is the capital and largest city in France. About 2.3 million people live in the city center (10 million in the greater Paris region).

Currency: Euro.

Nickname: The City of Light.

City Layout: Paris is sliced by the Seine River, with the Right Bank to the north and the Left Bank to the south (orient yourself by looking downstream—the Left Bank is to your left, the Right Bank to your right). The city is divided into 20 boroughs, called arrondissements.

Transportation Basics: The Métro is the most-used public transportation in Paris, with 16 lines, 300 stations, and nearly 5 million passengers each day. Mayor Anne Hidalgo, continuing a trend to reduce vehicular traffic, has called for a total ban on diesel cars by 2024, expanded traffic-free areas, and added more bike lanes. She has also proposed free public transit for residents. Today only 40 percent of Parisians own cars.

Tourist Tracks: Paris is the world's top tourist destination, attracting more than 30 million visitors a year. Of its 3,800 historical monuments, the most popular are the Louvre (more than 9 million people tour it each year) and the Eiffel Tower (more than 7 million). But Mona can't hold a candle to Mickey—Disneyland Paris gets 16 million visitors a year.

Culture Count: Most Parisians, including those of French ancestry, were born outside of the city—and roughly one in five residents of greater Paris was born outside France (and one in three has at least one immigrant parent). The city has significant populations from Africa, China, Eastern Europe, and the Middle East.

Famous Residents: Brigitte Bardot, Juliette Binoche, Carla Bruni, Sofia Coppola, Catherine Deneuve, Jean-Luc Godard, Rickie Lee Jones, Diane Kruger, Tony Parker, Roman Polanski, Mick Jagger, Kristin Scott Thomas, Audrey Tautou, and Emmanuel Macron.

produced many kings of England who spoke French. In 1328 King Charles IV died without an heir, and the Norman king of England tried to claim the throne of France, which led to more than a century of Franco-Anglo battles, called the Hundred Years' War. Rallied by the teenage visionary Joan of Arc in 1429, the French finally united north and south, and drove the English across the Channel in 1453. Modern France was born, with Paris as its capital.

Sights

- Notre-Dame Cathedral
- Sainte-Chapelle

- Cluny Museum (tapestries)
- Carnavalet Museum
- Sorbonne
- Latin Quarter

RENAISSANCE AND RELIGIOUS WARS (1500s)

A strong, centralized France emerged, with French kings setting Europe's standard. François I made Paris a cultural capital, inviting Leonardo and Mona Lisa to visit. Catholics and Protestants fought openly, with 2,000 Parisians slaughtered in the St. Bartholomew's Day Massacre in 1572. The Wars of Religion subsided for a while when the first Bourbon king, Henry IV, took the throne in 1589 after converting to Catholicism. In 1598, he signed the Edict of Nantes, which instituted freedom of religious worship.

Sights
- Louvre (palace and Renaissance art)
- Pont Neuf
- Place des Vosges
- Fontainebleau

LOUIS XIV, THE ABSOLUTE MONARCH (1600s)

Louis XIV solidified his power, neutered the nobility, revoked the Edict of Nantes, and moved the capital to Versailles, which also became the center of European culture. France's wealth sparked "enlightened" ideas that became the seeds of democracy.

Sights
- Versailles and Vaux-le-Vicomte
- Hôtel des Invalides
- Paintings by Nicolas Poussin and Claude Lorrain

DECADENCE AND REVOLUTION (1700s)

This was the age of Louis XV, Louis XVI, Marie-Antoinette, Voltaire, Jean-Jacques Rousseau, Maximilien de Robespierre, and Napoleon. A financial crunch from wars and royal excess drove the French people to revolt. On July 14, 1789, they stormed the Bastille. A couple of years later, the First French Republic arrested and then beheaded the king and queen. Thousands lost their heads—guillotined if suspected of hindering the Revolution's progress. A charismatic commoner promising stability rose amid the chaos: Napoleon Bonaparte.

Sights
- Versailles
- Place de la Concorde and Place de la Bastille

Typical Church Architecture

History comes to life when you visit a centuries-old church. Even if you wouldn't know your apse from a hole in the ground, learning a few simple terms will enrich your experience. Note that not every church has every feature, and a "cathedral" isn't a type of church architecture, but rather a designation for a church that's a governing center for a local bishop.

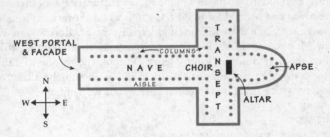

Aisles: Long, generally low-ceilinged arcades that flank the nave

Altar: Raised area with a ceremonial table (often adorned with candles or a crucifix), where the priest prepares and serves the bread and wine for Communion

Apse: Space behind the altar, sometimes bordered with small chapels

Barrel Vault: Continuous round-arched ceiling that resembles an extended upside-down U

Choir: Intimate space reserved for clergy and choir, located within the nave near the high altar and often screened off

Cloister: Covered hallways bordering a square or rectangular open-air courtyard, traditionally where monks and nuns got fresh air

Facade: Exterior of the church's main (west) entrance, usually highly decorated

Groin Vault: Arched ceiling formed where two equal barrel vaults meet at right angles

Narthex: Area (portico or foyer) between the main entry and the nave

Nave: Long central section of the church (running west to east, from the entrance to the altar) where the congregation sits or stands during the service

Transept: One of the two parts forming the "arms" of the cross in a traditional cross-shaped floor plan; runs north-south, perpendicularly crossing the east-west nave

West Portal: Main entry to the church (on the west end, opposite the main altar)

PAST & PRESENT

- Conciergerie
- Champs-Elysées
- Paintings by Watteau, Boucher, Fragonard, and David (Louvre)

ELECTED EMPERORS AND CONSTITUTIONAL KINGS (1800s)

Napoleon conquered Europe, crowned himself emperor, invaded Russia, was defeated on the battlefields of Waterloo, and ended up exiled to an island in the Atlantic. The monarchy was restored, but rulers toed the democratic line—or were deposed in the popular uprisings of 1830 and 1848. The latter uprising resulted in the Second French Republic, whose first president was  Napoleon's nephew. He rewrote the constitution with himself as Emperor Napoleon III, and presided over a wealthy, middle-class nation with a colonial empire in slow decline. The disastrous Franco-Prussian War in 1870 ended his reign, leading to the Third Republic. France's political clout was fading, even as Paris remained the world's cultural center during the belle époque—the "beautiful age."

Sights

- Arc de Triomphe
- Baron Haussmann's wide boulevards
- Eiffel Tower
- Les Invalides and Napoleon's Tomb
- Pont Alexandre III
- Grand Palais and Petit Palais
- Montmartre
- Opéra Garnier
- Paintings by Ingres and Delacroix (Louvre)
- Impressionist and Post-Impressionist paintings (Manet, Monet, Renoir, Degas, Toulouse-Lautrec, Cézanne, and so on) at the Orsay, Marmottan, and Orangerie museums

WAR AND DEPRESSION (1900-1950)

France began the turn of the 20th century as top dog, but two world wars with Germany (and the earlier Franco-Prussian War) wasted the country. France had millions of casualties in World War I, sank into an economic depression, and was easily overrun by Hit-

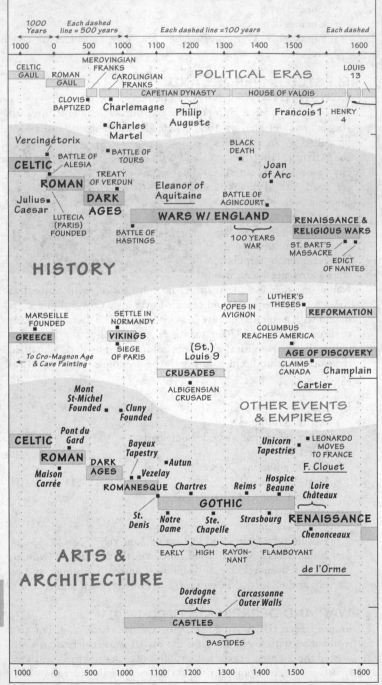

PAST & PRESENT

French History & Art Timeline

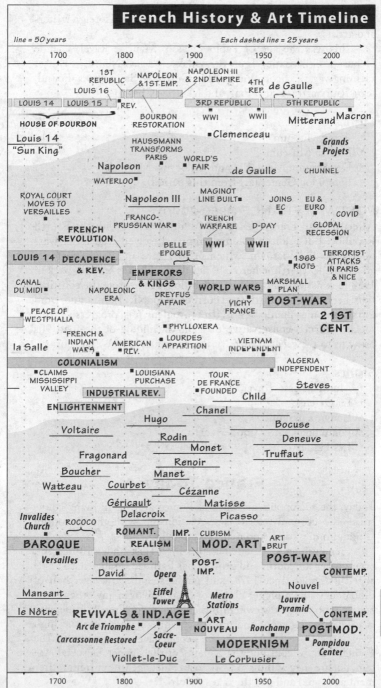

line = 50 years   Each dashed line = 25 years

1700   1800   1900   1950   2000

1ST REPUBLIC
NAPOLEON & 1ST. EMP.
NAPOLEON III & 2ND EMPIRE
4TH REP.
de Gaulle
LOUIS 16
REV.
LOUIS 14   LOUIS 15
3RD REPUBLIC   5TH REPUBLIC
HOUSE OF BOURBON
BOURBON RESTORATION
WWI   WWII   Mitterand   Macron

Louis 14
"Sun King"
HAUSSMANN TRANSFORMS PARIS
WORLD'S FAIR
Clemenceau
Grands Projets

Napoleon
WATERLOO
de Gaulle
CHUNNEL

ROYAL COURT MOVES TO VERSAILLES
Napoleon III
MAGINOT LINE BUILT
JOINS EC
EU & EURO
COVID

FRENCH REVOLUTION
FRANCO-PRUSSIAN WAR
TRENCH WARFARE
D-DAY
GLOBAL RECESSION

BELLE EPOQUE
WWI   WWII

LOUIS 14   DECADENCE & REV.
EMPERORS & KINGS
WORLD WARS
MARSHALL PLAN
1968 RIOTS
TERRORIST ATTACKS IN PARIS & NICE

CANAL DU MIDI
NAPOLEONIC ERA
DREYFUS AFFAIR
VICHY FRANCE
POST-WAR

PEACE OF WESTPHALIA
21ST CENT.

PHYLLOXERA
la Salle
"FRENCH & INDIAN" WARS
AMERICAN REV.
LOURDES APPARITION
VIETNAM INDEPENDENT

COLONIALISM
ALGERIA INDEPENDENT

CLAIMS MISSISSIPPI VALLEY
LOUISIANA PURCHASE
TOUR DE FRANCE FOUNDED
Steves

INDUSTRIAL REV.
Child

ENLIGHTENMENT
Chanel

Voltaire
Hugo
Bocuse

Fragonard
Rodin
Deneuve

Monet
Truffaut

Renoir

Boucher
Manet

Watteau
Courbet
Cézanne

Géricault
Matisse

Delacroix
Picasso

Invalides Church
ROCOCO

BAROQUE
ROMANT.
IMP.
CUBISM
ART BRUT

REALISM
MOD. ART
POST-WAR

Versailles
NEOCLASS.
POST-IMP.
CONTEMP.

David
Opera
Nouvel

Mansart
Eiffel Tower
Metro Stations
Louvre Pyramid
CONTEMP.

le Nôtre
REVIVALS & IND. AGE
ART NOUVEAU
Ronchamp
POSTMOD.

Arc de Triomphe
Sacre-Coeur
MODERNISM
Pompidou Center

Carcassonne Restored

Viollet-le-Duc
Le Corbusier

1700   1800   1900   1950   2000

ler in World War II. Paris, now dirt cheap, attracted foreign writers and artists.

This was the age of Pablo Picasso, Maurice Ravel, Claude Debussy, Erik Satie, Igor Stravinsky, Vaslav Nijinsky, Ernest Hemingway, F. Scott Fitzgerald, Gertrude Stein, Ezra Pound, Jean-Paul Sartre, Edith Piaf, and Maurice Chevalier.

Sights
- Army Museum
- Picasso Museum
- Deportation Memorial and Holocaust Memorial
- Pompidou Center (art from this period)

POSTWAR FRANCE (1950-2000)

After the war, France reestablished a democracy with the Fourth Republic. But France's colonial empire dissolved after bitter wars in Algeria and Vietnam, which helped mire an already unsteady government. Wartime hero Charles de Gaulle was brought back in 1958 to assist with France's regeneration. He rewrote the constitution, beginning the Fifth (and current) Republic. Immigrants from former colonies flooded Paris. The turbulent '60s, progressive '70s, socialist-turned-conservative '80s, and the middle-of-the-road '90s bring us to the *début de siècle*, or the beginning of the 21st century.

Sights
- Montparnasse Tower
- La Défense
- Louvre's pyramid
- Pompidou Center (modern art)
- Les Halles

France Today

Today, the sociopolitical issues in France are—as in many countries—the economy, terrorism, relationship with the European Union, immigration, and managing Covid.

French unemployment remains high (just under 10 percent, even higher for youth) and growth has flatlined. France hasn't balanced its books since 1974, and public spending, at over half of GDP, chews up a bigger chunk of output than in any other euro-zone country. The overwhelming challenge for French leadership is to address its economic problems while maintaining the high level of social services that French people have come to expect. The French want to continue the benefits of their generous social system, but are they willing to work to an older age (the current retirement age is 62) and pay the taxes required?

France also has its economic strengths: a well-educated workforce, an especially robust service sector and high-end manufacturing industry, and more firms big enough to rank in the global Fortune 500 than any other European country. Ironically, while France's economy may be one of the world's largest—and the French want all the creature comforts of a consumer economy—they remain skeptical about the virtues of capitalism and the work ethic. Globalization conflicts in a fundamental way with French values—many fear losing what makes their society unique in the quest for a bland, globalized world. Business conversation outside the office is generally avoided, as it implies a fascination with money that the French find vulgar. It's considered gauche even to ask what someone does for a living (in part because they think there's much more to a person than their occupation). In France, CEOs are not glorified as celebrities—chefs are.

The French believe that the economy should support social good, not vice versa, and that people are entitled to secure jobs from which they cannot be fired easily. This has produced a cradle-to-grave social security system of which the French are proud. But if you're considering starting a business in France, you're on the wrong track—taxes are *formidable* (figure a total small-business tax rate of around 66 percent—and likely to increase). And this job-security entitlement makes it difficult for employers to find motivated staff. You'll feel this impact in small hotels and restaurants where owners run themselves ragged trying to do everything themselves.

As part of the 27-member European Union, the "United States of Europe" that has successfully dissolved borders, France's governments have been decidedly pro-EU and critical to the EU's success. But many French are Euroskeptics, afraid that EU meddling threatens their job security and social benefits. The Brexit vote in 2016 focused attention on France. Would a Frexit follow? The EU can survive sans Britain but probably not sans France. For now, that possibility seems to have been shelved with President Macron, who is pro-EU.

French voters are notorious for their belief in the free market's heartless cruelty. France is routinely plagued with strikes, demonstrations, and slowdowns as workers try to preserve their rights in the face of a competitive global economy.

Meanwhile, immigration is shifting the country's ethnic and cultural makeup in ways that challenge French society. Ten percent of France's population is now of North African descent—mainly immigrants from former colonies. Many immigrants are Muslim, raising cultural questions in this heavily Catholic society with a history of official state secularism. In 2011 the government (quite controversially) made it illegal for women to wear a full, face-covering veil *(niqāb)* in public. Debates continue about whether banning the veil enforces democracy—or squelches diversity.

In 2015, Paris was hit with a double-whammy of Islamist terrorist attacks—at the offices of the satirical magazine *Charlie Hebdo*, and then at the Bataclan theater. In 2016, an attack in Nice shook the entire country. Armed soldiers now patrol rail stations and streets. The French have had to come to grips with the realization that many of the attackers were French citizens as well as immigrants. These attacks raised serious questions about immigration, policing, class divisions, and what it means to be French.

France is governed by a president elected by popular vote every five years. The president then selects the prime minister, who in turn chooses the cabinet ministers. Collectively, this executive branch is known as the *gouvernement*. The parliament consists of a Senate (348 seats) and Assemblée Nationale (577 seats).

In France, voters have an array of political parties to choose from, making compromise and coalition-building essential to keeping power. Even the biggest parties rarely get more than one-third of the seats in parliament. And, because the parliament can force the *gouvernement* to resign at any time, it's essential that the *gouvernement* work with them.

To understand the current political landscape and the most recent election, it's helpful to consider the 2012 and 2017 elections. (French elections last only several months, with just a few TV debates.)

In 2012, socialist François Hollande defeated center-right incumbent Nicolas Sarkozy. But when Hollande's term became fraught with scandal, rocked by terrorist events, and weighed down by a flat economy, Hollande opted against running for reelection in 2017. That left the field wide open.

The 2017 election was a wild ride, with events never seen before in France. Eleven candidates competed in the French version of a primary, reducing the field to two for the final vote. For the first time since de Gaulle, neither of the two finalists were from the traditional right and left parties. (Imagine a US presidential election sans Republican or Democratic candidates.) Emmanuel Macron, a centrist businessman, had no party affiliation and had never held elected office. Marine Le Pen represented the far-right National Front party, once a pariah party tarnished by accusations of anti-Semitism.

Le Pen rallied support by proposing to limit immigration and step back from the EU. Macron proposed a moderate stay-the-course plan that attracted both liberals and moderate conservatives. The tone of the debates was uncharacteristically nasty for genteel France. In the end, the French overwhelmingly chose the moderate path. Macron won with a whopping 66 percent of the vote. Still, Le Pen's result was the best yet for a National Front candidate.

Elected at 39 (and looking even younger), Macron became France's youngest leader since Napoleon Bonaparte. His success was completely unpredicted. He won as an outsider, representing a change from traditional party politics. (Sound familiar?)

After an almost flawless first year in office, Macron's second year was a different story. While he was internationally respected for his commitment to multilateralism and for combating climate change, his popularity among the French dropped from 64 percent to below 30 percent in 2018. The working class felt abandoned by Macron, calling him "the president of the rich" (thanks to more business-friendly policies). His proposal to fund climate-change initiatives by raising the tax on gasoline led to the first true crisis of his presidency: "yellow vest" anti-government protests. In late 2019 and early 2020, a four-month transportation strike created havoc throughout France. Shortly after, the Covid-19 pandemic shut down the country—and most of Europe. Macron's measures to combat Covid—including tough restrictions on residents leaving their homes, and severe limits on travel—did not increase his popularity, but he seems to have emerged as well as any nation's leader.

Macron approached the 2022 presidential election with a strong lead in the polls, running against a broad range of candidates. Once again, Macron and Le Pen emerged as the two finalists—a repeat of the 2017 election. Voters were faced with the same sharp contrasts in policies and personalities: calm and steady Macron, middle-of-the-road but leaning left and all-in for the EU; and rabble-rousing right-wing Le Pen, fashioning herself a bit after Donald Trump and wanting France out of the EU and NATO—and immigrants out of France (her role model: Viktor Orbán of Hungary).

The second and final vote happened on April 24, 2022. Macron was favored to win, as a majority of the other candidates put their support behind him, but the margin was close enough—and the stakes seemingly high enough—to make the election a nailbiter. In an eerily quiet city, with the lowest voter turnout in 50 years, Macron emerged again as the clear winner, with 58 percent of the vote. He's the first president to be reelected in 20 years.

For more about French history, consider Europe 101: History and Art for the Traveler *by Rick Steves and Gene Openshaw, available at Rick-Steves.com.*

PAST & PRESENT

PRACTICALITIES

This chapter covers the practical skills of European travel: how to get tourist information, pay for things, sightsee efficiently, find good-value accommodations, eat affordably but well, use technology wisely, and get between destinations smoothly. For more information on these topics, see RickSteves.com/travel-tips.

Travel Tips

Travel Advisories: Before traveling, check updated health and safety conditions, including restrictions for your destination, on the travel pages of the US State Department (www.travel.state. gov) and Centers for Disease Control and Prevention (www.cdc. gov/travel). The US embassy website for France is another good source of information (see below).

Covid Vaccine/Test Requirements: It's possible you'll need to present proof of vaccination against the coronavirus and/or a negative Covid-19 test result to board a plane to Europe or back to the US. Carefully check requirements for each country you'll visit well before you depart, and again a few days before your trip. See the websites listed above for current requirements.

ETIAS Registration: The European Union may soon require US and Canadian citizens to register online with the European Travel Information and Authorization System (ETIAS) before entering France and other Schengen Zone countries (quick and easy process). For the latest, check www.etiasvisa.com.

Tourist Information: The French national tourist office is a wealth of information. Before your trip, scan their website—http://us.france.fr. It has particularly good resources for special-interest travel and plenty of free-to-download brochures.

Paris' official TI website, www.parisinfo.com, offers practical information on hotels, special events, museums, children's activities, fashion, nightlife, and more.

In Paris, TI offices are almost extinct, and they aren't helpful enough to warrant a special trip anyway. The most handy and helpful locations are at the airports.

Emergency and Medical Help: For any emergency service—ambulance, police, or fire—call **112** from a mobile phone or landline (operators typically speak English). For hearing-assisted help for all services, dial 114. If you get sick, do as the French do and go to a pharmacist for advice. Or ask at your hotel for help—they'll know the nearest medical and emergency services.

Other Medical Services: These places have English-speaking staff—**American Hospital** (63 Boulevard Victor Hugo, in Neuilly suburb, +33 1 46 41 25 25, www.american-hospital.org); **Pharmacie des Champs** (84 Avenue des Champs-Elysées, Mo: George V, +33 1 45 62 02 41); and **Pharmacie Anglaise** (62 Avenue des Champs-Elysées, +33 1 43 59 82 30; both pharmacies open daily 9:00-24:00). For a list of **English-speaking doctors,** search on the US embassy's website: france.embassy.gov.au/pari/Engdoc.html.

SOS Médicins (SOS Doctors) has some English-speaking doctors who make house calls to hotels or homes (+33 1 47 07 77 77, www.sosmedecins-france.fr); **SOS Help** offers a telephone hotline with crisis/suicide prevention listening services in English (daily 15:00-23:00, +33 1 46 21 46 46, www.soshelpline.org); and **SOS Dentist** offers emergency dental assistance (daily, 87 Boulevard de Port-Royal, +33 1 43 37 51 00, contact@sos-dentaire.com). The **American Chiropractic Center** is at 119 Rue de l'Université (closed Sun, Mo: Invalides, +33 1 45 51 38 38, www.chiropractique.com).

Theft or Loss: To replace a passport, you'll need to go in person to an embassy or consulate (see next). If your credit and debit cards disappear, cancel and replace them (see "Damage Control for Lost Cards" on page 655). File a police report, either on the spot or within a day or two; you'll need it to submit an insurance claim for lost or stolen items, and it can help with replacing your passport or credit and debit cards. For more information, see RickSteves.com/help.

For other **lost property,** contact the Bureau des Objets Trouvés (Mon-Fri 8:30-17:00, closed Sat-Sun, at police station at 36 Rue des Morillons, Mo: Convention—on south end of line 12, +33 1 53 71 53 71).

US Consulates and Embassies: Appointment required. Dial +33 1 43 12 22 22 (2 Avenue Gabriel, to the left as you face Hôtel Crillon, Mo: Concorde, https://fr.usembassy.gov).

Canadian Consulate and Embassy: Appointment required. Dial +33 1 44 43 29 00 (130 Rue du Faubourg Saint-Honoré, Mo: Saint-Philippe-du-Roule, www.canadainternational.gc.ca/france).

Time Zones: France, like most of continental Europe, is generally six/nine hours ahead of the East/West Coasts of the US. The exceptions are the beginning and end of Daylight Saving Time: Europe "springs forward" the last Sunday in March (two weeks after most of North America), and "falls back" the last Sunday in October (one week before North America). For a handy time converter, use the world clock app on your phone or download one (see www.timeanddate.com).

Business Hours: In Paris, most smaller shops are open Monday through Saturday (10:00-12:00 & 14:00-19:00) and closed Sunday. These exceptions are open daily (no Sunday closure): large grocery stores, the Galeries Lafayette store near the Opéra Garnier, the Carrousel du Louvre underground shopping mall at the Louvre, and some shops near Sèvres-Babylone, along the Champs-Elysées, and in the Marais. Many small markets, *boulangeries* (bakeries), and street markets are open Sunday mornings until noon.

Sundays have the same pros and cons as they do for travelers in the US: Special events and weekly markets pop up (usually until about noon) and sightseeing attractions are generally open, while public transportation options are fewer, and there's no rush hour.

Watt's Up? Europe's electrical system is 220 volts, instead of North America's 110 volts. Most electronics (laptops, phones, cameras) and appliances (newer hair dryers, CPAP machines) convert automatically, so you won't need a converter, but you will need an adapter plug with two round prongs, sold inexpensively at travel stores in the US.

Discounts: Discounts for sights are generally not listed in this book. However, youths under 18 and students and teachers with proper identification cards (www.isic.org) can get discounts at many sights—always ask. Seniors age 65 and over may get the odd discount, but don't get your hopes up. To inquire about a senior discount, ask, *"Réduction troisième âge?"* (ray-dewk-see-ohn trwah-zee-ehm ahzh). Some discounts are available only to European citizens.

English-Language Churches in Paris

American Church (interdenominational): 65 Quai d'Orsay, Mo: Invalides, +33 1 40 62 05 00, www.acparis.org. For more information, see page 50.

American Cathedral (Episcopalian): 23 Avenue George V, Mo: George V, +33 53 23 84 00, www.americancathedral.org.

Unitarian Universalist Fellowship: 129 Rue Marcadet, Mo: Jules Joffrin, www.uuparis.org.

Scots Kirk (Church of Scotland): 17 Rue Bayard, Mo: Franklin D. Roosevelt, www.scotskirkparis.com.

St. George's Anglican Church: 7 Rue Auguste Vacquerie, Mo: George V or Kleber, +33 1 47 20 22 51, www.stgeorgesparis.com.

St. Joseph's Church (Roman Catholic): 50 Avenue Hoche, Mo: Etoile, +33 1 42 27 28 56, www.stjoeparis.org.

St. Michael's Church (Anglican): 5 Rue d'Aguesseau, Mo: Concorde or Madeleine, +33 1 47 42 70 88, www.saintmichaelsparis.org.

Online Translation Tips: Google's Chrome browser instantly translates websites; Translate.google.com and DeepL.com are also handy. The Google Translate app converts spoken or typed English into most European languages (and vice versa) and can also translate text it "reads" with your phone's camera.

Going Green: There's plenty you can do to reduce your environmental footprint when traveling. When practical, take a train instead of a flight within Europe, and use public transportation within cities. In hotels, use the "Do Not Disturb" sign to avoid daily linen and towel changes (or hang up your towels to signal you'll reuse them). Bring a reusable shopping tote and refillable water bottle (Europe's tap water is safe to drink). Skip printed brochures, maps, or other materials that you don't plan to keep—get your info online instead. To find out how Rick Steves' Europe is offsetting carbon emissions with a self-imposed carbon tax, see RickSteves.com/about-us/climate-smart.

Money

Here's my basic strategy for using money wisely in Europe. I pack the following and keep it all safe in my money belt.

Credit Card: You'll use your credit card for purchases both big (hotels, advance tickets) and small (little shops, food stands). Some European businesses have gone cashless, making a card your only

Exchange Rate

1 euro (€) = about $1.10

To convert prices in euros to dollars, add about 10 percent: €10 = about $11, €50 = about $55. Like the dollar, one euro is broken into 100 cents. Coins range from €0.01 to €2, and bills from €5 to €200.

Check www.oanda.com for the latest exchange rates.

payment option. A "tap-to-pay" or "contactless" card is the most widely accepted and simplest to use.

Debit Card: Use this at ATMs to withdraw a small amount of local cash. Wait until you arrive to get euros (European airports have plenty of ATMs); if you buy euros before your trip, you'll pay bad stateside exchange rates. While most transactions are by card these days, cash can help you out of a jam if your card randomly doesn't work, and can be useful to pay for things like tips and local guides.

Backup Card: Some travelers carry a third card (debit or credit; ideally from a different bank) in case one gets lost or simply doesn't work.

Stash of Cash: For an emergency reserve, in most of Europe bring dollars. But in France, consider bringing €200 (bring euros, as dollars can be hard to change in France).

BEFORE YOU GO

Know your cards. For credit cards, Visa and MasterCard are universal while American Express and Discover are less common. US debit cards with a Visa or MasterCard logo will work in any European ATM.

Go "contactless." Get comfortable using contactless pay options. Check to see if you already have—or can get—a tap-to-pay version of your credit card (look on the card for the tap-to-pay symbol—four curvy lines) and consider setting up your smartphone for contactless payment (see next section for details). Both options are widely used in Europe and are more secure than a physical credit card: Instead of recording your credit card number, a one-time encrypted "token" enables the purchase and expires shortly afterward.

Know your PIN. Make sure you know the numeric, four-digit PIN for each of your cards, both debit and credit. Request it if you don't have one, as it may be required for some purchases. Allow time to receive the information by mail—it's not always possible to obtain your PIN online or by phone.

Report your travel dates. Let your bank know that you'll be using your debit and credit cards in Europe, and when and where you're headed.

Adjust your ATM withdrawal limit. Find out how much you can withdraw daily and ask for a higher daily limit if you want to get more cash at once. Note that European ATMs will withdraw funds only from checking accounts, not savings accounts.

Find out about fees. For any purchase or withdrawal made with a card, you may be charged a currency conversion fee (1-3 percent) and/or a Visa or MasterCard international transaction fee (less than 1 percent). If you're getting a bad deal, consider getting a new card. Reputable no-fee cards include those from Capital One, as well as Charles Schwab debit cards. Most credit unions and some airline loyalty cards have low or no international transaction fees.

IN EUROPE
Using Credit Cards and Payment Apps

Tap-to-Pay or **Contactless Cards:** These cards have the usual chip and/or magnetic stripe, but with the addition of a contactless symbol. Simply tap your card against a contactless reader to complete a transaction—no PIN or signature is required. This is by far the easiest way to pay and has become the standard in much of Europe.

Payment Apps: Just like at home, you can pay with your smartphone or smartwatch by linking a credit card to an app such as Apple Pay or Google Pay. To pay, hold your phone near a contactless reader; you may need to verify the transaction with a face scan, fingerprint scan, or passcode. If you've arrived in Europe without a tap-to-pay card, you can easily set up your phone to work in this way.

Other Card Types: Chip-and-PIN cards have a visible chip embedded in them; rather than swiping, you insert the card into the payment machine, then enter your PIN on a keypad. In Europe, these cards have largely been supplanted by tap-to-pay cards, but you may be asked to use chip-and-PIN for certain purchases. **Swipe-and-sign** credit cards—with a swipeable magnetic stripe, and a receipt you have to sign—are increasingly rare.

Will My US Card Work? Usually, yes. On rare occasions, at self-service payment machines (such as transit-ticket kiosks, tollbooths, or fuel pumps), some US cards may not work. Usually a tap-to-pay card does the trick in these situations. Just in case, carry cash as a backup and look for a cashier who can process your payment if your card is rejected. Drivers should be prepared to move on to the next gas station if necessary. (In some countries, gas stations sell prepaid gas cards, which you can purchase with any US

PRACTICALITIES

card). When approaching a toll plaza or ferry ticket line, use the "cash" lane.

Using Cash

Cash Machines: European cash machines work just like they do at home—except they spit out local currency instead of dollars, calculated at the day's standard bank-to-bank rate. In most places, ATMs are easy to locate—in France ask for a *distributeur* (dee-stree-bew-tur). When possible, withdraw cash from a bank-run ATM located just outside that bank.

If your debit card doesn't work, try a lower amount—your request may have exceeded your withdrawal limit or the ATM's limit. If you still have a problem, try a different ATM or come back later.

Avoid "independent" ATMs, such as Travelex, Euronet, Moneybox, Your Cash, Cardpoint, and Cashzone. These have high fees, can be less secure, and may try to trick users with "dynamic currency conversion" (see next).

Dynamic Currency Conversion: When withdrawing cash at an ATM or paying with a credit card, you'll often be asked whether you want the transaction processed in dollars or in the local currency. Always refuse the conversion and *choose the local currency.* While DCC offers the illusion of convenience, it comes with a poor exchange rate, and you'll wind up losing money.

Exchanging Cash: Minimize exchanging money in Europe; it's expensive (you'll generally lose 5 to 10 percent). In a pinch you can find exchange desks at major train stations or airports. Banks generally do not exchange money unless you have an account with them.

Security Tips

Pickpockets target tourists, particularly those arriving in Paris—dazed and tired—carrying luggage in the Métro and city trains and stations. Keep your cash, credit cards, and passport secure in your money belt, and carry only a day's spending money in your front pocket or wallet.

Before inserting your card into an ATM, inspect the front. If anything looks crooked, loose, or damaged, it could be a sign of a card-skimming device. When entering your PIN, carefully block other people's view of the keypad.

Avoid using a debit card for purchases. Because a debit card pulls funds directly from your bank account, potential charges incurred by a thief will stay on your account while your bank investigates.

To access your accounts online while traveling, be sure to use a secure connection (see the "Tips on Internet Security" sidebar, later).

Damage Control for Lost Cards

If you lose your credit or debit card, report the loss immediately to the respective global customer-assistance centers. With a mobile phone, call these 24-hour US numbers: Visa (+1 303 967 1096), MasterCard (+1 636 722 7111), and American Express (+1 336 393 1111). From a landline, you can call these US numbers collect by going through a local operator.

You'll need to provide the primary cardholder's identification-verification details (such as birth date, mother's maiden name, or Social Security number). You can generally receive a temporary card within two or three business days in Europe (see RickSteves.com/help for more).

If you report your loss within two days, you typically won't be responsible for unauthorized transactions on your account, although many banks charge a liability fee.

TIPPING

Tipping *(donner un pourboire)* in France isn't as automatic and generous as it is in the US. For special service, tips are appreciated, but not expected. As in the US, the proper amount depends on your resources, tipping philosophy, and the circumstances, but some general guidelines apply.

Restaurants: At cafés and restaurants, a service charge is included in the price of what you order, and it's unnecessary to tip extra, though you can for helpful service. If paying with a credit card, be prepared to tip separately with cash or coins; credit card receipts don't often have a tip line. For details on tipping in restaurants, see "Eating," later.

Taxis: For a typical ride, round up your fare a bit (for instance, if the fare is €13, pay €14). If the cabbie hauls your bags and zips you to the airport to help you catch your flight, you might want to toss in a little more.

Services: In general, if someone in the tourism or service industry does a super job for you, a small tip of a euro or two is appropriate...but not required. If you're not sure whether (or how much) to tip, ask a local for advice.

GETTING A VAT REFUND

Wrapped into the purchase price of your French souvenirs is a value-added tax (VAT) of about 20 percent. You're entitled to get most of that tax back if you purchase more than €175 worth of goods at a store that participates in the VAT-refund scheme. Typically, you must ring up the minimum at a single retailer—you can't add up your purchases from various shops to reach the required amount. (If the store ships the goods to your US home, VAT is not assessed on your purchase.)

Getting your refund is straightforward...and worthwhile if you spend a significant amount.

At the Merchant: Have the merchant completely fill out the refund document, called a *bordereau de détaxe* (they'll ask for your passport; a photo of your passport usually works). Keep track of the paperwork and your original sales receipt. Note that you're not supposed to use your purchased goods before you leave Europe.

At the Border or Airport: Process your VAT document at your last stop in the European Union (such as at the airport) with the customs agent who deals with VAT refunds (allow plenty of extra time to deal with this process). At some airports, you'll have to go to a customs office to get your documents stamped and then to a separate VAT refund service (such as Global Blue or Planet) to process the refund. At other airports, a single VAT desk handles the whole thing. (Note that refund services typically extract a 4 percent fee, but you're paying for the convenience of receiving your money in cash immediately or as a credit to your card.) Otherwise, you'll need to mail the stamped refund documents to the address given by the merchant.

CUSTOMS FOR AMERICAN SHOPPERS

You can take home $800 worth of items per person duty-free, once every 31 days. Many processed and packaged foods are allowed, including cheeses, dried herbs, jams, baked goods, candy, chocolate, oil, vinegar, condiments, and honey. Fresh fruits and vegetables and most meats are not allowed, with exceptions for some canned items. As for alcohol, you can bring in one liter duty-free (it can be packed securely in your checked luggage, along with any other liquid-containing items).

To bring alcohol (or liquid-packed foods) in your carry-on bag on your flight home, buy it at a duty-free shop at the airport. You'll increase your odds of getting it onto a connecting flight if it's packaged in a "STEB"—a secure, tamper-evident bag. But stay away from liquids in opaque, ceramic, or metallic containers, which usually cannot be successfully screened (STEB or no STEB).

For details on allowable goods, customs rules, and duty rates, visit http://help.cbp.gov.

Sightseeing

Sightseeing can be hard work. Use these tips to make your visits to Paris' finest sights meaningful, fun, efficient, and painless.

MAPS AND NAVIGATION TOOLS

A good map is essential for efficient navigation while sightseeing. The maps in this book are concise and simple, designed to help

Covid Changes:
What to Expect Post-Pandemic

The Covid-19 pandemic caused many disruptions and changes to the way museums and other sights operate—some of which were temporary, others of which may turn out to be permanent. Depending on what's happening during your visit, hours may be modified; reservations may be required (or strongly recommended) to control crowd flow; and paper maps and audioguides may have been replaced by apps.

For any must-see sight on your list, check in advance on its official website (listed throughout this book) to fully understand the current situation. You may learn that it's required to prebook, for example, or you may be able to download an app so you'll have an up-to-date museum map and audioguide on your phone when you arrive.

you locate recommended destinations, sights, hotels, restaurants, and local TIs, where you can pick up more in-depth maps. More detailed maps are sold at newsstands and bookstores.

You can also use a mapping app on your mobile device, which provides turn-by-turn directions for walking, driving, and taking public transit. Google Maps, Apple Maps, and CityMaps2Go allow you to download maps for offline use; ideally, download the areas you'll need before your trip. For certain features, you'll need to be online—either using Wi-Fi or an international data plan.

PLAN AHEAD

Set up an itinerary that allows you to fit in all your must-see sights. For a one-stop look at opening hours, see the "Paris at a Glance" sidebar in the Sights in Paris chapter. Remember, the Louvre and some other museums are closed on Tuesday, and many others are closed on Monday (see the "Daily Reminder" in the Orientation chapter). Most sights keep stable hours, but you can easily confirm the latest by checking their websites. You can also find good information on many of Paris' sights online at Parisinfo.com.

Don't put off visiting a must-see sight—you never know when a place will close unexpectedly for a holiday, strike, or restoration. Many museums are closed or have reduced hours at least a few days a year, especially on holidays such as Christmas, New Year's, and Labor Day (May 1). A list of holidays is in the appendix; check for possible closures during your trip. In summer, some sights may stay open late. Off-season hours may be shorter.

Going at the right time helps avoid crowds. This book offers tips on the best times to see specific sights. Evening visits (when possible) are usually more peaceful, with fewer crowds. Late morning is usually the worst time to visit a popular sight.

If you plan to hire a local guide, reserve ahead by email. Popular guides can get booked up.

Study up. To get the most out of the self-guided tours and sight descriptions in this book, read them before you visit.

RESERVATIONS, ADVANCE TICKETS, AND PASSES

Many popular sights have long lines—not to get in, but to buy a ticket. Visitors who buy tickets online in advance (or who have a museum pass covering these key sights) can skip the line and waltz right in. Advance tickets are often timed-entry, reserving your spot on a certain date and time.

For some sights, buying ahead is required (tickets aren't sold at the sight). At others, buying ahead is smart to skip the line. At less crowded sights, advance tickets may be available but aren't needed. Use my advice in this book as a guide. Note any must-see sights that sell out long in advance and be prepared to buy tickets early.

Given how precious your vacation time is, I'd book in advance both where it's required (as soon as your dates are firm) and where it will avoid a long line (in some cases, you can do this even on the day of your visit). For Paris, to see the Louvre, Sainte-Chapelle, Orangerie, and Versailles, you must book tickets in advance (see page 56). It's also smart to reserve for the Eiffel Tower, Catacombs, and Conciergerie.

You'll generally be emailed an eticket with a QR or bar code, which you'll scan at the entrance (if you prefer, you can print it out). Look for the ticket-holders line rather than the ticket-buying line; you may still have to wait in a security line.

Another smart choice is to buy a Paris Museum Pass, which can save you money and speed you through lines at some covered sights. For details on the advance ticketing and the Paris Museum Pass, see the beginning of the Sights in Paris chapter.

AT SIGHTS

Here's what you can typically expect:

Entering: You may not be allowed to enter if you arrive too close to closing time. And guards start ushering people out well before the actual closing time, so don't save the best for last.

Many sights have a security check. Allow extra time for these lines. Some sights require you to check daypacks and coats. (If you'd rather not check your daypack, try carrying it tucked under your arm like a purse as you enter.)

At churches—which often offer interesting art (usually free) and a cool, welcome seat—a modest dress code (no bare shoulders or shorts) is encouraged though rarely enforced.

Photography: If the museum's photo policy isn't clearly posted, ask a guard. Generally, taking photos without a flash or tripod is allowed. Some sights ban selfie sticks; others ban photos altogether.

Audioguides and Apps: I've produced free, downloadable audio tours for my Historic Paris Walk and Rue Cler Walk, plus tours of the Louvre, Orsay Museum, Versailles, and Père Lachaise Cemetery. Look for the 🎧 in this book. For more on my audio tours, see page 24.

Some sights offer audioguides with worthwhile recorded descriptions in English. In some cases, you'll rent a device to carry around (if you bring your own plug-in earbuds, you'll enjoy better sound). Increasingly, museums and sights instead offer an app you can download with their audioguide (often free; check websites from home and consider downloading in advance as not all sights offer free Wi-Fi).

Temporary Exhibits: Museums may show special exhibits in addition to their permanent collection. Some exhibits are included in the entry price, while others come at an extra cost (which you may have to pay even if you don't want to see the exhibit).

Expect Changes: Artwork can be on tour, on loan, out sick, or shifted at the whim of the curator. Pick up a floor plan as you enter and ask museum staff if you can't find a particular item. Say the title or artist's name, or point to the photograph in this book and ask for its location by saying, *"Où est?"* (oo ay).

Services: Important sights usually have an on-site café or cafeteria (handy and air-conditioned places to rejuvenate during a long visit). The WCs at sights are free and generally clean.

Before Leaving: At the gift shop, scan the postcard rack or thumb through a guidebook to be sure you haven't overlooked something that you'd like to see. Every sight or museum offers more than what is covered in this book. Use the information I provide as an introduction—not the final word.

Sleeping

Accommodations in Paris are generally easy to find, if you book far enough ahead. Choose from one- to five-star hotels (two and three stars are my mainstays), bed-and-breakfasts (*chambres d'hôtes*, usually cheaper than hotels), hostels, and apartments.

Extensive and opinionated listings of good-value rooms are a major feature of this book's Sleeping section. Rather than list accommodations scattered throughout a town, I choose hotels in my favorite neighborhoods that are convenient to your sightseeing.

My recommendations run the gamut, from dorm beds to lux-

Sleep Code

Hotels in this book are categorized according to the average price of a standard double room without breakfast in high season.

$$$$	**Splurge:**	Most rooms over €300
$$$	**Pricier:**	€200-300
$$	**Moderate:**	€130-200
$	**Budget:**	€70-130
¢	**Backpacker:**	Under €70
RS%	**Rick Steves discount**	
*	**French hotel rating system** (0-5 stars)	

Unless otherwise noted, credit cards are accepted, hotel staff speak basic English, and free Wi-Fi is available. Comparison-shop by checking prices at several hotels (on each hotel's own website, on a booking site, or by email). For the best deal, *book directly with the hotel*. Ask for a discount if paying in cash; if the listing includes **RS%,** request a Rick Steves discount.

urious rooms with all the comforts. I like places that are clean, central, relatively quiet at night, reasonably priced, friendly, small enough to have a hands-on owner or manager, and run with a respect for French traditions. I'm more impressed by a handy location and a fun-loving philosophy than oversized TVs and a spa. Most of my recommendations fall short of perfection. But if I can find a place with most of these features, it's a keeper.

Book your accommodations as soon as your itinerary is set, especially if you want to stay at one of my top listings or if you'll be traveling during busy times. Reserving ahead is particularly important for Paris—the sooner, the better. Wherever you're staying, be ready for larger crowds in May and September and during these holiday periods: Easter weekend, Labor Day, Ascension weekend, Pentecost weekend, Bastille Day and the week during which it falls, and the winter holidays (mid-Dec–early Jan). Note that many holiday weekends fall in May, jamming French hotels. In August and at other times when business is slower, some Paris hotels offer lower rates to fill their rooms. Check hotel websites for the best deals. See the appendix for a list of major holidays and festivals in France.

RATES AND DEALS

I've categorized my recommended accommodations based on price, indicated with a dollar-sign rating (see sidebar). Room prices can fluctuate significantly with demand and amenities (size, views, room class, and so on), but relative price categories remain constant.

Booking Direct: Once your dates are set, compare prices at several hotels. You can do this by checking hotel websites and booking sites such as Hotels.com or Booking.com. After you've zeroed in on your choice, book directly with the hotel itself. This increases the chances that the hotelier will be able to accommodate special needs or requests (such as shifting your reservation). And when you book on the hotel's website, by email, or by phone, the owner avoids the commission paid to booking sites, giving them wiggle room to offer you a discount, a nicer room, or a free breakfast. French hotels recently won the right to undercut Booking.com and Hotels.com prices on their websites; virtually all offer lower rates if you book direct. If the price they quote is higher than the offer on a booking site, let the hotel know, and they'll usually adjust the rate.

Getting a Discount: Some hotels extend a discount to those who pay cash. And some accommodations offer a special discount for Rick Steves readers, indicated in this guidebook by the abbreviation **"RS%."** Discounts vary: Ask for details when you reserve. Generally, to qualify for this discount, you must book direct (not through a booking site), mention this book when you reserve, show it upon arrival, and sometimes stay a certain number of nights. In some cases, you may need to enter a discount code (which I've provided in the listing) in the booking form on the hotel's website. Rick Steves discounts apply to readers with either print or digital books. Understandably, discounts do not apply to promotional rates.

Room Taxes: Hotels in France must charge a daily tax *(taxe du séjour)* of about €1-4 per person per day (based on the number of stars the hotel has). Some hotels include it in their prices, but most add it to your bill.

TYPES OF ACCOMMODATIONS
Hotels

In this book, the price for a double room will normally range from €70 (very simple; toilet and shower down the hall) to €400 (grand lobbies, maximum plumbing, and the works), with most clustering around €150-250 (with private bathrooms).

Most hotels also offer single and triple rooms, and some offer larger rooms for four or more people (I call these "family rooms" in the listings). Some hotels can add an extra bed (for a small charge) to turn a double into a triple. A triple room is cheaper

Using Online Services to Your Advantage

From booking services to user reviews, online businesses play a greater role in travelers' planning than ever before. Take advantage of their pluses—and be wise to their downsides.

Booking Sites

Booking websites such as Booking.com and Hotels.com offer one-stop shopping for hotels. While convenient for travelers, they're both a blessing and a curse for small, independent, family-run hotels. Without a presence on these sites, small hotels become almost invisible. But to be listed, a hotel must pay a sizable commission.

Here's the work-around: Use the big sites to research what's out there, then book directly with the hotel by email or phone, in which case hotel owners are free to give you whatever price they like. Ask for a room without the commission markup (or ask for a free breakfast if not included, or a free upgrade). If you do book online, be sure to use the hotel's own website. French hotels now have the right to offer room rates on their site below those listed on third-party websites; most will give you lower rates by booking direct.

As a savvy consumer, remember: When you book with an online service, you're adding a middleman who takes a cut. To support small, family-run hotels whose world is more difficult than ever, book direct.

Short-Term Rental Sites

Rental juggernaut Airbnb (along with other short-term rental sites) allows travelers to rent rooms and apartments, often providing more value, space, and amenities than a cookie-cutter hotel. Airbnb fans appreciate feeling part of a real neighborhood and getting into a daily routine as "temporary Europeans." Depending on the host, Airbnb can provide an opportunity to get to know a local person and keep your money in the community; but beware: others are impersonally managed by large, absentee agencies.

than the cost of a double and a single. Three or four people can economize by requesting one big room.

The French have a simple hotel rating system based on amenities and rated by stars (indicated in this book by asterisks, from * through *****). One star is modest, two has most of the comforts, and three is generally a two-star with a fancier lobby and more elaborately designed rooms. Four-star places give a bit more comfort than those with three. Five stars probably offer more luxury than you'll have time to appreciate. Two-star-and-above hotels are required to have an English-speaking staff, though nearly all hotels I recommend have someone who speaks English.

Critics of Airbnb see it as a threat to "traditional Europe." Landlords can make more money renting to short-stay travelers, driving rents up—and local residents out. Traditional businesses are replaced by ones that cater to tourists. And the character and charm that made those neighborhoods desirable to tourists in the first place goes too. Some cities have cracked down, requiring owners to obtain a license and to occupy rental properties part of the year (and staging disruptive "inspections" that inconvenience guests).

As a lover of Europe, I share the worry of those who see residents nudged aside by tourists. But as an advocate for travelers, I appreciate the value Airbnb can provide in offering the chance to stay in a local building or neighborhood with potentially fewer tourists.

User Reviews

User-generated review sites and apps such as Yelp and TripAdvisor can give you a consensus of opinions about everything from hotels and restaurants to sights and nightlife. If you scan reviews of a restaurant or hotel and see several complaints about noise or a rotten location, you've gained insight that can help in your decision-making.

As a guidebook writer, my sense is that there is a big difference between the uncurated information on a review site and the vetted listings in a guidebook. A user review is based on the limited experience of one person, who stayed at just one hotel in a given city and ate at a few restaurants there. A guidebook is the work of a trained researcher who forms a well-developed basis for comparison by visiting many restaurants and hotels year after year.

Both types of information have their place, and in many ways, they're complementary. If something is well reviewed in a guidebook and it also gets good online reviews, it's likely a winner.

The number of stars does not always reflect room size or guarantee quality. One- and two-star hotels are less expensive, but some three-star (and even a few four-star) hotels offer good value, justifying the extra cost. Unclassified hotels (no stars) can be bargains...or depressing dumps.

Within each hotel, prices vary depending on the size of the room, whether it has a tub or shower, and the bed type (tubs and twins usually cost more than showers and double beds). If you have a preference, ask for it. Hotels often have more rooms with tubs (which the French prefer) and are inclined to give you one by de-

French Hotel-Room Lingo

Know your options. Hoteliers often don't mention the cheaper rooms—they assume you want a private bathroom or a bigger room. Here are the types of rooms and beds:

French	English
une chambre avec douche et WC	room with private shower and toilet
une chambre avec bain et WC	room with private bathtub and toilet
une chambre avec cabinet de toilette	room with a toilet (shower down the hall)
une chambre sans douche ni WC	room without a private shower or toilet
chambres communiquantes	connecting rooms (ideal for families)
une chambre simple, une single	a true single room
un grand lit	double bed (55 in. wide)
deux petits lits	twin beds (30-36 in. wide)
un lit queen-size	queen-size bed (63 in. wide)
un king size	king-size bed (usually two twins pushed together)
un lit pliant	folding bed
un berceau	baby crib
un lit d'enfant	child's bed

fault. You can save lots by finding the rare room without a private shower or toilet.

Most French hotels now have queen-size beds in double rooms—to confirm, ask, *"Avez-vous des lits queen-size?"* (ah-vay-voo day lee queen-size). Some hotels push two twins together under king-size sheets and blankets to make *le king-size*. If you'll take either twins or a double, ask for a generic *une chambre pour deux* (room for two) to avoid being needlessly turned away. Some hotels have a few family-friendly rooms that open up to each other *(chambres communiquantes)*.

Arrival and Check-In: Hotels and B&Bs are sometimes located on the higher floors of a multipurpose building with a secured door. In that case, look for your hotel's name on the buttons by the main entrance. When you ring the bell, you'll be buzzed in.

Hotel elevators are common, though small, and some older buildings still lack them. You may have to climb a flight of stairs to reach the elevator (if so, you can ask the front desk for help carrying your bags up).

The EU requires hotels to collect your name, nationality, and ID number. At check-in, the receptionist will normally ask for your passport and may keep it for several hours. If you're not comfortable leaving your passport at the desk, bring a copy to give them instead.

If you're arriving in the morning, your room probably won't be ready. Check your bag safely at the hotel and dive right into sightseeing.

In Your Room: Most hotel rooms have a TV and free Wi-Fi, which can vary in strength and quality. Room phones are fast becoming extinct.

Some places provide quilts as the only bed covering. While comfortable, they're warm in summers (forcing me to use air-conditioning)—ask the hotel for a sheet *(uhn drah)* for cooler sleeping.

Breakfast and Meals: Most hotels offer breakfast, but it's rarely included in the room rates—pay attention when comparing rates between hotels (though some offer free breakfast to Rick Steves readers or with direct booking—ask). The price of breakfast correlates with the price of the room: The more expensive the room, the more expensive the breakfast. This per-person charge rises with the number of stars the hotel has and can add up, particularly for families. While hotels hope you'll buy their breakfast, it's optional unless otherwise noted; to save money, head to a bakery or café instead.

Hoteliers uniformly detest it when people bring food into bedrooms. Dinner picnics are particularly frowned upon: Hoteliers worry about cleanliness, smells, and attracting insects. Be tidy and considerate.

Checking Out: While it's customary to pay for your room upon departure, it can be a good idea to settle your bill the day before, when you're not in a hurry and while the manager's in.

Hotelier Help: Hoteliers can be a good source of advice. Most know their city well and can assist you with everything from public transit and airport connections to calling an English-speaking doctor, or finding a good restaurant, a late-night pharmacy, or a self-service launderette *(laverie automatique,* lah-veh-ree oh-to-mah-teek).

Hotel Hassles: Even at the best places, mechanical breakdowns occur: sinks leak, hot water turns cold, toilets may gurgle or smell, the Wi-Fi goes out, or the air-conditioning dies when you need it most. Report your concerns clearly and calmly at the front desk.

If you find that night noise is a problem (if, for instance, your room is over a nightclub or facing a busy street), ask for a quieter room in the back or on an upper floor. To guard against theft in your room, keep valuables out of sight. Some rooms come with a safe, and other hotels have safes at the front desk. I've never both-

Making Hotel Reservations

Reserve your rooms as soon as you've pinned down your travel dates. For busy national holidays, it's wise to reserve far in advance (see the appendix).

Requesting a Reservation: For family-run hotels, it's generally best to book your room directly via email or phone. For business-class and chain hotels, or if you'd rather book online, reserve directly through the hotel's official website (not a booking website). Almost all of my recommended hotels take reservations in English.

Here's what the hotelier wants to know:

- Type(s) of room(s) you want and number of guests
- Number of nights you'll stay
- Arrival and departure dates, written European-style as day/month/year (for example, 18/06/23 or 18 June 2023)
- Special requests (en suite bathroom, cheapest room, twin beds vs. double bed, quiet room)
- Applicable discounts (such as a Rick Steves discount, cash discount, or promotional rate)

Confirming a Reservation: Most places will request a credit-card number to hold your room. If the hotel's website doesn't have a secure form where you can enter the number directly, share this info via a phone call.

Canceling a Reservation: If you must cancel, it's courteous—and smart—to do so with as much notice as possible, especially for smaller family-run places. Cancellation policies can be strict; read

ered using one and in a lifetime of travel, I've never had anything stolen from my room.

For more complicated problems, don't expect instant results. Above all, keep a positive attitude. Remember, you're on vacation. If your hotel is a disappointment, spend more time out enjoying the place you came to see.

Modern Hotel Chains: France is littered with ultramodern hotels. The clean and inexpensive Ibis Budget chain (about €55/room for up to three people), the more attractive and spacious standard Ibis hotels (€100-150 for a double), and the cushier Mercure and Novotel hotels (€150-300 for a double) are all run by the same company, Accor (www.accorhotels.com). Though hardly quaint, these can be a good value (look for deals on their websites), particularly when they're centrally located; I list several in this book. Other chains to consider are Kyriad, with moderate prices and good quality (www.kyriad.com) and the familiar-to-Americans Best Western (www.bestwestern.com). Château and Hotels Collection has more cushy digs (www.chateauxhotels.com).

From:	rick@ricksteves.com
Sent:	Today
To:	info@hotelcentral.com
Subject:	Reservation request for 19-22 July

Dear Hotel Central,

I would like to stay at your hotel. Please let me know if you have a room available and the price for:
• 2 people
• Double bed and en suite bathroom in a quiet room
• Arriving 19 July, departing 22 July (3 nights)

Thank you!
Rick Steves

the fine print before you book (many hotels require a 48-hour cancellation minimum for refunds). Many discount deals require prepayment and can be expensive to change or cancel.

Reconfirming a Reservation: Always call or email to reconfirm your room reservation a few days in advance. For *chambres d'hôtes* or very small hotels, I call again on my arrival day to tell my host what time to expect me (especially important if arriving late—after 17:00).

Phoning: For tips on calling hotels overseas, see page 690.

Bed & Breakfasts

Though B&Bs (*chambres d'hôtes*, abbreviated CH) are generally found in smaller towns and rural areas, some are available in Paris. See the end of the Sleeping in Paris chapter for a list of rental agencies that can help.

Short-Term Rentals

A short-term rental—whether an apartment, a house, or a room in a private residence—is a popular alternative, especially if you plan to settle in one location for several nights. For stays longer than a few days, you can usually find a rental that's comparable to—and cheaper than—a hotel room with similar amenities. Plus, you'll get a behind-the-scenes peek into how locals live.

Many places require a minimum stay and have strict cancellation policies. And you're generally on your own: There's no reception desk, breakfast, or daily cleaning service.

Finding Accommodations: Websites such as Airbnb, FlipKey, Booking.com, and VRBO let you browse a wide range of

Keep Cool

If you're visiting France in the summer, you'll want an air-conditioned room. Most hotel air-conditioners come with a remote control that generally has similar symbols and features: fan icon (click to toggle through wind power, from light to gale); temperature (20 degrees Celsius is comfortable); louver icon (choose steady airflow or waves); snowflake and sunshine icons (cold air or heat, depending on season); and clock ("O" setting: run X hours before turning off; "I" setting: wait X hours to start). When you leave your room for the day, do as the environmentally conscious Europeans do, and turn off the air-conditioning.

properties. Alternatively, rental agencies such as InterhomeUSA.com and RentaVilla.com can provide more personalized service (their curated listings are also more expensive).

The Sleeping in Paris chapter lists several Paris-focused rental agencies.

Before you commit, be clear on the location. I like to virtually "explore" the neighborhood using Google Street View. Also consider the proximity to public transportation, and how well connected the property is with the rest of the city. Ask about amenities (elevator, air-conditioning, laundry, Wi-Fi, parking, etc.). Reviews from previous guests can help identify trouble spots.

Think about the kind of experience you want: Just a key and an affordable bed...or a chance to get to know a local? Some hosts offer self check-in and minimal contact; others enjoy interacting with you. Read the description and reviews to help shape your decision.

Confirming and Paying: Many places require payment in full before your trip, usually through the listing site. Be wary of owners who want to conduct your transaction offline; this gives you no recourse if things go awry. Never agree to wire money (a key indicator of a fraudulent transaction).

Apartments or Houses: If you're staying in one place for several nights, it's worth considering an apartment or house (shorter stays aren't worth the hassle of arranging key pickup, buying groceries, etc.). Apartment or house rentals can be especially cost-effective for groups and families. European apartments, like hotel rooms, tend to be small by US standards. But they often come with laundry facilities and small, equipped kitchens, making it easier and cheaper to dine in.

Rooms in Private Homes: Renting a room in someone's home is a good option for those traveling alone, as you're more likely to find true single rooms—with just one single bed, and a price to match. These can range from air-mattress-in-living-room basic to plush-B&B-suite posh. While you can't expect your host to also be your tour guide—or even to provide you with much info—some are interested in getting to know the travelers who pass through their home.

Other Options: Swapping homes with a local works for people with an appealing place to offer (don't assume where you live is not interesting to Europeans). Good places to start are HomeExchange.com and LoveHomeSwap.com. To sleep for free, Couchsurfing.com is a vagabond's alternative to Airbnb. It lists millions of outgoing members who host fellow "surfers" in their homes.

Hostels

A hostel *(auberge de jeunesse)* provides cheap beds in dorms where you sleep alongside strangers for about €35 per night. Travelers of any age are welcome if they don't mind dorm-style accommodations and meeting other travelers. Most hostels offer kitchen facilities, guest computers, Wi-Fi, and a self-service laundry. Hostels almost always provide bedding, but the towel's up to you (though you can usually rent one). Family and private rooms are often available.

Independent hostels tend to be easygoing, colorful, and informal (no membership required; www.hostelworld.com). You may pay slightly less by booking directly with the hostel. **Official hostels** are part of Hostelling International (HI) and share an online booking site (www.hihostels.com). HI hostels typically require that you be a member or else pay a bit more per night.

Hip Hop Hostels is a clearinghouse for budget hotels and hostels in Paris. It's worth a look for its good selection of cheap accommodations (+ 33 1 48 78 10 00, www.hiphophostels.com).

Eating

The French eat long and well. Relaxed and tree-shaded lunches with a chilled rosé, three-hour dinners, and endless hours of sitting in outdoor cafés are the norm. Here, celebrated restaurateurs are as famous as great athletes, and mamas hope their babies will grow up to be great chefs. Cafés, cuisine, and wines should become a highlight of any French adventure: It's sightseeing  for your palate. Even if the rest of you is sleeping in a cheap hotel, let your taste buds travel first-class in France.

You can eat well without going broke—but choose carefully:

Restaurant Code

Eateries in this book are categorized according to the average cost of a typical main course. Drinks, desserts, and splurge items can raise the price considerably.

$$$$	**Splurge:** Most main courses over €40
$$$	**Pricier:** €30-40
$$	**Moderate:** €20-30
$	**Budget:** Under €20

In France, a crêpe stand or other takeout spot is **$**; a sit-down brasserie, café, or bistro with affordable *plats du jour* ranges from **$** to **$$**; a casual but more upscale restaurant is **$$$**; and a swanky splurge is **$$$$**.

You're just as likely to blow a small fortune on a mediocre meal as you are to dine wonderfully for €25. Read the information that follows and consider my restaurant suggestions in this book.

For listings in this guidebook, I look for restaurants that are convenient to your hotel and sightseeing. When restaurant-hunting, choose a spot filled with locals, not the place with the big neon signs boasting, "We Speak English and Accept Credit Cards." In Paris, restaurant lunches are a great value, as most places offer the same quality and similar selections for far less than at dinner. If you're on a budget or just like going local, try making lunch your main meal, then have a lighter evening meal at a café.

RESTAURANT PRICING

I've categorized my recommended eateries based on the average price of a typical main course, indicated with a dollar-sign rating (see sidebar). Expensive specialties, fine wine, appetizers, and dessert can significantly increase your final bill.

The categories also indicate the personality of a place: **Budget** eateries include street food, takeaway, order-at-the-counter shops, basic cafeterias, and bakeries selling sandwiches. **Moderate** eateries are nice (but not fancy) sit-down restaurants, ideal for a pleasant meal with good-quality food. Most of my listings fall in this category—great for a taste of the local cuisine at a reasonable price.

Pricier eateries are a notch up, with more attention paid to the setting, presentation, and (often inventive) cuisine. **Splurge** eateries are dress-up-for-a-special-occasion swanky—typically with an elegant setting, polished service, and pricey and refined cuisine.

BREAKFAST

Most hotels serve an optional breakfast, which is usually pleasant and convenient (generally €10-20, price rises proportionately with room cost). They almost all offer a buffet breakfast (cereal, yogurt, fruit, cheese, ham, croissants, juice, and hard-boiled eggs). Some add scrambled eggs and sausage. Before committing to breakfast, check to see if it's included in your room rate; if not, scan the offerings to be sure it's to your liking. Once committed, it's self-service and as much as you want. Coffee is often self-serve as well. If there's no coffee machine and you want to make your own *café au lait*, find the hot milk and mix it with your coffee. If your hotelier serves your coffee, ask for *café avec du lait*. For your basic American-style coffee (black and not too strong), ask for *café Américain*.

Breakfast is a great time to try the country's delightful array of breads, pastries, jams, and more. Many hotels and B&Bs take pride in serving these extremely fresh—often with a different selection each day.

If all you want is coffee or tea and a croissant, the corner café or bakery offers more atmosphere and is less expensive (though you get more coffee at your hotel). Go local at a café and ask for *une tartine* (ewn tart-een), a baguette slathered with butter or jam. If you crave eggs for breakfast, order *une omelette* or *œufs sur le plat* (fried eggs). Some cafés and bakeries offer worthwhile breakfast deals with juice, croissant, and coffee or tea for about €8-12 (for more on coffee and tea drinks, see the "Beverages" section, later).

To keep it cheap, pick up some fruit at a grocery store and pastries at your favorite *boulangerie* and have a picnic breakfast, then savor your coffee at a café bar *(comptoir)* while standing, like the French do.

PICNIC DINING AND FOOD TO GO

Whether going all out on a perfect Parisian picnic or simply grabbing a sandwich to eat on an atmospheric square, dining with the city as your backdrop can be one of your most memorable meals. For a list of places to picnic in Paris, see the sidebar in the Eating in Paris chapter.

Picnics

Great for lunch or dinner, French picnics can be first-class affairs and adventures in high cuisine. Be daring. Try the smelly cheeses, strange-looking pâtés, and minuscule yogurts. You'll find tasty €5 sandwiches, to-go salads, quiches, crêpes, and high-quality takeout at bakeries, charcuteries, and market stands (see "Assembling a Picnic," below).

Shopkeepers are accustomed to selling small quantities of produce. Get a succulent takeaway salad and ask for a fork. While single-use plastic cups and silverware are no longer allowed in France, biodegradable ones should be available at grocery stores.

Picnic Vocabulary

English	French
Please	*s'il vous plaît* (see voo play)
a fork	*une fourchette* (ewn foor-sheht)
a cup	*un gobelet* (uhn goh-blay)
a paper plate	*une assiette en carton* (ewn ah-see-eht ahn kar-tohn)
napkins	*les serviettes* (lay sehr-vee-eht)
a small container	*une barquette* (ewn bar-keht)
a knife	*un couteau* (uhn koo-toh)
a corkscrew	*un tire-bouchon* (uhn teer-boo-shohn)
sliced	*tranché* (trahn-shay)
a slice	*une tranche* (ewn trahnsh)
a small slice	*une petite tranche* (ewn puh-teet trahnsh)
more	*plus* (plew)
less	*moins* (mwan)
It's just right.	*C'est bon.* (say bohn)
That'll be all.	*C'est tout.* (say too)
Thank you.	*Merci.* (mehr-see)

Plastic bags may not be available at markets; bring or buy your own bag (cheap at stores) or daypack for carrying items.

If you need a knife or corkscrew, buy it cheap at a grocery shop or borrow one from your hotelier (but please don't picnic in your room, as French hoteliers uniformly detest this). Though drinking wine in public places is taboo in the US, it's *pas de problème* in France. Wine merchants sell chilled, picnic-friendly bottles that they'll happily open for you.

Scenic picnic sites are everywhere (for suggestions, see the Eating in Paris chapter).

Assembling a Picnic: Visit several small stores to put together a complete meal. Shop early, as many shops close from 12:00 or 13:00 to 15:00 for their lunch break. Say *"Bonjour madame/monsieur"* as you enter, then point to what you want and say, *"S'il vous plaît."* For other terminology you might need while shopping, see the sidebar.

At the *boulangerie* (bakery), buy some bread. A baguette usually does the trick, or choose from the many loaves of bread on display: *pain aux céréales* (whole grain with seeds), *pain de campagne* (country bread, made with unbleached bread flour), *pain complet* (wheat bread), or *pain de seigle* (rye bread). To ask for it sliced, say "*Tranché, s'il vous plaît.*"

At the *pâtisserie* (pastry shop, which is often the same place you bought the bread), choose a dessert that's easy to eat with your hands. My favorites are *éclairs* (*chocolat* or *café* flavored), individual fruit *tartes* (*framboise* is raspberry, *fraise* is strawberry, *citron* is lemon), and *macarons* (made of flavored cream sandwiched between two meringues).

At the *crémerie* or *fromagerie* (cheese shop), choose a sampling of cheeses *(un assortiment).* I usually get one hard cheese (like Comté, Cantal, or Beaufort), one soft cow's milk cheese (like Brie or Camembert), one goat's milk cheese (anything that says chèvre), and one blue cheese (Roquefort or Bleu d'Auvergne). Goat cheese usually comes in individual portions. For all other large cheeses, point to the cheese you want and ask for *une petite tranche* (a small slice). The shopkeeper will show you the size of the slice about to be cut, then look at you for approval. If you'd like more, say, "*Plus.*" If you'd like less, say "*Moins.*" If it's just right, say "*C'est bon!*"

At the **charcuterie** or *traiteur* (for deli items, prepared salads, meats, and pâtés), I like a slice of *pâté de campagne* (country pâté made of pork) and *saucissons secs* (dried sausages, some with pepper crust or garlic—you can ask to have it sliced thin

like salami). I get a fresh salad, too. Typical options are *carottes râpées* (shredded carrots in a tangy vinaigrette), *salade de betteraves* (beets in vinaigrette), and *céleri rémoulade* (celery root with a mayonnaise sauce). The food comes in takeout containers, and they may supply a biodegradable fork.

At a *cave à vin* you can buy chilled wines that the merchant is usually happy to open and recork for you.

At a **supermarché, épicerie,** or **magasin d'alimentation** (grocery store or minimart), you'll find biodegradable cutlery and glasses, paper plates, and napkins, plus drinks, chips, and a display of produce. Daily Monop' and Carrefour City stores—offering fresh salads, wraps, juices, and more at reasonable prices—are everywhere and convenient one-stop places for assembling a picnic.

To-Go Food

You'll find plenty of to-go options at *crêperies*, bakeries, and small stands. Baguette sandwiches, quiches, and pizza-like items are tasty, filling, and budget-friendly (about €5). Most grocery shops sell good and cheap packaged salads, wraps, sandwiches, and plastic containers of *carottes râpées* (shredded carrots), *salade de betteraves* (beets), and *céleri rémoulade* (celery root slaw).

Sandwiches: Anything served *à la provençale* has marinated peppers, tomatoes, and eggplant. A sandwich *à l'italienne* is a grilled *panini* (usually referred to as *pannini*). Here are some common sandwiches:

Fromage (froh-mahzh): Cheese only

Jambon beurre (zhahn-bohn bur): Ham and butter (a tasty, true French classic)

Jambon crudités (zhahn-bohn krew-dee-tay): Ham with tomatoes, lettuce, cucumbers, and mayonnaise

Fougasse (foo-gahs): Bread rolled up with salty bits of bacon, cheese, or olives

Poulet crudités (poo-lay krew-dee-tay): Chicken with tomatoes, lettuce, maybe cucumbers, and always mayonnaise

Saucisson beurre (soh-see-sohn bur): Thinly sliced sausage and butter

Thon crudités (tohn krew-dee-tay): Tuna with tomatoes, lettuce, and maybe cucumbers, but definitely mayonnaise

Quiche: Typical quiches you'll see at shops and bakeries are *lorraine* (ham and cheese), *fromage* (cheese only), *aux oignons* (with onions), *aux poireaux* (with leeks—my favorite), *aux champignons* (with mushrooms), *au saumon* (salmon), or *au thon* (tuna).

Crêpes: The quintessentially French thin pancake called a crêpe (rhymes with "step," not "grape") is filling, usually inexpensive, and generally quick. Place your order at the *crêperie* window or kiosk, and watch the chef in action. But don't be surprised if they don't make the crêpe for you from scratch; at some *crêperies*, they might premake a stack of crêpes and reheat them when they fill your order.

Crêpes generally are *sucrée* (sweet) or *salée* (savory). Technically, a savory crêpe should be made with a heartier buckwheat batter, and is called a *galette*. However, many cheap and lazy *crêperies* use the same sweet batter *(de froment)* for both their sweet-topped and savory-topped crêpes. A *socca* is a chickpea crêpe.

Standard crêpe toppings include cheese (*fromage;* usually Swiss-style Gruyère or Emmental), ham *(jambon)*, egg *(œuf)*, mushrooms *(champignons)*, chocolate, Nutella, jam *(confiture)*, whipped cream *(chantilly)*, apple jam *(compote de pommes)*, chestnut cream *(crème de marrons)*, and Grand Marnier.

RESTAURANT AND CAFE DINING

To get the most out of dining out in France, slow down. Give yourself time to dine at a French pace, engage the waiter, show you care about food, and enjoy the experience as much as the food itself. If you want a full meal, head to a restaurant or bistro, where you can choose from a two- to four-course set *menu* or order *à la carte*. If all you want is a salad, crêpe, bowl of soup, or other simple, quick meal, go to a café, a crêperie, or a takeout joint.

French waiters probably won't overwhelm you with friendliness. As their tip is already included in the bill (see "Tipping," below), there's less schmoozing than we're used to at home. Notice how hard they work. They almost never stop. Cozying up to clients (French or foreign) is probably the last thing on their minds. They're often stuck with client overload, too, because the French rarely hire part-time employees, even to help with peak times. To get a waiter's attention, try to make meaningful eye contact, which is a signal that you need something. If this doesn't work, raise your hand and simply say, *"S'il vous plaît"* (see voo play)—"please."

This phrase also works when you want to ask for the check. In French eateries, a waiter will rarely bring you the check unless you request it. To the French, having the bill dropped off before asking for it is *gauche*. But busy travelers are often ready for the check sooner rather than later. If you're in a hurry, ask for the bill when your server comes to clear your plates or checks in to see if you want dessert or coffee. To request your bill, say, *"L'addition, s'il vous plaît."* If you don't ask now, the wait staff may become scarce as they leave you to digest in peace. (For a list of other restaurant survival phrases, see the appendix.)

Note that all café and restaurant interiors are smoke-free. Today the only smokers you'll find are at outside tables, which—unfortunately—may be exactly where you want to sit.

Tipping: At cafés and restaurants, a 12-15 percent service charge is always included in the price of what you order *(service compris* or *prix net)*, but you won't see it listed on your bill. Unlike in the US, France pays servers a decent wage (a favorite café owner told me that his waiters earn more than some high school teachers). Because of this, most locals only tip a little, or not at all. When dining, expect reasonable, efficient service. If you don't get it, skip the tip. If you feel the service was good, tip a little—about 5 percent; maybe 10 percent for terrific service. To tell the waiter to keep the change when you pay, say *"C'est bon"* (say bohn), meaning "It's good." If you are using a credit card, leave your tip in cash—credit-card receipts don't even have space to add a tip. Never feel guilty if you don't leave a tip. Still, be aware that some waiters in areas popular with Americans may ask for a tip (knowing that Americans are accustomed to tipping generously). Don't feel pressured to tip in these circumstances. If you choose to, tip 10 percent or less.

Cafés and Brasseries

French cafés and brasseries provide user-friendly meals and a relief from sightseeing overload. They're not necessarily cheaper than many restaurants and bistros, and famous cafés on popular squares can be pricey affairs. Their key advantage is flexibility: They offer long serving hours, and you're welcome to order just a salad, a sandwich, or a bowl of soup, even for dinner. It's also OK to share starters and desserts, though not main courses.

Cafés and brasseries usually open by 7:00, but closing hours vary. Unlike some restaurants, which open only for dinner and sometimes for lunch, many cafés and all brasseries serve food throughout the day (usually with a limited menu during off hours), making them the best option for a late lunch or an early dinner. *Service Continu* or *Service Non-Stop* signs indicate continued service throughout the day.

Check the price list first, which by law should be posted. There are two sets of prices: You'll pay more for the same drink if you're seated at a table *(salle)* than if you're seated or standing at the bar or counter *(comptoir)*. (For tips on ordering coffee and tea, see the "Beverages" section, later.)

At a café or a brasserie, if the table is not set, it's fine to seat yourself and just have a drink. However, if it's set with a placemat and cutlery, you should ask to be seated and plan to order a meal. If you're unsure, ask the server before sitting down.

Ordering: A salad, crêpe, *croque monsieur,* or omelet is a fairly cheap way to fill up. Omelets come lonely on a plate with a basket of bread. Sandwiches, generally served day and night, are inexpensive, but most are very plain (*boulangeries* serve better ones). To get more than a piece of ham *(jambon)* on a baguette, order a *sandwich jambon crudités* (garnished with veggies). Popular sandwiches are

Vegetarians, Allergies, and Other Dietary Restrictions

Many French people think "vegetarian" means "no red meat" or "not much meat." If you're a strict vegetarian, be specific: Tell your server what you don't eat—and it can be helpful to clarify what you do eat. Write it out on a card and keep it handy.

But be reasonable. Think of your meal (as the French do) as if it's a finely crafted creation by a trained artist. The chef knows what goes well together, and substitutions are considered an insult to his training. Picky eaters should try their best to just take it or leave it.

However, French restaurants are willing to accommodate genuine dietary restrictions and other special concerns, or at least point you to an appropriate choice on the menu. These phrases might help:

French	English
Je suis végétarien/végétarienne. (zhuh swee vay-zhay-tah-ree-an/vay-zhay-tah-ree-ehn)	I am vegetarian.
Je ne peux pas manger de _____. (zhuh nuh puh pah mahn-zhay duh _____)	I cannot eat _____.
Je suis allergique à _____. (zhuh sweez ah-lehr-zheek ah_____)	I am allergic to _____.
Pas de_____, s'il vous plaît. (pah duh _____, see voo play)	No _____, please.

the *croque monsieur* (grilled ham-and-cheese) and *croque madame* (*monsieur* with a fried egg on top).

Salads are typically meal size and often can be ordered with warm ingredients mixed in, such as melted goat cheese, fried gizzards, or roasted potatoes. One salad is perfect for lunch or a light dinner. See the "French Cuisine" section later for a list of classic salads.

The daily special—*plat du jour* (plah dew zhoor)—is your fast, hearty, and garnished hot plate for about €12-20. At most cafés, feel free to order only *entrées* (which in French means the starter course); some find these lighter and more to their taste than a main course. A vegetarian can enjoy a tasty, filling meal by ordering two *entrées*.

Regardless of what you order, bread is free but almost never comes with butter; to get more bread, just hold up your basket and ask, *"Encore, s'il vous plaît?"*

Restaurants

Choose restaurants filled with locals. Consider my suggestions and your hotelier's opinion, but trust your instincts. If a restaurant doesn't post its prices outside, move along.

Most restaurants open for dinner at 19:00 (some at 18:30), and a few serve food nonstop from lunch until late (those places are identified in this book). Local favorites get crowded after 21:00. To minimize crowds, go early (by 19:30). Last seating at Parisian restaurants is usually about 22:00. Many restaurants close Sunday and/or Monday.

Tune into the quiet, relaxed pace of French dining. The French don't do dinner and a movie on date nights; they just do dinner. The table is yours for the night. Notice how quietly French diners speak in restaurants and how few mobile phones you see during a meal, and how this improves your overall experience. Go local.

Ordering: In French restaurants, you can choose something off the menu *(la carte)*, or you can order a multicourse, fixed-price meal (confusingly, called a *menu*). If you ask for *un menu* (instead of *la carte*), you'll get a fixed-price meal.

Ordering **à la carte** gives you the best selection. I enjoy going à la carte especially when traveling with others and eating family style (waiters are usually happy to accommodate this approach and will bring small extra plates). It's traditional to order an *entrée* (a starter—not a main dish) and a *plat principal* (main course), though it's becoming common to order only a *plat principal*—and maybe a dessert. *Plats* are generally more meat-based, while *entrées* usually include veggies. Multiple-course meals, while time-consuming (a positive thing in France), create the appropriate balance of veggies to meat. Elaborate meals may also have *entremets*—tiny dishes served between courses. Wherever you dine, consider the waiter's recommendations and anything *de la maison* (of the house), as long as it's not an organ meat (tripe, *rognons*, or andouillette).

Two people can split an *entrée* or a big salad (small-size dinner salads are usually not offered á la carte) and then each get a *plat principal*. At restaurants, it's inappropriate for two diners to share one main course. If all you want is a salad or soup, go to a café or brasserie.

Fixed-price *menus*—which usually include two, three, or four courses—are always a better deal than eating à la carte, providing you want several courses. At most restaurants offering fixed-price *menus*, the price for a two- or three-course *menu* is only slightly higher than a single main course from the à la carte list (though the main course is usually larger than the one you get with the fixed-price *menu*). With a three-course *menu* you'll choose a starter of soup, appetizer, or salad; select from three or four main courses with vegetables; and finish up with a cheese course and/or a choice

```
  ⛵    ︶︾          ☀

Restaurant  La Mer
 18, rue de la Galette, Paris

MENU TOURISTIQUE  €22

Entrée au choix (FIRST COURSE CHOICES)
• SOUPE DE POISSONS (FISH SOUP)
• 12 ESCARGOTS EN COQUILLE (SNAILS IN SHELL)
• SALADE NIÇOISE
• SUGGESTION DU CHEF

Plat au choix (SECOND COURSE CHOICES)
• PLATEAU FRUITS DU MER (PLATTER OF MIXED
                          COLD SEAFOOD)
• POISSON DU MARCHE (FISH FROM THE MARKET)
• POULET BASQUAISE (CHICKEN BASQUE STYLE)
• STEAK-FRITES, SAUCE A L'ECHALOTE (STEAK W/FRIES
                                    + SHALLOT SAUCE)

Dessert au choix (DESSERT CHOICES)
• FROMAGE (CHEESE)
• PATISSERIE DU JOUR (PASTRY OF THE DAY)
• GLACE OU SORBET (ICE CREAM OR SHERBET)
• CREME BRULEE

~ SERVICE  COMPRIS ~ (SERVICE INCLUDED)

       Merci et Bon Appetit!
```

of desserts. It sounds like a lot of food, but portions are a bit smaller with fixed-price *menus*, and what we cram onto one large plate they spread out over several courses. If you're dining with a friend, one person can get the full *menu* while the other can order just a *plat* (and share the *menu* courses). Also, many restaurants offer less expensive and less filling two-course *menus*, sometimes called *formules*, featuring an *entrée et plat*, or *plat et dessert*. Many restaurants have a reasonable *menu-enfant* (kid's meal).

Wine and other drinks are extra, and certain premium items add a few euros, clearly noted on the menu (*supplément* or *sup.*).

Lunch: If a restaurant serves lunch, it generally begins at 12:00 and goes until 14:30, with last orders taken at about 13:30. If you're hungry when restaurants are closed (late afternoon), go to a *boulangerie*, brasserie, or café (see previous section). Even fancy places usually have affordable lunch *menus* (often called *formules* or *plat de midi*), allowing you to sample the same gourmet cooking for a lot less than the price of dinner.

FRENCH CUISINE

You can be a galloping gourmet and try several types of French cuisine without ever leaving the confines of Paris. Most restaurants serve dishes from several regions, though some focus on a particular region's cuisine (see the sidebar for a list of specialty dishes by region). Among the listings in this book are restaurants specializing in food from Provence, Burgundy, Alsace, Normandy, Brittany, Dordogne, Languedoc, and the Basque region.

General styles of French cooking include *cuisine gastronomique* (classic, elaborately prepared, multicourse meals); *cuisine semi-gastronomique* or *bistronomie* (the finest-quality home cooking); *cuisine des provinces* (traditional dishes of specific regions); and *nouvelle cuisine* (a focus on smaller portions and closer attention to the texture and color of the ingredients). Sauces are a huge part of French cooking. In the early 20th century, the legendary French chef Auguste Escoffier identified five French "mother sauces" from which all others are derived: *béchamel* (milk-based white sauce), *es-*

French Specialties by Region

Burgundy: Considered by many to be France's best, Burgundian cuisine is peasant cooking elevated to an art. This wine region excels in *coq au vin* (chicken with wine sauce), *bœuf bourguignon* (beef stew cooked with wine, bacon, onions, and mushrooms), *œufs en meurette* (eggs poached in red wine), *escargots* (snails), and *jambon persillé* (ham with garlic and parsley).

Normandy and Brittany: Normandy specializes in cream sauces, sea salt, organ meats (sweetbreads, tripe, and kidneys—the "gizzard salads" are great), and seafood *(fruits de mer)*. Dairy products are big here. Try the *moules* (mussels) and *escalope normande* (veal in cream sauce). Brittany is famous for its oysters and crêpes. Both regions use lots of *cidre* (hard apple cider) in their cuisine.

Provence: The extravagant use of garlic, olive oil, herbs, and tomatoes makes Provence's cuisine France's liveliest. To sample it, order anything *à la provençale*. Among the area's spicy specialties are ratatouille (a thick mixture of vegetables in an herb-flavored tomato sauce), *brandade* (a salt cod, garlic, and cream mousse), aioli (a garlicky mayonnaise often served atop fresh vegetables), tapenade (a paste of puréed olives, capers, anchovies, herbs, and sometimes tuna), *soupe au pistou* (vegetable soup with basil, garlic, and cheese), and *soupe à l'ail* (garlic soup).

Riviera: The Côte d'Azur gives Provence's cuisine a Mediterranean flair. Local specialties are bouillabaisse (the spicy seafood

pagnole (veal-based brown sauce), *velouté* (stock-based white sauce), *hollandaise* (egg yolk-based white sauce), and *tomate* (tomato-based red sauce).

The following list of items should help you navigate a typical French menu. Galloping gourmets should bring a menu translator. The most complete (and priciest) menu reader around is *A to Z of French Food* by G. de Temmerman (look for the cheaper app). The *Marling Menu-Master* is also good. The *Rick Steves French Phrase Book,* with a menu decoder, works well for most travelers.

First Course (Entrée)

Crudités: A mix of raw and lightly cooked fresh vegetables, usually including grated carrots, celery root, tomatoes, and beets, often with a hefty dose of vinaigrette dressing. If you want the dressing on the side, say, *"La sauce à côté, s'il vous plaît"* (lah sohs ah koh-tay, see voo play).

Escargots: Snails cooked in parsley-garlic butter. You don't even have to like the snail itself. Just dipping your bread in garlic butter is more than satisfying. Prepared a variety of ways, the classic is *à la bourguignonne* (served in their shells).

stew/soup that seems worth the cost only for those with a sea-food fetish), *bourride* (a creamy fish soup thickened with aioli), and *salade niçoise* (described earlier, under "Salads").

Basque: Mixing influences from the mountains, sea, Spain, and France, it's dominated by seafood, tomatoes, and red peppers. Look for anything *basquaise* (cooked with tomatoes, eggplant, red peppers, and garlic), such as *thon* (tuna) or *poulet* (chicken). Try *piperade,* a dish combining peppers, tomatoes, garlic, and eggs (ham optional), and *ttoro,* a seafood stew and the Basque answer to bouillabaisse.

Alsace: The German influence is obvious—sausages, potatoes, onions, and sauerkraut. Look for *choucroute garnie* (sauerkraut and sausage—although it seems a shame to eat it in a fancy restaurant), the more traditionally Alsatian *Baeckeoffe* (potato, meat, and onion stew), *Rösti* (an oven-baked potato-and-cheese dish), fresh trout, foie gras, and *flammekueche* (a paper-thin pizza topped with bacon, onions, and sour cream).

Languedoc and Périgord: What Parisians call "Southwest cuisine" *(cuisine du sud-ouest)* is hearty peasant fare, using full-bodied red wines and lots of duck. Try *cassoulet* (white bean, duck, and sausage stew), *canard* (duck), *pâté de foie gras* (goose-liver pâté), *pommes sarladaise* (potatoes fried in duck fat), *truffes* (truffles, earthy mushrooms), and anything with *noix* (walnuts).

Foie gras: Rich and buttery in consistency—and hefty in price—this pâté is made from the swollen livers of force-fed geese (or ducks, in *foie gras de canard*). Put small chunks on bread—don't spread it, and never add mustard. For a real French experience, try this dish with a sweet white wine (such as a Muscat).

Huîtres: Oysters, served raw any month, are particularly popular at Christmas and on New Year's Eve, when every café seems to have overflowing baskets in their window.

Œuf mayo: A simple hard-boiled egg topped with a dollop of flavorful mayonnaise

Pâtés and *terrines:* Slowly cooked ground meat (usually pork, though game, poultry liver, and rabbit are also common) that is highly seasoned and served in slices with mustard and *cornichons* (little pickles). Pâtés are smoother than the similarly prepared but chunkier *terrines.*

Soupe à l'oignon: Hot, salty, filling, and easiest to find at cafés, French onion soup is a beef broth served with a baked cheese-and-bread crust over the top.

Salads (Salades)

With the exception of a *salade mixte* (simple green salad, often difficult to find), the French get creative with their *salades*. Here are some classics:

Salade de chèvre chaud: This mixed-green salad is topped with warm goat cheese on small pieces of toast.

Salade de gésiers: Though it may not sound appetizing, this salad with chicken gizzards (and often slices of duck) is worth a try.

Salade composée: "Composed" of any number of ingredients, this salad might have *lardons* (bacon), Comté (a Swiss-style cheese), Roquefort (blue cheese), *œuf* (egg), *noix* (walnuts), and *jambon* (ham, generally thinly sliced).

Salade gourmande: The "gourmet" salad varies by region and restaurant but usually features cured and poached meats served on salad greens with a mustard vinaigrette.

Salade niçoise: A specialty from Nice, this tasty salad usually includes greens topped with ripe tomatoes, raw vegetables (such as radishes, green peppers, celery, and perhaps artichoke or fava beans), tuna (usually canned), anchovy, hard-boiled egg, and olives.

Salade paysanne: You'll usually find potatoes *(pommes de terre)*, walnuts *(noix)*, tomatoes, ham, and egg in this salad.

Main Course (Plat Principal)

Duck, lamb, and rabbit are popular in France, and each is prepared in a variety of ways. You'll also encounter various stew-like dishes that vary by region. The most common regional specialties are described here.

Bœuf bourguignon: A Burgundian specialty, this classy beef stew is cooked slowly in red wine, then served with onions, potatoes, and mushrooms.

Cabillaud: Cod is France's favorite fish, and you'll find it on French menus. It's cooked in many ways that vary by region, but most commonly with butter, white wine, and herbs.

Confit de canard: A favorite from the southwest Dordogne region is duck that has been preserved in its own fat, then cooked in its fat, and often served with potatoes (cooked in the same fat). Not for dieters. (Note that *magret de canard* is sliced duck breast and very different in taste.)

Coq au vin: This Burgundian dish is rooster marinated ever so slowly in red wine, then cooked until it melts in your mouth. It's served (often family-style) with vegetables.

Daube: Generally made with beef, but sometimes lamb, this is a long and slowly simmered dish, typically paired with noodles or other pasta.

PRACTICALITIES

Escalope normande: This specialty of Normandy features turkey or veal in a cream sauce.

Gigot d'agneau: A specialty of Provence, this is a leg of lamb often grilled and served with white beans. The best lamb is *pré salé,* which means the lamb has been raised in salt-marsh lands (like at Mont St-Michel).

Le hamburger: This American import is all the rage in France. Cafés and restaurants serve it using local sauces, breads, and cheeses. It's fun to see their interpretation of this classic American dish.

Poulet rôti: Roasted chicken on the bone—French comfort food

Saumon and *truite:* You'll see salmon and trout *(truite)* dishes served in various styles. The salmon usually comes from the North Sea and is always served with sauce, most commonly a sorrel *(oseille)* sauce.

Steak: Referred to as *pavé* (thick hunk of prime steak), *bavette* (skirt steak), *faux filet* (sirloin), or *entrecôte* (rib steak), French steak is usually thinner and tougher than American steak and is always served with sauces (*au poivre* is a pepper sauce, *une sauce roquefort* is a blue-cheese sauce). Because steak is usually better in North America, I generally avoid it in France (unless the sauce sounds good). You will also see *steak haché,* which is a lean, gourmet hamburger patty served *sans* bun. When it's served as *steak haché à cheval,* it comes with a fried egg on top.

By American standards, the French undercook meats: Their version of rare, *saignant* (seh-nyahn), means "bloody" and is close to raw. What they consider medium, *à point* (ah pwan), is what an American would call rare. Their term for well-done, or *bien cuit* (bee-yehn kwee), would translate as medium for Americans (and overdone for the French).

Steak tartare: This wonderfully French dish is for adventurous types only. It's very lean, raw hamburger served with savory seasonings (usually Tabasco, capers, raw onions, salt, and pepper on the side) and topped with a raw egg yolk. This is not hamburger as we know it, but freshly ground beef.

Cheese Course *(Le Fromage)*

The cheese course is served just before (or instead of) dessert. It not only helps with digestion, it gives you a great opportunity to sample the tasty regional cheeses—and time to finish up your wine. Between cow, goat, and sheep cheeses, there are more than 350 different ones to try in France. Some restaurants will offer a cheese platter *(plateau de fromages),* from which you select a few different kinds. A good platter has at least four cheeses: a hard cheese (such as Cantal), a flowery cheese (such as Brie or Camembert), a blue or Roquefort cheese, and a goat cheese.

Cheeses most commonly served in Paris are Brie de Meaux (mild and creamy, from just outside Paris), Camembert (semi-creamy and pungent, from Normandy), chèvre (goat cheese with a sharp taste, usually from the Loire), and Roquefort (strong and blue-veined, from south-central France).

To sample several types of cheese from the cheese plate, say, *"Un assortiment, s'il vous plaît"* (uhn ah-sor-tee-mahn, see voo play). You'll either be served a selection of several cheeses or choose from a large selection offered on a cheese tray. If you serve yourself from the cheese tray, observe French etiquette and keep the shape of the cheese: Shave off a slice from the side or cut small wedges.

A glass of good red wine is a heavenly complement to your cheese course—but if you're eating goat cheese, do as the French do and opt for white wine.

Dessert (Le Dessert)

If you order espresso, it will always come after dessert. To have coffee with dessert, ask for *"café avec le dessert"* (kah-fay ah-vehk luh day-sayr). See the list of coffee terms next. Here are the types of treats you'll see:

Baba au rhum: Pound cake drenched in rum, served with whipped cream

Café gourmand: An assortment of small desserts selected by the restaurant, served with an espresso—a great way to sample several desserts

Crème brûlée: A rich, creamy, dense, caramelized custard

Crème caramel: Flan in a caramel sauce

Fondant au chocolat: A molten chocolate cake with a runny (not totally cooked) center. Also known as *moelleux* (meh-leh) *au chocolat.*

Fromage blanc: A light dessert similar to plain yogurt (yet different), served with sugar or herbs

Glace: Ice cream—typically vanilla, chocolate, or strawberry

Ile flottante: A light dessert consisting of islands of meringue floating on a pond of custard sauce

Mousse au chocolat: Chocolate mousse

Profiteroles: Cream puffs filled with vanilla ice cream, smothered in warm chocolate sauce

Riz au lait: Rice pudding

Sorbets: Light, flavorful, and fruity ices, sometimes laced with brandy

Tartes: Open-face pie, often filled with fruit

Tarte tatin: Apple pie like grandma never made, with caramelized apples, cooked upside down, but served upright

BEVERAGES

In stores, unrefrigerated soft drinks, bottled water, and beer are cheaper than cold drinks. Bottled water and boxed fruit juice are the cheapest drinks. Avoid buying drinks to-go at streetside stands; you'll pay far less in a shop.

In bars and at eateries, be clear when ordering drinks—you can easily pay €10 for an oversized Coke and €15 for a supersized beer at some cafés. When you order a drink, state the size in centiliters (don't say "small," "medium," or "large," because the waiter might bring a bigger drink than you want). For something small, ask for 25 *centilitres* (vant-sank sahn-tee-lee-truh; about 8 ounces); for a medium drink, order 33 cl (trahnte-trwah; about 12 ounces—a normal can of soda); a large is 50 cl (san-kahnt; about 16 ounces); and a super-size is one liter (lee-truh; about a quart—which is more than I would ever order in France). The ice cubes melted after the last Yankee tour group left.

Water, Juice, and Soft Drinks

The French are willing to pay for bottled water with their meal (*eau minérale;* oh mee-nay-rahl) because they prefer the taste over tap water. Badoit is my favorite carbonated water (*l'eau gazeuse;* loh gah-zuhz) and is commonly available. To get a free pitcher of tap water, ask for *une carafe d'eau* (ewn kah-rahf doh). Otherwise, you may unwittingly buy bottled water.

In France *limonade* (lee-moh-nahd) is Sprite or 7-Up. For a fun, bright, nonalcoholic drink of 7-Up with mint syrup, order *un diabolo menthe* (uhn dee-ah-boh-loh mahnt). For 7-Up with fruit syrup, order *un diabolo grenadine* (think Shirley Temple). Kids love the local orange drink, Orangina, a carbonated orange juice with pulp. They also like *sirop à l'eau* (see-roh ah loh), flavored syrup mixed with carbonated water.

For keeping hydrated on the go, hang on to your store-bought water bottle and refill. I drink tap water throughout France, filling up my bottle in hotel rooms.

Coffee and Tea

The French define various types of espresso drinks by how much milk is added. To the French, milk is a delicate form of nutrition: You need it in the morning, but as the day goes on, too much can upset your digestion. Therefore, the amount of milk that's added to coffee decreases as the day goes on. The average French person thinks a *café au lait* is exclusively for breakfast, and a *café crème* is only appropriate through midday. You're welcome to order a milk-

PRACTICALITIES

French Wine-Tasting 101

France is peppered with wineries and wine-tasting opportunities. For some, trying to make sense of the vast range of French wines can be overwhelming, particularly when faced with a no-nonsense winemaker or sommelier. Do your best to follow my tips, and don't linger if you don't feel welcome.

Winemakers and sommeliers are usually happy to work with you, but it helps to know what you like (drier or sweeter, lighter or full-bodied, fruity or more tannic, and so on). The people serving you may know those words in English, but you're wise to learn the key words in French.

French wines usually have a lower alcohol level than American or Australian wines. While Americans might like a big, full-bodied wine, most French prefer subtler flavors. They judge a wine by how well it pairs with a meal. The French enjoy sampling younger wines and divining how they will taste in a few years, allowing them to buy bottles at cheaper prices and stash them in their cellars. Americans want it now—for today's picnic.

At tastings, vintners and wine shops are hoping you'll buy a bottle or two (otherwise you may be asked to pay a small tasting fee). They understand that North Americans can't take much wine with them, but they hope you'll look for their wines when you're back home. Some places will ship wine—ask.

ier coffee drink later in the day, but don't be surprised if you get a funny look.

In cafés, stand at the bar to sip your drink and get the lowest prices. Before ordering at a table, check out the price list *(les prix de consommation)*, which should be prominently displayed. This shows the price of the most commonly ordered drinks *au comptoir* (at the counter) and *en salle* (seated at a table). I use the price of *un café* (shot of espresso) at the counter as a reference—if the price is about €2 or less, the place is likely to be reasonable. If given a choice between a small, medium, or large beverage, be aware that small is usually the norm and larger drinks can be crazy pricey.

By law, a waiter must give you a glass of tap water with your

Here are some phrases to get you started when wine-tasting:
Hello, madam/sir.
Bonjour, madame/monsieur.
(bohn-zhoor, mah-dahm/muhs-yuh)

We would like to taste a few wines.
Nous voudrions déguster quelques vins.
(noo voo-dree-ohn day-gew-stay kehl-kuh van)

We would like a wine that is ___ and ___.
Nous voudrions un vin ___ et ___.
(noo voo-dree-ohn uhn van ___ ay ___)

Fill in the blanks with your favorites from this list:

English	French
red	*rouge* (roozh)
white	*blanc* (blahn)
rosé	*rosé* (roh-zay)
light	*léger* (lay-zhay)
full-bodied	*robuste* (roh-bewst)
fruity	*fruité* (frwee-tay)
sweet	*doux* (doo)
tannic	*tannique* (tah-neek)
fine	*fin, avec finesse* (fan, ah-vehk fee-nehs)
ready to drink (mature)	*prêt à boire* (preh ah bwar)
not ready to drink	*fermé* (fair-may)
oaky or woody	*boisé* (bwah-zay)
from old vines	*de vieilles vignes* (duh vee-yay-ee veen-yuh)
sparkling	*pétillant* (pay-tee-yahn)

coffee or tea if you request it; ask for *"un verre d'eau, s'il vous plaît"* (uhn vehr doh, see voo play).

Here are some common coffee and tea drinks:

Café (kah-fay): Shot of espresso

Café allongé, a.k.a. *café long* (kah-fay ah-lohn-zhay; kah-fay lohn): Espresso topped up with hot water—like an Americano

Noisette (nwah-zeht): Espresso with a dollop of milk (best value for adding milk to your coffee)

Café au lait (kah-fay oh lay): Espresso mixed with lots of warm milk (used mostly for coffee made at home; in a café, order *café crème*)

Café crème (kah-fay krehm): Espresso with a sizable pour of steamed milk (closest thing you'll get to an American-style latte)

Grand crème (grahn krehm): Double shot of espresso with a bit more steamed milk (and often twice the price)

Décafféiné (day-kah-fee-nay): Decaf—available for any of the above

Thé nature (tay nah-tour): Plain tea

Thé au lait (tay oh lay): Tea with milk

Thé citron (tay see-trohn): Tea with lemon

Infusion (an-few-see-yohn): Herbal tea

Alcoholic Beverages

The legal drinking age is 18—at restaurants it's normal for wine to be served with dinner to teens.

Wine: Wines are often listed in a separate *carte des vins*. House wine is generally cheap and good enough (about €5/glass). Finer wines are harder to find by the glass. At a café, a carafe of house wine costs around €15. To order less expensive wine, ask for table wine *(vin de table)*.

Here are some important wine terms:

Vin de table (van duh tah-bluh): House wine

Verre de vin rouge (vehr duh van roozh): Glass of red wine

Verre de vin blanc (vehr duh van blahn): Glass of white wine

Pichet (pee-shay) or *carafe* (kah-rahf): Pitcher or carafe

Demi-pichet (duh-mee pee-shay): Half-carafe

Quart (kar): Quarter-carafe (ideal for one)

Bouteille (boo-teh-ee): Bottle

Demi-bouteille (duh-mee boo-teh-ee): Half-bottle

Beer: Local *bière* (bee-ehr) costs about €6 at a restaurant and is cheaper on tap (*une pression;* ewn pres-yohn) than in the bottle. France's best-known beers are Alsatian; try Kronenbourg or the heavier Pelfort (one of your author's favorites). Craft beers *(bière artisanale)* are very popular—Brittany produces some of the best, though all regions seem to be making craft beers these days.

Aperitifs: Champagne is a popular way to start your evening in France. For a refreshing before-dinner drink, order a *kir* (pronounced "keer")—a thumb's level of *crème de cassis* (black currant liqueur) topped with white wine (upgrade to a *kir royal* if you'd like it made with champagne). Also consider a glass of Lillet, a sweet, flowery fortified wine from Bordeaux. *Pastis,* the standard southern France aperitif, is a sweet anise (licorice) drink that comes on the rocks with a glass of water (cut it with water to taste). *Un Monaco* is a red drink made with beer, grenadine, and lemonade.

After Dinner: If you like brandy, try a *marc* (regional brandy—e.g., *marc de Bourgogne*) or an Armagnac, cognac's cheaper twin brother.

Staying Connected

One of the most common questions I hear from travelers is, "How can I stay connected in Europe?" The short answer? More easily and affordably than you might think.

The simplest solution is to bring your own device—phone, tablet, or laptop—and use it much as you would at home, following the money-saving tips below, such as getting an international plan or connecting to free Wi-Fi whenever possible. Another option is to buy a European SIM card for your mobile phone. Or you can use European landlines and computers to connect. More details are at RickSteves.com/phoning.

USING YOUR PHONE IN EUROPE

Here are some budget tips and options.

Sign up for an international plan. To stay connected at a lower cost, sign up for an international service plan through your carrier. Most providers offer a simple bundle that includes calling, messaging, and data. Your normal plan may already include international coverage (for example, T-Mobile's covers data and text, but not voice calls).

Before your trip, research your provider's international rates. Activate the plan a day or two before you leave, then remember to cancel it when your trip's over.

Use free Wi-Fi whenever possible. Unless you have an unlimited-data plan, save most of your online tasks for Wi-Fi (pronounced *wee-fee* in French). Most accommodations in Europe offer free Wi-Fi. Many cafés (including Starbucks and McDonald's) offer hotspots for customers; ask for the password when you buy something. You may also find Wi-Fi at TIs, city squares, major museums, public-transit hubs, important train stations, airports, and aboard trains and buses.

Minimize the use of your cellular network. The best way to make sure you're not accidentally burning through data is to put your device in "airplane" mode (which also disables phone calls and texts) and connect to Wi-Fi as needed. When you need to get online but can't find Wi-Fi, simply turn on your cellular network (or turn off airplane mode) just long enough for the task at hand.

Even with an international data plan, wait until you're on Wi-Fi to Skype or FaceTime, download apps, stream videos, or do other megabyte-greedy tasks. Using a navigation app such as Google Maps over a cellular network can require lots of data, so download maps when you're on Wi-Fi, then use the app offline.

Limit automatic updates. By default, your device constantly checks for a data connection and updates app content. Check your device's settings menu for ways to turn this off, and change your

How to Dial

Here's how to dial from anywhere in the US or Europe, using the phone number of one of my recommended Paris hotels as an example (01 47 05 25 45). If a number starts with 0, drop it when dialing internationally (except when calling Italy).

From a US Mobile Phone

Phone numbers in this book are presented exactly as you would dial them from a US mobile phone. For international access, press and hold 0 (zero) to get a + sign, then dial the country code (33 for France) and phone number.

▶ To call the Paris hotel from any location, dial +33 1 47 05 25 45.

From a US Landline

Replace + with 011 (US/Canada access code), then dial the country code (33 for France) and phone number.

▶ To call the Paris hotel from your home landline, dial 011 33 1 47 05 25 45.

From a European Landline

Replace + with 00 (Europe access code), then dial the country code (33 for France, 1 for the US) and phone number.

▶ To call the Paris hotel from a Spanish landline, dial 00 33 1 47 05 25 45.

▶ To call my US office from a French landline, dial 00 1 425 771 8303.

From One French Phone to Another

To place a domestic call (from a French landline or mobile), drop +33 and dial the phone number (including the initial 0).

▶ To call the Paris hotel from Nice, dial 01 47 05 25 45.

More Dialing Tips

Local Numbers: European phone numbers and area codes can vary in length and spacing, even within the same country. Mobile phones use separate prefixes (for instance, in France, Paris landline numbers begin with 01, and mobile numbers begin with 06 or 07).

Toll and Toll-Free Calls: It's generally not possible to dial European toll or toll-free numbers from a US mobile or landline (although you can sometimes get through using Skype). Look for a direct-dial number instead.

Calling the US from a US Mobile Phone, While Abroad: Dial +1, area code, and number.

More Phoning Help: See HowToCallAbroad.com.

email settings from "auto-retrieve" to "manual" (or from "push" to "fetch").

Use Wi-Fi calling and messaging apps. Skype, WhatsApp, FaceTime, and Google Meet are great for making free or low-cost voice calls or sending texts over Wi-Fi worldwide. Just log on to a Wi-Fi network, then connect with friends, family members, or local contacts who use the same service.

Buy a European SIM card. If you anticipate making a lot of local calls, need a local phone number, or your provider's international data rates are expensive, consider buying a SIM card in Europe to replace the one in your (unlocked) US phone or tablet. SIM cards are sold at department-store electronics counters, some newsstands (you may need to show your passport), and vending machines. If you need help setting it up, buy one at a mobile-phone shop. There are generally no roaming charges when using a European SIM card in other EU countries, but confirm when you buy.

WITHOUT A MOBILE PHONE

It's less convenient but possible to travel in Europe without a mobile device. You can make calls from your hotel and check email or get online using public computers.

Most **hotels** charge a fee for placing calls. Prepaid international phone cards *(cartes international)* are not widely used in France, but can be found at some newsstands, tobacco shops, and train stations.

Public computers are not always easy to find. Some hotels have one in their lobby for guests to use; otherwise you may find one at a public library (ask your hotelier or the TI for the nearest location). On a European keyboard, use the "Alt Gr" key to the right of the space bar to insert the extra symbol that appears on some keys. If you can't locate a special character (such as @), simply copy and paste it from a Web page.

MAIL

You can mail one package per day to yourself worth up to $200 duty-free from Europe to the US (mark it "personal purchases"). If you're sending a gift to someone, mark it "unsolicited gift." For details, visit www.cbp.gov, select "Travel," and search for "Know Before You Go."

The French postal service works fine, but for quick transatlantic delivery (in either direction), consider services such as DHL (DHL.com). French post offices are referred to as *La Poste* or sometimes the old-fashioned PTT, for "Post, Telegraph, and Telephone." Hours vary, though most are open weekdays 8:00-19:00 and Saturday morning 8:00-12:00. Stamps are also sold at *tabacs*. It costs about €1 to mail a postcard to the US. One convenient, if expensive, way to send packages home is to use the post office's Colissimo XL postage-paid mailing box. It costs €50-90 to ship boxes weighing 5-7 kilos (about 11-15 pounds).

Tips on Internet Security

Make sure that your device is running the latest versions of its operating system, security software, and apps. Next, ensure that your device and key programs (like email) are password-protected. On the road, use only secure, password-protected Wi-Fi. Ask the hotel or café staff for the specific name of their network, and make sure you log on to that exact one.

If you must access your financial info online, use a banking app rather than accessing your account via a browser, and use a cellular connection, not Wi-Fi. Never log on to personal finance sites on a public computer. If you're very concerned, consider subscribing to a VPN (virtual private network).

Transportation

If your trip will cover more of France than just Paris, you may need to take a long-distance train, rent a car, or fly. I give some specifics on trains and flights here. For more detailed information, see RickSteves.com/transportation.

TRAINS

France's SNCF rail system (short for Société Nationale Chemins de Fer) sets the pace in Europe. Its high-speed trains (TGV, tay zhay vay; *Train à Grande Vitesse*—also called "InOui") have inspired bullet trains throughout the world. The TGV, which requires a reservation, runs at 170-220 mph. Its rails are fused into one long, continuous track for a faster and smoother ride. The TGV has changed commuting patterns throughout France by putting most of the country within day-trip distance of Paris.

Any staffed train station has schedule information, can make reservations, and can sell tickets for any destination. For more on train travel, see RickSteves.com/rail.

Schedules

Schedules change by season, weekday, and weekend. Verify train times and frequencies shown in this book—online, go to Bahn. com (Germany's excellent all-Europe schedule site), or check locally at train stations. The French rail website is www.sncf.com; for online sales, go to http://oui.sncf.com. If you'll be traveling on long-distance trains without a rail pass, it's worth looking online, as advance-purchase discounts can be a great deal.

Bigger stations may have helpful information agents roaming the station (usually in bright red or blue vests) and at *Accueil* or *Information* offices or booths. Make use of their help; don't stand in a ticket line if all you need is a train schedule or to confirm a departure time.

Rail Passes

The single-country Eurail France Pass can be a good value for long-distance train travelers. Each day of use of your France Pass allows you to take as many trips as you want on one calendar day (you could go from Paris to Beaune in Burgundy, enjoy wine tasting, then continue to Avignon, stay a few hours, and end in Nice—though I wouldn't recommend it).

Rail passes are delivered electronically via email and must be activated through the Eurail Rail Planner app. Download the app before you leave home. To activate your pass, enter the following in the app: the pass number (provided in the rail pass email), your passport number, and pass activation date (your first day of travel using the pass). Before boarding any train with a digital pass, open the app and "register" the specific journey you're taking (regardless of whether the train requires seat reservations). The app then generates a barcode (or QR code) that the ticket inspector will scan.

Be aware that France's fast TGV and international trains require paid seat reservations (starting at €12). Particularly on international trains, places for rail-pass holders can be limited—which means trains may "sell out" for pass holders well before they've sold out for ticket buyers. Reserving these fast trains at least several weeks in advance is recommended (for strategies, see "Reservations," later).

You'll save money with the second-class version of the France Pass, but first class gives you more options when reserving popular TGV routes. A first-class pass also grants you access to "Salon des Grand Voyageurs" lounges in many bigger-city stations. These first-class lounges are more basic than airport lounges—but they often offer free coffee and water, Wi-Fi, WCs, and a place to charge your phone.

For most trips in France, buy second-class point-to-point tickets. Longer rides are where you can really save money with either a rail pass or advance-purchase ticket discounts.

If your trip extends beyond France, consider the **Eurail Global Pass,** covering most of Europe. If you buy two separate passes for neighboring countries, note that you'll use a travel day on each when crossing the border. For more detailed advice on figuring out the smartest rail-pass options for your train trip, visit RickSteves.com/rail.

Buying Tickets

Online: While there's no deadline to buy any train ticket, the fast, reserved TGV trains get booked up. Buy well ahead for any TGV you cannot afford to miss. Tickets go on sale four months in advance,

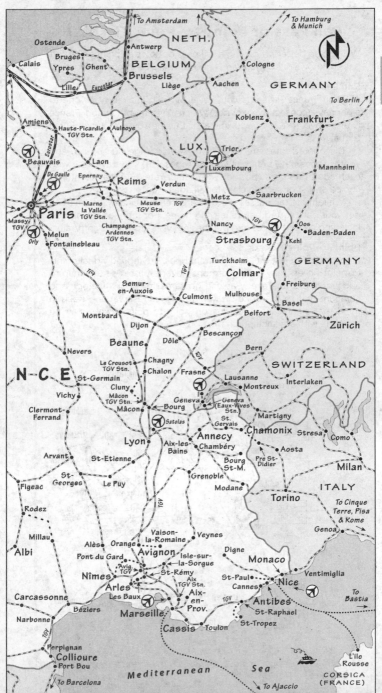

PRACTICALITIES

Rail Pass or Point-to-Point Tickets?

Will you be better off buying a rail pass or point-to-point tickets? It pays to know your options and choose what's best for your itinerary.

Rail Passes

A Eurail France Pass lets you travel by train in France for one to eight days (consecutively or not) within a one-month period. France is also covered (along with most of Europe) by the classic Eurail Global Pass.

Discounted rates are offered for seniors (age 60 and up) and youths (ages 12-27). Up to two kids (ages 4-11) can travel free with each adult-rate pass (but not with senior rates). All passes offer a choice of first or second class for all ages.

While most rail passes are delivered electronically, it's smart to get your pass sorted before leaving home. For more on rail passes, including current prices and purchasing, visit RickSteves.com/rail.

Point-to-Point Tickets

If you're taking just a couple of train rides, buying individual point-to-point tickets may save you money over a pass. Use this map to add up approximate pay-as-you-go fares for your itinerary, and compare that to the price of a rail pass plus reservations. Keep in mind that significant discounts on point-to-point tickets may be available with advance purchase.

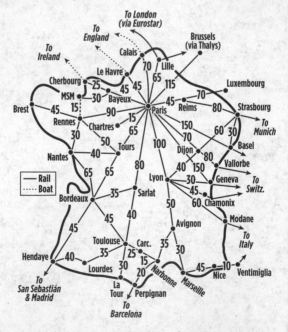

Map shows approximate costs, in US dollars, for one-way, second-class tickets on faster trains.

with a wide range of prices. The cheapest tickets sell out early and reservations for rail-pass holders also get more expensive as seats fill up.

To buy the cheapest advance-discount tickets (up to 60 percent less than full fare), visit http://oui.sncf.com three to four months ahead of your travel date. (A pop-up window may ask you to choose between being sent to the Rail Europe website or staying on the SNCF page—select "Stay.") Choose your train carefully, noting the departure and arrival stations and number of connections.

Some of the cheapest rates you'll see are for a no-frills version of TGV called OUIGO (www.ouigo.com). These run equally fast but have all second-class seating, luggage limits, seats assigned just a few days before departure—and early check-in is required. They sometimes use alternate stations (such as Marne-la-Vallée outside central Paris), and they don't accept rail passes. Most tickets are delivered electronically, and the site is easy to use.

Note that with either site, many US credit cards won't work unless your bank has certain security protocols set up, such as the "Verified by Visa," "MasterCard SecureCode," or "American Express SafeKey" programs. PayPal is accepted for just a few (nonrefundable) ticket types, not including OUIGO.

Aside from those two websites, US customers can order through a US agency, such as at RickSteves.com/rail, which does not sell OUIGO tickets; or Trainline (www.trainline.eu), which includes OUIGO departures (and accepts PayPal and Apple Pay). Both charge about the same rates (in euros or dollars).

Travelers have the option of saving tickets and reservations directly to their phones (choose "m-ticket"). For more details, see https://en.oui.sncf/en/mobile.

In France: You can buy train tickets in person at any train station, either from a staffed ticket window or from a machine. You can buy tickets on regional trains for a €10-60 surcharge depending on the length of your trip, but you must find the conductor immediately upon boarding; otherwise it's a €50 minimum charge.

The ticket machines available at most stations are great time savers when other lines are long. While most machines accept American chip cards if you know the PIN code, be prepared with euro coins and bills just in case. Some machines have English instructions, but for those that don't, here are the prompts. (Turn the dial or move the cursor to your choice, and press *"Validez"* to agree to each step.)

1. *Quelle est votre destination?* (What's your destination?)
2. *Billet Plein Tarif* (Full-fare ticket—yes for most.)
3. *1ère ou 2ème* (First or second class; normally second is fine.)
4. *Aller simple ou aller-retour?* (One-way or round-trip?)
5. *Prix en Euro* (The price should be shown if you get this far.)

Coping with Strikes

Going on strike (*en grève*) is a popular pastime in this revolution-happy country. Because bargaining between management and employees is not standard procedure, workers strike to get attention. Trucks and tractors block main roads and autoroutes (they call it Opération Escargot—"Operation Snail's Pace"), baggage handlers bring airports to their knees, and museum workers make artwork off-limits to tourists. Métro and train personnel seem to strike every year—probably during your trip. What does the traveler do? You could *jeter l'éponge* (throw in the sponge) and go somewhere less strike-prone (Switzerland's nice), or learn to accept certain events as out of your control. Strikes in France have become unpredictable in length, but if you're aware of them, you can usually plan around them. Your hotelier will know the latest (or can find out). Make a habit of asking your hotel receptionist about strikes. For a list of ongoing and upcoming strikes in France, check www.cestlagreve.fr.

Reservations

Reservations are required for any TGV or Intercité train, *couchettes* (sleeping berths) on night trains, and some other trains where indicated in timetables. You can reserve any train at any station any time before your departure. If you're buying a point-to-point ticket for a TGV or Intercité train, you'll reserve your seat when you purchase your ticket.

Popular TGV routes can fill up quickly. It's wise to book well ahead for any TGV, especially on the busy Paris-Avignon-Nice line. If the TGV trains you want are fully booked, ask about slower TER trains serving the same destination, as these don't require reservations.

If you're using a rail pass, reservations cost €12-20 for domestic travel, depending on the kind of train they're for and when you buy them. Seat reservations on international trains including Thalys, Eurostar, and international TGV routes usually range from €10 to €38, with the price depending on destination and class of service (and can cost up to €60 in first class on TGV Lyria trains to Swiss cities). These international routes allocate a very limited number of seats for rail-pass holders and accept only the Eurail Global Pass (no single-country passes).

Rail-pass holders can book TGV reservations directly at French stations up to departure, if still available, or book on Eurail's website (your account is linked with your pass in the Rail Planner app, though it's helpful to print your reservation as a back-up). Given the possible difficulty of getting TGV reservations with a rail pass, I recommend making those reservations online before you leave home.

Train Tips
At the Station

- Arrive at the station at least 30 minutes before your departure, when platform numbers are typically posted. Large stations have separate information *(accueil)* windows; at small stations the ticket office gives information.
- Small stations are minimally staffed; if there is no agent at the station, go directly to the tracks and look for the overhead sign that confirms your train stops at that track.
- Larger stations have platforms with monitors showing TGV layouts (numbered forward or backward) so you can figure out where your car *(voiture)* will stop on the long platform and where to board each car.
- Travelers with first-class tickets or rail passes can gain access to lounges at some stations (see "Rail Passes" earlier).

Validating Tickets, Reservations, and Rail Passes

- At major stations (including all Paris stations) you'll need to scan your ticket at turnstiles to access the tracks. Smaller stations without turnstiles continue to use the old system of validating your ticket in yellow machines near the platform or waiting area. Print-at-home tickets and etickets don't require validation.

- If you have a rail pass and your train requires a reservation, you may need to present your reservation QR code (in your Rail Planner app) for scanning before boarding the train. For all other trains, conductors will scan your code on board. Having a printed back-up or screenshot of your reservation code is helpful (in case Wi-Fi is spotty at the station and you can't use the app).

On the Train

- Before getting on a train, confirm that it's going where you think it is. For example, if you want to go to Chartres, ask the conductor or any local passenger, *"À Chartres?"* (ah shar-truh; meaning, "To Chartres?").
- Some longer trains split off cars en route. Make sure your train car is continuing to your destination by asking, for ex-

ample, *"Cette voiture va à Chartres?"* (seht vwah-tewr vah ah shar-truh; meaning, "This car goes to Chartres?").

- If a non-TGV train seat is reserved, it'll likely be labeled *réservé*, with the cities to and from which it is reserved.
- If you don't understand an announcement, ask your neighbor to explain: *"Pardon madame/monsieur, qu'est-ce qui se passe?"* (kehs kee suh pahs; "Excuse me, what's going on?").
- Verify with the conductor all the transfers you must make: *"Correspondance à Lyon?"* ("Must I transfer to get to Lyon?")
- To guard against theft, keep your bags in sight (directly overhead is ideal but rarely available—the early boarder gets the best storage space). If you must store them in the lower racks by the doors (available in most cars), pay attention at stops. Your bags are most vulnerable to theft before the train takes off and whenever it stops.
- Note your arrival time, so you'll be ready to get off.
- Use the train's free WCs before you get off.

TAXIS AND RIDE-BOOKING SERVICES

Most European taxis are reliable and reasonable. In many cities, two people can travel short distances by cab for little more than the cost of bus or subway tickets. If you like ride-booking services such as Uber, their apps usually work in Europe just like they do in the US: Request a car on your mobile phone (connected to Wi-Fi or data), and the fare is automatically charged to your credit card. In France, Uber services generally work in only the largest cities and are not much cheaper than taxis.

Blablacar is a popular long-distance ride-sharing service, connecting drivers with riders who can share the cost of gas, freeway tolls, and other expenses (www.blablacar.in). It's the cheapest way to get around France.

FLIGHTS

To compare flights, begin with an online travel search engine: Kayak is the top site for flights to and within Europe, easy-to-use Google Flights has price alerts, and Skyscanner includes many inexpensive flights within Europe. To avoid unpleasant surprises, before you book be sure to read the small print about refunds, changes, and the costs for "extras" such as reserving a seat, checking a bag, or printing a boarding pass.

Flights to Europe: Start looking for international flights about four to six months before your trip, especially for peak-season travel. Depending on your itinerary, it can be efficient and no more expensive to fly into one city and out of another. If your flight requires a connection in Europe, see our hints on navigating Europe's top hub airports at RickSteves.com/hub-airports.

Flights Within Europe: Flying between European cities is surprisingly affordable. If you're visiting one or more French cities on a longer European trip—or linking up far-flung French cities (such as Paris and Nice)—a flight can save both time and money. Before buying a long-distance train or bus ticket, first check the cost of a flight on one of Europe's airlines, whether a major carrier or a no-frills outfit like EasyJet or Vueling (which fly out of Charles de Gaulle and Orly airports) or Ryanair (which flies out of Beauvais Airport). Also check Air France for specials. Be aware that flying with a discount airline can have drawbacks, such as minimal customer service, time-consuming treks to secondary airports, and a larger carbon footprint than a train or bus.

Flying to the US and Canada: Because security is extra tight for flights to the US, be sure to give yourself plenty of time at the airport (see www.tsa.gov for the latest rules).

Resources from Rick Steves

Begin Your Trip at RickSteves.com

My mobile-friendly **website** is *the* place to explore Europe in preparation for your trip. You'll find thousands of fun articles, videos, and radio interviews; a wealth of money-saving tips for planning your dream trip; travel news dispatches; a video library of travel talks, my travel blog; our latest guidebook updates (RickSteves.com/update); and the free Rick Steves Audio Europe app. You can also follow me on Facebook, Instagram, and Twitter.

Our **Travel Forum** is a well-groomed collection of message boards where our travel-savvy community answers questions and shares their personal travel experiences—and our well-traveled staff chimes in when they can be helpful (RickSteves.com/forums).

Our **online Travel Store** offers bags and accessories that I've designed to help you travel smarter and lighter. These include my popular carry-on bags (which I live out of four months a year), money belts, totes, toiletries kits, adapters, guidebooks, and planning maps (RickSteves.com/shop).

Our website can also help you find the perfect **rail pass** for your itinerary and your budget, with easy, one-stop shopping for rail passes, seat reservations, and point-to-point tickets (RickSteves.com/rail).

Rick Steves' Tours, Guidebooks, TV Shows, and More

Small Group Tours: Want to travel with greater efficiency and less stress? We offer more than 40 itineraries reaching the best destinations in this book...and beyond. Each year about 30,000

PRACTICALITIES

travelers join us on about 1,000 Rick Steves bus tours. You'll enjoy great guides and a fun bunch of travel partners (with small groups of around 24 to 28 travelers). You'll find European adventures to fit every vacation length. For all the details, and to get our tour catalog, visit RickSteves.com/tours or call us at +1 425 608 4217.

Books: This book is just one of many books in my series on European travel, which includes country and city guidebooks, Snapshots (excerpted chapters from bigger guides), Pocket Guides (full-color little books on big cities), "Best Of" guidebooks (condensed, full-color country guides), and my budget-travel skills handbook, *Rick Steves Europe Through the Back Door.* A complete list of my titles—including phrase books, cruising guides, and travelogues on European art, history, and culture—appears near the end of this book.

TV Shows and Travel Talks: My public television series, *Rick Steves' Europe,* covers Europe from top to bottom with over 100 half-hour episodes—and we're working on new shows every year (watch full episodes on my website for free). My free online video library, Rick Steves Classroom Europe, offers a searchable database of short video clips on European history, culture, and geography (Classroom.RickSteves.com). And to raise your travel I.Q., check out the video versions of our popular classes (covering most European countries as well as travel skills, packing smart, cruising, tech for travelers, European art, and travel as a political act—RickSteves.com/travel-talks).

Audio Tours on My Free App: I've produced dozens of free, self-guided audio tours of the top sights in Europe. For those tours and other audio content, get my free **Rick Steves Audio Europe app,** an extensive online library organized by destination. For more on my app, see page 24.

Radio: My weekly public radio show, *Travel with Rick Steves,* features interviews with travel experts from around the world. It airs on 400 public radio stations across the US. An archive of programs is available at RickSteves.com/radio.

Podcasts: You can enjoy my travel content via several free podcasts. The podcast version of my radio show brings you a weekly, hour-long travel conversation. My other podcasts include a weekly selection of video clips from my public television show, my audio tours of Europe's top sights, and live recordings of my travel classes (RickSteves.com/watch-read-listen/audio/podcasts).

APPENDIX

Holidays and Festivals

This list includes selected festivals in Paris, plus national holidays observed throughout France. Many sights and banks close on national holidays—keep this in mind when planning your itinerary. Paris is lively with festivals and events throughout the summer and fall. Before planning a trip around a festival, verify the dates with the festival website, the Paris tourist office, or my "Upcoming Holidays and Festivals in France" web page (RickSteves.com/europe/france/festivals).

In Paris, hotels get booked up Easter weekend (note that Easter Monday is a holiday, and the weeks before and after are also busy), Labor Day, V-E Day, Ascension weekend, Pentecost weekend, Bastille Day and the week during which it falls, and the winter holidays (last half of December). Avoid leaving Paris at the beginning of one of these holiday weekends or returning at the end—you'll be competing with Parisians for seats on planes and trains, or fighting them in traffic on the roadways.

If you're in Paris during Christmas, see the Paris in Winter chapter for information on things to do. (Christmas week is generally quieter than the week of New Year's.)

Here are some major holidays and festivals in 2023 and 2024:

Jan 1	New Year's Day
Late March	Daylight Saving begins: March 26, 2023; March 31, 2024
March/April	Easter weekend (Good Friday-Easter Monday): April 7-10, 2023; March 29-April 1, 2024
May 1	Labor Day
May 8	V-E (Victory in Europe) Day
May	Ascension: May 18, 2023; May 9, 2024
May/June	Pentecost and Whit Monday: May 28-29, 2023; May 19-20, 2024
May (last Sunday)	Mother's Day in France
Late May-early June	French Open tennis tournament
May-June	St. Denis Festival (classical concerts by international artists; www.festival-saint-denis.com)
June (third Sunday)	Father's Day in France
June 21	Fête de la Musique (concerts and dancing in the streets; http://fetedelamusique.culturecommunication.gouv.fr)
July	Tour de France (national bicycle race culminating in Paris; www.letour.fr)
July 14	Bastille Day (fireworks, dancing, and revelry)
Mid-July-mid-Aug	Paris Neighborhoods Festival (theater, dance, and concerts around the city)
Mid-July-mid Aug	Paris Plages (ersatz beach along the Seine)
Aug 15	Assumption of Mary
Late Aug-mid-Sept	La Villette Jazz Festival (outdoor concerts; www.jazzalavillette.com)
Sept	Festival of Autumn (theater, dance, film, and opera performances; www.festival-automne.com)
Early Oct	Fête des Vendanges (grape harvest festival and parades in Montmartre; www.fetedesvendangesdemontmartre.com)
Late Oct	Daylight Saving ends: Oct 29, 2023; Oct 27, 2024
Nov 1	All Saints' Day
Nov 11	Armistice Day
Dec 25	Christmas Day
Dec 31	New Year's Eve

Books and Films

To learn more about France past and present, and specifically Paris, check out a few of these books or films. For kids' recommendations, see the Paris with Children chapter. To learn what's making news in France, you'll find *France 24 News* online at www.France24.com/en. To experience expat life in Paris from home, a fun website is www.secretsofparis.com.

Nonfiction

A to Z of French Food, a French to English Dictionary of Culinary Terms (G. de Temmerman, 1995). This is the most complete (and priciest) menu reader around—and it's beloved by foodies. You can find it cheaper in France (try FNAC department stores) or by downloading the app.

Almost French: Love and a New Life in Paris (Sarah Turnbull, 2003). Turnbull takes an amusing look at adopting a famously frosty city.

Americans in Paris: Life and Death Under Nazi Occupation (Charles Glass, 2009). Using stories from American expatriates, Glass transports readers back to Nazi-occupied Paris in the early 1940s.

The Art Lover's Guide to Paris (Ruby Boukabou, 2019). Pick up this guide for terrific, up-to-date information for enjoying Paris' art scene. It also lists dates of important art and photography festivals in Paris.

The Cambridge Illustrated History of France (Colin Jones, 1995). The political, social, and cultural history of France is explored in detail, accompanied by coffee-table-book pictures and illustrations.

A Corner in the Marais (Alex Karmel, 1998). After buying a flat in the Marais, the author digs into the history of the building—and the evolution of one of Paris' great neighborhoods.

The Course of French History (Pierre Goubert, 1988). Goubert provides a readable summary of French history.

Culture Shock! France (Sally Adamson Taylor, 2012). Demystify French culture—and the French people—with this good introduction.

Don't Be a Tourist In Paris (Vanessa Grall, 2017). This book, by the creator of a well-known blog called *Messy Nessy Chic* (https://book.messynessychic.com/), offers tips for finding lesser-known experiences in Paris.

The Flâneur (Edmund White, 2001). Reading this book is like wandering the streets of Paris with the author, who lived here for 16 years.

French or Foe? (Polly Platt, 1994). This best seller, along with its follow-up, *Savoir-Flair!*, is helpful (if somewhat dated) for interacting with the French and navigating the intricacies of their culture.

From Here, You Can't See Paris: Seasons of a French Village and Its Restaurant (Michael S. Sanders, 2002). Foodies may enjoy this book about a small-town restaurant where foie gras is always on the menu.

Half an Hour from Paris (Annabel Simms, 2018). Living in Paris since 1991, Simms offers insights for exploring the Paris countryside by train and discovering little-known travel gems.

How Paris Became Paris: The Invention of the Modern City (Joan DeJean, 2014). DeJean describes how Paris emerged from the Dark Ages to become the world's grandest city.

I'll Always Have Paris (Art Buchwald, 1996). The American humorist recounts life as a Paris correspondent during the 1940s and 1950s.

Into a Paris Quartier: Reine Margot's Chapel and Other Haunts of St. Germain (Diane Johnson, 2005). The author acquaints readers with the sixth arrondissement by recounting her strolls through this iconic neighborhood.

Is Paris Burning? (Larry Collins and Dominique Lapierre, 1964). Set in the last days of the Nazi occupation, this is the story of the French Resistance and how a German general disobeyed Hitler's order to destroy Paris.

La Seduction: How the French Play the Game of Life (Elaine Sciolino, 2011). Sciolino, former Paris bureau chief of the *New York Times*, gives travelers a fun, insightful, and tantalizing peek into how seduction is used in all aspects of French life—from small villages to the halls of national government.

A Moveable Feast (Ernest Hemingway, 1964). Paris in the 1920s as recalled by Hemingway.

My Life in France (Julia Child, 1996). The inimitably zesty chef recounts her early days in Paris.

The New Paris (Lindsey Tramuta, 2017). A writer based in Paris takes a fresh, personal look at the city, revealing new trends in food, drink, fashion, and design with eye-catching photos.

Paris Noir: African Americans in the City of Light (Tyler Stovall, 1996). Stovall explains why African Americans found Paris so freeing in the first half of the 20th century.

Paris to the Moon (Adam Gopnik, 2000). This collection of essays and journal entries explores the idiosyncrasies of life in France from a New Yorker's point of view. His literary anthology, *Americans in Paris,* is also recommended.

A Place in the World Called Paris (Steven Barclay, 1994). This anthology includes essays by literary greats from Truman Capote to Franz Kafka.

Sixty Million Frenchmen Can't Be Wrong (Jean-Benoit Nadeau and Julie Barlow, 2003). This is a must-read for anyone serious about understanding French culture, contemporary politics, and what makes the French tick.

The Sweet Life in Paris (David Lebovitz, 2009). Funny and articulate, pastry chef and cookbook author Lebovitz delivers oodles of food suggestions for travelers.

Travelers' Tales: Paris and *Travelers' Tales: France* (edited by James O'Reilly, Larry Habegger, and Sean O'Reilly, 2002). Notable writers explore Parisian and French culture.

Fiction

City of Darkness, City of Light (Marge Piercy, 1996). Three French women play pivotal roles behind the scenes during the French Revolution.

The Hotel Majestic (Georges Simenon, 1942). Ernest Hemingway was a fan of Simenon, a Belgian writer who often set his Inspector Maigret detective books, including this one, in Paris.

Le Divorce (Diane Johnson, 1997). An American woman visits her stepsister and husband in Paris during a time of marital crisis (also a 2003 movie with Kate Hudson).

Murder in the Marais (Cara Black, 1999). Set in Vichy-era Paris, private investigator Aimée Leduc finds herself at the center of a murder mystery.

Night Soldiers (Alan Furst, 1988). The first of Furst's gripping WWII espionage novels puts you right into the action in Paris.

Suite Française (Irène Némirovsky, 2004). Némirovsky, a Russian Jew who was living in France and died at Auschwitz in 1942, plunges readers into the chaotic WWII evacuation of Paris, as well as daily life in a small rural town during the ensuing German occupation.

A Tale of Two Cities (Charles Dickens, 1859). Dickens' gripping tale shows the pathos and horror of the French Revolution.

A Year in the Merde (Stephen Clarke, 2004). Englishman Paul West takes on life as a *faux* Parisian in this lighthearted novel that relies on some stereotypes.

Film and TV

Amélie (2001). A charming waitress searches for love in Paris.

Before Sunset (2004). Nine years after meeting on a train to Vienna, Jesse and Celine (played by Ethan Hawke and Julie Delpy) are reunited in Paris.

Breathless (1960). A Parisian petty thief (Jean-Paul Belmondo) persuades an American student (Jean Seberg) to run away with him in this classic of French New Wave cinema.

Children of Paradise (1945). This melancholy romance was filmed during the Nazi occupation of Paris.

Dangerous Liaisons (1988). This inside look at sex, intrigue, and revenge takes place in the last days of the French aristocracy in pre-Revolutionary Paris.

The Intouchables (2011). A quadriplegic Parisian aristocrat hires a personal caregiver from the projects, and an unusual and touching friendship ensues.

Jules and Jim (1962). François Truffaut, the master of the French New Wave, explores a decades-long love triangle in this classic.

La Vie en Rose (2007). Marion Cotillard won the Best Actress Oscar for this film about the glamorous and turbulent life of singer Edith Piaf, who famously regretted nothing (many scenes were shot in Paris).

Les Misérables (2012). A Frenchman trying to escape his criminal past becomes wrapped up in Revolutionary intrigues (based on Victor Hugo's 1862 novel).

Lost in Paris (2017). This funny, quirky film follows a young Canadian librarian who flies to Paris on a fluke and finds love while searching for her missing aunt.

Loving Vincent (2017). The first fully painted animated feature film, this movie follows an investigation into Vincent van Gogh's final days before his death in Auvers-sur-Oise.

Marie Antoinette (2006). Kirsten Dunst stars as the infamous and misunderstood French queen (with a Californian accent) at Versailles in this delicate little bonbon of a film.

Midnight in Paris (2011). Woody Allen's sharp comedy shifts between today's Paris and the 1920s mecca of Picasso, Hemingway, and Fitzgerald.

Moulin Rouge! (2001). Baz Luhrmann's fanciful musical is set in the legendary Montmartre nightclub.

Ridicule (1996). A nobleman navigates the opulent court of Louis XVI on his wits alone.

Ronin (1998). Robert De Niro stars in this crime caper, which includes a car chase through Paris and scenes filmed in Nice, Villefranche-sur-Mer, and Arles.

Three Colors trilogy (1990s). Krzysztof Kieślowski's stylish trilogy (*Blue, White,* and *Red*) is based on France's national motto—"Liberty, Equality, and Fraternity." Each features a famous French actress as the lead (*Blue,* with Juliette Binoche, is the best).

The Triplets of Belleville (2003). This surreal-yet-heartwarming animated film begins in a very Parisian fictional city.

Conversions and Climate

Numbers and Stumblers

- Europeans write a few of their numbers differently than we do: 1 = 1, 4 = 4, 7 = 7.
- In Europe, dates appear as day/month/year, so Christmas 2023 is 25/12/23.
- Commas are decimal points and decimals are commas. A dollar and a half is $1,50, one thousand is 1.000, and there are 5.280 feet in a mile.
- When counting with fingers, start with your thumb. If you hold up your first finger to request one item, you'll probably get two.
- What Americans call the second floor of a building is the first floor in Europe.
- On escalators and moving sidewalks, Europeans keep the left "lane" open for passing. Keep to the right.

Metric Conversions

A **kilogram** equals 1,000 grams (about 2.2 pounds). One hundred **grams** (a common unit at markets) is about a quarter-pound. One **liter** is about a quart, or almost four to a gallon.

A **kilometer** is six-tenths of a mile. To convert kilometers to miles, cut the kilometers in half and add back 10 percent of the original (120 km: 60 + 12 = 72 miles). One **meter** is 39 inches—just over a yard.

1 foot = 0.3 meter	1 square yard = 0.8 square meter
1 yard = 0.9 meter	1 square mile = 2.6 square kilometers
1 mile = 1.6 kilometers	1 ounce = 28 grams
1 centimeter = 0.4 inch	1 quart = 0.95 liter
1 meter = 39.4 inches	1 kilogram = 2.2 pounds
1 kilometer = 0.62 mile	32°F = 0°C

Clothing Sizes

When shopping for clothing, use these US-to-European comparisons as general guidelines (but note that no conversion is perfect).

Women: For pants and dresses, add 32 in France (US 10 = French 42). For blouses and sweaters, add 8 for most of Europe (US 32 = European 40). For shoes, add 30-31 (US 7 = European 37/38).

Men: For shirts, multiply by 2 and add about 8 (US 15 = European 38). For jackets and suits, add 10. For shoes, add 32-34.

Children: Clothing is sized by height—in centimeters (2.5 cm = 1 inch), so a US size 8 roughly equates to 132-140. For shoes up to size 13, add 16-18, and for sizes 1 and up, add 30-32.

Paris' Climate

First line, average daily high; second line, average daily low; third line, average days without rain. For more detailed weather statistics for destinations in this book (as well as the rest of the world), check Wunderground.com.

J	F	M	A	M	J	J	A	S	O	N	D
Paris											
43°	45°	54°	60°	68°	73°	76°	75°	70°	60°	50°	44°
34°	34°	39°	43°	49°	55°	58°	58°	53°	46°	40°	36°
14	14	19	17	19	18	19	18	17	18	15	15

APPENDIX

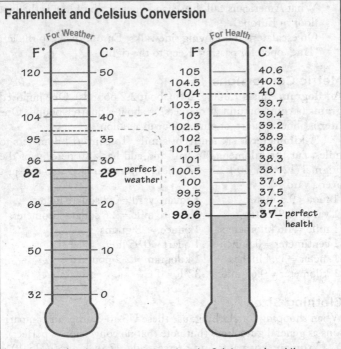

Fahrenheit and Celsius Conversion

Europe takes its temperature using the Celsius scale, while we opt for Fahrenheit. For a rough conversion from Celsius to Fahrenheit, double the number and add 30. For weather, remember that 28°C is 82°F—perfect. For health, 37°C is just right. At a launderette, 30°C is cold, 40°C is warm (usually the default setting), 60°C is hot, and 95°C is boiling. Your air-conditioner should be set at about 20°C.

Packing Checklist

Whether you're traveling for five days or five weeks, you won't need more than this. Pack light to enjoy the sweet freedom of true mobility.

Clothing

- ☐ 5 shirts: long- & short-sleeve
- ☐ 2 pairs pants (or skirts/capris)
- ☐ 1 pair shorts
- ☐ 5 pairs underwear & socks
- ☐ 1 pair walking shoes
- ☐ Sweater or warm layer
- ☐ Rainproof jacket with hood
- ☐ Tie, scarf, belt, and/or hat
- ☐ Swimsuit
- ☐ Sleepwear/loungewear

Money

- ☐ Debit card(s)
- ☐ Credit card(s)
- ☐ Hard cash (US $100-200)
- ☐ Money belt

Documents

- ☐ Passport
- ☐ Other required ID: Vaccine card/Covid test, entry visa, etc.
- ☐ Driver's license, student ID, hostel card, etc.
- ☐ Tickets & confirmations: flights, hotels, trains, rail pass, car rental, sight entries
- ☐ Photocopies of important documents
- ☐ Insurance details
- ☐ Guidebooks & maps

Electronics

- ☐ Mobile phone
- ☐ Camera & related gear
- ☐ Tablet/ebook reader/laptop
- ☐ Headphones/earbuds
- ☐ Chargers & batteries
- ☐ Phone car charger & mount (or GPS device)
- ☐ Plug adapters

Toiletries

- ☐ Basics: soap, shampoo, toothbrush, toothpaste, floss, deodorant, sunscreen, brush/comb, etc.
- ☐ Medicines & vitamins
- ☐ First-aid kit
- ☐ Glasses/contacts/sunglasses
- ☐ Face masks & hand sanitizer
- ☐ Sewing kit
- ☐ Packet of tissues (for WC)
- ☐ Earplugs

Miscellaneous

- ☐ Daypack
- ☐ Sealable plastic baggies
- ☐ Laundry supplies: soap, laundry bag, clothesline, spot remover
- ☐ Small umbrella
- ☐ Travel alarm/watch
- ☐ Notepad & pen
- ☐ Journal

Optional Extras

- ☐ Second pair of shoes (flip-flops, sandals, tennis shoes, boots)
- ☐ Travel hairdryer
- ☐ Picnic supplies
- ☐ Disinfecting wipes
- ☐ Water bottle
- ☐ Fold-up tote bag
- ☐ Small flashlight
- ☐ Mini binoculars
- ☐ Small towel or washcloth
- ☐ Inflatable pillow/neck rest
- ☐ Tiny lock
- ☐ Address list (to mail postcards)
- ☐ Extra passport photos

PRONOUNCING PARIS PLACE NAMES

When using the phonetics: Try to nasalize the n sound (let the sound come through your nose). Note that the "ahn" combination uses the "ah" sound in "father," but the "an" combination uses the "a" sound in "sack." Pronounce the "ī" as the long "i" in "light." If your best attempt at pronunciation meets with a puzzled look, just point to the place name on the list.

Arc de Triomphe ark duh tree-ohnf

arrondissement ah-rohn-dees-mohn

Art Nouveau ar noo-voh

Auvers-sur-Oise oh-vehr-sewr-wahz

Bateaux Mouches bah-toh moosh

Bon Marché bohn mar-shay

boulangerie boo-lahn-zheh-ree

Carnavalet kar-nah-val-eh

Champ de Mars shahn duh mar

Champs-Elysées shahn-zay-lee-zay

Chantilly shahn-tee-yee

charcuterie shar-kew-tuh-ree

Chartres shar-truh

château(x) shah-toh

Cité see-tay

Cité des Sciences see-tay day see-ahns

Conciergerie kon-see-ehr-zhuh-ree

Contrescarpe kohn-truh-scarp

droguerie droh-guh-ree

Ecole Militaire ay-kohl mee-lee-tair

Egouts ay-goo

Fauchon foh-shohn

Fontainebleau fohn-tehn-bloh

fromagerie froh-mah-zhuh-ree

Galeries Lafayette gah-luh-ree lah-fay-yet

gare gar

Gare d'Austerlitz gar doh-stehr-leets

Gare de l'Est gar duh lehst

Gare de Lyon gar duh lee-ohn

Gare du Nord gar dew nor

Gare St. Lazare gar san lah-zahr

Giverny zhee-vayr-nee

Grand Palais grahn pah-lay

Grande Arche de la Défense grahnd arsh duh lah day-fahns

Hôtel de Sully oh-tehl duh soo-lee

Ile de la Cité eel duh lah see-tay

Ile St. Louis eel san loo-ee

Jacquemart-André zhahk-mar-ahn-dray

jardin zhar-dan

Jardin des Plantes zhar-dan day plahnt

Jeu de Paume juh duh pohm

La Coulée Verte lah koo-lay vehrt

La Madeleine lah mah-duh-lehn

Le Hameau luh ah-moh

Les Halles lay zahl

Les Invalides lay-zan-vah-leed

Loire lwahr

L'Orangerie loh-rahn-zhuh-ree

Louvre loov-ruh

Marais mah-ray

Marché aux Puces mar-shay oh pews

Marmottan mar-moh-tahn

Métro may-troh

Monge mohnzh

Montmartre mohn-mart

Montparnasse mohn-par-nas

Moulin Rouge moo-lan roozh

musée mew-zay

Musée de l'Armée mew-zay duh lar-may

Musée d'Orsay mew-zay dor-say

Notre-Dame noh-truh-dahm

Opéra Garnier oh-pay-rah gar-nee-ay

Orangerie oh-rahn-zhuh-ree

Orsay or-say

palais pah-lay

Palais de Justice pah-lay duh zhew-stees

Palais Royal pah-lay roh-yahl

Parc de la Villette park duh lah vee-leht

Parc Monceau park mohn-soh

Père Lachaise pehr lah-shehz

Petit Palais puh-tee pah-lay

Pigalle pee-gahl

place plahs

Place Dauphine plahs doh-feen

Place de la Bastille plahs duh lah bah-steel

Place de la Concorde plahs duh lah kohn-kord

Place de la République plahs duh lah ray-pew-bleek

Place des Vosges plahs day vohzh

Place du Tertre plahs dew tehr-truh

Place St. André-des-Arts plahs san tahn-dray-day-zart

Place Vendôme plahs vahn-dohm

Pompidou pohn-pee-doo

pont pohn

Pont Alexandre III pohn ah-lehks-ahn-druh trwah

Pont Neuf pohn nuhf

quai kay

Rive Droite reev drwaht

Rive Gauche reev gohsh

Rodin roh-dan

rue rew

Rue Cler rew klehr

Rue Daguerre rew dah-gehr

Rue des Rosiers rew day roz-ee-ay

Rue Montorgueil rew mohn-tor-goy

Rue Mouffetard rew moof-tar

Rue de Rivoli rew duh ree-voh-lee

Sacré-Cœur sah-kray-kur

Sainte-Chapelle sant-shah-pehl

Seine sehn

Sèvres-Babylone seh-vruh bah-bee-lohn

Sorbonne sor-buhn

St. Germain-des-Prés san zhehr-man-day-pray

St. Julien-le-Pauvre san zhew-lee-an-luh-poh-vruh

St. Séverin san say-vuh-ran

St. Sulpice san sool-pees

Tour Eiffel toor ee-fehl

Trianon tree-ahn-ohn

Trocadéro troh-kah-day-roh

Tuileries twee-lay-ree

Vaux-le-Vicomte voh-luh-vee-komt

Venus de Milo veh-news duh mee-loh

Versailles vehr-sī

French Survival Phrases

When using the phonetics, try to nasalize the <u>n</u> sound.

Good day.	Bonjour.	bohn-zhoor
Mrs. / Mr.	Madame / Monsieur	mah-dahm / muhs-yuh
Do you speak English?	Parlez-vous anglais?	par-lay-voo ah<u>n</u>-glay
Yes. / No.	Oui. / Non.	wee / noh<u>n</u>
I understand.	Je comprends.	zhuh koh<u>n</u>-prah<u>n</u>
I don't understand.	Je ne comprends pas.	zhuh nuh koh<u>n</u>-prah<u>n</u> pah
Please.	S'il vous plaît.	see voo play
Thank you.	Merci.	mehr-see
I'm sorry.	Désolé.	day-zoh-lay
Excuse me.	Pardon.	par-doh<u>n</u>
No problem.	Pas de problème.	pah duh proh-blehm
It's good.	C'est bon.	say boh<u>n</u>
Goodbye.	Au revoir.	oh ruh-vwahr
one / two / three	un / deux / trois	uh<u>n</u> / duh / trwah
four / five / six	quatre / cinq / six	kah-truh / sa<u>n</u>k / sees
seven / eight	sept / huit	seht / weet
nine / ten	neuf / dix	nuhf / dees
How much is it?	C'est combien?	say koh<u>n</u>-bee-a<u>n</u>
Write it?	Ecrivez?	ay-kree-vay
Is it free?	C'est gratuit?	say grah-twee
Included?	Inclus?	a<u>n</u>-klew
Where can I buy / find...?	Où puis-je acheter / trouver...?	oo pwee-zhuh ah-shuh-tay / troo-vay
I'd like / We'd like...	Je voudrais / Nous voudrions...	zhuh voo-dray / noo voo-dree-oh<u>n</u>
...a room.	...une chambre.	ewn shah<u>n</u>-bruh
...a ticket to ___.	...un billet pour ___.	uh<u>n</u> bee-yay poor ___
Is it possible?	C'est possible?	say poh-see-bluh
Where is...?	Où est...?	oo ay
...the train station	...la gare	lah gar
...the bus station	...la gare routière	lah gar root-yehr
...tourist information	...l'office du tourisme	loh-fees dew too-reez-muh
Where are the toilets?	Où sont les toilettes?	oo soh<u>n</u> lay twah-leht
men / women	hommes / dames	ohm / dahm
left / right	à gauche / à droite	ah gohsh / ah drwaht
straight	tout droit	too drwah
pull / push	tirez / poussez	tee-ray / poo-say
When does this open / close?	Ça ouvre / ferme à quelle heure?	sah oo-vruh / fehrm ah kehl ur
At what time?	À quelle heure?	ah kehl ur
Just a moment.	Un moment.	uh<u>n</u> moh-mah<u>n</u>
now / soon / later	maintenant / bientôt / plus tard	ma<u>n</u>-tuh-nah<u>n</u> / bee-a<u>n</u>-toh / plew tar
today / tomorrow	aujourd'hui / demain	oh-zhoor-dwee / duh-ma<u>n</u>

In a French Restaurant

I'd like / We'd like...	Je voudrais / Nous voudrions... zhuh voo-dray / noo voo-dree-ohn
...to reserve...	...réserver... ray-zehr-vay
...a table for one / two.	...une table pour un / deux. ewn tah-bluh poor uhn / duh
Is this seat free?	C'est libre? say lee-bruh
The menu (in English), please.	La carte (en anglais), s'il vous plaît. lah kart (ahn ahn-glay) see voo play
service (not) included	service (non) compris sehr-vees (nohn) kohn-pree
to go	à emporter ah ahn-por-tay
with / without	avec / sans ah-vehk / sahn
and / or	et / ou ay / oo
breakfast / lunch / dinner	petit déjeuner / déjeuner / dîner puh-tee day-zhuh-nay / day-zhuh-nay / dee-nay
special of the day	plat du jour plah dew zhoor
specialty of the house	spécialité de la maison spay-see-ah-lee-tay duh lah may-zohn
appetizers	hors d'œuvre or duh-vruh
first course (soup, salad)	entrée ahn-tray
main course (meat, fish)	plat principal plah pran-see-pahl
bread / cheese	pain / fromage pan / froh-mahzh
sandwich / soup	sandwich / soupe sahnd-weech / soop
salad	salade sah-lahd
meat / chicken	viande / poulet vee-ahnd / poo-lay
fish / seafood	poisson / fruits de mer pwah-sohn / frwee duh mehr
fruit / vegetables	fruit / légumes frwee / lay-gewm
dessert	dessert day-sehr
mineral water	eau minérale oh mee-nay-rahl
tap water	l'eau du robinet loh dew roh-bee-nay
(orange) juice	jus (d'orange) zhew (doh-rahnzh)
coffee / tea / milk	café / thé / lait kah-fay / tay / lay
wine / beer	vin / bière van / bee-ehr
red / white	rouge / blanc roozh / blahn
glass / bottle	verre / bouteille vehr / boo-tay
Cheers!	Santé! sahn-tay
More. / Another.	Plus. / Un autre. plew / uhn oh-truh
The same.	La même chose. lah mehm shohz
The bill, please.	L'addition, s'il vous plaît. lah-dee-see-ohn see voo play
Do you accept credit cards?	Vous prenez les cartes? voo pruh-nay lay kart
tip	pourboire poor-bwahr
Delicious!	Délicieux! day-lees-yuh

For more user-friendly French phrases, check out *Rick Steves' French Phrase Book* or *Rick Steves' French, Italian & German Phrase Book*.

INDEX

INDEX

MAP INDEX

MAP INDEX

Explore Europe

At ricksteves.com you can browse through thousands of articles, videos, photos and radio interviews, plus find a wealth of money-saving travel tips for planning your dream trip. And with our mobile-friendly website, you can easily access all this great travel information anywhere you go.

TV Shows

Preview the places you'll visit by watching entire half-hour episodes of *Rick Steves' Europe* (choose from all 100 shows) on-demand, for free.

ricksteves.com

your travel dreams into affordable reality

Radio Interviews

Enjoy ready access to Rick's vast library of radio interviews covering travel tips and cultural insights that relate specifically to your Europe travel plans.

Travel Forums

Learn, ask, share! Our online community of savvy travelers is a great resource for first-time travelers to Europe, as well as seasoned pros.

Travel News

Subscribe to our free Travel News e-newsletter, and get monthly updates from Rick on what's happening in Europe.

Classroom Europe®

Check out our free resource for educators with 500 short video clips from the *Rick Steves' Europe* TV show.

Audio Europe™

Pack Light and Right

Gear up for your next adventure at ricksteves.com

Light Luggage

Pack light and right with Rick Steves' affordable, custom-designed rolling carry-on bags, backpacks, day packs and shoulder bags.

Accessories

From packing cubes to moneybelts and beyond, Rick has personally selected the travel goodies that will help your trip go smoother.

Rick Steves has

Save time and energy

This guidebook is your independent-travel toolkit. But for all it delivers, it's still up to you to devote the time and energy it takes to manage the preparation and logistics that are essential for a happy trip. If that's a hassle, there's a solution.

Rick Steves Tours

A Rick Steves tour takes you to Europe's most interesting places with great

great tours, too!

guides and small groups. We follow Rick's favorite itineraries, ride in comfy buses, stay in family-run hotels, and bring you intimately close to the Europe you've traveled so far to see. Most importantly, we take away the logistical headaches so you can focus on the fun.

Join the fun

This year we'll take thousands of free-spirited travelers—nearly half of them repeat customers—along with us on 50 different itineraries, from Athens to Istanbul. Is a Rick Steves tour the right fit for your travel dreams?

Find out at ricksteves.com, where you can also check seat availability and sign up. Europe is best experienced with happy travel partners. We hope you can join us.

A Guide for Every Trip

BEST OF GUIDES

Full-color guides in an easy-to-scan format. Focused on top sights and experiences in the most popular European destinations

Best of England
Best of Europe
Best of France
Best of Germany
Best of Ireland
Best of Italy
Best of Scotland
Best of Spain

COMPREHENSIVE GUIDES

City, country, and regional guides printed on Bible-thin paper. Packed with detailed coverage for a multi-week trip exploring iconic sights and venturing off the beaten path

Amsterdam & the Netherlands
Barcelona
Belgium: Bruges, Brussels,
  Antwerp & Ghent
Berlin
Budapest
Croatia & Slovenia
Eastern Europe
England
Florence & Tuscany
France
Germany
Great Britain
Greece: Athens & the Peloponnese
Iceland
Ireland
Istanbul
Italy
London
Paris
Portugal
Prague & the Czech Republic
Provence & the French Riviera
Rome
Scandinavia
Scotland
Sicily
Spain
Switzerland
Venice
Vienna, Salzburg & Tirol

HE BEST OF ROME

, Italy's capital, is studded with
n remnants and floodlit fountain
s. From the Vatican to the Colos-
with crazy traffic in between, Rome
derful, huge, and exhausting. The
, the heat, and the weighty history

of the Eternal City where Caesars walked
can make tourists wilt. Recharge by taking siestas, gelato breaks, and after-dark
walks, strolling from one atmospheric
square to another in the refreshing evening air.

Rick Steves books are available from your favorite bookseller.
Many guides are available as ebooks.

POCKET GUIDES
Compact color guides for shorter trips

Amsterdam
Athens
Barcelona
Florence
Italy's Cinque Terre
London
Munich & Salzburg

Paris
Prague
Rome
Venice
Vienna

SNAPSHOT GUIDES
Focused single-destination coverage

Basque Country: Spain & France
Copenhagen & the Best of Denmark
Dublin
Dubrovnik
Edinburgh
Hill Towns of Central Italy
Krakow, Warsaw & Gdansk
Lisbon
Loire Valley
Madrid & Toledo
Milan & the Italian Lakes District
Naples & the Amalfi Coast
Nice & the French Riviera
Normandy
Northern Ireland
Norway
Reykjavík
Rothenburg & the Rhine
Sevilla, Granada & Southern Spain
St. Petersburg, Helsinki & Tallinn
Stockholm

CRUISE PORTS GUIDES
Reference for cruise ports of call

Mediterranean Cruise Ports
Scandinavian & Northern European
  Cruise Ports

Complete your library with...

TRAVEL SKILLS & CULTURE
*Study up on travel skills and gain
insight on history and culture*

Europe 101
Europe Through the Back Door
Europe's Top 100 Masterpieces
European Christmas
European Easter
European Festivals
For the Love of Europe
Italy for Food Lovers
Travel as a Political Act

PHRASE BOOKS & DICTIONARIES
French
French, Italian & German
German
Italian
Portuguese
Spanish

PLANNING MAPS
Britain, Ireland & London
Europe
France & Paris
Germany, Austria & Switzerland
Iceland
Ireland
Italy
Scotland
Spain & Portugal

Credits

RESEARCHER
For help with this edition, Rick, Steve, and Gene relied on...

Virginie Moré

After living for 10 years in Los Angeles, Montana, and Florida, Virginie has been back in France for a few years. Originally from Brittany, she now lives in southern Burgundy with her husband Olivier, where they run an eco-friendly guesthouse. Along with doing book research, she teaches Americans about French culture and history while leading Rick Steves' Europe tours and guiding small private groups in this beautiful, off-the-beaten-path wine region.

ACKNOWLEDGEMENTS
Thank you to Risa Laib for her 25-plus years of dedication to the Rick Steves guidebook series.

Avalon Travel
Hachette Book Group
1700 Fourth Street
Berkeley, CA 94710

Printed in Canada by Friesens.
24th Edition. First printing September 2022.

ISBN 978-1-64171-479-2

For the latest on Rick's talks, guidebooks, tours, public television series, and public radio show, contact Rick Steves' Europe, 130 Fourth Avenue North, Edmonds, WA 98020, +1 425 771 8303, RickSteves.com, rick@ricksteves.com.

Rick Steves' Europe
Managing Editor: Jennifer Madison Davis
Assistant Managing Editor: Cathy Lu
Editors: Glenn Eriksen, Suzanne Kotz, Rosie Leutzinger, Teresa Nemeth, Jessica Shaw, Carrie Shepherd
Editorial & Production Assistant: Megan Simms
Researcher: Virginie More
Graphic Content Director: Sandra Hundacker
Maps & Graphics: Orin Dubrow, David C. Hoerlein, Lauren Mills, Mary Rostad

Avalon Travel
Senior Editor and Series Manager: Madhu Prasher
Associate Managing Editor: Jamie Andrade
Editor: Rachael Sablik
Proofreader: Maggie Ryan
Indexer: Stephen Callahan
Production & Typesetting: Lisi Baldwin, Rue Flaherty, Jane Musser
Cover Design: Kimberly Glyder Design
Maps & Graphics: Kat Bennett

COLOR MAPS

Paris • West Paris • East Paris • Paris Metro • Paris, Normandy & the Loire

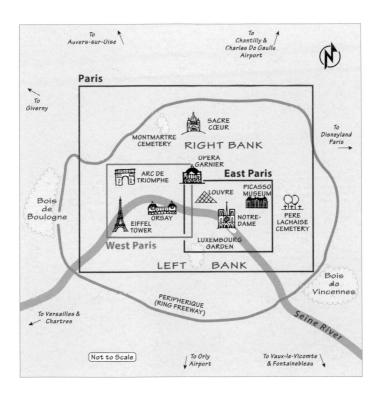

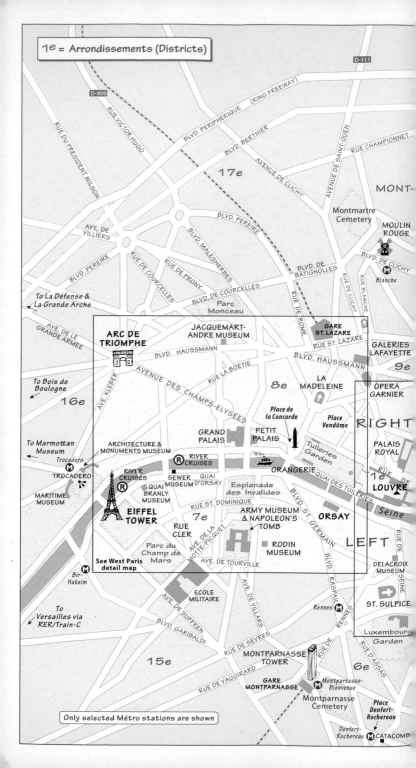

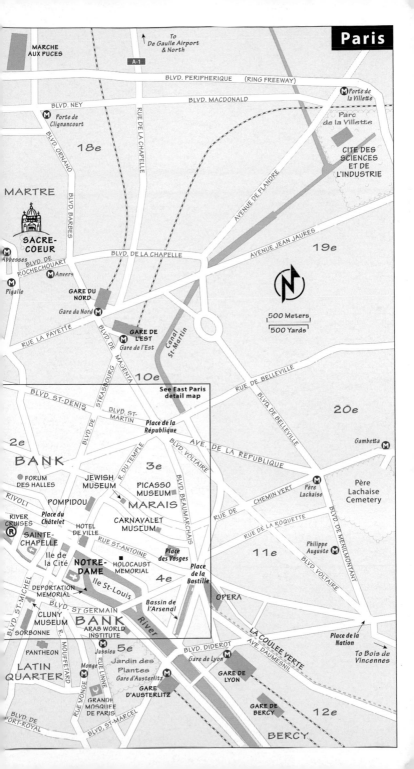

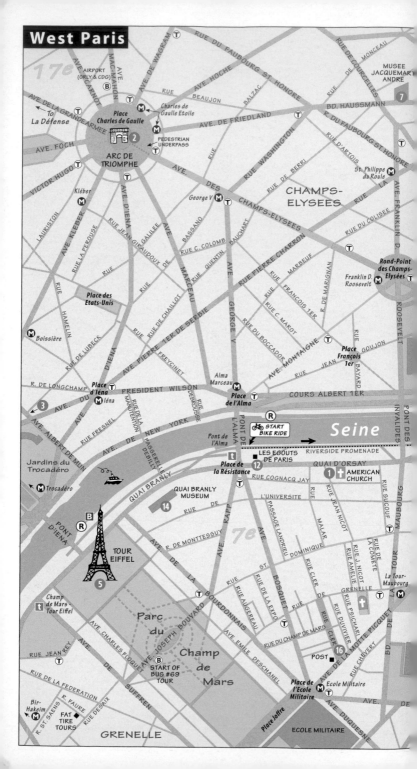

West Paris

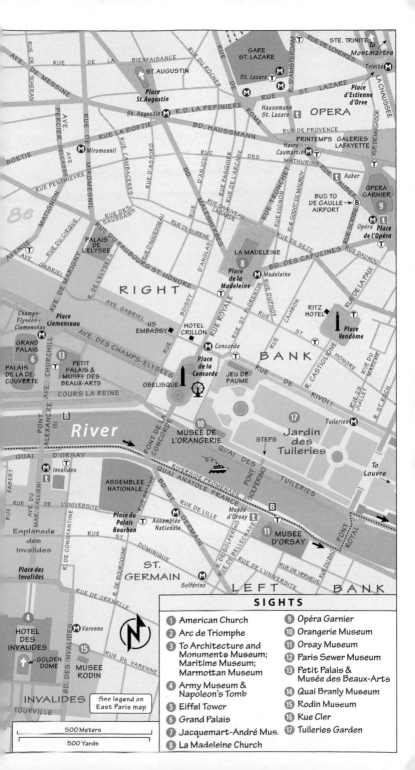

SIGHTS

1. American Church
2. Arc de Triomphe
3. To Architecture and Monuments Museum; Maritime Museum; Marmottan Museum
4. Army Museum & Napoleon's Tomb
5. Eiffel Tower
6. Grand Palais
7. Jacquemart-André Mus.
8. La Madeleine Church
9. Opéra Garnier
10. Orangerie Museum
11. Orsay Museum
12. Paris Sewer Museum
13. Petit Palais & Musée des Beaux-Arts
14. Quai Branly Museum
15. Rodin Museum
16. Rue Cler
17. Tuileries Garden

See legend on East Paris map

500 Meters

500 Yards

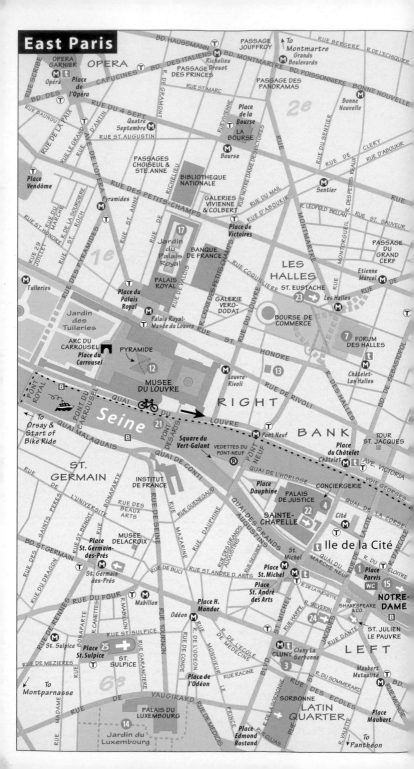

East Paris

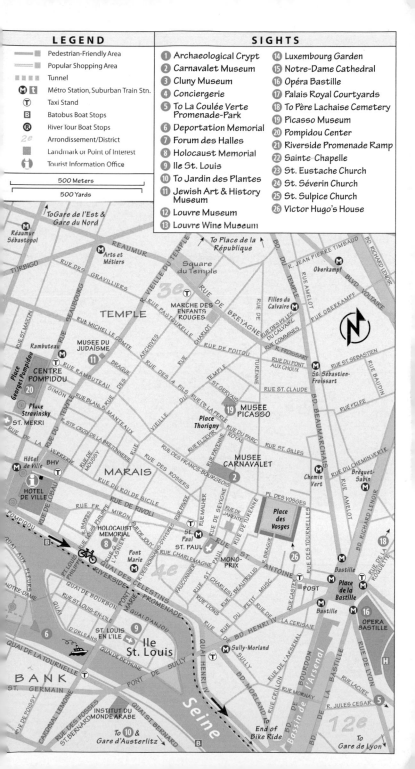

LEGEND

▬▬▪	Pedestrian-Friendly Area
═══▪	Popular Shopping Area
▪▪▪▪	Tunnel
M **t**	Métro Station, Suburban Train Stn.
T	Taxi Stand
B	Batobus Boat Stops
R	River Tour Boat Stops
2e	Arrondissement/District
▪	Landmark or Point of Interest
⊕	Tourist Information Office

500 Meters

500 Yards

SIGHTS

1. Archaeological Crypt
2. Carnavalet Museum
3. Cluny Museum
4. Conciergerie
5. To La Coulée Verte Promenade-Park
6. Deportation Memorial
7. Forum des Halles
8. Holocaust Memorial
9. Ile St. Louis
10. To Jardin des Plantes
11. Jewish Art & History Museum
12. Louvre Museum
13. Louvre Wine Museum
14. Luxembourg Garden
15. Notre-Dame Cathedral
16. Opéra Bastille
17. Palais Royal Courtyards
18. To Père Lachaise Cemetery
19. Picasso Museum
20. Pompidou Center
21. Riverside Promenade Ramp
22. Sainte-Chapelle
23. St. Eustache Church
24. St. Séverin Church
25. St. Sulpice Church
26. Victor Hugo's House

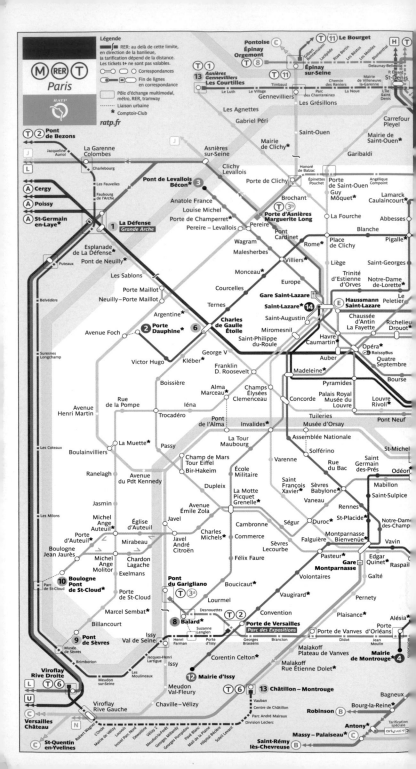

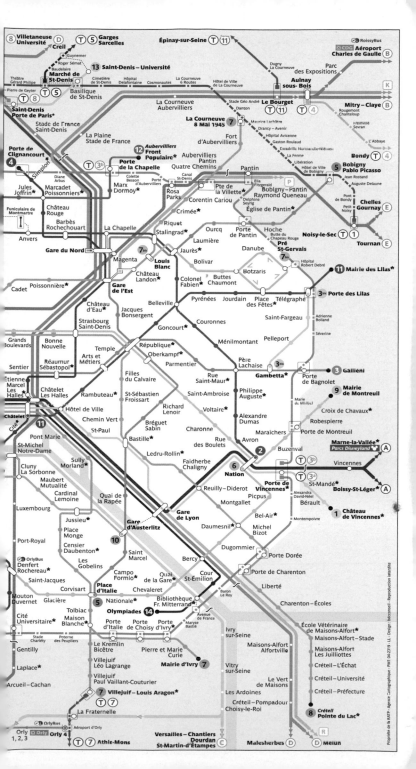

Paris, Normandy & the Loire

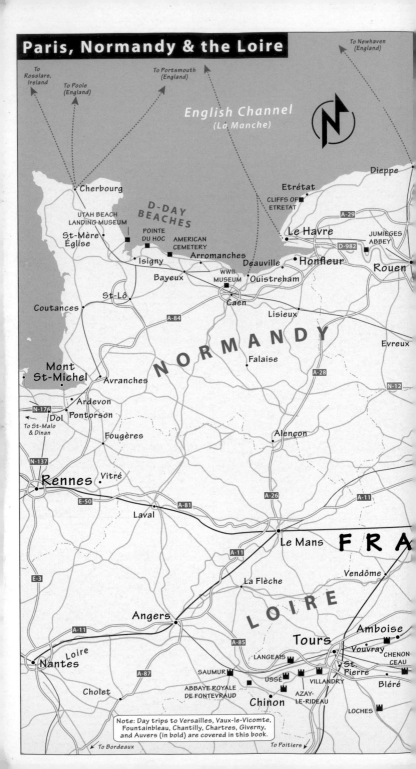

To Newhaven (England)

To Rosslare, Ireland

To Poole (England)

To Portsmouth (England)

English Channel
(La Manche)

N

Dieppe

Cherbourg

Etrétat

CLIFFS OF ETRETAT

D-DAY BEACHES

UTAH BEACH LANDING MUSEUM

St-Mère Église

POINTE DU HOC

AMERICAN CEMETERY

Isigny

Arromanches

Deauville

Le Havre

A-29

JUMIEGES ABBEY

D-982

Honfleur

Rouen

Bayeux

WWII MUSEUM

Ouistreham

St-Lô

Caen

Coutances

Lisieux

N O R M A N D Y

Evreux

A-84

Falaise

A-28

N-12

Mont St-Michel

Avranches

N-17A

Ardevon

Dol

Pontorson

To St-Malo & Dinan

Alençon

Fougères

N-137

Rennes

Vitré

E-50

A-81

A-26

A-11

Laval

Le Mans

F R A

E-3

La Flèche

Vendôme

L O I R E

Angers

A-11

Amboise

A-85

Tours

Vouvray

CHENONCEAU

LANGEAIS

Nantes

A-87

SAUMUR

USSE

VILLANDRY

St. Pierre

Bléré

ABBAYE ROYALE DE FONTEVRAUD

Cholet

Loire

Chinon

AZAY-LE-RIDEAU

LOCHES

Note: Day trips to Versailles, Vaux-le-Vicomte, Fountainbleau, Chantilly, Chartres, Giverny, and Auvers (in bold) are covered in this book.

To Bordeaux

To Poitiers

More for your trip!
Maximize the experience with Rick Steves as your guide

Guidebooks
Make side trips smooth and affordable with Rick's France and Provence & the French Riviera guides

Phrase Books
Rely on Rick's French Phrase Book & Dictionary

Rick's TV Shows
Preview your destinations with a variety of shows covering Paris

Rick's Audio Europe™ App
Get free self-guided audio tours for Paris' top sights

Small Group Tours
Take a lively, low-stress Rick Steves tour through Paris

For all the details, visit ricksteves.com